W9-COL-840

TREATIES AND ALLIANCES OF THE WORLD

KEESING'S PUBLICATIONS (LONGMAN GROUP LIMITED)

Siegler & Co. KG., Bonn-Vienna-Zürich

TREATIES
AND
ALLIANCES
OF THE
WORLD

An International Survey Covering

Treaties in Force and Communities of States

CHARLES SCRIBNER'S SONS

New York

RESEARCH REPORTS PREPARED BY KEESING'S ARCHIVES

1. *The Arab-Israeli Conflict*
2. *The Cultural Revolution in China*
3. *The Sino-Soviet Dispute*
4. *Race Relations in the USA 1954–1968*
5. *South Vietnam: A Political History 1954–1970*
6. *Africa Independent: A Study of Political Developments*
7. *Disarmament: Negotiations and Treaties 1946–1971*
8. *Germany and Eastern Europe Since 1945*
9. *Pakistan: From 1947 to the Creation of Bangladesh*

Copyright © 1974, 1968 Keesing's Publications
(Longman Group Ltd.)

Library of Congress Cataloging in Publication Data
Main entry under title:

Treaties and alliances of the world.

"The bulk of the information . . . can be found
in Keesing's contemporary archives."
1. Alliances. 2. Treaties. I. Keesing's contemporary archives.
JX4005.T72 1974   341.3′7   73–15927
ISBN 0-684–13650–3

Copyright under the Berne Convention
All rights reserved. No part of this book may be reproduced
in any form without the permission of
Charles Scribner's Sons.

3 5 7 9 11 13 15 17 19 C|C 20 18 16 14 12 10 8 6 4 2

Printed in the United States of America

CONTENTS

DIAGRAMS AND TABLES ix
LIST OF MAPS xi
PREFACE TO THE
  SECOND EDITION xiii
INTRODUCTION xv

1 Early International Agreements and Their Later
Expansion 1

THE DECLARATION OF PARIS OF 1856 1
THE GENEVA CONVENTIONS OF THE INTERNATIONAL
  RED CROSS 1
THE HAGUE CONVENTIONS OF 1899 AND 1907 2
THE GENEVA PROTOCOL 3
CONVENTIONS ON INTELLECTUAL PROPERTY 3
CONCORDATS 4

2 World War II: Treaties and Agreements on Territorial
Changes, Frontiers, and Other Matters Arising out of the
War 6

THE YALTA AND POTSDAM CONFERENCES 6
PEACE TREATIES 7
THE AUSTRIAN STATE TREATY 8
THE FRANCO-GERMAN TREATY ON THE SAAR 9

3 The United Nations 10

HISTORY 10
THE CHARTER 11
THE CONVENTION ON THE PREVENTION AND PUNISHMENT
  OF THE CRIME OF GENOCIDE 14
THE UNIVERSAL DECLARATION OF HUMAN RIGHTS AND
  THE COVENANTS ON HUMAN RIGHTS 15
THE DECLARATION ON THE ELIMINATION OF
  DISCRIMINATION AGAINST WOMEN 17
OTHER U.N. CONVENTIONS 17
THE GENERAL ASSEMBLY AND BODIES RESPONSIBLE TO IT 19
THE SECURITY COUNCIL 23
THE TRUSTEESHIP COUNCIL 23

THE ECONOMIC AND SOCIAL COUNCIL (ECOSOC)   24
SPECIAL BODIES FUNCTIONING UNDER AUTHORITY OF
   ECOSOC   25
THE INTERNATIONAL COURT OF JUSTICE   25
THE SECRETARIAT AND SECRETARY-GENERAL   26
OTHER BODIES WITHIN THE FRAMEWORK OF THE U.N.   26
SPECIALIZED AGENCIES AND THE IAEA   27
MEMBERSHIP OF THE U.N. AND RELATED AGENCIES   32

4   Treaties and Agreements on Nuclear Weapons and Co-operation in Antarctica, on the Seabed, and in Outer Space 37

ANTARCTIC TREATY   37
NUCLEAR TEST-BAN TREATY   37
NUCLEAR NON-PROLIFERATION TREATY   38
SEABED ARMS CONTROL TREATY   38
AGREEMENTS ON A COMMUNICATIONS SATELLITE SYSTEM   39
OUTER SPACE TREATY   39
AGREEMENT ON RESCUE AND RETURN OF ASTRONAUTS   40
CONVENTION ON INTERNATIONAL LIABILITY   40

5   Europe: Steps Toward Integration Among Non-Communist States 41

THE BRUSSELS TREATY AND WESTERN EUROPEAN UNION   41
THE COUNCIL OF EUROPE   43
BENELUX   48
THE NORDIC COUNCIL   50
THE EUROPEAN COMMUNITIES   51
   The European Coal and Steel Community (ECSC)   53
   The European Economic Community (EEC)   55
   Euratom   74
THE EUROPEAN FREE TRADE ASSOCIATION (EFTA)   77
EUROPEAN CO-OPERATION IN OTHER SPHERES   79
BILATERAL TREATIES AND AGREEMENTS IN WESTERN
   EUROPE   84

6   The Organization for Economic Co-operation and Development (OECD) 85

THE OEEC   85
THE OECD   85

7   The North Atlantic Treaty Organization (NATO) 93

8   The Communist World 113

INTERNATIONAL COMMUNIST ORGANIZATIONS   113
   Soviet-Yugoslav Reconciliation   119

THE WARSAW PACT   119
OTHER TREATIES OF COMMUNIST STATES   122
COUNCIL FOR MUTUAL ECONOMIC ASSISTANCE
  (COMECON or CMEA)   129

9   East-West Treaties of 1970–72 133

10   The Commonwealth: Commonwealth Regional Group-
    ings and the Treaties of Great Britain 140

THE COMMONWEALTH   140
COMMONWEALTH REGIONAL GROUPINGS   144
TREATIES OF GREAT BRITAIN   145

11   The French Community ("Communauté") 148

12   The Americas 151

PAN-AMERICANISM AND THE FIRST REGIONAL SECURITY
  ARRANGEMENTS   151
THE ORGANIZATION OF AMERICAN STATES (OAS)   153
THE ORGANIZATION OF CENTRAL AMERICAN STATES (OCAS)   165
LATIN AMERICAN PARLIAMENT   167
LATIN AMERICAN FREE TRADE ASSOCIATION (LAFTA)   168
OTHER REGIONAL AGREEMENTS IN LATIN AMERICA   169
BILATERAL AGREEMENTS IN LATIN AMERICA   170
DEFENSE TREATIES OF THE U.S.A.   170
OTHER BILATERAL U.S. AGREEMENTS   175
THE 26 INDEPENDENT STATES IN THE AMERICAS   175
DEPENDENT TERRITORIES IN THE AMERICAS   176

13   The Middle East 177

THE ARAB LEAGUE   177
THE CONSTANTINOPLE CONVENTION ON FREE NAVIGATION
  OF THE SUEZ CANAL   182
CENTRAL TREATY ORGANIZATION (CENTO)   182

14   Africa 186

THE ORGANIZATION OF AFRICAN UNITY (OAU)   186
REGIONAL ORGANIZATIONS IN AFRICA   188
BILATERAL TREATIES IN AFRICA   191
GROUPINGS IN AFRICA   191

15   South and East Asia and the Pacific Area 194

AUSTRALIAN-NEW ZEALAND AGREEMENT (ANZAC)   194

ANZUS PACT 194
AUSTRALIA-NEW ZEALAND FREE TRADE AREA 195
SOUTHEAST ASIA TREATY ORGANIZATION (SEATO) 195
BILATERAL MUTUAL DEFENSE TREATIES OF THE U.S.A. 198
THE GENEVA AGREEMENTS ON INDO-CHINA 200
TREATIES AMONG NATIONS OF SOUTH AND EAST ASIA 203
ASIAN DEVELOPMENT BANK 204
ASIAN AND PACIFIC COUNCIL (ASPAC) 205
ASSOCIATIONS OF SOUTHEAST ASIAN COUNTRIES 205
MEKONG RIVER DEVELOPMENT 206
DEPENDENT TERRITORIES IN THE PACIFIC AREA AND
 SOUTHEAST ASIA 207

16 The "Third World": Attempts at Achieving a Union 208

THE BANDUNG CONFERENCE 208
CONFERENCES OF NON-ALIGNED COUNTRIES 209
AFRO-ASIAN SOLIDARITY COUNCIL 210
AFRO-ASIAN ORGANIZATION FOR ECONOMIC CO-OPERATION
 (AFRASEC) 211
LATIN AMERICAN SOLIDARITY ORGANIZATION 212

Supplementary Developments, January–September 1973 213

Abbreviations of Main Organizations and Groupings 226

        INDEX 227

DIAGRAMS AND TABLES

THE UNITED NATIONS—

Organs 20–21

Membership 34–36

NON-COMMUNIST COUNTRIES IN EUROPE facing 42

WESTERN EUROPEAN UNION—

Organs 43

COUNCIL OF EUROPE—

Organs facing 43

ORGANIZATION FOR ECONOMIC CO-OPERATION AND DEVELOPMENT—

Structure 88–89

NORTH ATLANTIC TREATY ORGANIZATION—

The North Atlantic Council 98–99

Military Organs 100–101

U.S. Military Assistance Agreements Under the Mutual Security Act of 1951 110–111

COMMONWEALTH—

Dependent Territories of Britain 140

Independent Countries Within the Commonwealth 141

FRENCH COMMUNITY—

Bilateral Agreements with France 149

THE AMERICAS—

The 26 Independent States in the Americas 175

Dependent Territories in the Americas 176

AFRICA—

Dependent Territories 191

Groupings of Independent States 192–193

PACIFIC AREA—

Dependent Territories 207

MAPS

NATO and WARSAW PACT MEMBER-STATES 94

EUROPE:

Brussels Pact and Western European Union Member-States 42

Council of Europe Member-States 46

Benelux and Nordic Council 51

Member-States and Associate Member-States of the European Economic Community (EEC) and of the European Free Trade Area (EFTA) 56

European Members of the Organization for Economic Co-operation and Development (OECD) 87

Member-States of the Warsaw Pact 123

AMERICA:

Member-States of the Organization of American States (OAS), of the Organization of Central American States (OCAS), and of the Latin American Free Trade Area (LAFTA) 165

MIDDLE EAST and NORTH AFRICA:

Member-States of CENTO and of the Arab League 183

AFRICA:

Dependent Territories 187

Associate Members of the EEC 74

Member-States of the Joint African and Malagasy Organization (OCAM) and of the *Conseil de l'Entente* 190

Independent Member-States of the Commonwealth 187

SOUTHEAST ASIA and the PACIFIC:

SEATO, ANZUS, and U.S. and British Defense Agreements 199

PREFACE TO THE SECOND EDITION

Since the publication of the first edition of this book, a significant feature in the development of international relations was expressed by President Nixon in his first State of the Union message on Jan. 22, 1970, when he said of the relations between the United States and the Communist Powers:

"We are moving with precision and purpose from an era of confrontation to an era of negotiation. Our concern . . . is to avoid a catastrophic collision and to build a solid basis for peaceful settlement of our differences."

It has therefore been necessary, in updating the contents of this book, to add a new chapter on those treaties so far concluded in the movement toward increasing negotiation between the Western world and Communist Powers.

Jan. 1, 1973.

INTRODUCTION

The ascendancy of the Nation State in modern history appears to be nearing its peak. There are now more than 140 independent States. To this number the completion of the decolonization process and possible secessions are likely to add no more than a handful in the next few years.

Political fragmentation has brought with it the need for a host of bilateral agreements and multilateral treaties as well as for larger groupings, mainly of a regional nature, in the shape of military alliances and economic communities.

At the same time, the urge to reach mutual understanding and agreement on a wider and even global scale—beginning with the conventions of the 19th century on specific matters such as the law of the sea, rules of warfare, intellectual property, and postal communications—led to the founding of the League of Nations in 1919. The League, in which the U.S.A. took no part, failed, however, to stem aggression by Japan in Asia from 1930 onwards and by Italy in Ethiopia in 1935, and it succumbed to the stresses leading to the outbreak of World War II. A new attempt to reach a universal *modus vivendi* among States has been made with the establishment of the United Nations as the successor to the League of Nations.

This survey is designed to present the state of affairs with regard to groupings of States and their principal treaties with each other in force at Jan. 1, 1973. In addition to those mentioned in this survey, there are altogether a few thousand, mainly bilateral, agreements on such matters as trade, economic and technical aid, cultural relations, and extradition.

A survey of this kind was first published by Siegler & Co. KG, Verlag für Zeitarchive, the eleventh edition of this work showing the state of affairs as at Feb. 28, 1973.

Additional information has been supplied by the U.N. Information Center in London, the External Relations Division of the OECD, and the Directorate of Information of the Council of Europe in Strasbourg. Their permission to use material supplied is gratefully acknowledged.

The U.S. State Department has issued a list of treaties and international agreements of the United States under the title "Treaties in Force," its latest edition showing those in force on Jan. 1, 1972.

The bulk of the information given in this survey, and in many cases the full text of the documents involved, can be found in *Keesing's Contemporary Archives*. Citations from this source, given in square brackets, refer to the consecutive pagination of the Archives starting from July 1, 1931, and continuing to the present day.[1]

In the supplement to be found on pages 213–225, the contents of this book have been updated to Sept. 30, 1973.

---

[1] The Archives are available on subscription, and subscribers can also obtain any of the 18 back volumes for the years 1931 to 1972.

TREATIES AND ALLIANCES OF THE WORLD

1

Early International Agreements and Their Later Expansion

THE DECLARATION OF PARIS OF 1856

The Congress of Paris, attended by representatives of the leading European Powers, in 1856 adopted the Declaration of Paris designed to assimilate the provisions of the maritime law of individual States in the event of war. After being signed by Austria, Britain, France, Prussia, Russia, Sardinia, and Turkey, the Declaration was eventually adhered to by all civilized States except Bolivia, the U.S.A., Uruguay, and Venezuela.

The Declaration provided for:

(*a*) the continued prohibition of privateering (i.e. warfare by privately armed vessels under a commission from the State);

(*b*) acceptance of the principle that a neutral flag covers enemy goods except contraband of war, and that neutral goods—again except contraband of war—are not liable to confiscation under an enemy flag; and

(*c*) the principle that blockades, in order to be binding, must be effective—i.e. maintained "by forces sufficient to prevent access to the enemy coast line." (This provision on blockades was repeated in the Declaration of London of February 1909, which was, however, never ratified.)

THE GENEVA CONVENTIONS OF THE INTERNATIONAL RED CROSS

1. The first Geneva Convention, signed by delegates from 16 European countries in Geneva in 1864, established the principle that sick and wounded combatants in war should be respected and cared for irrespective of their nationality; that the personnel caring for them, as well as buildings, equipment, and transport used for their care, should be protected, and that a distinctive emblem—the Red Cross (to which the Red Crescent for Moslem countries and the Red Lion and Sun in Persia were added later)—should be the symbol of their community. This protection was to be claimed only in respect of medical personnel, buildings, equipment, and transport operating as part of the Medical Services of the Armed Forces of the belligerents.

2. The second Geneva Convention of 1906 extended the above principles to maritime warfare and included shipwrecked persons among those to be protected.

3. The third Geneva Convention of 1929 contained amendments to the earlier Conventions arising out of experiences during World War I and incorporated provisions from a Prisoners of War Convention of the same year. This provided for information bureaus in the belligerent countries to circulate information on prisoners of war, and to safeguard their interests through a neutral Power, whose representatives were allowed to visit prisoner of war camps and to question prisoners.

At the outbreak of World War II the Geneva Conventions had not been signed by a number of States, including Japan and the Soviet Union.

4. Further Conventions were drafted at an International Red Cross conference in Stockholm held Aug. 23–30, 1948. These included:

(*a*) A *Convention on the Protection of Civilians in Wartime.*

This convention (*a*) recommends the immediate designation in peacetime of "security zones" (which will be recognized by signatory belligerents in wartime) for the wounded, children under 15, pregnant mothers and mothers with children under 7, and persons over 65, without discrimination on racial, national, religious, or political grounds; (*b*) provides, in addition, for the setting up of "neutral zones" in actual fighting areas to which the sick and injured, as

1]

well as all non-combatant civilians, may be removed; (c) grants special protection from attack to civilian hospitals marked with the Red Cross sign, as well as to transports of sick and injured; (d) prohibits the sending of "protected persons" (i.e. all those who in the case of war or occupation come under the rule of a Power whose nationality they do not possess, or those who in the case of civil war do not take part in hostilities) to, or their retention in, areas subject to warlike actions; their misuse for the safeguarding of certain areas or military operations; physical or mental torture and similar practices to obtain information; collective punishment, reprisals, and the destruction of property if not necessitated by military operations; and the taking of hostages; (e) prohibits also, in the case of occupation, deportations, evacuations not required for military reasons, and conscription of "protected persons" for combatant units or auxiliary forces, or their voluntary recruitment, and allows conscription for work only to safeguard public services, as well as laying down specific rules concerning labor conditions, hygiene and sanitary measures, the prevention of epidemics, etc., in occupied countries; (f) makes the occupying Power in wartime responsible for feeding the civilian population, prohibits the removal of food if there is any shortage, and likewise prohibits the transfer of part of the occupying Power's own civilian nationals to occupied territory; (g) grants analogous protection to aliens in belligerent countries, who are given the right to return to their home country unless a special court set up to examine these cases orders their retention for cogent security reasons, the court having also to make a decision as to whether the alien concerned is to be placed under supervision or to be detained, all proceedings being subject to the ordinary guarantees of law; (h) provides, as far as civilian internment camps are concerned, that internees must be grouped according to nationality, language, and habits, that family members should not be separated and parents be entitled to have their children with them, that internment and P.O.W. camps must be separated, and that internees must not be forced to work unless they choose; detailed provisions also deal with housing and sanitary conditions in such camps, protection against air attack and war operations, feeding, postal communications, receipt of gift parcels, censorship, etc.; (i) empowers the representatives of the Protecting Power to visit any place where there are "protected persons" and to talk to them personally without observers; (k) lays down that the free passage of medical supplies and, in the case of children and pregnant mothers, of food and clothing, must be allowed by belligerents even if destined for civilians of an enemy country. [9536A]

This Convention was to apply also in inter-State conflicts where one of the belligerents did not recognize the existence of a formal state of war, including civil, colonial, and religious wars.

(b) A *Convention on the Treatment of Prisoners of War*. It amends the 1929 Convention to enable prisoners of war to receive collective relief assignments; pledges signatories to give them adequate rations to keep them in good health (instead of "rations equal to those of their captors," as previously); and extends the application of the 1929 Convention to include not only members of the armed forces and civilians openly bearing arms in defense against enemy forces, but also members of military organizations or resistance movements fighting an occupying Power, provided they wear armlets or other visible signs and carry arms openly (the existing requirement of a uniform being dropped). [9536A]

(c) A *Convention on Relief of the Wounded and Sick in Armies of the Field*.

(d) A *Convention adapting the principles of the Geneva Convention of 1906 to maritime warfare*.

These Conventions were approved in Geneva on Aug. 12, 1949, by the representatives of 58 countries—although only a minority of these signed all of them. [10198B]

THE HAGUE CONVENTIONS OF 1899 AND 1907

1. At an international conference held at The Hague in 1899 on the initiative of Czar Nicholas II of Russia and attended by representatives of 26 nations (which included the U.S.A. and Mexico), a number of conventions were adopted, and declarations issued, limiting methods of warfare and providing for peaceful settlement of disputes.

The first of the conventions adopted concerned the laws and customs of war. In this connection the conference issued three declarations prohibiting (a) the discharge of projectiles from balloons; (b) the use of asphyxiating gases; and (c) the use of expanding bullets.

Further, a Convention for the Pacific Settlement of International Disputes established the Hague Permanent Court of Arbitration, the forerunner of the International Court of Justice (see below under United Nations).

2. A second international conference, held at The Hague from June 15 to Oct. 18, 1907, and attended by representatives of 44 countries, revised and renewed the 1899 conventions (though without renewing the declarations on asphyxiating gases and expanding bullets).

In a Convention on Prisoners of War it laid down rules, largely already in practice, on their treatment.

In accordance with this Convention, prisoners of war must be humanely treated, protected from violence, not subjected to reprisals, and supplied with reasonable nourishment as well as medical and sanitary facilities. They are regarded as being in the power of the Government of the captors, and not in that of the captors themselves; their personal belongings (other than arms and military papers) remain their own; they may not be detained in a convict prison; the captor

State may utilize their labor, except in the case of officers, with payment according to rank and ability, but they may not be engaged in excessive work or any tasks relating to military operations.

Prisoners of war need not give any other information than their true name and rank, but these they must give under penalty of losing normal prisoner of war advantages. The Convention also provides for exchange procedure.

The conference also adopted ten new conventions: a Convention Respecting the Limitation of Force for the Recovery of Contract Debts, and nine others dealing with (a) the need for a declaration of war, i.e. "previous and explicit warning, in the form either of a reasoned declaration of war or of an ultimatum with a conditional declaration"; (b) the rights and duties of neutrals in war on land; (c) the status of enemy merchant vessels at the outbreak of war; (d) the conversion of merchant vessels into warships; (e) the laying of automatic submarine contact mines; (f) bombardment by naval forces; (g) the right of capture in maritime war; (h) the setting-up of an international prize court; and (i) the rights and duties of neutral Powers in maritime war.

THE GENEVA PROTOCOL

A Protocol prohibiting the use in war of asphyxiating, poisonous, and other gases, and of bacteriological methods of warfare, was signed at Geneva on June 17, 1925. Twenty-nine countries signed the Protocol originally, the Soviet Union adhering in 1928.

The United States, though adhering to the Protocol in 1925, has not to date ratified it; however, it was announced on Nov. 25, 1969, that the Protocol would be submitted to the U.S. Senate for ratification.

CONVENTIONS ON INTELLECTUAL PROPERTY

1. The Convention of the Union of Paris for the Protection of Industrial Property

This Convention, approved on March 20, 1883, and revised at The Hague (on Nov. 6, 1925), in London (on June 2, 1934), and in Lisbon (Oct. 31, 1958), gave inventors' patents protection in foreign countries by providing that patent applications in the other member-countries should apply from the same date as the patent application in the inventor's home country. By 1965 a total of 68 countries were parties to these

Conventions; they included the Soviet Union but not China.

2. Copyright Conventions

(a) THE BERNE COPYRIGHT CONVENTION OF 1886

This Convention was adhered to by 41 countries (mostly European, with only Brazil and Canada from the Western Hemisphere), and was revised in Paris in 1896, in Berlin in 1908, in Rome in 1928, and in Brussels in 1948.

The Brussels revision of 1948 extended the protection previously given to authors of works of literature, art, and music to the spheres of film, radio, television, and allied arts, and laid down that disputes between countries on the interpretation or application of the Convention were to be submitted to the International Court of Justice.

(b) There were also several Pan-American Conventions among Western Hemisphere countries, the most important being the Buenos Aires Convention of 1910 with 15 adherents, including the U.S.A.

(c) THE UNIVERSAL COPYRIGHT CONVENTION

Under the auspices of UNESCO (see page 28), a conference held in Geneva from Aug. 25 to Sept. 7, 1952, resulted in the signing by representatives of 35 countries, of a Universal Copyright Convention, the principal provisions of which were:

(i) Each signatory country undertakes to give to foreign works the same copyright protection as that given to works of its own nationals. The terms of protection will be not less than the life of the author and 25 years after his death.

(ii) All existing formalities of registration and legal deposit will be eliminated, and will be replaced by a simple system under which the letter "C" will be imprinted within a circle on each copy of the works protected, accompanied by the author's name and the date of the first publication.

(iii) Translation rights will also be covered, and during a minimum period of 7 years authors will have the exclusive right to publish translations of their works, or to authorize the making and publication of such translations.

By June 1969 the Universal Copyright Convention had been ratified by 58 countries. The Convention does not supersede the Berne Convention, which remains binding upon its members. [12639B]

3. Stockholm Conference on Intellectual Property

A Conference held in Stockholm from June 12 to July 14, 1967, and attended by representatives of 132 countries (including the Soviet Union and other Communist countries), created a World Organization for Intellectual Property with three organs: (*a*) a General Assembly of representatives of all member-States; (*b*) a co-ordinating committee with consultative and executive functions; and (*c*) a permanent secretariat designated as the International Bureau for Intellectual Property, to be located in Geneva. The provisions of the Paris and Berne Conventions (see above under 1 and 2) were adapted to the new organization.

The Conference also adopted, *inter alia,* a protocol (proposed by Sweden) giving preferential rights to those developing countries which are members of the Berne Copyright Convention.

This protocol authorized these countries: (*a*) to translate into their own language and publish, without permission by its author and immediately after publication of the original, "any book to be used for teaching, study, and research in all fields of education"; (*b*) to translate and publish literary and artistic works similarly 3 years or more after their original publication (though reprinting of such books in the original language remained subject to the existing copyright regulations); and (*c*) to pay, in all these cases, royalties to authors in accordance with the developing countries' own rates.

The protocol was applicable only against a country of origin which had agreed to its provisions. Of the developing countries, India is the most prominent member of the Berne Convention, while most other developing countries are not members.

The protocol was adopted without dissent, but with Britain abstaining, and the British Government did not sign it.

4. 1971 Revision of Universal and Berne Copyright Conventions

The Universal Copyright Convention was revised at a conference of 46 countries—the contracting parties to the Convention—in Paris, July 5–24, 1971, by the addition of three new articles:

(i) Defining "non-industrialized countries" and the period of preferential treatment to be granted to them for their needs in teaching, scholarship, and research;

(ii) reducing the 7-year period for authors' exclusive rights to translation of their work [see 2(c)(iii) above] in the case of editions to be used for teaching, scholarship, or research to 3 years for works published in a widely used language, and to 1 year in the case of a little-used language—subject to a ban on exports of such translations; and

(iii) enabling any national of a contracting country to obtain a license, under certain conditions, for reproduction, for the purpose of "systematic instruc-

tional activities," of a work of which the first issue had not been distributed within a specified period.

At the same time the Berne Convention of 1886 was modified so as to give non-industrialized countries the same advantages as they had under the Universal Convention.

CONCORDATS

Concordats are treaties concluded between the Pope, as Head of the Roman Catholic Church, and secular Governments on matters concerning the interests of Roman Catholic citizens, especially in education, and property of the Catholic Church.

Among over 20 such Concordats signed since the end of World War I were the following:

1. The Lateran Treaty, signed by the Cardinal Secretary of State of the Vatican and Benito Mussolini, then Head of the Italian Government, on Feb. 11, 1929, embodied recognition by the Government of Italy of the sovereignty of the Vatican City State, and provided for compensation by the Italian State for Church property seized in 1870.

2. A Concordat concluded with Bavaria in 1924 was expressly reaffirmed in the 1946 Constitution of the *Land* of Bavaria.

3. The Concordat concluded with Nazi Germany on July 20, 1933, was ruled by the German Federal Constitutional Court in 1957 to be still in force though not binding on *Länder* (i.e. federal units of West Germany) in regard to school legislation.

4. A new Concordat was subsequently concluded between the Vatican and the *Land* of Lower Saxony on Feb. 26, 1965, covering provisions for the establishment and maintenance of Roman Catholic schools, a grant-in-aid toward salaries of ministers of religion, and the setting up of a Roman Catholic Theological Faculty at the *Land's* university in Göttingen. [*20884A*]

5. The Concordat with Portugal, signed on May 7, 1940, included an acknowledgment by the State of the intangible character of church marriage, as well as provisions confirming the Church's possession of property and the appointment of Bishops by the Pope with their formal nomination by the Head of the State. [*4088C*]

6. The Concordat with Spain, signed on Aug. 27, 1953, embodied a number of previous agreements concluded between the Holy See and the Government of General Franco.

This Concordat provided *inter alia* for:

(*a*) a reaffirmation by the Spanish Government that the Roman Catholic religion was the sole religion of the Spanish people—while the Holy See recognized the validity of the article in the Spanish Constitution which laid down that no person should be molested for holding and practicing other religious beliefs;

(*b*) admission of the Spanish language as an official language (equally with Latin) in cases of beatification and canonization;

(*c*) the appointment of a second Spanish assessor in the Supreme Court of the Roman Rota—giving Spain, as the only country, two seats in the Court instead of one;

(*d*) appointment of Bishops and Archbishops, as previously agreed, from a list proposed by the Head of the Spanish State;

(*e*) exemption of the clergy from military service and of Church property from taxation. [*13201B*]

Other agreements concluded by the Catholic Church and a secular Government have been entered upon by Church leaders in their respective countries.

These include the agreement concluded between Archbishop Grosz of Kalocsa and the Hungarian State on Aug. 30, 1950, by which the Bishops undertook to "recognize and support the Constitution and State order of the Hungarian People's Republic." [*11259A*]

2

World War II: Treaties and Agreements on Territorial Changes, Frontiers, and Other Matters Arising Out of the War

During and after World War II the Allied Powers, in a series of treaties and agreements, determined their proposed treatment of the countries of the Axis Powers after the conclusion of hostilities. The most important conferences, at which such agreements were reached, were the Yalta Conference and the Potsdam Conference of 1945.

THE YALTA CONFERENCE

At this conference, held in Yalta (Crimea), Feb. 4–11, 1945, Churchill, Roosevelt, and Stalin confirmed previous agreements on the occupation of Germany.

These agreements included acceptance of a proposal made by the European Advisory Commission of the Allied Powers at the Second Quebec Conference of September 1944; France, as a fourth occupying power, now associated herself with this proposal. It involved (a) Allied administration of Germany in British, French, Soviet, and United States occupation zones; and (b) the control of Berlin by the four Allied Powers.

Further decisions reached at Yalta were:

1. Britain and the U.S.A. would support membership in the United Nations General Assembly for the Soviet republics of the Ukraine and Byelorussia, in addition to the Soviet Union itself.

2. Under the terms of a secret protocol, the Soviet Union would enter the war against Japan "within two or three months" after the surrender of Germany, and the Western Powers would in return (a) recognize the independence of Outer Mongolia and (b) agree to the transfer to the Soviet Union of Southern Sakhalin, adjacent islands, and the Kurile Islands, as well as to her recovery of certain rights in the Far East which Russia had lost in the war against Japan in 1904–5. [6991A]

THE POTSDAM CONFERENCE

At the Potsdam Conference, held July 17–Aug. 2, 1945, Clement Attlee (then British Prime Minister), Stalin, and President Truman agreed *inter alia* on the following points:

1. Germany was not to be partitioned, but to be treated as a single economic unit with certain central administrative departments, though with a program of decentralization to be carried out.

2. Britain and the U.S.A. would support, at the eventual peace settlement, the Soviet annexation of the northern half of East Prussia (including Königsberg).

3. "Pending the final delimitation of Poland's western frontier," the "former German territories" east of the Oder and Neisse Rivers and the former free city of Danzig were to be left under Polish administration and should not be considered as part of the Soviet zone of occupation in Germany.

4. Peace treaties should be concluded with Bulgaria, Finland, Hungary, Italy, and Romania.

5. The remaining German population in Poland, Czechoslovakia, and Hungary was to be transferred to Germany. [7361A]

Decisions by the Allied Control Council

Allied policy on Germany was implemented by the Allied Control Council, consisting of the Supreme Commanders of the British, French, Soviet, and U.S. Armed Forces.

On June 5, 1945, the Allied Control Council declared that the four Allied Governments would "hereafter determine the boundaries of Germany or any part thereof and the status of Germany or of any area at present being part of Germany." It also established the occupation of Berlin by all four Powers and its government by an inter-Allied Kommandatura. [7227A]

(The Kommandatura was, however, dissolved by the Soviet commandant on July 1, 1948, an event from which dates the division of the city into East Berlin and West Berlin.) [9393A]

On March 1, 1947, the Allied Control Council decreed that "the Prussian State, which from its early days has been a promoter of militarism and reaction in Germany, has *de facto* ceased to exist." [8481F]

The Western Powers subsequently reached agreements which led to the establishment of the German Federal Republic (often referred to as West Germany), without a peace settlement having been reached with Germany as a whole.

1. A 6-Power conference agreed in London on June 2, 1948, on the structure of a German Federal Government for the British, French, and U.S. occupation zones; an Allied occupation statute; an economic merger of the French zone with the U.S. and British zones (which had already been merged in a "bi-zone" on Jan. 1, 1947); and the establishment of an international coal and steel authority. [9309A]

2. The Paris agreements of Oct. 23, 1954, gave full sovereign status to the German Federal Republic as from May 5, 1955, and also gave it membership in NATO (see also Western European Union, page 41) [13869A]

PEACE TREATIES

The first peace treaty concluded by the Allied nations with an ex-enemy country was signed by Britain and India on the one hand and the Kingdom of Siam (now Thailand) on the other on Jan. 1, 1946.

The preamble stated *inter alia* that the British and Indian Governments had taken note of the fact that the Siamese Government had already repudiated the declaration of war against the British Empire made in 1942. The treaty nullified all Siamese acquisitions of British territories (in Malaya and Burma) made during the War; provided for Siamese collaboration in all international security arrangements approved by the U.N., especially those relating to Southeast Asia; and provided for the restoration of diplomatic, economic, and commercial links between the parties. Siam also undertook not to construct a canal across the Kra Isthmus (linking the Indian Ocean and the Gulf of Siam) without British consent. [7695A]

Peace treaties between the Allied and Associated Powers on the one hand and Bulgaria, Finland, Hungary, Italy, and Romania were signed in Paris on Feb.

10, 1947. All these treaties contained provisions for reparations and imposed limitations on the armed forces of the countries concerned and in particular prohibited their possession or construction of atomic weapons. [8442A]

All five peace treaties came into force on Sept. 16, 1947, after the instruments of ratification had been deposited as required in the treaties. [8827C]

Bulgaria

The Bulgarian peace treaty confirmed Bulgaria's frontiers as those of Jan. 1, 1941, i.e. as including the Southern Dobruja ceded by Romania in August 1940. It further stipulated *inter alia:* "Navigation on the Danube shall be free and open for the nationals, commercial vessels, and goods of all States."

Finland

Under the Finnish peace treaty Finland confirmed the cession to the Soviet Union of the province of Petsamo (which meant that Finland no longer had direct access to the Arctic Ocean and the Soviet Union obtained a common frontier with Norway). The peace treaty also confirmed the frontier changes of the Moscow Peace Treaty of 1940, whereby the Soviet Union acquired the Karelian Isthmus, Viborg, and other territories west of Lake Ladoga. Renouncing her right (under the terms of the 1940 treaty) of leasing the Hangö peninsula, the Soviet Union obtained a 50-year lease of the Porkkala-Udd area (S.W. of Helsinki) for the establishment of a Soviet naval base. [8517A]

(The Porkkala base, however, was evacuated by the Soviet Union in 1955 after a 20-year extension of the Soviet-Finnish treaty of friendship and mutual assistance of 1948—see page 126). [14460A]

Italy

The Italian peace treaty provided for the demarcation of Italy's frontiers with her neighbors, including the Free Territory of Trieste set up by the treaty, and involving cessions: (*a*) to France, of several areas in the Alps, among them the Little St. Bernard Pass and the Mont Cenis plateau; (*b*) to Yugoslavia, to Zara and islands off the Dalmatian coast; and (*c*) to Greece, of the Dodecanese Islands (in the Eastern Mediterranean). Italy also renounced all rights to Libya, Eritrea, and Italian Somaliland, and recognized the independence of Albania and of Ethiopia.

The treaty also incorporated an agreement on South Tyrol reached by the Austrian and Italian Governments on Sept. 5, 1946, providing full equality of rights with Italian-speaking inhabitants to German-speaking inhabitants of Bolzano Province and of bilingual townships in Trento Province. *[8465A]*

A new treaty, giving extended rights to the German-speaking inhabitants of South Tyrol, was concluded between Austria and Italy and initialed in Vienna on Dec. 2, 1969. *[23845A]*

The status of the Free Territory of Trieste was ended under the terms of an agreement initialed in London on Oct. 5, 1954, whereby Italy obtained most of its northern part (known as Zone A) including the city and port of Trieste, and Yugoslavia its southern part (Zone B), together with about 5 square miles of Zone A. *[13821A]* The agreement was implemented Oct. 25–29, 1954. *[13858A; 13999A]*

Hungary

The Hungarian peace treaty re-established Hungary's frontiers as those of Jan. 1, 1938. This meant the reversion of Transylvania to Romania and of Eastern Slovakia to Czechoslovakia; and confirmation of the transfer of Ruthenia to the Soviet Union—which had obtained this territory from Czechoslovakia under the terms of a treaty of June 29, 1945. Hungary also ceded several villages near Bratislava to Czechoslovakia. The treaty contained the same provisions for navigation on the Danube as the Bulgarian peace treaty. *[8152B]*

Romania

The Romanian peace treaty defined Romania's frontiers as those of Jan. 1, 1941 (i.e. including Transylvania) but with the cession of Bessarabia and the Bukovina to the Soviet Union and of the Southern Dobruja to Bulgaria. It also contained the clause on freedom of navigation on the Danube. *[8483A]*

Japan

A peace treaty with Japan was signed in San Francisco on Sept. 8, 1951, by all Allied Powers represented at a 52-nation conference except Czechoslovakia, Poland, and the Soviet Union. The conference was not attended by Burma, India, and Yugoslavia. *[11721A]*

The treaty came into force on April 28, 1952, after the instruments of ratification had been deposited in Washington by the U.S.A. and Japan and by 9 out of 13 other countries specified in the treaty.

Under the terms of this treaty Japan recognized the independence of Korea; renounced all claims to Korea, Formosa, and the Pescadores, the Kurile Islands and South Sakhalin, and the Pacific Islands formerly mandated to Japan by the League of Nations. Japan also agreed to the proposal to place under the U.N. trustee-

ship system, with the U.S.A. as the sole administering authority, the Ryukyu Islands (S. of 29° N.), the Bonin Islands, the Volcano Islands, Marcus Island, and some smaller islands. *[11681A]*

The treaty contained no specific definition of reparations to be made by Japan.

The Governments of both Communist China and Nationalist China took no part in the conclusion of the Japanese peace treaty.

Under an agreement signed on April 5, 1968, by the U.S.A. and Japan, the Bonin and Volcano Islands, together with Rosario, Parece, and Marcus Islands, were returned to Japan.

The agreement also provided that the U.S.-Japanese Security Treaty (see page 199) would apply to the islands after their return to Japan; that the U.S.A. would continue to use two radio stations on Iwo Jima (the largest of the Bonin Islands) and Marcus Island under the U.S.-Japanese Status of Forces Agreement; but that all other installations and sites on the islands would be transferred to Japan. *[22762C]*

An agreement on the transfer of sovereignty over the Ryukyu Islands to Japan was signed on June 17, 1971, and after ratification of the agreement both in Japan and in the U.S.A. the reversion of the islands to Japanese jurisdiction took place on May 15, 1972.

The agreement accordingly amended the relevant article of the San Francisco Peace Treaty, but at the same time laid down that Japan would grant the United States, as from the date of entry into force of the agreement, the use of "facilities and areas" in the Ryukyu Islands in accordance with the 1960 Treaty of Mutual Co-operation and Security (see page 199). These included the Kadena Air Force base on Okinawa, though the Japanese Government's approval was required for air or ground military operations to be launched by the U.S.A. *[24715A; 25285A]*

Germany

No peace treaty has been concluded between the Allies of World War II and Germany.

THE AUSTRIAN STATE TREATY

The Austrian State Treaty, which ended more than ten years of Allied occupation of Austria, preceded by seven years of German occupation, was signed at the Belvedere Palace in Vienna on May 15, 1955, by the Foreign Ministers and Ambassadors in Vienna of the four occupying Powers (Soviet Union, Britain, U.S.A., and France), and by the Austrian Foreign Minister.

Its main operative clauses are as follows:

Art. 1. Re-establishment of Austria as a Free and Independent State. The Allied and Associated Powers recognize that Austria is re-established as a sovereign, independent and democratic state.

Art. 2. Maintenance of Austria's Independence. The Allied and Associated Powers declare that they will respect the independence and territorial integrity of Austria as established under the present treaty.

Art. 3. Recognition by Germany of Austrian Independence. The Allied and Associated Powers will incorporate in the German peace treaty provisions for securing from Germany the recognition of Austria's sovereignty and independence and the renunciation by Germany of all territorial and political claims in respect of Austria and Austrian territory.

Art. 4. Prohibition of Anschluss. (1) The Allied and Associated Powers declare that political or economic union between Austria and Germany is prohibited. Austria fully recognizes its responsibilities in this matter and shall not enter into political or economic union with Germany in any form whatsoever. . . .

Art. 5. Frontiers of Austria. The frontiers of Austria shall be those existing on January 1, 1938. . . .

Art. 8. Democratic Institutions. Austria shall have a democratic government based on elections by secret ballot and shall guarantee to all citizens free, equal, and universal suffrage, as well as the right to be elected to public office without discrimination as to race, sex, language, religion, or political opinion. . . .

Art. 13. Prohibition of Special Weapons. (1) Austria shall not possess, construct, or experiment with (*a*) any atomic weapons, (*b*) any other major weapon adaptable now or in the future to mass destruction and defined as such by the appropriate organ of the U.N., (*c*) any self-propelled or guided missiles or torpedoes, or apparatus connected with their discharge or control, (*d*) sea mines, (*e*) torpedoes capable of being manned, (*f*) submarines or other submersible craft, (*g*) motor torpedo-boats, (*h*) specialized types of assault craft, (*i*) guns with a range of more than 30 kilometers, (*j*) asphyxiating, vesicant, or poisonous materials or biological substances in quantities greater than, or of types other than, are required for legitimate civil purposes. . . .

Other articles deal with the rights of minority groups and the security of Human Rights. Most clauses, however, were of only transitional significance, dealing with matters immediately arising from the war.

Following the signature of the Treaty, the Austrian Foreign Ministry published the text of a resolution on Austria's permanent neutrality, which was passed as a constitutional law by the *Nationalrat* (Austrian Lower House) on Oct. 26, 1955, and came into force on Nov. 5, 1955.

Its significant paragraphs were as follows:

(1) With the object of the lasting and perpetual maintenance of her independence from without and the inviolability of her territory, as well as in the interest of maintaining internal law and order, Austria declares of her own free will her perpetual neutrality, and is resolved to maintain and defend it with all means at her disposal.

(2) Austria, in order to secure these objectives, will join no military alliances and will not permit the establishment of military bases of foreign States on her territory. [*14193A*]

THE FRANCO-GERMAN TREATY ON THE SAAR

The importance of the Saar region, the status of which was in dispute for decades, rests on its rich deposits of coal. After World War I the Saar came under the administration of the League of Nations. From 1920 to 1935 France possessed the rights to exploit the Saar coal fields, but in 1935, after a plebiscite, the region reverted to Germany. After World War II the Saar was first a *Land* within the French zone of Germany, and later, under a new Constitution ratified in November 1947, an autonomous State having an economic union with France. An agreement between France and the German Federal Republic on the future status of the Saar, of October 1954, was rejected in a referendum a year later. A final treaty settling the future of the Saar region was signed by France and West Germany in Luxemburg on Oct. 27, 1956. The treaty provided for the political incorporation of the Saar into the German Federal Republic on Jan. 1, 1957, and full economic re-integration with Germany by Dec. 31, 1959. Until that date the Franco-Saar customs union would remain in force and the Saar would retain French currency. For 25 years France would purchase from the Saar a total of 90,000,000 tons of coal; a special Franco-German organization would be set up to handle Saar coal supplies. [*15165A*]

The Saar territory duly became part of the German Federal Republic at midnight of Dec. 31, 1956. On June 25, 1959, the French and Federal German Governments agreed that the Saar should be fully incorporated economically in the German Federal Republic by July 6, 1959. [*16909B*]

3

The United Nations

SEAT: New York

EUROPEAN OFFICE: Geneva

MEMBERS: see table, pages 34–36

HISTORY

The United Nations came into being during World War II as a collaboration of the Allied nations against the Axis powers (Germany, Italy, and Japan).

The Atlantic Charter

The first steps toward the working out of a program of principles and policy—later to take shape as the Charter of the United Nations—were taken by President Roosevelt of the United States and the British Prime Minister, Winston Churchill, in August 1941. After a meeting between the two, on board ship in the Atlantic, a joint declaration of principles was issued on Aug. 14, 1941. This declaration, generally referred to as the *Atlantic Charter,* ran as follows:

The President of the United States and the Prime Minister, Mr. Churchill, representing H.M. Government in the United Kingdom, being met together, deem it right to make known certain common principles in the national policies of their respective countries on which they base their hopes for a better future for the world.

1. Their countries seek no aggrandizement, territorial or other.

2. They desire to see no territorial changes that do not accord with the freely expressed wishes of the peoples concerned.

3. They respect the right of all peoples to choose the form of Government under which they will live; and they wish to see sovereign rights and self-government restored to those who have been forcibly deprived of them.

4. They will endeavor, with due respect for their existing obligations, to further enjoyment by all States, great or small, victor or vanquished, of access, on equal terms, to the trade and to the raw materials of the world which are needed for their economic prosperity.

5. They desire to bring about the fullest collaboration between all nations in the economic field, with the object of securing for all improved labor standards, economic advancement, and social security.

6. After the final destruction of Nazi tyranny, they hope to see established a peace which will afford to all nations the means of dwelling in safety within their own boundaries, and which will afford assurance that all the men in all the lands may live out their lives in freedom from fear and want.

7. Such a peace should enable all men to traverse the high seas and oceans without hindrance.

8. They believe all of the nations of the world, for realistic as well as spiritual reasons, must come to the abandonment of the use of force. Since no future peace can be maintained if land, sea, or air armaments continue to be employed by nations which threaten, or may threaten, aggression outside of their frontiers, they believe, pending the establishment of a wider and permanent system of general security, that the disarmament of such nations is essential. They will likewise aid and encourage all other practicable measures which will lighten for peace-loving peoples the crushing burden of armament.   [*4739A*]

The Atlantic Charter was referred to in a joint declaration of the 26 Allied nations at war with Germany, Italy, and Japan, signed on Jan. 1, 1942. The declaration stated that the Governments of the Allies, "having subscribed to a common program of purposes and principles embodied in the joint declaration . . . known as the Atlantic Charter, being convinced that complete victory over their enemies is essential to defend life, liberty, independence, and religious freedom, and to preserve human rights and justice in their own lands as well as in other lands," pledged themselves to employ their full resources against the enemy and to make no separate armistice or peace.   [*4957A*]

Dumbarton Oaks Conference

A 4-Power conference was held at Dumbarton Oaks, near Washington, Aug. 21–Oct. 7, 1944, to establish the framework of a postwar international security organization. The participants in the talks were the United States, Britain, the Soviet Union, and China.

At the close of the conference it was stated that 90 percent agreement had been reached by the four Powers. The proposals contained in their draft for a post-war international security organization, were largely embodied in the later Charter of the United Nations (see below). They dealt with the maintenance of international peace and security, and established most of the main organs of the United Nations, namely the General Assembly, the Security Council, the International Court of Justice, and the Economic and Social Council. [6868A]

The Yalta Conference

At the tripartite summit conference held at Yalta in the Crimea Feb. 4–11, 1945 (see page 6), the participants—the United States, Britain, and the Soviet Union—agreed, *inter alia,* that a conference of the United Nations should be called to meet at San Francisco on April 25, 1945. The question of voting procedure within the new organization, which had not been settled at Dumbarton Oaks, was resolved at the Yalta Conference. [6991A]

The San Francisco Conference

The United Nations Conference on International Organization (UNCIO) was held at San Francisco from April 25 to June 25, 1945. It was sponsored by the U.S.A., Britain, the Soviet Union, and China. France, although she refused an invitation to become a sponsor, participated in all meetings of the sponsoring Powers on a basis of full equality, forming one of the so-called "Big Five."

The three most controversial issues discussed at the conference were: (1) the question of the veto power of the "Big Five" and voting procedure in the Security Council; (2) the question of the integration of regional pacts and arrangements into the general framework of world security; (3) the question of trusteeship over dependent areas and backward peoples. All three questions were finally satisfactorily settled, although the solution of the first took several weeks.

THE UNITED NATIONS CHARTER

The Charter of the United Nations was signed on June 26, 1945, at the end of the San Francisco Conference. It entered into force on Oct. 24, 1945.

The contents of the Charter are described, with extracts, below.

PREAMBLE

We, the peoples of the United Nations,
Determined to save succeeding generations from the scourge of war, which twice in our lifetime has brought untold sorrow to mankind;
to reaffirm faith in fundamental human rights, in the dignity and worth of the human person, and in the equal rights of men and women and of nations large and small;
to establish conditions under which justice and respect for obligations arising from treaties and other sources of international law can be maintained;
to promote social progress and better standards of life in larger freedom;
to practice tolerance and live together in peace with one another as good neighbors;
to unite our strength to maintain international peace and security;
to ensure, by the acceptance of principles and the institution of methods, that armed force shall not be used, save in the common interest;
to employ international machinery for the promotion of the economic and social advancement of all peoples;
have resolved to combine our efforts to accomplish these aims, have agreed to the present Charter of the United Nations, and do hereby establish an international organization to be known as the United Nations.

CHAPTER 1
Purposes

Art. 1. The purposes of the United Nations are:
1. To maintain international peace and security, and to that end: to take effective collective measures for the prevention and removal of threats to the peace and for the suppression of acts of aggression or other breaches of the peace, and to bring about by peaceful means, and in conformity with the principles of justice and international law, adjustment or settlement of international disputes or situations which might lead to a breach of the peace;
2. To develop friendly relations among nations based on respect for the principle of equal rights and self-determination of peoples, and to take other appropriate measures to strengthen universal peace;
3. To achieve international co-operation in solving international problems of an economic, social, cultural or humanitarian character, and in promoting and encouraging respect for human rights and for the fundamental freedoms for all without distinction of race, sex, language, or religion; and
4. To be a center for harmonizing the actions of nations in the attainment of these common ends.

Principles

Art. 2. The organization and its members, in pursuit of the purposes stated in Art. 1, shall act in accordance with the following principles:
1. The organization is based on the principle of the sovereign equality of all its members.
2. All members shall fulfil in good faith the obligations assumed by them in accordance with the Charter.
3. All members shall settle their international disputes by peaceful means in such a manner that international peace, security, and justice are not endangered.
4. All members shall refrain in their international relations from the threat or use of force against the territorial integrity or political independence of any member or State, or in any other manner inconsistent with the purposes of the United Nations.
5. All members shall give the United Nations every assistance in any action it takes in accordance with the provisions of the Charter, and shall refrain from giving assistance to any state against which the United Nations is taking preventive or enforcement action.

6. The organization shall ensure that States not members act in accordance with these principles so far as may be necessary for the maintenance of international peace and security.

7. Nothing in the Charter shall authorize the United Nations to intervene in matters which are essentially within the domestic jurisdiction of any State, or shall require the members to submit such matters to settlement under the present Charter; but this principle shall not prejudice the application of enforcement measures under Chapter 7.

Chapter 2 deals with the conditions of membership and provides for the suspension or expulsion from the organization of erring members.

Chapter 3 enumerates the main organs, and provides for universal eligibility to serve on them.

Chapter 4 gives details of the composition, functions and powers of, and procedure in the General Assembly (see page 20).

Important provisions on voting are:

Art. 18. Decisions of the General Assembly on important questions shall be made by a two-thirds majority of those present and voting. These questions shall include: recommendations with respect to the maintenance of international peace and security; the election of non-permanent members of the Security Council; the election of members of the Economic and Social Council; the election of members of the United Nations which are to designate the members on the Trusteeship Council . . . ; the admission of new members to the United Nations; the expulsion of members; the suspension of the rights and privileges of members; questions relating to the operations of the trusteeship system; and budgetary questions. . . .

Art. 19. A member in arrears in the payment of its financial contributions to the organization shall have no vote if the amount of arrears equals or exceeds the amount of the contributions due from it for the preceding 2 full years. The General Assembly may, nevertheless, permit such a member to vote if it is satisfied that the failure to pay is due to conditions beyond the member's control.

Chapter 5 gives details of the composition and responsibility of the Security Council and of its procedure. Amendments to the Charter, which came into force on Aug. 31, 1965, affected Articles 23 and 27 of this chapter, raising the membership of the Council from 11 to 15, and the number of affirmative votes to carry decisions from 7 to 9 (see page 23).

CHAPTER 6
Pacific Settlement of Disputes

Art. 33. 1. The parties to any dispute whose continuance is likely to endanger the maintenance of international peace and security shall, first of all, seek a solution by negotiation, inquiry, mediation, conciliation, arbitration, judicial settlement, resort to regional agencies or arrangements, or other peaceful means of their own choice.

2. The Security Council shall, when it deems necessary, call upon the parties to settle their dispute by such means.

Art. 34. The Security Council may investigate any dispute, or any situation which might lead to international friction or give rise to a dispute, in order to determine whether its continuance is likely to endanger the maintenance of international peace and security.

Art. 35. 1. Any member of the United Nations may bring any dispute or situation of the nature referred to in Art. 34 to the attention of the Security Council or the General Assembly.

2. A State which is not a member of the United Nations may bring to the attention of the Security Council or the General Assembly any dispute to which it is a party, if it accepts in advance, for the purposes of the dispute, the obligations of pacific settlement provided in the Charter.

3. The proceedings of the General Assembly in respect of matters brought to its attention under this article will be subject to the provisions of Art. 11 and 12 (see page 20).

CHAPTER 7
Action with Respect to Threats to the Peace, Breaches of the Peace and Acts of Aggression

Art. 39. The Security Council shall determine the existence of any threat to the peace, breach of the peace, or act of aggression, and shall make recommendations, or decide what measures shall be taken in accordance with Art. 41 and 42, to maintain or restore international peace and security.

Art. 40. In order to prevent an aggravation of the situation, the Security Council may, before making the recommendations or deciding upon the measures provided for in Art. 41, call upon the parties concerned to comply with such provisional measures as it deems necessary or desirable. Such provisional measures shall be without prejudice to the rights, claims, or position of the parties concerned. The Security Council shall duly take account of failure to comply with such provisional measures.

Art. 41. The Security Council may decide what measures not involving the use of armed force are to be employed to give effect to its decisions, and may call upon members of the United Nations to apply such measures. These may include complete or partial interruption of economic relations and of rail, sea, air, postal, telegraphic, radio, and other means of communication, and the severance of diplomatic relations.

Art. 42. Should the Security Council consider that measures provided for in Art. 41 would be inadequate, or have proved to be inadequate, it may take such action by air, sea, or land forces as may be necessary to maintain or restore international peace and security. Such action may include demonstrations, blockade, and other operations by air, sea, or land forces of members of the United Nations.

Art. 43. 1. All members of the United Nations, in order to contribute to the maintenance of international peace and security, undertake to make available to the Security Council, on its call and in accordance with a special agreement or agreements, armed forces, assistance, and facilities, including rights of passage, necessary for the purpose of maintaining international peace and security.

2. Such agreement or agreements shall govern the numbers and types of forces, their degree of readiness and general location, and the nature of the facilities and assistance to be provided.

3. The agreement or agreements shall be negotiated as soon as possible on the initiative of the Security Council. They shall be concluded between the Security Council and member States or between the Security Council and groups of member States, and shall be subject to ratification by the signatory States.

Art. 45. In order to enable the United Nations to take urgent military measures, members shall hold immediately available national air force contingents for combined international enforcement action. The strength and degree of readiness of these contingents, and plans for their combined action, shall be determined, within the limits laid down in the special agreement or agreements referred to in Art. 43, by the Security Council with the assistance of the Military Staff Committee.

Art. 48. 1. The action required to carry out the decisions of the Security Council for the maintenance of international peace and security shall be taken by all the members of the United Nations, or by some of them, as the Security Council may determine.

2. Such decisions shall be carried out by the members of the United Nations directly and through their action in the appropriate international agencies of which they are members.

Art. 50. If preventive or enforcement measures against any State are taken by the Security Council, any other State, whether a member of the United Nations or not, which finds itself confronted with special economic problems arising from the carrying out of those measures, shall have the right to consult the Security Council with regard to a solution of those problems.

Art. 51. Nothing in the present Charter shall impair the inherent right of individual or collective self-defense, if an armed attack occurs against a member of the organization, until the Security Council has taken the measures necessary to maintain international peace and security. Measures taken by members in the exercise of this right of self-defense shall be immediately reported to the Security Council and shall not in any way affect the authority and responsibility of the Security Council to take at any time such action as it may deem necessary in order to maintain or restore international peace and security.

CHAPTER 8
Regional Arrangements

Art. 52. 1. Nothing in the present Charter precludes the existence of regional arrangements or agencies for dealing with such matters relating to the maintenance of international peace and security as are appropriate for regional action, provided that such arrangements or agencies and their activities are consistent with the purposes and principles of the organization.

2. The members of the United Nations entering into such arrangements or constituting such agencies shall make every effort to achieve peaceful settlement of local disputes through such regional arrangements or agencies before referring them to the Security Council.

3. The Security Council should encourage the development of peaceful settlement of local disputes through such regional arrangements or agencies either on the initiative of the States concerned or by reference from the Security Council.

4. This Article in no way impairs the application of Art. 34 and 35.

Art. 53. 1. The Security Council shall, where appropriate, utilize such arrangements or agencies for enforcement action under its authority. But no enforcement action shall be taken under regional arrangements or by regional agencies without the authorization of the Security Council, with the exception of measures against any enemy State, as described below, or in regional arrangements directed against renewal of aggressive policy on the part of any such State, until such time as the organization may, on request of the governments concerned, be charged with the responsibility for preventing further aggression by such a State.

2. The term "enemy State" applies to any State which during the second World War has been an enemy of any signatory of the Charter.

CHAPTER 9
International Economic and Social Co-operation

Art. 55. With a view to the creation of conditions of stability and well-being which are necessary for peaceful and friendly relations among nations, based on respect for the principle of equal rights and self-determination of peoples, the United Nations shall promote:

(*a*) Higher standards of living, full employment, and conditions of economic and social progress and development;

(*b*) Solutions of international economic, social, health, and related problems and international cultural and educational co-operation; and

(*c*) Universal respect for, and observance of, human rights and fundamental freedoms for all without distinction as to race, sex, language, or religion.

Chapter 10 gives details of the composition, functions and powers of, and procedure in the Economic and Social Council (see page 124). Under the amendments to the Charter of Aug. 31, 1965, the membership of the Council was raised from 18 to 27. [*21057A*]

CHAPTER 11
Declaration Regarding Non-Self-Governing Territories

Art. 73. Members of the United Nations which have or assume responsibilities for the administration of territories whose peoples have not yet attained a full measure of self-government recognize the principle that the interests of the inhabitants of these territories are paramount, and accept as a sacred trust the obligation to promote to the utmost the well-being of the inhabitants of these territories, and, to this end:

(*a*) to ensure, with due respect for the culture of the peoples concerned, their political, economic, social, and educational advancement, their just treatment, and their protection against abuses;

(*b*) to develop self-government, to take due account of the political aspirations of the peoples, and to assist them in the progressive development of their free political institutions, according to the particular circumstances of each territory and its peoples and their varying stages of advancement;

(*c*) to further international peace and security;

(*d*) to promote constructive measures of development, to encourage research, and to co-operate with one another and with appropriate international bodies with a view to the practical achievement of the social, economic, and scientific purpose set forth in this paragraph; and

(*e*) to transmit regularly to the Secretary-General for information purposes, subject to such limitations as security and constitutional considerations may require, statistical and other information of a technical nature relating to economic, social, and educational conditions in the territories for which they are respectively responsible, other than those territories to which Chapters 12 and 13 apply.

CHAPTER 12
International Trusteeship System

Art. 75. The United Nations shall establish under its authority an international trusteeship system for the administration and supervision of such territories as may be placed thereunder by subsequent individual agreements. These territories are hereafter referred to as 'trust territories.'

Art. 76. The basic objectives of the trusteeship system shall be:

(*a*) to further international peace and security;

(*b*) to promote the political, economic, social, and educational advancement of the inhabitants of the trust territories, and their progressive development toward self-government or independence as may be appropriate to the particular circumstances of each territory and its peoples and the freely expressed wishes of the peoples concerned, and as may be provided by the terms of each trusteeship agreement;

(*c*) to encourage respect for human rights and for fundamental freedoms for all without distinction as to race, sex, language, or religion, and to encourage recognition of the interdependence of the peoples of the world; and

(*d*) to ensure equal treatment in social, economic, and commercial matters for all members of the United Nations and their nationals, and also equal treatment for the latter in the administration of justice, without prejudice to the attainment of the foregoing objectives. . . .

Art. 77. 1. The trusteeship system shall apply to such territories in the following categories as may be placed thereunder by means of trusteeship agreements:

(*a*) Territories now held under mandate;

(*b*) Territories which may be detached from enemy States as a result of the second World War; and

(*c*) Territories voluntarily placed under the system by States responsible for their administration.

2. It will be a matter for subsequent agreement as to which territories in the foregoing categories will be brought under the trusteeship system and upon what terms.

Art. 78. The trusteeship system shall not apply to territories which have become members of the United Nations, relationship among which should be based on respect for the principle of sovereign equality.

Art. 79. The terms of trusteeship for each territory to be placed under the trusteeship system, including any alteration or amendment, shall be agreed upon by the States directly concerned, including the mandatory power in the case of territories held under mandate by a member of the United Nations. . . .

Chapter 13 deals with the composition, functions and powers of, and procedure in the Trusteeship Council (see page 23).

Chapter 14 deals with the International Court of Justice (see page 25).

Chapter 15 deals with the Secretariat and includes details of the functions of the Secretary-General (see page 26).

Chapter 16 contains miscellaneous provisions, including:

Art. 103. In the event of a conflict between the obligations of the members of the United Nations under the Charter and any other international obligations to which they are subject, their obligations under the Charter shall prevail.

Art. 105. 1. The organization shall enjoy in the territory of each of its members such privileges and immunities as are necessary for the fulfilment of its purposes.

2. Representatives of the members of the United Nations and officials of the organization shall similarly enjoy such privileges and immunities as are necessary for the independent exercise of their functions in connection with the organization.

Chapter 17 provides for certain transitional security arrangements.

Chapter 18 gives the procedure for the adoption of amendments to the Charter, and provides for the convening of a conference for the purpose of reviewing the Charter.

Chapter 19 contains provisions on the ratification and signature of the Charter. [7425A]

The principles of the U.N. Charter incorporated those of the Pact of Paris (or Briand-Kellogg Pact), proposed by the United States, signed in Paris on Aug. 27, 1928, accepted by 15 Governments and subsequently ratified by 63 States.

This Pact consisted of two paragraphs as follows:

Art. 1. The High Contracting Parties solemnly declare in the name of their peoples that they condemn recourse to war for the solution of international controversies, and renounce it as an instrument of national policy in their relations with one another.

Art. 2. The High Contracting Parties agree that the settlement or solution of all disputes or conflicts of whatever nature or of whatever origin they may be, which may arise among them, shall never be sought except by pacific means.

The Paris Pact was binding only upon the parties to it.

THE CONVENTION ON THE PREVENTION AND PUNISHMENT OF THE CRIME OF GENOCIDE

This Convention, adopted by the U.N. General Assembly on Dec. 9, 1948, provided *inter alia* as follows:

Art. 1. The Contracting Parties confirm that genocide, whether committed in time of peace or of war, is a crime under international law which they undertake to prevent and punish.

Art. 2. Genocide means any of the following acts committed with intent to destroy, in whole or part, a national, ethnical, racial, or religious group:

(*a*) Killing members of the group;

(*b*) Causing serious bodily or mental harm to members of the group;

(*c*) Deliberately inflicting on the group conditions of life calculated to bring about its physical destruction in whole or part;

(d) Imposing measures intended to prevent births within the group;

(e) Forcibly transferring children of the group to another group.

Art. 3. The following acts shall be punishable:

(a) Genocide;

(b) Conspiracy to commit genocide;

(c) Direct and public incitement to commit genocide;

(d) Attempt to commit genocide;

(e) Complicity in genocide.

Art. 4. Persons committing genocide or any of the other acts enumerated in Art. 3 shall be punished, whether they are constitutionally responsible rulers, public officials, or private individuals.

Art. 5. The Contracting Parties undertake to enact, in accordance with their respective constitutions, the necessary legislation to give effect to the provisions of the Convention, and, in particular, to provide effective penalties for persons guilty of genocide or any of the other acts enumerated in Art. 3.

Art. 6. Persons charged with genocide or any of the other acts enumerated in Art. 3 shall be tried by a competent tribunal of the State in the territory of which the act was committed, or by such international penal tribunal as may have jurisdiction with respect to such Contracting Parties as shall have accepted the jurisdiction of such tribunal.

Art. 7. Genocide and the other acts enumerated in Art. 3 shall not be considered as political crimes for the purpose of extradition. The Contracting Parties pledge themselves in such cases to grant extradition in accordance with their laws and treaties in force.

Art. 8. Any Contracting Party may call upon the competent organs of the United Nations to take such action under the U.N. Charter as they consider appropriate for the prevention and suppression of acts of genocide or any of the other acts enumerated in Art. 3.

Art. 9. Disputes between the Contracting Parties relating to the interpretation, application, or fulfilment of the Convention, including those relating to the responsibility of a State for genocide or any of the other acts enumerated in Art. 3, shall be submitted to the International Court of Justice at the request of any of the parties to the dispute. [*Page 9700*]

The Convention came into force on Jan. 12, 1951. [*11336C*]

THE UNIVERSAL DECLARATION OF HUMAN RIGHTS AND THE COVENANTS ON HUMAN RIGHTS

The U.N. General Assembly on Dec. 10, 1948, adopted, by 48 votes to none (with 8 abstentions by the Communist member-States, South Africa, and Saudi Arabia), the Universal Declaration of Human Rights, the first international Bill of Rights in human history.

The Declaration is worded as follows:

PREAMBLE

Whereas recognition of the inherent dignity and of the equal and inalienable rights of all members of the human family is the foundation of freedom, justice, and peace in the world;

whereas disregard and contempt for human rights have resulted in barbarous acts which have outraged the conscience of mankind, and the advent of a world in which human beings shall enjoy freedom of speech and belief and freedom from fear and want has been proclaimed as the highest aspiration of the common people;

whereas it is essential, if man is not to be compelled to have recourse, as a last resort, to rebellion against tyranny and oppression, that human rights should be protected by the rule of the law;

whereas it is essential to promote the development of friendly relations between nations;

whereas the people of the United Nations have in the Charter reaffirmed their faith in fundamental human rights, in the dignity and worth of the human person, and in the equal rights of men and women, and have determined to promote social progress and better standards of life in larger freedom;

whereas Member-States have pledged themselves to achieve, in co-operation with the United Nations, the promotion of universal respect for and observance of human rights and fundamental freedoms;

whereas a common understanding of these rights and freedoms is of the greatest importance for the full realization of this pledge;

The General Assembly proclaims this Universal Declaration of Human Rights as a common standard of achievement for all peoples and nations, to the end that every individual and every organ of society, keeping this Declaration constantly in mind, shall strive by teaching and education to promote respect for these rights and freedoms, and by progressive measures, national and international, to secure their universal and effective recognition and observance, both among the peoples of Member-States themselves and among the peoples of territories under their jurisdiction.

Art. 1. All human beings are born free and equal in dignity and rights. They are endowed with reason and conscience, and should act towards one another in a spirit of brotherhood.

Art. 2. Everyone is entitled to all the rights and freedoms set forth in this Declaration, without distinction of any kind, such as race, color, sex, language, religion, political or other opinion, national or social origin, property, birth, or other status.

Furthermore, no distinction shall be made on the basis of the political, jurisdictional, or international status of the country or territory to which a person belongs, whether it be independent, trust, non-self-governing or under any other limitation of sovereignty.

Art. 3. Everyone has the right to life, liberty, and security of person.

Art. 4. No one shall be held in slavery or servitude; slavery and the slave trade shall be prohibited in all their forms.

Art. 5. No one shall be subjected to torture or to cruel, inhuman, or degrading treatment or punishment.

Art. 6. Everyone has the right to recognition everywhere as a person before the law.

Art. 7. All are equal before the law, and are entitled without any discrimination to equal protection of the law. All are entitled to equal protection against any discrimination in violation of this Declaration and against any incitement to such discrimination.

Art. 8. Everyone has the right to an effective remedy by the competent national tribunals for acts violating the fundamental rights granted him by the Constitution or by law.

Art. 9. No one shall be subjected to arbitrary arrest, detention, or exile.

Art. 10. Everyone is entitled in full equality to a fair and public hearing by an independent and impartial tribunal, in the determination of his rights and obligations and of any criminal charge against him.

Art. 11. (1) Everyone charged with a penal offense has the right to be presumed innocent until proved guilty according to law in a public trial at which he has had all the guarantees necessary for his defense.

(2) No one shall be held guilty of any penal offense on account of any act or omission which did not constitute a penal offense, under national or international law, at the time when it was committed. Nor shall a heavier penalty be imposed than the one that was applicable at the time the penal offense was committed.

Art. 12. No one shall be subjected to arbitrary interference with his privacy, family, home, or correspondence, nor to attacks upon his honor and reputation. Everyone has the right to the protection of the law against such interference or attacks.

Art. 13. (1) Everyone has the right to freedom of movement and residence within the borders of each State.

(2) Everyone has the right to leave any country, including his own, and to return to his country.

Art. 14. (1) Everyone has the right to seek and enjoy in other countries asylum from persecution.

(2) This right may not be invoked in the case of prosecutions genuinely arising from non-political crimes or from acts contrary to the purposes and principles of the United Nations.

Art. 15. (1) Everyone has the right to a nationality.

(2) No one shall be arbitrarily deprived of his nationality nor denied the right to change his nationality.

Art. 16. (1) Men and women of full age, without any limitation due to race, nationality, or religion, have the right to marry and to found a family. They are entitled to equal rights as to marriage, during marriage, and at its dissolution.

(2) Marriage shall be entered into only with the free and full consent of the intending spouses.

(3) The family is the natural and fundamental group unit of society, and is entitled to protection by society and the State.

Art. 17. (1) Everyone has the right to own property alone as well as in association with others.

(2) No one shall be arbitrarily deprived of his property.

Art. 18. Everyone has the right to freedom of thought, conscience, and religion. This right includes freedom to change his religion or belief, and freedom, either alone or in community with others, and in public or private, to manifest his religion or belief in teaching, practice, worship, and observance.

Art. 19. Everyone has the right to freedom of opinion and expression. This right includes freedom to hold opinions without interference and to seek, receive, and impart information and ideas through any media and regardless of frontiers.

Art. 20. (1) Everyone has the right to freedom of peaceful assembly and association.

(2) No one may be compelled to belong to an association.

Art. 21. (1) Everyone has the right to take part in the Government of his country, directly or through freely chosen representatives.

(2) Everyone has the right of equal access to public service in his country.

(3) The will of the people shall be the basis of the authority of Government; this will shall be expressed in periodic and genuine elections which shall be by universal and equal suffrage, and shall be held by secret vote or by equivalent free voting procedures.

Art. 22. Everyone, as a member of society, has the right to social security and is entitled to the realization, through national effort and international co-operation and in accordance with the organization and resources of each State, of the economic, social, and cultural rights indispensable for his dignity and the free development of his personality.

Art. 23. (1) Everyone has the right to work, to free choice of employment, to just and favorable conditions of work, and to protection against unemployment.

(2) Everyone, without any discrimination, has the right to equal pay for equal work.

(3) Everyone who works has the right to just and favorable remuneration, ensuring for himself and his family an existence worthy of human dignity, and supplemented, if necessary, by other means of social protection.

(4) Everyone has the right to form and to join trade unions for the protection of his interests.

Art. 24. Everyone has the right to rest and leisure, including reasonable limitation of working hours and periodic holidays with pay.

Art. 25. (1) Everyone has the right to a standard of living adequate for the health and well-being of himself and his family, including food, clothing, housing, and medical care and necessary social services, and the right to security in the event of unemployment, sickness, disability, widowhood, old age, or other lack of livelihood in circumstances beyond his control.

(2) Motherhood and childhood are entitled to special care and assistance. All children, whether born in or out of wedlock, shall enjoy the same social protection.

Art. 26. (1) Everyone has the right to education. Education shall be free, at least in the elementary and fundamental stages. Elementary education shall be compulsory. Technical and professional education shall be made generally available, and higher education shall be equally accessible to all on the basis of merit.

(2) Education shall be directed to the full development of the human personality and to the strengthening of respect for human rights and fundamental freedoms. It shall promote understanding, tolerance, and friendship among all nations, racial or religious groups, and shall further the activities of the United Nations for the maintenance of peace.

(3) Parents have a prior right to choose the kind of education that shall be given to their children.

Art. 27. (1) Everyone has the right freely to participate in the cultural life of the community, to enjoy the arts, and to share in scientific advancement and its benefits.

(2) Everyone has the right to the protection of the moral and material interests resulting from any scientific, literary, or artistic production of which he is the author.

Art. 28. Everyone is entitled to a social and international order in which the rights and freedoms set forth in this Declaration can be fully realized.

Art. 29. (1) Everyone has duties to the community in which alone the free and full development of his personality is possible.

(2) In the exercise of his rights and freedoms, everyone shall be subject only to such limitations as are determined

by law solely for the purpose of securing due recognition and respect for the rights and freedoms of others, and of meeting the just requirements of morality, public order, and the general welfare in a democratic society.

(3) These rights and freedoms may in no case be exercised contrary to the purposes and freedoms set forth herein.

Art. 30. Nothing in this Declaration may be interpreted as implying for any State, group, or person any right to engage in any activity or to perform any act aimed at the destruction of any of the rights and freedoms set forth herein. [*9699A*]

In implementation of the Declaration, the U.N. General Assembly unanimously adopted, on Dec. 13, 1967, (*a*) an International Covenant on Economic, Social, and Cultural Rights; (*b*) an International Covenant on Civil and Political Rights, and (*c*) an Optional Protocol to the latter.

The Covenant under (*a*), consisting of 31 articles, recognized, *inter alia,* the right to work, to social security, to adequate standards of living, to freedom from hunger, and to health and education. It provided that States parties to the Covenant would report to the U.N. Economic and Social Council on the measures adopted and progress made toward the realization of these rights.

The Covenant under (*b*), consisting of 53 articles, provided, *inter alia,* for the right to life, liberty, security, and privacy; for the right to a fair trial and to freedom from arbitrary arrest; for freedom of thought, conscience, and religion; and for freedom of association. Other Articles provide for freedom of consent to marriage, the protection of children, and the preservation of the cultural, religious, and linguistic heritage of minorities. It was laid down that the implementation of this Covenant would be supervised by a Human Rights Committee consisting of 18 persons elected by the States acceding to the Covenant.

The Optional Protocol empowered the Human Rights Committee to receive and consider communications from individuals claiming to be victims of a violation by a State party to the Covenant of any of the rights set forth in the Covenant. [*21930A*]

Arising out of the Declaration of Human Rights, a Convention on the Nationality of Married Women was approved by the U.N. General Assembly in 1957 against the votes of Egypt and Syria and with 24 abstentions (including the U.S.A.). [*Page 15509*]

THE DECLARATION ON THE ELIMINATION OF DISCRIMINATION AGAINST WOMEN

The U.N. General Assembly on Nov. 7, 1967, adopted by 111 votes to nil, with 11 countries absent, a Declaration on the Elimination of Discrimination against Women.

The Declaration proclaimed *inter alia* that women should have equal rights with men in the political sphere and in the field of civil law, in economic and social life, and in education at all levels. It called for the abolition of all laws and customs which had the effect of discriminating against women and of all practices based on the idea of the inferiority of women; for the prohibition of child marriage and of betrothal of girls before puberty; and for measures to combat traffic in women and exploitation of prostitution. Among rights enumerated were those of a wife to retain her nationality if married to an alien; to have free choice of a husband; and to enjoy equality of treatment with men in respect of work of equal value. [*22584A*]

OTHER U.N. CONVENTIONS

Supplementary Convention on the Abolition of Slavery, the Slave Trade, and Institutions and Practices Similar to Slavery

A United Nations convention on slavery, based on the 1951 report of a 4-member committee appointed by the Secretary-General in 1949 at the request of the Economic and Social Council, was designed to supplement a League of Nations convention of 1926. The Supplementary Convention on the Abolition of Slavery, the Slave Trade, and Institutions and Practices Similar to Slavery was adopted and opened for signature in September 1956 and has been in force since April 30, 1957. By the end of October 1967, 70 nations had ratified or acceded to it.

The U.N. convention differs from the earlier one in dealing with a number of institutions and practices similar to slavery in their effect. The institutions and practices outlawed by the 1956 Convention are debt bondage, serfdom, marriage by payment or inheritance, and the exploitation of child labor.

The convention advocates the prescribing of minimum ages of marriage, and the registration of marriages. It also provides for the punishment of persons participating in the slave trade, and of persons guilty of enslaving another person or of inducing another person to give himself or a dependent into slavery. Provision is made for the co-operation of States parties to the convention to give effect to its provisions, and for the communication to the U.N. Secretary-General of laws, regulations, and administrative measures enacted or put into effect to implement the provisions of the convention. The convention applies to all non-self-governing, trust, colonial, and other non-metropolitan territories for the international relations of which any State party is responsible.

Conventions on the Law of the Sea

A U.N. Conference on the Law of the Sea held in Geneva from Feb. 24 to April 28, 1958, adopted, after preparation by the International Law Commission, four Conventions and a Protocol on compulsory settlement of disputes, but reached no agreement on the maximum width of territorial waters and the maximum limits of exclusive fishing rights.

(a) The *Convention on the Territorial Sea and the Contiguous Zone* defined the "Territorial Sea"; laid down the right of "innocent passage" through the territorial sea; limited the "contiguous zone" of the high seas to an area up to 12 miles from the shore baselines; and authorized the coastal State to prevent infringements of its Customs, fiscal, immigration, or sanitary regulations committed within its territory or territorial sea and to punish such infringements.

(b) The *Convention on the High Seas* proclaimed the freedom of the high seas (including the freedom to fly over them) and the right of land-locked States to have free access to the sea; granted each State the right to determine conditions for the grant of its nationality to ships; gave immunity from the jurisdiction of any State other than the flag State to warships and other non-commercial Government vessels on the high seas; and enjoined States to ensure safety at sea, to prevent slave trade and piracy, and to prevent pollution of the sea.

(c) The *Convention on Fishing and Conservation of the Living Resources of the High Seas* provided *inter alia* for agreement on conservation measures and for arbitration procedure in the event of disputes.

(d) The *Convention on the Continental Shelf* gave coastal States exclusive rights to exploit universal and other non-living resources as well as "sedentary" living organisms (e.g. oysters) of the continental shelf, i.e. "the seabed and subsoil of the submarine areas adjacent to the coast, but outside the area of the territorial sea, up to the point where the waters above are 200 meters deep, or beyond that limit if the depth allows exploitation of natural resources." The boundary of the coastal shelf adjacent to any State lying opposite another State on the same shelf was to be determined by mutual agreement or, failing such agreement, would be the median line.

(e) The *Protocol on Settlement of Disputes* provided for compulsory jurisdiction of the International Court of Justice in disputes arising out of the interpretation or application of any Convention on the Law of the Sea (except as covered by the arbitration procedure under (c) above), as well as for arbitration or conciliation where both parties agreed to this procedure instead of resorting to the International Court of Justice. [16411A]

Convention on the Non-Applicability of Statutory Limitations to War Crimes and Crimes Against Humanity

A *Convention on the Non-Applicability of Statutory Limitations to War Crimes and Crimes against Humanity,* drafted in the Third (Social, Humanitarian, and Cultural) Committee of the U. N. General Assembly, was adopted by the Assembly on Nov. 26, 1968, by 58 votes to 7 (Australia, El Salvador, Honduras, Portugal, South Africa, United Kingdom, and United States), with 36 abstentions.

In its Preamble, the Convention affirmed "the principle that there is no period of limitation for war crimes and crimes against humanity," and in one of its Articles the States parties to the Convention undertook "to ensure that statutory or other limitations shall not apply to the prosecution and punishment" of such crimes.

The Convention entered into force on Nov. 11, 1970, after ratification by 10 countries (all of them Communist States). [23196; 24296D]

Convention on the Prohibition and Destruction of Bacteriological Weapons

The U. N. General Assembly adopted on Dec. 16, 1971, by 110 votes to none, with 1 abstention, a resolution commending for signature a draft *Convention on the Prohibition of the Development, Production, and Stockpiling of Bacteriological (Biological) and Toxin Weapons and on their Destruction,* which had been submitted to it by the Conference of the Committee on Disarmament.

The convention provided *inter alia:*

Art. 1. Each State party to this convention undertakes never in any circumstances to develop, produce, stockpile, or otherwise acquire or retain:
(a) Microbial or other biological agents or toxins, whatever their origin or method of production, of types and in quantities that have no justification for prophylactic, protective, or other peaceful purposes;
(b) Weapons, equipment, or means of delivery designed to use such agents or toxins for hostile purposes or in armed conflict.
Art. 2. Each State party to this convention undertakes to destroy, or to divert to peaceful purposes, as soon as possible but not later than nine months after the entry into force of the convention, all agents, toxins, weapons, equipment, and means of delivery specified in Article 1 . . . , which are in its possession or under its jurisdiction or control. In imple-

menting the provisions of this Article all necessary precautions shall be observed to protect populations and the environment.

Art. 8. Nothing in this convention shall be interpreted as in any way limiting or detracting from the obligations assumed by any State under the Protocol . . . signed at Geneva on June 17, 1925.

The Convention was signed on April 10, 1972, by the Soviet Union, Britain, and the United States, about 70 other countries signing on the same day. [252374]

THE GENERAL ASSEMBLY

The General Assembly, the main deliberative organ of the United Nations, is composed of delegations representing all the member countries of the U.N. Each delegation comprises not more than five full representatives with their five deputies and any number of advisers and experts.

The General Assembly meets regularly once a year in ordinary session, but a special session may be convened at the request of the Security Council or of a majority of Assembly members.

Each member has one vote. Decisions on important questions are adopted by a two-thirds majority; other questions are decided by a simple majority. The decisions of the General Assembly are binding only for those States which have voted for them.

The General Assembly is empowered to discuss and make recommendations on all questions which fall within the scope of the U.N. Charter. Under Article 12 of the Charter, however, "while the Security Council is exercising in respect of any dispute or situation the functions assigned to it in the present Charter, the General Assembly shall not make any recommendations with regard to that dispute or situation unless the Security Council so requests." On Nov. 3, 1950, the plenary session of the General Assembly adopted a plan of the U.S. Government (the "United Action for Peace" Resolution), by which, at the request of any seven members of the Security Council, the General Assembly can be called in emergency session if the Security Council is prevented, through exercise of the veto, from taking action in any case "where there appears to be a threat to the peace, breach of the peace or act of aggression." [11069A]

The General Assembly is led by a President, who is elected for each session, and a number of Vice Presidents.

Committees

The seven main committees of the General Assembly, on which all U.N. members have the right of representation, are:

(1) Political and Security Committee.
(2) Economic and Financial Committee.
(3) Social, Humanitarian, and Cultural Committee.
(4) Trusteeship Committee.
(5) Administrative and Budgetary Committee.
(6) Legal Committee.
(7) Special Political Committee (set up to aid the first Committee).

These committees consider questions referred to them by the General Assembly, and prepare draft resolutions for submission to the Assembly.

There are two procedural committees, the 25-man General (Steering) Committee and the 9-man Credentials Committee, and two principal standing committees, these being a 12-man Advisory Committee on Administrative and Budgetary Questions and a 10-man Committee on Contributions.

Under the American "United Action for Peace" Resolution of Nov. 3, 1950 (see above), two special committees were set up: a *Peace Observation Commission,* whose 14 members include the 5 permanent members of the Security Council; and a 14-member *Collective Measures Committee* to study "the measures which might be used and the resources, including armed forces, which are or might be made available to the United Nations in order to maintain international peace and security."

Another permanent subsidiary committee is the 25-member *International Law Commission,* which meets annually to discuss the development and codification of international law. The General Assembly also sets up *ad hoc* committees from time to time in accordance with the world situation.

Nuclear and Conventional Disarmament

Since 1946 the United Nations has created a series of commissions and committees to consider the question of world disarmament.

The first of these, the *Atomic Energy Commission,* was approved by the General Assembly in January 1946. Its creation was followed, a year later, by the setting up of a *Commission for Conventional Armaments* under a resolution of the Security Council passed on Feb. 13, 1947. These two commissions were superseded by a new Disarmament Commission approved by a plenary session of the General Assembly in January 1952. Its 12 members were the 11 nations represented in the Security Council together with Canada.

In November 1957 the General Assembly approved the enlargement of the Disarmament Commission from 12 to 25 members, and a year later, in November 1958, the Commission was reconstituted to in-

THE UNITED NATIONS

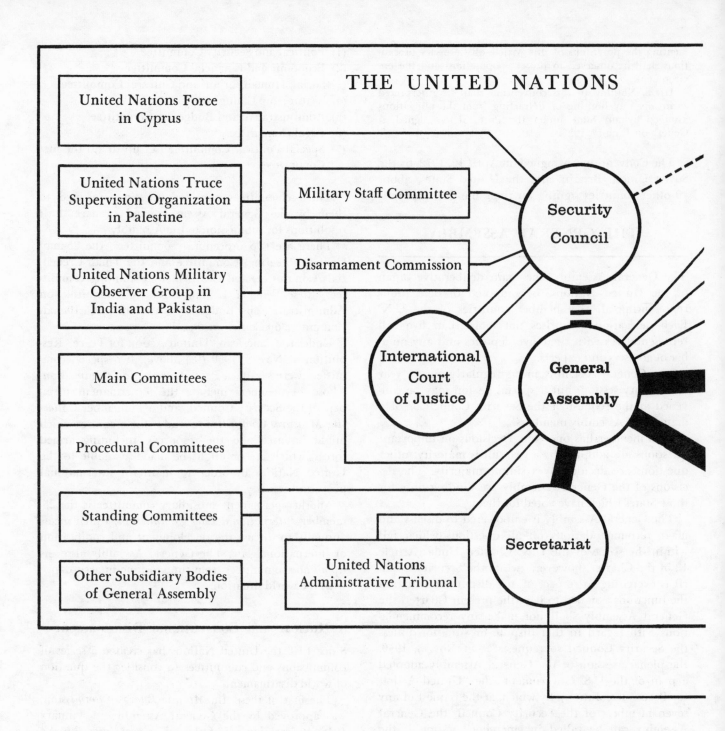

United Nations Force in Cyprus

United Nations Truce Supervision Organization in Palestine

United Nations Military Observer Group in India and Pakistan

Main Committees

Procedural Committees

Standing Committees

Other Subsidiary Bodies of General Assembly

Military Staff Committee

Disarmament Commission

United Nations Administrative Tribunal

Security Council

International Court of Justice

General Assembly

Secretariat

THE SPECIALIZED

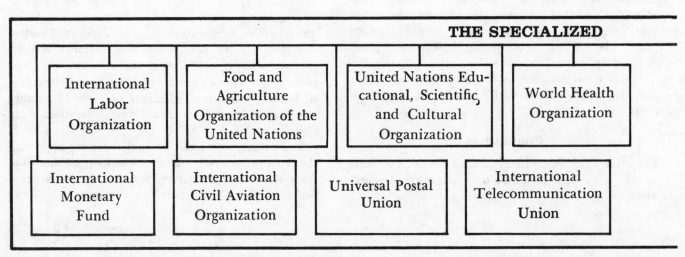

International Labor Organization

Food and Agriculture Organization of the United Nations

United Nations Educational, Scientific, and Cultural Organization

World Health Organization

International Monetary Fund

International Civil Aviation Organization

Universal Postal Union

International Telecommunication Union

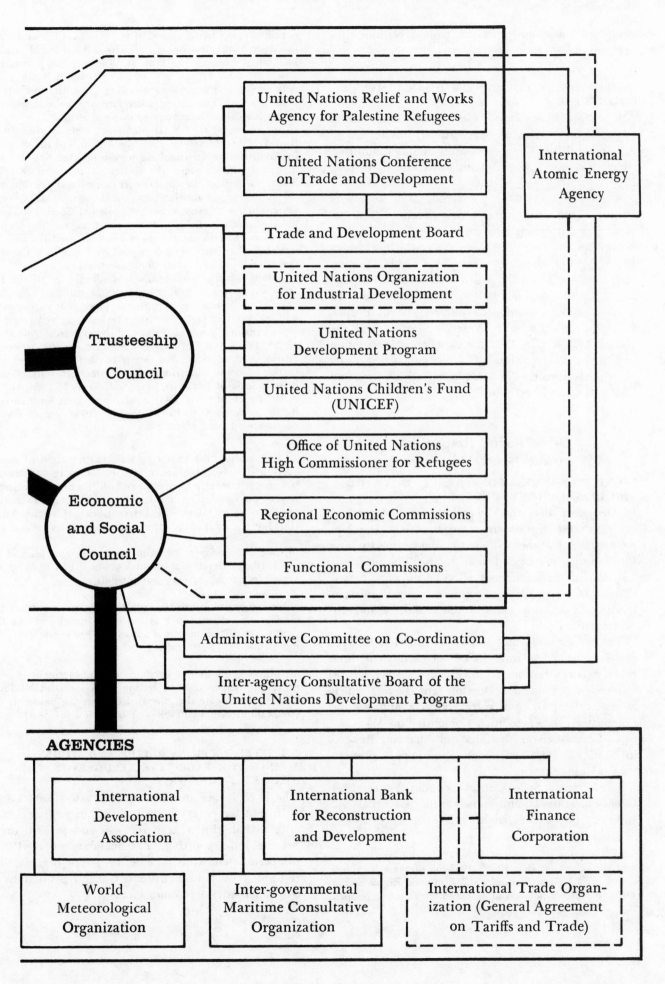

United Nations Relief and Works Agency for Palestine Refugees

United Nations Conference on Trade and Development

Trade and Development Board

United Nations Organization for Industrial Development

United Nations Development Program

United Nations Children's Fund (UNICEF)

Office of United Nations High Commissioner for Refugees

Regional Economic Commissions

Functional Commissions

International Atomic Energy Agency

Trusteeship Council

Economic and Social Council

Administrative Committee on Co-ordination

Inter-agency Consultative Board of the United Nations Development Program

AGENCIES

International Development Association

International Bank for Reconstruction and Development

International Finance Corporation

World Meteorological Organization

Inter-governmental Maritime Consultative Organization

International Trade Organization (General Agreement on Tariffs and Trade)

clude all the members of the United Nations, this being its present form.

EVOLUTION OF THE GENEVA DISARMAMENT COMMITTEE

A *10-Power Disarmament Committee,* comprising 5 Eastern and 5 Western bloc nations, was set up in September 1959. The negotiations of this committee, which was not a U.N. organ, broke down in June 1960.

A joint resolution of the U.S.A. and the Soviet Union on the setting up of a new *18-nation Disarmament Committee* was adopted by the General Assembly on Dec. 20, 1961. The Committee, which is formed by 5 NATO countries (Britain, Canada, France, Italy, and the U.S.A.), 5 Warsaw Pact countries (Bulgaria, Czechoslovakia, Poland, Romania, and the U.S.S.R.) and 8 uncommitted countries (Brazil, Burma, Ethiopia, India, Mexico, Nigeria, Sweden, and the United Arab Republic), is in almost continuous session in Geneva. France, although a member of the Committee, has boycotted its work from its inception, and takes no part in its activities.

Other Bodies Responsible to the General Assembly

1. UNITED NATIONS CONFERENCE ON TRADE AND DEVELOPMENT (UNCTAD)

In December 1964 the General Assembly agreed to establish the U.N. Conference on Trade and Development, which had met in Geneva from March to June 1964, as one of its permanent organs. The principal function of the conference is to encourage international trade, particularly between countries at different levels of development and with different social and economic systems.

The conference, which has its headquarters in Geneva, is convened at intervals of not more than three years. Between sessions its work is carried out by the 55-member Trade and Development Board, which meets at least twice a year. Four committees—the Committee of Commodities, Committee on Manufactures, Committee on Invisibles and Financing Related to Trade, and Committee on Shipping—implement the work of the Board.

The 77 developing countries represented at the 1964 Geneva meetings became known as the "Group of 77," and this group later expanded to 96 members.

At a meeting of Ministers from 71 developing countries held in Algiers on Oct. 10–24, 1967, 63 of these Ministers signed the "Algiers Charter of the Economic Rights of the Third World," which was to be presented to the developed

nations. The Charter stated that between 1953 and 1966 the share of the developing countries in total world exports had fallen from 27 per cent to 19.3, and the purchasing power of their export earnings by one-tenth, while their debt service payments were equaling the entire amount of loans granted. The Charter therefore urged the implementation of a comprehensive programme of action.

At the second UNCTAD conference, held in New Delhi from Feb. 1 to March 29, 1968, the demands of the developing countries for increased aid were supported by the Communist countries (with the Soviet Minister for Foreign Trade calling on the capitalist countries and the international lending institutions to provide more aid as "compensation for damage caused by colonial domination and neo-colonialist policies"). Representatives of the United States and Britain, on the other hand, stressed the difficulties of further increasing their countries' large aid commitments in times of balance-of-payments crises.

Among the numerous resolutions adopted by the conference was one setting a new target for transfers from developed to developing countries at 1 per cent of the gross national product (as against the previously agreed target of 1 per cent of the national income). Newly elected members of the Trade and Development Board comprised representatives of 22 African and Asian countries, 18 developed market-economy countries, 9 Latin American nations, and 6 from Socialist countries. [*20581A; 22564A; 22893A*]

At the third UNCTAD conference, held in Santiago (Chile) between April 13 and May 21, 1972, some 40 resolutions were adopted, including:

(*a*) one urging "the widest possible participation of developed and developing countries" in "a more satisfactory system of monetary co-operation," with strong representation of the developing countries in a proposed "Committee of Twenty" to advise the International Monetary Fund (IMF) on a reform of the international monetary system;

(*b*) one asking for relief, both by donor-countries and by the IMF, for developing countries, which had suffered adverse effects from currency realignments;

(*c*) one containing recommendations for special treatment of 25 countries regarded as the "least developed" of the "third world," i.e. mainly those with a *per capita* gross domestic product of $100 or less; and

(*d*) others containing suggestions on improvements to existing aid systems and on setting up a special UNCTAD body to investigate the effects of debt-service payments on economic growth in developing countries. [*25376A*]

2. UNITED NATIONS RELIEF AND WORKS AGENCY FOR PALESTINE REFUGEES IN THE NEAR EAST (UNRWA)

The U.N. Relief and Works Agency was founded in 1950 as a temporary body to bring immediate assistance to Palestinian Arab refugees and to help them become self-supporting. The mandate of UNRWA has been extended to June 30, 1975. The organization is headed by a Commissioner-General assisted by a 9-member Advisory Commission.

3. UNITED NATIONS COMMISSION FOR THE UNIFICATION AND REHABILITATION OF KOREA (UNCURK)

Established in October 1950, UNCURK was given the task of trying to bring about an independent, democratic and unified Korea. The commission, the members of which are Australia, the Netherlands, Pakistan, the Philippines, Thailand, and Turkey, meets about four times a year. Chile withdrew from UNCURK on Nov. 18, 1970.

THE SECURITY COUNCIL

The Security Council functions continuously, and its decisions are binding on all members of the United Nations. The Council is composed of 15 members, 5 of whom—Britain, China, France, the U.S.S.R., and the U.S.A.—are permanent. The remaining 10 members are elected by the General Assembly, normally to serve a term of two years. Each member-State of the Council holds the Presidency for one month, the rotation following the English alphabetical order.

Each member has one vote. Decisions on important (non-procedural) questions must be carried by 9 affirmative votes, but any one of the permanent members, exercising the right of veto, can prevent the adoption of a decision. Procedural matters may be decided by the affirmative votes of any nine members.

The Security Council has "primary responsibility for the maintenance of international peace and security," and to this end it acts for all U.N. members (Article 24 of the U.N. Charter). The tasks of the Security Council include the pacific settlement of international disputes (Articles 33–38), determination of the existence of any threat to the peace, breach of the peace or act of aggression, and, where necessary, the carrying out of preventive or enforcement measures of a political, economic, or military nature through some or all U.N. members (Articles 39–45). Under Article 26 of the Charter the Security Council is also "responsible for formulating plans . . . for the establishment of a system for the regulation of armaments."

In all questions of a military nature the Council is aided by a Military Staff Committee, consisting of the Chiefs of Staff of the five permanent members of the Security Council.

Peace-Keeping Bodies Responsible to the Security Council

1. UNITED NATIONS TRUCE SUPERVISION ORGANIZATION (UNTSO)

Originally formed to maintain the 1949 Armistice Agreements between Israel on the one hand and the Arab nations of Egypt, Lebanon, Jordan, and Syria on the other, the United Nations Truce Supervision Organization now has the task of supervising the cease-fire line established at the end of the 6-day Arab-Israeli war of June 1967. Its headquarters are in Jerusalem.

2. UNITED NATIONS MILITARY OBSERVER GROUP FOR INDIA AND PAKISTAN (UNMOGIP)

Established in 1949, UNMOGIP is responsible for supervising the Indian-Pakistani cease-fire line along the Kashmir border. The Group is staffed by Military Observers and civilian specialists.

3. UNITED NATIONS COMMAND IN SOUTH KOREA

The United Nations Military Command in Korea was set up in July 1950 to assist the Republic of Korea (South Korea) in defending itself against attack. The U.N. Force originally consisted of troops from 16 nations under the command of the U.S.A., but is now reduced almost entirely to U.S. troops, whose function is to supervise the armistice of July 1953.

4. UNITED NATIONS PEACE-KEEPING FORCE IN CYPRUS (UNFICYP)

The U.N. Force in Cyprus was set up in March 1964, initially for three months. Repeated extensions of the mandate have, however, kept UNFICYP in existence up to the present. Its purpose is to keep the peace between the Greek and Turkish communities in the island.

THE TRUSTEESHIP COUNCIL

The Trusteeship Council, which has its headquarters in New York, is concerned with the supervision of the administration of U.N. Trust Territories. Its objectives are to aid the political, economic, social, and educational development of these territories towards self-government or independence, and to promote the welfare of their inhabitants.

Only two territories still remain under the trusteeship system, these being New Guinea (administered by Australia) and the Trust Territory of the Pacific Islands (administered by the U.S.A.). The 20-year-old U.N. trusteeship agreement on Nauru terminated on Jan. 31, 1968, when the island achieved full independence. [22500A]

The members of the Trusteeship Council are the administering countries, whose membership is permanent, and an equal number of nonadministering countries, who are elected by the General Assembly to serve

Waterloo Local Schools

on the Council for periods of three years. The Council meets annually.

For the supervision of the administration of New Guinea the Trusteeship Council is responsible to the General Assembly, but in the case of the Trust Territory of the Pacific Islands, which has been designated a strategic area, the Council operates under the authority of the Security Council. [22500A]

THE ECONOMIC AND SOCIAL COUNCIL (ECOSOC)

The Economic and Social Council is responsible for co-ordinating the United Nations' policy in the economic, social, cultural, and humanitarian fields.

Its functions are:

(1) to make studies of, and reports and recommendations on, world co-operation in these fields;

(2) to promote the observance and pursuit of human rights and fundamental freedoms for all;

(3) to convene international conferences;

(4) to consult with the Specialized Agencies (see below) and co-ordinate their activities;

(5) to consult with non-governmental organizations which are concerned with ECOSOC matters.

The General Assembly decided on Dec. 20, 1971, by 105 votes to 2 (France and Great Britain) and with 15 abstentions, to enlarge the Council from 27 to 54 members and to amend Article 61 of the Charter accordingly.

Under the amendment, the General Assembly each year elects 18 members to the Council for a term of 3 years (though transitional measures would be applied for elections during the first 3 years after the increase in membership). Of the Council's 54 members, 14 were to be from African States; 11 from Asian States; 10 from Latin American States; 13 from Western European and other States; and 6 from Socialist States of Eastern Europe. [25134]

Most of the work of ECOSOC is carried out through functional and regional commissions. The following are the functional commissions:

Statistical Commission.
Population Commission.
Social Commission.
Commission on Human Rights.
Commission on the Status of Women.
Commission on Narcotic Drugs.

The regional commissions are the following:

Economic Commission for Europe (ECE).
Economic Commission for Asia and the Far East (ECAFE).
Economic Commission for Latin America (ECLA).
Economic Commission for Africa (ECA).

The Council also has the following five standing committees:

Technical Assistance Committee.
Committee on Housing, Building, and Planning.
Council Committee on Non-Governmental Organizations.
Executive Committee of the U.N. High Commissioner for Refugees.
Advisory Committee on the Application of Science and Technology to Development.

Commodity Producers' Agreements

Under the sponsorship of ECAFE, the Asian Coconut Community was formed on Oct. 16, 1968, by Ceylon (Sri Lanka), India, Indonesia, Malaysia, the Philippines, Singapore, and Thailand. [23138B]

During the 27th session of ECAFE on April 21, 1971, an agreement was signed by India, Indonesia, and Malaysia establishing a Pepper Community, to come into effect early in 1972. [25244C]

As the result of a conference of representatives from Iraq, Iran, Kuwait, Saudi Arabia, and Venezuela held in Baghdad, Sept. 10–14, 1960, it was announced on Sept. 24 of that year that an *Organization of Petroleum Exporting Countries* (OPEC) was to be set up with the 5 above countries as its initial members. Qatar became a member in January 1961, Indonesia and Libya in June 1962, Abu Dhabi in November 1967, Algeria in July 1969, and Nigeria in July 1971. While supplying about 85 per cent of the world's oil exports outside the Soviet bloc, OPEC does not include the two largest single oil-producing countries—the Soviet Union and the United States.

The main object of OPEC is to increase the share of revenue accruing to the oil-exporting countries, and among agreements concluded between OPEC member-countries and oil companies that of Tehran, concluded on Feb. 14, 1971, by Abu Dhabi, Iran, Iraq, Kuwait, Qatar, and Saudi Arabia, provided for "security of supply and stability in financial arrangements for the five-year period 1971–75."

An agreement setting up an *Organization of Arab Petroleum Exporting Countries* (OAPEC) to represent the special interests of Arab nations was signed on Jan.

9, 1968, in Beirut. Its initial members—Kuwait, Libya, and Saudi Arabia—were joined in May 1970 by Abu Dhabi, Algeria, Bahrain, Dubai, and Qatar. Dubai withdrew in December 1972.

The new organization, which would be concerned with the economic and commercial rather than the political interests of its members, would respect the existing charter of OPEC.   [24647A]

An *International Coffee Organization,* set up at a conference of coffee-producing countries in Rio de Janeiro in January 1958, concluded a number of International Coffee Agreements (annually between 1958 and 1962, and for five-year periods from Dec. 27, 1963, and from Dec. 30, 1968). The Organization fixed export quotas, agreed on an "indicator price range," and took other measures to bring supply and demand more into line with one another. The 1968 agreement had 41 coffee-exporting and 20 importing members. [23119D; 22929A; 22966A]

A five-year *International Sugar Agreement,* fixing major basic export tonnages for sugar-exporting countries for the first three years, and providing for annual export quotas and for a floor-price to be observed by importing countries, entered into force on June 17, 1969.

The previous Agreement—negotiated in 1958, to run for five years from Jan. 1, 1959, and to include all exporting countries—had lapsed because of a disruption in the market caused by the cessation of trade between Cuba and the U.S.A. in 1961.

The new agreement was, however, accepted only by a limited number of countries, and in particular not by the U.S.A. and the EEC. [16462B; 23180A; 23447A]

SPECIAL BODIES FUNCTIONING UNDER THE AUTHORITY OF ECOSOC AND THE GENERAL ASSEMBLY

1. United Nations Development Program (UNDP)

The U.N. Development Program was formed in November 1965 by the merger of the U.N. Special Fund and the Expanded Program of Technical Assistance. Functioning under the joint authority of ECOSOC and the General Assembly, the UNDP supports pre-investment projects in developing countries. The fields of activity of the UNDP include development planning, agricultural and industrial productivity, education, health, and public and social services; the work is carried out through the various Specialized Agencies of the United Nations (see page 27).

The two organs of the UNDP are the Governing Council, whose 37 members include both developed and developing countries, and the Inter-Agency Consultative Board, composed of the U.N. Secretary-General and the Executive Heads of the Specialized Agencies.

2. United Nations High Commissioner for Refugees (UNHCR)

The office of U.N. High Commissioner for Refugees was created in 1950. The High Commissioner is responsible to ECOSOC and the General Assembly for the "international protection" of refugees. His mandate does not, however, cover refugees who have the same rights and obligations as nationals of their country of residence, or who receive assistance from other U.N. agencies.

The activities of the High Commissioner include efforts to facilitate the naturalization of refugees and to improve their legal status; repatriation; local integration by helping refugees to become self-supporting; and resettlement through emigration. An important task of the UNHCR is to supervise the application of the 1951 Convention determining the status of refugees, this being the principal legal document dealing with the question.   [12074A]

The High Commissioner is elected by the General Assembly on the recommendation of the Secretary-General. He is assisted by a Deputy High Commissioner. A 30-member Executive Committee of the High Commissioner's Program directs the policy of the Program at its twice-yearly meetings.

The High Commissioner's Office in Geneva has four departments, which deal with operations, legal questions, administration and finance, and external relations. There are also 29 Branch Offices and 12 Correspondents or Special Representatives away from headquarters.

THE INTERNATIONAL COURT OF JUSTICE

The principal judicial organ of the United Nations is the International Court of Justice, which sits at The Hague. It functions in accordance with a statute annexed to the Charter of the United Nations, and is permanently in session.

The 15 judges who comprise the Court are elected for nine years by both the General Assembly and the Security Council. Five new judges are elected every three years. In addition to possessing first-class legal qualifications the judges must be men of high moral character. No two judges may be of the same nationality, and the Court should include representatives of all the main legal systems of the world.

FUNCTIONS AND POWERS

The International Court is not authorized to hear cases brought by individuals. Those States which may submit a dispute are all the members of the United Nations with the addition of Liechtenstein, San Marino, and Switzerland.

The Court has jurisdiction over all cases referred to it by the parties to the Statute, and also over matters specially provided for in the U.N. Charter and in treaties in force. In addition, 47 States which are parties to the Statute have voluntarily recognized the compulsory jurisdiction of the Court in relation to States accepting the same obligation and over certain specified classes of international disputes.

Should a party to a case refuse to comply with the judgment of the Court, the other party may have recourse to the Security Council, which may decide upon measures to give effect to the judgment.

The Court may give advisory opinions on legal questions to the General Assembly, the Security Council, and other organs of the United Nations if requested to do so.

THE SECRETARIAT AND SECRETARY-GENERAL

The general administration of the United Nations is the responsibility of the Secretariat in New York, headed by the Secretary-General.

The Secretary-General is elected by the General Assembly, on the recommendation of the Security Council, for a period of five years. The Secretary-General acts as the U.N.'s chief administrative officer at all meetings of the General Assembly, the Security Council, the Economic and Social Council, and the Trusteeship Council. Among his duties are the preparation of an annual report which he submits to the General Assembly, and a general vigilance over the international scene, so that he may bring to the attention of the Security Council any situations which he considers to be a threat to international peace.

The following departments and institutions are included within the Secretariat:

Department of Political and Security Council Affairs.
Department of Economic and Social Affairs.
United Nations Conference on Trade and Development (see page 22).
Department of Trusteeship Affairs and Non-Self-Governing Territories.

Office of Public Information.
Office of Conference Services.
Office of General Services.
United Nations' Development Program (see page 25).
United Nations Children's Fund (UNICEF) (see below).
United Nations Institute for Training and Research (UNITAR) (see page 26).
United Nations Industrial Development Organization (UNIDO) see page 27).

EUROPEAN OFFICE OF THE U.N.

The European Secretariat of the United Nations has its office at Geneva. It is headed by a Director-General and a Deputy Director, who are responsible to the Secretary-General in New York.

OTHER BODIES WITHIN THE FRAMEWORK OF THE UNITED NATIONS

1. United Nations Children's Fund (UNICEF)

Headquarters: New York

The United Nations Children's Fund is an operating agency of the United Nations, founded in December 1946 to aid mothers and children in need as a result of the devastation of war.

The work of UNICEF is carried out in conjunction with WHO, FAO, and UNESCO (see below under "Specialized Agencies"), and is now mainly directed towards aiding children and young people in developing countries through health, nutrition, and social welfare projects.

The decision-making organ of UNICEF is its 30-member Executive Board, which meets annually. There is also a Secretariat, staffed by members of the U.N. Secretariat.

2. United Nations Institute for Training and Research (UNITAR)

Headquarters: New York

The United Nations Institute for Training and Research was inaugurated in March 1965. It was created, as an autonomous body within the framework of the U.N., to train personnel—particularly from developing countries—for service with member-governments and organizations of the U.N. Another of UNITAR's functions is to study major questions relating to the promotion of economic and social development and the maintenance of international peace and security.

A Board of Trustees, whose members are appointed by the U.N. Secretary-General to sit for two years, directs the policy of the organization. Meetings of the Board take place twice a year and are attended, where appropriate, by representatives of the Specialized Agencies. An Administrative and Financial Committee assists the Board. The direction and general administration of the Institute are the responsibility of an Executive Director.

3. United Nations Industrial Development Organization (UNIDO)

Headquarters: at present New York; eventually Vienna

The United Nations Industrial Development Organization was established in November 1966, to function as an autonomous organization within the U.N.

It is the objective of UNIDO to promote and accelerate the industrialization of the developing countries through the mobilization of national and international resources. Its work takes the form of both operational activities and programs of research and study.

UNIDO's principal organ is the Industrial Development Board, whose members represent both developed and developing countries. Meetings are held annually. The administrative and research activities of UNIDO are the responsibility of a permanent Secretariat headed by an Executive Director.

SPECIALIZED AGENCIES AND THE IAEA

The United Nations Specialized Agencies are independent international organizations, which function in co-operation with the U.N. under agreements made with an ECOSOC Committee. They have responsibilities in a wide variety of fields. Membership of the Specialized Agencies is not restricted to the members of the United Nations (see table on pages 34–6).

1. International Bank for Reconstruction and Development (IBRD)

Headquarters: Washington

The International Bank for Reconstruction and Development, or World Bank as it is commonly designated, was set up in December 1945 to assist in the economic development of member-nations by making loans to governments and private enterprises for productive purposes. The Bank's main objectives are to facilitate the investment of capital and to promote

private foreign investment; to further the balanced growth of international trade; and to maintain equilibrium in the balance-of-payments of its members.

The capital of the Bank is derived from the members' subscriptions, the amount of each subscription being based on the country's economic resources. The Bank acquires additional funds by borrowing in world capital markets, and by selling some of its loans to private investors.

The powers of the Bank are vested in the Board of Governors, on which each of the member-nations is represented by one Governor. A body of 20 Executive Directors, to which the Board has delegated most of its power, meets monthly. The President of the Bank, who is also the Chairman of Executive Directors, is responsible for conducting the business of the Bank. [10181A]

2. International Monetary Fund (IMF)

Headquarters: Washington

Established at the same time as the World Bank, the International Monetary Fund exists primarily to promote stability and international co-operation in the fields of trade and monetary exchange. Members may purchase foreign exchange from the Fund to make short-term or medium-term payments. Each member is assigned a quota which determines its subscription, its voting power, and the amount of foreign exchange which it may purchase. In addition to making available foreign exchange the Fund provides financial advice to its members on request.

The organs of the Fund are the Board of Governors, on which each member is represented by a Governor and an alternate, and a 20-member Board of Executive Directors. [10181A]

The establishment of the IMF and the IBRD (see above) had been agreed upon at a conference held in Bretton Woods (New Hampshire), July 1–22, 1944, and attended by representatives of 44 countries.

A "Group of Ten" comprising the 10 strongest industrial countries outside the Communist world (Belgium, Britain, Canada, France, Western Germany, Italy, Japan, the Netherlands, Sweden, and the United States) agreed on Jan. 8, 1962, to "stand ready to lend their currencies to the Fund up to specified amounts when the Fund and these countries consider that supplementary resources are needed to forestall or cope with an impairment of the international monetary system." [18537A] The Group of Ten was also joined as an observer by Switzerland, which is not a member of the IMF.

The Fund's Articles of Agreement were amended in June 1968 so as to create a new facility of "Special

Drawing Rights" (SDRs), which came into force on July 28, 1969. The SDRs would be distributed among participating countries according to their Fund quotas and would entitle the countries concerned to make drawings of currency unconditionally to meet balance-of-payments difficulties. The SDRs would be additional to the Fund's normal stand-by and drawing arrangements, which would continue to be operated subject to certain conditions as before.

The IMF announced on July 28, 1972, the establishment of a Committee of the Board of Governors on Reform of the International Monetary System and Related Issues (the "Committee of Twenty"), representing both developed and developing countries. Its aim would be to "provide a forum in which momentum can be maintained at a high policy-making level for all aspects of reform of the international monetary system."

The Committee of Twenty met for the first time on Sept. 28, 1972. [*25388A; 25566B*]

3. International Finance Corporation (IFC)

Headquarters: Washington

The International Finance Corporation, an affiliate of the World Bank, came into being in July 1956. The function of the IFC is to encourage the growth of productive private enterprises in less developed areas by investing in undertakings on reasonable terms and without government guarantee, by recruiting private capital, and by supplying experienced management. The share of capital subscribed by the IFC's members is supplemented by a loan provided by the World Bank.

The IFC is served by a President, an Executive Vice-President and a Deputy Executive Vice-President. Its Directors are drawn from the Executive Directors of the World Bank. [*15098A*]

4. International Development Association (IDA)

Headquarters: Washington

Like the IFC, the International Development Association is an affiliate of the World Bank. It was created in September 1960 and began operations in November 1960. Its function is to provide loans, on flexible terms, to finance important development projects in less developed areas. The IDA may—unlike the World Bank —finance projects which are not directly productive. Its main aims are to promote economic development, increase productivity, and raise standards of living.

The greater part of the Association's funds is de-

rived from members' subscriptions, but supplementary resources include transfers from the World Bank. The IDA is operated concurrently with the World Bank by the same officers and staff.

5. International Labor Organization (ILO)

Headquarters: Geneva

The International Labor Organization, which has existed since 1919, became the first Specialized Agency of the United Nations in 1946. Its main function is to promote international standards of acceptable labor conditions. It also provides technical assistance in such fields as productivity and management development, manpower organization, labor conditions, small-scale industries and handicrafts, and social security.

The principal organ of the ILO is the International Labor Conference, which meets annually and is attended by delegations from the member-nations. The delegations generally comprise two government delegates, one delegate representing employers and one representing workers. The other organs of the ILO are the International Labor Office, which is its secretariat, and the Governing Body, an executive council meeting at least three times a year. The 48-member Governing Body is formed by 24 representatives of governments, 12 representatives of employers, and 12 workers' representatives.

Two institutions founded by the ILO are the International Institute for Labor Studies, set up in March 1960 in Geneva as an advanced educational and research institute, and the International Center for Advanced Technical and Vocational Training, established in March 1963 in Turin, Italy.

The ILO has approved some 120 conventions and more than 100 recommendations, forming an international labor code intended to serve as a guideline for Governments. Member-countries are committed to conventions after ratification, and have to submit to the ILO periodical reports on their implementation.

6. United Nations Educational, Scientific, and Cultural Organization (UNESCO)

Headquarters: Paris

UNESCO came into being in November 1945. The basic purpose of the organization is to promote international collaboration in the fields of education, science, and culture, and through this, to foster and strengthen universal respect for the human rights and fundamental freedoms affirmed in the Charter of the United Nations.

The work of UNESCO includes the documentation of information of all kinds; the extension of free and compulsory education; the improvement of facilities for vocational and technical training and for higher education; the promotion of scientific research; the preservation of the world's cultural heritage in books, works of art, and historical and scientific monuments; and the improvement of all means of communication in order to encourage the free flow of ideas and knowledge.

The organs of UNESCO are a General Conference of the member-nations, meeting every two years; a 30-member Executive Board which meets at least twice a year to prepare the organization's program; and a Secretariat. National Commissions and Co-operating Bodies within the member-countries serve to co-ordinate the work of UNESCO with national efforts in the same fields.

7. Food and Agriculture Organization (FAO)

Headquarters: Rome

The Food and Agriculture Organization was formally set up at Quebec in October 1945. Its principal aims are to raise levels of nutrition and standards of living; to improve efficiency in production and distribution of food and agricultural products; and to improve the conditions of rural populations. FAO serves to provide its member-governments with information and technical advice on questions relating to agriculture, forestry, fisheries, nutrition, and home economics.

The supreme organ of FAO is the Conference of all the member-nations, which sits every two years. Between sessions of the Conference the work of the organization is carried on by a 31-member Council, meetings of which are normally held twice a year and after each Conference session. There is also a Secretariat headed by a Director-General.

The World Food Program (WFP), a joint U.N.–FAO enterprise, was established in 1963 to provide aid, in the form of food, to less developed countries. It is hoped, through this aid, to encourage social and economic development projects in the countries to which it is provided.

The organization of the WFP consists of a 24-member Inter-Governmental Committee (12 members elected by FAO and 12 by ECOSOC) and a joint U.N.–FAO Administrative Unit headed by an Executive Director.

8. World Health Organization (WHO)

Headquarters: Geneva

The World Health Organization was established in April 1948. Its aim is to raise the standard of health of all peoples to the highest possible level through, *inter alia*, health education; the promotion of work to eradicate disease; the promotion of maternal and child health welfare; the fostering of mental health activities; and the improvement of environmental hygiene and sanitation. WHO provides its members with both advisory services and technical assistance.

The supreme organ of WHO is the World Health Assembly, which meets annually to decide on a program of world health. Other organs are the 24-man Executive Board which meets at least twice a year, and the Secretariat.

9. International Civil Aviation Organization (ICAO)

Headquarters: Montreal

The International Civil Aviation Organization formally came into being in April 1947, although the agreement for its creation had been concluded at the Chicago conference on civil aviation held Nov. 1–Dec. 6, 1944. [7069A]

The main functions of the ICAO are to study the problems of international civil aviation, and to establish international standards and regulations for civil aviation. The organization encourages the use of safety measures, and promotes the use of new techniques and equipment.

The two organs of the ICAO are the Assembly of all the member-nations, which meets every three years, and the 27-member Council, which is the executive organ and remains almost continuously in session.

A *Convention on Offenses and Certain Other Acts Committed on Board Aircraft,* opened for signature in Tokyo on Sept. 14, 1963, came into force on Dec. 4, 1969, after it had been ratified by 12 countries (including the U.S.A., Denmark, Italy, Mexico, Norway, the Philippines, Portugal, Sweden, and the United Kingdom).

The Convention laid down rules on jurisdiction over aircraft, also for extradition purposes, and defined the authority of the aircraft commander. All parties to the Convention undertook to take all appropriate measures, in cases of hijacking, to restore control of the aircraft to its lawful commander. [22480A]

A *Convention for the Suppression of Unlawful Seizure of Aircraft,* concluded by a Diplomatic Conference on Air Law under ICAO auspices in The Hague on Dec. 16, 1970, entered into force on Oct. 14, 1971, after it had been ratified by 10 countries (including Bulgaria, Hungary, Israel, Japan, Norway, Sweden, Switzerland, and the U.S.A.).

The Convention defined unlawful seizure, or attempt at seizure, of civil aircraft as an offense and committed each contracting State to make the offense punishable by severe penalties. It also defined the jurisdiction of contracting States and laid down procedure against offenders, including their possible extradition to another contracting State. The Convention further required offenses to be reported to the

ICAO; it enjoined the contracting States to submit any disputes to arbitration; and it authorized them to appeal, if necessary, to the International Court of Justice. [24456A; 25026A]

A *Convention for the Suppression of Unlawful Acts Against the Safety of Civil Aviation* was adopted by a Diplomatic Conference on Air Law under ICAO auspices in Montreal on Sept. 23, 1971.

The Convention defined offenses against the safety of civil aircraft and committed contracting States to make such offenses punishable by severe penalties; to take all necessary measures to establish its jurisdiction; and to take offenders into custody.

Other provisions of the Convention were similar to those of the Convention for the Suppression of Unlawful Seizure of Aircraft (see above). [25026A]

10. Inter-Governmental Maritime Consultative Organization (IMCO)

Headquarters: London

The Inter-Governmental Maritime Consultative Organization was formally established on Jan. 13, 1959. The main functions of the Organization are to promote inter-governmental co-operation in matters of regulation and practice affecting international shipping, and to encourage the highest standards of safety at sea; to remove discriminatory action affecting international shipping; and to examine unfair restrictive practices by shipping.

IMCO has consultative and advisory functions. Its organs are the Assembly, composed of representatives of all the member-countries as well as various observers, and meeting every two years; the 16-member Council, which meets about twice a year; the 14-member Maritime Safety Committee, meeting at least once a year; and the Secretariat, headed by the Secretary-General.

An *International Convention on the Safety of Life at Sea,* revising the 1948 convention which had entered into force in 1952, was signed on July 17, 1960, by 34 countries, 6 more signing during the following month. The convention dealt with safety of navigation, provisions for nuclear ships, and carriage of dangerous goods.

At the seventh meeting of the IMCO Assembly, Oct. 5–15, 1971, amendments were adopted to the convention, rendering mandatory the observance of traffic-routing schemes approved by IMCO, including a scheme for traffic separation in the Dover Strait. [9509D; 18017A; 25496A]

Conventions on Oil Pollution

1. An *International Convention for the Prevention of Pollution of the Sea by Oil,* banning the discharging into the sea of crude oil, fuel oil, diesel oil, and lubricating oil within specified zones, came into force for tankers on July 26, 1958, and for dry cargo ships on July 26, 1961. Amendments to this convention were signed in 1962, 1969, and 1971. [13598C; 18784A; 23708A]

(Further progress toward international control of oil pollution was made when on Aug. 9, 1972, the British Government announced agreements with France and Belgium on co-operation in the surveillance of oil slicks in the English Channel area.)

2. An *International Convention Relating to Intervention on the High Seas in Cases of Oil Pollution Casualties* was adopted at the end of a conference held by IMCO from Nov. 10 to 29, 1969. The convention dealt with the right of a coastal State to protect its own interests when a casualty occurred on the high seas which might damage those interests.

3. At the same conference, an *International Convention on Civil Liability for Oil Pollution Damage* was adopted, providing that the owner of a ship from which polluting oil escaped would be held liable for any pollution damage caused, and at a complementary conference held Nov. 29–Dec. 18, 1971, another agreement resulted, known as the *Convention on the Establishment of an International Fund for Compensation for Oil Pollution Damage.* The fund was designed to offer compensation in cases of large-scale pollution where the terms of provisions for civil liability were inadequate to cover the damage incurred. It was also complementary to the Tanker Owners' Voluntary Agreement for Liability for Oil Pollution (Tovalop), which came into effect on Oct. 6, 1969, and was renewed in October 1971 for a further three years. [23708A; 25637A]

4. A *Convention on the Prevention of Marine Pollution by Dumping* was adopted at an intergovernmental conference held in London, Oct. 30–Nov. 13, 1972, and attended by representatives of 81 Governments and observers from 12 other countries. The Soviet Union participated, but the People's Republic of China was absent.

The main aim of the convention is to prevent indiscriminate disposal at sea of waste chemicals and minerals, on the understanding that the sea's capacity to assimilate waste and to regenerate natural resources is not unlimited. The dumping of certain categories of waste will be prohibited or subject to permit.

At the close of the conference the convention had been initialed by 57 countries. [25637A]

11. World Meteorological Organization (WMO)

Headquarters: Geneva

The World Meteorological Organization became operative as a U.N. Specialized Agency in April 1951, although the Convention of the organization had been in effect since March 1950. The main purpose of the WMO is to encourage international co-operation in meteorology through the establishment of networks of stations for meteorological observations; through the promotion of a standardization of observations and uniform publication of statistics; and through co-ordination of research and training in meteorology.

The supreme organ of the WMO is the World Meteorological Congress held every four years and attended by representatives of all the members of the organization. The executive organ is the Executive Committee, whose 21 members include the Presidents of the six Regional Associations. The Executive Committee meets at least once a year. There is also a Secretariat, which is responsible for general administration. The six Regional Associations are for Africa, Asia, South America, North and Central America, the South-West Pacific, and Europe.

12. International Telecommunication Union (ITU)

Headquarters: Geneva

The International Telecommunication Union originated in 1865 as the International Telegraph Union, and came into being under its present title in January 1934. The ITU became a U.N. Specialized Agency in November 1947. Its main functions are to promote international co-operation in telecommunications, and to encourage the development of radio, telegraph, and telephone installations with their efficient operation at the lowest possible rates.

The supreme organ of the ITU is the Plenipotentiary Conference of all the members, which meets every five years. Other organs are the 29-member Administrative Council, which meets once a year, and the General Secretariat. Administrative Conferences are held from time to time in accordance with technical requirements.

Other bodies within the framework of the ITU are the International Frequency Registration Board (IFRB); the International Telegraph and Telephone Consultative Committee (CCITT); and the International Radio Consultative Committee (CCIR).

13. Universal Postal Union (UPU)

Headquarters: Berne

The Universal Postal Union was established in Berne (Switzerland) in 1874, when the first International Postal Convention was signed, creating the General Union of Posts (which changed its name to UPU in 1878).

The Convention was based on five principles:

(*a*) For the purposes of postal communication all member-States formed a single territory. This means that in effect every member-State has the full use of postal services throughout the world.

(*b*) Uniformity of postage rates and units of weight. After World War I this principle of a uniform rate was changed to that of a maximum and a minimum rate.

(*c*) Classification of mail matter into letters, postcards, and "other matter," with detailed rules for their distinction.

(*d*) The making of definite payments by the country dispatching mail for the use of services of other countries—except the country of destination (it being assumed that the traffic in either direction is approximately equal).

(*e*) A universal system of registration and compensation.

A parcel post agreement was concluded by 19 countries in 1880.

The legislative body and supreme organ of the UPU is the Congress, meeting every five years. The remaining organs of the Union are the 27-member Executive Council, which meets annually; the Consultative Committee on Postal Studies, on which all the member-countries of the UPU are represented; and the International Bureau, which is the general administrative organ.

14. General Agreement on Tariffs and Trade (GATT)

Headquarters: Geneva

The General Agreement on Tariffs and Trade is a multilateral trade agreement concluded in October 1947 at the 23-nation U.N. Conference on Trade and Employment, held in Geneva from April 10 to Oct. 30, 1947.

One of the main purposes of this conference was to draft a charter for a proposed International Trade Organization (ITO). The provisions of GATT were intended to be superseded by the ITO Charter as soon as the latter should come into force. Although a final text of the ITO Charter was approved at the subsequent Havana Conference on Trade and Employment (Nov. 21, 1947–March 24, 1948), it has never been ratified. Thus, GATT—originally intended as an interim institution—has developed into a permanent international instrument for the regulation of world trading practices.

The aims of GATT are to raise standards of living, to ensure full employment, to develop resources, to expand the production and exchange of goods, and to promote economic development.

The members of GATT (81 contracting parties and 15 other members) meet in session once a year. Matters arising between sessions are dealt with by a Council of Representatives, and there is also a Secretariat, composed of trade specialists and administrative staff.

Conferences on the reduction and stabilization of tariffs are held at irregular intervals, as a result of which tariffs have been reduced on goods accounting for around half the world's trade.

An International Trade Center, to provide information and advice to developing countries, was established in Geneva in May 1964.   [13388A]

The principal achievements of GATT include world-wide tariff reductions agreed upon:

(a) in the "Dillon Round" of 1960–62, under which many customs tariffs were reduced by an average of 20 per cent between the U.S.A. and the EEC, between the U.S.A. and Britain, between Britain and the EEC, and between the U.S.A. and other countries, with all bilateral concessions being granted to all other GATT member-countries under the "most-favored-nation" principle, and

(b) in the "Kennedy Round" of 1963–67, in which the "linear approach" for tariff reductions "across the board," instead of item-by-item bargaining for different commodities, was applied for the first time; this approach eventually led to a reduction of tariffs for industrial goods, carried out in agreed stages, averaging over 30 percent on trade between the participating countries, and reaching up to 50 percent in many cases.   [18793A; 22641A; 22741B; 23823A; 24408A]

International Atomic Energy Agency (IAEA)

Headquarters: Vienna

The International Atomic Energy Agency came officially into existence in July 1957. The Agency submits reports to the General Assembly, to ECOSOC, to the Security Council, and to other U.N. organs where appropriate, thus differing from the Specialized Agencies, which report only to ECOSOC.

Membership of the IAEA is open to all members of the United Nations and the Specialized Agencies.

The principal aim of the IAEA is to accelerate and enlarge the contribution of atomic energy to peace, health, and prosperity throughout the world. The work of the Agency includes the establishment of a system of safeguards against the use, for any military purpose, of special fissionable and other materials which it has made available; the exchange of technical information; the preparation of international regulations for transport of radioactive materials and disposal of radioactive waste; provision of training facilities; and the application of techniques using atomic energy to agriculture, medicine, and hydrology.

The IAEA has established a number of institutions: a laboratory for physics, chemistry, and agriculture at Seibersdorf in Austria; a laboratory for medical physics and hydrology in Vienna; an International Center for Theoretical Physics at Trieste; and a Nuclear Data Unit in Vienna.

The Agency's principal organs consist of a General Conference of all the member-nations, which meets annually; a 25-member Board of Governors meeting about four times a year and acting as the Agency's executive organ; and a Director-General, who heads a secretariat divided into departments for Technical Assistance, Technical Operations, Research and Life Sciences, Safeguards and Inspection, and Administration. There is also a 10-man Scientific Advisory Committee of nuclear experts.

MEMBERSHIP OF THE UNITED NATIONS AND RELATED AGENCIES

The following table lists the members of the United Nations, its Specialized Agencies and the International Atomic Energy Agency, and the Contracting Parties to the General Agreement on Tariffs and Trade, as of September 1, 1973.

The complete names of the organizations included in this table are:

UN	United Nations
IAEA	International Atomic Energy Agency
ILO	International Labor Organization
FAO	Food and Agriculture Organization of the United Nations
UNESCO	United Nations Educational, Scientific, and Cultural Organization
WHO	World Health Organization
BANK	International Bank for Reconstruction and Development
IFC	International Finance Corporation
IDA	International Development Association
FUND	International Monetary Fund
ICAO	International Civil Aviation Organization
UPU	Universal Postal Union
ITU	International Telecommunication Union
WMO	World Meteorological Organization
IMCO	Inter-Governmental Maritime Consultative Organization
GATT	General Agreement on Tariffs and Trade

In this list the countries shown below appear as follows:

Cambodia as Khmer Republic;
Ceylon as Sri Lanka;
Congo (Brazzaville) as Congo;
Congo (Kinshasa) as Zaïre;

Eastern Germany as German Democratic Republic;
Great Britain (Britain) as United Kingdom;
Madagascar as Malagasy Republic;
Nationalist China (Formosa) as Taiwan;
Persia as Iran;
Republic of Ireland as Ireland;
Rumania as Romania;
Siam as Thailand;
Soviet Union as Union of Soviet Socialist Republics;
South Korea as Republic of Korea;
South Vietnam as Republic of Vietnam;
South Yemen as People's Democratic Republic of
   Yemen;
Tanzania as United Republic of Tanzania;
The Vatican as Holy See;
Western Germany as Federal Republic of Germany.

Membership

Countries which have not applied for U.N. membership are Andorra, the Federal Republic of Germany, Liechtenstein, Monaco, Nauru, San Marino, Sikkim, Switzerland, and the Vatican.

Of these countries, three are, in foreign relations, represented by other countries: Andorra by France, Liechtenstein by Switzerland, and Sikkim by India.

The Federal Republic of Germany had not applied because it expected any application to be vetoed in the Security Council by the Soviet Union unless the German Democratic Republic were admitted at the same time. However, in a document accompanying the "Basic Treaty" signed in December 1972 between the two German States (see page 136) it was stated that steps would be taken in due course for the application of the two States at approximately the same time.

Switzerland has refrained from applying because it regards any sanctions imposed under Chapter VII of the U.N. Charter (such as the mandatory sanctions imposed against Rhodesia on Dec. 16, 1966) as being in conflict with its status of neutrality.

Applications refused were those by South Korea and South Vietnam (both vetoed by the U.S.S.R.) and by North Korea and North Vietnam (both failing to gain the necessary number of affirmative votes in the Security Council).

The question of U.N. membership of the People's Republic of China was the subject of a vote at almost every session of the U.N. General Assembly since 1950. The United States, however, announced on Jan. 21, 1951, that it recognized the Nationalist Chinese Government in Taiwan (Formosa) as the only legal representative of China, and until 1960 the U.S.A. succeeded in having discussion of the Chinese membership question deferred. From 1961 onwards the question of the admission of the People's Republic was, at the instance of the United States, judged to be an "important" one to be decided upon only by a two-thirds majority in accordance with the U.N. Charter. It was not until 1970 that an Albanian move to give the People's Republic of China a seat in the United Nations obtained a simple majority in the General Assembly. On Oct. 15, 1971, however, the General Assembly adopted by 76 votes to 35, with 17 abstentions and three delegations absent, an Albanian resolution appointing the People's Republic of China to the Chinese seat in all its functions and to exclude the Taiwan Government, as having usurped these rights, from the organization. (The Government of Taiwan was thus the first to be expelled from the United Nations.) The People's Republic subsequently took its seat in all U.N. organs, including that of a permanent member of the Security Council, and in some of the Specialized Agencies. [24941A; 24988A]

The table of membership follows.

Country	UN	IAEA	ILO	FAO	UNESCO	WHO	BANK	IFC	IDA	FUND	ICAO	UPU	ITU	WMO	IMCO	GATT
Afghanistan	X	X	X	X	X	X	X	X	X	X	X	X	X	X	—	—
Albania	X	X	—	—	X	X	X	—	—	—	—	X	X	X	X	7
Algeria	X	X	X	X	X	X	X	—	—	X	X	X	X	X	X	7
Argentina	X	X	X	X	X	X	X	X	X	X	X	X	X	X	X	X
Australia	X	X	X	X	X	X	X	X	X	X	X	X	X	X	X	X
Austria	X	X	X	X	X	X	X	X	X	X	X	X	X	X	—	X
Bahrain	X	—	—	X	X	X	X	—	—	X	X	—	—	—	—	7
Bangladesh	—	X	X	X	X	X	X	—	X	X	X	X	X	X	—	X
Barbados	X	—	X	X	X	X	—	—	—	X	X	X	X	X	—	X
Belgium	X	X	X	X	X	X	X	X	X	X	X	X	X	X	X	X
Bhutan	X	—	—	—	—	—	—	—	—	—	—	X	X	—	—	—
Bolivia	X	X	X	X	X	X	X	X	X	X	X	X	X	X	—	—
Botswana	X	—	X	—	—	X	X	—	X	X	X	X	X	X	—	7
Brazil	X	X	X	X	X	X	X	X	X	X	X	X	X	X	X	X
Bulgaria	X	X	X	X	X	X	—	—	—	—	X	X	X	X	—	X
Burma	X	X	X	X	X	X	X	—	X	X	X	X	X	X	—	X
Burundi	X	—	X	X	X	X	X	—	X	X	X	X	X	X	—	X
Byelorussia	X	X	X	—	X	X	—	—	.	—	—	X	X	X	—	—
Cameroon	X	X	X	X	X	X	—	X	X	X	X	X	X	X	—	X
Canada	X	X	X	X	X	X	X	X	X	X	X	X	X	X	X	X
Central African Republic	X	—	X	X	X	X	—	X	X	X	X	X	X	X	—	X
Chad	X	—	X	X	X	X	X	X	X	X	X	X	X	X	—	X
Chile	X	X	X	X	X	X	X	X	X	X	X	X	X	X	X	X
China	X	X	X	X	X	X	—	—	—	—	X	X	X	X	—	—
Colombia	X	X	X	X	X	X	X	X	X	X	X	X	X	X	—	X
Congo	X	—	X	X	X	X	X	—	X	X	X	X	X	X	—	X
Costa Rica	X	X	X	X	X	X	X	X	X	X	X	X	X	X	—	X
Cuba	X	X	X	X	X	X	—	—	—	—	X	X	X	X	X	X
Cyprus	X	X	X	X	X	X	X	X	X	X	X	X	X	X	—	X
Czechoslovakia	X	X	X	X	X	X	—	—	—	—	X	X	X	X	—	X
Dahomey	X	—	X	X	X	X	X	—	X	X	X	X	X	X	—	X
Denmark	X	X	X	X	X	X	X	X	X	X	X	X	X	X	X	X
Dominican Republic	X	X	X	X	X	X	X	X	X	X	X	X	X	X	X	X
Ecuador	X	X	X	X	X	X	X	X	X	X	X	X	X	X	X	—
Egypt	X	X	X	X	X	X	X	X	X	X	X	X	X	X	X	X
El Salvador	X	X	X	X	X	X	X	X	X	X	X	X	X	X	—	—
Equatorial Guinea	X	—	X	—	—	X	—	X	X	—	X	X	—	X	—	7
Ethiopia	X	X	X	X	X	X	X	X	X	X	X	X	X	X	—	7
Federal Republic of Germany	—	X	X	X	X	X	X	X	X	X	X	X	X	X	—	X
Fiji	X	—	—	X	—	X	X	X	X	X	X	X	X	—	—	7
Finland	X	X	X	X	X	X	X	X	X	X	X	X	X	X	X	X
France	X	X	X	X	X	X	X	X	X	X	X	X	X	X	X	X
Gabon	X	X	X	X	X	X	X	X	X	X	X	X	X	X	—	X
Gambia	X	—	—	X	—	X	X	—	—	X	X	—	—	—	—	X
German Democratic Republic	—	—	—	—	X	X	—	—	—	—	—	—	—	—	—	—
Ghana	X	X	X	X	X	X	X	X	X	X	X	X	X	X	X	X
Greece	X	X	X	X	X	X	X	X	X	X	X	X	X	X	X	X
Guatemala	X	X	X	X	X	X	X	X	X	X	X	X	X	X	—	X
Guinea	X	—	X	X	X	X	X	—	X	X	X	X	X	X	—	—
Guyana	X	—	X	X	X	X	X	—	X	X	X	X	X	X	—	—
Haiti	X	X	X	X	X	X	X	X	X	X	X	X	X	X	X	X
Holy See	—	X	—	—	X	—	—	—	—	—	—	X	X	—	—	—
Honduras	X	—	X	X	X	X	X	X	X	X	X	X	X	X	X	—
Hungary	X	X	X	X	X	X	—	—	—	—	X	X	X	X	X	—
Iceland	X	X	X	X	X	X	X	X	X	X	X	X	X	X	X	X
India	X	X	X	X	X	X	X	X	X	X	X	X	X	X	X	X
Indonesia	X	X	X	X	X	X	X	X	X	X	X	X	X	X	X	X

Country	UN	IAEA	ILO	FAO	UNESCO	WHO	BANK	IFC	IDA	FUND	ICAO	UPU	ITU	WMO	IMCO	GATT
Iran	X	X	X	X	X	X	X	X	X	X	X	X	X	X	X	—
Iraq	X	X	X	X	X	X	X	X	X	X	X	X	X	X	—	—
Ireland	X	X	X	X	X	X	X	X	X	X	X	X	X	X	·	X
Israel	X	X	X	X	X	X	X	X	X	X	X	X	X	X	X	X
Italy	X	X	X	X	X	X	X	X	X	X	X	X	X	X	X	X
Ivory Coast	X	X	X	X	X	X	X	X	X	X	X	X	X	X	X	X
Jamaica	X	X	X	X	X	X	X	—	X	X	X	X	X	X	—	X
Japan	X	X	X	X	X	X	X	X	X	X	X	X	X	X	X	X
Jordan	X	X	X	X	X	X	X	X	X	X	X	X	X	X	X	—
Kenya	X	X	X	X	X	X	X	X	X	X	X	X	X	X	—	X
Khmer Republic	X	X	X	X	X	X	X	—	X	X	X	X	X	X	X	7
Kuwait	X	X	X	X	X	X	X	X	X	X	X	X	X	X	X	X
Laos	X	—	X	X	X	X	X	—	X	X	X	X	X	X	—	—
Lebanon	X	X	X	X	X	X	X	X	X	X	X	X	X	X	X	—
Lesotho	X	—	—	X	X	X	X	X	X	X	X	—	X	X	—	7
Liberia	X	X	X	X	X	X	X	X	X	X	X	X	X	X	X	—
Libya	X	X	X	X	X	X	X	X	X	X	X	X	X	X	X	—
Liechtenstein	—	X	—	—	—	—	—	—	—	—	—	X	X	—	—	—
Luxemburg	X	X	X	X	X	X	X	X	X	X	X	X	X	X	—	X
Malagasy Republic	X	X	X	X	X	X	X	X	X	X	X	X	X	X	X	X
Malawi	X	—	X	X	X	X	X	X	X	X	X	X	X	X	—	X
Malaysia	X	X	X	X	X	X	X	X	X	X	X	X	X	X	X	X
Maldives	X	—	—	X	—	X	—	—	—	—	—	X	X	—	X	7
Mali	X	X	X	X	—	X	X	—	X	X	X	X	X	X	X	7
Malta	X	—	X	X	X	X	X	—	X	X	X	X	X	—	X	X
Mauritania	X	—	X	X	X	X	X	X	X	X	X	X	X	X	X	X
Mauritius	X	—	X	X	X	X	X	X	X	X	X	X	X	X	X	X
Mexico	X	X	X	X	X	X	X	X	X	X	X	X	X	X	X	X
Monaco	—	X	—	—	X	X	X	—	—	—	—	X	X	X	—	—
Mongolia	X	—	X	—	X	X	—	—	—	—	X	X	X	X	—	—
Morocco	X	X	X	X	X	X	X	X	X	X	X	X	X	X	X	X
Nauru	—	—	—	—	—	—	—	—	—	—	—	X	X	—	—	—
Nepal	X	—	X	X	X	X	X	X	X	X	X	X	X	X	—	—
Netherlands	X	X	X	X	X	X	X	X	X	X	X	X	X	X	X	X
New Zealand	X	X	X	X	X	X	X	—	X	X	X	X	X	X	X	X
Nicaragua	X	—	X	X	X	X	X	X	X	X	X	X	X	X	—	X
Niger	X	X	X	X	X	X	X	—	X	X	X	X	X	X	—	X
Nigeria	X	X	X	X	X	X	X	X	X	X	X	X	X	X	X	X
Norway	X	X	X	X	X	X	X	X	X	X	X	X	X	X	X	X
Oman	X	—	—	X	X	X	X	X	X	X	—	X	X	—	—	—
Pakistan	X	X	X	X	X	X	X	X	X	X	X	X	X	X	X	X
Panama	X	X	X	X	X	X	X	X	X	X	X	X	X	X	X	—
Paraguay	X	X	X	X	X	X	X	X	X	X	X	X	X	X	—	—
People's Democratic Republic of Yemen	X	—	X	X	X	X	X	—	X	X	X	X	X	X	—	7
Peru	X	X	X	X	X	X	X	X	X	X	X	X	X	X	X	X
Philippines	X	X	X	X	X	X	X	X	X	X	X	X	X	X	X	—
Poland	X	X	X	X	X	X	—	X	—	—	X	X	X	X	X	X
Portugal	X	X	X	X	—	X	X	X	X	—	X	X	X	X	X	X
Qatar	X	—	X	X	X	X	X	—	—	X	X	X	—	—	—	7
Republic of Korea	—	X	—	X	X	X	X	X	X	X	X	X	X	X	X	X
Republic of Vietnam	—	X	X	X	X	X	X	X	X	X	X	X	X	X	X	—
Romania	X	X	X	X	X	X	X	—	—	X	X	X	X	X	X	X
Rwanda	X	—	X	X	X	X	X	—	X	X	X	X	X	X	—	X
San Marino	—	—	—	—	—	—	—	—	—	—	—	X	—	—	—	—
Saudi Arabia	X	X	—	X	X	X	X	X	X	X	X	X	X	X	X	—

35]

Country	UN	IAEA	ILO	FAO	UNESCO	WHO	BANK	IFC	IDA	FUND	ICAO	UPU	ITU	WMO	IMCO	GATT
Senegal	X	X	X	X	X	X	X	X	X	X	X	X	X	X	—	X
Sierra Leone	X	X	X	—	X	X	X	X	—	X	X	X	X	X	X	X
Singapore	X	—	X	—	X	X	X	—	X	X	X	X	X	X	X	—
Somalia	X	—	X	X	X	X	X	X	X	X	X	X	X	X	—	—
South Africa	X	X	—	—	X	X	X	X	X	X	X	X	X	X	X	X
Spain	X	X	X	X	X	X	X	X	X	X	X	X	X	X	X	X
Sri Lanka	X	X	X	X	X	X	X	X	X	X	X	X	X	X	X	X
Sudan	X	X	X	X	X	X	X	X	X	X	X	X	X	X	—	—
Swaziland	X	—	—	X	—	—	X	X	X	X	—	X	X	—	—	7
Sweden	X	X	X	X	X	X	X	X	X	X	X	X	X	X	X	X
Switzerland	—	X	X	X	X	X	—	—	—	X	X	X	X	X	X	X
Syria	X	X	X	X	X	X	X	X	X	X	X	X	X	X	X	—
Taiwan	—	—	—	—	—	X	X	X	X	X	—	—	—	X	—	—
Thailand	X	X	X	X	X	X	X	X	X	X	X	X	X	X	—	—
Togo	X	—	X	X	X	X	X	X	X	X	X	X	X	X	—	X
Tonga	—	—	—	—	—	—	—	—	—	—	—	X	X	—	—	7
Trinidad and Tobago	X	—	X	X	X	X	X	X	X	X	X	X	X	X	X	X
Tunisia	X	X	X	X	X	X	X	X	X	X	X	X	X	X	X	7
Turkey	X	X	X	X	X	X	X	X	X	X	X	X	X	X	X	X
Uganda	X	X	X	X	X	X	X	X	X	X	X	X	X	X	—	X
Ukraine	X	X	X	—	X	X	—	—	—	—	X	X	X	X	—	—
Union of Soviet Socialist Republics	X	X	X	—	X	X	—	—	—	—	X	X	X	X	X	—
United Arab Emirates	X	—	X	—	—	X	—	—	—	X	—	—	—	—	—	—
United Kingdom	X	X	X	X	X	X	X	X	X	X	X	X	X	X	X	X
United Republic of Tanzania	X	—	X	X	X	X	X	X	X	X	X	X	X	X	—	X
United States	X	X	X	X	X	X	X	X	X	X	X	X	X	X	X	X
Upper Volta	X	—	X	X	X	X	X	—	X	X	X	X	X	X	X	X
Uruguay	X	X	X	X	X	X	X	X	—	X	X	X	X	X	X	X
Venezuela	X	X	X	X	X	X	X	X	—	X	X	X	X	X	—	—
Western Samoa	—	—	—	—	—	X	—	—	—	X	—	—	—	—	—	—
Yemen	X	—	X	X	X	X	X	X	X	X	X	X	X	X	—	—
Yugoslavia	X	X	X	X	X	X	X	X	X	X	X	X	X	X	X	X
Zaïre	X	X	X	X	X	X	X	X	X	X	X	X	X	X	X	X
Zambia	X	X	X	X	X	X	X	X	X	X	X	X	X	X	—	7
Totals	132	103	123	126	129¹	135²	121	97	111	125	122	146³	142⁴	136⁵	79⁶	83

¹ UNESCO has 1 associate member: British Eastern Caribbean Group.

² WHO has 2 associate members: Papua New Guinea, Rhodesia.

³ The 146 members of UPU include the following not listed in the table: Netherlands Antilles and Surinam; Overseas Territories for the international relations of which the Government of the United Kingdom of Great Britain and Northern Ireland are responsible; Portuguese Provinces in East Africa, Asia, and Oceania; Portuguese Provinces in West Africa; Spanish Territory in Africa; whole of the Territories of the United States of America, including the Trust Territory of the Pacific Islands; whole of the Territories represented by the French Overseas Post and Telecommunication Agency.

⁴ The 142 members of ITU include the following not listed in the table: Group of Territories represented by the French Overseas Post and Telecommunication Agency; Overseas Territories for the international relations of which the Government of the United Kingdom of Great Britain and Northern Ireland are re-

sponsible; Portuguese Overseas Provinces; Rhodesia; Spanish Province in Africa; Territories of the United States of America.

⁵ The 136 members of WMO include States and 13 Territories maintaining their own meteorological services. Besides those listed in the table, the members are: Bahamas, British Caribbean Territories, Comoro Islands, French Polynesia, French Territory of the Afars and the Issas, Hong Kong, Netherlands Antilles, New Caledonia, Portuguese East Africa, Portuguese West Africa, St. Pierre and Miquelon, Rhodesia, Surinam.

⁶ IMCO has 1 associate member: Hong Kong.

⁷ The 83 Contracting Parties to GATT include Rhodesia, not listed in the table. Any additional countries, marked ⁷ in the table, have the following forms of special relationship: *Acceded provisionally:* Tunisia; *applying GATT de facto pending final decision as to their future commercial policy:* Algeria, Bahrain, Botswana, Equatorial Guinea, Fiji, Khmer Republic, Lesotho, Maldives, Mali, People's Democratic Republic of Yemen, Qatar, Swaziland, Tonga, Zambia.

4

Treaties and Agreements on Nuclear Weapons and Co-operation in Antarctica, on the Seabed, and in Outer Space

Leading members of the United Nations have initiated agreements over wide areas in respect of scientific co-operation as well as the limitation of nuclear warfare or of nuclear tests.

ANTARCTIC TREATY

On Dec. 1, 1959, a 30-year treaty was signed in Washington at the end of a 12-nation conference on peaceful international scientific co-operation in Antarctica. The 12 original signatories were Argentina, Australia, Belgium, Britain, Chile, France, Japan, New Zealand, Norway, South Africa, the Soviet Union, and the United States, who have subsequently been joined by Czechoslovakia, Denmark, and Poland. The treaty came into force on June 23, 1961.

The main provisions of the treaty are summarized below:

Art. 1. Antarctical shall be used for peaceful purposes only. The contracting parties are forbidden to establish military bases in the area, to carry out military maneuvers, or to test any kind of weapons.

Art. 2. Freedom of scientific investigation and co-operation toward that end should be maintained.

Art. 3. Scientific information and personnel should be exchanged by the contracting parties.

Art. 4. Nothing contained in the treaty may be interpreted as a renunciation, denial, or support of a claim to territorial sovereignty in Antarctica. No new claim to territorial sovereignty may be asserted while the treaty is in force.

Art. 5. Any nuclear explosions in Antarctica and the disposal there of radioactive waste shall be prohibited.

Art. 6. The provisions of the treaty apply to the land area south of 60 degrees South latitude.

Art. 7. Each contracting party has the right to send observers to carry out inspections in Antarctica. Notification must be given of all expeditions and stations in Antarctica.

Art. 8. Observers and scientific personnel in Antarctica are subject to the jurisdiction of their own country.

Art. 9. The contracting parties shall meet at suitable intervals to consult together on measures for the furtherance of the principles and objectives of the treaty. [*17159A*]

In February 1972 the treaty's 12 original signatories concluded an agreement on the protection of seals in the Antarctic, including those in the open sea or on floating ice. [*25166A*]

NUCLEAR TEST-BAN TREATY

A treaty banning all nuclear tests except those held underground was signed in Moscow on Aug. 5, 1963, by the United States, the Soviet Union, and Britain.

The most important provisions of the treaty are:

Art. 1. 1. Each of the parties to this treaty undertakes to prohibit, to prevent, and not to carry out any nuclear weapon test explosion, or any other nuclear explosion, at any place under its jurisdiction or control:

(*a*) In the atmosphere; beyond its limits, including outer space; or under water, including territorial waters or high seas; or

(*b*) In any other environment if such explosion causes radioactive debris to be present outside the territorial limits of the State under whose jurisdiction or control such explosion is conducted. It is understood in this connection that the provisions of this sub-paragraph are without prejudice to the conclusion of a treaty resulting in the permanent banning of all nuclear test explosions, including all such explosions underground, the conclusion of which, as the parties have stated in the preamble to this treaty, they seek to achieve.

2. Each of the parties to this treaty undertakes furthermore to refrain from causing, encouraging, or in any way participating in the carrying out of any nuclear weapon test explosion, or any other nuclear explosion, anywhere, which would take place in any of the environments described, or have the effect referred to, in paragraph 1 of this Article.

Art. 4. This treaty shall be of unlimited duration. Each party shall, in exercising its national sovereignty, have the right to withdraw from the treaty if it decides that extraordinary events, related to the subject matter of this treaty, have jeopardized the supreme interest of its country. It shall give notice of such withdrawal to all other parties to the treaty three months in advance.

A joint statement issued by the three Powers at the time of signature expressed the hope that other States would adhere to the treaty. From Aug. 8, 1963, the treaty was open for signature in all three capitals (Washington, Moscow, and London). By the date of the treaty's entry into force (Oct. 10, 1963) 105 nations had signed it, most of them in all three capitals. Of the States which have refused to sign, the most important are the People's Republic of China and France; other Governments which did not sign the treaty included those of Albania, Cambodia, Cuba, Guinea, North Korea, and North Vietnam. [*19553A; 19789A*]

NOTE: A Treaty for the Prohibition of Nuclear Weapons in Latin America (the "Treaty of Tlatelolco") was signed by 21 Latin American countries on Feb. 14, 1967, and approved by the U.N. General Assembly on Dec. 5, 1967. The treaty is not yet in force and is therefore not dealt with here. [*22505A; 25682B*]

NUCLEAR NON-PROLIFERATION TREATY

The Treaty on the Non-Proliferation of Nuclear Weapons, adopted by the U.N. General Assembly on June 12, 1968, came into force on March 5, 1970, by which date a total of 47 countries had deposited instruments of ratification.

The main provisions of the treaty are:

Art. 1. Each nuclear-weapon State party to the treaty undertakes not to transfer to any recipient whatsoever nuclear weapons or other nuclear explosive devices or control over such weapons or explosive devices directly, or indirectly; and not in any way to assist, encourage, or induce any non-nuclear-weapon State to manufacture or otherwise acquire nuclear weapons or other nuclear explosive devices, or control over such weapons or explosive devices.

Art. 3. (1) Each non-nuclear State party to the treaty undertakes to accept safeguards, as set forth in an agreement to be negotiated and concluded with the International Atomic Energy Agency . . . , for the exclusive purpose of

verification of the fulfilment of its obligations assumed under this treaty with a view to preventing diversion of nuclear energy from peaceful uses to nuclear weapons or other nuclear explosive devices. . . .

(2) Each State party to the treaty undertakes not to provide: (*a*) source or special fissionable material, or (*b*) equipment or material especially designed or prepared for the processing, use, or production of special fissionable material, to any non-nuclear-weapon State for peaceful purposes, unless the source or special fissionable material shall be subject to the safeguards required by this Article.

Art. 4. (1) Nothing in this treaty shall be interpreted as affecting the inalienable right of all the parties to the treaty to develop research, production, and use of nuclear energy for peaceful purposes without discrimination. . . .

Art. 7. Nothing in this treaty affects the right of any group of States to conclude regional treaties in order to assure the total absence of nuclear weapons in their respective territories.

The treaty was signed on July 1, 1968, by Britain, the Soviet Union, and the United States, 56 other countries signing on the same day. Two of the nuclear Powers—France and the People's Republic of China—have to date not signed the treaty. [*22787A; 23965A*]

Following the signature of the treaty by five countries of the European Communities—Belgium, Western Germany, Italy, Luxemburg, and the Netherlands—the European Commission began negotiations with the IAEA on an inspection agreement as stipulated in Article 3, with the objective of reaching agreement on how the Euratom control system, as previously applied, could be adapted and verified by the Agency in accordance with the treaty requirements.

The Council of Ministers on Sept. 25, 1972, approved the text of the agreement. A total of 30 similar agreements had by that time been concluded between the IAEA and signatories of the treaty, and a further 20 were in the course of negotiation.

SEABED ARMS CONTROL TREATY

A Treaty on the Prohibition of the Emplacement of Nuclear Weapons and Other Weapons of Mass Destruction on the Seabed and the Ocean Floor and in the Subsoil thereof, which had been submitted to the U.N. General Assembly by the Conference of the Committee on Disarmament, was signed on Feb. 11, 1971, by Britain, the Soviet Union, and the United States. By the time of its entry into force on May 18, 1972, a total of 34 countries had deposited instruments of ratification, while another 5 had signed the treaty but not yet ratified it.

The parties to the treaty undertook not to place on the seabed "any nuclear weapons or any other types of weapons of mass destruction as well as structures, launching installations, or any other facilities specifically designed for storing, testing, or using such weapons." [24501A]

AGREEMENTS ON A COMMUNICATIONS SATELLITE SYSTEM

Two agreements on the establishment of an international communications satellite system were signed in Washington on Aug. 20, 1964, by the United States, Britain, and 9 other countries. The first, an inter-governmental agreement, outlined the general organizational principles of the system, while the second agreement, concluded between the "designated communications entities of each country" (e.g. the U.S. Communications Satellite Corporation) dealt with the commercial, financial, and technical operations, and provided for the setting up of a management committee. By Jan. 1, 1967, a total of 55 States, including the Vatican, had adhered to the treaties.

The provisions of the inter-governmental treaty included the following:

(a) The design, development, construction, and establishment of satellites, and the ground installations for their control, would be a co-operative international enterprise. The telecommunications ground stations would be owned by the countries or groups of countries in which they were located.

(b) The U.S. Communications Satellite Corporation (COMSAT) would be responsible for the management of the satellite system, and would bear the greatest part of the cost.

(c) Part ownership of the system would be open to any member of the International Telecommunication Union (see page 31).

(d) The agreements would be of an interim character and would remain in force until 1969, when a conference would be held to consider the establishment of permanent arrangements.

A supplementary agreement on arbitration was concluded in Washington on June 4, 1965. [20614A]

The International Telecommunications Satellite Consortium (Intelsat) set up under these agreements had by July 1972 a total of 83 members. [25411A]

An agreement on the establishment of an international space communications organization to be known as Intersputnik was signed in Moscow on Nov. 15, 1971, by Bulgaria, Cuba, Czechoslovakia, Eastern Germany, Hungary, Mongolia, Poland, Romania, and the Soviet Union. Intersputnik would be open to accession by all countries and would co-ordinate its activities with the International Telecommunications Union and with the other organizations concerned with the use of communications satellites. [24944A]

OUTER SPACE TREATY

It was disclosed at the United Nations on Dec. 8, 1966, that agreement had been reached on the first international treaty governing space exploration. The treaty, officially designated the "Treaty on the Principles of the Activity of States in the Exploration and Use of Outer Space Including the Moon and Other Celestial Bodies," was unanimously approved by the U.N. General Assembly on Dec. 19, 1966. It was signed by the United States, the Soviet Union, and Britain in their respective capitals on Jan. 27, 1967, and by the date of its entry into force (Oct. 10, 1967), it had been signed in Washington, London, or Moscow by a total of 93 nations. [22362A]

The main provisions of the treaty are:

Art. 1. The exploration and use of outer space, including the moon and other celestial bodies, shall be carried out for the benefit and in the interests of all countries, irrespective of their degree of economic or scientific development, and shall be the province of all mankind.

Outer space, including the moon and other celestial bodies, shall be free for exploration and use by all States without discrimination of any kind, on a basis of equality and in accordance with international law, and there shall be free access to all areas of celestial bodies.

There shall be freedom of scientific investigation in outer space, including the moon and other celestial bodies, and States shall facilitate and encourage international co-operation in such investigation.

Art. 2. Outer space, including the moon and other celestial bodies, is not subject to national appropriation by claim of sovereignty, by means of use or occupation, or by any other means.

Art. 3. States parties to the treaty shall carry on activities in the exploration and use of outer space, including the moon and other celestial bodies, in accordance with international law, including the Charter of the United Nations, in the interest of maintaining international peace and security and promoting international co-operation and understanding.

Art. 4. States parties to the treaty undertake not to place in orbit around the earth any objects carrying nuclear weapons or any other kinds of weapons of mass destruction, install such weapons on celestial bodies, or station such weapons in outer space in any other manner.

The moon and other celestial bodies shall be used by all States parties to the treaty exclusively for peaceful purposes. The establishment of military bases, installations, and fortifications, the testing of any type of weapons, and the conduct of military maneuvers on celestial bodies shall be forbidden. The use of military personnel for scientific research or for any other peaceful purposes shall not be prohibited. The use of any equipment or facility necessary for peaceful exploration of the moon and other celestial bodies shall also not be prohibited.

Art. 9. In the exploration and use of outer space, including the moon and other celestial bodies, States parties to the treaty shall be guided by the principle of co-operation and mutual assistance and shall conduct all their activities in outer space, including the moon and other celestial bodies, with due regard to the corresponding interests of all other States parties to the treaty. . . . [21791A]

AGREEMENT ON RESCUE AND RETURN OF ASTRONAUTS

An Agreement on the Rescue of Astronauts, the Return of Astronauts and the Return of Objects Launched into Outer Space was approved by the U.N. General Assembly on Dec. 19, 1967, by 115 votes to none, with no abstentions.

Under this agreement, which had been worked out by the United States and the Soviet Union in co-operation with a 28-nation Committee on Outer Space of the U.N. General Assembly, signatories were bound to render "all possible assistance to astronauts in the event of accident, distress, emergency, or unintended landing." The agreement also provided for safe and prompt return of astronauts and space objects, and reimbursement of expenses to the launching State, as well as for notification of unplanned landings by space travelers or spacecraft.

The agreement entered into force on Dec. 3, 1968, after ratification by Britain, the Soviet Union, and the United States. [22539A; 23192A]

CONVENTION OF INTERNATIONAL LIABILITY

The U.N. General Assembly approved on Nov. 29, 1971, by 93 votes to none with 4 abstentions (Canada, Iran, Japan, and Sweden) a Convention on International Liability for Damage Caused by Space Objects. [25192A; 25133]

5

Europe: Steps Toward Integration Among Non-Communist States

THE BRUSSELS TREATY AND WESTERN EUROPEAN UNION

Members of Western European Union: Belgium, Britain, France, German Federal Republic, Italy, Luxemburg, the Netherlands.

The Brussels Treaty, signed on March 17, 1948, by representatives of Belgium, Britain, France, Luxemburg, and the Netherlands, was a treaty of collective military aid and economic and social co-operation.

The Development of Western Union

The basis of the Brussels Treaty, or Western Union, was the Treaty of Dunkirk, an Anglo-French treaty of alliance signed on March 4, 1947. By this treaty the two signatories were pledged to give mutual support in the event of renewed German aggression, and to take common action should either Party be prejudiced by the failure of Germany to fulfil any of her economic obligations. [8463A]

On March 4, 1948, a conference of representatives of Belgium, Britain, France, Luxemburg, and the Netherlands opened in Brussels to draft a 5-nation treaty implementing proposals for Western Union earlier put forward by Ernest Bevin, the British Foreign Secretary. The 50-year Treaty was signed two weeks later.

Main Provisions of the Brussels Treaty

In a preamble to the Treaty the signatories included among their aims: the strengthening of economic, social, and cultural ties; the co-ordination of efforts to create a firm basis for European economic recovery, and mutual assistance in maintaining international peace and security.

Article 4 of the Treaty provided for mutual automatic military assistance in the event of an armed attack in Europe. Article 7 created a Consultative Council to discuss matters dealt with in the Treaty. [9157A]

Western European Union (WEU)

The Brussels Treaty was amended and expanded through the so-called Paris Agreements, which were signed on Oct. 23, 1954, and came into force on May 5, 1955. The decisions embodied in the Paris Agreements had been reached at a 9-power conference held in London from Sept. 28 to Oct. 3, 1954, after the breakdown of plans for the creation of a European Defense Community.

Among the Paris Agreements was a series, signed by representatives of Belgium, Britain, Canada, France, the German Federal Republic, Italy, Luxemburg, the Netherlands, and the United States (the 9 powers which attended the London Conference), dealing with the accession of Italy and the German Federal Republic to the Brussels Treaty Organization. The Organization itself, in its new and expanded form, was renamed the Western European Union.

Others of the Paris Agreements made provision for the ending of the occupation regime in West Germany, for the restoration of sovereignty to the German Federal Republic, and for the entry of the latter into NATO. [13809A; 13850A]

The Revised Brussels Treaty

Those documents of the Paris Agreements which are relevant to the formation of the WEU comprise four Protocols and a resolution on the production and standardization of armaments.

Protocol I amended the Brussels Treaty of 1948 to permit the entry of the German Federal Republic and

Signatories of the Brussels Pact

Adherents to W.E.U. under the Paris Agreements

Italy into the Treaty Organization. The system of mutual automatic assistance in case of attack was extended to the two new entrants. The Consultative Council set up under the original Treaty was given powers of decision and renamed the Council of Western European Union.

Protocol II laid down the maximum strength of land and air forces to be maintained in Europe at the disposal of the Supreme Allied Commander of NATO by each of the member-countries of the WEU in peace-time. The contribution of naval forces to NATO by each of the WEU countries would be determined annually. Regular inspections would be held by the Supreme Allied Commander, Europe, to ensure that the limits were observed. A special article recapitulated an undertaking by Britain not to withdraw or diminish her forces in Europe against the wishes of the majority of her partners. In 1957 Britain was given permission, by the WEU Council, to withdraw some of her forces from West Germany.

Protocol III embodied resolutions on the control of armaments on the European mainland. The German Federal Republic was forbidden to manufacture atomic, biological, or chemical weapons, and stocks of such weapons in other countries of continental Europe were to be strictly controlled. In addition, Germany undertook not to manufacture long-range and guided missiles, influence mines, warships, and strategic bombers unless the competent NATO Supreme Commander should recommend any change in the ruling.

Protocol IV set up an Agency for the Control of Armaments and defined its functions, these being mainly to enforce the provisions of Protocol III. [*Page 13871*]

Later Decisions of the WEU

The most important decisions taken at subsequent meetings of the WEU have concerned amendments to Protocol III of the revised Brussels Treaty.

The first such decision was taken at a meeting of the Permanent Council on April 23, 1958, when West Germany's request to manufacture short-range, anti-tank, guided missiles with only conventional warheads was approved. [*16238A*]

On Oct. 21, 1959, the Council of the WEU removed the restriction on the construction of ground-to-air and air-to-air anti-aircraft missiles by Germany. [*Page 17850*]

Between May 1961 and October 1963, the WEU approved a number of revisions to the permitted limits on West German naval construction. On May 24, 1961, the Council of the WEU raised the tonnage limit for eight West German destroyers to 6,000 tons (double the existing general limit), and permitted the German Federal Republic to build fleet auxiliary vessels of up to 6,000 tons and to manufacture influence mines for port protection. [*Page 18443*]

On Oct. 19, 1962, the WEU announced its agreement to increase from 350 to 450 tons the limit for West German submarines "to fufil NATO requirements." [*Page 19396*] A year later, on Oct. 9, 1963, the WEU Permanent Council agreed to raise the tonnage limit for West German submarines from 450 to 1,000 tons, and to allow six submarines of the latter size to be built in the German Federal Republic. [*19684C*]

Co-operation Between EEC and WEU

On July 11, 1963, the Council of Ministers of the EEC (comprising all the member-countries of the WEU except Britain) agreed that regular tri-monthly Ministerial meetings of the WEU should be held, and that the item "exchange of views on the European economic situation" should always appear on the agenda. The European Commission (see page 52) takes part in these economic discussions. [*Page 19803*]

Temporary French Withdrawal from Ministerial Council

France withdrew from meetings of the WEU Ministerial Council on Feb. 19, 1969, and did not return to them until June 5, 1970.

France's withdrawal followed (*a*) discussions by the Council on Oct. 21–22, 1968, and Feb. 6–7, 1969, of

NON-COMMUNIST COUNTRIES IN EUROPE

Communities and Regional Groups

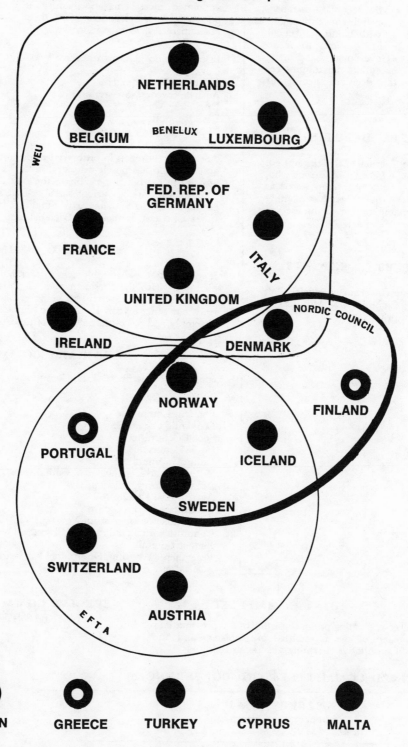

WEU

NETHERLANDS

BELGIUM   BENELUX   LUXEMBOURG

FED. REP. OF
GERMANY

FRANCE

ITALY

UNITED KINGDOM

NORDIC COUNCIL

IRELAND   DENMARK

NORWAY

FINLAND

PORTUGAL

ICELAND

SWEDEN

SWITZERLAND

E F T A

AUSTRIA

SPAIN   GREECE   TURKEY   CYPRUS   MALTA

Member countries of the Council of Europe are represented by black spots

COUNCIL OF EUROPE

COMMITTEE OF MINISTERS
(The Council's Executive Organ)

consisting of Foreign Ministers of 17 member-States. Authorized to conclude conventions and agreements, to decide with binding effect all matters of internal organization, to make recommendations to Governments, and to be informed on their execution. Unanimity required on all important decisions affecting all member-States.

MINISTERS' DEPUTIES

consisting of the permanent delegates of member-States of the Council of Europe who, since March 1952, have been empowered to deal with most of the routine work at monthly meetings in the name of the Committee of Ministers.

COMMITTEES OF EXPERTS

consisting of higher Government officials and appointed by the Committee of Ministers to deal with specified problems.

CONSULTATIVE ASSEMBLY

consisting of 140 members elected by their national Parliaments or appointed, most being also members of their own Parliaments. Political parties in each delegation reflect their relative strength in the national Parliament.   Composition:

Britain, France, German Federal Republic, Italy	18 each
Turkey	10
Belgium, Netherlands	7 each
Austria, Sweden, Switzerland	6 each
Denmark, Norway	5 each
Irish Republic	4
Cyprus, Iceland, Luxemburg, Malta	3 each

The Assembly meets in ordinary session in at least two parts (spring and autumn) and has purely advisory, no legislative powers. The Committee of Ministers is not responsible to the Assembly, but merely reports to it. The deputies of the various member-States have formed parliamentary groups according to their party affiliations, irrespective of their nationality (i.e. a Christian-Democratic, Socialist, and Liberal group).

STANDING COMMITTEE

representing the Assembly when it is not in session, consisting of 35 members (with the President and Vice-Presidents of the Assembly and the Chairmen of Committees being *ex-officio* members) and meeting at least four times a year. Its task is to prepare the work of the Consultative Assembly and to co-ordinate that of the Committees.

ORDINARY COMMITTEES

consisting of members of the Consultative Assembly

	Number of Members
Political Committee	33
Economic Committee	33
Social Committee	33
Legal Committee	33
Cultural Committee	33
Scientific and Technological Committee	33
Local Authorities Committee	33
Agricultural Committee	26
Committee for Procedure	26
Committee for Interests of Non-represented Nations	22
Committee for Population and Refugees	18
Budget Committee	18
Permanent Working Group for Parliamentary and Public Relations	18

JOINT COMMITTEE

co-ordinating organ consisting of 8 representatives each of the Committee of Ministers and the Consultative Assembly meeting as required

SPECIAL COMMITTEES
(appointed as required)

MIXED COMMITTEES AND CONFERENCES

SECRETARIAT
Secretary-General
(appointed by the Consultative Assembly)

Political Department

Meetings Dept. Administration

Press and Information Department

Human Rights Directorate

Studies

Legal Affairs   External Affairs   Technical Services

EUROPEAN COMMISSION OF HUMAN RIGHTS

(on which each member-State is represented by one member elected by the Committee of Ministers)

EUROPEAN COURT OF HUMAN RIGHTS

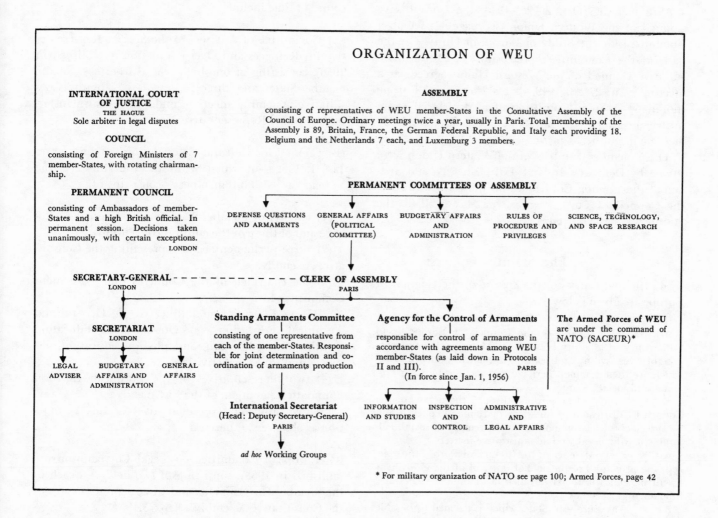

ORGANIZATION OF WEU

INTERNATIONAL COURT OF JUSTICE
THE HAGUE
Sole arbiter in legal disputes

COUNCIL

consisting of Foreign Ministers of 7 member-States, with rotating chairmanship.

PERMANENT COUNCIL

consisting of Ambassadors of member-States and a high British official. In permanent session. Decisions taken unanimously, with certain exceptions.
LONDON

ASSEMBLY

consisting of representatives of WEU member-States in the Consultative Assembly of the Council of Europe. Ordinary meetings twice a year, usually in Paris. Total membership of the Assembly is 89, Britain, France, the German Federal Republic, and Italy each providing 18. Belgium and the Netherlands 7 each, and Luxemburg 3 members.

PERMANENT COMMITTEES OF ASSEMBLY

| DEFENSE QUESTIONS AND ARMAMENTS | GENERAL AFFAIRS (POLITICAL COMMITTEE) | BUDGETARY AFFAIRS AND ADMINISTRATION | RULES OF PROCEDURE AND PRIVILEGES | SCIENCE, TECHNOLOGY, AND SPACE RESEARCH |

SECRETARY-GENERAL – – – – – – – – – – – – **CLERK OF ASSEMBLY**
LONDON — PARIS

SECRETARIAT
LONDON

| LEGAL ADVISER | BUDGETARY AFFAIRS AND ADMINISTRATION | GENERAL AFFAIRS |

Standing Armaments Committee

consisting of one representative from each of the member-States. Responsible for joint determination and co-ordination of armaments production

Agency for the Control of Armaments

responsible for control of armaments in accordance with agreements among WEU member-States (as laid down in Protocols II and III).
PARIS
(In force since Jan. 1, 1956)

The Armed Forces of WEU are under the command of NATO (SACEUR)*

International Secretariat
(Head: Deputy Secretary-General)
PARIS

| INFORMATION AND STUDIES | INSPECTION AND CONTROL | ADMINISTRATIVE AND LEGAL AFFAIRS |

ad hoc Working Groups

* For military organization of NATO see page 100; Armed Forces, page 42

---

the "Harmel Plan"—a proposal made by M. Pierre Harmel, the Belgian Foreign Minister, for co-operation between the European Community and Britain in the fields of foreign, defense, technological and monetary policy, and (*b*) a meeting held by the WEU Permanent Council, against France's wishes and without her participation, for discussions on the Middle East situation. [*23265A; 24040A*]

THE COUNCIL OF EUROPE

The Council of Europe, a political organization of European States, came into being on May 5, 1949, when its Statute was signed by the ten founding members

(see page 48). The Statute came into force on Aug. 3, 1949.

History

In December 1947, the four principal movements in the campaign for European unity—the British United Europe Movement, the French Council for United Europe, the Independent League for European Co-operation, and the European Union of Federalists—united to form the "International Committee of Movements for European Unity." [*9317A*]

This Committee organized a "Congress of Europe" held at The Hague, May 7–10, 1948. Here resolutions stressing the need for political, economic, and social collaboration in Europe were adopted. On Oct. 25,

1948, at a meeting in Brussels of the International Committee of Movements for European Unity, it was announced that the Committee would be enlarged to include all bodies working for European unity, and would be renamed the "European Movement." [9602D]

At a meeting, Oct. 25–26, 1948, the Consultative Council of the Western Union (see page 41) set up a Committee for the Study of European Unity. On the basis of the Committee's preparatory work the Consultative Council of the Western Union agreed, at a meeting, Jan. 27–28, 1949, that a Council of Europe should be created, "consisting of a Ministerial Committee meeting in private, and a Consultative Body meeting in public." [9765A]

The 5 member-countries of the Western Union were joined by Denmark, Ireland, Italy, Norway, and Sweden at the London Conference on the Constitution of the Council of Europe where, on May 5, 1949, the Statute was signed. [9973A]

The Statute

The principal clauses of the Statute of the Council of Europe are given below:

Art. 1.—(a) The aim of the Council of Europe is to achieve a greater unity between its Members for the purpose of safeguarding and realizing the ideals and principles which are their common heritage and facilitating their economic and social progress.

(b) This aim shall be pursued through the organs of the Council by discussion of questions of common concern and by agreements and common action in economic, social, cultural, scientific, legal, and administrative matters.

Art. 3.—Every Member of the Council of Europe must accept the principles of the rule of law and of the enjoyment by all persons within its jurisdiction of human rights and fundamental freedoms.

Art. 4.—Any European State, which is deemed to be able and willing to fulfil the provisions of Art. 3, may be invited to become a Member of the Council of Europe by the Committee of Ministers.

By a revision of this Article the Consultative Assembly must now be consulted before the issue of an invitation to join the Council.

Art. 10.—The organs of the Council of Europe are: (i) the Committee of Ministers; (ii) the Consultative Assembly. Both these organs shall be served by the Secretariat of the Council of Europe.

Art. 11.—The seat of the Council of Europe is at Strasbourg.

Others articles of the Statute deal with the functions and activities of the various organs of the Council, with matters of finance, and with the privileges and immunities to be enjoyed by representatives of Members of the Council of Europe in the territories of Members of the Council. [9973A]

Committees of Experts

Permanent committees of experts established in the course of time include:

(A) Committee of Advisers to the Special Representative for Refugees and Over-Population (established in 1956), consisting of one high official from each of the member-States and three representatives of the Consultative Assembly meeting under the chairmanship of the Special Representative.

(B) Council for Cultural Co-operation (established on Jan. 1, 1962)—of which Spain and the Holy See (the Vatican) are also full members—consisting of:

(1) experts of member-States of the Council of Europe and of those of the cultural conventions;
(2) three parliamentarians representing the Consultative Assembly;
(3) the chairmen of the Council's four Permanent Committees for:
(a) Higher Education and Research, (b) General and Technical Education, (c) Out-of-School Education (youth, adult education, and physical education and sport), and (d) Film Activities;
(4) two representatives of the European Cultural Foundation (an organ of the EEC); and
(5) two additional representatives of this Foundation as observers, if necessary.

(C) European Committee on Legal Co-operation (established in 1963), consisting of two delegates each of the member-Governments and three representatives of the Consultative Assembly. [20158A]

Permanent Conferences Organized by the Consultative Assembly

A number of conferences of a non-governmental character, created by the Consultative Assembly, have developed into more or less permanent institutions. They include:

(A) *European Conference of Local Authorities*, meeting every two years and consisting of the same number of elected local government representatives from member-countries as the latters' representatives in the Consultative Assembly, while non-member-countries may send observers (as has been done by Finland, Israel, and Yugoslavia). It has drawn up a Charter, approved by the Committee of Ministers in January 1961, aimed at securing the participation of local authorities in the work of the Council of Europe. A joint commission of this conference and the Consultative Assembly on improvement of the European territory was created by the Assembly on Sept. 26, 1961, and another joint committee promotes inter-municipal exchanges. [*Page 20161*]

(B) *Professional Conference on Alcoholic Beverages,* organized by the Agricultural Committee of the Consultative Assembly. The Conference, which first met on April 4–5, 1960, and has subsequently met from time to time, considers questions related to the production and marketing of alcoholic beverages.

(C) *European Conference on Road Safety,* an *ad hoc* conference organized by the Economic Committee of the Assembly, held its first session, April 12–14, 1962.

(D) *European Conference on Air Pollution,* called by the Committee of Ministers on the initiative of the Social Committee of the Assembly. The Conference first met, June 24–July 1, 1964 [*Page 20161*]

Permanent Inter-Governmental Conferences

Permanent inter-government conferences associated with the Council of Europe include the following:

(A) *European Civil Aviation Conference,* set up by the International Civil Aviation Organization (ICAO) on the initiative of the Council of Europe. Its first session took place from Nov. 29 to Dec. 16, 1955, and subsequent sessions have been held generally every two years. Members of the Conference are the member-countries of the Council of Europe with the exception of Cyprus and Malta and with the addition of Finland, Portugal, and Spain. [*15122A*]

(B) *European Conference of Ministers of Justice,* organized on the initiative of the European Committee for Crime Problems (a Committee of the Council of Europe). The Conference first met in June 1961, and subsequent sessions have been held at intervals of roughly two years. The delegates to the Conference are the Justice Ministers of the member-countries of the Council of Europe.

(C) *European Conference of Ministers of Education.* The first Conference of European Ministers of Education, held at The Hague in November 1959, took place within the framework of WEU. In 1960, however, the Council of Europe took over responsibility for the Conference.

(D) *Governmental Conference on European Public Services.* After the dissolution in 1962 of the Council of Europe's Consultative Committee formed to study problems related to public services in Europe, a governmental conference was called to deal with these problems. The Conference, which first met, Nov. 5–6, 1963, is attended by representatives of 23 Governments and 16 international organizations.

Conventions and Agreements

Of the many conventions and agreements on various aspects of European co-operation which have been concluded by the Council of Europe, the most important are the European Convention for the Protection of Human Rights and Fundamental Freedoms, and the European Social Charter.

1. HUMAN RIGHTS

The European Convention for the Protection of Human Rights and Fundamental Freedoms, signed in Rome on Nov. 4, 1950, and in force since Sept. 3, 1953, differs from the United Nations' Declaration on Human Rights of 1948 (see page 15), in that it sets up machinery for the examination of complaints of any violation of human rights and fundamental freedoms on the part of signatories to the Convention. These decision-taking bodies are the European Commission of Human Rights and the European Court of Human Rights.

All member-countries of the Council of Europe except Switzerland and Malta have signed the Convention and, of the signatories, all except France have ratified it.

The principal provisions relating to specific human rights are given below:

Art. 2. (1) Everyone's right to life shall be protected by law. No one shall be deprived of his life intentionally save in the execution of a sentence of a court following his conviction of a crime for which this penalty is provided by law. . . .

Art. 3. No one shall be subjected to torture or to inhuman or degrading treatment or punishment.

Art. 4. (1) No one shall be held in slavery or servitude.

(2) No one shall be required to perform forced or compulsory labor.

Art. 5. (1) Everyone has the right to liberty and security of person. . . .

Art. 6. (1) In the determination of his civil rights and obligations, or of any criminal charge against him, everyone is entitled to a fair and public hearing within a reasonable time by an independent and impartial tribunal established by law. . . .

Art. 7. (1) No one shall be held guilty of any criminal offense on account of any act or omission which did not constitute a criminal offense under national or international law at the time when it was committed. Nor shall a heavier penalty be imposed than the one that was applicable at the time the criminal offense was committed. . . .

Art. 8. (1) Everyone has the right to respect for his private and family life, his home, and his correspondence. . . .

Art. 9. (1) Everyone has the right to freedom of thought, conscience, and religion. . . .

Art. 10. (1) Everyone has the right to freedom of expression. . . .

Art. 11. (1) Everyone has the right to freedom of peaceful assembly and to freedom of association with others. . . .

Art. 12. Men and women of marriageable age have the right to marry and to found a family. . . .

Art. 14. The enjoyment of the rights and freedoms set forth in this Convention shall be secured without discrimination on any ground such as sex, race, color, language, religion, political or other opinion, national or social origin, association with a national minority, property, birth, or other status. . . . [11341A]

The Fourth Protocol to the Convention, opened for signature on Sept. 16, 1963, provides for freedom from imprisonment for inability to fulfil a contractual obligation; freedom of movement and residence; freedom from exile; and a guarantee against the collective expulsion of exiles. [20158A]

The European Commission of Human Rights is composed of a number of representatives equal to that of the High Contracting Parties to the Convention. It is competent to receive petitions from Governments or individuals claiming violation of the provisions of the Convention. Before the Commission could begin to exercise its powers, which it did on July 5, 1955, its competence to receive individual petitions had to be recognized by a minimum of six signatory countries.

After it has examined a petition and tried to bring about a settlement, the Commission submits a report to the Committee of Ministers of the Council of Europe, which then decides, by a majority of two-thirds of its members, whether there has been a violation of the Convention. In some cases, however, the matter is referred to the Court of Human Rights.

The European Court of Human Rights consists of a number of judges equal to that of the members of the Council of Europe. Under Article 56 of the Convention, the Court of Human Rights could come into being only when eight of the High Contracting Parties had declared acceptance of the Court's compulsory jurisdiction. The Icelandic and Austrian declarations of acceptance on Sept. 3, 1958, brought the total of acceptances up to the required number.

The Court functions through a Chamber composed of seven judges. Only the Commission of Human Rights and the Governments of the High Contracting Parties to the Convention may bring a case before the Court, and then only after the Commission has acknowledged the failure of efforts to reach a friendly settlement. The judgment of the Court is final. [11341A]

The original provisions of the Convention dealing with the Commission and Court of Human Rights have been amended by the Second and Third Protocols, which were opened for signature on May 6, 1963. The Second Protocol gives the Court of Human Rights advisory powers in legal matters concerning the Convention, while the Third Protocol amends the original Convention to accelerate and simplify procedure before the Commission of Human Rights. [20158A]

2. PEACEFUL SETTLEMENT OF DISPUTES

The European Convention for the Peaceful Settlement of Disputes was signed in Strasbourg on April 29, 1957, by all member-States of the Council of Europe except Austria and Turkey, and came into force on April 30, 1958, for those countries which had ratified it.

Under this Convention the signatories agreed to submit to the International Court of Justice all international legal disputes which might arise between them. For other disputes the Convention provided for the establishment of a 5-member Conciliation Commission whenever requested by a party to a dispute, and also for an Arbitral Tribunal for such disputes as remained unresolved within one month after the end of the conciliation procedure.

(In an agreement concluded between Austria and Italy on July 17, 1971, the provisions of the Convention were made retroactive to before the date of its entry into force for these two countries.) [24747A]

3. THE EUROPEAN SOCIAL CHARTER

In order to provide protection for social rights, as the Convention for Human Rights protects civil and political rights, a Charter was drawn up by a Social Committee of experts in collaboration with the International Labor Office, the Consultative Assembly of the

Council of Europe, and employers and trade union organizations. After approval by the Committee of Ministers, the Charter was signed on Oct. 18, 1961, by 13 member-countries of the Council of Europe. Signatories to date are Austria, Belgium, Britain, Denmark, France, German Federal Republic, Greece, Ireland, Italy, Luxemburg, Netherlands, Norway, Sweden, and Turkey. The Charter came into effect on Feb. 26, 1965.

In Part I of the Charter, the signatory Governments "accept as the aim of their policy, to be pursued by all appropriate means, both national and international in character, the attainment of conditions in which the following rights and principles may be effectively realized:

"(1) Everyone shall have the opportunity to earn his living in an occupation freely entered upon.

"(2) All workers have the right to just conditions of work.

"(3) All workers have the right to safe and healthy working conditions.

"(4) All workers have the right to a fair remuneration sufficient for a decent standard of living for themselves and their families.

"(5) All workers and employers have the right to freedom of association in national or international organizations for the protection of their economic and social interests.

"(6) All workers and employers have the right to bargain collectively.

"(7) Children and young persons have the right to a special protection against the physical and moral hazards to which they are exposed.

"(8) Employed women, in case of maternity, and other employed women as appropriate, have the right to a special protection in their work.

"(9) Everyone has the right to appropriate facilities for vocational guidance with a view to helping him choose an occupation suited to his personal aptitude and interests.

"(10) Everyone has the right to appropriate facilities for vocational training.

"(11) Everyone has the right to benefit from any measures enabling him to enjoy the highest possible standard of health attainable.

"(12) All workers and their dependents have the right to social security.

"(13) Anyone without adequate resources has the right to social and medical assistance.

"(14) Everyone has the right to benefit from social and welfare services.

"(15) Disabled persons have the right to vocational training, rehabilitation, and resettlement, whatever the origin and nature of their disability.

"(16) The family as a fundamental unit of society has the right to appropriate social, legal, and economic protection to ensure its full development.

"(17) Mothers and children, irrespective of marital status and family relations, have the right to appropriate social and economic protection.

"(18) The nationals of any one of the Contracting Parties have the right to engage in any gainful occupation in the territory of any one of the others on a footing of equality with the nationals of the latter, subject to restrictions based on cogent economic or social reasons.

"(19) Migrant workers who are nationals of a Contracting Party and their families have the right to protection and assistance in the territory of any other Contracting Party."

Parts II and III of the Charter, comprising 38 Articles, lay down procedures for the application of the above principles, and include provisions for (i) derogations in time of war or emergency; (ii) the partial or complete application of the Charter by a signatory Government to non-metropolitan territories for whose international relations it is responsible; and (iii) the granting to refugees of "treatment as favorable as possible." Acceptance of Part I of the Charter (the statement of aims) and of a specified minimum of individual Articles was laid down as a requirement for ratification by a signatory Government. [20158A]

Other Conventions and Agreements in Force

SOCIAL AND MEDICAL QUESTIONS

	Opened for signature:
Interim Agreements on Social Security	Dec. 11, 1953
Convention and Protocol on Social and Medical Assistance	Dec. 11, 1953
Agreement on Exchange of War Disabled for Medical Treatment	Dec. 13, 1955
Agreement on Exchange of Therapeutic Substances of Human Origin (creation of European "Blood Bank")	Dec. 15, 1958
Agreement on Duty-free Importation of Medical, Surgical, and Laboratory Equipment	April 28, 1960
Agreement for Mutual Assistance in Special Medical Treatment and Climatic Facilities	May 14, 1962
Agreement for Exchange of Blood Reagents	May 14, 1962
Agreement on the Issue to Civil and Military War Disabled of International Vouchers for the Repair of Prosthetic and Orthopaedic Appliances	Dec. 17, 1962

CULTURAL QUESTIONS

Convention on Equivalence of Diplomas for Admission to Universities	Dec. 11, 1953
European Cultural Convention (aimed "to foster among the nationals of all members . . . the study of the languages, history, and civilization of the others and of the civilization which is common to them all.")	Dec. 19, 1954
Convention on Equivalence of Periods of University Studies	Dec. 15, 1956

Agreement on Program Exchanges by Means of Television Films	Dec. 15, 1958
Convention on Academic Recognition of University Qualifications	Dec. 14, 1959
Agreements for Protection of Television Broadcasts	June 22, 1960

AGREEMENTS ON OTHER MATTERS

Convention Relating to Formalities Required for Patent Applications	Dec. 11, 1953
Convention on International Classification of Patents	Dec. 19, 1954
Convention on Establishment (laying down common rules for the treatment of nationals of member-states on an equal footing when residing in each other's countries)	Dec. 13, 1955
Convention for Peaceful Settlement of Disputes	April 29, 1957
Convention on Extradition	Dec. 13, 1957
Agreement on Regulations Governing Movement of Persons Between States	Dec. 13, 1957
Convention on Mutual Assistance in Criminal Matters	April 20, 1959
Agreement on Abolition of Visas for Refugees	April 20, 1959
Agreement on Travel by Young Persons on Collective Passports	Dec. 16, 1961

[*20158A*]

Member-Countries of the Council of Europe

The 10 founding members of the Council were Belgium, Britain, Denmark, France, Ireland, Italy, Luxemburg, the Netherlands, Norway, and Sweden. The following 8 countries joined the Council subsequently: Greece and Turkey in August 1949; Iceland in March 1950; German Federal Republic in May 1951; Austria in April 1956; Cyprus in April 1961; Switzerland in May 1963; and Malta in January 1965. Greece withdrew from membership on Dec. 12 1969.

This decision followed the release by the Council on Sept. 25, 1969, of a report by the *rapporteur* of the Consultative Assembly (Mr. Max van der Stoel of the Netherlands Labour Party), who described the regime set up in Greece on April 21, 1967, as "undemocratic, illiberal, authoritarian, and repressive." This report had been followed by a move, supported by at least 11 of the Council's members, to suspend Greece from membership until democratic and constitutional conditions had been restored in that country. [*23773A*]

BENELUX

Members: Belgium, Luxemburg, the Netherlands

The Benelux Economic Union Treaty, establishing an Economic Union between Belgium, the Netherlands, and Luxemburg, was signed on Feb. 3, 1958, at The Hague by the Prime Ministers of the three countries. The Treaty came into effect on Nov. 1, 1960.

The purposes of the Economic Union were defined as the free mutual movement of persons, goods, services and capital; the co-ordination of national economic policies; and the pursuance of a common trade policy toward third countries.

History

The formal signing of the treaty represented the successful culmination of 14 years of work aimed at the economic union of the three countries.

As long ago as Sept. 5, 1944, the Governments of Belgium, Luxemburg, and the Netherlands—then in exile in London—signed a treaty establishing Benelux. It was not until Jan. 1, 1948, however, that the London agreement, involving measures to introduce a common customs tariff *vis-à-vis* third countries and to abolish import duties in mutual trade relations, could come into force. The organs provided for in the London agreement—a Customs Regulation Council, a Trade Treaties Council, and an Economic Union Council—were set up at the same time.

At a ministerial conference in Luxemburg in October 1949 the three countries concluded the so-called Pre-Union Treaty, as an introductory stage to a full-fledged Economic Union. Under this treaty, the exchange of goods between the three countries was made progressively free from quantitative restrictions, except for a special arrangement for agricultural products, and the three countries undertook not to change this liberalization of their mutual trade except by common agreement.

A period of instability for Benelux in the early 1950s was followed on July 24, 1953, by a protocol which laid down that the member-countries would in future coordinate their economic and social policies. A further protocol was signed on Dec. 9, 1953, under which the three countries started concluding joint trade agreements with third countries.

Further steps in the extension of economic co-operation between the Benelux countries included (*a*) the treaty of July 8, 1954, which largely liberalized the mutual exchange of capital; (*b*) a protocol signed on May 3, 1955, on the progressive harmonization of their agricultural policies within a seven-year period; and

(c) the setting-up of a common labor market under interim regulations in April 1957, as a transitional stage in the implementation of a Labor Treaty which had been signed on June 7, 1955.

An agreement of Nov. 5, 1955, provided for the establishment of an Interparliamentary Benelux Advisory Council (see below).

The Economic Union Treaty was formally initialed on Sept. 17, 1957, by the Foreign Ministers of Belgium, the Netherlands, and Luxemburg, and submitted to the Benelux Interparliamentary Advisory Council which approved it in November 1957. On July 1, 1960, shortly before the Treaty came into force, passport controls were abolished for nationals of the Benelux countries traveling between those countries. Foreigners traveling across the inner frontiers of the three countries could also, from that date, obtain a Benelux visa.

From Nov. 1, 1960, all remaining customs duties within the Benelux frontiers were abolished, and from Jan. 1, 1961, all trade agreements with third countries were to be concluded by Benelux as an entity. It was established that, by November 1965, all remaining obstacles to the free flow of goods among the three countries should be eliminated.

The Treaty

The principal provisions of the Treaty are summarized below:

Free Movement of Persons. The nationals of the three member-countries will be free to move within the whole territory of the Economic Union, and the nationals of each member-country will enjoy in the other two countries the same treatment as is accorded to the nationals of those countries.

Free Exchange of Goods, Capital, and Services. Trade between the three countries will be free from all import duties, taxes, or levies, as well as from any import or export restrictions of a quantitative, qualitative, or currency nature; capital movements from one country to the other will also be free; the exchange of services will be subject to the same principles as merchandise trade.

Co-ordination of Economic, Financial, and Social Policies. The three Governments will jointly consult on their national economic policies with a view to creating the necessary conditions for the economic integration of their countries.

Co-ordinated and Joint Action toward Third Countries. In addition to co-ordinating their internal economic policies, member-countries will also consult each other to determine the Union's attitude at meetings of international bodies and in matters relating to regional economic integration, or in relation to matters with third countries, insofar as these matters affect the aims of the Union. There will also be common policy to cover trade and payments with third countries.

The two principal provisions of Part IV laid down (1) that the scope of the Treaty would be limited to the territories of the member-countries in Europe, although the interests of Belgian and Dutch overseas territories could be safeguarded in trade agreements concluded with third countries; (2) that the Treaty would be concluded for a period of 50 years, but could be tacitly extended by further 10-year terms unless any of the parties wished to terminate it by giving advance notice of one year.

Institutions of the Union

THE COMMITTEE OF MINISTERS
This Committee, consisting of 9 members (3 from each member-country), is the directing body of the Union, being charged with the implementation of the Treaty and the taking of the necessary measures to that end. Decisions must be taken by unanimous vote and be binding on the three Governments. The Committee also gives directives to the bodies operating under it, and maintains contact with the Advisory Interparliamentary Council.

INTERPARLIAMENTARY COUNCIL
Consisting of 21 members each from Belgium and the Netherlands and 7 from Luxemburg, the Interparliamentary Council (first established on Nov. 5, 1955) advises on questions of closer economic, political, cultural, and legal co-operation between the three countries.

COUNCIL OF THE ECONOMIC UNION
This body, which functions under the Committee of Ministers as a co-ordinator of the other institutions, consists of three chairmen appointed by each of the member-Governments, and of representatives of the committees similarly designated by member-Governments.

COMMITTEES AND SPECIAL COMMITTEES
There are 7 committees: (1) on foreign economic relations; (2) on monetary and financial questions; (3) on industry and commerce; (4) on agriculture, foodstuffs, and fisheries; (5) on customs duties and taxes; (6) on transport; and (7) on social questions.

There are also 5 special committees for (1) co-ordination and statistics; (2) comparing the budgets of public and semi-public institutions; (3) public tenders; (4) public health; and (5) for the "trading middle class" (i.e. small and medium businesses).

All these committees are empowered to make proposals to the directing organs of the Union; they also possess executive and supervisory powers regarding the administration of decrees by the member-Governments.

SECRETARIAT-GENERAL
Established at Brussels, it is directed by a Netherlander, its organization and powers agreeing broadly with those of the Secretariat-General already existing under the Customs Agreement of 1944.

JOINT SERVICES

The Committee of Ministers is empowered to institute joint services if a need for these should arise.

ECONOMIC AND SOCIAL CONSULTATIVE COUNCIL

This body (whose members are appointed by the three Governments) gives advice—at the request of the Committee of Ministers or on its own initiative—on matters directly related to the operation of the Union.

BOARD OF ARBITRATORS

The original Board of Arbitrators set up to discuss disputes over the application of the Treaty has been superseded by a Court of Arbitration. A convention concerning the establishment of such a court was adopted during a meeting of the Interparliamentary Council at The Hague on Feb. 22, 1964. Composed of three judges from each of the Benelux countries, the Court supervises the execution of the Benelux Agreements. [16044A]

THE NORDIC COUNCIL

Members: Denmark, Finland, Iceland, Norway, Sweden

A new organ of Scandinavian regional co-operation, the Nordic Council, consisting of Parliamentary and Ministerial representatives of Denmark, Norway, Sweden, and Iceland, was formally inaugurated in Copenhagen on Feb. 12, 1953. The setting up of such a Council—first advocated in 1938 by the then Danish Foreign Minister—had been recommended by the Nordic Interparliamentary Union at a meeting in Stockholm in August 1951.

The proposals, put forward by a drafting committee set up by the Nordic Interparliamentary Union's Council in November 1951, were adopted at a meeting of the Interparliamentary Union's Council in Stockholm on Dec. 5, 1951. They were finally approved at a meeting on March 16, 1952, attended by the Foreign Ministers of Denmark, Norway, and Sweden, and the Icelandic Minister in Copenhagen.

The constitution and functions of the Nordic Council are summarized below:

Membership. The four participating countries would be represented by 16 members from each of the Danish, Norwegian, and Swedish Parliaments and 5 from the Icelandic *Althing.* The Prime Ministers and Foreign Ministers of the member countries, as well as other Ministers, would also be able to attend all meetings but would have no voting power. It was provided that Finland could enter the Council whenever she wished, and this she in fact did on Oct. 28, 1955.

Functions. In its relations with the Parliaments of the participating countries, the functions of the Nordic Council would be purely advisory, and would be aimed at "stimulating initiative and shaping opinion," though its decisions would have no binding character. It would, however, develop the existing co-operation between the Scandinavian countries; would aim at co-ordinating their legislation wherever desirable; would, as far as possible, try to bring about uniformity in administrative practice as far as the status of their citizens was concerned; would deal with all such questions where there was a possibility of co-ordinated action; would submit suitable proposals to the Governments concerned; and would stimulate joint initiative. The sovereignty of the participating countries would not be affected.

Meetings. The Nordic Council would meet at least once a year in ordinary session. It would set up permanent secretariats in each capital which would carry out joint investigations on behalf of the Council and function as information centers. [12787C]

Further resolutions were passed at subsequent sessions of the Council.

FIRST SESSION (FEB. 20–21, 1953)

At its first meeting the Nordic Council set up committees to deal with economic, cultural, social, and legal matters, and a further one to deal with questions of communications. Recommendations of the committees adopted by the Council included the relaxation and eventual abolition of all passport and currency controls for inter-Scandinavian travel by nationals of the Council's member-countries, and an increase in economic, social, cultural, and postal co-operation.

SECOND SESSION (AUG. 9–18, 1954)

At its second session the Council passed resolutions to prepare for the establishment of a Nordic common market and to inquire into the possibility of eliminating inter-Scandinavian customs duties and trade restrictions. [13777A]

FIFTH SESSION (FEBRUARY, 1957)

At the Nordic Council's fifth session it was decided to found a Nordic Institute of Theoretical Atomic Physics in Copenhagen, and to foster co-operation between the Nordic states (with the exception of Finland) in the practical use of atomic energy.

TENTH SESSION (MARCH, 1962)

At the end of the Nordic Council's tenth session, held in Helsinki, a treaty of Nordic Co-operation, known as the Helsinki Convention, was initialed by the Council's 5 member-nations. The principal subjects covered by the Convention, which summarized the results of all Nordic co-operation since 1953, were as follows:

Cultural Co-operation. Uniformity of vocational training, mutual recognition of the validity of academic degrees and other examinations throughout the area, and joint planning of educational and research centers.

Juridical Co-operation. Mutual law enforcement, making judgments given by courts in one country enforceable also in the others, and co-operation in jurisprudence.

Social Co-operation. Co-operation of labor exchanges throughout the area; unification of vocational guidance; co-ordination of measures to protect workers; and social benefits and welfare measures in each member-country to be the same for citizens of the other countries as for its own citizens—the aim of all these measures being the continuation of the existing single labor market.

Economic Co-operation. Mutual consultation on economic policy, with emphasis on the possibility of parallel measures; co-ordination of production and investment, and promotion of direct arrangements between private enterprises in two or more of the Nordic countries; maximum possible freedom of capital investment in the Nordic area; mutual consultation on questions of international trade policy; joint development measures for regions belonging to two or more member-countries, if economically desirable; co-operation in trying to find joint solutions on payments and foreign exchange questions; co-ordination of customs legislation; simplification of customs rules to facilitate mutual commercial exchanges; maximum facilities for border traffic; collaboration in projects to assist under-developed countries; and co-ordination of statistics.

Communications. Co-operation in the construction of communications, and joint measures relating to safety of road traffic. [18877A]

EIGHTEENTH SESSION (FEB. 7–12, 1970)

The Nordic Council approved at its eighteenth session, held in Reykjavik, a draft treaty on the establishment of a customs union and other measures of economic co-operation between Denmark, Finland, Norway, and Sweden (Nordek), which had been signed by officials of these countries in Stockholm on Feb. 4, 1970.

The draft treaty provided *inter alia* for (a) the establishment of a common external tariff for industrial products imported from third countries, which would bring Nordic tariffs roughly into line with the common external tariff of the EEC; (b) long-term agricultural co-operation; (c) a sys-

Members of Benelux

Members of the Nordic Council

tem of price stabilization for fish; (d) financial and other co-operation; and (e) common institutions, including a Ministerial Council.

However, no progress was made with the draft treaty's implementation after the Finnish Government had declared (on Jan. 12, 1970) that it reserved the right to withdraw if any of the three other Governments began talks with another European organization —as Denmark and Norway subsequently did in applying for accession to the EEC (see page 58). [24047A]

THE EUROPEAN COMMUNITIES

Members: Belgium, France, German Federal Republic, Italy, Luxemburg, the Netherlands
Also, from Jan. 1, 1973: Britain, Denmark, Republic of Ireland
Associate Members: (see separate listing under each of the Communities)

The three European Communities—European Coal and Steel Community (ECSC), European Economic Community (EEC), and European Atomic Energy Community (Euratom)—were formed under separate treaties and, until July 1967, were directed by separate organs, while sharing a common European Parliament and Court of Justice. A treaty providing for the merger of the High Authority of the ECSC, the Commission of the EEC, and the Commission of Euratom, and the merger of the Councils of Ministers of all three, was signed on April 8, 1965, the mergers coming into effect on July 1, 1967. [20775A; 22217A]

Common Organs

1. COUNCIL OF MINISTERS
The common Council of Ministers fulfils the same functions as did the separate organs of the three Communities, and exercises its rights and obligations under the same conditions as provided for in the treaties for each Community.

Each member-State is represented by a member of its Government, usually the Minister of Foreign Affairs, Finance, Agriculture, or Economics, according to the subject to be discussed.

The basic function of the Council of Ministers is to co-ordinate the economic policies of the member-countries within the framework of the three treaties for the Communities, and to make decisions for the implementation of the treaties.

Most decisions of the Council are taken by a simple majority vote, but in certain cases the treaties require a unanimous vote or a qualified majority. For a qualified majority the votes are as follows: Britain, France, Italy and the German Federal Republic have 10 votes each; Belgium and the Netherlands have 5 votes each; Denmark and Ireland 3 each; and Luxemburg 2.

Where the treaties require a previous proposal of the Commission (see below), at least 41 out of the 58 votes are needed to carry a decision, but in all other cases the 12 votes must include a favorable vote by at least 6 of the member-countries.

The Council is authorized to request the Commission to examine proposals which may be submitted to it, and to make studies toward the achievement of the common objectives.

2. EUROPEAN COMMISSION

The new joint Commission of the EEC, the ECSC, and Euratom is known as the European Commission. It exercises its rights and obligations under the same conditions as provided for in the treaties of the Communities for their individual organs.

The membership of the Commission was in May 1970 reduced from 14 to 9—two each from France, the German Federal Republic, and Italy, and one each from Belgium, Luxemburg, and the Netherlands—but was increased to 13 on Jan. 1, 1973, when Britain, Denmark, and Ireland joined the Communities. The members are appointed by the Governments of the member-States, but they are independent and neither solicit nor accept instructions from their Governments. Each member is responsible for a particular sphere of economic activity.

Decisions of the Commission are taken by simple majority vote. The work of the Communities is directed by the Commission through four variously binding types of decision: (a) regulations, which are compulsory and directly applicable in any member-State; (b) directives, under which member-States are obliged to achieve a particular result but are free to choose their own ways and means; (c) decisions, which are obligatory on the parties concerned; and (d) recommendations and opinions, which have no binding force.

The functions of the Commission are to supervise the application of the treaties and of measures adopted within their framework; to make proposals to the Council which the latter cannot amend except by unanimous vote; to formulate opinions and recommendations on matters within the scope of the treaties; to take decisions for which it has authority; and to publish an Annual General Report.

On its inception the European Commission formed the following seven groups: for general economy; for industry; for agriculture; for external relations and development aid; for social affairs; for membership applications and requests for association; and for administration.

3. EUROPEAN PARLIAMENT

The European Parliament was set up under the treaties establishing the EEC and Euratom, and superseded the existing Assembly of the ECSC. Its main function is to supervise the work of the Commission and to discuss the latter's Annual General Report, to which it may propose amendments.

The 198 seats in the European Parliament are allotted to members of the national Parliaments of the 9 member-countries in the following proportions: 36 members each from France, Italy, the German Federal Republic, and Britain; 14 each from Belgium and the Netherlands; 10 each from Denmark and Ireland; and 6 from Luxemburg. Seating in the Parliament is according to political, not national, groupings.

Meetings of the Parliament are held in Strasbourg eleven times a year, the opening session always taking place in October. It can meet in extraordinary session at the request of the Commission, the Council of Ministers, or a majority of its own members.

The European Parliament has no executive powers, but guides the work of the Communities through the expression of resolutions and opinions. Members are entitled to request information on all aspects of the Communities from the Commission and the Council of Ministers. The Parliament can, by a two-thirds majority, enforce the resignation of the Commission.

Twelve Standing Committees of the European Parliament deal respectively with:

Political Affairs.
Economic Affairs.
Finance and Budget.
Agriculture.
Social Affairs and Health.
External Economic Relations.
Legal Affairs.
Energy, Research, and Nuclear Affairs.
Transport.
Association with Greece.
Association with Turkey.
Relations with African Countries and Madagascar.

4. COURT OF JUSTICE

The task of the Court of Justice is to safeguard the law in the interpretation and application of the treaties setting up the Communities.

The Court is composed of nine Judges jointly appointed by the member-Governments, and four Advocates General. The President of the Court is appointed by the Judges from among their members.

The jurisdiction of the Court covers the settlement of all disputes within the Communities. The Court is the final arbiter on the legality of decisions—other than recommendations or opinions—of the executive. It hears appeals on the part of the executive or of a member-State on grounds of incompetence, violation of essential rules of procedure, infringement of the treaties or of any rule implementing them, or an abuse of power. Any person or legal entity may, under the same terms, appeal against a decision which affects him.

Other matters which come under the jurisdiction of the Court include compensation for damage, and disputes between the Communities and their employees.

Advisory Committees

Consultative Committee of the ECSC

The European Coal and Steel Community's Consultative Committee has a minimum membership of 30 and a maximum membership of 51. Its members, who are appointed by the Council of Ministers for a 2-year term, include producers, workers, dealers, and consumers.

Under the terms of the ECSC treaty the advice of the Consultative Committee must be sought by the Commission in certain cases before a decision can be reached. It may also be consulted on any other relevant matter.

Economic and Social Committee

An Economic and Social Committee, which is common to the EEC and Euratom, assists the Council of Ministers and the Commission in an advisory capacity. It must be consulted on certain matters specified in the treaties.

The 144 members of the Committee represent the 9 member-States in the following proportions: France, Italy, the German Federal Republic, and Britain, 24 each; Belgium, and the Netherlands, 12 each; Denmark and Ireland, 9 each; Luxemburg, 6.

Headquarters of the Communities

By a decision of the Council of Ministers, coming into effect at the same time as the treaty on the merger of the three executives, it was agreed that:

(1) Brussels, Luxemburg, and Strasbourg would remain the working seats of the Community as long as no final choice of a single capital had been made.
(2) Brussels would be the seat of the new single Community Executive and the consultative bodies attached to it; meetings of the Council of Ministers would also be held there except during three months of the year.
(3) Luxemburg would be the meeting-place of the Council of Ministers during April, June, and October each year. It would also retain the Secretariat of the European Parliament and the Court of Justice of the European Communities, and would become the seat of other legal or quasi-legal bodies which might be set up, including any body with legal jurisdiction in the patents field.
(4) Strasbourg would continue to be the meeting-place of the European Parliament.
(5) Luxemburg would also become the seat of the financial institutions, viz. (a) the European Investment Bank, at present in Brussels; (b) the financial services of the former High Authority of the Coal and Steel Community dealing with the ECSC levy and with loans to the coal and steel industries in member-countries; (c) any other similar bodies which might be created; (d) a liaison office to facilitate relations between the European Investment Bank (which promotes economic development within the Community) and the European Development Fund (which is responsible for Community aid to overseas countries). The Monetary Committee of the European Economic Community would sit either in Luxemburg or in Brussels.

(6) Certain other services of the Communities would be transferred to, or remain in, Luxemburg in order to ensure that the *status quo* was maintained in terms of the number of European civil servants in that city. These services would be: (a) the Community Statistical Offices, at present divided between Brussels and Luxemburg; (b) the Joint Publications Office; (c) services dealing with workers' health and the dissemination of scientific knowledge attached to Euratom. [20775A]

The European Coal and Steel Community (ECSC)

The European Coal and Steel Community was set up under a 50-year treaty, providing for the institution of a common market by the abolition of import and export duties, subsidies, and other restrictive practices on the movement of coal and steel between the participating countries. The Community is financed by a levy of 0.25 percent on the value of production.

CREATION OF THE ECSC

On May 9, 1950, the French Foreign Minister, Robert Schuman, issued a declaration approved by the French Cabinet, proposing the creation of a single authority to control the production of coal and steel in France and West Germany. The organization would be open for membership to other European countries and would be associated with the United Nations. This plan, known as the "Schuman Plan," represented the first step toward a federation of Europe, since it proposed that individual nations should entrust part of their sovereignty to a supra-national authority. It was felt that economic co-operation in Europe, particularly between France and Germany, which had long been traditional enemies, would form a firm basis for later political federation.

A 6-nation conference for the pooling of the coal and steel resources of Western Europe under a supranational authority, as put forward in the Schuman Plan, was held in Paris, June 20–27, 1950, and attended by delegations from France, West Germany, Italy, Belgium, Luxemburg, and the Netherlands (the "Six"). Negotiations on the drafting of a treaty for the proposed Community continued throughout the following nine months, culminating in the signing in Paris, on April 18, 1951, of a Joint Declaration formally setting up the European Coal and Steel Community. The treaty entered into force on July 25, 1952, and the High Authority (created as the principal organ of the Community) began operations on Aug. 10, 1952. [*10701A; 11905A*]

Britain was an associate member of the ECSC until Dec. 31, 1972.

The Treaty

The character, aims, and functions of the ECSC are contained in Articles 1–6 of the treaty.

Art. 1. By the present Treaty the High Contracting Parties institute among themselves a European Coal and Steel Community, based on a common market, common objectives, and common institutions.

Art. 2. The mission of the European Coal and Steel Community is to contribute to economic expansion, the development of employment, and the improvement of the standard of living in the participating countries through the institution, in harmony with the general economy of the member-States, of a common market as defined in Art. 4.

The Community must progressively establish conditions which will in themselves assure the most rational distribution of production at the highest possible level of productivity, while safeguarding the continuity of employment and avoiding the creation of fundamental and persistent disturbances in the economies of the member-States.

Art. 3. Within the framework of their respective powers and responsibilities, the institutions of the Community should: (*a*) see that the common market is regularly supplied, taking account of the needs of third countries; (*b*) assure to all consumers in comparable positions within the common market equal access to the sources of production; (*c*) seek the establishment of the lowest prices which are possible without requiring any corresponding rise either in the prices charged by the same enterprises in other transactions or in the price-level as a whole in another period, while at the same time permitting necessary amortization and providing normal possibilities of remuneration for capital invested; (*d*) see that conditions are maintained which will encourage enterprises to expand and improve their ability to produce and to promote a policy of rational development of natural resources, avoiding inconsiderate exhaustion of such resources; (*e*) promote the improvement of the living and working conditions of the labor force in each of the industries under its jurisdiction so as to make possible the equalization of such conditions in an upward direction; (*f*) further the development of international trade and see that equitable limits are observed in prices charged on external markets; (*g*) promote the regular expansion and the modernization of production, as well as the improvement of its quality, under conditions which preclude any protection against competing industries, except where justified by illegitimate action on the part of such industries or in their favor.

Art. 4. The following were recognized to be incompatible with the common market for coal and steel, and were therefore "abolished and prohibited" within the Community: (*a*) import and export duties, or charges with an equivalent effect, and quantitative restrictions on the movement of coal and steel; (*b*) measures or practices discriminating among producers, buyers, or consumers, specifically as concerned prices, delivery terms and transportation rates, as well as measures or practices which hampered the buyer in the free choice of his supplier; (*c*) subsidies or State assistance, or special charges imposed by the State, in any form whatsoever; (*d*) restrictive practices tending toward the division of markets or the exploitation of the consumer.

Art. 5. The Community would accomplish its mission with "limited direct intervention," and to this end it would: "enlighten and facilitate the action of the interested parties" by collecting information, organizing consultations, and defining general objectives; place financial means at the disposal of enterprises for their investments and participate in the expenses of readaptation; assure the establishment, maintenance, and observance of normal conditions of competition, and take direct action with respect to production and the operation of the market only when circumstances made it absolutely necessary; publish the justifications for its action and take the necessary measures to ensure observance of the rules set forth in the Treaty. The institutions of the Community should carry out these activities with "as little administrative machinery as possible" and in close co-operation with the interested parties.

Art. 6. Provided that the Community should have "juridical personality" and that it should enjoy, in its international relationships, "the juridical capacity necessary to the exercise of its functions and the attainment of its ends."

Arts. 7–45 are concerned with the institutions of the Community—the High Authority, the Assembly, the Council, and the Court—the functions of which have since been taken over by the European Commission, the European Parliament, the joint Council of Ministers, and the European Court of Justice respectively (see pages 51–2).

Arts. 46–75 contain the technical details for the realization of the objectives of the treaty. The remaining provisions are concerned, *inter alia,* with such general matters as the privileges and immunity of the Community in the territory of member-States, settlements of disputes, and relations with other international organizations. [*11905A*]

Among the documents accompanying the Treaty was a Convention on Transitional Provisions, setting forth the measures necessary for the creation of the common market. These covered a five-year period from the creation of the common market for coal.

DEVELOPMENTS
ECSC Common Market
The Common Market between the 6 member-countries of the ECSC was opened for coal, iron ore, and scrap on Feb. 10, 1953; for steel on May 1, 1953; and for special steels on Aug. 1, 1954. The market came into full operation on Feb. 10, 1958, when the five-year transitional period of its formation came to an end. By this time all barriers to trade in coal and steel—such as customs duties, currency restrictions, and quantitative restrictions—had been abolished, all subsidies had been eliminated and discriminatory practices abol-

ished, and a harmonized external tariff for the whole Community had been introduced.

Trade and Production
In the initial period after the formation of the ECSC the production of all commodities covered by the ECSC treaty (coal, coke, iron ore, pig iron, crude steel, and finished rolled products) rose considerably, as also did the volume of trade among Community countries and between Community countries and other countries. Since 1957, however, the coal industry has declined, although steel production has continued to rise. Between 1952 and 1965 Community steel production rose from 41,900,000 tons to 86,000,000 tons.

Labor Aid
The Community plays an active part in overcoming the social problems within its sphere of activity. It has evolved adaptation schemes to protect workers against the risk of unemployment, these being particularly applicable to workers in the coal industry; has carried out programs of house-building to accommodate workers; has developed vocational training and research in industrial health and medicine; and has made loans for industrial development in certain areas.

AGREEMENTS OF THE ECSC
ECSC and Switzerland

(A) CONSULTATION AGREEMENT
Under this agreement, signed on May 7, 1956, the High Authority undertook, *inter alia,* to consult Switzerland before introducing any allocation system for the Community's coal, steel, iron ore, or scrap production. Switzerland, on her part, undertook to consult with the High Authority before taking any measures affecting trade between her and the Community. A permanent joint committee was set up to supervise the implementation of the agreement.

(B) AGREEMENT ON TRANSPORT CHARGES
Signed on July 28, 1956, this agreement provided for (i) the introduction of international through-rates for coal and steel traffic between Community countries across Swiss territory; (ii) the abolition of Swiss terminal charges and other handling fees for such traffic; and (iii) the formation of a Joint Transport Committee. [*15025A*]

The European Economic Community (EEC)

Associated Mediterranean States: Cyprus, Greece, Malta, Morocco, Tunisia, Turkey

Associated African States (under the Yaoundé Convention): Burundi, Cameroon, Central African Republic, Chad, Congo (Brazzaville), Dahomey, Gabon, Ivory Coast, Madagascar, Mali, Mauritania, Mauritius, Ni-

ger, Rwanda, Senegal, Somalia, Togo, Upper Volta, Zaïre

Associated East African States (under the Arusha Convention): Kenya, Tanzania, Uganda

Associated Overseas Territories: Comoro Islands, French Austral Lands, French Guiana, French Polynesia, Guadeloupe, Martinique, Netherlands Antilles, New Caledonia, French Territory of the Afars and Issas (formerly French Somaliland), Réunion, St. Pierre et Miquelon, Surinam, Wallis and Futuna Islands

EFTA Countries with Special Relations Agreements: Austria, Portugal, Sweden, Switzerland (see page 79). The EEC, or Common Market as it is frequently termed, formed the second stage in the economic integration of the "Six." Whereas the first step in this direction, the ECSC, restricted the common market of the six nations to coal, steel, and iron ore, the EEC includes all items of trade.

CREATION OF THE EEC
The Foreign Ministers of the six ECSC nations met at Messina, June 2–4, 1955, to discuss certain proposals for further European economic integration which had been put forward by the three Benelux countries on May 20, 1955.

The Benelux proposals called for (*a*) the establishment of a "common organization" to study development plans for a European network of roads, canals, and railways, and for the co-ordination of civil aviation policies; (*b*) the study of methods of co-ordinating power policy in Europe; (*c*) the creation of a "common authority" for the development of atomic energy for peaceful purposes, with the pooling of investment funds, technical knowledge, and research facilities; and (*d*) the progressive integration of the national economies of the 6 member-countries and the harmonization of economic, financial, and social policies. To implement this program the Benelux Governments proposed that a conference should be called to work out (*a*) a treaty on the pooling of transport, power, and atomic energy; (*b*) a treaty on general economic integration; and (*c*) a treaty defining the European institutions necessary to carry out the program.

At the end of their meeting the Foreign Ministers adopted the "Messina Resolution," which included a plan for the creation of "a common European market free from all customs barriers and quantitative restrictions," to be realized by stages. The six Ministers also envisaged the creation of a joint organization having "the responsibility and the facilities" for ensuring the development of atomic energy for peaceful purposes. An Intergovernmental Committee was set up to study the problems raised and to prepare draft treaties. [*Page 15030*]

The final drafts of the treaties establishing the EEC and Euratom were completed by the Intergovernmental Committee on March 9, 1957, and were signed in Rome by Belgium, France, the German Federal Republic, Italy, Luxemburg, and the Netherlands on March 25, 1957. Both came into force on Jan. 1, 1958.

The EEC Treaty

The main provisions of the treaty setting up the European Economic Community (the Treaty of Rome) are summarized below.

AIMS

In the preamble to the treaty, the six signatory countries declared their intention of establishing "the foundations of an enduring and closer union between European peoples" by gradually removing the economic effects of their political frontiers. A common market and a common external tariff (customs union) would be established for all goods; common policies would be devised for agriculture, transport, labor mobility, and important sectors of the economy; common institutions would be set up for economic development; and the overseas territories and possessions of member-States would be associated with the new Community for an experimental five-year period. All these measures would have one "essential aim"—the steady improvement in the conditions of life and work of the peoples of the member-countries.

The tasks of the Community were defined in Article 1 of the Treaty as the achievement of a harmonious development of the economy within the whole Community, a continuous and balanced economic expansion, increased economic stability, a more rapid improvement in living-standards, and closer relations between the member-countries.

PROGRESSIVE IMPLEMENTATION OF COMMON MARKET—PROCEDURE DURING TRANSITIONAL PERIOD

One of the principal characteristics of the process of creating a Common Market would be its irrevocable character —i.e. once the process had been set in motion, the ultimate aim would have to be achieved. This constituted an important safeguard for the member-countries inasmuch as their sacrifices in adjusting themselves to the new conditions would not be in vain, and would not involve a risk of a complete standstill and a subsequent return to the previous status after a number of years. The change from one stage to the next would thus in principle take place automatically.

The Common Market would be progressively established in three stages within a transitional period of 12 years, which might be extended to 15 years. Within the basic 12-year period there would be three stages, each lasting in principle four years. However, if at the end of the first four years the Council of Ministers and the Commission were not unanimously agreed that the objectives of that stage had been essentially accomplished, the stage would automatically be extended for one year. At the end of the fifth year there would be another one-year extension on the same condition, whilst at the end of the sixth year (when the decision of the Council of Ministers would no longer require unanimity but would be taken by a weighted majority) a further extension could be granted only if a request by a member-State for such an extension was recognized as justified by an *ad hoc* arbitration tribunal of three members appointed by the Council of Ministers.

The second and third stages could either be prolonged or shortened by unanimous decision of the Council of Ministers, subject to the maximum limit of 15 years for the whole transitional period.

REMOVAL OF TARIFFS AND QUANTITATIVE RESTRICTIONS—DEVELOPMENT OF AGRICULTURE

The European Economic Community would be based on a Customs Union covering the whole trade of member-countries and entailing (a) a prohibition on imposing import or export duties or similar levies between member-countries; (b) the introduction of a common tariff on imports from non-Community countries; (c) the abolition of all quantitative import and export restrictions and other similar measures between member-countries. The free exchange of goods within the Community would apply not only to goods produced in the member-countries but also to those which had been imported by a member-country from outside the Community, and on which customs duties had been paid on entry. The only exception from the application of the common customs tariff *vis-à-vis* non-Community countries would be in the case of goods landed in a free trade zone where each member-country could apply its own customs tariff.

Internal Tariffs

Tariff restrictions on trade between member-countries would have to be abolished entirely by the end of the transitional period at the latest.

All export duties and similar levies on goods destined for other Community countries would be abolished not later than the end of the first stage.

External Tariffs

A common tariff on imports from non-Community countries would be established in full not later than the end of the transitional period.

Quantitative Restrictions

All quantitative restrictions on trade within the Community would be progressively eliminated by a series of quota increases. (This procedure differed from the one applied by the OEEC, which provided for the immediate complete removal of import quotas in respect of a growing range of individual products.)

Thus, one year after the coming into force of the Treaty, the member-States would convert all their existing bilateral import quotas into global quotas in favor of all other member-countries, without any discrimination between them. All these global import quotas would then be increased annually by at least 20 per cent as regards their overall value, and by at least 10 per cent as regards each individual product; bigger increases would be made in the case of quotas amounting initially to less than 3 per cent of the domestic output of a given product.

Agriculture

Agricultural products would be included in the Common Market, although a special regime would apply in view of the different social structure of agriculture in the various member-countries, which made it impossible to introduce a completely liberalized market.

A common agricultural policy would be implemented in the course of the transitional period, aiming at increased agricultural productivity, safeguarding an adequate standard of living for the agricultural population, stabilization of agricultural markets, an assurance of adequate supplies, and fair prices for consumers.

A Joint Organization of agricultural markets would be created, but, because of the diversity of market conditions for individual products, this development would not take place under prearranged rules but through decisions of the organs of the Community, varying from case to case.

FREEDOM OF MOVEMENT FOR LABOR, SERVICES, AND CAPITAL—JOINT TRANSPORT POLICY

Labor, Settlement, Services, and Capital

The free circulation of labor, services, and capital, as well as the right to settle, work, and trade anywhere in the Community, would be fully established by the end of the transitional period.

All restrictions on the right to settle freely in any member-country, or the right of nationals of any member-country to set up agencies, branches, or subsidiary companies in the territory of another, would be gradually removed during the transitional period.

All restrictions on the offering of services by insurance companies, banks, finance houses, the wholesale and retail trade, and by members of the professions would be gradually removed within the Community during the transitional period.

Existing restrictions on the movement of capital between the Community countries would be progressively removed. As far as was necessary for the proper working of the Common Market, restrictions on current payments relating to the movement of capital (e.g. interest, dividends, rents, premiums) would be completely abolished not later than the end of the first stage of the transitional period.

Transport

The Council of Ministers would establish a joint transport policy and common rules for international transport within or through the Community, covering rail, road, and inland water transport.

COMMON POLICIES

To ensure free and equal competition within the Community, common rules and policies would be introduced in the member-countries as summarized below.

Common Rules

Any agreement or association preventing, restraining, or distorting competition within the Community would be forbidden—e.g. agreements or associations directly or indirectly fixing prices; regulating or controlling production, investment, or technical development; sharing markets; requiring the acceptance of additional goods besides those needed by the customer; or providing for discriminatory conditions of supply.

Dumping practices by any member-country within the Common Market would be prohibited.

Unless otherwise provided by the Treaty, State subsidies (of whatever kind) which distorted or threatened to distort competition would be prohibited.

Economic Policy

Member-countries would harmonize their general economic, foreign exchange, and foreign trade policies.

The general economic policies of member-countries would be regarded as a matter of joint interest, and the countries concerned would consult each other as well as the Commission on the measures which should be taken to meet changing circumstances.

A common external trade policy would be established by the end of the transitional period.

The common external trade policy after the end of the transitional period would cover the application of a common customs tariff; the joint conclusion of trade and customs agreements; the unification of trade liberalization measures; the working-out of common export policies; and the joint application of protective measures, e.g. against dumping or subsidies by non-Community countries.

Social Policy

The EEC Commission would promote the coordination of the social policies of member-countries, with particular reference to employment, labor legislation, conditions of work, vocational training, social security, prevention of industrial accidents and occupational diseases, health protection, trade union rights, and collective bargaining between employers and employed.

PROVISIONS FOR ASSOCIATION AND FUTURE MEMBERSHIP

The overseas territories of Belgium, France, Italy, and the Netherlands would be associated with the Community. A special convention annexed to the Treaty laid down the details of this association for the initial five-year period.

Any other European country could apply for membership in the Community; the terms of its admission, and any consequential amendments of the Treaty which might become necessary, would be agreed between the original member-countries and the applicant country.

Agreements might also be concluded with another country or group of countries for their association with the Community, based on certain mutual rights and obligations, joint action, and special procedures. Similar agreements of association might be entered into with international organizations.

The treaty was concluded for an unlimited period. [15951A]

Institutions of the EEC

European Investment Bank

The European Investment Bank was set up under the Treaty of Rome as an independent legal entity. Its members are the Governments of the 9 Common Market member-countries.

The function of the Bank is to promote a common investment policy within the Community, thus contributing to the smooth development of the Common Market. The Bank grants, on a non-profit basis, loans or guarantees for (1) projects in under-developed regions; (2) the modernization, reorganization or extension of already established enterprises; and (3) new enterprises of joint interest to several member-countries which, because of their size or special character, would be difficult to finance by a single member-country.

The powers of the European Investment Bank are vested in a Board of Governors, usually consisting of the Finance Ministers of the member-countries. The executive organ is a Board of Directors, comprising 12 members and 12 alternate members, appointed by the Board of Governors for five years. France, Germany, and Italy each nominate 3 members and 3 alternate members, the Benelux countries jointly nominate 2 members and 2 alternate members, and the Commission nominates 1 of each. There is also a Management Committee, consisting of a President, two Vice Presidents, and a Director General.

The initial authorized capital of the Bank was 1,000,000,000 units of account (u.a.) of the European Monetary Agreement, with France and the German Federal Republic each contributing 30 percent, Italy 24 percent, Belgium 8.65 percent, Netherlands 7.15 percent, and Luxemburg 0.2 percent. (Contributions by new members are given on page 60.) The EEC Council of Ministers decided on April 26, 1971, that the Bank's authorized capital should be raised to 1,500,000,000 u.a., the additional amount to be provided by the 9 member-countries in the same proportions as the initial capital. [24824]

European Social Fund

The European Social Fund was created under the Treaty of Rome to facilitate employment and the mobility of labor within the Community. By improving opportunities of employment the Social Fund helps to raise the standard of living in the Common Market countries.

At the request of a member-State the Fund pays 50 percent of the cost incurred by that country or any of its public bodies in (a) retraining or granting resettlement allowances to workers who have become unemployed as a result of Common Market activities, and (b) granting aid to workers temporarily forced to work for a short time or suspended as a result of changes in production in the undertaking employing them, so that these workers may maintain their standard of living pending the restoration of their full employment.

The Fund is administered by the EEC Commission assisted by a committee consisting of representatives of member-Governments, trade unions, and employers' associations.

The Council of Ministers on Nov. 26, 1970, approved proposals for changing the Social Fund into a "dynamic instrument" of a common employment policy. The major change under the new reforms would be to enable an increasing proportion of the Fund's budget to help workers directly affected, or likely to be affected, by the execution of Community policies.

The Council decided on the same date to establish a Standing Committee on Employment to provide a forum for co-operation between the Council, the Commission, employers, and unions. The Committee held its first meeting in Brussels on March 18, 1971. [Page 24823]

European Development Fund

The Convention on the Association of Overseas Territories of Belgium, France, Italy, and the Netherlands, which accompanied the Treaty of Rome, provided for the establishment of a special Development Fund. The purpose of the Fund is to promote the economic and social development of the territories and countries associated with the EEC. Much of the aid granted is devoted to projects in the fields of education, health, and rural development.

Enlargement of the Community

At the end of protracted negotiations on the enlargement of the European Community—which in the case of Britain had been conducted over a period of more than 10 years—a Treaty of Accession to the European Communities (the Treaty of Brussels) was signed in Brussels on Jan. 22, 1972, by the Prime Ministers of Britain, Denmark, the Republic of Ireland, and Norway.

The three principal documents making up the treaty were:

(a) The "Treaty concerning the accession of the Kingdom of Denmark, Ireland, the Kingdom of Norway and the United Kingdom of Great Britain and Northern Ireland to the European Economic Community and the European Atomic Energy Community."

(b) The "Decision of the Council of the European Communities of Jan. 22, 1972, concerning the accession of the Kingdom of Denmark, Ireland, the Kingdom of Norway and the United Kingdom of Great Britain and Northern Ireland to the European Coal and Steel Community."

(c) The "Act concerning the conditions of accession and the adjustments to the treaties," covering under a number of heads the negotiations between Britain, Ireland, Denmark, and Norway with the Six over the previous 18 months. Unlike (a) and (b), which were relatively short documents, (c) was an Act of great complexity and detail, embodying 161 Articles and with numerous annexes.

As regards (a) and (b), a separate procedure was required for accession to the European Economic Community and Euratom on the one hand, and to the European Coal and Steel Community on the other, because of legal differences between the original treaties—the Treaties of Rome and the Treaty of Paris respectively.

The Treaty on accession contained the following provisions:

Art. 1. (1) The Kingdom of Denmark, Ireland, the Kingdom of Norway and the United Kingdom of Great Britain and Northern Ireland hereby become members of the European Economic Community and of the European Atomic Energy Community and Parties to the Treaties establishing these Communities as amended or supplemented.

(2) The conditions of admission and the adjustments to the Treaties establishing the European Economic Community and the European Atomic Energy Community necessitated thereby are set out in the Act annexed to this Treaty. The provisions of that Act concerning the European Economic Community and the European Atomic Energy Community shall form an integral part of this Treaty.

(3) The provisions concerning the rights and obligations of the member-States and the powers and jurisdiction of the institutions of the Communities as set out in the Treaties referred to in paragraph 1 shall apply in respect of this Treaty.

Art. 2. This Treaty will be ratified by the High Contracting Parties in accordance with their respective constitutional requirements. The instruments of ratification will be deposited with the Government of the Italian Republic by Dec. 31, 1972, at the latest.

This Treaty will enter into force on Jan. 1, 1973, provided that all the instruments of ratification have been deposited before that date and that all the instruments of accession to the European Coal and Steel Community are deposited on that date.

If, however, the States referred to in Article 1(1) have not all deposited their instruments of ratification and accession in due time, the Treaty shall enter into force for those States which have deposited their instruments. . . .

The Decision of the Council contained provisions as follows:

Art. 1. (1) The Kingdom of Denmark, Ireland, the Kingdom of Norway and the United Kingdom of Great Britain and Northern Ireland may become members of the European Coal and Steel Community by acceding, under the conditions laid down in this Decision, to the Treaty establishing that Community, as amended or supplemented.

(2) The conditions of accession and the adjustments to the Treaty establishing the European Coal and Steel Community necessitated thereby are set out in the Act annexed to this Decision. The provisions of that Act concerning the European Coal and Steel Community shall form an integral part of this Decision.

(3) The provisions concerning the rights and obligations of the member-States and the powers and jurisdiction of the institutions of the Community as set out in the Treaty referred to in paragraph 1 shall apply in respect of this Decision.

Art. 2. The instruments of accession of the Kingdom of Denmark, Ireland, the Kingdom of Norway and the United Kingdom of Great Britain and Northern Ireland to the European Coal and Steel Community will be deposited with the Government of the French Republic on Jan. 1, 1973.

Accession will take effect on Jan. 1, 1973, provided that all the instruments of accession have been deposited on that date and that all the instruments of ratification of the Treaty concerning Accession to the European Economic Community and the European Atomic Energy Community have been deposited before that date.

If, however, the States referred to in the first paragraph of this Article have not all deposited their instruments of accession and ratification in due time, accession shall take effect for the other acceding States. . . . [*25101A*]

The Act on condition of accession provided *inter alia* for the following adjustments:

(a) An increase in the membership of the European Parliament from 142 to 208, with the additional 66 members being 36 from Britain and 10 each from Denmark, Ireland, and Norway;

(b) enlargement of the Council of Ministers from 6 to 10 members;

(c) enlargement of the Commission from 9 to 14 members, by the addition of 2 from Britain and 1 each from the other three applicant countries;

(d) the appointment to the Social and Economic Committee of 24 representatives from Britain and 9 each from Denmark, Ireland, and Norway; and

(e) an increase in the number of Judges in the Court of Justice from 7 to 11, and the appointment of an additional Advocate-General, with a change in their rota so that every three years either five Judges and one Advocate-General or six Judges and two Advocates-General are newly appointed.

The 161 Articles of the Act specified the transitional arrangements agreed upon in the negotiations leading to the conclusion of the Treaty.

During a transitional period of five years the new member-countries undertook:

(a) to reduce customs barriers and non-tariff obstacles for industrial products between them and the old members of the Community in five phases at 20 percent per annum;

(b) to adopt the Community's common external tariff at the end of the five-year period by adjustment in four phases of 40 percent on Jan. 1, 1974, and 20 percent on Jan. 1 of the three succeeding years.

In regard to agriculture the new member-countries adopted the Community system of support under the Common Agricultural Policy, with adjustments to full Community price levels in six steps over the five-year transitional period.

From Jan. 1, 1973, the new member-States were to contribute to the Community's budget by payments derived from agricultural levies, customs duties, and part of the revenue from value-added tax at the following percentage rates of the total budget:

	1973	1974	1975	1976	1977
Britain	8.64	10.85	13.34	16.02	18.92
Denmark	1.099	1.382	1.698	2.040	2.408
Ireland	0.272	0.342	0.421	0.505	0.596
Norway	0.754	0.947	1.164	1.398	1.650

These contributions would not reach their final full extent until Jan. 1, 1980.

The new members were expected to contribute to the capital and reserves of the European Investment Bank as follows: Britain 30 percent; Denmark 4 percent; Norway 3 percent; Ireland 1 percent. Britain also undertook to apply a phased reduction to sterling reserves in London and gradually to stabilize official sterling holdings so as to be compatible with the long-term objectives of economic and currency union.

Transitional agreements were later reached for sugar, dairy products, and fisheries.

Britain was in May–June 1971 permitted to import sugar until the end of 1974 at the quantities and prices specified in the Commonwealth Sugar Agreement; after 1974 special sugar interests were to be safeguarded in an agreement with the countries concerned.

Britain's butter and cheese imports from New Zealand were to be reduced over a period of five years. [24837A]

In regard to fisheries, it was agreed in December 1971 that until Dec. 31, 1982, member-States might restrict fishing in their territorial waters to vessels of their own nationality, with the normal 6-mile zone being in certain areas extended to 12 miles. For the years after 1982 the Council of Ministers would have to examine what agreement could be concluded. [25203A]

Approval of Enlargement in Britain, Denmark, and Ireland—Rejection in Norway

In Britain, the European Communities Bill, providing for the United Kingdom's entry into the European Economic Community, was given a second reading in the House of Commons on Feb. 17, 1972, by 309 votes (304 Conservatives and 5 Liberals) to 301 (279 Labour members, 15 Conservatives, 6 Independents, and 1 Liberal), with 8 abstentions and 3 members absent. The Bill passed its third reading in the House of Commons on July 13, 1972, by 301 votes (296 Conservatives and 5 Liberals) to 284 (264 Labour members, 16 Conservatives, and 4 Independents), with 4 Conservatives and 13 Labour members abstaining. In the House of Lords the Bill was approved by far larger majorities—189 votes to 19 at its second reading on July 26, and 161 votes to 21 at its third reading on Sept. 20.

The Bill became law on Oct. 17, 1972.

In Denmark, ratification of the Treaty of Accession was approved by Parliament on Sept. 8, 1972, by 272 votes to 95, with 1 blank vote. Denmark's entry into the Community was also approved in a referendum on Oct. 3 by 1,958,115 votes (63.3 percent of the votes cast) to 1,135,691 (36.7 percent), with 11,907 blanks and 7,409 other invalid papers, in a 90.1 percent poll.

Royal Assent was given to the ratification on Oct. 11, 1972.

In the Republic of Ireland, the necessary amendment to the Constitution, enabling the Republic to become a member of the European Communities, was approved by the *Dail* (Lower House of Parliament) on Jan. 26, and by the Senate on March 8, 1972. As required by the Constitution, the proposal to amend it was submitted to a popular referendum on May 10, 1972, with the result that 1,041,880 voters (83 per cent of those voting) voted for the amendment, and 211,888 (17 percent) against it, in a 71 percent poll—so that those in favor constituted over 58 percent of the electorate, and those against about 12 percent.

The Bill was signed by President de Valera on June 8, 1972.

In Norway the decision to join the European Communities was, under the Norwegian Constitution, subject to a three-quarters' majority in the *Storting* (Parliament) being in favor; the Government, which did not command a parliamentary majority, did not expect to gain the required support in Parliament and decided to seek the people's approval of entry in a referendum (which is not provided for in the Norwegian Constitution), in the expectation that a popular majority in favor of entry would enable it subsequently to obtain the necessary parliamentary majority. In the event, the referendum held on Sept. 24–25, 1972, resulted in 1,099,389 votes (53.5 percent of the poll) being cast against entry and 956,043 (or 46.5 percent) in favor, in a 77.6 percent poll.

The Norwegian Government consequently informed the representatives of the European Community's member-countries in Brussels on Sept. 26 that Norway was withdrawing its participation in the consultative negotiating committees, and it was officially announced on the same day that the Government had decided not to submit a proposal for membership of the European Communities to the *Storting*.

Norway's failure to ratify the Treaty of Accession necessitated a number of amendments to the Treaty and its attendant documents, and these amendments were subsequently made, including the deletion of special protocols previously agreed upon with the Norwegian Government, and the reduction in the number of Judges at the Court of Justice to 9 (instead of the 11 previously envisaged).

Approval of Ratification by the Six—Accession of Britain, Denmark, and Ireland

In France, ratification of the Treaty of Accession by the French President was approved in a referendum held throughout metropolitan France and the French overseas departments and territories on April 23, 1972, the official result being as follows:

	Actual figure	Percentage of electorate	Percentage of valid votes
"Yes" votes	10,847,554	36.37	68.31
"No" votes	5,030,934	16.87	31.68
Blank or spoilt papers	2,086,119	6.99	—
Abstentions	11,855,857	39.75	—

[25261A]

Ratification of the treaty was approved in Belgium by the Senate on June 30, 1972, and by the Chamber of Deputies on Dec. 8; in Western Germany by the *Bundestag* on June 21 and by the *Bundesrat* on July 7; in Italy by the Chamber of Deputies on Dec. 5 and by the Senate on Dec. 19; in Luxemburg by the Parliament on Dec. 20; and in the Netherlands by the Second Chamber of the States-General on Sept. 14 and by the First Chamber on Nov. 14.

Britain, Denmark, and the Republic of Ireland became members of the European Communities on Jan. 1, 1973, in accordance with the provisions of the Treaty of Accession. [25645A]

Progress of the EEC

Progressive Implementation of the Common Market

The progressive implementation of the Common Market in three four-year stages, as envisaged in the Treaty of Rome, proceeded without prolonging any of the stages as provided for in the Treaty. The most critical changeover was that from the first to the second stage which took place on Jan. 14, 1962. On this date, after a series of 45 meetings, the Council of Ministers finally reached unanimous agreement on a common policy for agriculture, without which the French Government had refused to agree to the move into the second stage of the Common Market's transitional period.

During the first stage of the Treaty a unanimous decision of the Council of Ministers was required for the settlement of most issues, only a limited number of questions being decided by a qualified majority vote. The application of a qualified majority vote was extended in the second stage, when the unanimous vote was retained only on important questions of economic union and common policies, including the following:

(1) The co-ordination of legislative provisions restricting on grounds of *ordre public* the right of establishment of foreign nations (Article 56.2);

(2) The co-ordination of legislative provisions concerning the engagement in and exercise of non-wage-earning activities (Article 57.2);

(3) The co-ordination of exchange policies (Article 70.1);

(4) The authorization of certain State aids (Article 93.2);

(5) The harmonization of legislation on turnover tax (Article 99);

(6) Decisions on general measures concerning policy relating to economic trends (Article 103.2);

(7) The extension or curtailment of the second stage or third stage (Article 8.5);

(8) The social security of migrant workers (Article 51);

(9) The renewal of the Treaty of Association with the Overseas Territories (Article 136);

(10) The possible extension of the transport provisions to sea and air transport (Article 84.2);

(11) The admission to the Common Market of new members or associates (Articles 237 and 238). [18975A]

The third stage of implementation of the Treaty, which began on Jan. 1, 1966, saw yet a further extension of the application of the qualified majority vote, the unanimous vote being retained only on the 11 issues listed above.

Acceleration of Economic Integration

From the middle of 1959 economic and political conditions within the Community improved to such an extent that adherence to the program of economic integration laid down in the Treaty of Rome was no longer necessary. On May 12, 1960, the Council of Ministers therefore agreed on a plan to speed up implementation of the Treaty from Jan. 1, 1961.*

---

* In connection with its decision of May 12, 1960, to accelerate the reduction of customs duties between member-countries and the adjustment of their duty rates to a common external tariff (see above), the Council of Ministers issued on the same date a "declaration of intention" to carry out such an acceleration also in all other spheres of economic integration, especially in the implementation of social measures, notably vocational training of employees, their freedom to accept employment anywhere, the application of social security schemes, and equal pay for men and women.

Customs duties within the European Economic Community were reduced on Jan. 1, 1962, by a further 10 percent, making a total of 40 percent for industrial products, 35 percent for non-liberalized agricultural products, and 30 percent for agricultural products liberalized since the formation of the Community. The 40 percent reduction had been made in four stages of 10 percent each on Jan. 1, 1959; July 1, 1960; Jan. 1, 1961; and Jan. 1, 1962. The reduction of duty for each industrial product by a minimum of 25 percent, which was the target under the Treaty of Rome in the first stage of the transitional period up to Jan. 1, 1962, had therefore been substantially exceeded.

The European Economic Community took its first step toward a common external tariff policy on Dec. 31, 1960, i.e. the alignment of individual national tariffs with the proposed common tariff. The Treaty of Rome originally set the date for this at Dec. 31, 1961 (the end of the first transitional period), but the Council of Ministers decided on May 12, 1960, to bring it forward by one year, i.e. to Dec. 31, 1960. The Treaty specified that where individual duties were higher or lower than the common tariff rate by not more than 15 percent, the common tariff rate was to be introduced at the first stage of alignment; in other cases the individual rates were to be increased or decreased toward the level of the common tariff by 30 percent of the difference between the common tariff rate and the individual national rate. For the first move on Dec. 31, 1960, which applied only to industrial products while agricultural commodities were expressly excluded, the Community modified the basis of calculation by requiring the alignment to be carried out toward the rates shown in the common tariff nationally reduced by 20 percent. The downward alignment of national rates on the common tariff, as calculated on this basis, was subject to the proviso that the resultant rate must not be less than that shown in the common tariff before the national 20 percent reduction.

At its meeting of May 15, 1962, the Council of Ministers decided also to bring forward the second stage of adjustment between national tariffs and the common external tariff, this time by 18 months, i.e. from Dec. 31, 1965 (the end of the second stage), to July 1, 1963. From the latter date, therefore, a second 30 percent alignment would come into force, reducing the difference between national tariffs and the common external tariff by 60 percent.

Further Tariff Reductions
Customs duties on industrial and agricultural goods were reduced by 10 percent on July 1, 1963, Jan. 1, 1965, and Jan. 1, 1966. By the last-named date there had been a total reduction of 80 percent on industrial

goods, 65 percent on non-liberalized agricultural goods, and 60 percent on agricultural goods liberalized since the establishment of the Community. A further lowering of customs duties in the industrial sector took place on July 1, 1967, when duties were reduced by another 5 percent, bringing the total reduction up to 85 percent. The final abolition of these duties came into force on July 1, 1968, thereby completing the Customs Union in the industrial sector. [18975A; 21885A]

Formation of a Common Agricultural Policy
The principal cause of disagreement within the EEC has been agricultural policy.

In 1960 the EEC Commission proposed the formation of a common agricultural policy based on common prices, a single fund for price supports, and joint import levies. It was not until Jan. 14, 1962, however, that an agreement for the first stage of a common agricultural policy for the EEC was adopted by the Council of Ministers.

Policy Objectives. The main objectives of the common policy for agriculture were outlined as follows:
(a) To balance supply and demand within the Community and externally by influencing supply by such measures as more regional specialization, stockpiling, and structural reforms, and increasing demand by improving the quality of products.
(b) To provide farmers with a fair income by structural and regional improvements, the consolidation of holdings, electricity supplies, better transport and farming methods, information services, and education.
(c) To stabilize the market by protecting farmers from speculative price fluctuations while not insulating them from the influence of long-term movements in world markets.
(d) To ensure equitable supplies to consumers by enabling the processing industries to find external outlets at reasonable or competitive prices, and by preventing prices from being fixed on the basis of marginal production costs.

Products. The regulations adopted by the Ministers applied to grain, pigmeat, eggs, poultry, fruit and vegetables, and wine. Fundamental decisions were also taken on the remaining major farm products (rice, beef and veal, dairy produce, and sugar) and a time-table was set for the publication of the full regulations on all these items in 1962. The products covered constituted over 46 per cent of the total inter-Community trade in farm produce.

Transition Period. A seven-year transition period pending the full implementation of the common policy was fixed from July 1, 1962, to Dec. 31, 1969, but a decision to shorten this period to six years could be taken in the third year.

Other clauses of the agreement provided for common quality standards, harmonization of prices, and a system of levies. The agreement also provided for the setting up of five Management Committees for grain, pigmeat, eggs and poultry, fruit and vegetables, and wine respectively.

The common agricultural policy would be financed

by a Guidance and Guarantee Fund consisting, for the first three years, of financial contributions by the member-States. As soon as a common market system for agricultural products should come into force the Community expenditure would be directly financed by receipts from levies on imports from non-member-countries.

The common marketing organizations for grain, pigmeat, eggs and poultry, fruit and vegetables, and wine came into operation on July 30, 1962. Agreement on other agricultural marketing organizations was reached on Dec. 23, 1963. [18975A]

An important agreement on cereal prices was reached by the Council of Ministers on Dec. 15, 1964. The Ministers agreed on the settling of common prices for cereals, to be effective from July 1, 1967, and they also agreed to establish a common fund to help in harmonizing agriculture throughout the Community. The agreement was based on a set of proposals presented by the Commission to the Council of Ministers in November 1963. This plan set target prices for the whole community for all cereals, and provided for compensation from the EEC budget for farmers who would thereby suffer loss of income. [20829A]

The Crisis over Agricultural Policy
At its meeting on Dec. 15, 1964, the Council of Ministers asked the EEC Commission for proposals, to be presented before April 1, 1965, on how the common agricultural policy should be financed for the period 1965–70.

The Commission accordingly submitted its proposals to the Council on April 1, 1965. These covered not only the renewal of levies on agricultural goods but also proposed that both these levies and industrial import duties should be paid into the EEC fund. As these receipts represented enormous amounts and constituted the EEC's financial resources, the Commission proposed that the European Parliament should be strengthened by being given powers to determine the Community's revenue, and that it should also receive wider powers over the Community's budget.

The Commission's scheme was considered by the Council of Ministers at a meeting in Brussels which opened on June 28, 1965, under the chairmanship of M. Couve de Murville, the French Foreign Minister.

M. Couve de Murville immediately rejected the Commission's proposals, maintaining that political conditions had been imposed by the Commission which were totally unacceptable to France, and that the sole question to be settled was the renewal of levies after the expiration of the existing agricultural finance regulations on June 30, 1965.

Following the breakdown on July 2, 1965, of talks between the Foreign Ministers of the Six, the French Government announced on July 5, that it was withdrawing its representatives from a number of the Commission's working committees. France also boycotted the next meeting of the Council of Ministers on July 26–27, 1965, and did not in fact meet again with the other five EEC member-States until January 1966. The main issues on which France felt unable to co-operate with her fellow-members of the EEC were (1) the granting to the Commission of significant supra-national authority, in particular of a budget of its own, financed from agricultural levies and customs duties, and (2) the application of majority decisions, to which France could not agree on matters of importance.

These questions were discussed at the two Council meetings held in Luxemburg on Jan. 17–18 and Jan. 28–29, 1966. On the question of the powers of the Commission, the Council adopted a number of points for improving its relations with the Commission.

These included the following:

(1) The Commission should consult the member-Governments at the appropriate level before submitting proposals for Community action of particular importance to the Council.
(2) Commission proposals should not be made known to the European Parliament or the public before their submission to the Council.
(3) The executive powers granted to the Commission in any policy field should be precisely formulated, leaving no room for its discretion.
(4) The Council should exercise a closer control over the Commission's budget.

The question of majority decisions was solved as follows:

(1) When issues very important to one or more member-countries are at stake, the members of the Council will try, within a reasonable time, to reach solutions which can be adopted by all members of the Council, while respecting their mutual interests, and those of the Community, in accordance with Article 2 of the Treaty. (This article aims at approximating the economic policies of EEC members to create a common market.)
(2) The French delegation considers that, when very important issues are at stake, discussion must be continued until unanimous agreement is reached.
(3) The six delegations note that there is a divergence of views on what should be done in the event of a failure to reach complete agreement.
(4) They consider that this divergence does not prevent the Community's work being resumed in accordance with normal procedure.

On Feb. 2, 1966, the Commission issued a communiqué stating that the Community would resume its normal activities.

1966 Agreement on Agricultural Policy
Following the French delegation's return to the conference table, the Foreign Ministers decided at Luxemburg on Jan. 31, 1966, to proceed with all speed in an

effort to reach agreement on the common agricultural policy and the industrial customs union, including the completion of a common external tariff. Accordingly, at their meeting on May 11 the Ministers agreed on details of the Farm Fund and set July 1, 1968, as the target date for the coming into force of complete common markets for both industrial and agricultural goods. Finally, following a further series of meetings which opened on July 21 and lasted four days and two nights, full agreement was reached on the outstanding agricultural questions and also on the common external tariff for industrial goods. [21591A]

Between 1966 and 1970 agreement was reached on common organization of markets in most agricultural sectors and also with respect to fisheries. [24167A; 24821A; 25248A]

The Mansholt Plan for "Agriculture 1980"

The European Commission presented to the Council of Ministers on Dec. 10, 1968, a 10-year plan on agricultural reform drawn up by Dr. Sicco Mansholt (Netherlands), then the Commission's Vice-President.

The Mansholt Report proposed a radical restructuring of farming in the European Community with the dual aim of raising the living standards of farmers and agricultural workers and of halting the persistent increase in the cost of the common agricultural policy.

To this end the report proposed:

(a) a reduction in the emphasis on market and price policies, and priority for the removal of economic and legislative barriers which made it difficult to increase the size of farms and to improve the mobility of labor;

(b) a reduction in the acreage of farmland within the EEC; and

(c) encouragement and acceleration of the existing drift of workers from the land to the towns, so that the total of persons in agricultural employment would be reduced from an estimated 10,000,000 to 5,000,000 by 1980, or from 14 to 6 percent of the working population (while in 1950 it had been 28 and in 1960 21 percent).

Dr. Mansholt explained on Dec. 10, 1968, that the objective was to reduce the EEC's total annual expenditure on support for farm prices after 1980 to no more than $750,000,000 (as against $2,300,000,000 for 1968–69).

The program meant that farmers would be invited to collectivize their farms on a voluntary basis; there would be massive education and retraining of workers leaving the land, as well as capital disbursement to those leasing their land to new "modern farms" in order to enable them to set up in business outside farming.

The Commission estimated the cost of implementing

the proposals at an average $2,500,000,000 per annum. [23629A]

After a series of debates which began in January 1969 on the above plan, the principal measures establishing a 10-year program of reforms were decided upon by the Council of Ministers at a meeting on March 24, 1972. The reforms, together with details of the farm prices to be applied in the 1972–73 season, were accepted on March 28, 1972, by the 4 prospective member-countries.

The three directives adopted applied to farm modernization, retirement pensions, and retraining schemes. Member-Governments were required to implement the agreed measures through their national legislation by April 1973, although in practice it was expected that relatively few fundamental changes would be necessary as most Governments, with the exception of Italy, had already moved toward a common position in the areas concerned. Nevertheless, the measures represented the first successful attempt to broaden the common agricultural policy beyond the limitations of price measures only. New members of the Community would adjust their own legislation to the requirements of the directives within one year of accession and subject to minor adjustments made during consultations between the Community countries and Britain, Ireland, Norway, and Denmark.

No estimate was made of the total cost of the reforms agreed upon by the Council, as the details and scale of their implementation would be the responsibility of national Governments, but the cost over five years to the European Agricultural Guidance and Guarantee Fund (EAGGF) was calculated at 830,000,000 u.a. [25248A]

FINANCING OF AGRICULTURAL GUIDANCE AND GUARANTEE FUND

After lengthy discussions, agreement was reached on financing the EAGGF. For the two years 1965–66 and 1966–67 the cost of the common agricultural policy would be met entirely by percentage contributions from the member-countries to the Fund. From July 1, 1967 onwards, 90 percent of the levies on imports of footstuffs would be handed over by the member-Governments to the European Fund. This would, in fact, cover some 45 percent of the Fund's expenditure, and the remainder of the cost would be paid from the national exchequers of the member-countries in the following proportions:

	1965–66 (percent)	1966–67 (percent)	1967 onwards (percent)
Belgium	7.95	7.95	8.1
Germany	31.67	30.83	31.2
France	32.58	29.26	32.0
Italy	18.00	22.00	20.3
Luxemburg	0.22	0.22	0.2
Netherlands	9.58	9.74	8.2

After two further Council meetings, June 28–July 1 and July 13–14, 1966, final agreement on the outstanding problems of the common agricultural policy was reached at the end of the July 21–24 meeting and was formalized on July 26.

During the meeting the Commission put further proposals to the Ministers on July 21 and July 24: (i) concerning the establishment of common agricultural principles for the three remaining product groups—fruit and vegetables, sugar, fats and oils; and (ii) for fixing common prices for milk and dairy products, beef and veal, sugar, rice, oilseeds, and olive oil. [21731A]

Agreement was also reached by the Council of Ministers on Feb. 5–7, 1970, on a regulation for financing the common agricultural policy as from Jan. 1, 1971, provided the preconditions for the coming into force of the arrangements replacing the contributions by member-countries to the Community by the Community's own revenues had been met by that date. When the regulations became effective, the Guarantee Section of the Agricultural Fund would take over complete financing responsibility from the national Governments. From Jan. 1, 1972, the Guidance Section would receive a maximum allocation of $285,000,000 per annum; this amount could be increased by a weighted-majority vote of the Council after consultation with the European Parliament. [24167A]

Developments in Other Fields

Labor

On July 20, 1960, the EEC Commission sent a formal recommendation to member-States on the fulfilment of the principle of equal pay for men and women in return for equal work. The Council approved the reduction of the maximum differences to 15 percent by June 30, 1962, and to 10 percent by June 30, 1963, with their complete elimination by Dec. 31, 1964.

The first regulations on the free movement of workers within the Community came into force on Sept. 1, 1961. These were superseded by new regulations effective from May 4, 1964. The principal changes were as follows:

Abandonment of Priority for Home Labor Market

The new regulations provided, in principle, for equal right of access to employment throughout the Community territory for all wage-earners, and particularly seasonal and frontier workers, who had previously not been covered by any regulation regarding free movement.

To prevent the balance of the labor market from being upset in certain regions, or the aggravation of crises in certain occupations, a member-State, if it should consider such action necessary, might provisionally maintain or reinstate priority for the home labor market with specific limits (i.e. lay down that any available vacancies on the national labor market should be filled within three weeks by the domestic administration from its own nationals, but that after this period offers of employment should be transmitted to the other Community countries). A member-State must inform the Commission of its decision, giving its reasons for taking such action.

Prolongation of Employment Rights

The period of "assimilation" of foreign workers in the country of employment (making them eligible for any employment within the Community) was reduced from four to two years. A foreign-worker who had been in regular employment for two years and who subsequently returned to his country of origin would retain for two years afterwards the rights acquired under the provision for prolongation of employment.

Eligibility of Workers for Election to Representative Bodies in Places of Employment

Hitherto, foreign workers had enjoyed the right to vote for but not the right to election to representative bodies in the firm in which they were working. Under the new regulations foreign workers could be elected to these bodies provided they satisfied the same conditions as national workers and had worked for the firm for three years.

Admission of Foreign Workers' Families

The earlier regulations allowed the worker the right to be accompanied or joined by his wife and children under the age of 21. Under the new regulations this right was extended to all dependent relatives and any other relative living in the worker's home. Admission of a worker's family would continue to depend on whether he could house them in a manner regarded as normal for local workers in the area where he was employed. [18975A, 20829A]

Freedom of Establishment and Freedom to Supply Services

A program of gradually abolishing restrictions on setting up businesses and supplying services was adopted by the Council of Ministers on Oct. 25, 1961.

The program envisaged the abolition of discriminations based on nationality, hitherto restricting access to numerous activities as follows:

(1) by Dec. 31, 1963, for the textile, footwear, paper, basic chemicals, and metalworking industries, and for the wholesale trade, banking, and dealings in property;

(2) by Dec. 31, 1965, for retail distribution, department stores, and the food industry;

(3) by Dec. 31, 1967, for pharmacies (chemists), veterinary surgeons, insurance agents, and transport;

(4) by Dec. 31, 1969, for education, film production, and publicity material.

Certain general principles on freedom of establishment and freedom to supply services were approved by the Council of Ministers at its meeting in November 1963. They included the following:

(1) Self-employed people who wished to establish themselves or supply services in another member-country had the right to membership in Chambers of Commerce and professional associations in that country, and would be eligible to hold office in these organizations provided that such officers would not exercise public authority.

(2) Where specific qualifications were required for certain occupations, the host country would only be able to require that the applicant had passed a supplementary examination if the practice of a profession was subject to special conditions.

(3) Persons who supplied services would have the right to be accompanied by members of their staff in the country in which the service was performed. [18975A; 20829A]

Freedom of Movement for Capital

On May 12, 1960, the Council of Ministers approved a directive on freedom of movement for capital, which entered into force on June 27, 1960.

It established:

(1) unconditional freedom of capital movements connected with the freeing of trade in goods, of services, and of the movement of persons, and also with the free exercise of the right to establishment;

(2) unconditional and irreversible freedom for sale and purchase of stocks and shares quoted in the Community stock markets;

(3) conditional freedom with regard to the issuing and placing of stocks and shares on capital markets, and for the purchase of unquoted stocks and shares. Any Community country might, however, maintain or reimpose existing restrictions if their abolition was likely to hinder the achievement of its economic policy objectives.

The German Federal Republic, Belgium, and Luxemburg were not required to take any further liberalization measures in this respect since their foreign currency legislation already went beyond the obligations imposed by the Community directive. [18975A]

Development of a Common Transport Policy

On Feb. 27, 1962, the Council of Ministers asked the Commission to present detailed proposals for a common transport policy for roads, railways, and inland waterways. The program, which was submitted on June 1, 1962, was based on the principles of equality of treatment; financial independence; freedom of action for transport enterprises; free choice by the user of the means of transport; and co-ordination of investment. [18975A]

An actual common transport policy was not agreed upon by the Council of Ministers until June 22, 1965. The Community transport system was intended to regulate competition in all sectors by the progressive introduction of fixed-rate limits in two separate stages.

During the first stage—1966 to 1969—only commercial transport between member-countries would be subject to EEC regulations. Upper and lower tariff limits would be published for certain classes of road and rail traffic, though contracts could be made outside these rates under certain circumstances provided the details were published. Non-binding reference limits would be fixed for water transport, but contracts made outside these limits would also be published.

In the second stage—1969 to 1972—the reference limit system would be extended to certain categories of national and international traffic of heavy goods (the Council had still to decide on a definition) and also on other forms of national transport. By 1970, therefore, almost all road transportation and a significant part of rail goods traffic in the Common Market would be covered by a strict system of rate control, while a more flexible system would apply to all waterborne traffic and the remaining section of railway traffic, though probably to only a small part of road haulage.

The Ministers also agreed that during the two stages of the program the harmonization of national regulations affecting their transport sectors should be achieved and an attempt made to reach a common position on competition questions, including subsidies for national railways. [21885A]

Competition Policy

Following a decision of the Council of Ministers, on Dec. 19, 1961, to adopt a common anti-trust policy, detailed regulations on monopolistic practices were approved by the Council on Feb. 6, 1962.

The regulations (1) reaffirmed Articles 85–86 of the Treaty of Rome, which places a general ban on agreements, decisions, and concerted practices of an anticompetitive character; (2) required all such agreements, decisions, and practices already in force to be registered with the Commission by Nov. 1, 1962, if they had been made or agreed between more than two participants, and by Feb. 1, 1963, if between two participants; (3) laid down that all agreements etc. entered into after the coming into force of the regulations must be notified to the Commission; (4) exempted, however, from the stipulations under (2) and (3) certain types of agreements, decisions, and concerted practices; (5) gave the Commission power with regard to provision of information, control, and, in the cases where the rules were not observed, the imposition of penalties and fines.

It was stated that the rules would apply in principle also to transport, though they might be modified by the common transport policy; that they would apply to agriculture only in so far as they did not affect the aims of the common agricultural policy; and that they applied to oil but not to coal, for which the European Coal and Steel Community was responsible. [18975A]

On March 14, 1967, the EEC Commission adopted a

regulation on block exemption for some 30,000 exclusive dealing agreements between manufacturers and distributors, which had been notified to the Commission in accordance with the regulations of Feb. 6, 1962. Under each of these agreements, which was between a manufacturer and a dealer, the dealer could acquire a sole right of re-sale of products in a specific area of the Community. The new regulation came into force on May 1, 1967.   [22217A]

The achievement of the customs union in July 1968 was followed by rapid development of competition policy with the aim of maintaining the free trade facilitated by the removal of tariff barriers. The application of the relevant Articles of the Treaty of Rome and of the 1962 regulations was carried out by means of further block exemptions for certain business agreements and also by means of a series of test cases, designed to identify restrictive business practices which the Commission judged to be in contravention of the Community rules.

On July 29, 1968, the Commission published a list of forms of co-operation between small and medium-sized companies which it actively encouraged, and illustrated its intentions by a number of individual decisions with respect to certain forms of agreement. In parallel with this action the Commission also took a number of decisions forbidding various forms of cartels and in July 1969 for the first time imposed fines against members of two cartels.

The decisions to impose fines and, in one of the two cases, to act against companies based outside the Community, were upheld by the Court of Justice in July 1970 and in July 1972. On Dec. 16, 1972, the Commission announced that it had imposed fines totaling 9,000,000 units of account on members of a sugar cartel, the heaviest penalty thus far inflicted to enforce competition policy.

The first interpretation of Community competition policy with regard to Article 86 (dealing with abuse of a dominant position) was made with a decision against the West German performing rights society on June 2, 1971, and was followed by a further decision against an American metal container company on Dec. 13, 1971. The latter decision was the first in which the Commission had attempted to define Article 86 of the Rome Treaty as an instrument for controlling economic concentrations.

Common Turnover Tax System

On Feb. 9, 1967, the Council of Ministers adopted two directives on the harmonization of the turnover tax system in member-countries, to be completed by Jan. 1, 1970. The system adopted by the Six was the "value-added" system (VAT), by which only the value added to a product at different stages of production is liable to taxation, as opposed to the "cascade" system, by which the whole value of the product at different stages of production is taxed.   [22217A]

The system was adopted by 3 member-countries—France, Western Germany, and the Netherlands—before the deadline; by Luxemburg on Jan. 1, 1970; by Belgium on Jan. 1, 1971; and by Italy on Jan. 1, 1973. VAT had already been in force in Denmark since 1967; was introduced in Ireland on Nov. 1, 1972; and will come into force in Britain on April 1, 1973.   [25716A]

Agreements of Association with the EEC

A. GREECE

The first agreement on an associate membership in the EEC was signed by representatives of Greece and the six Common Market countries on July 9, 1961, and came into effect on Nov. 1, 1962.

The principal provisions of the agreement are given below:

Under Article 238 of the Treaty of Rome, Greece became associated with the EEC on the basis of a customs union, with the prospect of incorporation into the Community when the progress of her economy would allow her to assume fully the obligations deriving from the Treaty of Rome.

Greece would reduce her tariffs over a transitional period of 12 years, at the end of which the customs union would become fully effective. This would not, however, apply to most industrial goods produced in Greece, for which the transitional period of tariff reduction would be 22 years. It was estimated that the 22-year transition period would apply to roughly one-third of Greek imports from the Community.

Tariff reductions which had already taken place among the six EEC member-countries would automatically apply to Greek products on the entry into force of the agreement; any further reductions would also apply.

Greece accepted the tariffs of the EEC's common external tariff scale. Goods imported from third countries would thus, at the end of the transitional period, be subject to a common external tariff in Greece and the six Common Market countries.

Quantitative restrictions would be progressively eliminated between Greece and the EEC, the process to be completed by the end of the 22-year transitional period.

Special agricultural provisions ensured that Greek agricultural products would receive equal treatment with similar products of the Six through harmonization of the agricultural policies of the signatory countries. Greece could, however, decline to implement the harmonization policy for a particular product if this ran contrary to her interests.

The agreement also provided for the establishment of a common economic policy, taking into account the needs and resources of Greece. The common policy would cover movement of workers, services, and capital; vocational training and exchange of young workers; tax legislation; currency policy; transport systems; and the rules of competition.

A special protocol provided for loans to Greece of up to $125,000,000 to be used during the first five years of the Agreement.

A Council of the Association was set up to supervise the application of the Agreement. It consists of members of the Council of Ministers and of the Commission on the one hand, and of members of the Greek Government on the other. Each side has one vote and decisions are taken on the basis of unanimity. [18168A]

Developments

The principal developments under the Association Agreement between the EEC and Greece are given below.

(a) *Tariffs.* The internal tariff reductions introduced within the Community on Jan. 1, 1966, were extended to Greek products, but more favorable treatment was accorded to Greece's key export products, raisins, and tobacco.

On Nov. 1, 1965, Greece reduced her customs duties for imports from the EEC by 30 percent for most products (20 or 10 percent for other products subject to a slower reduction rate). On the same date Greece began to align her tariffs for imports from third countries on those of the Community.

(b) *Harmonization of Agricultural Policies.* At a meeting of the Council of Association on June 16, 1964, it was agreed that the agricultural policies of the Community and of Greece would have to be harmonized in two stages:

(i) During the first stage Greece would be allowed the levies and other machinery of the common agricultural policy without application of the price structure;

(ii) in the second stage Greece would progressively align her agricultural prices and protection levels on those prevailing in the EEC and would open her markets to Community farm exports. Agricultural assistance from the U.S.A. would have to be discontinued.

Although November 1964 was the original date laid down in the Association Agreement by which agreement on harmonization of agricultural policies should be reached, no agreement has yet been reached on a timetable for the plan.

(c) *Development Aid.* By mid-1966 loans amounting to $38,800,000 had been granted to Greece, most of the money being used for infrastructure projects. [21885A]

After the Greek military coup of April 1967, the EEC applied only those provisions of the agreement and of any later decisions which involved clearly defined obligations, and there were no fresh negotiations for new financial assistance after Oct. 31, 1967. [24170]

B. TURKEY

An agreement on Turkey's associate membership in the EEC was signed in Ankara on Sept. 12, 1963, and entered into force on Dec. 1, 1964.

Like the Agreement of Association between the EEC and Greece this agreement provided for Turkey's becoming a full member of the EEC when her economic progress should permit this.

The objective of the agreement—the continuous strengthening of the economic and commercial relations between Turkey and the EEC—would be attained by stages.

1. During a 5-year preparatory stage Turkey, with the assistance of the EEC, would continue her efforts to strengthen her economic and commercial position. The assistance would take the form of (a) tariff quotas, to be gradually increased, allowing Turkey to sell specified amounts of tobacco, raisins, dried figs, and hazelnuts in the Common Market; and (b) loans for economic development granted through the European Investment Bank.

2. The second or transitional stage, lasting a maximum of 12 years, would see the gradual establishment of a customs union between Turkey and the EEC. Although the details would depend on the situation at the end of the initial phase of the agreement, a framework for the trade and economic arrangements in the second stage was laid down. Under the arrangements, which would cover all trade, Turkey would be expected to adopt the common customs tariff, and to bring her economic policy with regard to free movement of persons, transport policy, and rules of competition into line with that of the EEC.

3. The third or definitive stage would be based on a full customs union, including a common external tariff.

The application of the Agreement is supervised by a Council of the Association, the members of which are drawn from the Council of Ministers, the Commission, the Governments of the Nine, and the Turkish Government. [20829A]

Developments

The main developments under the Agreement of Association between the EEC and Turkey took the form of quota increases for Turkish tobacco, raisins, dried figs, and hazelnuts as provided for in the initial stage of the Agreement. The largest such increases were agreed upon by the Council of the Association on Nov. 23, 1966.

By Dec. 31, 1965, Turkey had received loans amounting to more than $50,000,000 from the European Investment Bank, the money being devoted mainly to infrastructure projects.   [21885A]

A supplementary protocol agreed on July 22, 1970, and signed on Nov. 23, 1971, regulated the transition from the preparatory to the second (transitional) stage. Under an interim agreement, pending ratification of the above protocol, but in any case valid only until Sept. 30, 1972, Turkish industrial goods (except petroleum products and certain textile goods) were able to enter EEC countries without tariff or quantitative restrictions from Sept. 1, 1971, and about 90 percent of Turkey's agricultural exports were granted preferential treatment. In return Turkey would start to apply tariff reductions for industrial goods from the EEC.

An annex to the protocol provided for loans of $220,000,000 over 5 years and a 10-year schedule as from 1976 for the free movement and social rights of Turkish workers employed in the EEC. [24171, 24823]

C. AFRICAN STATES AND MADAGASCAR

The first Convention on the Association of Overseas Territories with the EEC, annexed to the Treaty of Rome (see page 56), expired on Dec. 31, 1962. Before this date a number of independent African States which had formerly been French, Belgian, or Italian colonies expressed a wish to continue the association under a new agreement. After protracted negotiations the new Convention of Association between the EEC and associated African States and Madagascar was signed at Yaoundé (Cameroon) on July 20, 1963. The Yaoundé Convention, as it was known, entered into force on June 1, 1964. The 18 associated African States are listed on page 55, together with Mauritius, a signatory of the Second Yaoundé Convention.

The principal provisions of the Yaoundé Convention were the following.

Exports from the associated States to the EEC member-countries would be subject to the same gradual elimination of duties and expansion of quotas as applied within the Community. Certain tropical products would enter Common Market countries duty-free, and the common external tariff would operate at reduced rates for these products.

Not later than six months after the Convention's entry into force, the associated States would extend the same tariff treatment to products originating in all EEC countries, and would gradually abolish quantitative restrictions. In certain cases, however, duties might still be applied by associated States to products from the Community when such duties corresponded to the requirements of their development, industrialization or budget.

The object of the Convention—to foster the economic and social development of the associated States—would be achieved through the European Development Fund and the European Investment Bank.

The provisions on establishment, service, payments, and capital were based on the principle of reciprocal non-discrimination against individuals and companies.

The Convention would be valid for five years, but could be terminated at six months notice by any of the associated States with respect to the Community or vice versa.

The institutions of association, set up under the Convention are (a) the Council of Association, composed of members of the Community's Council of Ministers and Commission, and a member of the Government of each associated State; (b) the Parliamentary Conference of the Association, consisting of members of the European Parliament and of the Parliaments of the associated States; and (c) the 5-member Court of Arbitration of the Association.   [20829A]

The Second Yaoundé Convention, renewing the Convention of 1963 with modifications, was signed on July 29, 1969, after protracted negotiations.

Difficulties had arisen through criticism by the African States of the divergent results of the first convention; they pointed out that their exports to the EEC had risen by less than 1 percent between 1964 and 1966, and had fallen by 1 percent in 1967, whereas EEC exports to the African countries had increased by some 10 percent in 1966–67. The Associated States also expressed dissatisfaction with the allocation of aid from the European Development Fund, which had shown only a small increase in "genuine aid" against a high relative increase in loans.

The second Convention, due to expire not later than Jan. 31, 1975, provided:

(a) that the EEC would grant to agricultural imports from the Associated States a more favorable treatment than before, while continuing the complete exemption from customs duty of imports of non-agricultural products from these States;

(b) that aid of $918,000,000 (to be supplied through the European Development Fund in the form of grants totaling $748,000,000 and loans on favorable terms of $80,000,000, and through the European Investment Bank as loans totaling $90,000,000) would be provided to the Associated States for the 5-year period of the new

Convention—the Associated States having previously requested a total of $1,500,000,000;

(c) that of the total grants, from $65,000,000 to $80,000,000 should be set aside as a "disaster fund" to be used in emergencies, including severe falls in export prices; and

(d) that African companies should have a 15 percent advantage in tendering for certain EEC-financed projects. [23631]

An agreement providing for the accession of Mauritius to the Yaoundé Convention was signed in Port Louis on May 12, 1972.

D. OVERSEAS TERRITORIES AND DEPARTMENTS

A number of Netherlands overseas territories and French overseas territories and *départements* (listed on page 55) were associated with the EEC through an Association Decision valid for five years from June 1, 1964. In respect of the Netherlands Antilles, the association arrangements came into effect on Oct. 1, 1964. [20829A]

These arrangements were extended in June 1969 for another five years, during which the European Development Fund would make grants of $62,000,000 and loans of $10,000,000, and the European Investment Bank loans of $10,000,000, to these territories. [23632]

E. NIGERIA

At the time of the signature of the Yaoundé Convention the member-States of the EEC expressed their readiness to negotiate with any other African countries wishing to become associated with the Common Market, if the economic structure and production of those countries should be comparable to those of the associated States.

On this basis a separate agreement was concluded with Nigeria on July 16, 1966. The agreement was valid until May 31, 1969—the date on which the first Yaoundé Convention expired—but it never came into force. [21885A]

F. THE EAST AFRICAN COMMUNITY

A first Association Agreement between the EEC and Kenya, Tanzania, and Uganda had been drawn up in Brussels on June 13, 1968, after three years of protracted negotiations, and signed at Arusha (Tanzania) on July 26.

Apart from the abolition of customs duties on many East African exports to EEC countries, it also provided for East African non-discrimination and most-favored-nation treatment of EEC countries in respect of the right to settle, freedom of services, and payments.

This agreement, however, had not been ratified by all the EEC member-countries before the expiry, on May 31, 1969, of the first Yaoundé Convention, to which it was linked, and had therefore never come into effect. Negotiations for the renewal of the agreement with certain modifications took place in Brussels from June 30 to July 10, 1969.

In its final form the new Arusha Convention, which followed the same pattern as the one signed in July 1968, provided that the EEC would suspend customs duties and quantitative restrictions on imports of all East African products except for cloves, coffee, and canned pineapples, which competed with exports of the 18 Associated States and for which tariff quotas were fixed at 56,000 tons per annum for coffee, 860 tons for tinned pineapple, and 100 tons for cloves. In return Kenya, Tanzania, and Uganda granted the EEC member-countries tariff preferences varying between 2 and 8 percent on 58 products, affecting 6.5 percent of the total imports of the three East African countries, and 10 percent of their imports from the EEC countries.

The new agreement was for five years, was to run parallel to the second Yaoundé Convention, and would therefore also expire on Jan. 31, 1975. [23632]

G. MOROCCO AND TUNISIA

Agreements of association between the EEC and Morocco and Tunisia, to be valid for five years, were signed on March 31 and March 28, 1969, respectively. The main provisions of these agreements, which came into force on Sept. 1, 1969, were as follows:

Morocco and Tunisia would benefit from tariff-free and quantitatively unrestricted entry for most of their industrial exports to the EEC; the latter, however, reserved the right to reintroduce tariffs on certain refined oil products if the exports by the two countries to the EEC exceeded 100,000 tons. For agricultural products, the EEC made a number of concessions, and in particular granted an 80 percent duty preference for citrus fruits, provided certain price requirements were fulfilled.

In return, Morocco would, *inter alia,* make tariff reductions of 25 percent on certain EEC products, and Tunisia would, for 40 percent of its imports from the EEC, grant tariff reductions equivalent to 70 percent of the preference given to imports from France. [23631]

H. MALTA

An association agreement between Malta and the EEC was approved by the EEC Council of Ministers on Nov. 26, 1970, and signed on Dec. 5. It came into force on April 1, 1971, and was aimed at the completion of a customs union by 1981 in two 5-year stages.

During the first stage the EEC would grant Malta a 70 percent reduction in customs duties on industrial products, except petroleum and some textiles which would remain subject to quotas. Malta would reduce its import duties on EEC products by 15 percent on April 1, 1971; 10 percent at the start of the third year of the agreement; and another 10 percent at the start of the fifth year. In the second stage Malta would reduce these duties by at least a further 35 percent. [24824]

I. CYPRUS

An association agreement between Cyprus and the European Economic Community was signed on Dec. 19, 1972, providing for reciprocal tariff reductions on industrial and agricultural products during the course of a first stage ending on June 30, 1977.

For industrial products the EEC agreed to make an immediate 70 percent reduction in tariffs, while Cyprus undertook to reduce its tariffs by 35 percent in three steps over a four year period. In the agricultural sector EEC tariffs would be cut by 40 percent with regard to citrus fruits, while carobs would enter the EEC duty-free. In addition, special arrangements were made for continuing Cypriot exports of sherry to the United Kingdom and Ireland for a two-year period and within quota limitations.

Trade Agreements with Non-Members

Various agreements have been signed between the EEC and countries outside the Community, as follows:

1. A three-year agreement between the EEC and **Iran,** signed on Oct. 14, 1963, and in force since Dec. 1, 1963, provided *inter alia* for temporary reductions in the EEC's common external tariff for products of special importance to Iran's economy (such as carpets, dried grapes, and apricots) and fixed a tariff quota for raisins imported by the EEC from Iran (at 15 percent of such imports from non-member and non-associated countries). The agreement was amended in 1967 and extended for a further three years from Dec. 1, 1970. [20833; 24824]

2. A trade agreement between the EEC and **Israel,** signed on June 4, 1964, in force since July 1, 1964, for a three-year period with a possible extension. No formal extension was approved, although certain special trade arrangements between Israel and the EEC were continued.

A new trade agreement, for five years, signed on June 29, 1970, provided for mutual tariff reductions as from Oct. 1, 1970.

These agreements included provisions for a 40 percent reduction in the EEC tariff for citrus and other fruit from Israel, and an immediate 30 percent reduction on a wide range of industrial products, with fur-

ther 5 percent annual reductions so as to reach a total of 50 percent by Jan. 1, 1974. These measures were expected to benefit about 55 percent of Israel's industrial exports to the EEC, and about 80 percent of her agricultural exports. Israel granted tariff preferences ranging from 5 to 30 percent by 1974 for about half of her industrial and agricultural imports from the EEC subject to duties. [24171]

3. An agreement on trade and technical co-operation between the Community and its member-countries on the one hand and **Lebanon** on the other, signed on May 21, 1965. The agreement was valid for a period of three years and has since been renewed several times, the latest extension being on July 13, 1972, for a further period of one year pending the conclusion of a more comprehensive preferential trade agreement.

4. A trade agreement with **Yugoslavia,** signed on March 19, 1970, and in force from May 1, 1970, provided for most-favored-nation treatment between the two sides; an acceleration of the import duty concessions proposed under the Kennedy Round (see page 32); concessions for Yugoslav beef exports; and the establishment of a mixed commission to carry out the agreement. [24171]

5. A trade agreement with **Spain,** signed on June 29, 1970, and in force from Oct. 1, 1970, envisaged preferential arrangements which would within a reasonable time lead to a customs union. The agreement covered about 95 percent of the EEC's industrial imports from Spain subject to tariffs, and 62 percent of agricultural imports, as well as about 61 percent of Spanish imports from the EEC. For most industrial goods from Spain the tariff reductions would be 30 percent initially; 50 percent from Jan. 1, 1972; 60 percent from Jan. 1, 1973; and 70 percent from Jan. 1, 1974. [24171]

6. The first trade agreement of the EEC with a Latin American country was that with **Argentina,** signed in Brussels on Nov. 8, 1971, for a three-year period from Jan. 1, 1972.

This non-preferential agreement, providing for mutual most-favored-nation treatment, afforded Argentina tariff advantages for frozen beef exports to the EEC; it also provided for duty-free imports of Argentine industrial and processed farm goods within the EEC's "generalized preferences" scheme for developing nations, which came into effect from July 1, 1971 (see above). The agreement would be implemented by a joint commission set up between Argentina and the EEC and charged with examining possible further tariff concessions.

7. An agreement with the **United States,** formally approved by the EEC member-countries on Feb. 11,

1972, after consultation with the four applicant countries (Denmark, Great Britain, Ireland, and Norway) temporarily reduced EEC import duties on U.S. oranges and grapefruit; provided for increased EEC stockpiling of U.S. wheat, and for the U.S. withdrawal of 18,000,000 acres from feed grain production and 8,000,000 acres from wheat production in 1972–73; and envisaged further mutual consultations to avoid undesirable changes in trade patterns.

8. A preferential trade agreement between the Community and **Egypt** was signed in Brussels on Dec. 18, 1972, providing for a series of reciprocal tariff reductions on industrial products and additional Community concessions on Egyptian exports of certain agricultural products.

The five-year agreement would enter into force on March 1, 1973, when EEC tariffs on industrial products would be reduced by 45 percent while Egyptian tariffs would be reduced by 30 percent. The Community preference would be increased to 55 percent on Jan. 1, 1974, while the Egyptian preference would increase to 40 percent on the same date and to 50 percent on Jan. 1, 1975. Community concessions for Egyptian agricultural products would include a 40 percent preference for citrus fruits.

Tariff Preferences for Developing Countries
The Council of Ministers decided on March 30, 1971, to introduce as from July 1, 1971, general tariff preferences in favor of manufactured and semi-manufactured goods exported to the EEC by 91 developing countries, involving the abolition of duties on such exports as well as on certain processed agricultural products—within certain limits.

These limits included the imposition of "ceilings" on imports of manufactures from developing countries and the limitation of preferences for the most competitive of the developing countries so as to reserve a substantial quota for the less developed ones.

Monetary Agreements
The European Commission on Feb. 12, 1969, sent to EEC member-Governments a proposal—the so-called "Barre plan" (named after the Commission's Vice-President, M. Raymond Barre)—for co-ordination of economic policies and monetary co-operation.

Under this plan, each member-country undertook to place part of its reserves at the disposal of the others, and in the event of difficulties any member might call on its partners for assistance within a ceiling to be fixed subsequently. Joint consultations would then be held with a view to re-establishing equilibrium. If no agreement could be reached, the receiving country's indebtedness should not exceed three months, but if agreement was reached the credits might be renewed or converted into medium-term assistance, all such arrangements having to be accompanied by increased co-ordination of economic policies.

The Council of Ministers approved the plan on March 4, 1969, with the proviso that the arrangements should be between the various central banks rather than between the Governments. [23447; 23630]

Community Budget
Following a conference of the member-countries' Heads of State or Government at The Hague, Dec. 1–5, 1969, the Council of Ministers reached agreement on Dec. 22, 1969, on the Communities' budget as follows:

From Jan. 1, 1971, all receipts from levies would be allocated to the Communities, and there would be a similar gradual allocation of the receipts from customs duties from the same date. Any deficit during an interim period would be covered by national contributions according to an agreed scale, and after the interim period these contributions would be replaced by receipts corresponding to a uniform rate of the harmonized value added tax (VAT).

As from the adoption of the 1975 budget the European Parliament would have powers to amend, by a majority vote of its members, any draft budget submitted by the Council of Ministers, although any amendment of the VAT rate would have to remain within the limit set by the Council's decree introducing this tax. Any amendments made by the European Parliament might be altered by the Council by a qualified majority vote; any such alterations by the Council could be changed by the European Parliament by a decision of a majority of its membership and subject to three-fifths of the votes cast being in favor; the Parliament would thus adopt the budget in its final form, but if Parliament failed to reach a decision within a fixed period, the budget would stand as drawn up by the Council.

Procedures for the European Parliament's control of the budget were approved by the Council on April 22, 1970. [24167A]

Progress Toward Economic and Monetary Union
With a view to achieving complete economic and monetary union of the EEC member-countries by December 1980, the Council endorsed in February 1971 plans for the first of three stages for this scheme. The details were contained in the so-called Werner Report, drawn up by a working party under the chairmanship of M. Pierre Werner, the Luxemburg Prime Minister and Minister of Finance.

The final part of this report, completed on Oct. 8, 1970, restated the objectives of economic and monetary union as affirmed by the Hague conference of EEC Heads of State and Government in December 1969.

The report made it clear that the proposed union would mean that the principal decisions of economic policy would be taken at Community level, and that the necessary powers would therefore be transferred from the national plane to the Community plane, which would entail the progressive development of political co-operation. In the long run, the report said, this development was bound to lead to political union.

The proposed monetary union would imply, the report continued, "the total and irreversible convertibility of currencies, the elimination of margins of fluctuation in rates of exchange, the irrevocable fixing of parity ratios and the total liberation of movements of capital."

The Community's center of decision would be politically responsible to a European Parliament.

The report also laid down procedures for the first stage of this program, covering three years as from Jan. 1, 1971.

After adopting the above plan on Feb. 9, 1971, the Council defined its objectives in a resolution, approved on March 22, 1971, and including the following details:

At the end of the three-stage, 10-year plan, the Community would be:

(a) "an area within which persons, goods, services and capital can circulate freely . . . without leading to structural and regional disequilibrium . . .";

(b) "an individual monetary unit within the international system, . . . comprising a Community organization of the central banks"; and

(c) in possession of institutions empowered to ensure the management of economic and monetary union "subject to the deliberations and control" of the European Parliament.

The resolution also laid down what measures would have to be taken within the first three-year stage. These included the establishment of Community rules determining the uniform assessment of the Value Added Tax; harmonization in the application, assessment, and collection of excise duties; and harmonization of other taxes. It was also stressed that "the Community must progressively adopt common positions in monetary relations with third countries and international organizations."

At the same time the Council took a number of decisions which, *inter alia,* established target figures for the six EEC member-countries, including percentages for average annual rates of (a) price increases (ranging from 2 to 3.3 percent); (b) growth in the gross national product (ranging from a minimum of 2.6 percent for Luxemburg to a maximum of 6.2 percent for Italy);

and (c) unemployment (of up to 3 percent for Italy).

Another decision by the Council involved approval for a four-year scheme (later renewable every five years) for providing medium-term financial aid for member-countries which might be in, or threatened by, balance-of-payments difficulties—this decision being an implementation of the "Barre plan" of 1969 (see above).

At their meeting on Feb. 8–9, 1971, the EEC Ministers of Foreign Affairs and Finance agreed, at a request by the German Federal Republic, to an "escape clause," under which, if progress in the harmonization of the economic policies of the member-countries was in the view of one or more members insufficient and further negotiations to reach an agreed solution of the outstanding problems remained unsuccessful, it would become possible for dissatisfied members to demand, by Dec. 31, 1975, the termination of the various measures of monetary co-operation although it was agreed, on French insistence, that the decision not to widen the fluctuation margins between Community currencies could not be revoked.   [*24781A*]

The Council of Ministers on March 21, 1972, formally approved an agreement in principle on the implementation of the 1971 resolution on economic and monetary union (see above). The main element of the agreement was that by July 1, 1972, at the latest, the maximum margin of fluctuation between the currencies of any two member-States would be fixed at 2.25 percent, while the longer-term aim was the complete elimination of any fluctuation margin.   [*25423A*]

At a Summit meeting of the Nine held in Paris on Oct. 19–20, 1972, decisions on economic and monetary policy were outlined in a communiqué as follows:

(1) "The Heads of State or of Government reaffirm the determination of the member-States of the enlarged European Communities irreversibly to achieve the economic and monetary union, confirming all the elements of the instruments adopted by the Council and by the representatives of member-States on March 22, 1971, and March 21, 1972 (see above).

"The necessary decisions should be taken in the course of 1973 so as to allow the transition to the second stage of the economic and monetary union on Jan. 1, 1974, and with a view to its completion not later than Dec. 31, 1980."

(2) A European Monetary Co-operation Fund, administered by the Committee of Governors of Central Banks, would be set up before April 1, 1973.

(3) The need was stressed to co-ordinate more closely the economic policies of the Community, priority being given to the fight against inflation and a return to price stability.

(4) Member-States should work on agreed guidelines for the general reform of the international monetary system. *[Page 25541]*

Moves Toward Political Unification

After the Hague conference of EEC Heads of State and Government of December 1969 had agreed to an examination of "the best way of achieving progress in the matter of political unification" a group of Foreign Ministry officials under the chairmanship of Vicomte Etienne Davignon subsequently prepared two reports, the final version of the second report being adopted by the EEC Foreign Ministers on Oct. 27, 1970.

Listing the objects of a united Europe, the Davignon Report stated that it should be "based on a common heritage of respect for the liberty and rights of man and bring together democratic States with freely elected Parliaments."

Proposals made in the report were *inter alia* that Foreign Ministers should meet at least once every six months; conferences of Heads of State or Government should be held when deemed desirable; and "in the event of a serious crisis or special urgency" there should be extraordinary consultation between the member-States' Governments. The ministerial meetings should be prepared by a Political Committee, and the Council's President-in-office should, once a year, provide the European Parliament with a progress report on the work done in this field. *[24821A]*

At the Summit conference of Heads of Government or of State of the Nine held in Paris in October 1972, a communiqué was issued setting out the future policies of the enlarged Community. Member-countries agreed as follows:

(1) to create before Dec. 31, 1973, a Regional Development Fund;

(2) to draw up by Jan. 1, 1974, action programs in the fields of social policy, industrial, scientific and technological policy, and environmental policy;

(3) to define guidelines for external relations with developing countries and with Eastern Europe. In this field the Community also attached major importance to the multilateral negotiations in the context of GATT in which it will participate.

(4) With regard to foreign policy, Foreign Ministers would in future meet four times a year instead of twice as hitherto, and would prepare a second stage report on political integration by June 30, 1973.

(5) Support would be given to measures aimed at clarifying relationships between Community institutions and member-States, and practical steps toward this end would be taken before June 30, 1973.

(6) The meeting requested the institutions of the Community to draw up a report by the end of 1975 on the incorporation before the end of the decade of "the whole complex of the relations of member-States into a European union." *[25537A]*

European Atomic Energy Community (EAEC or Euratom)

For the events leading up to the creation of the European Atomic Energy Community, see "European Economic Community," page 55ff.

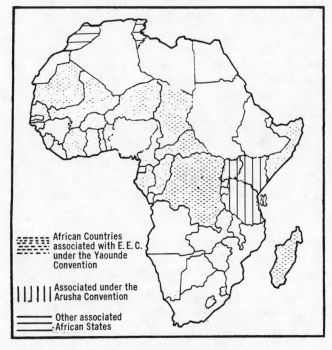

African Countries associated with E.E.C. under the Yaounde Convention

Associated under the Arusha Convention

Other associated African States

The Euratom Treaty

The aims of the Community were defined in the preamble as the raising of living standards in the member-countries and the promotion of trade with non-Community countries. The tasks of Euratom were defined in Article 1 of the Treaty as the creation, within a short period, of the technical and industrial conditions necessary to utilize nuclear discoveries, and especially to produce nuclear energy on a large scale. This result would be achieved by joint measures of the member-countries and through the activities of the institutions of the Community.

The main functions of Euratom, as laid down in the treaty, can be summarized as follows:

(1) The promotion, facilitation, and co-ordination of research in member-countries, and the execution of a research program of its own; (2) the dissemination of information on atomic energy, and the acquisition of information on all patents, patent applications and working models of inventions which would be useful to the Community; (3) the establishment of a code of

basic standards governing personal safety against dangers resulting from ionizing radiation; (4) the promotion of a planned development of investments by public and private undertakings in the nuclear energy fields; and (5) the formation of Community undertakings for the development of nuclear industry within Euratom.

Other significant provisions of the Treaty are as follows:

Supplies

A joint policy would be pursued with regard to the supply of ores, raw materials, and special fissile matter on the basis of the principle of equal access to resources. For this purpose the Commission would set up a Commercial Agency which would be a corporate body, vested with financial independence and able to conduct its affairs according to business rules, but controlled by the Commission. The Agency (the majority of whose capital would have to be owned by the Community and the member-countries) would possess (i) an option to purchase any of the materials in question produced in member-States; and (ii) the exclusive right to conclude contracts for the purchase or sale of such materials outside the Community.

The Commission would be entitled to make recommendations regarding prospecting and the exploitation of mines, and might participate financially in such activities. Member-States would be required to send the Commission annual reports on prospecting, reserves, and mining investments.

Security

The Commission would be required to ensure (i) that ores, raw materials, and special fissile matter were not diverted from their intended use as declared by their consumers; and (ii) that arrangements for their supply, and any special control measures accepted by the Community in an agreement with a non-Community State or international organization, were observed.

To this end, the Commission would:

(a) Request declarations from all the undertakings concerned describing the basic technical characteristics of their equipment;

(b) request statements of all transactions in order to facilitate accounting of ores, raw materials and special fissile matter;

(c) insist, if necessary, on all surplus special fissile matter temporarily not in use being placed in deposit;

(d) arrange for its inspectors to carry out checks and, where necessary, impose sanctions ranging from a warning to the complete withdrawal of raw materials or special fissile matter.

Ownership of Special Fissile Matter

All special fissile matter would be the property of the Community. Member-States, undertakings or individuals, however, would be entitled to the widest possible utilization and consumption of the special fissile matter which had legitimately come into their possession.

Common Market in Nuclear Materials

A common market in nuclear materials would be set up, involving the following obligations on member-countries:

(a) To introduce, one year after the coming into force of the Treaty, a common customs tariff for nuclear minerals, materials and products imported from non-Community countries;

(b) to repeal between each other, after the same one-year period, all import and export duties and taxes on such minerals, materials, and products (the non-European territories of member-States being entitled, however, to continue to levy duties and taxes of a purely fiscal character);

(c) to apply the procedure laid down in the Common Market Treaty for the gradual abolition of internal tariffs and quantitative import restrictions between member-countries, and for the introduction of a uniform customs tariff, to all other products which might be used in the nuclear industry;

(d) to admit nationals of the other member-countries, without discrimination, to all posts and occupations requiring qualifications in the nuclear sphere, as well as to participation in the construction of nuclear undertakings;

(e) to set up an insurance scheme covering risks arising from the use of atomic energy;

(f) to facilitate the transfer between member-countries of capital needed for nuclear projects, and to permit the transfer to other member-countries of payments in connection with nuclear transactions and employment in nuclear industries or research. [15927A]

Implementation of the Treaty

Nuclear Research

A Joint Research Center, set up under the Euratom Treaty, includes four important establishments for nuclear research.

These are:

1. The Nuclear Research Center at Ispra (Italy), transferred by Italy to Euratom under an agreement signed on July 22, 1959;

2. The Central Nuclear Measurements Bureau at Geel (Belgium);

3. The Transuranium Elements Institute at Karlsruhe (German Federal Republic);

4. The General Purpose Center at Petten (Netherlands).

Euratom has signed several hundred research contracts with public and private undertakings in the 9 member-countries of the Community. Under these contracts the Community contributes both finance and personnel. One of the most important such agreements is with the Belgian Nuclear Study Center at Mol, whose high-neutron-flux reactor (BR-2) for the testing of materials is jointly operated by the Center and by Euratom, the latter bearing two-thirds of the running costs. Other fields of research covered by such agreements include fast-breeder and high temperature gas reactors, nuclear ship propulsion, and the uses of nuclear energy in agriculture and medicine.

Part of Euratom's research program is carried out

in conjunction with that of the European Nuclear Energy Agency of the OECD (see pages 91–2). In particular Euratom is participating in the ENEA's Dragon project. The Community also co-operates with the International Atomic Energy Agency of the United Nations (see page 32). [18610A]

Information on the various research projects with which Euratom is concerned is disseminated through an atomic information and documentation center.

Following the completion of a second five-year research program in December 1967, the member-States failed to agree on a further multiannual program, and research continued at a reduced level by means of a series of five interim annual programs until the end of 1972. During this period the emphasis in Euratom research shifted from participation in the development of future generations of nuclear power reactors to more basic studies in the nuclear field and also to work in other scientific sectors.

Promotion of the Atomic Energy Industry

Euratom has adopted a number of measures by which it promotes the development of the peaceful uses of atomic energy in Europe.

These include:

(1) The creation of the common market for nuclear materials and equipment (in operation since Jan. 1, 1959);

(2) the introduction of the freedom of movement within the Community for technical workers in the atomic energy industry;

(3) the preparation of an insurance convention under which the Community as a whole will have third-party coverage for damages arising out of the atomic energy industry;

(4) financial assistance for power reactor projects in return for access to all planning, constructional, and operational information;

(5) the creation of a special bureau (Eurisotop) to provide information on the use of radio isotopes in industry.

Supplies, Health, and Security

A Supply Agency, as provided for in the Treaty, came into operation on June 1, 1960. This Agency, which is a commercially-operating independent department attached to the Commission, has an option to purchase any ores, raw materials, and special fissile matter produced in the member-countries, and has the exclusive right to conclude contracts for the purchase or sale of such materials outside the Community.

To protect workers in the atomic energy industry, and also the rest of the population, Euratom has drawn up a code of basic health standards (February 1959). The code, which has been made binding on the Governments of the Six, has been incorporated in the national legislation of each of the member-countries of the Community. The regulations, whose coverage includes X-ray installations and the use of radioactive materials in the manufacture of household goods and cosmetics, represented the first attempt anywhere to set up a comprehensive legal system to cover radiation health risks. [16574A]

A security control system to supervise the proper use of ores, raw materials, and special fissile materials, as provided for in the Treaty, has been set up by the Commission. The control system is binding on the Governments of the Six. (NOTE: Euratom has no control over nuclear materials or installations intended for military purposes.)

Agreements with Non-Member Countries

Agreements made by Euratom with non-member countries concerning the peaceful uses of atomic energy are as follows:

(1) *Euratom—U.S.A.* Under a joint power development agreement signed on Nov. 8, 1958, the U.S. Government pledged technical and financial help in the construction and running of six to eight power-producing reactors with a total capacity of 1,000,000 kilowatts. The agreement made provision for the collaboration of the U.S.A. and Euratom in a ten-year nuclear research and development program. A revision to this agreement, on July 9, 1962, provided for the loan of fissile materials for the joint program, whereas such materials had previously been sold to Euratom by the U.S.A. [16574A]

(2) *Euratom—Britain.* An agreement on collaboration in developing nuclear energy for peaceful purposes was signed by Euratom and Britain in February 1959. Under it a standing committee for co-operation was set up. Aspects of nuclear research in which the two parties have co-operated include (i) the study of controlled thermo-nuclear reactions for peaceful purposes; (ii) fast-breeder reactor techniques, and (iii) advanced gas-cooler reactor systems. [16574A; 17141C]

The original 10-year agreement was extended for another two years on Feb. 4, 1969. [23261C]

(3) *Euratom—Canada.* Two agreements with Canada were signed on Oct. 5, 1959. An outline agreement concluded with the Canadian Government laid down the conditions under which Canada and Euratom would exchange nuclear data, materials, and equipment between individuals and corporations. The sec-

ond agreement, a technical agreement between Euratom and Atomic Energy of Canada Ltd., provided for a joint research and development program in the use of reactors powered by uranium fuel moderated by heavy water. [*17141C*]

(4) *Euratom—Brazil*. A 20-year agreement for co-operation between Euratom and Brazil in the peaceful uses of atomic energy was signed on June 9, 1961. The agreement covered exchange of information on research and development; means of health protection; installations and equipment; utilization of minerals, raw materials, special fissile matter, and nuclear fuels and radio-isotopes; exchange of personnel; and the granting of patent licenses. [*18610A*]

(5) *Euratom—Argentina*. A similar agreement to that between Euratom and Brazil was concluded between Euratom and Argentina on Sept. 4, 1962. [*18974A*]

Atomic Energy Co-operation Agreements

India and Egypt, September 1962	[*18922D*]
India and U.S.A., July 1963	[*18563A*]
India and Canada, Nov. 15, 1963	[*19866A*]
Britain and Japan, March 6, 1968	[*22979C*]
Britain and Norway, March 1968	[*22979C*]
Britain and Finland, May 24, 1968	[*23424A*]
Britain, Western Germany, and Netherlands,	
Nov. 25, 1968	[*23088C*]
Dec. 19, 1969	[*23806B*]
Britain and Pakistan, July 26, 1970	[*24296A*]
Belgium and Pakistan, Oct. 9, 1970	[*24296A*]
Western Germany and India, Oct. 5, 1971	[*24884C*]

THE EUROPEAN FREE TRADE ASSOCIATION (EFTA)

Members: Austria, Iceland, Norway, Portugal, Sweden, Switzerland
Associate Member: Finland

The European Free Trade Association (EFTA)—an organization comprising Austria, Iceland, Norway, Portugal, Sweden, and Switzerland, and until Dec. 31, 1972, Britain and Denmark—formally came into being on May 3, 1960, following the ratification of the Treaty of Stockholm (signed between Dec. 29, 1959 and Jan. 4, 1960). This Treaty established the Association and laid down its aims, functions, procedure, and organization.

History

The first definite moves toward the creation of a European free trade area, comprising the six Common Market countries and the eleven other members of the

OEEC (Organization for European Economic Co-operation, see page 85), were made at Ministerial meetings of the OEEC on Feb. 13, March 8, and Oct. 17, 1957. At the last-mentioned meeting a resolution was unanimously passed expressing the Council's "determination to secure the establishment of a European free trade area which would comprise all member-countries of the Organization (i.e. the OEEC); which would associate, on a multilateral basis, the European Economic Community with the other member-countries; and which, taking fully into consideration the objectives of the European Economic Community, would in practice take effect parallel with the Treaty of Rome." [*17613A*]

Discussions were continued throughout the next year, but little progress was made because of the French Government's opposition to some aspects of the free trade area as proposed in a working paper then being considered. A complete breakdown in negotiations finally took place at a session of the Inter-Governmental Committee of the OEEC on Nov. 13–14, 1958, when the French Minister of Information stated that the French Cabinet saw no possibility of establishing a free trade area on the lines proposed, since there were no provisions for a common external tariff nor for harmonization of social and economic systems.

With the imminent threat of an economic rift between the Common Market members of the OEEC and the eleven other member-countries, a conference of senior trade officials of the so-called "Outer Seven" countries (Austria, Britain, Denmark, Norway, Portugal, Sweden, and Switzerland) was held on Dec. 1–2, 1958, at Geneva.

A statement was issued after the meeting by the chairman of the conference, Dr. Schaffner (of the Swiss Ministry of Economics), which (1) expressed the identity of views of the Governments represented on both the short-term and long-term objectives of the free trade area negotiations with the six EEC countries; (2) reaffirmed their intention to pursue their efforts to find a satisfactory formula of multilateral association between the Six and the other members of the OEEC. [*Page 17614*]

A further meeting of experts of the "Outer Seven" countries was held on March 17–18, 1959, at Saltsjö-baden, Sweden. The delegates decided that the Hall-stein Report—a memorandum of the EEC Commission on possible measures to overcome the crisis between the two economic groups in Europe—did not constitute a satisfactory basis for negotiations with the Common Market countries. It was decided that investigations into the possibilities of stimulating trade between the "Outer Seven" countries, by the gradual removal of tariffs and quantitative import restrictions, should be opened.

These investigations led to a meeting of experts of the "Outer Seven" countries to draw up a plan for a "trading association." The draft plan was examined by Ministers at a meeting in Stockholm on July 20–21, 1959, and it was finally announced that the Ministers would recommend to their Governments "that a European Free Trade Association among the seven countries should be established."

The Convention

The Convention of the European Free Trade Association was drafted between Oct. 8 and Nov. 5, 1959, and initialed at a Ministerial meeting in Stockholm on Nov. 20, 1959. On Dec. 12, 1959, the seven EFTA States decided on the establishment of a permanent Secretariat which, it was subsequently announced, would have its headquarters in Geneva. [17613A]

Art. 2 of the Convention of the European Free Trade Association described the Association's objectives as (a) "to promote within the Area of the Association and within each member-State a sustained expansion of economic activity, full employment, increased productivity and the rational use of resources, financial stability, and a continuous improvement in living standards"; (b) to secure that trade between member-States took place in conditions of fair competition; (c) to avoid significant disparity in the supply of raw materials; and (d) to contribute to the harmonious development and expansion of world trade.

Art. 3 laid down that as from the dates shown below no member-State might apply an import duty on any product at a level exceeding the percentage of the basic duty as applied by that country on Jan. 1, 1961—or March 1, 1960, in the case of Denmark—as follows:

Percentage of basic duty

July 1, 1960	..	..	80 percent
Jan. 1, 1962	..	..	70 percent
July 1, 1963	..	..	60 percent
Jan. 1, 1965	..	..	50 percent
Jan. 1, 1966	..	..	40 percent
Jan. 1, 1967	..	..	30 percent
Jan. 1, 1968	..	..	20 percent
Jan. 1, 1969	..	..	10 percent

All import duties were to be eliminated by Jan. 1, 1970.

Each member-State declared its willingness to apply import duties at lower levels if it considered that its economic and financial position and the position of the sector concerned so permitted.

(The actual rate of tariff reduction is shown in the following table:

Percentage of basic duty

Jan. 1, 1960	80 percent
Jan. 1, 1961	70 percent
March 1—Sept. 1, 1962	60 percent
Oct. 31—Dec. 31, 1962	50 percent
Dec. 31, 1963	40 percent
Jan. 1, 1965	30 percent
Dec. 31, 1965	20 percent
Jan. 1, 1967	0 percent

The first decision to accelerate tariff reductions was made at a meeting of the Ministerial Council in Geneva Feb. 14–16, 1961. At the Council's meeting in Lisbon May 9–11, 1963, it was decided that the tariff reduction should be complete by Dec. 31, 1966. Almost all remaining tariffs and quotas on trade in industrial goods between the seven EFTA countries were in fact abolished with effect from Dec. 31, 1966, with only a few exceptions under special arrangements.)

Art. 4. Goods would qualify for Area tariff treatment if (a) they had been wholly produced within the Area of the Association, or (b) they had been produced by certain processes within the Area of the Association (the "process rule"), or (c) not more than 50 percent of their value consisted of non-Area materials (the "percentage rule"). Provision was made for certain materials of which there were large imports from outside the Area (i.e. basic materials) to be treated as if they had originated from within the area.

The main provisions of the remainder of the Convention are summarized below:

Safeguards

Member-countries will be free to take action which they consider necessary for the protection of their essential security interests and, consistently with their other international obligations, their balance of payments. In certain circumstances a member-State may also take special safeguarding action where the application of the Convention leads to serious difficulties in a particular sector of industry.

Competition

The Convention contains provisions to ensure that the benefits which are expected from the removal of tariffs and quotas are not nullified through the use of other measures by Governments, public undertakings, or private industries. These include provisions about subsidies, restrictive business practices, and discriminatory restrictions against nationals of member-States wishing to establish businesses anywhere in the area.

Agriculture and Fish

Special arrangements have been made for agricultural goods and fish and other marine products. The objective is to facilitate reasonable reciprocity to those member-States whose economies depend to a great extent on agricultural or fish exports. Arrangements have also been concluded between several member-countries in respect of trade in agricultural goods.

The Council

The Convention establishes a Council charged with the general oversight of the application of the Convention and with the task of considering what further action should be taken to promote the objectives of the Association and to facilitate close association with other countries or groups of countries. The Council is empowered to establish relationships with other international organizations. Each member-State has one vote on the Council. Decisions and recommendations are to be made by unanimous vote where new obligations are involved. On a wide range of issues, and particularly in dealing with any complaints which may be made by member-States, decisions will be by majority vote.

Consultation and Complaints

The procedure for consultation and complaints is an important part of the Convention, and a member-country may refer to the Council any case in which it considers that a benefit conferred upon it by the Convention or an objective of the Association is being or may be frustrated. Member-States intend to pursue economic and financial policies in a manner which will promote the objectives of the Association, and to exchange views about them from time to time.

Extension

The council is empowered to make arrangements for the accession of other countries, and member-States may propose the extension of the Convention to cover non-European territories for which they are responsible.

After the Danish Government had proposed, in December 1967, that the Convention should be made applicable to the Faroe Islands, this territory was included in the EFTA area as from Jan. 1, 1968.

Annex on Portugal
Special arrangements concerning Portugal were contained in Annex G of the Convention. By these arrangements Portugal was permitted to apply a slower rate of import duty reduction than other EFTA members. The planned reduction of the percentage of the basic duty was to 50 percent by 1970. An accelerated rate of duty reduction was provided for in the case of exporting industries.

Finnish Association with EFTA
Under an agreement signed in Helsinki on March 27, 1961, Finland became associated with EFTA. The agreement, which entered into force on June 26, 1961, contained special provisions in favor of Finland in order to prevent conflict with the provisions of her existing trade treaty with the Soviet Union. [*18251A*]

Yugoslav Observers
It was announced on Dec. 11, 1967, that it had been agreed that Yugoslavia could send observers to EFTA technical meetings, including those on double taxation, patents, and probably customs.

Iceland's Accession
Iceland became a full member of EFTA, and also a party to the Finland-EFTA agreement, on March 1, 1970.

Iceland's protective import duties on EFTA industrial products were reduced immediately by 30 percent, with seven further annual reductions by 10 percent to follow from Jan. 1, 1974, so that all such tariffs would be abolished by Jan. 1, 1980. [*23872A*]

Special Relations Agreements
Following the withdrawal of Britain and Denmark from EFTA on Jan. 31, 1972, Special Relations Agreements entered into force between four of the seven remaining members or associates of EFTA—Austria, Portugal, Sweden, and Switzerland—on the one hand and the EEC on the other, thus inaugurating a program of tariff reductions and other measures which would lead to a free trade area embracing the 13 countries involved.

The agreements, concluded in Brussels on July 22, 1972, provided for the gradual achievement of free trade in industrial goods between the 6 original members of the EEC and Ireland on the one hand and each of the 6 EFTA countries which had not applied for full EEC membership on the other, while at the same time preserving the existing free trade among all countries which were members of EFTA at the time of signature of the agreements, including Britain, Norway, and Denmark. The agreements differed fundamentally from the terms reached for full membership with the other three EFTA countries and Ireland in that the 6 countries would have no power of decision in Community affairs, and they would not take part in any institutions except in a joint executive committee which would meet twice a year to manage the free trade arrangements.

The free trade area will be further extended when (1) the Finnish Government has signed the terms of a Special Relations Agreement initialed in July 1972 but not formally signed by the end of that year; (2) a similar agreement has been negotiated by Norway with the Communities, following the Norwegian decision not to become a full member (see page 60); and (3) the Icelandic Parliament has approved the agreement signed in July 1972 with the Communities. [*25645A*]

EUROPEAN CO-OPERATION IN OTHER SPHERES

European Conference of Ministers of Transport (ECMT)

Members: Austria, Belgium, Britain, Denmark, France, German Federal Republic, Greece, Ireland, Italy, Luxemburg, the Netherlands, Norway, Portugal, Spain, Sweden, Switzerland, Turkey, and Yugoslavia

The European Conference of Ministers of Transport (ECMT) was set up at a conference of Transport Ministers from a number of European countries, held in Brussels between Oct. 12 and 17, 1953. The aim of the organization is to achieve the best use and most economical development of the means of transport for inter-European communications.

Organs

The organs of the ECMT are:

(1) A Council of Ministers, composed of the Ministers of Transport of the member-countries, meeting at least once a year.

(2) A Committee of Deputies, composed of officials of the member-countries acting as the Ministers' deputies. The Committee, which meets six times a year, prepares —with the assistance of a number of specialized subsidiary bodies—the material to be discussed at meetings of the Council of Ministers.

(3) A Secretariat, which is responsible for the everyday administration of the Conference.

Although it is an autonomous institution, the ECMT works in close co-operation with other international organizations, in particular with the OECD, the Council of Europe, and the United Nations Economic Commission for Europe (ECE). [*13315D; 13935B*]

Eurocontrol

At a meeting in Rome on June 9–10, 1960, the Aviation Ministers of the Six approved a draft convention and protocol for a unified air-traffic control system for Western Europe (Eurocontrol). The convention was signed in Brussels on Dec. 13, 1960, by the Six and Britain. [*17486B; 17822D; 19462B*]

Eurofima

The first European company for the financing of purchases of railway rolling-stock was created at a meeting of the European Conference of Ministers of Transport Oct. 18–20, 1955, when the Convention formally establishing the company (known as Eurofima) was signed.

The function of the company, which was formally constituted for 50 years on Nov. 20, 1956, is to obtain rolling-stock for shareholding railway administrations on the most favorable possible terms. The present Eurofima shareholders are the national railway administrations in Austria, Belgium, Denmark, France, the German Federal Republic, Greece, Italy, Luxemburg, the Netherlands, Norway, Portugal, Spain, Swe-

den, Switzerland, Turkey, and Yugoslavia. [*14357A; 14531C*]

European Organization for Nuclear Research (CERN)

Members: Austria, Belgium, Britain, Denmark, France, German Federal Republic, Greece, Italy, the Netherlands, Norway, Sweden, Switzerland
Observers: Poland, Turkey, Yugoslavia

History

On May 8, 1952, a European Council for Nuclear Research was set up under the auspices of UNESCO, as a result of an agreement signed by Denmark, France, West Germany, Greece, Italy, the Netherlands, Sweden, Switzerland, and Yugoslavia on Feb. 15, 1952. Norway and Belgium later adhered to the agreement. [*12116A; 12391C*]

At a meeting on June 21, 1952, the Council decided to build a nuclear research institute which would house two of the world's largest particle accelerators—a proton-cyclotron and a synchro-cyclotron. The project would be a co-operative venture. On Oct. 6, 1962, the Council decided that the European Nuclear Research Laboratory should be sited at Geneva. [*12485B*]

The preparation of a convention transforming the European Council for Nuclear Research into a full international organization took place at meetings of the Council in January, March, and June 1953. The Convention of the European Organization for Nuclear Research (Conseil Européen pour la Recherche Nucléaire, or CERN) was signed in Paris on July 1, 1953, by representatives of Belgium, Britain, Denmark, France, West Germany, Greece, Italy, the Netherlands, Norway, Sweden, Switzerland, and Yugoslavia. It entered into force on Sept. 29, 1954.

The Convention

The functions of the Organization are defined in the basic program outlined in the Convention.

These are "the construction and operation of an international laboratory for research on high energy particles, including work in the field of cosmic rays" and "organizing and sponsoring international co-operation in nuclear research, including co-operation outside the laboratory." Specifically, mention is made of co-operative work in nuclear physics and cosmic rays, the promotion of contacts between and interchange of scientists, the dissemination of information, the provision of advanced training for research workers, and collaboration with national research institutes.

The work is carried out on a purely theoretical basis and solely for non-military purposes, and its results are published for general distribution.

Provision is made for the entry into the Organization of other States by the unanimous vote of the existing member-States.

The funds to finance the Organization are provided by the member-States on a relative scale based on their average net national incomes.   [13223A]

The Organs

The governing body of CERN is the Council, on which each member-State is represented by two delegates. The Council meets at least once a year to determine policy, approve plans, and adopt the budget. The Council is assisted by a 12-member Committee of the Council, a Scientific Policy Committee, and a Finance Committee.

The executive body is a Board of Directors, consisting of the Director-General (appointed by the Council) and the Directors of the seven divisions within the Organization.

Developments

The construction program undertaken by CERN was completed in 1961, the foundation-stone for the laboratory at Meyrin near Geneva having been laid on June 10, 1955. The installations include a 600 million electron volt synchro-cyclotron, which entered into operation on Aug. 17, 1957, and a 30,000 million electron volt proton-synchrotron, brought into operation in November 1959. These two machines form the basis of CERN's experimental research program, which is primarily concerned with high-energy particles. The experiments are conducted by mixed teams of scientists from the member-countries of the Organization.

The organization's Council decided on Feb. 19, 1971, that a 300,000 million electron volt particle accelerator (proton-synchrotron) for high-energy nuclear physics should be built on a site adjacent to CERN's existing installations at Meyrin.   [24508A]

Under an agreement of October 1965 the area of the CERN laboratory was extended across the Swiss border into France.

On June 16, 1960, it was announced that an agreement had been made with the U.S.S.R. for the exchange of scientists from CERN with scientists from the Nuclear Research Center at Dubna near Moscow. [17637B]

In 1963 Yugoslavia withdrew from membership of CERN, but remained associated with the Organization as an observer. Poland and Turkey also became observers in 1963. Spain withdrew from membership on Dec. 31, 1968.

European Launcher Development Organization (ELDO)

Members: Australia, Belgium, France, German Federal Republic, Italy, the Netherlands
Observers: Britain, Denmark, Switzerland

Formation

On a British and French initiative a conference was convened at Strasbourg, Jan. 30–Feb. 2, 1961, to discuss the "technical and financial possibilities" of developing a European earth-satellite launcher in preparation for "the possible use of satellites for various purposes." No decision on the setting up of such an organization was reached at this conference, but at a further conference, held in London Oct. 30–Nov. 3, 1961, plans for launching a European space vehicle were approved. The countries attending the London conference were the present ELDO members with the addition of Spain (which later decided not to participate).

The Convention establishing the European Launcher Development Organization (ELDO) was signed on April 12, 1962, and entered into force on March 2, 1964.   [17935A, 18712A]

Program

The original ELDO program (ELDO-A) covered the development and construction of a three-stage satellite-launching vehicle. The work involved in the program was distributed among the ELDO member-countries as follows: Britain, France, and the German Federal Republic would be responsible for the first, second, and third stages of the rocket respectively; Italy would be responsible for the first series of satellite test vehicles, Belgium for ground guidance stations, and the Netherlands for long-range telemetry; development firings would be made at Woomera, Australia. [18712A]

In April 1966 the ELDO Secretariat proposed a modification of the ELDO-A program to make possible the placing in orbit of a synchronous telecommunications satellite. This revised program—to be known as ELDO-PAS—would require two additional stages and an equatorial launching site. The necessity for a modified program arose from a dispute between Britain and the rest of the ELDO membership concerning the cost (which had more than doubled) and direction of the ELDO program.

After indicating the possibility of her withdrawal from ELDO at the beginning of June 1966, Britain decided to remain within the organization following agreement, at an ELDO Ministerial meeting, that the costs of the organization should be more equitably distributed.

At a Ministerial conference in Paris July 7–8, 1966, the following revised arrangements for ELDO were adopted:

(1) The ELDO-A program would be completed with the addition of ELDO-PAS.

(2) A new scale of contributions would be introduced from Jan. 1, 1967, to cover all remaining work. Under this Britain would pay 27 percent, West Germany also 27 percent, France 25 percent, Italy 12 percent, and Belgium and the Netherlands each 4½ percent; Australia would remain a member on the existing basis of supplying facilities at Woomera.

(3) An overall ceiling of commitments for participating States would be fixed at about $330,000,000.

(4) Kourou, in French Guiana, would be used as an operational equatorial launching site, but test firings would continue to be made from Woomera.

(5) The following steps would be taken to improve the management of ELDO and the technical and financial control of its programs: (*a*) contracts would be placed directly by the Secretariat on the basis, wherever possible, of tenders and fixed prices; (*b*) separate project management directorates would be established; (*c*) inspectors would be appointed; and (*d*) there would be annual reviews of projects.

(6) Problems of co-ordinating space policies in Europe would be examined. [*22113A*]

The British Government announced on April 16, 1968, that it would make no further contribution to ELDO after the completion of existing commitments in 1971.

The Government explained that further ELDO programs could not be justified because of their "prohibitive" costs and the fact that their potential applications were "both limited and speculative." ELDO launcher firings made at Woomera in 1967–70 were failures, and so was one made at Kourou on Nov. 5, 1971. [*22796A; 25706A*]

Organization

The governing body of ELDO is the Council, on which each member-country is represented by two delegates. The Council approves the program of research, development, and construction, and directs the distribution of the work among the member-countries. It is assisted by a Scientific and Technical Committee, and a Finance Committee.

The Secretariat is responsible for administration and finances, for external relations, and for the execution of the organization's program of work.

European Space Research Organization (ESRO)

Members: Belgium, Britain, Denmark, France, German Federal Republic, Italy, the Netherlands, Spain, Sweden, Switzerland
Observers: Austria, Norway

Formation

A European space-research conference, convened by CERN, the European Organization for Nuclear Research, was held at Meyrin near Geneva Nov. 28–Dec. 2, 1960. The countries represented were all the present members of ESRO with the exception of Spain and with the addition of Norway. The conference set up a Preparatory Commission to consider the structure, financing, and scientific program of a proposed European space-research organization. This Commission finally approved a draft Convention for ESRO in February 1962. Details of the Convention, which was signed on June 14, 1962, and entered into force on March 21, 1964, were not made public. [*17935A; 18712A*]

Program

The first program of work for ESRO covers an eight-year period. It includes the firing of considerable numbers of fully-instrumented vertical sounding-rockets; the launching, from the fourth year, of two fully-instrumented satellites in near-earth orbits; the launching, from the fifth year, of four highly eccentric orbit satellites; the launching, from the sixth year, of two fully-instrumented space probes or large satellites; and the eventual launching of several large astronomical satellites.

The first of 300 sounding-rockets, to be launched to aid research into solar radiation, magnetic fields, and cosmic rays, was fired from Sardinia in July 1964.

On Jan. 19, 1967, a four-year ESRO program of satellite launchings was announced. The first attempted launching, which took place on May 29, 1967, was a failure. However, the *2B* spacecraft was successfully launched into orbit on May 17, 1968. [*22113A; 22796A*]

Organization

The principal organ of ESRO is the Council, which consists of two representatives from each member-country. It meets at least twice a year to consider the administrative and financial affairs of the Organization, and to decide the scientific and technical policy. The Council is assisted by an Administrative and Financial Committee and a Scientific and Technical Committee.

The work of the Organization is directed by a Director-General assisted by an internationally-staffed Secretariat. Scientific, Technical, and Administrative Directorates act in an advisory capacity.

Installations

The following installations have been established under ESRO:

The Space Technology Center (ESTEC) at Noordwijk in the Netherlands, which is responsible for the technical research connected with the launching program.

The Space Research Laboratory (ESLAB) at Noordwijk, which co-ordinates the various projects of ESRO's program.

The Data Center (ESDAC) at Darmstadt in the German Federal Republic.

The Sounding-Rocket Launching Range (ESRANGE) at Kiruna in Arctic Sweden. Operational since 1966.

The Space Research Institute (ESRIN) at Frascati in Italy, which carries out theoretical research on the physical and chemical phenomena of space.

The Tracking and Telemetry Network (ESTRACK) to track and communicate with satellites. The four stations of the network are at Fairbanks (Alaska), Ny-Alesund in Spitsbergen, Port Stanley (Falkland Islands), and Redu in Belgium.

Co-operation with Countries Outside ESRO

In September 1965 ESRO made agreements with Norway on the building and operation of a telemetry station in Spitsbergen (see above). The first agreement, between ESRO and the Norwegian Government, covered the construction and conditions of operation of the station; the second, between ESRO and the Norwegian Technical and Scientific Research Council, covered the operation of the station. An important condition of the agreements was that the station should be used for purely scientific and peaceful ends. [21061B]

Co-operation with the United States has taken the form of a "Memorandum of Agreement" signed in July 1964 with the U.S. National Aeronautics and Space Administration (NASA). An agreement on the launching of an ESRO satellite by a U.S. Delta rocket was signed on March 8, 1967, in implementation of this Memorandum.

In November 1966 ESRO signed an agreement with the U.S. Government for the building of the space-tracking station at Fairbanks, Alaska. [22113A]

Finance

ESRO is financed by contributions from its member-countries in proportions as shown below:

	Percent		Percent
Belgium	4.42	Italy	11.17
Britain	25.00	The Netherlands	4.24
Denmark	2.21	Spain	2.66
France	19.14	Sweden	5.17
German Federal		Switzerland	3.43
Republic	22.56		

Merging of ELDO and ESRO

At a meeting in Brussels on July 22–24, 1970, of the European Space Conference—a continuing ministerial conference established on Dec. 13, 1966, and comprising representatives from the members of ELDO, ESRO, and the European Conference on Satellite Communications (CETS)—a decision was reached to merge ELDO and ESRO.

At a further meeting of the ESC in Brussels on Dec. 20, 1972, it was agreed to form a European Space Agency, to be established before the beginning of 1974 and to incorporate ELDO and ESRO. [24706A]

North Sea Continental Shelf

Treaties on the Delimitation of the North Sea Continental Shelf between the Federal Republic of Germany and Denmark, and between the Federal Republic and the Netherlands, were signed in Copenhagen and The Hague on Jan. 28, 1971, ratification documents being exchanged in Bonn and London on Nov. 7, 1972. The provisions of the treaties settled a dispute on which the International Court of Justice had delivered judgment on Feb. 20, 1969. [24718A]

Declarations and Conventions on Environment Problems

1. A *Declaration on the Management of the Natural Environment of Europe* was adopted on Feb. 12, 1970, by a European Conservation Conference convened in Strasbourg by the Council of Europe and attended by the Council's 17 members as well as by representatives of 10 other countries (Canada, Czechoslovakia, Finland, Israel, Liechtenstein, Portugal, Romania, Spain, the United States, and Yugoslavia).

The declaration laid down guidelines for the "rational use and management of the environment"; for the harmonization of legislation for safeguarding the environment; and for co-operation between public authorities, industry, and conservationists. [24107A]

2. A *Declaration on the Problem of Sea Pollution* was issued by the Consultative Assembly of the Council of Europe on Sept. 24, 1970, calling on member-Governments to "take forthwith drastic measures" to end pollution of the sea which threatened "directly the very life of the sea and . . . put in question the survival of humanity as a whole." [24343B]

3. A *Convention Against Marine Pollution,* designed to prevent sea pollution by the dumping of waste from ships and aircraft, was signed in Oslo on Feb. 15, 1972, by Belgium, Denmark, Finland, France, Western Germany, Iceland, the Netherlands, Norway, Portugal, Spain, Sweden, and the United Kingdom.

The area covered by the convention comprised the high seas and territorial waters of the northeast Atlantic and part of the Arctic area, its western boundary being the longitude of Greenland and its southern boundary the latitude of the Straits of Gibraltar. The convention provided for the establishment of an international supervisory commission. [25166B]

BILATERAL TREATIES AND AGREEMENTS IN WESTERN EUROPE

1. France and Western Germany
A treaty of co-operation between France and the German Federal Republic was signed on Jan. 22, 1963. The treaty, which provided for the co-ordination of the policies of the two countries in foreign affairs, defense, information, and cultural affairs, entered into force on July 2, 1963.

The principal provisions are summarized below.

There would be regular meetings of the Heads of State, Foreign and Defense Ministers, and Chiefs of Staff of the two countries. An inter-ministerial commission would be set up in each country to supervise questions of co-operation. Under the program of co-operation set forth in the treaty, the two Governments undertook to "consult each other before taking any decision on all major questions of foreign policy."

In the sphere of defense the treaty provided for the setting up of Franco-German operational research institutes, for the exchange of personnel between the two armed forces, and for the organization of joint activities in the field of armaments.

The cultural program outlined in the treaty included: the extension of reciprocal language-teaching; the adoption of arrangements for equivalent values of periods of education, examinations, degrees, and diplomas; and an increase in co-operation in scientific research.

Except for the clauses concerning defense, the treaty also applies to West Berlin. [19209A]

2. France and Spain
A five-year military co-operation agreement was signed in Madrid on June 22, 1970, and was automatically renewable for two years unless six months' notice was given by either side. It provided for close co-operation in defense and armaments, involving joint defense exercises, exchanges of personnel and units, and collaboration in respect of equipment, "including missiles, munitions, and spare parts." [24141A]

6

The Organization for Economic Co-operation and Development (OECD)

MEMBERS: Australia, Austria, Belgium, Britain, Canada, Denmark, Finland, France, German Federal Republic, Greece, Iceland, Ireland, Italy, Japan, Luxemburg, the Netherlands, Norway, Portugal, Spain, Sweden, Switzerland, Turkey, U.S.A.
SPECIAL STATUS: Yugoslavia (see page 87)

The OEEC

The basis of European economic co-operation after World War II was the so-called Marshall Plan, a program of American economic aid to Europe, first put forward by the U.S. Secretary of State, George C. Marshall, in a speech at Harvard on June 5, 1947. In this speech Marshall called on the European nations themselves to unite in planning their economic rehabilitation and in forming a joint program of reconstruction. [*8659A*]

On July 5, 1947, Britain and France invited 22 European nations to send delegations to a European Economic Conference, where a program of the resources and needs of Europe would be drawn up. This conference, when it opened on July 12, 1947, was attended by Britain, France, and 14 of the countries invited, viz. Austria, Belgium, Denmark, Greece, Iceland, Ireland, Italy, Luxemburg, the Netherlands, Norway, Portugal, Sweden, Switzerland, and Turkey. The conference approved the creation of a Committee of Economic Co-operation, on which all 16 nations would be represented, to draw up a report for the U.S. Government on European availabilities and requirements on the basis of information freely supplied by the participating countries. [*8711A*]

The report of the Committee of Economic Co-operation, which was signed in Paris on Sept. 22, 1947, contained an outline of the European Recovery Program, a four-year program of reconstruction which was to form the basis of the Marshall Plan (1948–51). The report also contained the suggestion that a permanent organization of the 16 nations participating in the European Recovery Program (ERP) should be set up. [*8955A*]

At a further conference of the 16 nations, held in Paris March 15–16, 1948, a working party was set up to draft a convention for European economic co-operation. Under this convention, signed on April 16, 1948,

by representatives of the 16 ERP countries and also by military representatives for the Anglo-American and French zones of Germany, the Organization for European Economic Co-operation (OEEC) was established. [*9201A; 9221A*]

The membership of the OEEC eventually reached 18 with the accession of the German Federal Republic in October 1949, and of Spain in July 1959. In addition the U.S.A. and Canada participated in the work of the OEEC as associate members; Yugoslavia took a full part in certain OEEC activities; and Finland sent observers to certain of the organization's committees. [*10270A; 10920A*]

The OECD

A Special Economic Committee, comprising representatives from Belgium, Britain, Canada, Denmark, France, the German Federal Republic, Greece, Italy, the Netherlands, Portugal, Sweden, Switzerland, and the U.S.A., and also from the Commission of the European Economic Community (EEC), met in Paris Jan. 12–13, 1960. At this meeting it was decided, *inter alia*, that a new improved organization for economic co-operation should be formed. As a preliminary measure, a four-man group—the "Group of Four on Economic Organization"—was appointed to study the matter and make recommendations.

The Group published its report on April 20, 1960. The report said that economic co-operation between Western Europe and North America since the end of the Second World War, especially through the OEEC, had achieved "extraordinary progress"; that this co-operation should be continued and extended; that the targets envisaged in the Marshall Plan had been reached but that new problems "no less pressing" had arisen; and that the richer nations had a responsibility toward the poorer countries. The report recommended that an Organization for Economic Co-operation and

Development, in which Canada and the U.S.A. would participate as full members, should be established with the aim of promoting "within the framework of free political institutions" policies designed: (1) to facilitate the attainment of the highest sustainable economic growth, while maintaining financial stability and high levels of employment, and thus to contribute to the development of the world economy and the promotion of world trade on a multilateral and non-discriminatory basis; and (2) to contribute to sound economic growth in areas in the process of economic development, both in member-countries and elsewhere, by appropriate means, including the encouragement of the flow of development capital to those areas."

Representatives of the 18 members of the OEEC, and of the U.S.A., Canada, and the Commission of the EEC met in Paris on May 24–25, 1960, and again on July 22–23, 1960, to discuss a draft convention for the proposed OECD. At the second meeting the broad outlines of the draft convention were agreed upon, and a preparatory committee was then charged with completing the final draft. This meeting also approved the setting up of a trade committee within the OECD, its functions being defined as the confrontation of general trade policies and practices; the examination of specific trade problems affecting members; and the examination of other short-term and long-term trade problems. [*17907A*]

The Convention

The final draft of the Convention of the Organization for Economic Co-operation and Development was signed on Dec. 14, 1960, by the 18 full members of the OEEC and by Canada and the U.S.A. It entered into force on Sept. 30, 1961.

The preamble and a summary of the principal articles of the Convention are given below:

PREAMBLE

Considering that economic strength and prosperity are essential for the attainment of the purposes of the United Nations, the preservation of individual liberty, and the increase of general well-being;

Believing that they can further these aims most effectively by strengthening the tradition of co-operation which has evolved among them;

Recognizing that the economic recovery and progress of Europe, to which their participation in the OEEC has made a major contribution, have opened new perspectives for strengthening that tradition and applying it to new tasks and broader objectives;

Convinced that broader co-operation will make a vital contribution to peaceful and harmonious relations among the peoples of the world;

Recognizing the increasing interdependence of their economies;

Determined by consultation and co-operation to use more effectively their capacities and potentialities so as to promote the highest sustainable growth of their economies and improve the economic and social well-being of their peoples;

Believing that the economically more advanced nations should co-operate in assisting to the best of their ability the countries in process of economic development;

Recognizing that the further expansion of world trade is one of the most important factors favoring the economic development of countries and the improvement of international economic relations; and

Determined to pursue these purposes in a manner consistent with their obligations in other international organizations or institutions in which they participate or under agreements to which they are a party;

The signatories of the Convention agree on the following provisions for the reconstitution of the Organization for European Economic Co-operation as the Organization for Economic Co-operation and Development:—

Art. 1. The aims of the OECD shall be to promote policies designed:

(*a*) to achieve the highest sustainable economic growth and employment and a rising standard of living in member-countries, while maintaining financial stability, and thus to contribute to the development of the world economy;

(*b*) to contribute to sound economic expansion in member as well as non-member countries in the process of economic development; and

(*c*) to contribute to the expansion of world trade on a multilateral, non-discriminatory basis, in accordance with international obligations.

Art. 2. In pursuit of these aims, the members agree that they will, both individually and jointly,

(*a*) promote the efficient use of their economic resources;

(*b*) in the scientific and technological field, promote the development of their resources, encourage research, and promote vocational training;

(*c*) pursue policies designed to achieve economic growth and internal and external financial stability and to avoid developments which might endanger their economies or those of other countries;

(*d*) pursue their efforts to reduce or abolish obstacles to the exchange of goods and services and current payments, and maintain and extend the liberalization of capital movements; and

(*e*) contribute to the economic development of both member and non-member countries in the process of economic development by appropriate means and in particular by the flow of capital to those countries, having regard to the importance to their economies of receiving technical assistance and of securing expanding export markets.

Art. 3. The members therefore agreed that they would

(*a*) keep each other informed and furnish the Organization with the information necessary for the accomplishment of its tasks;

(*b*) consult together on a continuing basis, carry out studies, and participate in agreed projects; and

(*c*) co-operate closely, and where appropriate take co-ordinated action.

Art. 5. In order to achieve its aims, the OECD might:

(*a*) take decisions which, except as otherwise provided, shall be binding on all the members;

(*b*) make recommendations to members; and

European Members of the OECD
Special Relationship with the OECD

(c) enter into agreements with members, non-member-States, and international organizations.

Art. 6. Unless the Organization otherwise agrees unanimously for special cases, decisions shall be taken and recommendations shall be made by mutual agreement of all the members.

Each member shall have one vote. If a member abstains from voting on a decision or recommendation, such abstention shall not invalidate the decision or recommendation, which shall be applicable to the other members but not to the abstaining member.

No decision shall be binding on any member until it has complied with the requirements of its own constitutional procedures. The other members may agree that such a decision shall apply provisionally to them.

Art. 7–9. A Council composed of all the members should be set up as the executive body of the Organization and might meet in sessions of Ministers or of Permanent Representatives. It would designate each year a Chairman to preside at its ministerial sessions, and two Vice-Chairmen, and might establish an Executive Committee and "such subsidiary bodies as required for the achievement of the aims of the Organization." A Chairman could be re-elected only for two consecutive terms.

Art. 10–11. A Secretary-General responsible to the Council would be appointed by it for a term of five years, and would be assisted by one or more Deputy or Assistant Secretaries-General appointed by the Council on his recommendation. He would serve as Chairman of the Council meeting at sessions of Permanent Representatives; would assist the Council in all appropriate ways; might submit proposals to the Council or to any other body of the Organization; and would appoint the staff required in accordance with organizational plans approved by the Council. Staff regulations would be subject to Council approval.

Having regard to the international character of the Organization, the Secretary-General, the Deputy or Assistant Secretaries-General, and the staff shall neither seek nor re-ceive instructions from any of the members or from any Government or authority external to the Organization.

Art. 12. Upon such terms and conditions as the Council may determine, the Organization may (a) address communications to non-member States or organizations; (b) establish and maintain relations with non-member States or organizations; and (c) invite non-member Governments or organizations to participate in activities of the Organization.

Art. 13 and Supplementary Protocol No. 1 provided that representation in the OECD of the European Communities established by the Treaty of Paris of April 18, 1951 and the Treaty of Rome of March 25, 1957, should be determined in accordance with the institutional provisions of those Treaties, and that the Commissions of the EEC and of the European Atomic Energy Community (Euratom), as well as the High Authority of the European Coal and Steel Community, should take part in the work of the OECD.

Art. 15. When this Convention comes into force, the reconstitution of the OEEC shall take effect, and its aims, organs, powers, and name shall thereupon be as provided herein. The legal personality possessed by the OEEC shall continue in the Organization, but decisions, recommendations, and resolutions of the OEEC shall require approval of the Council to be effective after the coming into effect of this Convention.

Art. 19 and Supplementary Protocol No. 2 set out the legal capacity of the Organization and the privileges, exemptions, and immunities of the Organization, its officials and representatives.

In addition to the two Supplementary Protocols (see above), a Protocol was signed dealing with the revision of the Convention for European Economic Co-operation of April 16, 1948.

Under this Protocol, the members of the OEEC, "desirous that the aims, organs, and powers of the OEEC be re-defined and that the Governments of Canada and the U.S.A. be members of that Organization as reconstituted," agreed (a) that the Convention should be revised and replaced by the Convention on the OECD; (b) that the Protocol should come into force together with the Convention on the OECD, and that the Convention for European Economic Co-operation should cease to have effect as regards any signatory of the Protocol when the Convention on the OECD came into force. [17907A]

Japan became a full member of the OECD on April 28, 1964; Finland on Jan. 28, 1969; and Australia on June 7, 1971, bringing the membership to 23.

Special Status

Yugoslavia has the status of a full member in the following fields of activity: comparison of economic policies; science and technology; agriculture and fisheries; technical assistance; and productivity. In all other fields she has observer status.

Institutions of the OECD

1. European Monetary Agreement
The European Monetary Agreement, signed Aug. 5, 1955, came into operation on Dec. 27, 1958. It super-

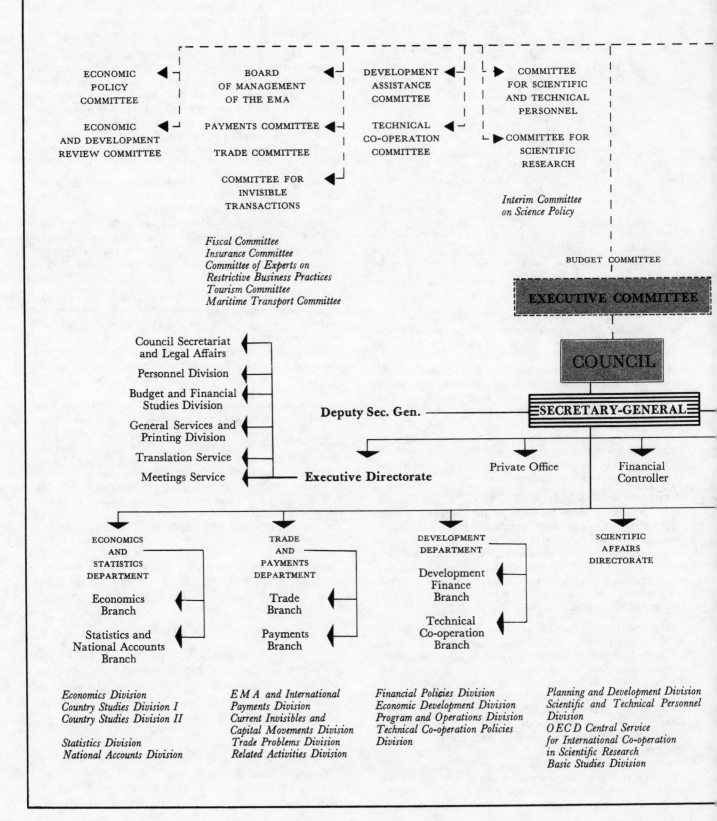

ECONOMIC POLICY COMMITTEE

ECONOMIC AND DEVELOPMENT REVIEW COMMITTEE

BOARD OF MANAGEMENT OF THE EMA

PAYMENTS COMMITTEE

TRADE COMMITTEE

COMMITTEE FOR INVISIBLE TRANSACTIONS

DEVELOPMENT ASSISTANCE COMMITTEE

TECHNICAL CO-OPERATION COMMITTEE

COMMITTEE FOR SCIENTIFIC AND TECHNICAL PERSONNEL

COMMITTEE FOR SCIENTIFIC RESEARCH

Interim Committee on Science Policy

Fiscal Committee
Insurance Committee
Committee of Experts on Restrictive Business Practices
Tourism Committee
Maritime Transport Committee

BUDGET COMMITTEE

EXECUTIVE COMMITTEE

COUNCIL

SECRETARY-GENERAL

Deputy Sec. Gen.

Council Secretariat and Legal Affairs

Personnel Division

Budget and Financial Studies Division

General Services and Printing Division

Translation Service

Meetings Service

Executive Directorate

Private Office

Financial Controller

ECONOMICS AND STATISTICS DEPARTMENT

Economics Branch

Statistics and National Accounts Branch

TRADE AND PAYMENTS DEPARTMENT

Trade Branch

Payments Branch

DEVELOPMENT DEPARTMENT

Development Finance Branch

Technical Co-operation Branch

SCIENTIFIC AFFAIRS DIRECTORATE

Economics Division
Country Studies Division I
Country Studies Division II

Statistics Division
National Accounts Division

E M A and International Payments Division
Current Invisibles and Capital Movements Division
Trade Problems Division
Related Activities Division

Financial Policies Division
Economic Development Division
Program and Operations Division
Technical Co-operation Policies Division

Planning and Development Division
Scientific and Technical Personnel Division
O E C D Central Service for International Co-operation in Scientific Research
Basic Studies Division

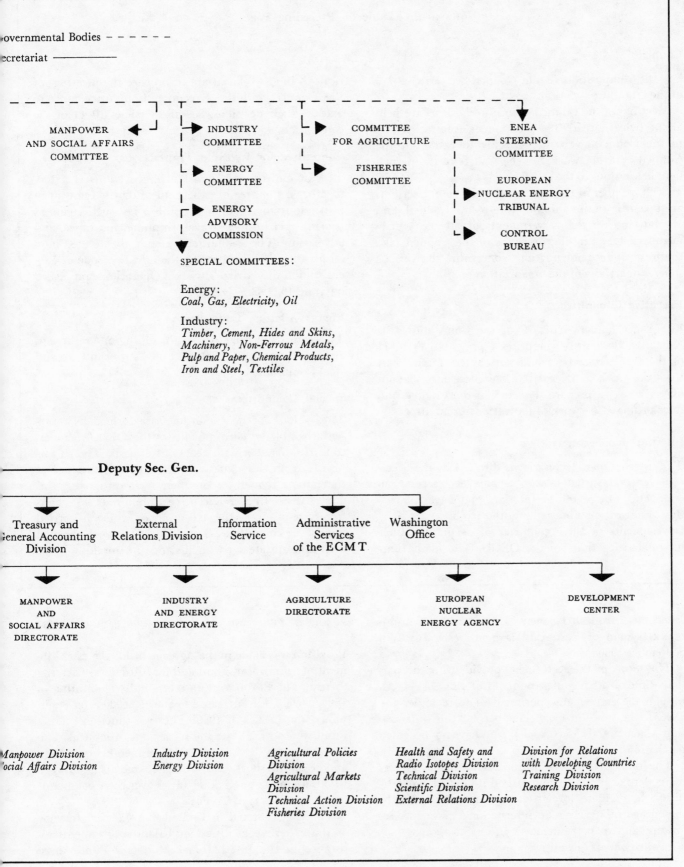

overnmental Bodies – – – – –

ecretariat ───────

MANPOWER
AND SOCIAL AFFAIRS
COMMITTEE

INDUSTRY
COMMITTEE

COMMITTEE
FOR AGRICULTURE

ENEA
STEERING
COMMITTEE

ENERGY
COMMITTEE

FISHERIES
COMMITTEE

EUROPEAN
NUCLEAR ENERGY
TRIBUNAL

ENERGY
ADVISORY
COMMISSION

CONTROL
BUREAU

SPECIAL COMMITTEES:

Energy:
Coal, Gas, Electricity, Oil

Industry:
*Timber, Cement, Hides and Skins,
Machinery, Non-Ferrous Metals,
Pulp and Paper, Chemical Products,
Iron and Steel, Textiles*

───────── **Deputy Sec. Gen.**

Treasury and
General Accounting
Division

External
Relations Division

Information
Service

Administrative
Services
of the ECM T

Washington
Office

MANPOWER
AND
SOCIAL AFFAIRS
DIRECTORATE

INDUSTRY
AND ENERGY
DIRECTORATE

AGRICULTURE
DIRECTORATE

EUROPEAN
NUCLEAR
ENERGY AGENCY

DEVELOPMENT
CENTER

*Manpower Division
Social Affairs Division*

*Industry Division
Energy Division*

*Agricultural Policies
Division
Agricultural Markets
Division
Technical Action Division
Fisheries Division*

*Health and Safety and
Radio Isotopes Division
Technical Division
Scientific Division
External Relations Division*

*Division for Relations
with Developing Countries
Training Division
Research Division*

Reproduced by permission of the Head of the External Relations Division of the OECD (25.9.67.)

Notes to the Table on Preceding Pages

Council

For the composition of the Council see Articles 7–9 of the OECD Convention.

Meetings of the Council at ministerial level are held about twice a year. The Permanent Representatives to the Council, who meet weekly to carry out the Council's current work, are the leaders of the permanent delegations to the OECD.

Each member of the Council has one vote. Decisions are taken by the unanimous vote of the Council, and are binding on the Governments of all the OECD members. Less binding decisions of the Council take the form of recommendations concerning the various spheres of activity of the organization.

Executive Committee

Established under Article 9 of the Convention, the Executive Committee comprises representatives of 11 of the OECD member-countries, elected annually by the Council. The Executive Committee meets about once a week to prepare the work of the Council and to co-ordinate the work of the various Committees.

International Secretariat

The international Secretariat is directed by the Secretary-General assisted by two Deputy Secretaries-General. The staff of the Secretariat, who have international status, are under the authority of neither the Governments of their countries of origin nor their national delegations to the OECD. The main func-tions of the Secretariat are to prepare the meetings of the Council and the Executive Committee, and to execute their decisions. See also Articles 10–11 of the convention.

Committee for Invisible Transactions

The Committee for Invisible Transactions is a ten-member committee of experts to study the removal of restrictions to trade in invisibles, i.e. such items as tourism and business travel, shipping, insurance, and advertising. The Committee is responsible to the Council for the administration of the OECD's Code of Liberalization of Current Invisible Operations, published on June 15, 1962. [*18929C*]

Energy Advisory Commission

This consists of nine experts, including one representative each from the U.S.A. and the European Coal and Steel Community.

Special Committees

The various special committees are formed by representatives of the Governments of the OECD member-countries together with economic experts. Their function is to provide data to the Executive Committee at the latter's request or on their own initiative. This data is used by the Executive Committee as a basis for its resolutions, the execution of which is carried out by the committees. The committees work through their appropriate departments and directorates.

---

seded the European Payments Union (EPU), a multi-lateral system of European payments established in September 1950.

The terms of the Agreement provided for the participation of all member-countries of the OEEC. Although the Agreement continued in force under the OECD, the non-European members of this organization (Canada, the U.S.A., and Japan) have not become parties to it.

The objectives of the European Monetary Agreement were to promote multilateral trade and convertibility; to regulate foreign exchange transactions; to discourage bilateralism in international payments relations; and to help members in any temporary balance-of-payments difficulties.

EUROPEAN FUND AND MULTILATERAL CLEARING SYSTEM

Provision was made in the Agreement for the establishment of a European Fund and a Multilateral Clearing System. The European Fund, originally amounting to $600,000,000, was increased to $607,500,000 after Spain joined the OEEC in 1959. The two functions of the Fund were to facilitate the settlement of monthly balances between the Central Banks of member-countries, and to grant short-term credits to member-countries who were in temporary difficulties over their balance of payments. [*14374A; 16605A*]

The OECD stated in December 1972 that, in view of the extensive facilities for balance-of-payments assistance in the International Monetary Fund, there was no longer any need for a special fund to provide credits to member-countries, and the European Fund was accordingly to be liquidated and the European Monetary Agreement terminated on Dec. 31, 1972. [25680A]

The main features of the EMA other than the European Fund—namely examination of monetary and financial questions and the exchange guarantee—are covered in new arrangements which entered into force on Jan. 1, 1973, and which include (1) an agreement between the Central Banks of 18 member-countries establishing an exchange guarantee on the working balances held by these banks in each other's national currencies; and (2) the creation within the OECD of a new Committee for Monetary and Foreign Exchange Matters, in which all 23 OECD countries are represented. [25680A]

2. Nuclear Energy Agency (formerly European Nuclear Energy Agency—ENEA)

The Statute of the European Nuclear Energy Agency (ENEA) was adopted by the OEEC on Dec. 20, 1957, and the Agency came officially into existence on Feb. 1, 1958. The ENEA was created as a specialized agency within the framework of the OEEC to co-ordinate nuclear research and development for peaceful purposes as carried out by member-countries. When the OEEC was superseded by the OECD in September 1961, the ENEA was taken over by the new organization.

Full membership of the Agency is confined to the European members of the OECD, with the exception of Japan which became a full member on May 17, 1972. Canada and the U.S.A. are associate members.

The ENEA changed its name to the Nuclear Energy Agency in May 1972.

The Agency is governed by a Steering Committee, a Secretariat headed by a Director-General and a Deputy Director-General, and a top-level Group on Co-operation in Research.

FUNCTIONS

Among the functions of the NEA are the promotion of joint undertakings and common services by the member-countries (see below); co-ordination of research and production programs in the field of nuclear energy; the establishment of committees of international experts in certain fields (see table, pages 88–9); the harmonization of national legislation concerning atomic energy, particularly for the safeguarding of health, the prevention of accidents, third-party liability, and atomic risk insurance; and the examination of the contribution to be made by nuclear energy to Europe's expanding energy demands. [16039A]

EUROCHEMIC

One of the principal NEA joint undertakings, EUROCHEMIC (European Company for Chemical Processing of Irradiated Fuels), is an international shareholding company which came into existence simultaneously with the Agency. The Company's plant for the treatment of irradiated fuels, located at Mol in Belgium, was finally completed in July 1966. The shareholders in EUROCHEMIC are the Austrian, Belgian, Danish, West German, Netherlands, Norwegian, Swiss, and Turkish Governments, and Atomic Energy Authorities in France, Italy, Portugal, Spain, and Sweden. [16039A]

On the initiative of Eurochemic a *Société de Fluoration de l'Uranium* (SFU) was formed on Oct. 21, 1969, by governmental organizations and private industry in eight European countries—Belgium, Denmark, France, Western Germany, Italy, the Netherlands, Norway, and Sweden. [23675B]

THE HALDEN REACTOR

The Experimental Boiling Heavy Water Reactor at Halden in southern Norway was built by the Norwegian *Institutt for Atomenergi*. It became a joint undertaking under the ENEA in June 1958, and a research and development program was initiated in July 1958. This program, completed early in 1964, was succeeded by a further program of specialized research and development work, scheduled for completion at the end of 1969; further extensions of the program, the latest having been announced in June 1972, provide for its continuation until Dec. 31, 1975.

Participants in the program are atomic energy institutions or authorities in Britain, Denmark, Finland, Italy, Japan, the Netherlands, Norway, and Sweden; the Swiss Government; and a West German industrial group working in agreement with the Federal Ministry of Scientific Research. The Austrian Atomic Energy Study Company and the U.S. Atomic Energy Commission participate as associate members. [16241A]

THE "DRAGON" PROJECT

The "Dragon" High Temperature Reactor Project at Winfrith Heath in Dorset (southwest England) was constructed under a 12-nation agreement, signed on March 23, 1959, by representatives of the British Atomic Energy Authority; Euratom (comprising Belgium, France, the German Federal Republic, Italy, Luxemburg, and the Netherlands); the atomic energy authorities of Denmark, Norway, and Sweden; and the Governments of Austria and Switzerland.

Under an agreement signed in December 1962, the original five-year program of the Project was extended until March 31, 1967. An offer by the British Government to pay 86.6 percent of the cost of the project was accepted by the ENEA in December 1967, making possible the continuation of the program throughout 1968.

The Project has since been extended several times, the latest extension announced in December 1972 enabling it to continue until March 31, 1976.

The reactor's maximum design output of 20 thermal megawatts was reached for the first time on April 24, 1966. [16654A; 16730D]

THE SEIBERSDORF PROJECT

A program of research on food irradiation is being carried out at the Seibersdorf Nuclear Research Center in Austria, under an agreement concluded in September 1964 between the NEA, the IAEA, and the Austrian Atomic Energy Study Company. The six-year program was initiated in January 1965.

COMMON SERVICES

The two principal common services of the NEA are the Neutron Data Compilation Center at the Saclay *Centre d'Etudes Nucléaires* in France; and the NEA Computer Program Library at the Euratom Joint Research Establishment at Ispra in Italy.

CONVENTIONS

A convention on security control was signed by the OEEC Council on Dec. 20, 1957.

The basic rules of this security control closely follow those defined in the statute of the International Atomic Energy Agency and the Euratom Treaty. They provide for an examination of all plants subject to control; a system of quantitative control for nuclear fuel; on-the-spot supervision by international inspectors; and, in cases of non-observance, the possibility of imposing penalties by a majority vote. Provision is made for an international tribunal to settle certain disputes to which the exercise of control may give rise. [16039A]

An important convention providing for uniform rules on third-party liability in the field of nuclear energy was signed in Paris on July 29, 1960, and came into force on April 1, 1968. [22634A]

The convention is designed to ensure that the effects of a nuclear incident do not stop at political or geographical boundaries, and that claimants may proceed with their claims against any reactor operator in any of the signatory countries. The liability of reactor operators for any damage caused by the escape of radioactive material from nuclear installations is absolute in the sense that there is liability without any need to prove fault or blame on the part of the reactor owner; liability will cover all incidents occurring both in connection with the installations and in the course of transport of radioactive substances.

A supplementary convention was signed in Brussels in January 1963, extending the maximum limit of compensation. [17588A]

3. Development Assistance Committee (DAC)

The Special Economic Committee which met in Paris Jan. 12–13, 1960 (see also page 85), adopted a resolution on the formation of a Development Assistance Group to co-ordinate aid to under-developed countries.

The founder-members of the Group were Belgium, Britain, Canada, France, the German Federal Republic, Italy, Japan, Portugal, the U.S.A., and the EEC Commission. The Netherlands joined later in 1960.

In a communiqué of Dec. 14, 1960, it was stated that, on the inception of the OECD, the Development Assistance Group would be constituted as an organ of the OECD to be known as the Development Assistance Committee (DAC). The present members of the DAC are Australia, Austria, Belgium, Britain, Canada, Denmark, the EEC Commission, France, the German Federal Republic, Italy, Japan, the Netherlands, Norway, Portugal, Sweden, Switzerland, and the U.S.A. [17907C; 18924A; 19433A; 20709A; 20954A; 21244D]

The main objectives of the DAC are to examine ways of increasing the volume of development assistance; to assess the indebtedness of the less-developed countries and the appropriate terms of assistance; and to co-ordinate assistance efforts, both capital and technical.

The DAC works primarily through the Annual Aid Review, a systematic and detailed examination of each member-country's program of aid, taking in the volume, financial terms, geographical distribution, purposes and techniques of the assistance. Meetings of the DAC are also held to discuss specific subjects connected with development aid.

4. OECD Development Center

Set up early in 1963, the Development Center is a scientifically independent body within the OECD. Its functions are to carry out research on important economic problems faced by developing countries; to give advanced training to senior officials from developing countries; and to provide for the exchange and supply of information on relevant matters. [19433A]

7

The North Atlantic Treaty Organization (NATO)

MEMBERS: Belgium, Britain, Canada, Denmark, France, the German Federal Republic, Greece, Iceland, Italy, Luxemburg, the Netherlands, Norway, Portugal, Turkey, U.S.A.

The North Atlantic Treaty was signed on April 4, 1949, to provide for the collective defense and security of the Western world through an international organization.

Origin

The necessity for the creation of a defense alliance of Western Powers became apparent soon after the end of World War II. The tension which had arisen between the Allied Nations of Western Europe and the Soviet bloc came to a head in 1948 with the Communist *coup d'état* in Czechoslovakia and the Soviet blockade of Berlin. [*9145A; 9337A*]

In addition, the authority of the United Nations, as guardian of world peace and security, had shown itself to be severely restricted by the use of the veto in the Security Council, which precluded the settlement of many important questions.

In the years immediately following the War the Soviet Union formed a close network of military alliances in Eastern Europe. In answer to this Belgium, Britain, France, Luxemburg, and the Netherlands created their own defense system in the Western Union, based on the Brussels Treaty of March 17, 1948 (see page 41). It was, however, apparent that, without the participation of the U.S.A., such an alliance would in no way counterbalance the defense system of Eastern Europe.

The Vandenberg Resolution

The principles upon which the U.S.A. would be willing to join a defensive alliance of Western nations were set out in a resolution introduced in the U.S. Senate Foreign Relations Committee by Senator Vandenberg, the Republican Party's foreign affairs specialist, and approved on May 19, 1948. The resolution committed the United States, in principle, to military assistance to regional alliances and other collective arrangements entered into within the framework of the United Nations. It was stressed, however, that the U.S.A. would not enter into any "automatic commitments"; that any action associating the U.S.A. with defense pacts such as the Western Union would require Congressional approval; and that any regional defense arrangements must provide for the "continuous and effective self-help" of the countries concerned before the question of U.S. participation could be considered. [*9306B*]

A report commending the policy outlined in the Vandenberg Resolution was formally adopted by the Senate Foreign Relations Committee on May 27, 1948, and approved by the full Senate on June 11.

The report declared that "certainty in advance concerning the intentions of the U.S.A. should constitute a vital factor in deterring aggression," and stressed that regional alliances or other "collective arrangements" should be promised the "association and help" of the U.S.A., subject to final approval by Congress, if they guaranteed among themselves "continuous and effective self-help and mutual aid." Senator Vandenberg, speaking on the necessity for a plain declaration by the U.S.A. that aggression would mean war, declared: "The experience of World War I and World War II suggests that the best deterrent to aggression is the certainty that immediate and effective counter-measures will be taken against those who violate the peace. The principle of individual and collective self-defense is fundamental to the independence and integrity of the members of the U.N. This is recognized in Art. 51. By reaffirming now its allegiance to this principle, the U.S.A. would take an important step in the direction of removing any dangerous uncertainties that might mislead potential aggressors. Such a re-affirmation is directed against no one and threatens no one. It is directly solely against aggression."

The report pointed out that peace-loving people everywhere were "concerned over the present inability

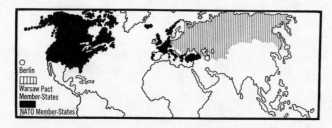

Berlin
Warsaw Pact Member-States
NATO Member-States

of the U.N. to assure international peace" and were troubled by the excessive use of the veto and the failure of arms control, and went on: "The present sense of insecurity in many parts of the world retards and hampers the efforts which the U.S.A. is making to promote international economic recovery. It is clear that the security aspects of world economic recovery cannot be ignored. The people of the world look to the U.S.A., as the strongest free nation, for leadership in making the United Nations an effective instrument for peace and security." [9360D]

The North Atlantic Treaty

On the basis of the Vandenberg Resolution negotiations were opened in July 1948 between the members of the Western Union on the one hand and the U.S.A. and Canada on the other. Further exploratory talks on the proposed North Atlantic Alliance were held in December 1948 and January 1949, but it was only after several weeks of discussions that, in March 1949, the final draft treaty was agreed upon by the U.S.A., Canada, Belgium, Britain, France, Luxemburg, the Netherlands, and Norway (which had taken part in the later stages of the negotiations). The treaty was signed on April 4, 1949, by the 8 nations listed above and by Denmark, Iceland, Italy, and Portugal, which had received invitations to join the pact.

Later adherents to the North Atlantic Treaty were Greece and Turkey (Feb. 18, 1952), and the German Federal Republic (May 5, 1955). [9399B; 9765A; 9869A; 9901A]

The Treaty

The text of the North Atlantic Treaty, which entered into force on Aug. 24, 1949, is given below:

PREAMBLE

The parties to this treaty reaffirm their faith in the purposes and principles of the U.N. Charter and their desire to live in peace with all peoples and all Governments.

They are determined to safeguard the freedom, common heritage, and civilization of their peoples, founded on the principles of democracy, individual liberty, and the rule of law.

They seek to promote stability and well-being in the North Atlantic area.

They are resolved to unite their efforts for collective defense for the preservation of peace and security.

They therefore agree to this North Atlantic treaty.

Art. 1. The parties undertake, as set forth in the U.N. Charter, to settle any international disputes in which they may be involved by peaceful means in such a manner that international peace and security and justice are not endangered, and to refrain in their international relations from the threat or use of force in any manner inconsistent with the purposes of the United Nations.

Art. 2. They will contribute toward the further development of peaceful and friendly international relations by strengthening their free institutions, by bringing about a better understanding of the principles upon which these institutions are founded, and by promoting conditions of stability and well-being. They will seek to eliminate conflict in their international economic policies and will encourage economic collaboration between any or all of them.

Art. 3. In order more effectively to achieve the objectives of this treaty, the parties, separately and jointly, by means of continuous and effective self-help and mutual aid, will maintain and develop their individual and collective capacity to resist armed attack.

Art. 4. They will consult together whenever, in the opinion of any of them, the territorial integrity, political independence, or security of any of them is threatened.

Art. 5. They agree that an armed attack against one or more of them in Europe or North America shall be considered an attack against them all, and consequently agree that, if such an armed attack occurs, each of them, in exercise of the right of individual or collective self-defense recognized by Art. 51 of the U.N. Charter, will assist the party or parties so attacked by taking forthwith, individually and in concert with the other parties, such action as it deems necessary, including the use of armed force, to restore and maintain the security of the North Atlantic area. Any such armed attack, and all measures taken as a result thereof, shall immediately be reported to the Security Council. Such measures shall be terminated when the Security Council has taken the measures necessary to restore and maintain international peace and security.

Art. 6. For the purpose of Art. 5 an armed attack on one or more of the parties is deemed to include an armed attack on the territory of any of them in Europe or North America, on the Algerian Departments of France, on the Occupation forces of any party in Europe, on the islands under the jurisdiction of any party in the North Atlantic area north of the Tropic of Cancer, or on the vessels or aircraft in this area of any of the parties. [9869A]

To provide for the accession to NATO of Greece and Turkey, Article 6 was reworded in a protocol to the treaty (signed on Oct. 22, 1951) as follows:

For the purpose of Art. 5 an armed attack on one or more of the parties is deemed to include an armed attack—(i) on the territory of any of the parties in Europe or North America, on the Algerian Departments of France, on the territory of Turkey, or on the islands under the jurisdiction of any of the parties in the North Atlantic area north of the Tropic of Cancer; (ii) on the forces, vessels, or aircraft of any of the parties, when in or over these territories or any other area in Europe in which Occupation forces of any of the parties were stationed on the date when the treaty entered into force, or the Mediterranean Sea, or the North Atlantic area north of the Tropic of Cancer. [*11764A*]

In January 1963 the clauses of this Article referring to the Algerian Departments of France were recognized by the North Atlantic Council as having become inapplicable since July 3, 1962 (the date of Algerian independence). [*Page 19394*]

Art. 7. The treaty does not affect, and shall not be interpreted as affecting, in any way the rights and obligations under the Charter of the parties which are members of the United Nations, or the primary responsibility of the Security Council for the maintenance of international peace and security.

Art. 8. Each party declares that none of the international engagements now in force between it and any other of the parties or any third State is in conflict with the provisions of the treaty, and undertakes not to enter into any international engagement in conflict with the treaty.

Art. 9. The parties hereby establish a Council, on which each of them shall be represented, to consider matters concerning the implementation of the treaty. The Council shall be so organized as to be able to meet promptly at any time. It shall set up such subsidiary bodies as may be necessary; in particular, it shall establish immediately a Defense Committee, which shall recommend measures for the implementation of Arts. 3 and 5.

Art. 10. The parties may, by unanimous agreement, invite any other European State in a position to further the principles of the treaty, and to contribute to the security of the North Atlantic area, to accede to the treaty. Any State so invited may become a party to the treaty by depositing its instrument of accession with the U.S. Government.

Art. 11. The treaty shall be ratified and its provisions carried out by the parties in accordance with their respective constitutional processes. Instruments of ratification shall be deposited as soon as possible with the U.S. Government. The treaty shall enter into force between the States which have ratified it as soon as the ratifications of the majority of the signatories, including those of Belgium, Canada, France, Luxemburg, the Netherlands, the United Kingdom, and the United States, have been deposited, and shall come into effect with respect to other States on the date of deposit of their ratifications.

Art. 12. After the treaty has been in force for 10 years, or at any time thereafter, the parties shall if any of them so requests, consult together for the purpose of reviewing the treaty, having regard for the factors then affecting peace and security in the North Atlantic area, including the development of universal as well as regional arrangements under the U.N. Charter for the maintenance of international peace and security.

Art. 13. After the treaty has been in force for 20 years, any party may cease to be a party 1 year after notice of denunciation has been given to the U.S. Government.

Art. 14. The treaty, of which the English and French texts are equally authentic, shall be deposited in the archives of the U.S. Government. Copies will be transmitted to the Governments of the other signatories. [*9869A*]

A Protocol to the North Atlantic Treaty on the Accession of the Federal Republic of Germany formed one of the Paris Agreements of Oct. 23, 1954 (see also Western European Union, page 41). The document was signed by the 14 North Atlantic Treaty countries. A Resolution of Association, welcoming and recapitulating a Declaration made by the Federal Republic of Germany and a Joint Declaration issued by the United States, British, and French Governments at the London Nine-Power Conference of Sept. 28–Oct. 3, 1954 (see also Western European Union, page 41), was signed at the same time. The German Declaration ran as follows:

The German Federal Republic has agreed to conduct its policy in accordance with the principles of the United Nations Charter.

Upon her accession to the North Atlantic Treaty and the Brussels Treaty, the German Federal Republic declares that she will refrain from any action inconsistent with the strictly defensive character of the two treaties. In particular, the German Federal Republic undertakes never to have recourse to force to achieve the reunification of Germany or the modification of the present boundaries of the German Federal Republic, and to resolve by peaceful means any disputes which may arise between the Federal Republic and other States. [*Page 13812; 13869A*]

In the tripartite Joint Declaration the three Governments, after stating their resolution to devote their efforts to the strengthening of peace in accordance with the U.N. Charter, declare that:

(1) They consider the Government of the Federal Republic as the only German Government freely and legitimately constituted, and therefore entitled to speak for Germany as the representative of the German people in international affairs.

(2) In their relations with the Federal Republic they will follow the principles set out in Article 2 of the U.N. Charter.

(3) A peace settlement for the whole of Germany, freely negotiated between Germany and her former enemies, which should lay the foundation of a lasting peace, remains an essential aim of their policy. The final determination of the boundaries of Germany must await such a settlement.

(4) The achievement through peaceful means of a fully free and unified Germany remains a fundamental goal of their policy.

(5) The security and welfare of Berlin and the maintenance of the position of the three Powers there are regarded by the three Powers as essential elements of the peace of the free world in the present international situation. Accordingly they will maintain armed forces within the territory of Berlin as long as their responsibilities require it. They therefore reaffirm that they will treat any attack against Berlin from any quarter as an attack upon their forces and themselves.

(6) They will regard as a threat to their own peace and safety any recourse to force which, in violation of the principles of the U.N. Charter, threatens the integrity and unity of the Atlantic Alliance or its defensive purposes. In the event of any such action the three Governments will consider the offending Government as having forfeited its rights to any guarantee and any military assistance provided for in the North Atlantic Treaty and its protocols. They will act in accordance with Article 4 of the North Atlantic Treaty with a view to taking other measures which may be appropriate. [*Page 13812*]

North Atlantic Council

The supreme authority of the Atlantic Alliance is the North Atlantic Council, a political assembly composed of representatives of the Governments of the 15 member-countries. The council meets at the level of Ministers or of Permanent Representatives.

Ministerial meetings, which are generally held twice a year, are attended by Ministers for Foreign Affairs, Defense, or Economic Affairs from each of the member-countries. The agenda of each meeting determines which Ministers should attend. Member-countries are occasionally represented by their Heads of State.

The Council functions continuously at the level of Permanent Representatives who are of ambassadorial rank and who lead national delegations accredited to NATO. The Permanent Representatives meet at least once a week.

The Chairman of the Council, at both Ministerial and Permanent Representatives' level, is the Secretary General of NATO. The presidency, held by the Foreign Minister of each member-country in turn, rotates annually.

Council Committees

Much of the work of the North Atlantic Council is carried out through permanent and temporary committees, which give advice and make recommendations on technical matters.

Development of Nato

I.   1949–1955

The first phase of NATO's existence, roughly covering the period from its inception to the mid-1950s, saw the evolution of the organization's complex military and civilian structure.

The first meeting of the NATO Council, set up under Article 9 of the North Atlantic Treaty, was held on Sept. 17, 1949. The Council, which consisted of the Foreign Ministers of the member-countries, decided to set up a Defense Committee. This Committee, to be composed of the Ministers of Defense of the NATO countries, was to have the initial function of drawing up unified defense plans for the North Atlantic area.

Other bodies formed at this meeting were a Military Committee, composed of high military representatives of each member-country, to advise on military matters; a Standing Group, comprising one representative each of Britain, France and the U.S.A., to provide military information and guidance; and five Regional Planning Groups to prepare plans for the defense of each region (Northern Europe, Western Europe, Southern Europe, the Western Hemisphere and the North Atlantic). [*10236A*]

At its second session, held on Nov. 18, 1949, the Council created a Defense Financial and Economic Committee, and a Defense Production Board. The function of the latter was to promote the co-ordinated production, standardization, and further technical development of armaments. [*10713A*]

Two important organizational decisions were made at the fourth session of the Council (the second at Ministerial level), held May 15–18, 1950. It was decided to form a Permanent Council of Deputies to the Foreign Ministers, and to create a North Atlantic Planning Board for Ocean Shipping. [*10713A*]

In December 1950, after a meeting of the Foreign and Defense Ministers of the 12 NATO countries, it was announced that arrangements had been completed for an integrated defense force under centralized control and command, to which all the participating Governments would contribute contingents. The Supreme Headquarters Allied Powers in Europe (SHAPE) was set up in Paris in 1951.

In May 1951 a reorganization of the North Atlantic Council was announced. The Defense Committee and Defense Financial and Economic Committee (see above) ceased to exist as separate organs, but were incorporated in the North Atlantic Council, which thus became the sole Ministerial body of NATO. Henceforth the Ministerial Council might be formed by Foreign, Defense or Finance Ministers according to the agenda of the meeting. The functions of the Council of Deputies were defined as being to co-ordinate and guide all other permanent organs of NATO, and to exchange views on political matters within the scope of the Treaty. A new body set up at this time was the Financial and Economic Board to make recommendations on financial and economic matters. [*11513A*]

At a meeting of the North Atlantic Council in September 1951 it was agreed, *inter alia,* to support the entry into NATO of Greece and Turkey. A Temporary Committee of the Council (TCC) was set up to study the problems of reconciling the requirements for the fulfilment of a militarily acceptable defense plan with the realistic politico-economic capabilities of the member-countries. The final report of the TCC was adopted by the Council at its session in February

1952, after which the Committee was wound up. On the basis of the report the Council agreed on a "definite program of measures to increase defensive strength in following years." Organizational changes agreed upon were the creation of the post of Secretary-General to head a unified international Secretariat, and the formation of a North Atlantic Council in permanent session through the appointment of permanent representatives. The Council would assume the functions hitherto performed by the Council of Deputies, the Defense Production Board, and the Financial and Economic Board. [*11755A; 12049A*]

Early 1952 also saw the formation of the other two main NATO military commands: the Atlantic Ocean Command, headed by the Supreme Allied Commander Atlantic (SACLANT); and the Channel Command, headed by the Allied Commander-in-Chief Channel (CINCHAN).

In the same year the North Atlantic Council agreed upon close association with the proposed European Defense Community (EDC) of Belgium, France, the German Federal Republic, Italy, Luxemburg, and the Netherlands. After the French rejection of the EDC treaty in August 1954, however, the integration of the German Federal Republic into a defense system of the West had to be reconsidered. The results of these considerations, carried out at the 9-power London conference of September 1954, were embodied in the Paris Agreements which included the protocol on the entry of Western Germany into NATO (see page 7). [*11037A; 11693A; 13797A; 13869A*]

The first inter-parliamentary conference of NATO member-countries was held in Paris in July 1955. It was recalled, at the meeting, that one of the purposes of NATO was to contribute to the economic, social, and cultural developments of the peoples of the Atlantic community which, it was stated, "would be facilitated by closer relations between the members of the representative Assemblies of the different countries." Annual meetings of NATO Parliamentarians have since taken place. [*14365A*]

2. 1956–1965

In the decade from 1955 to 1965 the actual structure of NATO underwent relatively little alteration, the main developments within the organization being an increase in its political role, and the improvement and adaptation of its defensive system.

Political Development

At a North Atlantic Council meeting in May 1956 it was decided, *inter alia,* to set up a committee of three Ministers (known as the "three wise men") to examine "ways and means to improve and extend NATO co-operation in non-military fields and develop greater unity within the Atlantic community." The report of this committee, which was adopted by the Council on Dec. 13, 1956, recommended full and timely consultation between NATO member-Governments on issues of common concern. The following points were given as a guideline to such consultation:

(1) Members should inform the Council of any development which significantly affected the Alliance. They should do this not merely as a formality but as a preliminary to effective political consultation.

(2) Both individual member-Governments and the Secretary-General should have the right to raise for discussion in the Council any subject which was of common NATO interest, and not of a purely domestic character.

(3) A member-Government should not, without adequate advance consultation, adopt firm policies or make major political announcements on matters which significantly affected the alliance or any of its members, unless circumstances made such prior consultation obviously and demonstrably impossible.

(4) In developing their national policies, members should take into consideration the interests and views of other Governments—particularly those most directly concerned—as expressed in NATO consultation, even where no community of view or consensus of opinion had been reached in the Council.

(5) Where consensus had been reached, it should be reflected in the formation of national policies. When for national reasons the consensus was not followed, the Government concerned should offer an explanation to the Council. It was even more important that, where an agreed and formal recommendation had emerged from the Council's discussions, Governments should give it full weight in any national actions or policies related to the subject of that recommendation.

(6) To strengthen the process of consultation it was recommended that at each spring meeting the Foreign Ministers should make an appraisal of the political progress of the Alliance and consider the lines along which it should advance.

(7) To prepare for this discussion, the Secretary-General should submit an annual report analyzing the major political problems of the Alliance; reviewing the extent to which member-Governments had consulted and co-operated in such problems; and indicating the problems and the possible developments which might require consultation, so that difficulties might be resolved and positive and constructive initiatives taken.

(8) To assist the permanent representatives (of member-countries) and the Secretary-General in discharging their responsibilities for political consultation, a committee of political advisers from each delegation should be constituted under the Council, aided when necessary by specialists.

Settlement of Members' Disputes. It was further recommended that NATO members should submit any dispute between them which had not proved capable of direct settlement to "good offices" procedures under NATO before resorting to any other international agency. Exceptions to this procedure would be legal questions which could be dealt with more appropriately by a judicial tribunal, or economic questions which could more appropriately be dealt with in the specialized economic organizations.

All member-countries, as well as the Secretary-General,

COMMITTEES

Permanent Committees include:

Committee of Political Advisers

Armaments Committee

Economic Committee

Defense Review Committee

Science Committee

Infrastructure Committee
(connected with fundamental and applied research)

Senior Civil Emergency Planning Committee

Committee for European Airspace
Co-ordination

Committee for Pipelines

Committee for Information and Cultural Affairs

Civil and Military Budget Committees

Defense Planning Committee (established 1963)

Nuclear Defense Affairs Committee (established 1966), composed of Defense Ministers of all NATO countries except France, Iceland, and Luxemburg, and a Nuclear Planning Group (also established 1966) of seven or eight members with periodical changes in composition

Committee on the Challenges of Modern Society.

There are also *Temporary Committees* and *Working Groups*.

North Atlantic Council

The supreme authority of the Atlantic Alliance is the North Atlantic Council, a political assembly composed of representatives of the Governments of the 15 member-countries. The council meets at the level of Ministers or of Permanent Representatives.

Ministerial meetings, which are generally held twice a year, are attended by Ministers for Foreign Affairs, Defense, or Economic Affairs from each of the member-countries. The agenda of each meeting determines which Ministers should attend. Member-countries are occasionally represented by their Heads of State.

The Council functions continuously at the level of Permanent Representatives who are of ambassadorial rank and who lead national delegations accredited to NATO. The Permanent Representatives meet at least once a week.

The Chairman of the Council, at both Ministerial and Permanent Representatives' level, is the Secretary-General of NATO. The presidency, held by the Foreign Minister of each member-country in turn, rotates annually.

Council Committees

Much of the work of the North Atlantic Council is carried out through permanent and temporary committees, which give advice and make recommendations on technical matters.

Civilian Agencies responsible to the Council:

Central Europe Pipeline System (CEPS)

NATO Air Defense Ground Environment System Organization (NADGE)

NATO Maintenance and Supply Organization (NAMSO)

NATO Integrated Communications System Organization (NICSO)

Further Agencies are:

NATO Hawk Production and Logistics Organization (NHPLO)

NATO Multi-Role Combat Aircraft Development and Production Management Organization (NAMMO)

INTERNATIONAL SECRETARIAT

Secretary-General and Chairman of the North Atlantic Council
assisted by a Deputy Secretary-General

Administration

Private Office

Legal Adviser

Office of the Executive Secretary acting as Secretary to the Council and ensuring co-ordination of the Committees' activities.

Office of Security, responsible for the overall co-ordination of security within NATO and for providing advice and guidance on NATO security matters.

Office of Council Operations and Communications with two Directorates:

1. The Council Operations Directorate concerned with operations of the NATO Headquarters in the areas of crisis management, planning and conduct of high-level exercises, and the operation of the NATO Situation Center;

2. The Communications and Electronics Directorate charged with the responsibility for the co-ordination of the overall policy aspects of NATO's civil and military communications.

The office also includes a section responsible for the co-ordination of European Air Space.

Office of Administration, whose director is responsible for the general administration of the International Staff; the preparation and presentation of the annual budget; as head of the Personnel Services, for co-ordinating personnel management and policy guidance for NATO's civilian staff; for the Conference Linguistic Service and the security and maintenance of the Headquarters; and for the supervision of the Statistics Service.

Financial Controller, an independent office—the Financial Controller being appointed by the Council.

COUNCIL

MILITARY ORGANS (see pages 100–101)

Divisions

each under an Assistant Secretary-General

I. Political Division
with three separate Directorates:

1. Political Affairs Directorate
   with responsibility for

   (a) preparation of political discussions of the Council and of the Committee of Political Advisers;
   (b) preparation of notes and reports on political subjects for the Secretary-General and the Council;
   (c) political liaison with member-countries' delegations;
   (d) liaison with other international organizations.

2. Economic Directorate
   with similar functions for all economic questions having political or defense implications of concern to NATO; it also maintains contact with international economic organizations.

3. Information Directorate
   with responsibility for

   (a) informing public opinion on the aims and achievements of NATO;
   (b) assisting member-Governments to widen public understanding of NATO activities through periodicals, films, radio and television programs, publications, and exhibitions;
   (c) arranging group visits to NATO headquarters and participating in the organization of special courses and seminars on NATO matters for young people.

The Division also has a Press Service, whose head is responsible for daily press reviews and press cutting services to the Secretariat.

II. Division of Defense Planning and Policy
with three separate Directorates:

1. Force Planning;
2. Nuclear Planning;
3. Civil Emergency Planning.

The Division has responsibility for

(a) Preparation of the discussions of the Council, Defense Planning Committee, Nuclear Defense Affairs Committee, and Nuclear Planning Group;
(b) Preparation of the work of the Defense Review Committee, Senior Civil Emergency Planning Committee, and Nuclear Planning Group Staff;
(c) Development of draft proposals for political directives to the NATO Military Authorities or for guidance to national authorities;
(d) Study of the non-military aspects of relevant problems arising from the application of such political directives or guidance as approved by the Council or Defense Planning Committee;

(e) Study of the overall financial and economic aspects of defense by country, within the framework of the plans proposed by the NATO Military Authorities, and the national defense budgets; analysis and costing by Services of the countries' defense programs;
(f) Provision of advice for the Secretary-General;
(g) Liaison with the delegations of member countries and with the International Military Staff;
(h) Liaison with other international organizations as necessary.

III. Division of Defense Support
with three separate Directorates
with responsibility for

(a) The promotion of the most efficient use of the resources of the Alliance for the equipment and support of its forces. This task especially involves:
   —The encouragement of co-operation between nations in research, development, and production and standardization of weapons and equipment and their supply and maintenance within the framework of the defense plans of the Alliance.
   —The organization of exchanges of information which may lead to such equipment.
   —The study of logistic problems including the operation of the NATO Pipeline System, the NATO Maintenance and Supply Organization, etc.
(b) To assure technical and financial supervision of the NATO Infrastructure program.
(c) Participation in the process of Defense Reviews on matters within the responsibility and competence of the Division.

IV. Scientific Affairs Division
with the following responsibilities:

(a) to advise the Secretary-General on scientific matters of interest to NATO;
(b) to ensure liaison in the scientific field with the military and civil authorities of NATO, with agencies in the member countries responsible for implementation of science policies and with international organizations having scientific affiliations;
(c) to direct the activities of the working groups created by the Science Committee, and in general to implement the decisions of the Science Committee and its working groups;
(d) to chair the Committee on the Challenges of Modern Society (CCMS), provide secretarial services for that committee, and liaison between the International Staff and the pilot projects.

MILITARY COMMITTEE
consisting of the Chiefs of Staff of member-countries except France (and Iceland, represented by a civilian).
Exercises authority over

—Allied Communications Security Agency (ACSA)

—Allied Long Lines Agency (ALLA)

—Allied Naval Communications Agencies

—Allied Radio Frequency Agency (ARFA)

—Advisory Group for Aerospace Research and Development (AGARD)

—Military Agency for Standardization (MAS)

—NATO Defense College

—SACLANT Anti-Submarine Warfare Research Center

—SHAPE Technical Center

and other specialized agencies

Allied Command Europe (ACE)
covering Europe from the North Cape to the Mediterranean and from the Atlantic to the eastern border of Turkey— except Britain and Portugal

Supreme Allied Commander Europe
(SACEUR): Headquarters
(SHAPE): Mons (Belgium)

—Northern Europe Command
   (AFNORTH): Kolsaas (Norway)

—Central Europe Command
   (AFCENT): Brunssum (Netherlands)

—Southern Europe Command
   (AFSOUTH): Naples (Italy)

   Southern Europe Naval Command
      (NAVSOUTH): Naples

   Maritime Air Forces Mediterranean
   (MARAIRMED)

—U.K. Air Defense Region Command:
   Stanmore (U.K.)

—Allied Command Europe Mobile Force
   Seckenheim (Germany)

Military Committee

The highest military authority of NATO is the Military Committee, the presidency of which rotates annually among the member-countries according to the English alphabetical order. The Chairman is elected by the Military Committee for a period of two to three years.

The Military Committee meets at the level of Chiefs of Staff at least twice a year. Between these meetings the Com-mittee functions in permanent session at the level of Permanent Military Representatives appointed by their Chiefs of Staff. The Committee is assisted by an integrated International Military Staff.

Contact between the Military Committee and the North Atlantic Council takes place through a Military Committee Representative, who attends meetings of the Council to communicate to it the advice and recommendations of the Military Committee.

OF NATO

COMMANDS

Allied Command Atlantic (ACLANT)
covering the Atlantic Ocean from the North Pole to the Tropic of Cancer and from the coastal waters of North America to those of Europe and Africa, including Portugal but excluding the Channel and the British Isles

Supreme Allied Commander Atlantic (SACLANT). Headquarters: Norfolk, Va. (U.S.A.)

Allied Command Channel (ACCHAN)
covering the English Channel and the southern North Sea*

advised by **Channel Committee**
consisting of the Naval Chiefs of Staff of Belgium, Britain, and the Netherlands

HEADQUARTERS: Northwood (U.K.)

Canada–United States Regional Planning Group
covering the Canada–United States region. Meets alternately in Washington and Ottawa

- - - - - (*Command held by C.-in-C. Eastern Atlantic)

Western Atlantic Command: Norfolk, Va.	**Eastern Atlantic Command:** Northwood (U.K.)	**Striking Fleet Atlantic Command**	**Submarine Allied Command Atlantic:** Norfolk, Va.	**Iberian Atlantic Command (IBERLANT)** Lisbon	**Standing Naval Force Atlantic (STANAVFORLANT)** Afloat

- Submarine Force Western Atlantic Area Command

- Ocean Sub-Area Command

- Canadian Atlantic Sub-Area Command

- Bermuda Command

- Azores Command

- Greenland Command

- Eastern Atlantic Area

- Commander Maritime Air Eastern Atlantic Area

- Commander Northern Sub-Area

- Commander Maritime Air Northern Sub-Area

- Commander Central Sub-Area

- Commander Maritime Air Central Sub-Area

- Commander Submarine Force Eastern Atlantic Area

- Island Commanders of Iceland and the Faroes

- Commander Carrier Striking Force

- Commanders Carrier Striking Groups I and II

- Island Command of Madeira

had the right and the duty to bring to the Council's attention matters which in their opinion might threaten the solidarity or effectiveness of the Alliance. The Secretary-General should be empowered to offer his good offices informally to the parties to a dispute and, with their consent, "to initiate or facilitate procedures of inquiry, mediation, conciliation, or arbitration." For this purpose, he should be able to use the assistance of not more than three permanent representatives chosen by him in each instance.

While approving the report, the United States informed the North Atlantic Council that it could not subject its policies or actions throughout the world to prior consultation within NATO. [15285A]

A NATO Political Committee was formed in January 1957, meeting once a week to discuss questions of political interest to the members of the Atlantic Alliance.

At the Ministerial meeting of the North Atlantic Council held in December 1959 in Paris, proposals were adopted for long-term planning, to cover the following ten years, on the objectives of the Alliance in the political, military, scientific, and economic fields and in regard to arms control. [17199A]

An "Atlantic Convention," attended by 98 delegates (private citizens appointed by their Governments) of all NATO member-countries, was held in Paris between Jan. 8 and Jan. 20, 1962, to make recommendations for the further political development of the Atlantic Community. The Convention finally adopted the "Declaration of Paris," calling for "the creation of a true Atlantic Community within the next decade." The Declaration included recommendations for the creation of new political, judicial, and cultural organs, for the harmonization of political, military, and economic policy on matters affecting the Atlantic Community as a whole, and for closer economic co-operation with developing countries. The Declaration was endorsed by the Parliamentarians' Conference in November 1962, but its proposals have not yet been adopted by the North Atlantic Council. [18758A]

Military and Defense Developments

From Dec. 16 to 19, 1957, the Heads of Government of the NATO countries met in conference in Paris. Their most important decision was to establish stocks of nuclear warheads in the Treaty area, and to place intermediate-range ballistic missiles (IRBMs) at the disposal of the Supreme Allied Commander Europe (SACEUR). They also decided to set up a Science Committee composed of qualified representatives of each NATO country, and to appoint a scientist of outstanding qualifications as Science Adviser to the Secretary-General of NATO.

In December 1957 the United States stated its willingness to participate in a NATO atomic stockpile,

and also to make available to other NATO members intermediate-range ballistic missiles for deployment according to the plans of SACEUR. Each country concerned would have to make a separate agreement with the U.S. with respect to material, training of personnel, and other necessary arrangements. [15965A] Agreements on co-operation in the field of atomic weapons were signed by the U.S.A. with Britain, Canada, France, the German Federal Republic, Greece, the Netherlands, and Turkey in May 1959. A similar agreement was signed with Italy in December 1960.

On March 2, 1960, it was announced by SACEUR that a multi-national Allied task force, to be equipped with both conventional and atomic weapons, would be established. The constituent units would be brought together occasionally for joint training, but would generally remain with their national formations. The multi-national task force came officially into existence in June 1961, when it comprised five reinforced infantry battalions.

Meanwhile, a new Anti-Submarine Warfare Research Center at La Spezia, Italy, had been formally inaugurated in May 1959. This was completely reorganized to receive full NATO support as an international military organization in January 1963. The building of a NATO Missile Training Range in Crete was approved in April 1960. [17845A]

Nuclear Force for NATO

At a Ministerial Council meeting held in Athens in May 1962, the United States made two important announcements on defense matters: (1) that it would not remove or diminish its nuclear stockpiles in Europe without prior consultation; and (2) that five *Polaris* Submarines would be immediately committed to NATO (these had already been promised in December 1960). At this meeting the Council decided to set up a special committee of all member-countries "to receive and exchange information about NATO's nuclear defenses." [18758A]

In December 1962 President Kennedy of the United States and the British Prime Minister, Harold Macmillan, met at Nassau, where they signed an agreement on U.S. provision of *Polaris* missiles to Britain. In a joint statement issued at the time the two Heads of State put forward a suggestion for a NATO multilateral nuclear force, which would initially consist of some part of the force already in existence. "This would include allocations from U.S. strategic forces, from U.K. Bomber Command, and from tactical nuclear forces now held in Europe. Such forces would be assigned as part of a NATO nuclear force and targeted in accordance with NATO plans." [19173A]

At the Ministerial Council meeting in Ottawa in

May 1963 it was decided to set up such a multi-national nuclear force by reorganizing the nuclear forces already assigned to SACEUR. The principle steps approved by the Council were: (1) the assignment of the British V-bomber force and three U.S. *Polaris* submarines to SACEUR; (2) the appointment by SACEUR of a Deputy responsible to him for nuclear affairs; (3) arrangements for broader participation by NATO officers in nuclear activities in Allied Command, Europe, and in co-ordination of operational planning; and (4) fuller information to national authorities. The Ministerial Council also directed the Council in Permanent Session to undertake studies toward a satisfactory balance between nuclear and conventional forces. [*19525A*]

At the Kennedy-Macmillan meeting at Nassau in December 1962 (cf. above) the U.S. President put forward a plan for the formation of a mixed-manned seaborne nuclear force to be assigned to NATO and to which non-nuclear Powers could contribute. Discussions on the technical details of such a force were opened in October 1963 and continued throughout 1964. In addition, the United States made available a destroyer for an experiment in mixed manning which began in May 1964. No agreement on the mixed-manned nuclear force (MLF) has, however, been concluded, as the New British Labour Government opposed the idea of a mixed-manned nuclear surface fleet. Britain proposed, as an alternative, an Atlantic Nuclear Force (ANF) comprising the British V-bomber force; a British fleet of *Polaris* submarines; at least an equal number of U.S. *Polaris* submarines; and some kind of mixed-manned or jointly-owned element in which the non-nuclear Powers could participate. [*20525A; 20703A*]

New Committees
It was announced on Aug. 25, 1964, that a NATO Defense Research Directors' Committee had been set up with the aim of attempting to "establish a more direct relevance between science and the military needs" of the Organization. It would supplement the work of the NATO Science Committee (established in 1957, see above), which devoted most of its activities to civilian science.

At a NATO Defense Ministers' meeting in Paris on May 31–June 1, 1965, the U.S. Defense Secretary Robert McNamara proposed the creation of a "select Committee" of a few member-countries to study ways of extending nuclear planning and consultation within the Alliance. This proposal led, in November 1965, to the creation of a ten-member "special committee" of Defense Ministers, i.e. the Defense Ministers of all NATO countries except France, Luxemburg, Norway,

Portugal, and Iceland (which has none). The Committee set up three working Groups to deal with Communications, Data Exchange, and Nuclear Planning. [*20255A; 21601A*]

3. 1966–1967
The year 1966–67 saw the withdrawal of France from the military side of NATO, and the subsequent removal of all NATO installations from French soil.

French Withdrawal from NATO
French opposition to the integrated military Organization was already of several years' standing, the French President, General de Gaulle, having repeatedly affirmed since 1959 that, although she was in favor of the Atlantic Alliance, France could no longer support an integrated defense system which deprived her of sovereignty over her own military forces.

In March 1959 the French Mediterranean Fleet was withdrawn from the integrated command, and French naval units were withdrawn from the Atlantic and Channel Commands from Jan. 1, 1964. In April 1964 the French Government gave formal notification of the withdrawal of all French naval officers serving in NATO naval command posts or on NATO naval staffs. [*16961A; 19525A; 20062C*]

In February and March 1966 the French Government made it clear that France intended to withdraw completely from the integrated Organization, while remaining a member of the Atlantic Alliance. She was, however, ready to conclude arrangements for liaison between French and NATO forces, and also to retain French forces in the German Federal Republic under new terms. [*21601A*]

On March 29, 1966, the French Government, in an *aide-mémoire* to the other NATO members, set a timetable for France's withdrawal. The withdrawal of French forces in West Germany from NATO command, and of French personnel from Allied commands and staffs, was timed for July 1, 1966; the removal of SHAPE, AFCENT, and the NATO Defense College from French territory was to be carried out by April 1, 1967; and the withdrawal of most U.S. and Canadian military installations was also to be completed by April 1, 1967. This timetable was, in fact, adhered to. [*Page 21609*]

On Sept. 7, 1966, France stated her intention of stopping her financial contributions to the military budget from Jan. 1, 1967, but expressed a wish to continue participation in the NATO Air Defense Ground Environment System, or NADGE, an automatic air defense system due for completion in 1971; in SHAPE's technical research center at The Hague; in the anti-submarine warfare center at La Spezia; and in the management organization of the *Hawk* missile (produced by a consortium of five European NATO countries). At the end of September France withdrew from the NATO Military Committee. [22123A; Page 22177]

Removal of NATO Institutions from French Territory

(1) *SHAPE.* The new headquarters of SHAPE, near Mons in southern Belgium, were officially opened by the Supreme Allied Commander Europe on March 31, 1967.

(2) *AFCENT.* The headquarters of Allied Forces Central Europe were removed from Fontainebleau to Brunssum, a site in the Netherlands province of Limburg, at the beginning of April 1967.

(3) *NATO Defense College.* Formerly located at the Ecôle Militaire in Paris, the NATO Defense College opened its first session in the Palazzo Fondiaria, on the outskirts of Rome, on Jan. 18, 1967.

(4) *NATO Council.* In October 1966 it was decided to move the headquarters of the Council from Paris to Brussels.

Reorganization of Military Structure

The Standing Group, which was formed in 1949 was abolished on July 1, 1966, as a result of France's withdrawal from NATO's military organization (see above). It was replaced by a temporary international staff.

The removal of the Military Committee from Washington to Brussels was authorized in November 1966.

The Allied Land Forces Central Europe (LANDCENT) and Allied Air Forces Central Europe (AIRCENT) lost their individual identity to be merged with AFCENT from Nov. 15, 1966. [22123A]

Changes in the naval organization which were made in 1966–67 were as follows:

(1) In January 1966 the Commander-in-Chief Eastern Atlantic assumed the additional NATO post of Commander-in-Chief Channel.

(2) On Feb. 22, 1967, a new Command, the Iberian Command Atlantic (IBERLANT), was inaugurated. IBERLANT, based in Lisbon, is attached to Allied Command Atlantic.

(3) Another new Command, Naval Command South (NAVSOUTH), was inaugurated on June 5, 1967. This Command, responsible to the Commander-in-Chief Allied Forces Southern Europe, replaced the Commander-in-Chief Allied Forces Mediterranean. [22176A]

4. 1968–1971

In 1968–1971 the NATO Council's decisions were designed to counteract growing Soviet power both on the continent of Europe and in the Mediterranean, and any proposals for a reduction of armed forces were treated with reserve.

The NATO Nuclear Planning Group declared on April 19, 1968, that the deployment of an anti-ballistic missile system in Europe was not justified at that time, although developments in that field should be kept under constant review. [22808A]

On June 25, 1968, the Council issued a Declaration on Mutual and Balanced Force Reductions, in which its Ministers affirmed that "the overall military capability of NATO should not be reduced except as part of a pattern of mutual force reductions balanced in scope and timing." At the same time they agreed that "it was desirable that a process leading to mutual force reductions should be initiated."

The Ministers also decided that, in view of the recent expansion of Soviet activity in the Mediterranean, measures should be taken to enhance the effectiveness and co-ordination of allied surveillance in that area. [22808A]

The Brussels Council meeting of Nov. 15–16, 1968, was strongly influenced by the Soviet invasion of Czechoslovakia on Aug. 20–21, 1968.

The Ministers' communiqué stated *inter alia:* "World opinion has been profoundly shocked by this armed intervention carried out against the wishes of the Government and people of Czechoslovakia. . . . The contention of the Soviet leadership that there exists a right of intervention in the affairs of other States deemed to be within a so-called 'Socialist Commonwealth' runs counter to the basic principles of the U.N. Charter [and] is dangerous to European security. . . . Applied to Germany [these] policies . . . would be contrary to the Four-Power agreements relating to Germany as a whole." In this context the Ministers reaffirmed "the determination of the Alliance to persevere in its efforts to contribute to a peaceful solution of the German question based on the free decision of the German people and on the interests of European security," and they reiterated their Governments' non-recognition of the German Democratic Republic.

In response to the Soviet action, the Ministers declared:

"The quality, effectiveness, and deployment of NATO's forces will be improved in terms of both manpower and equipment in order to provide a better capability for defense as far forward as possible. The quality of reserve forces will also be improved and their ability to mobilize rapidly will be increased.

"Renewed attention will be directed to the provision of reinforcements for the flanks and the strengthening of local forces there.

"The conventional capability of NATO's tactical air forces will be increased. Certain additional national units will be committed to the major NATO Commanders. Specific measures have been approved within these categories of action for improving the conventional capability of NATO's forces."

They added: "Prospects for mutual balanced force reductions have suffered a severe setback."

At a meeting of the Defense Planning Committee on Nov. 14, 1968, increased military contributions by member-Governments were announced by Defense Ministers of most member-countries. [23070A]

The Canadian Government, on the other hand, decided in April 1969 to reduce the size of Canadian forces in Europe. [23403A]

The Defense Planning Committee approved on Dec. 3, 1969, provisional political guidelines for the initial defensive use of tactical nuclear weapons, as drawn up by the Nuclear Planning Group in November. The Group had also completed a review of procedures for consultation on the possible use of nuclear weapons in defense of NATO. [23750A]

On May 27, 1970, the Council issued a further Declaration on Mutual and Balanced Force Reductions, calling for exploratory talks by interested States and stating *inter alia* that any reduction agreed upon should include "stationed and indigenous forces and their weapons systems in the area concerned," with "adequate verification and controls." [24032A]

A European Defense Improvement Program was announced in Brussels on Dec. 1, 1970, after a meeting of Defense Ministers of the European NATO member-countries except France, Iceland, and Portugal. Based on the assumption that U.S. forces in Europe would be maintained "at substantially current levels," the program comprised a "special European scheme" involving a contribution of about $420,000,000 toward the acceleration and extension of (*a*) the NATO Integrated Communications System (NICS) and (*b*) aircraft survival measures to improve the ability of NATO Air Forces to survive enemy strikes on their bases.

At its meeting on Dec. 3–4, 1970, the Council discussed in detail a comprehensive study "AD-70" setting out the problems for Allied Defense in the 1970s, with NATO's approach to security continuing to be "based on the twin concepts of defense and *détente*," and with the "special military and political role of U.S. forces in Europe as an irreplaceable contribution to the common defense." [24348A]

The Defense Planning Committee, in a communiqué issued on May 28, 1971, stated *inter alia* that, in view of "the continuing increase in real terms in the allocation of resources to military and military-related programs by the Soviet Union and other Warsaw Pact countries," and "in order to continue providing modern and sufficient nuclear and conventional forces and to improve the situation in the important areas high-lighted in the AD-70 Study, some overall increase in defense outlay was needed." The Committee had therefore given the NATO Military Authorities the necessary guidance for the planning period 1973–78.

Command Changes
A Standing Naval Force Atlantic (STANAVFOR-LANT), consisting of destroyers and frigates, under the overall command of SACLANT and responsible, when in European waters, to CINCHAN and C.-in-C. Eastern Atlantic, was established at Portland (U.K.) on Jan. 13, 1968.

A new command called Maritime Air Forces Mediterranean (MARAIRMED), subordinated to Allied Naval Forces Southern Europe (NAVSOUTH), was inaugurated in Naples on Nov. 21, 1968. [23070A]

The Council's Defense Planning Committee decided on May 28, 1969, that NATO's Military Authorities should establish a naval on-call force for the Mediterranean, the concept of which had been approved by the Council on Jan. 16, 1969. [23403A]

It was announced at NATO headquarters in Brussels on Aug. 20, 1971, that in accordance with the wishes of the Government of Malta and also with long-term planning aims agreed upon in 1965, the headquarters of Allied Naval Forces, Southern Europe, should be moved from Malta to Naples. [25008B]

NATO Air Defense System
A programing and training center forming part of a computerized underground control point for NATO's air defense system, was opened at Glons (Belgium) on April 9, 1968, for eventual incorporation in NADGE.

NATO Communications Satellite
The first NATO communications satellite, *NATO-1*, was launched from Cape Kennedy (U.S.A.) on March 20, 1970; it was to link NATO headquarters in Brussels, national capitals, and NATO land and sea commands. [24032A]

Committee on Challenges of Modern Society
The Council decided on Nov. 6, 1969, upon a proposal made by President Nixon on April 10, to establish a Committee on the Challenges of Modern Society to consider problems of the human environment, and at its first meeting on Dec. 8–10, 1969, the new Committee recommended pilot studies to be carried out on road safety, disaster relief, air and water pollution, and problems of individual and group motivations in a modern industrial society, as well as of the transmission of scientific knowledge to the decision-making sectors of government. [23750A]

Defense Expenditure
In a table published by NATO on Dec. 8, 1971, the Alliance's defense expenditure (in million U.S. dollars) for the years 1969–71 was given as follows:

	1969 Actual	1970 Actual	1971 Forecast
Total Europe	23,251	24,553	26,723
Total North America	83,199	79,733	79,697
Total NATO	106,450	104,286	106,420

[*25018*]

5. 1972 Decision to Prepare for European Security Conference

At the Council's meeting on May 30–31, 1972, Ministers welcomed the signing by the United States and the Soviet Union of the Treaty on the Limitation of Anti-Ballistic Missile Systems and the interim agreement on certain measures with respect to the limitation of strategic offensive arms (see page 137). Ministers also noted with satisfaction that the treaties between the Federal Republic of Germany on the one hand and the Soviet Union and Poland on the other (see page 133) would shortly enter into force. Ministers similarly welcomed recent agreements on Berlin. "In the light of these favorable developments," Ministers agreed to enter into multilateral conversations for the preparation of a Conference on Security and Co-operation in Europe. [*25361A*]

Economic Problems Related to NATO

Under Article 2 of the North Atlantic Treaty the signatories undertake to "seek to eliminate conflict in their international economic policies and . . . encourage economic collaboration between any or all of them." Economic problems fall within the sphere of NATO in so far as they affect defense planning.

The Temporary Committee of the Council (TCC) set up in September 1951 (see page 96) laid down the two principles on which must rest the expansion of individual and collective capacity to resist armed aggression: the equitable distribution of the financial burden of rearmament among member-countries; and the necessity for a sound economic and social basis if a country is to be able to sustain defense expenditures.

The TCC set up the procedure of the Annual Review, under which the defense plans of each NATO country are examined in detail, together with the resources which are to be allocated to them. This shows whether or not the defense efforts of all the NATO members are comparable, taking into account the economic state of each country. The findings of the Annual Review are not binding on Governments, although they have considerable moral force.

The Committee of Three on NATO co-operation in non-military fields (see page 97), set up in May 1956, concluded that "it would serve no useful purpose for NATO to duplicate the functions of other international organizations concerned with various forms of economic co-operation." It did, however, recommend the establishment of a committee of economic advisers, which came into being in February 1957. [*15285A*]

The NATO Heads of Government, meeting in December 1957 (see page 102), decided that the Council "shall from time to time, and in the spirit of Article 2 of the Treaty, review economic trends and assess economic progress, and may make suggestions for improvements either through existing organizations or by the efforts of individual countries, or in special cases by new initiatives."

In May 1962 the Ministerial Council agreed that NATO members in a position to do so should establish means of providing economic aid to Greece and Turkey, the least developed of the NATO countries. The matter was raised in July 1962, at a meeting of the Council of the Organization for Economic Co-operation and Development (OECD), of which all NATO countries are also members, and two working-parties on the long-term development problems of Greece and Turkey were set up. [*18758A; 18880A*]

Survey of Agreements Basic to the NATO Structure

1. NORTH ATLANTIC TREATY AND SUBSEQUENT ACCESSIONS

(*a*) North Atlantic Treaty between Belgium, Britain, Canada, Denmark, France, Iceland, Italy, Luxemburg, the Netherlands, Norway, Portugal, and U.S.A., signed on April 4, 1949 (for text see page 94).

(*b*) Protocol to the North Atlantic Treaty on the accession of Greece and Turkey, signed on Oct. 22, 1951.

(*c*) Protocol to the North Atlantic Treaty on the accession of the Federal Republic of Germany, signed on Oct. 23, 1954.

(*d*) Resolution of the North Atlantic Council on Implementation of Section IV of the Final Act of the London Conference, signed Oct. 23, 1954. This document, one of the Paris Agreements, provided for the placing of the armed forces of the NATO countries stationed on the Continent of Europe under the authority of the Supreme Allied Commander Europe (SACEUR); the location and integration of the forces; closer co-ordination of logistics; the right of inspection of forces in Europe by SACEUR; and the indefinite duration of the North Atlantic Treaty.

(*e*) Resolution of Association with the Tripartite Declaration of Oct. 3, 1954, signed on Oct. 23, 1954 (see page 41).

2. AGREEMENTS ON THE STATUS OF THE NORTH ATLANTIC TREATY ORGANIZATION

(a) Agreements on the Status of the North Atlantic Treaty Organization, National Representatives, and the International Staff, signed Sept. 20, 1951.

(b) Agreements between the U.S.A. and the North Atlantic Treaty Organization, pursuant to Article 19 of the Agreement on the Status of the North Atlantic Treaty Organization, signed: (i) Sept. 29, 1951; (ii) July 23, 1958.

3. AGREEMENTS ON THE STATUS OF FORCES

(a) Agreement between member-States of the North Atlantic Treaty on the Status of Their Forces, signed June 19, 1951.

(b) Agreement between the U.S.A. and Canada relating to the application of the NATO Status of Forces Agreement to the U.S. forces in Canada, signed April 28 and 30, 1952, in effect since Sept. 27, 1953.

(c) Agreements concluded between the U.S.A. and Turkey relating to implementation of the NATO Status of Forces Agreement, signed: (i) June 23, 1954; (ii) July 21, 1955.

(d) Agreement on the status of NATO forces stationed in Germany, signed Aug. 3, 1959 (in effect for Germany since July 1, 1963).

4. AGREEMENTS ON THE STATUS OF INTERNATIONAL MILITARY HEADQUARTERS

(a) Agreement concerning the employment by the International Military Headquarters of U.S. nationals, signed Feb. 25, 1953.

(b) Agreement concluded by the United States regarding the Headquarters of the Supreme Allied Commander Atlantic, signed Oct. 22, 1954 (operative since April 10, 1954).

(c) Agreement between the Government of the Turkish Republic and the Supreme Allied Commander Europe, signed Feb. 22, 1956.

(d) Agreement between the Government of the Italian Republic and SACEUR regarding special conditions of establishment and operation on Italian territory of International Military Headquarters which are or might be located there, signed July 26, 1961.

(e) Agreement between the Government of the Kingdom of the Netherlands and SACEUR regarding special conditions of establishment and operation on Dutch territory of International Military Headquarters, signed May 25, 1964.

5. AGREEMENTS SIGNED IN THE FRAMEWORK OF NATO

(a) Agreement between the 15 member-countries for co-operation regarding atomic information, signed June 18, 1964 (approved by the North Atlantic Council on April 13, 1955).

(b) Agreement concluded by the 15 member-countries for the mutual safeguarding of secrecy of inventions relating to defense, for which applications for patents have been made, signed Sept. 21, 1960.

Military Assistance Agreements Concluded by the U.S.A. with NATO Partners

On Oct. 6, 1949, the U.S. President signed the Mutual Defense Assistance Act of 1949 providing for military aid from the U.S.A. to the signatory Governments of the North Atlantic Treaty. An amended form of this Act, known as the Mutual Security Act, was passed in 1951.

Bilateral agreements between the U.S.A. and NATO member-countries, within the framework of the Mutual Security Act of 1951, can be broadly classified into the following categories: mutual defense agreements including military aid; agreements relating to the assurances required under the Mutual Security Act; facilities assistance agreements; offshore procurements agreements; agreements for the return of military equipment; agreements allowing members of the Land, Naval and Air Force Missions to act as a military Advisory Group, and agreements relating to military missions; mutual security military sales agreements; and weapons production agreements.

The most important of such agreements still in force are given in tabular form on pages 110–11, the date by which they are indicated being the date of entry into force. An asterisk indicates an emendation of the immediately preceding agreement.

Agreements Relating to Defense Concluded Between NATO Countries

The NATO defense system has been strengthened by the many agreements concluded between the various NATO countries. The agreements which fall within the framework of the U.S. Mutual Aid Program are given separately above. Other U.S. defense agreements with NATO countries may be found in the chapter "Defense Treaties of the U.S.A.," page 170.

Agreements among the other NATO countries are given below.

A. AGREEMENTS CONCLUDED BY BRITAIN WITH:

1. *Belgium and Canada:* on transit and stationing in Belgium of Canadian forces, signed March 30, 1953; in force July 29, 1953.

2. *Belgium:* on the establishment of a military base at Campine, Nov. 12, 1952.

3. *Denmark:* relating to the Agreement on the Status of Forces of June 19, 1951 (see previous page), Oct. 8, 1956.

4. *German Federal Republic:* (a) on British bases in the German Federal Republic, Sept. 9, 1952; Oct. 15 and 18, 1954; May 22 and 31, 1957.
(b) Relating to the Convention on Foreign Forces stationed in Germany (see below), April 11, 1957.
(c) On the maintenance cost of British forces stationed in Germany, June 7, 1957; Oct. 3, 1958; April 28, 1967.

5. *The Netherlands:* relating to the Convention on Foreign Forces stationed in Germany (see below), June 11 and 13, 1956. Extension signed on June 7, 1957.

6. *Turkey:* on the sale of destroyers to Turkey, Aug. 16, 1957. Amended on Jan. 12, 1959.

B. AGREEMENTS CONCLUDED BY CANADA WITH:

1. *Belgium and Britain* (see above under "Agreements concluded by Britain").

2. *Denmark:* on aircrew training for NATO, April 17, 1957. Renewed on March 25, 1960; extended on June 30, 1964.

3. *France:* (a) pursuant to the Convention on Foreign Forces stationed in Germany: April 19, 1955; Jan. 26, 1956.
(b) On the exchange of defense-science information, May 25, 1962.

4. *German Federal Republic:* on the training of German aircrews in Canada, Sept. 17 and Dec. 10, 1956.

5. *Greece:* on the exchange of defense-science information, July 17 and 18, 1962.

6. *The Netherlands:* on the extension of the NATO aircrew training program, April 12 and 13, 1957.

7. *Norway:* (a) on the transfer of three *Prestonian* class frigates to Norway, July 1, 1958;
(b) on the continuation of Canada's NATO air training program, June 30, 1964;
(c) on the exchange of information on defense, May 24, 1960.

C. AGREEMENTS CONCLUDED BY FRANCE WITH:

1. *Belgium and Luxemburg:* on co-operation between the three countries for internal defense, July 25, 1959.

2. *Canada* (see above).

3. *German Federal Republic:* (a) on logistics and training of German forces, Oct. 25, 1960;
(b) on co-operation in the field of political, economic, defense, cultural and scientific matters, Jan. 22, 1963 (see page 84).

4. *Portugal:* on the setting up, by France, of a tracking station for ballistic missiles in the Azores, April 9, 1964.

D. AGREEMENTS CONCLUDED BY THE GERMAN FEDERAL REPUBLIC.

1. *Convention on relations between the Three Powers* (the U.S.A., Britain, and France) and the German Federal Republic and related conventions, signed May 26, 1952. Amended by the Paris Agreements of Oct. 23, 1954.

For bilateral agreements pursuant to these conventions see above under "Agreements concluded by Britain" and "Agreements concluded by Canada."

2. *Agreements with the Netherlands* on (a) cost of maintenance of Dutch forces in the Federal Republic, July 10, 1957;
(b) reparations for damage caused by Dutch military units stationed in Germany, Jan. 29, 1957.

3. *Agreement with Norway* on the delivery of armament spare parts, Oct. 30, 1957.

4. *Agreement with Britain* on the development and production of a howitzer, Aug. 9, 1968.   [*22867*]

5. *Agreement with Portugal* on West German use of Beja air base, announced on Dec. 27, 1968.
An earlier agreement on training and storage facilities for West German forces in Portugal had been concluded on June 12, 1964.   [*20259; 23138A*]

E. AGREEMENTS CONCLUDED BY BELGIUM WITH:

1. *Luxemburg and France* (see above under "Agreements concluded by France").

2. *Luxemburg:* on an alarm network, Feb. 19 and 21, 1955.

Important Agreements Related to Military Bases and Nuclear Weapons

The more significant defense agreements between NATO partners are described below.

1. U.S.A.-BRITAIN

During 1948 the U.S.A. and Britain concluded an agreement on the use of air bases in Eastern England by the U.S. Strategic Air Command. Details of this agreement were, however, not made public. In 1952, after a meeting in Washington between President Truman and the British Prime Minister, Winston Churchill, it was stated that "the use of these bases in an emergency would be a matter for joint decision by H.M. Government and the U.S. Government in the light of the circumstances prevailing at the time." [11945A]

An agreement relating to the supply by the U.S.A. to Britain of intermediate-range ballistic missiles was signed on Feb. 22, 1958. In the agreement it was stressed that the arrangements were made "in consonance with the North Atlantic Treaty and in pursuance of the Mutual Defense Assistance Agreement of Jan. 27, 1950." Although ownership of the missiles would eventually pass to Britain, all nuclear warheads would remain "in full U.S. ownership, custody and control." The decision to launch the missiles would be a matter for joint decision by the two Governments. [16063A]

In 1960 the U.S.A. and Britain concluded an informal agreement under which the British Government agreed to provide facilities for U.S. *Polaris* nuclear submarines at a floating-base in Holy Loch on the Clyde (Scotland). [17726A]

On Dec. 21, 1962, a joint communiqué was issued by President Kennedy and the British Prime Minister, Harold Macmillan, after their meeting at Nassau where, *inter alia,* the question of nuclear missiles was discussed. The communiqué announced that the U.S. Government would make available to Britain, "on a continuing basis," *Polaris* missiles without warheads; that Britain would provide the necessary submarines; and that these forces, together with at least equal U.S. forces, would be made available for inclusion in a NATO multilateral nuclear force. An agreement on the terms of sale by the United States of up to 100 *Polaris* missiles in Britain was signed on April 6, 1963. The *Polaris* agreement superseded an earlier agreement, concluded during 1960, for the development of the *Skybolt* missile by the U.S. Government for the joint use of the U.S. and British air forces. [19173A; 19389A]

2. U.S.A.-CANADA

On Aug. 16, 1963, it was announced that Canada and the United States had reached agreement on "the conditions under which nuclear warheads will be made available for Canadian forces engaged in North American defense and assigned to NATO." The terms of the agreement were not made public, but it was stated that stockpiles of nuclear warheads would be stored at Canadian bases under Canadian command and control, but would remain under U.S. custody. The warheads could only be used operationally with the joint authorization of the U.S. and Canadian Governments.

Before the conclusion of this agreement the storage of U.S. nuclear warheads on Canadian territory had been the subject of political controversy in Canada. [19615B]

3. U.S.A.-ITALY

On March 30, 1959, it was announced that an agreement between the U.S.A. and Italy had been signed in Rome, under which the Italian armed forces would be equipped with American intermediate-range ballistic missiles. Italian personnel would receive training in the use of the missiles, but the nuclear warheads would remain under U.S. control. It was stressed that any decision to use the missiles and warheads would need the approval of both the Italian Government and SHAPE. [16907A]

4. U.S.A.-TURKEY

A similar agreement on the supply of IRBMs to Turkey came into force on Oct. 29, 1959. Other agreements concluded with Turkey were as follows:

Agreement relating to the implementation of the NATO agreement on status of forces of June 19, 1951: June 23, 1954.

Agreement of co-operation: March 5, 1959 (see page 183). [16748A]

Agreement relating to the introduction of modern weapons into NATO defense forces in Turkey. Exchange of notes Sept. 18 and Oct. 28, 1959; entry into force Oct. 28, 1959.

Agreement for the establishment of a facility for repairing and rebuilding M-12 range finders in Turkey; Nov. 30, 1959.

Agreement on a weapons production program: March 2, 1960.

Under an agreement between the United States and Turkey, signed in Ankara on July 3, 1969, and replacing over 50 earlier agreements concluded since 1959, Turkey's absolute sovereignty over all military installations in Turkey was emphasized; the agreement also laid down that Turkey would not lease or rent territory to the U.S.A., or exclude Turkish personnel from bases, and that Turkey would, within the general framework of NATO defense policies, have co-determination with the U.S.A. on the number of U.S. troops and their weapons and equipment to be stationed in Turkey. [23484C]

Agreement on with	Military Assistance	Assurances Required	Facilities Assistance	Offshore Procurement	Return of Equipment	
Belgium	March 30, 1950 June 3, 1971* June 28, 1971*	Jan. 7, 1952	April 19, 1963	June 18, 1953 July 22, 1954 July 22, 1954 May 13, 1954* July 19, 1954*	March 10, 1955 July 7, 1961	
Britain	Jan. 27, 1950	Jan. 8, 1952			May 13, 1957 Dec. 30, 1958* Nov. 10, 1961* Aug. 28, 1963	
Denmark	Jan. 27, 1950	Jan. 8, 1952		June 8, 1954	April 28, 1952 Sept. 12, 1960*	
France	Jan. 27, 1950	Jan. 5, 1952			Sept. 23, 1955	
German Federal Republic	Dec. 27, 1955	Dec. 28, 1951		Feb. 7, 1957	Dec. 27, 1955 March 9, 1961* May 25, 1962	
Greece	June 20, 1947	Jan. 7, 1952		Dec. 24, 1952 July 30, 1954 Oct. 14, 1954* Nov. 12, 1954*	Jan. 7, 1952 April 18, 1961*	
Iceland		Jan. 8, 1952				
Italy	Jan. 27, 1950	Jan. 7, 1952		March 31, 1954	Dec. 14, 1951 Sept. 7, 1960*	
Luxemburg	March 28, 1950 May 27, 1971* June 10, 1971*	Jan. 8, 1952		Sept. 30, 1955 Sept. 30, 1955 May 10, 1954* July 16, 1954*	July 7, 1954 March 4, 1960* June 10, 1960*	
Netherlands	Jan. 27, 1950	Jan. 8, 1952		July 30, 1954	Nov. 26, 1953 Aug. 10, 1960* Aug. 13, 1960*	
Norway	Feb. 24, 1950 Nov. 23, 1971* Dec. 16, 1971*	Jan. 8, 1952			Dec. 28, 1950 June 26, 1953 Sept. 1, 1960* Jan. 14, 1961*	
Portugal	Jan. 5, 1951	Jan. 8, 1952			July 9, 1952 Sept. 15, 1960*	
Turkey	July 12, 1947 June 23, 1954*	Jan. 7, 1952	Nov. 30, 1959	June 29, 1955	May 26, 1955 Aug. 10, 1962*	

ASSISTANCE AGREEMENTS

Military Assistance Advisory Group	Mutual Security Military Sales	Weapons Production	Other matters
		April 22, 1960	
		June 29, 1962	
Dec. 12, 1956		April 12, 1960	
	Jan. 30, 1958	Sept. 19, 1960	Oct. 28, 1958: Transfer of special tools.
	Nov. 23, 1953 Oct. 8, 1956 June 15, 1960* Oct. 24, 1960* Nov. 24, 1961*	May 27, 1960	Dec. 12, 1956: 1) Training of army personnel. 2) Training of navy personnel. Dec. 10, 1957: Transfer of three air bases.
		Feb. 15, 1960 June 3, 1960*	Oct. 12, 1953: Military Facilities. Sept. 7, 1956: Status of U.S. Forces. U.S. arms supplies to Greece, suspended after the Greek military coup of April 1967, were fully resumed in September 1970, their value being up to $56,000,000 over a two-year period. [24238B]
			Dec. 10, 1954: Sale of certain military equipment.
		July 7, 1960	July 8, 1955: Facilities for overhaul and repair of jet engines in Turin, Italy.
		March 24, 1960	Dec. 14, 1954: Establishment of Air Defense Technical Center.
April 13, 1954		Feb. 13, 1960 April 26, 1960* Sept. 16, 1960*	Feb. 26, 1970: Safeguarding of classified information. Nov. 5, 1971: Establishment and operation of OMEGA navigational station, Bratland.
		Sept. 26, 1960	
		March 2, 1960	March 5, 1959: Co-operation.

5. U.S.A.-PORTUGAL

An agreement between the U.S.A. and Portugal was signed on Sept. 6, 1951, defining the facilities in the Azores granted by Portugal to the U.S.A. for the purposes of the common defense. Under the agreement these facilities were integrated into the NATO framework. The agreement was extended on Nov. 15, 1957, until the end of 1962, and was again provisionally extended on Jan. 4, 1963.

The lease of a U.S. air base in the Azores under the U.S.-Portuguese agreement of Jan. 5, 1951, was on Nov. 15, 1957, extended to Dec. 31, 1962, and on Jan. 4, 1963, until a new lease was agreed. A new agreement was subsequently signed in Brussels on Dec. 9, 1971, granting the U.S.A. the continued use until Feb. 4, 1974, of air and naval bases on the island of Terceira, in the Azores, in return for economic assistance to Portugal by the U.S.A. [25239B]

6. U.S.A.-GREECE

An agreement giving American forces the use of air and naval bases in Greece, and authorizing the U.S.A. to develop Greek roads and railways for military purposes under the NATO defense pact, was signed on Oct. 12, 1953. This agreement was partially abrogated by the agreement on the status of U.S. forces in Greece of Sept. 7, 1956. [13204C]

7. U.S.A.-ICELAND

A new agreement between the U.S.A. and Iceland on the presence of U.S. defense forces in Iceland was announced on Dec. 6, 1956. Under the agreement an Iceland Defense Standing Group was set up to consult on the defense needs of Iceland and NATO in general, and to prepare for the training of Icelandic personnel to man the U.S. bases. In 1960 the U.S. forces in Iceland were reduced to leave only Air Force and Navy personnel at the air base and the radar installations. [15300B; 17190D]

8. BRITAIN-FRANCE

An Anglo-French military air transit agreement was signed on April 19, 1948. It governed flights by military aircraft over both countries and their servicing at British and French airfields. [9223B]

9. ROCKET TRAINING CENTER IN CRETE

On June 11, 1964, eight NATO countries—Belgium, Denmark, France, the German Federal Republic, Greece, the Netherlands, Norway, and the U.S.A.—signed an agreement on the building of a rocket training center in Crete, to be completed in 1965. Turkey, which had wished the center to be built on Turkish territory, refused to sign the agreement. [20255A]

The center, including a guided-missile firing range at Akrotiri, was completed and taken over by NATO on May 17, 1968. [22808A]

10. U.S. AGREEMENTS ON DEFENSE USES OF ATOMIC ENERGY

The United States has concluded agreements for co-operation on uses of atomic energy for mutual defense purposes with the following NATO member-countries, the dates given being those on which the agreements entered into force:

Belgium	Sept. 5, 1962.
Britain	Aug. 4, 1958; extended and amended May 7, 1959; Sept. 27, 1968; Oct. 16, 1969.
Canada	July 27, 1959.
France	July 20, 1959, and Oct. 9, 1961.
Germany (Federal Republic)	July 27, 1959.
Greece	Aug. 11, 1959.
Italy	May 24, 1961.
Netherlands	July 27, 1959.
Turkey	July 27, 1959.

In addition agreements for co-operation regarding atomic information for mutual defense purposes have been concluded with the following countries:

Australia	Aug. 14, 1957.
Canada	July 22, 1955; amended May 22, 1959.

8

The Communist World

INTERNATIONAL COMMUNIST ORGANIZATIONS

The Comintern (1917–1943)

The Comintern, the Third (Communist) International, was founded in 1919 by Lenin in Moscow. The First International had been founded in 1864 by Karl Marx and Friedrich Engels, but broke up in 1874 on account of internal dissensions. The Second International was formed in 1889, but collapsed on the outbreak of war in 1914. The Comintern served as a roof organization of the Communist parties of the world, the individual national Communist parties being in effect sections of the world revolutionary Communist party.

On June 8, 1943, the Presidium of the Executive Committee of the Communist International met to dissolve the Comintern formally with the approval of the majority of world Communist parties and without any of the existing sections of the Communist International having raised any objections to the dissolution.

The proposal for the dissolution of the Comintern, as put before the Executive Committee at a meeting on May 15, 1943, was worded as follows:

1. The Communist International, as the directing center of the international working-class movement, is to be dissolved.

2. The sections of the Communist International are to be freed from the obligations of their rules and regulations and from the decisions of the congress of the Communist International.

3. The Presidium calls on all supporters of the Communist International to concentrate their energies on wholehearted support for and active participation in the war of liberation waged by the peoples and States of the anti-Hitlerite coalition for the speediest defeat of the deadly enemy of the working-class—German Fascism and its associates and vassals. [*5789A; 5817B*]

The Cominform (1947–1956)

On Oct. 5, 1947, it was announced that the Communist parties of Bulgaria, Czechoslovakia, France, Hungary, Italy, Poland, Romania, the Soviet Union, and Yugoslavia had decided to set up a Communist Information Bureau (the Cominform), with its headquarters in Belgrade. Its purpose was stated to be to "organize the exchange of experience" and "where necessary to co-ordinate the activities of the Communist parties on the basis of mutual agreement." [*8864A*]

On June 28, 1948, it was disclosed that Yugoslavia had been expelled from the Cominform on grounds, *inter alia,* of deviation from Marxism-Leninism, of nationalism, and of hostility toward the Soviet Union. [*9381A*]

The official announcement of the dissolution of the Cominform appeared on April 18, 1956, signed by the eight national Communist parties which formed the membership of the organization. It was stated that the eight had unanimously agreed that the Cominform had "exhausted its function."

The International Communist Conferences of 1957 and 1960

Since the dissolution of the Cominform in 1956 there has been no co-ordinating body for the Communist parties in various countries. Conferences held in 1957 and 1960 failed to preserve the unity of the Communist movement.

THE 1957 CONFERENCE

This conference, which was held in Moscow Nov. 14–16, issued the "Moscow Declaration" approved by 12 parties:—the Communist parties of the U.S.S.R., China, Bulgaria, and Czechoslovakia, the Polish United Workers' Party, the Hungarian Socialist Workers' Party, the Romanian Workers' Party, the Socialist

Unity Party in East Germany, the Albanian Party of Labour, the (North) Korean Party of Labour, the Working People's Party of (North) Vietnam, and the Mongolian People's Revolutionary Party. [*Page 15901*]

This declaration, drawn up without the participation of the Yugoslav League of Communists, was expressly rejected by the latter on Dec. 7, 1957.

The declaration consisted of four sections:

(1) Denunciation of "Imperialism"

This section described the U.S.A. as "the center of world reaction"; accused "American, British, French, and other imperialists and their stooges" of waging wars in various parts of the world; blamed the "aggressive imperialist forces" for their "flat refusal" to reduce armaments or prohibit nuclear weapons; attacked NATO, SEATO, and "West German militarism and revanchism"; and asserted that "the cause of peace is upheld by . . . the invincible camp of Socialist countries headed by the Soviet Union." It added that other "powerful peace forces" were "the peace-loving countries of Asia and Africa taking an anti-imperialist stand"; the "international working class and above all its vanguard, the Communist Party"; the "liberation movement of the peoples of colonies and semi-colonies"; the "peoples of the European countries which have proclaimed neutrality"; and "the peoples of Latin America." This section also affirmed that the 12 Communist parties signing the declaration adhered to the "Leninist principles of peaceful coexistence . . . which . . . coincide with the Five Principles put forward jointly by China and India and with the program adopted at the Bandung conference of Afro-Asian countries" (see page 208).

(2) Co-operation Between Communist Countries

The Declaration described the principles, upon which collaboration among the Communist states should be constructed, in these terms:

"The Socialist countries base their relations on principles of complete equality, respect for territorial integrity, State independence and sovereignty, and non-interference in one another's affairs. These are vital principles. However, they do not exhaust the essence of the relations among them. Fraternal mutual aid is part and parcel of these relations. . . . The Socialist States also advocate all-round expansion of economic and cultural relations with all other countries, provided they desire it, on a basis of equality, mutual benefit, and non-interference in internal affairs. . . ."

(3) "Revisionism" and "Sectarianism"

In this section the "international phenomena" of "revisionism," "sectarianism," and "dogmatism" were attacked, and it was claimed that Marxism-Leninism, "deriving from historical materialism," was a "world outlook reflecting the universal law of development of nature, society, and human thinking" and was "valid for the past, present, and future."

The declaration continued: "In condemning dogmatism, the Communist parties believe that the main danger at present is revisionism—in other words, right-wing opportunism as a manifestation of bourgeois ideology paralyzing the revolutionary energy of the working-class and demanding the preservation or restoration of capitalism. However, dogmatism and sectarianism can also be the main danger at different phases of development in one party or another. It is for each Communist party to decide what danger threatens it more at a given time. . . . Modern revisionism seeks to smear the teaching of Marxism-Leninism, declares that it is 'out-moded,' and alleges that it has lost its significance for social progress. . . . The revisionists deny the historical necessity for a proletarian revolution and the dictatorship of the proletariat during the period of transition from capitalism to Socialism; reject the principles of proletarianism; and call for the rejection of the Leninist principles of party organization and democratic centralism. Above all, they call for the transformation of the Communist party from a militant revolutionary party into some kind of debating society. . . ."

(4) Relations with Non-Communist Parties were the subject of still another section:

". . . The working class and its vanguard—the Marxist-Leninist Party—seek to achieve the Socialist revolution by peaceful means. . . . In a number of capitalist countries the working-class today has the opportunity—given a united working-class and people's front, or other workable forms of political co-operation between the different parties and organizations—to unite a majority of the people, win power without civil war, and ensure the transfer of the basic means of production to the hands of the people . . . [The] . . . working-class . . . can secure a firm majority in parliament, transform parliament from an instrument serving the class interests of the bourgeoisie into an instrument serving the working people, launch a non-parliamentary mass struggle, smash the resistance of the reactionary forces, and create the necessary conditions for the peaceful realization of the Socialist revolution. . . .

"In the event of the ruling classes resorting to violence against the people, the possibility of non-peaceful transition to Socialism should be borne in mind. Leninism teaches, and experience confirms, that the ruling classes never relinquish power voluntarily. In this case the degree of bitterness and the forms of the class struggle will depend not so much on the proletariat as on the resistance put up by the reactionary circles. . . . The possibility of one or another way to Socialism depends on the concrete conditions in each country. . . .

"In the struggle for winning power and building Socialism, the Communist parties seek co-operation with the Socialist parties. Although right-wing Socialist Party leaders are doing their best to hamper this co-operation, there are increasing opportunities for co-operation between Communists and Socialists on many issues. The ideological differences between the Communist and Socialist parties should not keep them from establishing unity of action on the many pressing issues that confront the working-class movement. . . ." [*Page 15901*]

THE 1960 CONFERENCE

This, the largest conference since the Seventh World Congress of the Communist International held in 1935, was attended by delegations of 81 countries, excluding Yugoslavia, whose League of Communists had not been invited. The Conference was not attended by Chairman Mao Tse-tung of the Chinese Communist Party, nor by Signor Palmiro Togliatti, general secretary of the Italian Communist Party—although both these parties were represented by delegations.

The 1960 Conference was faced with the possibility of a split in the international Communist movement as the result of the controversy between the Soviet and Chinese parties on questions of theory and policy. The main issues of this controversy may be summarized as follows:

(1) The Soviet party upheld the view, put forward by Mr. Khrushchev at its 20th congress in 1956, that Lenin's theory of the inevitability of war under capitalism was no longer valid because of the growing strength of the Socialist bloc, the neutral policy pursued by many former colonial countries, and the strength of "anti-war" movements in capitalist countries. Chinese spokesmen, on the other hand, maintained that it was a "naive illusion" to think that war could be avoided before capitalism had been abolished.

(2) The Soviet party emphasized that nuclear war would prove equally disastrous to all concerned, and used this argument in favor of peaceful coexistence between countries with different social systems. The Chinese Communists, however, maintained that China could survive a nuclear war and that a third world war would result in further victories for Communism.

(3) The Chinese Communists rejected the policy of peaceful coexistence as involving a rejection of the class struggle and an attitude of "peace at any price."

(4) The Chinese Communists also rejected as "very wrong" the view that nationalist movements in colonial and underdeveloped countries might possibly endanger world peace and should therefore not necessarily be supported by the Soviet Union and international Communism.

(5) Soviet theoreticians contended that in underdeveloped countries Communists should ally themselves with the "bourgeoisie" in the struggle for national independence, which would prepare the way for the transition to Socialism. The Chinese Communists, however, declared in August 1960: "If we view the movement led by the bourgeoisie in colonial countries as the mainstream of the national liberation movement and give full support to it, while ignoring, or expressing contempt for, the anti-imperialist struggle waged by the revolutionary masses, it will in fact mean the adoption of bourgeois viewpoints."

(6) The Chinese Communists did not accept the Soviet view, then expressed by Mr. Khrushchev, that in certain countries it was possible for Communist Parties to attain power by parliamentary means without violent revolution.

(7) Against the accepted Marxist theory that intensive industrialization was an essential prerequisite for the transition from Socialism to full Communism, the Chinese Communists contended that agricultural expansion was "the one essential base."

(8) The Chinese party continued to uphold the assertion of the 1957 Moscow declaration (see above) that "revisionism" was "the main danger" to the international Communists movement and rejected the Soviet party's relaxation (since 1959) of its campaign against the "revisionism" of the Yugoslav Communists.

The declaration of the Moscow conference published on Dec. 5, 1960, reflected the Soviet view, although with some concessions made in its wording to the Chinese position. It contained the following significant passages:

War and Peace. "The aggressive nature of imperialism has not changed, but real forces have appeared that are capable of foiling its plans of aggression. War is not fatally inevitable. . . . World war can be prevented by the joint efforts of the world Socialist camp, the international working class, the national liberation movement, all the countries opposing war, and all peace-loving forces. . . . The policy of peaceful coexistence is also favored by a definite section of the bourgeoisie of the developed capitalist countries, which takes a sober view of the relationship of forces and of the dire consequences of a modern war. . . . But should the imperialist maniacs start war, the peoples will sweep capitalism out of existence and bury it. . . .

"The near future will bring the forces of peace and Socialism new successes. The U.S.S.R. will become the leading industrial Power of the world. China will become a mighty industrial State. The Socialist system will be turning out more than half the world's industrial product. The peace zone will expand. . . . In these conditions a real possibility will have arisen of excluding world war from the life of society even before Socialism achieves complete victory on earth, with capitalism still existing in a part of the world. . . .

"Peaceful coexistence of countries with different social systems does not mean conciliation of the Socialist and bourgeois ideologies. On the contrary, it implies intensification of the struggle of the working class, of all the Communist parties, for the triumph of Socialist ideas. But ideological and political disputes between States must not be settled through war. . . ."

Colonial and Under-developed Countries. "Communists have always recognized the progressive, revolutionary significance of national liberation wars. . . . The peoples of the colonial countries win their independence both through armed struggle and by non-military methods, depending on the specific conditions in the country concerned. . . .

"The urgent tasks of national rebirth facing the countries that have shaken off the colonial yoke cannot be effectively accomplished unless a determined struggle is waged against imperialism and the remnants of feudalism by all the patriotic forces of the nation, united in a single national democratic front. . . . The alliance of the working class and the peasantry is the most important force in winning and defending national independence, accomplishing far-reaching democratic transformations, and ensuring social progress. . . . The extent to which the national bourgeoisie participates in the liberation struggle depends to no small degree upon its strength and stability. . . . In present conditions the national bourgeoisie of the colonial and dependent countries unconnected with imperialist circles is objectively interested in the accomplishment of the principal tasks of the anti-imperialist, anti-feudal revolution, and therefore retains the capacity of participating in the revolutionary struggle against imperialism and feudalism. In that sense it is progressive. But it is unstable, and is inclined to compromise with imperialism and feudalism. . . .

"The Socialist countries are true and sincere friends of the peoples fighting for liberation and of those who have thrown off the imperialist yoke. While rejecting on principle any interference in the internal affairs of young national States, they consider it their internationalist duty to help the peoples in strengthening their independence. . . ."

Moving on to another major area of international Communist policy, the declaration also called for joint action on a national and international scale between Communist and Social Democratic parties in support of complete disarmament under international control, the abolition of military bases on foreign soil, assistance to the nationalist movements in colonial and dependent countries, and the improvement of living standards.

Forms of Transition to Socialism. "The imperialist reactionaries," the declaration continued, "intimidate the masses by alleging that the Communists need wars between States to overthrow the capitalist system and establish a Socialist system. The Communist parties emphatically reject this slander. The fact that both World Wars, which were started by the imperialists, ended in Socialist revolutions by no means implies that the way to social revolution is necessarily through world war. . . . The choice of its social system is the inalienable right of the people of each country. Socialist revolution is not an item of export, and cannot be imposed from without. . . .

"Today in a number of capitalist countries the working class, headed by its vanguard, has the opportunity . . . to unite a majority of the people, win State power without civil war, and ensure the transfer of the basic means of production to the hands of the people. . . . The working class can defeat the reactionary anti-popular forces, secure a firm majority in Parliament, . . . and create the necessary conditions for peaceful realization of the Socialist revolution. . . . In the event of the exploiting classes resorting to violence against the people, the possibility of non-peaceful transition to Socialism should be borne in mind. . . . The actual possibility of the one or the other way of transition to Socialism

in each individual country depends on the concrete historical conditions."

Revisionism and Dogmatism. After condemning "the personality cult, which shackles creative thought and initiative," the declaration denounced "the Yugoslav variety of international opportunism" and asserted that "further exposure of the leaders of the Yugoslav revisionists, and active struggle to safeguard the Communist and working-class movement from the anti-Leninist ideas of the Yugoslav revisionists, remains an essential task of the Marxist-Leninist parties." It repeated the formula of the 1957 declaration that "revisionism . . . remains the main danger" but that "dogmatism and sectarianism in theory and practice can also become the main danger at some stage of development of individual parties," and called for "a determined struggle" against both. In conclusion, the declaration referred to the Soviet party as "the universally recognized vanguard of the world Communist movement," and described the decisions of its 20th congress as initiating "a new stage in the world Communist movement." [*17897A*]

The 1961 Conference—Intensification of Sino-Soviet Dispute

During 1961 China concluded agreements with Albania providing for increased trade between the two countries and including a declaration on the two Governments' "complete agreement on ideological questions." During the same year Albania's relations with the Soviet Union began to deteriorate, and at the 22nd congress of the Soviet Communist Party, Oct. 17–31, 1961, Mr. Krushchev openly broke with Albania, alleging that its leaders had "begun to depart from the common agreed line of the Communist movement of the whole world on major issues" and were "using the same methods as were current in our country at the time of the personality cult" (i.e. under Stalin).

The break between the U.S.S.R. and China was widened at this congress, with Chou En-lai (the Chinese Foreign Minister) leaving Moscow before the end of the conference after blaming the Soviet party for "laying bare a dispute between fraternal parties or fraternal countries, openly in the face of the enemy" —which, he said, was "not a serious Marxist-Leninist attitude."

The congress was followed by the breaking-off of diplomatic relations between the U.S.S.R. and Albania and open expression of support for Albania by the Chinese Communist Party in December 1961.

During the years 1962–64 the Sino-Soviet conflict intensified. The Chinese Government disapproved of Mr. Khrushchev's approaches to Yugoslavia in May 1962; of his compromise with the U.S.A. over the Cuban issue in October 1962; and of Soviet military aid given to India in the Sino-Indian War of October–November 1962.

On June 14, 1963, the Chinese party approved a letter to the Soviet party, in which it put forward "25 points" for discussion at talks to be held in Moscow. These points included:

(3) "If the general line of the international Communist movement is one-sidedly reduced to 'peaceful coexistence,' 'peaceful competition,' and 'peaceful transition,' this is to violate the revolutionary principles of the 1957 declaration and the 1960 statement. . . .

(4) "The fundamental contradictions in the contemporary world . . . are: the contradiction between the Socialist camp and the imperialist camp; the contradiction between the proletariat and the bourgeoisie in the capitalist countries; the contradiction between the oppressed nations and imperialism; and the contradictions among imperialist countries and among monopoly capitalist groups. . . .

(5) "The following erroneous views should be repudiated . . . : (a) the view which blots out the class content of the contradiction between the Socialist and imperialist camps . . . ; (b) the view which recognizes only the contradiction between the Socialist and imperialist camps . . . ; (c) the view which maintains . . . that the contradiction between the proletariat and the bourgeoisie can be resolved without a proletarian revolution in each country and that the contradiction between the oppressed nations and imperialism can be resolved without revolution . . . ; (d) the view which denies that the development of the inherent contradictions in the contemporary capitalist world inevitably leads to a new situation in which the imperialist countries are locked in an intense struggle, and asserts that the contradictions among the imperialist countries can be reconciled or even eliminated by 'international agreements among the big monopolies'; and (e) the view which maintains that the contradiction between the two world systems of Socialism and capitalism will automatically disappear in the course of 'economic competition,' . . . and that a 'world without wars,' a new world of 'all-round co-operation,' will appear. . . .

(9) "The oppressed nations and peoples of Asia, Africa, and Latin America are faced with the urgent task of fighting imperialism and its lackeys. . . . In these areas extremely broad sections of the population refuse to be slaves of imperialism. They include not only the workers, peasants, intellectuals, and petty bourgeoisie, but also the patriotic national bourgeoisie and even certain kings, princes, and aristocrats. . . . The proletariat and its party must . . . organize a broad united front against imperialism. . . . The proletarian party should maintain its ideological, political, and organizational independence and insist on the leadership of the revolution. The proletarian party and the revolutionary people must learn to master all forms of struggle, including armed struggle. . . . The policy of the proletarian party should be . . . to unite with the bourgeoisie, in so far as they tend to be progressive, anti-imperialist, and anti-feudal, but to struggle against their reactionary tendencies to compromise and collaborate with imperialism and the forces of feudalism. . . .

(10) "In the imperialist and capitalist countries the proletarian revolution and the dictatorship of the proletariat are essential. . . . It is wrong to refuse to use parliamentary and other legal forms of struggle when they can and should be used. However, if a Marxist-Leninist party falls into legalism or parliamentary cretinism, confining the struggle within the limits permitted by the bourgeoisie, this will inevitably lead to renouncing the proletarian revolution and the dictatorship of the proletariat.

(11) "Marx and Lenin did raise the possibility that revolutions may develop peacefully. But, as Lenin pointed out, the peaceful development of revolution is an opportunity 'very seldom to be met with in the history of revolution.' As a matter of fact, there is no historical precedent for peaceful transition from capitalism to Socialism. . . . The proletarian party must never base its thinking, its policies for revolution, and its entire work on the assumption that the imperialists and reactionaries will accept peaceful transformation. . . .

(14) ". . . Certain persons now actually hold that it is possible to bring about 'a world without weapons, without armed forces, and without wars' through 'general and complete disarmament' while the system of imperialism and of the exploitation of man by man still exists. This is sheer illusion. . . .

(15) "The emergence of nuclear weapons does not and cannot resolve the fundamental contradictions in the contemporary world, does not and cannot alter the law of class struggle, and does not and cannot change the nature of imperialism and reaction. It cannot, therefore, be said that with the emergence of nuclear weapons the possibility and the necessity of social and national revolutions have disappeared, or that the basic principles of Marxism-Leninism, and especially the theories of proletarian revolution and the dictatorship of the proletariat . . . have become outmoded. . . .

(21) "Relations between Socialist countries, whether large or small, and whether more developed or less developed economically, must be based on the principles of complete equality. . . .

(22) "If the principle of independence and equality is accepted in relations among fraternal parties, then it is impermissible for any party to place itself above others, to interfere in their internal affairs, and to adopt patriarchal ways in relations with them. . . ."

The central committee of the Soviet party answered the above "25 points" on July 14, 1963.

In their reply the Soviet party blamed the Chinese for having themselves caused the deterioration in relations and described their views as "erroneous." In particular, the Soviet party claimed that the Chinese "obviously underestimated the whole danger of nuclear war," and also the importance of "the struggle for disarmament." The Soviet party emphasized that "the nuclear bomb does not distinguish between the imperialists and working people" and that it would not be possible, as suggested by Mao Tse-tung, "to build a bright future on the ruins of a destroyed imperialism."

The Soviet party also accused the Chinese leaders of "organizing and supporting various anti-party groups of renegades," including dissident Communist groups in various countries, and of having "pushed the Albanian leaders on to the road of open struggle against the Soviet Union."

Following bitter polemics in the press of the two countries, the Chinese party rejected on May 7, 1964, a Soviet proposal for a world conference to be held in the autumn of 1964 to end the dispute.

After Mr. Khrushchev's removal from office on Oct.

14, 1964, the dispute was aggravated by disagreements on Communist policy on Vietnam during 1965. The Chinese party refused to attend a meeting of Communist parties in Moscow in March 1965 and also to send a delegation to the 23rd Soviet party congress in March–April 1966.

During the period of the "Great Proletarian Cultural Revolution" in China the conflict was further intensified, and on Dec. 13, 1966, the Soviet party for the first time condemned the policy of "Mao Tse-tung and his group," whose actions, it said, had "nothing in common with Marxism-Leninism" and "objectively" assisted imperialism. Further fierce criticism of Mao Tse-tung and his policies followed in the Soviet press from February 1967 onward.

The Soviet invasion of Czechoslovakia on Aug. 20–21, 1968, was condemned by Chou En-lai on Aug. 23 as "the most barefaced and typical specimen of Fascist power politics played by the Soviet revisionist clique against its so-called allies"—a clique which had, he claimed, "degenerated into a gang of social-imperialists and social-Fascists." At the same time Chinese statements strongly denounced the Dubcek regime in Czechoslovakia for its "revisionism" and its failure to organize armed resistance to the invasion.

The "Brezhnev Doctrine"

Mr. Brezhnev, the First Secretary of the Soviet Communist Party, in an address to a Polish United Workers' Party congress in Warsaw on Nov. 12, 1968, put forward the doctrine of "limited sovereignty" in an attempt to justify the Soviet intervention in Czechoslovakia.

Mr. Brezhnev declared *inter alia*:

"When internal and external forces that are hostile to Socialism try to turn the development of some Socialist country toward the restoration of a capitalist regime, when Socialism in that country and the Socialist community as a whole is threatened, it becomes not only a problem of the country concerned, but a common problem and concern of all Socialist countries. Naturally, an action such as military assistance to a fraternal country designed to avert the threat to the social system is an extraordinary step, dictated by necessity." Such a step, he added, "may be taken only in case of direct actions of the enemies of Socialism within a country and outside it, actions threatening the common interests of the Socialist camp."

In China, Marshal Lin Piao commented on the theory on April 1, 1969, in his report to the ninth congress of the Chinese Communist Party, and prophesied that the Soviet Government would be overthrown by its own people.

"Since Brezhnev came to power," he said, ". . . the Soviet revisionist renegade clique has been practicing social-imperialism and social-Fascism more frantically than ever. Inter-

nally, it has intensified its suppression of the Soviet people and speeded up the all-round restoration of capitalism. Externally, it has stepped up its collusion with U.S. imperialism and its suppression of the revolutionary struggles of the people of various countries, intensified its control over and its exploitation of various East European countries and the People's Republic of Mongolia, and intensified its threat of aggression against China. . . .

"In order to justify its aggression and plunder, the Soviet revisionist renegade clique trumpets the so-called theory of 'limited sovereignty,' the theory of 'international dictatorship,' and the theory of 'Socialist community.' What does all this stuff mean? It means that your sovereignty is 'limited,' while his is unlimited. . . . We firmly believe that the proletariat and the broad masses of the people in the Soviet Union, with their glorious revolutionary tradition, will surely rise and overthrow this clique consisting of a handful of renegades."

In another passage of his report, in which he reaffirmed the party's views on the inevitability of war, Marshal Lin Piao opposed the "social-imperialist" countries (i.e. the U.S.S.R.) to the Socialist countries (i.e. China and Albania), and suggested that a conflict existed in the former between the proletariat and the "bourgeoisie," implying that the U.S.S.R. had ceased to be a Socialist country.

Mr. Brezhnev, however, denied during a visit to Yugoslavia on Sept. 22, 1971, that the so-called "doctrine of limited sovereignty" existed. The story of this "doctrine," he said, had been circulated by forces intent upon "driving a wedge between Yugoslavia and the U.S.S.R.," and it was not worth wasting time on denying "these slanderous inventions."

The Sino-Soviet dispute was further aggravated by Chinese claims on Soviet territory, arising out of the fact that large areas formerly under Chinese suzerainty had been annexed by Czarist Russia between 1858 and 1881.

These areas included over 75,000 square miles north and west of Lake Balkhash, ceded to Russia in 1864 and 1881; 230,000 square miles of territory north of the river Amur, acquired by Russia under the Treaty of Aigun (1858); and 150,000 square miles east of the Ussuri river, incorporated into the Russian Empire under the Treaty of Peking (1860).

China regarded these treaties as being two of nine "unequal treaties" which were forced upon the Chinese Empire between 1842 and 1901. These also included the 1881 Treaty of St. Petersburg confirming Russia's annexations of 1864; the 1895 Treaty of Shimonoseki, under which Japan obtained control of Taiwan (Formosa) and the Pescadores; and an 1898 Convention on the expansion of the territory of Hong Kong.

In addition, the Soviet Union and China disagreed on the exact demarcation of their common frontier, and boundary negotiations were intermittently conducted by the two Governments from 1964 onward without reaching final conclusions.

Meanwhile armed clashes had taken place along the

border between March and August 1969, and the press and radio on both sides continued their polemics from time to time.

Despite their dispute, negotiations between the two Governments led to (a) an agreement concluded on Aug. 8, 1969, on navigation on the Amur and Ussuri rivers, and (b) a trade and payments agreement concluded on Nov. 22, 1970.

The 1969 Conference

A further conference of Communist parties in Moscow on June 5–17, 1969, with 66 of the 75 parties taking part, approved a document entitled "Tasks at the present stage of the struggle against imperialism and united action of the Communist and Workers' parties and all anti-imperialist forces."

Mr. Brezhnev declared on June 7: "We cannot afford to ignore the divergences existing in the Communist movement today." In particular, he attacked the Chinese Communist Party for classifying as "revisionists" the "overwhelming majority of the Socialist countries and Communist parties" and for organizing "subversive splinter groups" against these parties. He also accused Maoism of calling for war, instead of for a struggle against war, and of directing its spearhead of foreign policy chiefly "against the Soviet Union and the other Socialist countries."

During the conference the Soviet intervention in Czechoslovakia in August 1968 was criticized by representatives of the British, Italian, Spanish, and Swedish Communist parties.

The document finally approved by the conference (a) reaffirmed the Communist movement's support for the policy of peaceful coexistence of States with different social systems, which did "not contradict the right of any oppressed people to fight for its liberation" (in which context the document called for "all-round support for the heroic Vietnamese people . . . in order to compel U.S. imperialism to withdraw its interventionist troops from Vietnam"); (b) expressed the view that the Communist countries made their "primary contribution to the struggle against capitalism" by their economic development, though it emphasized that this did not mean abandonment of support for revolutionary movements; (c) accepted the possibility of a peaceful transition to Socialism in certain countries, while accepting the use of force as inevitable in others; and (d) asserted that there was "no leading center of the international Communist movement" (thus in effect repudiating the 1960 Moscow conference statement that the Soviet party was "the universally recognized vanguard of the world Communist movement." See page 115). [23437A]

Soviet–Yugoslav Reconciliation

Following an improvement in relations between Yugoslavia and China (as well as Albania) and also between Romania and China during 1971, the Soviet Union's relations with both Yugoslavia and Romania underwent a period of tension. Romania was excluded from a meeting of the Communist Party leaders of the Warsaw Pact countries and Mongolia in the Crimea on Aug. 2, 1971.

However, following an "unofficial friendly visit" to Yugoslavia by Mr. Brezhnev on Sept. 22–25, 1971, Soviet-Yugoslav relations were again placed on a basis of "equality and mutual respect" and "non-interference in internal affairs," as expressed in a Belgrade Declaration of 1955 and a Moscow Declaration of 1956, which had ended the period of Soviet-Yugoslav "hostility" since Yugoslavia's expulsion from the Cominform. The reconciliation was confirmed during a visit to Moscow by President Tito on July 5–10, 1972. [24933A; 25368A]

THE WARSAW PACT

The Eastern European Mutual Assistance Treaty, or Warsaw Pact as it is generally known, is the equivalent, in Communist Eastern Europe, of NATO in the West. The 20-year treaty of friendship, co-operation, and mutual assistance was signed in Warsaw on May 14, 1955, by Albania, Bulgaria, Czechoslovakia, East Germany, Hungary, Poland, Romania, and the Soviet Union, who form the present membership. It came into force in the following month. [14249A]

History

The first move toward a military alliance of the Communist Bloc countries in Europe was made at a conference held in Moscow from Nov. 29 to Dec. 2, 1954, and attended by the eight countries listed above. At this conference on "the safeguarding of peace and collective security in Europe," the London and Paris Agreements establishing the Western European Union and providing for West Germany's entry into NATO (see page 41), were condemned as encouraging a revival of German militarism. A declaration published at the end of the conference stated that, if the Paris Agreements were ratified, the countries represented at the Moscow Conference would again meet "to adopt measures for safeguarding their security." [13936A]

On March 21, 1955, agreement was announced between the eight nations on the principles of a mutual defense treaty and the organization of a unified command. [14111D]

Six days after the Paris Agreements came into force, representatives of the eight nations met again in Warsaw, where they signed a treaty of mutual assistance, and decided on the creation of a unified military command for their armed forces with the exception of those of East Germany.

The Mutual Assistance Treaty

The preamble to the treaty reiterates the criticism of the Paris Agreements as creating a danger of renewed war through the re-militarization of West Germany. The principal provisions of the treaty are:

Art. 1. The contracting parties undertake, in accordance with the U.N. Charter, to refrain in their international relations from the threat or use of force, and to settle their international disputes by peaceful means so as not to endanger international peace and security.

Art. 2. The contracting parties declare their readiness to take part, in a spirit of sincere co-operation, in all international undertakings designed to safeguard international peace and security, and to use all their energies for the realization of these aims. Moreover, they will work for the adoption, in agreement with other States desiring to co-operate in this matter, of effective measures toward a general reduction of armaments and the prohibition of atomic, hydrogen, and other weapons of mass destruction.

Art. 3. The contracting parties will consult among themselves on all important international questions relating to their common interests. In the interests of organizing their joint defense, and of upholding peace and security, the contracting parties will immediately consult together whenever, in the opinion of any of them, there has arisen the threat of an armed attack on one or several States that are signatories of the treaty.

Art. 4. In the event of an armed attack in Europe on one or several States that are signatories of the treaty by any State or group of States, each party to this treaty shall, in the exercise of the right to individual or collective self-defense in accordance with Article 51 of the U.N. Charter, render the State or States so attacked immediate assistance, individually and in agreement with other States that are parties to this treaty, by all the means it may consider necessary, including the use of armed force. The parties to this treaty shall immediately consult among themselves on the necessary joint measures to be adopted for the purpose of restoring and upholding international peace and security.

In accordance with the U.N. Charter, the Security Council shall be advised of the measures taken on the basis of this Article. These measures shall be stopped as soon as the Security Council has taken the necessary steps to restore and uphold international peace and security.

Art. 5. The contracting parties have agreed to set up a joint command for their armed forces, which shall be placed under this command by agreement among the parties, and which shall function on the basis of jointly defined principles. They will also take other agreed measures to strengthen their defensive capacity, in order to safeguard the peaceful labor of their peoples, to guarantee the inviolability of their frontiers and territories, and to provide safeguards against possible aggression.

Art. 6. For the purpose of holding the consultations provided for in the treaty, and for considering problems arising out of the implementation of this treaty, a Political Consultative Committee shall be formed in which each State that is a party to this treaty shall be represented by a member of the government, or any other specially appointed representative. This committee may set up any auxiliary organs which may be necessary.

Art. 7. The contracting parties undertake not to participate in any coalitions and alliances, and not to conclude any agreements, the purposes of which would be at variance with those of the present treaty. They declare that their obligations under existing international treaties are not at variance with the provisions of the present treaty.

Art. 8. The contracting parties will act in a spirit of friendship and co-operation with the object of furthering and strengthening the economic and cultural relations between them, adhering to the principles of mutual respect for their independence and sovereignty, and of non-interference in their internal affairs.

Art. 9. This treaty may be acceded to by other States—irrespective of their social and State systems—who declare their readiness to assist the efforts of the peace-loving States for the purpose of safeguarding the peace and security of nations. [*14249A*]

Art. 11. Should a system of collective security be established in Europe, and a General European Treaty of Collective Security be concluded for this purpose, for which the contracting parties will unswervingly strive, the present treaty shall cease to be operative from the day the General European Treaty enters into force.

Formation of Unified Military Command

The decisions of the eight nations relating to the creation of a unified military command were contained in a separate statement declaring *inter alia* that:

(*a*) Questions relating to the joint force would be considered by the Political Consultative Committee set up by the Warsaw Treaty.

(*b*) Ministers of Defense and military leaders would have command of the armed forces of each State allotted to the joint armed forces, and would act as deputies of the Commander-in-Chief.

(*c*) A General Staff, with its headquarters in Moscow, would include representatives of the General Staffs of all the participating countries.

(*d*) Deployment of the joint armed forces in the territories of member-States would be carried out "in accordance with the requirements of mutual defense and by agreement between these States."

(*e*) The participation of the German Democratic Republic would be examined later.

At the first meeting of the Political Consultative Committee on Jan. 27–28, 1956, it was decided to incorporate contingents of a new East German Army in the joint command of the Warsaw Treaty Powers.

The Political Consultative Committee

Other important decisions taken at the first meeting of the Political Consultative Committee related to the organization of the Committee itself. It was decided that (a) the Committee would meet as often as necessary, but at least twice a year (meetings have, in fact, been less frequent); and (b) two subsidiary bodies—a Permanent Commission to make recommendations on foreign policy, and a Secretariat—should be set up.

Delegations sent by member-countries to the Political Consultative Committee generally include the First Secretary of the Party, the Chairman of the Council of Ministers, the Minister of Defense, and the Foreign Minister of each country. [14704A]

The Political Consultative Committee decided in Budapest on March 17, 1969, to endorse new statutes on:

(a) the permanent committee of member-countries' Defense Ministers;

(b) the joint supreme command;

(c) the appointment of deputy supreme commanders from the national general staffs to the joint supreme command;

(d) participation of generals and other officers from member-countries in the various commands of the armed forces in proportion to the member-countries' share in the combined forces; and

(e) the establishment of a co-ordinating authority for warfare and types of armament. [23261A]

Subsequent Developments

Membership
Although the membership of the Warsaw Treaty Organization has not formally changed since the treaty's inception in 1955, one member, Albania, did not participate in the activities of the Organization after the severance of relations with the Soviet Union in 1961, and announced its withdrawal from the Warsaw Pact on Sept. 12, 1968, on the ground that by the Soviet invasion of Czechoslovakia on Aug. 20–21, 1968, the Pact had been turned "from a treaty of defense against imperialist aggression into an aggressive treaty against the Socialist countries themselves." [22944A]

Hungary briefly withdrew from the Warsaw Pact on Oct. 31, 1956, at the time of the popular uprising in Hungary, but returned to the organization under the Soviet-oriented Government which replaced the revolutionary Government after the insurrection had been put down. [15189A]

Strength of Forces
According to the British Defense White Paper published on Feb. 19, 1970, the Warsaw Pact forces in Europe numbered 500,000 officers and men in the member-countries' navies, over 3,000,000 in their armies, and over 1,000,000 in air and rocket forces. There were some 30 Soviet divisions and 1,900 tactical aircraft permanently stationed in Czechoslovakia, the German Democratic Republic, Hungary, and Poland, and the Soviet western fleet included about 250 submarines (some nuclear-powered), nearly 400 strike and reconnaissance aircraft and 90 sizable surface ships. [23944A]

Declarations and Communiqués
A considerable number of declarations and communiqués have been issued by the Political Consultative Committee, embodying the views of the Warsaw Pact Organization. The most significant of these are listed below:

January 1956. A joint declaration, issued after the meeting held on Jan. 27–28, contained the recommendations that neither East nor West Germany should possess atomic weapons, and that NATO and the Warsaw Treaty Powers should sign a collective security treaty. [14704A]

May 1958. Documents published after the meeting on May 24 included the draft of a proposed non-aggression pact between the Warsaw Treaty Organization and NATO. [16301A]

August 1961. On Aug. 13 the text of a communiqué was issued in which the member-countries of the Warsaw Pact "addressed to the . . . Government of the German Democratic Republic a proposal to establish such control on the borders of West Berlin as would securely block the way for subversive activities against the Socialist countries," thus advocating the building of the wall between East and West Berlin. [*Page 18275*]

July 1966. Two important declarations were issued after the meeting of July 4–6:

(a) Declaration on Strengthening Peace and Security in Europe. This included proposals for the recognition of peaceful coexistence; for the relaxation of military tension in Europe, toward which all military alliances should be simultaneously dissolved; for the setting-up of nuclear-free zones; for a German peace settlement; and for a general European conference on European co-operation and security.

(b) Declaration on the Aggression of the U.S.A. in Vietnam (see page 125). [21651A]

OTHER TREATIES OF COMMUNIST STATES

East European Agreements

Prior to the conclusion of the Warsaw Pact the Soviet Union had concluded bilateral agreements with Czechoslovakia, Yugoslavia, and Poland, and after 1947, the U.S.S.R. made similar bilateral agreements with Romania, Hungary, and Bulgaria.

Later, the Warsaw Pact was supplemented by treaties on the stationing of Soviet troops in East European countries and by bilateral treaties of friendship and mutual assistance concluded among members of the Warsaw Treaty Organization.

Under the Warsaw Treaty the air defenses of the Soviet Union are extended to the other East European countries, whose forces are provided with advanced air defense radar systems, surface-to-air missiles, and fighter interceptors. Nuclear warheads and weapons, however, are kept in Soviet hands.

Bilateral Agreements of the U.S.S.R.
Concluded before 1950
Earlier bilateral treaties between the U.S.S.R. and East European countries, although not formally abrogated, have been superseded by the Warsaw Pact and new bilateral agreements of 1966.

These were the "Treaties of Friendship, Co-operation, and Mutual Assistance" between the U.S.S.R. and:

CZECHOSLOVAKIA	(Dec. 12, 1943)	
YUGOSLAVIA	(April 11, 1945, abrogated by the U.S.S.R. on Sept. 28, 1949)	[6153A] [7168C; 10291A]
POLAND	(April 21, 1945)	[7206A]
ROMANIA	(Feb. 4, 1948)	[9118A]
HUNGARY	(Feb. 18, 1948)	[9118A]
BULGARIA	(March 18, 1948)	[9171B]

In addition to these treaties there is an agreement on Political Co-operation and Economic Aid concluded with Albania on April 17, 1957 (of unlimited duration).

Bilateral Agreements Concluded among East European States, all of 20 Years' Duration

		Abrogated by:	on:
POLAND AND YUGOSLAVIA	March 18, 1946	POLAND	Sept. 9, 1949 [7823B]
CZECHOSLOVAKIA AND YUGOSLAVIA	May 9, 1946	CZECHOSLO-VAKIA	Oct. 4, 1949 [7899B]
ALBANIA AND YUGOSLAVIA	July 10, 1946	YUGOSLAVIA	Nov. 13, 1949 [8016E]
POLAND AND CZECHOSLOVAKIA*	March 10, 1947		[8510C]
BULGARIA AND YUGOSLAVIA	Nov. 27, 1947	BULGARIA	Oct. 1, 1949 [8975A]
HUNGARY AND YUGOSLAVIA	Dec. 8, 1947	HUNGARY	Sept. 30, 1949 [9045C]
BULGARIA AND ALBANIA	Dec. 16, 1947		[9045C]
YUGOSLAVIA AND ROMANIA	Dec. 19, 1947	ROMANIA	Oct. 2, 1949 [9045C]
BULGARIA AND ROMANIA*	Jan. 16, 1948		[9118A]
ROMANIA AND HUNGARY*	Jan. 24, 1948		[9118A]
CZECHOSLOVAKIA AND BULGARIA*	April 23, 1948		[9271B]
BULGARIA AND POLAND	May 29, 1948		[9312D]
HUNGARY AND POLAND*	June 18, 1948		[9118A]
BULGARIA AND HUNGARY*	July 19, 1948		[9434B]
ROMANIA AND CZECHOSLOVAKIA*	July 21, 1948		[9434B]
POLAND AND ROMANIA*	Jan. 26, 1949		[9795B]
CZECHOSLOVAKIA AND HUNGARY*	April 16, 1949		[9945A]

* Renewed, see page 124.

Treaties on Stationing of Soviet Troops in Four East European Countries
Treaties on the stationing of Soviet troops, in amplification of the Warsaw Pact, were concluded by the U.S.S.R. in 1956–57 with:

(a) *Poland* on Dec. 17, 1956; [15275B]

(b) the *German Democratic Republic* on March 12, 1957; [15500C]

(c) *Romania* on April 15, 1957 [15538B] (but, as decided by the Political Consultative Committee of the Warsaw Pact in Moscow on April 24, 1958, all Soviet troops were withdrawn from Romania in that year) [16301A; 16350C]; and

(d) *Hungary* on May 27, 1957. [15644C]

While the treaty with Hungary was of unlimited duration, the three others were limited to the period during which Soviet troops would be stationed in the country concerned, or until the conclusion of a new agreement by the contracting partners.

The treaties were similar in content, that with Poland specifying *inter alia* that: (1) the numbers and locations of Soviet troops in Poland would be defined by special agreements between the two countries; (2) no troop movements outside these locations would be permitted without Polish authorization; (3) Soviet troops in Poland, and their families, would have to respect Polish law and would be subject to the Polish courts; (4) persons committing crimes against Soviet military personnel would bear the same responsibility as for crimes committed against the Polish forces; (5) the Soviet Government would pay for any material damage which might be caused by the actions or negligence of Soviet military personnel in Poland; (6) the Polish Government, in return, could compensate the U.S.S.R. for damage to Soviet property caused by Polish nationals; (7) any disputes would be examined by a Mixed Commission; (8) the two Governments would appoint representatives to deal with any current problems arising out of the presence of Soviet troops in Poland.

The agreement stressed that "the temporary stay of Soviet troops in Poland can in no way affect the sovereignty of the Polish State and cannot lead to any interference in the domestic affairs of Poland." [*15275B*]

Soviet–Czechoslovak Treaty

Following the invasion of Czechoslovakia on Aug. 20, 1968, by troops of the Soviet Union and three other Warsaw Pact member-States, a treaty on the "temporary" stationing of Soviet troops in Czechoslovakia was signed in Prague on Oct. 16, 1968, and came into effect on Oct. 18 after ratification by the two countries.

Article 1 of the treaty stated that the Soviet troops would "remain temporarily on the territory of the C.S.R in order to ensure the security of the countries of the Socialist community against the increasing revanchist strivings of the West German militarist forces." [*23025A*]

Important Treaties Concluded by East Germany

1. Agreement on the Oder-Neisse Frontier

On June 7, 1950, it was announced that agreement had been reached, between the Polish and East German Governments, on the recognition of the Oder-Neisse line as the permanent frontier between East Germany and Poland. This agreement was implemented on July 6, 1950, when a frontier demarcation agreement was signed at the town of Görlitz on the River Neisse. [*10804A; 10876A*]

2. Soviet-East German Treaty of 1955

By this treaty, which was signed on Sept. 20, 1955, and came into force on Oct. 6, 1955, the U.S.S.R. recognized East Germany as a sovereign State. The main provisions are given below:

Art. 1. Both Governments "solemnly confirmed" that their relations were based "on complete equality of rights, mutual respect of sovereignty, and non-interference in domestic affairs." In accordance with this principle, East Germany was henceforth "free to decide questions concerning its internal and foreign policy, including its relations with the German Federal Republic as well as its relations with other States."

Art. 4. (*a*) The Soviet forces at present stationed in East Germany under international (i.e. four-Power) agreements would continue to be stationed there temporarily with the approval of the Government of the German Democratic Republic, and on conditions to be settled by an additional agreement between the two Governments.

(*b*) Soviet forces stationed in East Germany would not interfere in the internal affairs of the German Democratic Republic or in the social and political life of the country.

Art. 5. Both Governments were agreed that it was "their main aim to bring about a peaceful settlement for the whole of Germany by means of appropriate negotiations." To this end they would "make the necessary efforts toward a settlement by a peace treaty and toward the restoration of the unity of Germany on a peaceful and democratic basis." [*14451A*]

At the same time it was agreed that East Germany would take over responsibility for the control of its frontiers and of lines of communications between West Germany and West Berlin crossing East German territory.

123]

Bilateral Treaties of Friendship and Mutual Assistance between the U.S.S.R. and East European States and among the Latter, concluded since 1964

Partners	Date of Signature	Duration (years)	Automatic Extension
U.S.S.R. AND GERMAN DEMOCRATIC REPUBLIC	June 12, 1964	20	once for 10 years [20138A]
U.S.S.R. AND POLAND	April 8, 1965	20	every 5 years [20713A]
POLAND AND CZECHOSLOVAKIA	March 1, 1967	20	once for 5 years [21981A]
POLAND AND GERMAN DEMOCRATIC REPUBLIC	March 15, 1967	20	once for 10 years [21981A]
CZECHOSLOVAKIA AND GERMAN DEMOCRATIC REPUBLIC	March 17, 1967	20	once for 10 years [21981A]
POLAND AND BULGARIA	April 6, 1967	20	every 5 years [22049A]
U.S.S.R. AND BULGARIA	May 12, 1967	20	every 5 years [22049A]
HUNGARY AND GERMAN DEMOCRATIC REPUBLIC	May 18, 1967	20	once for 10 years [22089B]
BULGARIA AND GERMAN DEMOCRATIC REPUBLIC	Sept. 7, 1967	20	once for 10 years [22300A]
U.S.S.R. AND HUNGARY	Sept. 7, 1967	20	every 5 years [22263A]
BULGARIA AND CZECHOSLOVAKIA	April 26, 1968	20	every 5 years [22690C]
POLAND AND HUNGARY	May 16, 1968	20	every 5 years [22736A]
HUNGARY AND CZECHOSLOVAKIA	June 14, 1968	20	every 5 years
ROMANIA AND CZECHOSLOVAKIA	Aug. 16, 1968	20	every 5 years [22892]
HUNGARY AND BULGARIA	July 10, 1969	20	every 5 years [23519A]
U.S.S.R. AND CZECHOSLOVAKIA	May 6, 1970	20	every 5 years [23987A]
U.S.S.R. AND ROMANIA	July 7, 1970	20	every 5 years [24096A]
POLAND AND ROMANIA	Nov. 12, 1970	20	every 5 years [24314A]
BULGARIA AND ROMANIA	Nov. 19, 1970	20	every 5 years [24539A]
HUNGARY AND ROMANIA	Feb. 24, 1972	20	every 5 years [25171A]
ROMANIA AND GERMAN DEMOCRATIC REPUBLIC	May 12, 1972	20	once for 5 years [25457A]

The Treaties concluded by the German Democratic Republic contain references to (a) rejection of the German Federal Republic's claim to represent the whole of Germany, and (b) recognition of West Berlin as "an independent political unit" (i.e. not part of the German Federal Republic). Other provisions contained in the various bilateral treaties are: a reference to the principles of peaceful coexistence and those of the U.N. Charter; guarantees of the postwar frontiers in Europe (including the Oder-Neisse frontier between Germany and Poland and the frontier between East and West Germany); rejection of the 1938 Munich Agreement on Czechoslovakia as "invalid *ab initio*"; a refusal to permit access to nuclear weapons by the German Federal Republic; in the event of an armed attack on either of the contracting parties, immediate assistance, including military aid; and an undertaking to "communicate and consult with one another on all important international problems which concern them."

The bilateral treaties concluded by the Soviet Union since 1967, contrary to Article 4 of the Warsaw Treaty, do not limit the obligation of mutual assistance to an attack in Europe but call for all-round military assistance against aggression by "any State or combination of States."

Other Treaties of East European Countries
Treaties of Friendship and Co-operation were concluded between:

CZECHOSLOVAKIA AND CAMBODIA on Nov. 27, 1960;
CZECHOSLOVAKIA AND YEMEN on April 4, 1964;
BULGARIA AND YEMEN on April 9, 1964;
EAST GERMANY AND TANZANIA on May 17, 1964;
HUNGARY AND YEMEN on May 20, 1964.

A Treaty of Friendship and Mutual Aid was concluded between BULGARIA AND MONGOLIA on July 23, 1967. [22180B]

A 20-year Treaty of Friendship and Co-operation between the GERMAN DEMOCRATIC REPUBLIC AND MONGOLIA was signed on Sept. 12, 1968, replacing an earlier treaty of Aug. 22, 1957. [22979A]

Bilateral Treaties Between the U.S.S.R. and Asian Communist Countries

Since before World War II the Soviet Union has concluded a number of treaties with Asian Communist countries.

1. Treaties with Mongolia
Both the first and the most recent of such agreements were made with the People's Republic of Mongolia:

(a) Ten-year Treaty of Mutual Assistance, signed on March 28, 1936. [2051F]

(b) Twenty-year Treaty of Friendship and Mutual Assistance, signed on Feb. 27, 1946. [7765E]

(c) Twenty-year Treaty of Friendship, Co-operation and Mutual Assistance, signed on Jan. 15, 1966. [21209A]

2. Treaties with the People's Republic of China

(*a*) Thirty-year Treaty of Friendship, Alliance, and Mutual Assistance, signed on Feb. 14, 1950. [*10540A*]

(*b*) Agreements on political co-operation, signed on Oct. 12, 1954. The agreements were concluded for five years with automatic extension for further periods of five years. [*13855A*]

In view of the Sino-Soviet ideological dispute, these treaties must be regarded as defunct.

3. Treaty with North Korea

Treaty of Friendship, Co-operation, and Mutual Assistance, signed on July 6, 1961, for the duration of ten years. [*18246A*]

These Soviet treaties of friendship and mutual assistance, although they each contain clauses relating to the particular country forming the second party, have certain provisions in common. These are:

(*a*) Automatic mutual assistance in the event of one of the parties being an object of armed attack.

(*b*) An agreement not to conclude any alliance directed against the other party.

(*c*) An agreement on mutual consultation on all important international problems affecting the common interests of both.

(*d*) The development and consolidation of economic and cultural ties between the two countries.

Agreements on the Support of North Vietnam

The countries of the Communist Bloc have expressed their support for the Democratic Republic of Vietnam in multilateral and bilateral declarations. Practical support takes the form of short-term agreements—generally contained within the framework of the declarations—by which North Vietnam is to be given aid, mainly of a financial and economic nature. Although the exact content of these agreements is not known, they are generally concerned with the supplying of industrial products and equipment (both probably of a military nature) to North Vietnam on favorable terms.

The most important declarations and agreements are given below:

1. "Declaration on the Aggression of the U.S.A. in Vietnam"

This declaration was issued by the countries of the Warsaw Treaty Organization at a meeting of the Political Consultative Committee (see page 121) in Bucharest on July 4–6, 1966. [*21651A*]

The declaration said: "The parties to the Warsaw Treaty: (1) most resolutely warn the Government of the United States of the responsibility it assumes before mankind by continuing and expanding this war for all the unforeseeable consequences that may arise from this for the United States itself, among others; (2) are rendering and will go on rendering the Democratic Republic of Vietnam ever-increasing moral and political support and every kind of assistance, including economic help and assistance with the means of defense, materials, equipment, and experts which are needed to repulse victoriously the American aggression, taking the requirements of the new phase of the war in Vietnam into due account; (3) declare their readiness, if the Government of the Democratic Republic of Vietnam requests it, to allow their volunteers to go to Vietnam in order to help the Vietnamese people in their struggle against the American aggressors. . . ." [*Page 21771*]

2. Agreements between the U.S.S.R. and North Vietnam

Economic aid agreements between the Soviet Union and North Vietnam were signed on July 12, 1965, and Dec. 21, 1965. In January 1966 a new agreement on Soviet aid to North Vietnam was signed, as stated in the communiqué issued after the visit of a Soviet delegation to North Vietnam Jan. 7–13, 1966. [*Pages 21351; 21355*]

Further agreements signed in Moscow on Nov. 28, 1968, provided for "considerable" supplies to Vietnam by the Soviet Union, including armaments and equipment "necessary for the strengthening of the defense potential of the Democratic Republic of Vietnam and the development of its economy." [*23107D*]

On Oct. 15, 1970, similar agreements, including also the granting of long-term credits, were signed in Moscow. [*23639A*]

3. Agreement between the Soviet Union and the People's Republic of China

Following Soviet complaints early in 1967 of Chinese interference with Soviet military equipment intended for North Vietnam, the Soviet Union and China signed an agreement at the beginning of March 1967, whereby Soviet aid passing through China would be handed over to North Vietnamese representatives at the Soviet frontier instead of at the North Vietnamese frontier as previously. [*Page 22633*]

4. Agreements between other East European countries and North Vietnam

Agreements to supply economic aid to North Vietnam were made by:

POLAND	on June 12, 1965;
BULGARIA	on June 21, 1965;
HUNGARY	on Dec. 28, 1965;
EASTERN GERMANY	on Dec. 30, 1965. [*Page 21351*]

Bilateral Treaties Between the U.S.S.R. and Non-Communist Countries

1. Treaty of Friendship, Co-operation, and Mutual Assistance with Finland

Signed on April 6, 1948, the treaty was concluded for 10 years. A protocol extending the treaty for a further 20 years was signed on Sept. 19, 1955, and it is automatically renewable for 5-year periods after 1975, unless abrogated by one party one year before the date of expiration.

The treaty differs from other treaties of mutual assistance made by the Soviet Union, in that the obligation to intervene with military assistance in the event of aggression by a third party is restricted to the U.S.S.R. Finland is obliged only to fight any aggression on her own territory.

The main provisions of the treaty are given below.

Art. 1. In the event of Finland or the Soviet Union, across the territory of Finland, becoming the object of military aggression on the part of Germany or any State allied to the latter, Finland, loyal to her duty as an independent State, will fight to repulse the aggression. In doing so, she will direct all the forces at her disposal to the defense of the inviolability of her territory on land, on sea, and in the air, acting within her boundaries in accordance with her obligations under the present treaty with the assistance, in case of need, of the Soviet Union or jointly with the latter.

In the cases indicated above, the Soviet Union will render Finland the necessary assistance, in regard to the granting of which the parties will agree between themselves.

Art. 6. The parties undertake to observe the principles of mutual respect for their State sovereignty and independence, as well as of non-interference in the domestic affairs of the other State. [*9228A*]

On July 20, 1970, the Treaty was extended for another 20 years (i.e. until 1990), and on April 20, 1971, a further treaty was signed in Moscow on economic, technical, and industrial co-operation between the two countries. [*24115B; 24707A*]

2. Treaties with Iran

(*a*) Soviet-Iranian Treaty signed on Feb. 26, 1921

This treaty, between Iran and the Russian Socialist Federative Soviet Republic (RSFSR), consists of a preamble, 26 articles, and an exchange of Notes.

The provisions of the treaty included: Russian renunciation of all privileges which Iran had allowed Czarist Russia; the annulling of all treaties concerning Iran made by the former Russian regime with third powers; the opening of the Caspian Sea to Iran, in return for which Iran conceded fishing rights to the RSFSR; the restoration to validity of Iran's frontiers of 1881; and the cancellation of debts arising out of Czarist loans.

The most significant articles of the treaty are Articles 5 and 6. In Article 5 the two Governments agreed: (1) not to permit the creation or presence on their territory of any organization or group hostile to the RSFSR, Iran, or their allies; (2) not to permit any third party to import into, or convey through, the territory of either of the partners to the treaty any materials which could be used against the other partner; (3) to prevent, with all the means at their command, the presence of any military forces of a third power on their territory, in case the presence of such forces could be interpreted as a threat to the borders, the interests or the security of the other partner to the treaty.

Article 6 read as follows:

If a third party should attempt to carry out a policy of usurpation by means of armed intervention in Iran, or if such Power should desire to use Iran's territory as a base of operations against Russia, or if a foreign Power should threaten the frontiers of Federal Russia (i.e. the RSFSR) or those of its allies, and if the Iranian Government should not be able to put a stop to such menace after having been called upon to do so by Russia, Russia shall have the right to advance her troops into the interior of Iran for the purpose of carrying out the military operations necessary for its defense.

In the exchange of notes Iran asked for clarification of Articles 5 and 6. The clarification given by the RSFSR read as follows:

"Articles 5 and 6 are intended to apply only to cases in which preparations have been made for a considerable armed attack upon Russia, or the Soviet Republics allied to her, by the partisans of the regime which has been overthrown (i.e., the Czarist regime), or by its supporters among the foreign Powers which are in a position to assist the enemies of the Workers' and Peasants' Republics and at the same time to possess themselves, by force or by underhand methods, of part of Iran's territory."

(*b*) Amended Soviet-Iranian treaty signed on Oct. 1, 1927

This new treaty embodied the clarification of Articles 5 and 6 of the 1921 treaty, and also included a new Article providing for the neutrality of either party should the other be involved in conflict with one or several powers.

During Soviet-Iranian negotiations for a non-aggression treaty from Jan. 29 to Feb. 11, 1959, Iran requested the annulment of Articles 5 and 6 of the 1921 treaty, as being no longer applicable to the situation. The Iranian request was, however, refused by the U.S.S.R., and on this point—and others—the negotiations broke down. [*16769A*]

3. Treaty with Afghanistan

A Treaty of Neutrality and Non-Aggression was concluded between the Soviet Union and Afghanistan in 1931. On Dec. 18, 1955, the treaty was extended for ten years, and on Aug. 6, 1965, it was extended for a further ten years. [*Page 14606; 20938A*]

4. Spitsbergen Treaty with Norway
Under a treaty between the Soviet Union and Norway, concluded on Feb. 9, 1920, Spitsbergen, or Svalbard (to the north of Norway) was made a demilitarized area "unable to be used for war purposes." [*21061B*]

5. Treaty with Egypt
A Treaty of Friendship and Co-operation between the Soviet Union and the United Arab Republic was signed on May 27, 1971, for fifteen years and automatically renewable every five years unless one year's notice of termination was given by one of the parties. It came into force on July 1, 1971.

The Treaty provided, *inter alia,* that the two countries would "continue with the utmost determination to exert efforts toward achieving and ensuring a lasting and just peace in the Middle East in accordance with the aims and principles of the U.N. Charter." At the same time it stated that both countries would "continue to develop co-operation in the military field," and added: "Such co-operation will provide specifically for assistance in the training of U.A.R. military personnel and in mastering the arms and equipment supplied to the U.A.R. with a view to strengthening its capacity to eliminate the consequences of the aggression as well as increasing its ability to resist aggression in general." [*24284A; 24704C*]

Notwithstanding this treaty, all Soviet military personnel and advisers, estimated to number 20,000, were withdrawn from Egypt in July 1972 at the request of the Egyptian Government, announced on July 18. [*25397A*]

6. Treaty with India
A 20-year Treaty of Peace, Friendship, and Co-operation between the Soviet Union and India, automatically renewable for five-year periods unless either party gave prior notice of termination, was signed in New Delhi on Aug. 9, 1971.

The Treaty included the following articles:

Art. 2. Guided by the desire to contribute in every possible way toward ensuring the lasting peace and security of their peoples, the High Contracting Parties declare their determination to continue efforts to preserve and strengthen peace in Asia and throughout the world, end the arms race, and achieve general and complete disarmament, covering both nuclear and conventional weapons, under effective international control.

Art. 3. Guided by their devotion to the noble ideal of equality of all peoples and States, irrespective of race or creed, the High Contracting Parties condemn colonialism and racialism in all their forms and manifestations and reaffirm their determination to strive for their final and complete elimination.

The High Contracting Parties will co-operate with other States in achieving these aims and support the just aspirations of the peoples in their struggle against colonialism and racial domination.

Art. 4. The Union of Soviet Socialist Republics respects India's policy of non-alignment and reaffirms that this policy is an important factor for maintaining world peace and international security and for lessening tensions in the world.

The Republic of India respects the peaceful policy of the U.S.S.R. aimed at strengthening friendship and co-operation with all peoples.

Art. 8. In accordance with the traditional friendship established between the two countries, each of the High Contracting Parties solemnly declares that it will not enter into or participate in any military alliances directed against the other party.

Each High Contracting Party undertakes to refrain from any aggression against the other party and not to allow the use of its territory for the commission of any act that might inflict military damage on the other High Contracting Party.

Art. 9. Each High Contracting Party undertakes to abstain from giving any assistance to any third party that engages in an armed conflict with the other party. In the event of either party being subjected to attack or threat thereof, the High Contracting Parties shall immediately enter into mutual consultations with a view to eliminating this threat and taking appropriate effective measures to ensure the peace and security of their countries.

Art. 10. Each High Contracting Party solemnly declares that it will not enter into any commitment, secret or public, with one or more States which is incompatible with the present treaty. Each High Contracting Party further declares that no commitment exists, nor shall any be entered into between itself or any other State or States that might cause military damage to the other party.

In a communiqué issued at the time when the Treaty was signed the Indian Minister of External Affairs referred to "a heavy burden . . . placed on India by the influx of more than seven million refugees" from East Pakistan, and India's "gratitude for the Soviet Union's understanding of the problem," as shown by an appeal by President Podgorny to the President of Pakistan in April 1971.

The Treaty was ratified in New Delhi on Aug. 9 and in Moscow on Aug. 13, 1971. [*24773A; 24820B*]

7. Treaty with Iraq
A 15-year Treaty of Friendship and Co-operation between the Soviet Union and Iraq, automatically renewable for periods of five years, was signed in Baghdad on April 9, 1972.

Article 1 of the treaty provided for all-round co-operation in the political, economic, trade, scientific, technical, and other fields "on the basis of respect for State sovereignty, territorial integrity, and non-interference in one another's internal affairs."

In Article 4 both countries condemned "imperialism and colonialism in all their forms and manifestations" and undertook to "continue to wage an undeviating struggle against imperialism and Zionism. . . ."

Article 8 laid down that "in the event of situations which threaten the peace of either of the sides or create a threat to peace or the danger of a violation of peace" both countries would "immediately contact each other with the aim of co-ordinating their positions. . . ."

In Article 9 the two sides undertook to "continue to develop co-operation in the strengthening of their defense capabilities."

In Article 10 each of the two sides declared that it would "not enter into alliances or take part in any groupings of States or actions or undertakings" directed against the other side, and would "not permit the use of its territory for any act capable of doing military harm to the other side." [25201A]

The treaty came into force after the exchange of ratification documents in Moscow on July 20, 1972.

Bilateral Treaties Concluded by the People's Republic of China

Treaties with Asian Neighbors

Since 1950 the People's Republic of China has concluded a number of border-treaties, non-aggression pacts, and treaties of friendship with its neighbors in Asia, thus securing and safeguarding its position within Asia.

		Date
1. TIBET. Agreement whereby Tibet recognized China's suzerainty, and China, Tibet's autonomy. (The enforced reintegration of Tibet in 1959 nullified this agreement.)		May 23, 1951 [11610A; 16797A]
2. DEMOCRATIC REPUBLIC OF VIETNAM. Treaty of Friendship and Good Neighborly Relations.		July 7, 1955
3. BURMA. (a) Treaty of Friendship and Non-aggression; (b) Agreement on the settlement of border problems;		Jan. 28, 1960 [17278D; 17749A]
(c) Boundary treaty (incorporating (b) and full details of frontier line).		Oct. 1, 1960
4. THE MONGOLIAN PEOPLE'S REPUBLIC. (a) Treaty of Friendship and Mutual Economic Aid; (b) Frontier agreement.		May 31, 1960 Dec. 26, 1962
5. NEPAL. (a) Agreement on settlement of border problems; (b) Treaty of Peace and Friendship; (c) Boundary Treaty.		March 21, 1960 April 28, 1960 Oct. 5, 1961 [17380A; 17743A; 19024A]
6. AFGHANISTAN. (a) Treaty of Friendship and Non-aggression; (b) Border Treaty.		Aug. 27, 1960 Nov. 24, 1963 [17638C; 19761E]

	Date
7. CAMBODIA. Treaty of Friendship and Non-aggression.	Dec. 19, 1960 [18013A]
8. DEMOCRATIC PEOPLE'S REPUBLIC OF KOREA. Treaty of Friendship, Co-operation, and Mutual Assistance. This treaty is similarly worded to the treaties of mutual assistance made by the U.S.S.R. with Mongolia, the People's Republic of China, and North Korea.	July 11, 1961 [18246A]
9. PAKISTAN. (a) Border treaty. This provides for the possibility that, on the settlement of the Kashmir dispute between India and Pakistan, the region covered by the treaty may come under other than Pakistani rule.	March 2, 1963 [19427A]
(b) Protocol on the final demarcation of the frontier.	March 26, 1965 [20694A]

Treaties with European Communist Countries (other than the U.S.S.R.)

The People's Republic of China has concluded a number of treaties of friendship with European Communist States, but in view of the present split of the Communist world into Soviet and Chinese camps (see page 115ff) these treaties, except those with Albania, are probably now worthless.

The treaties, originally valid for ten years and to be automatically extended for a further ten years if neither party should abrogate them, are with:

1. THE GERMAN DEMOCRATIC REPUBLIC	Dec. 25, 1955	[14675A]
2. CZECHOSLOVAKIA	Aug. 27, 1957	
3. HUNGARY	May 6, 1959	

A number of economic agreements were signed by the Albanian and Chinese Governments in 1960 and 1961. An agreement on Chinese technical and scientific aid to Albanian industry was concluded on Oct. 24, 1960, and agreements providing for increased trade and a Chinese loan to Albania were signed on Feb. 3, 1961. [18042A]

Treaties with Other Countries

	Date	
1. GUINEA	Sept. 13, 1960	[18387E]
2. INDONESIA	April 1, 1961	
3. GHANA	Aug. 18, 1961	[18350A]
4. YEMEN	June 9, 1964	[20529A]
5. CONGO (BRAZZAVILLE)	Oct. 2, 1964	[20695A]
6. MALI	Nov. 3, 1964	
7. TANZANIA	Feb. 20, 1965	[20754A]

These treaties of friendship are all similar in content and wording. The treaty with Tanzania opens with a preamble in which the two parties state their desire to consolidate and develop their friendship and to "fight the forces of imperialism." In the principal article of the treaty they undertake to guide their mutual relations by "the Five Principles of mutual respect for sovereignty and territorial integrity, mutual non-aggression, non-interference in each other's internal affairs, equality and mutual benefit, and peaceful coexistence." (See "Bandung Conference," page 208.) Other provisions are for economic and cultural relations, and for peaceful consultation on any question concerning both parties.

Under subsequent Sino-Tanzanian agreements, China sent to Tanzania (a) some 13,000 technicians to work on the construction of a railway line from Tanzania to the copperbelt in Zambia, as agreed in July 1970 [24151B], and

(b) military equipment, including tanks and aircraft. China also undertook to build in Tanzania a naval base, for which the foundation stone was laid in May 1971. [24746A]

China has also had military aid agreements with the Congo (Brazzaville) since 1970. [24724A]

COUNCIL FOR MUTUAL ECONOMIC ASSISTANCE (COMECON OR CMEA)

Members: Bulgaria, Cuba, Czechoslovakia, German Democratic Republic, Hungary, Mongolian People's Republic, Poland, Romania, Soviet Union
Associate Member: Yugoslavia

The decision to establish a Council for Mutual Economic Assistance was made at an economic conference held in Moscow in January 1949 and attended by representatives of Bulgaria, Czechoslovakia, Hungary, Poland, Romania, and the Soviet Union. These countries were the founder-members of the Council for Mutual Economic Assistance (or Comecon as it is generally known), the creation of which was officially announced on Jan. 25, 1949. The purpose of Comecon would be "the exchange of experience in the economic field, and mutual assistance in regard to raw materials, foodstuffs, machinery, equipment, etc." Each of the participating countries would be equally represented on the Council.

It was further stated that the Council would be open for membership to "other countries in Europe which share its principles and desire broad economic co-operation with the countries already represented in it." [9768B]

Albania was admitted to membership in February 1949, but left the Council in 1961 as a result of ideological differences. The German Democratic Republic

entered in October 1950, and the Mongolian People's Republic in June 1962. Mongolia entered Comecon under an amendment to the Charter (see below) permitting the admission of non-European countries to membership. [9832D; 11007B; 18896A; 19186B]

Yugoslavia was admitted to partial membership under an agreement concluded on Sept. 17, 1964. By the terms of this agreement, Yugoslavia would be able to share in the work of Comecon, on a basis of equality and mutual benefit, in the fields of foreign trade, currency and financial relations, ferrous and non-ferrous metallurgy, engineering, the chemical industry, and the co-ordination of scientific and technical research. Yugoslavia's participation became effective on April 24, 1965. [20422A; 20758D]

The COMECON Charter

At its 12th session in December 1959, the Council drafted a Charter, which was signed on Dec. 14, 1959 and came into force on April 13, 1960.

A summary of the Charter is given below:

In the preamble the signatories state their determination "to continue developing all-round economic co-operation on the basis of the consistent implementation of the international socialist division of labor in the interests of building Socialism and Communism in their countries and ensuring a lasting peace throughout the world." They also state their "readiness to develop economic relations with all countries, irrespective of their social and State systems."

Art. 1. The purpose of the CMEA is to facilitate, by uniting and co-ordinating the efforts of the Council's member-countries, the planned development of the national economy, acceleration of economic and technical progress in these countries, a rise in the level of industrialization in countries with less developed industries, uninterrupted growth of labor productivity, and a steady advance of the welfare of the peoples in the Council's member-countries.

Art. 2 deals with membership of the CMEA. Membership is open to any European country sharing the Council's aims and principles. Any member-country may leave the Council with six months' notice. This article was amended at the 16th session of the Council, when admission to membership was extended to non-European countries.

Art. 3 states the functions of the CMEA to be to:
(a) "organize all-round economic, scientific and technical co-operation of all the Council's member-countries in the most rational use of their natural resources and acceleration of the development of their productive forces"; and
(b) "assist the Council's member-countries in elaborating and carrying out joint measures for:
(i) the development of the industry and agriculture of the Council's member-countries; (ii) the development of transport . . . ; (iii) the most efficient use of principal capital investments allocated by the Council's member-countries for the development of the mining and manufacturing industries and for the construction of major projects which are of interest to two countries or more;

(iv) the development of trade and exchange of services between the Council's member-countries and between them and other countries; (v) the exchange of scientific and technical achievements and advanced production experience."

Art. 4 states that "recommendations shall be made on questions of economic, scientific, and technical co-operation" and on "decisions on organizational and procedural matters." Recommendations and decisions apply only to those members who have declared an interest in the question from which they arise.

Art. 5 names the constituent organs of the Council as the Session of the Council; the Conference of Members' Representatives (since replaced by the Executive Committee); the Standing Commissions; and the Secretariat.

Arts. 6, 7, 8 and 9 give details of the composition and functions of the organs of the Council.

The remaining articles deal with the Council's international relations and financial arrangements, and with such matters as the ratification and amending of the Charter.

Organization of the Council

Summit Conferences
Since June 1962 the first secretaries of the Central Committees of the Communist and Workers' Parties and the Heads of Government of the member-countries of Comecon have met in conference from time to time to discuss the expansion and consolidation of economic co-operation among Comecon countries. At these summit conferences the general lines of Comecon's work are laid down. [18896A]

Session of the Council
The supreme permanent organ of Comecon is the Session of the Council, which meets at least once a year in the capital of each member-country in turn, the host-country providing the chairman for each Session. The program of work discussed at the summit conferences is here determined in greater detail. Recommendations, which must be passed unanimously, are put into effect by inter-governmental agreements.

Executive Committee
The Executive Committee was set up at the 16th Session of the Council on July 7, 1962. It consists of Deputy Prime Ministers of the Comecon member-countries, their deputies, and advisers. Meetings are held at least every two months, the function of the Committee being to co-ordinate national economic development plans and to supervise collaboration in scientific and technical research. A branch of the Executive Committee is the Bureau for Common Questions of Economic Planning, in which each Comecon country is represented by the Deputy Chairman of the State Planning Organization. [18896A]

Secretariat
The Secretariat consists, at present, of the Secretary of the Council and six Deputy Secretaries. It is responsible for preparation of material for the Council, the Committee, and the Permanent Commissions, and for the drafting of reports and the compiling of statistics.

Permanent Commissions
Twenty-three Permanent Commissions were set up at various times to study different aspects of Comecon's work. All the Comecon member-countries are represented on each of the committees and sub-committees of the Permanent Commissions.

The Commissions are listed below, together with their date of foundation and present headquarters.

Agriculture	(May 1956; Sofia)
Forestry	(May 1956; Bucharest)
Power	(May 1956; Moscow)
Coal Industry	(May 1956; Warsaw)
Machine Building	(May 1956; Prague)
Oil and Gas	(May 1956; Bucharest)
Ferrous Metals	(May 1956; Moscow)
Non-ferrous Metals	(May 1956; Budapest)
Chemical Industry	(May 1956; Berlin)
Wood, Cellulose, Paper	(May 1956; Budapest)
Transport	(June 1958; Warsaw)
Construction	(June 1958; Berlin)

Light Industry	(July 1963; Prague)	Created as a single commission in December, 1958
Food Industry	(July 1963; Sofia)	
Economic Questions	(1958; Moscow)	
Foreign Trade	(May 1959; Moscow)	
Peaceful Uses of Atomic Energy	(Sept. 1960; Moscow)	
Standardization	(June 1962; Berlin)	
Co-ordination of Scientific and Technical Research	(June 1962; Moscow)	
Statistics	(June 1962; Moscow)	
Finance and Currency	(Dec. 1962; Moscow)	
Radio and Electronics Industries	(July 1963; Budapest)	
Geology	(July 1963; Ulan-Bator)	

The creation of a Permanent Commission for Posts and Telecommunications was decided upon by the Council at its 25th Session held in Bucharest, July 27–29, 1971.

The Permanent Commission for the Co-ordination of Scientific and Technical Research was at the same time replaced by a Committee for Scientific and Technical Co-operation, and a Committee for Co-operation in the Sphere of Planning was also set up. [24978A]

International Investment Bank

An International Investment Bank, with its seat in Moscow, was set up on July 10, 1970, by 7 countries as founder-members (Bulgaria, Czechoslovakia, the German Democratic Republic, Hungary, Mongolia, Poland, and the Soviet Union). [24137A] Romania became a member of the bank on Jan. 12, 1971. [245-56B]

Starting operations on Jan. 1, 1971, with initial capital subscriptions totaling 175,000,000 rubles (to be increased by another 175,000,000 rubles in 1972 and a total of 650,000,000 in later years), the bank was to concentrate resources for capital construction and for co-ordinated expenditure through the granting of long- and medium-term credits. Membership subscriptions were based on the volume of members' exports in mutual trade turnover, with the Soviet Union providing nearly 40 percent and Eastern Germany about 17.6 percent of the capital. The bank was also authorized to use loans and investments from third countries.   [24556B]

International Bank for Economic Co-operation

An International Bank for Economic Co-operation, formed by Comecon's eight member-countries with an initial capital of 60,000,000 rubles (to be increased to 300,000,000 rubles within five years) came into being on Jan. 1, 1964.   [19911A]

Other Institutions

Other permanent bodies created by the Council are a Working Party for the Co-ordination and Delivery of Finished Articles (founded probably in 1959) and a Central Dispatcher Administration (founded in 1962).

A Standardization Institute was established in 1964, its function being the creation of a progressive standardization of industrial products among the Comecon member-countries.   [19911A]

The creation of an International Institute of Economic Problems of the World Socialist System was approved by Comecon's Executive Committee on July 24, 1970.

Division of Labor

The work of Comecon is largely based on the principle of the division of labor. In Sessions of the Council from 1956 to 1961 a number of plans were approved for specialization, in various industries, among the Comecon countries. At the Session of the Council from Dec. 12–15, 1961, the draft of the "Fundamental Principles of International Socialist Division of Labor" was adopted. The details of the document were published on June 17, 1962. Described as "a planned and consciously molded process, which takes into consideration the objectively operating economic laws of Socialism," the Principles are contrasted with the competitive system of capitalist international division. All later resolutions of Comecon in the field of the division of labor are based on this document.

"Complex Program"

The Council published on Aug. 7, 1971, a "Complex Program for the Further Deepening and Improvement of Co-operation and Development of the Socialist Economic Integration of the CMEA Member-Countries."

The purpose of the program was stated to be "the promotion of the growth of the economic power of the Socialist world system and the strengthening of the economic system of each country." Socialist economic integration, however, was to take place on the basis of "complete voluntariness" and would not be linked with the creation of supra-national organs. There would be intensified co-operation in planning, with joint forecasts for energy, petrochemicals, and automative systems in the period 1971–75, and also in joint research projects in science and technology.

The program further provided for a new form of trading, i.e. trade in non-quota goods which would not need to be balanced bilaterally but would, for clearing purposes, be counted in the total trade of the respective countries.

The "transferable rouble" (the collective currency used for accounting in the internal Comecon clearing accounts but not transferable otherwise) was to be strengthened so as to attain "real transferability" and be used in clearings with non-Comecon countries, and new parities would be established between the currencies of the member-States and in relation to the "transferable ruble."

The proposed increased co-operation was to include the creation of a network of express trains and of long-distance roads, joint shipping enterprises, and the introduction of standardized container transport systems.

The negotiations on the "Complex Program" during the Council's 25th session in Bucharest, July 27–29, 1971, revealed "serious controversy on questions of integration," and, in particular, strong reservations on any surrender of a country's sovereignty to Comecon were expressed by Romania.   [24978A]

Scientific Co-operation

The Eastern Joint Institute for Nuclear Research at Dubna (U.S.S.R.)
A preliminary agreement on the establishment of an Eastern Joint Institute for Nuclear Research, made on March 26, 1956, was implemented on July 12, 1956. The members of the joint Institute are Albania, Bulgaria, Czechoslovakia, the German Democratic Republic, Hungary, North Korea, the Mongolian People's Republic, Poland, Romania, the Soviet Union, and the Democratic Republic of Vietnam. The People's Republic of China, formerly a member, withdrew its scientists in July 1966.

On its inception the Joint Institute comprised the former Institute of Nuclear Problems and Electrophysical Laboratory of the Soviet Academy of Sciences. Its equipment included one synchrotron generating 10,000,000,000 electron volts and another generating 680,000,000 electron volts. Other sections of the Institute, which have come into operation since its establishment, are the Laboratory of High Energies, which began operating in 1957; the Laboratory of Neutron Physics, equipped with an experimental fast neutron pulse reactor (in operation since 1960); and a Laboratory of Nuclear Reactions equipped with a cyclotron for accelerating multicharged ions (also coming into operation in 1960). The Joint Institute also has a Computing Center and a Radiochemical Laboratory.

The supreme authority of the Joint Institute is the Committee of Government Plenipotentiaries, the members of which are the heads of the atomic energy authorities of the member-countries. The Committee is responsible for policy and finance. The program of work is the responsibility of a Scientific Council, while the practical administration is carried out by a Management consisting of a Director, two Vice-Directors and an Administrative Manager. *[14987D]*

Other Scientific Centers

Agreements signed in Moscow on April 28, 1971, provided for the establishment of seven new scientific centers to study such matters as new chemical compounds, prevention of pollution, control of weeds and agricultural pests, automated systems for medical institutions, anti-corrosion measures, research in biological physics, and uses of timber. *[24595A]*

Admission of Cuba

At the Council's 26th session, held in Moscow July 10–12, 1972, Cuba was unanimously admitted as a full member of Comecon.

In the communiqué issued at the end of the session, it was stated that from 1970 to 1971 the Comecon member-countries had increased their national income by 6.3 percent; their industrial output by 7.8 percent; their transactions in "transferable rubles" by 11 percent; and their foreign trade by 8.3 percent, that with the rest of the world having risen by 8.5 percent.

Increasing Participation by Yugoslavia

At the same time the Yugoslav Federal Prime Minister signed a protocol on the undertaking of joint projects between Comecon member-countries and Yugoslavia. *[25402A]*

9

East-West Treaties of 1970-72

In the pursuit of a policy of negotiation rather than confrontation between Western Governments and those of Communist countries, a number of treaties and agreements designed to increase *détente* and to normalize relations were concluded in 1970–72.

1. Western Germany and Soviet Union

A treaty on the renunciation of the use of force in relations between the West German and Soviet Governments was signed in Moscow on Aug. 12, 1970.

The operative Articles of the Treaty were as follows:

Art. 1. The Union of Soviet Socialist Republics and the Federal Republic of Germany regard the maintenance of international peace and the achievement of the relaxation of tension as a major objective of their policies.

They affirm their desire to promote the normalization of the situation in Europe and the development of peaceful relations between all European States, and in so doing proceed from the actual situation existing in this region.

Art. 2. The Federal Republic of Germany and the U.S.S.R. shall be guided in their mutual relations, as well as in matters concerning the safeguarding of European and international security, by the aims and principles set out in the Charter of the United Nations. Accordingly, they will settle their disputes exclusively by peaceful means and undertake, in accord with Article 2 of the U.N. Charter, to refrain from the threat of force or the use of force in any matters affecting security in Europe and international security, as well as in their mutual relations.

Art. 3. In conformity with the foregoing aims and principles set out above, the U.S.S.R. and the Federal Republic of Germany share the realization that peace in Europe can only be maintained if no one disturbs the present frontiers.

They undertake to respect the territorial integrity of all States in Europe within their existing frontiers;

They declare that they have no territorial claims whatsoever against anybody, and will not assert such claims in the future;

They regard as inviolable now and in the future the frontiers of all States in Europe as they are on the date of the signing of this treaty, including the Oder-Neisse line, which forms the western frontier of the Polish People's Republic, and the frontier between the Federal Republic of Germany and the German Democratic Republic.

Art. 4. The present Treaty between the U.S.S.R. and the Federal Republic of Germany does not affect any bilateral or multilateral treaties and agreements previously concluded by them.

Art. 5. The present Treaty is subject to ratification and shall come into force on the date of exchange of the instruments of ratification, which will take place in Bonn.

The West German Government, also on Aug. 12, published the following letter sent by the West German Foreign Minister to his Soviet counterpart:

In connection with today's signature of the Treaty between the Federal Republic of Germany and the Union of Soviet Socialist Republics, the Government of the Federal Republic of Germany has the honor to state that this Treaty does not conflict with the political objective of the Federal Republic of Germany to work for a state of peace in Europe in which the German nation will recover its unity in free self-determination.

The West German Government simultaneously advised the Governments of Britain, France, and the U.S.A. that it had been made clear in the negotiations that the Treaty did not affect the rights of the Four Powers "reflected in the known treaties and agreements" (i.e. the Potsdam agreements).

The West German Government also advised the Governments of Britain, France, and the U.S.A. that its Foreign Minister had declared:

The question of the rights of the Four Powers is in no way connected with the Treaty which the Federal Republic of Germany and the Union of Soviet Socialist Republics intend to conclude, and is not affected by it.

It added that the Soviet Foreign Minister had declared:

The question of the rights of the Four Powers will also not be affected by the Treaty which the Union of Soviet Socialist Republics and the Federal Republic of Germany intend to conclude. This is the attitude of the Soviet Government in this matter.

The treaty was ratified in Western Germany on May 23, 1972, coming into force on the following day, and by the Presidium of the Supreme Soviet on May 31.

2. Western Germany and Poland

A treaty normalizing relations between the Federal Republic of Germany and Poland was published on Nov. 20, 1970, the two Governments having agreed as follows:

Art. 1. (1) The Federal Republic of Germany and the People's Republic of Poland state in mutual agreement that the existing boundary line, the course of which is laid down in Chapter IX of the Decisions of the Potsdam Conference of Aug. 2, 1945, as running from the Baltic Sea immediately west of Swinemünde, and thence along the Oder River to the confluence of the western Neisse River and along the western Neisse to the Czechoslovak frontier, shall constitute the western State frontier of the People's Republic of Poland.

[The Polish text defined Poland's western frontier as "running from the Baltic Sea immediately west of Swinoujscie and thence along the Odra River to the confluence of the Lusatian Nysa river and along the Lusatian Nysa to the Czechoslovak frontier."]

(2) They reaffirm the inviolability of their existing frontiers now and in the future and undertake to respect each other's territorial integrity without restriction.

(3) They declare that they have no territorial claims whatsoever against each other and that they will not assert such claims in the future.

Art. 2. (1) The Federal Republic of Germany and the People's Republic of Poland shall in their mutual relations, as well as in matters of ensuring European and international security, be guided by the purposes and principles embodied in the Charter of the United Nations.

(2) Accordingly they shall, pursuant to Articles 1 and 2 of the U.N. Charter, settle all their disputes exclusively by peaceful means and refrain from any threat or use of force in matters affecting European and international security and in their mutual relations.

Art. 3. (1) The Federal Republic of Germany and the People's Republic of Poland shall take further steps toward full normalization and a comprehensive development of their mutual relations, of which the present treaty shall form the solid foundation.

(2) They agree that a broadening of their co-operation in the sphere of economic, scientific, technological, cultural, and other relations is in their mutual interest.

Art. 4. The present treaty shall not affect any bilateral or multilateral international arrangements previously concluded by either Contracting Party or concerning them.

Art. 5. The present treaty is subject to ratification and shall enter into force on the date of exchange of the instruments of ratification, which shall take place in Bonn.

The Treaty was signed in Warsaw on Dec. 7, 1970, by Herr Brandt, the German Federal Chancellor, and Mr. Cyrankiewicz, the President of Poland.

The treaty was ratified by Western Germany on May 23, 1972, and by the Polish Council of State on May 26, 1972.

Simultaneously with the approval of this treaty and of that concluded between the German Federal Government and the Soviet Union of Aug. 12, 1970, the parties represented in the Bundestag (the West German Lower House of Parliament) adopted, with only five abstentions, a resolution specifying that the treaties did not affect "the [German people's] inalienable right to self-determination" and declaring: "The policy of the Federal Republic of Germany, which aims at a peaceful restoration of national unity within the European framework, is not inconsistent with the treaties." The resolution also reiterated the Bundestag's view that "the final settlement of the German question as a whole" was "still outstanding," but emphasized that the Federal Republic advocated the normalization of relations with the German Democratic Republic.

It was only after agreement on the above resolution that the Opposition (of the Christian Democratic and Christian Social Unions) decided to abstain from voting on the treaties rather than against their approval.

3. Canada and Soviet Union

A Protocol on Consultations signed in Moscow on May 19, 1971, provided for regular consultation between the two countries on "important international problems of mutual interest . . . with the aim of facilitating a relaxation of tension, the development of co-operation, and the strengthening of security," and for such consultation to be held "without delay" in "the event of a situation which, in the opinion of the two Governments, endangers the maintenance of peace or involves a breach of the peace." [24675A]

4. Four-Power Agreement on Status of Berlin

Talks between the Ambassadors of Britain, France, and the United States to the German Federal Republic and the Soviet Ambassador to the German Democratic Republic led to the conclusion of an agreement on Berlin, the first part of which was signed on Sept. 3, 1971.

The four Powers agreed "to promote the elimination of tension" in the area, to settle disputes solely by peaceful means, and to "respect their individual and joint rights and responsibilities." They declared that transit traffic between West Berlin and the Federal Republic would be "unimpeded," "facilitated so as to take place in the most simple and expeditious manner" and "receive preferential treatment."

The agreement reiterated that the Western sectors of Berlin continued "not to be a constituent part of the Federal Republic of Germany and not to be governed by it."

The Government of the U.S.S.R. declared: "Communications between the Western sectors of Berlin and areas bordering on these sectors and those areas of the German Democratic Republic which do not border on these sectors will be improved. Permanent residents of the Western sectors will be able to travel to and visit such areas for compassionate, family, religious, cultural, or commercial reasons, or as tourists, under conditions comparable to those applying to other persons entering these areas. . . ."

On the status of West Berlin the three Western Powers agreed as follows:

(1) The ties between the Western sectors of Berlin and the Federal Republic of Germany will be maintained and developed, taking into account that these sectors continue not to be a constituent part of the Federal Republic of Germany and not to be governed by it. The provisions of the Basic Law of the Federal Republic of Germany and of the Constitution operative in the Western sectors of Berlin which contradict the above have been suspended and continue not to be in effect.

(2) The Federal President, the Federal Government, the Bundesversammlung [joint session of Parliament], the Bundesrat [Upper House], and the Bundestag [Lower House], including their committees and Fraktionen [Parliamentary party groups], as well as other State bodies of the Federal Republic of Germany, will not perform in the Western sectors of Berlin constitutional or official acts which contradict the provisions of paragraph (1).

(3) The Government of the Federal Republic of Germany will be represented in the Western sectors of Berlin to the authorities of the three Governments and to the Senate by a permanent liaison agency.

On the question of diplomatic representation the three Western Powers declared:

The Governments of the French Republic, the United Kingdom, and the United States of America maintain their rights and responsibilities relating to the representation abroad of the interests of the Western sectors of Berlin and their permanent residents, including those rights and responsibilities concerning matters of security and status both in international organizations and in relations with other countries.

The three Governments will authorize the establishment of a Soviet consulate-general in the Western sectors of Berlin accredited to the appropriate authorities of the three Governments.

In a final Quadripartite Protocol the four Governments agreed that they would proceed on the basis that the agreements and arrangements concluded between the competent German authorities would enter into force simultaneously with the quadripartite agreement.

The Protocol itself would enter into force on the date of signature. It was finally signed in West Berlin on June 3, 1972. [24813A; 25355A]

5. Other Berlin Agreements

Further Agreements on Berlin were signed in 1971 as follows:

(a) An agreement on transit traffic between the Federal Republic of Germany and West Berlin, concluded by the West and East German Governments and signed in Bonn on Dec. 17, 1971;

(b) an agreement between the Senate of West Berlin and the German Democratic Republic on "Facilitation and Improvement of Traveling and Visiting," signed in East Berlin on Dec. 19, 1971;

(c) an agreement between the Senate of West Berlin and the German Democratic Republic on the "Settlement of the Question of Enclaves by Exchange of Territories," also signed in East Berlin on Dec. 19, 1971. [25095A]

6. France and Soviet Union

In a document laying down "The Principles of Co-operation between the U.S.S.R. and France," signed in Paris on Oct. 29, 1971, the two Governments declared that their co-operation was based on reciprocity of advantages, was not directed against the interests of any people, and did not affect commitments of either country in respect of third States. In the event of situations creating a threat to peace, both Governments would "immediately contact each other with the object of concerting their positions on all aspects of those situations" and on steps which would make it possible to cope with them (as agreed in a protocol signed in Paris on Oct. 13, 1970). Both sides would co-operate closely in Europe, together with other States concerned, "in the maintenance of peace and the pursuit of *détente,* and in the strengthening of security, peaceful relations, and co-operation of all European States, on the basis of unswerving respect for the following principles: inviolability of the present frontiers, non-interference in internal affairs, equality, independence, and renunciation of the use or threat of force." Both parties would also work for "general and complete disarmament, and first of all nuclear disarmament," and "the overcoming of the division of the world into military-political groupings." [24957A; 24360A]

7. Western Germany and Eastern Germany

(a) A "Treaty between the Federal Republic of Germany and the German Democratic Republic on Questions of Traffic" was initialed in Bonn on May 12, 1972, and came into force on May 26.

The contracting States undertook "to the greatest possible extent to allow, to facilitate, and to organize as expeditiously as possible the traffic in and through their sovereign territories, corresponding to normal international practice on the basis of reciprocity and non-discrimination." Traffic would be subject to the law of the State in which it occurred, as far as the treaty did not provide otherwise.

The treaty included provisions for road and rail traffic and inland navigation. The text was supplemented by protocol notes, which stated that "at the proper time" further discussions on passenger and goods traffic would take place, as well as negotiations on an air traffic agreement. A "Notification of the G.D.R. on Travel Facilitations" stated that at the invitation of the G.D.R. citizens of Western Germany would be permitted to visit the G.D.R.

The treaty was approved by the Bundestag (Lower House) on Sept. 22, with no opposing votes and with 9 abstentions; unanimous approval was given by the Bundesrat (Upper House) on Oct. 6. The East German Volkskammer approved the treaty on Oct. 16, and the treaty came into force on the following day. [25355A]

Simultaneously with the traffic treaty a number of new East German travel regulations came into force, setting out conditions under which citizens of the two German States might be permitted to visit the other.

(b) After the signing of the above traffic treaty, the State Secretaries of the German Federal Republic and the German Democratic Republic succeeded in negotiating the terms of a "Basic Treaty" establishing the basis of relations between the two German States, which was initialed on Nov. 8, 1972, and signed on Dec. 21. The two Governments agreed as follows:

Art. 1. The F.R.G. and the G.D.R. will develop normal good-neighborly relations with each other on the basis of equality of rights.

Art. 2. The F.R.G. and the G.D.R. will let themselves be guided by the aims and principles which are laid down in the Charter of the United Nations, in particular those of the sovereign equality of all States, respect for independence, sovereignty and territorial integrity, the right of self-determination, the protection of human rights, and non-discrimination.

Art. 3. In accordance with the Charter of the United Nations, the F.R.G. and the G.D.R. will solve their differences solely by peaceful means and refrain from the threat of force or the use of force. They affirm the inviolability, now and in the future, of the border existing between them, and pledge themselves to unrestricted respect for each other's territorial integrity.

Art. 4. The F.R.G. and the G.D.R. proceed on the assumption that neither of the two States can represent the other internationally or act in its name.

Art. 5. The F.R.G. and the G.D.R. will promote peaceful relations among the European States and contribute to security and co-operation in Europe. They support the efforts toward a reduction of armed forces and armaments in Europe provided this does not adversely affect the security of the parties concerned. With a view to achieving general and complete disarmament under effective international control, the F.R.G. and the G.D.R. will support efforts serving international security and designed to bring about arms limitation and disarmament, in particular in the field of nuclear arms and other weapons of mass destruction.

Art. 6. The F.R.G. and the G.D.R. proceed from the principle that the sovereign power of each of the two States is confined to its [own] State territory. They respect the independence and sovereignty of each of the two States in its internal and external affairs.

Art. 7. The F.R.G. and the G.D.R. declare their readiness, in the course of the normalization of their relations, to settle practical and humanitarian questions. They will conclude agreements in order—on the basis of this treaty and for their mutual advantage—to develop and promote co-operation in the economic field, science and technology, transport, juridical relations, posts and telecommunications, public health, culture, sport, the protection of the environment and in other spheres. . . .

Art. 8. The F.R.G. and the G.D.R. will exchange permanent representative missions. They will be established at the seat of the respective Governments. Practical questions connected with the establishment of the missions will be settled separately.

Art. 9. The F.R.G. and the G.D.R. are agreed that bilateral and multilateral international treaties and agreements previously concluded by or concerning them are not affected by this treaty.

In a Supplementary Protocol it was proposed to set up a commission of representatives of the two Governments to "examine and, so far as is necessary, renew or supplement the demarcation of the border existing between the two States" and to "compile the necessary documentation on the line of the border."

In separate declarations on the Protocol the Federal Republic stated that questions of nationality had not been settled by the treaty, and the German Democratic Republic stated that it proceeded on the assumption that the treaty would facilitate a settlement of these matters.

The documents were accompanied by a series of exchanges of letters and declarations:

(1) In the course of the normalization of relations after the entry into force of the treaty, the Government of the G.D.R. would take steps for the settlement of questions related to (a) problems arising out of the separation of families; (b) the improvement of border and tourist passenger traffic; and (c) the improvement of non-commercial merchandise traffic.

(2) With the entry into force of the treaty the following improved arrangements would take effect:

Reunion of Families. Married couples would be reunited and parents who were in need of the care of their children could rejoin them, the same applying in the case of grandparents and grandchildren. In special cases the contraction of marriages would be permitted.

Travel Arrangements. These comprised (a) an extension of the list of urgent family matters, in the case of which East German citizens might be permitted to pay visits to Western Germany; (b) the inclusion of half-brothers and half-sisters having the same mother among those East German citizens entitled to apply for permission to pay visits to Western Germany in cases of urgent family matters; (c) the extension of the procedure for the issuing of visas in transit traffic between Western Germany and West Berlin to other transit traffic by rail and inland navigation; and (d) the possibility of breaks in transit journeys (with the exception of Berlin traffic).

(3) At the time of the entry into force of the treaty, four additional border crossing-points on the frontier between Eastern and Western Germany would be opened for passenger traffic.

(4) Each side took note that the other would initiate the necessary measures to seek membership of the United Nations; both Governments would inform each other of the date of their application.

(5) The Federal Government stated in a declaration that after the reassembly of the Bundestag [after the forthcoming general election] it would take steps for the creation of the necessary internal preconditions for application for West German membership of the United Nations. The leaders of both delegations declared that the above-mentioned reciprocal notification had as its objective that both applications should take place at approximately the same time.

(6) A "declaration on signing" stated that both Governments had agreed that in the course of the normalization of relations between the two States they would consult each other on questions of mutual interest, in particular on those which were of importance for the safeguarding of peace in Europe.

Talks between the British, French, and U.S. Ambassadors in Western Germany and the Soviet Ambassador to the G.D.R. on the maintenance of the rights and responsibilities of the four Powers in Germany after the conclusion of the basic treaty and the entry of the two German States into the United Nations opened in West Berlin on Oct. 23, 1972.

The text of the joint declaration agreed upon by them and published on Nov. 9 was worded as follows:

The Governments of the United Kingdom of Great Britain and Northern Ireland, the French Republic, the Union of Soviet Socialist Republics, and the United States of America, having been represented by their Ambassadors who held a series of meetings in the building formerly occupied by the Allied Control Council, are in agreement that they will support the applications for membership in the United Nations, when submitted, by the Federal Republic of Germany and the German Democratic Republic, and affirm in this connection that this membership shall in no way affect the rights and responsibilities of the four Powers and the corresponding related quadripartite agreements, decisions, and practices.

8. United States and Soviet Union

During a visit to Moscow by President Nixon, May 22–29, 1972, a Treaty on the Limitation of Anti-Ballistic Missile Systems, an Interim Agreement on Certain Measures with respect to the Limitation of Strategic Offensive Arms, and six different co-operation agreements were signed by the two sides.

The Treaty on the Limitation of Anti-Ballistic Missile Systems, signed on May 26, was the culmination of two and a half years of talks on strategic arms limitation (SALT) held between the two Governments. The treaty, concluded for an unlimited duration, consisted of 16 articles, including the following:

Art. 1. (1) Each party undertakes to limit anti-ballistic missile (ABM) systems and to adopt other measures in accordance with the provisions of this treaty.

(2) Each party undertakes not to deploy ABM systems for a defense of the territory of its country and not to provide a base for such a defense, and not to deploy ABM systems for defense of an individual region except as provided for in Article 3 of this treaty.

Art. 2. (1) For the purpose of this treaty an ABM system is a system to counter strategic ballistic missiles or their elements in flight trajectory currently consisting of:

(a) ABM interceptor missiles, which are interceptor missiles constructed and deployed for an ABM role, or of a type tested in an ABM mode;

(b) ABM launchers, which are launchers constructed and deployed for launching ABM interceptor missiles; and

(c) ABM radars, which are radars constructed and deployed for an ABM role, or of a type tested in an ABM mode.

(2) The ABM system components listed in paragraph 1 of this Article include those which are: (a) operational; (b) under construction; (c) undergoing testing; (d) undergoing overhaul, repair or conversion; or (e) mothballed.

Art. 3. Each party undertakes not to deploy ABM systems or their components except that:

(a) Within one ABM system deployment area having a radius of 150 kilometers and centered on the party's national capital, a party may deploy: (1) no more than 100 ABM launchers and no more than 100 ABM interceptor missiles at launch sites; and (2) ABM radars within no more than six ABM radar complexes, the area of each complex being circular and having a diameter of no more than three kilometers; and

(b) within one ABM system deployment area having a radius of 150 kilometers and containing ICBM silo launchers, a party may deploy: (1) no more than 100 ABM launchers and no more than 100 ABM interceptor missiles at launch sites; (2) two large phased-array ABM radars comparable in potential to corresponding ABM radars operational or under construction on the date of signature of the treaty in an ABM system deployment area containing ICBM silo launchers; and (3) no more than 18 ABM radars each having a potential less than the potential of the smaller of the above-mentioned two large phased-array ABM radars.

Art. 4. The limitations provided for in Article 3 shall not apply to ABM systems or their components for development or testing, and located within current or additionally agreed test ranges. Each party may have no more than a total of 15 ABM launchers at test ranges.

Art. 5. (1) Each party undertakes not to develop, test, or deploy ABM systems or components which are sea-based, space-based, or mobile land-based.

(2) Each party undertakes not to develop, test, or deploy ABM launchers for launching more than one ABM interceptor missile at a time from each launcher, nor to modify deployed launchers to provide them with such a capability, nor to develop, test, or deploy automatic or semi-automatic or other similar systems for rapid reload of ABM launchers.

Art. 6. To enhance assurance of the effectiveness of the limitations on ABM systems and their components provided by this treaty, each party undertakes:

(a) Not to give missiles, launchers, or radars, other than ABM interceptor missiles, ABM launchers, or ABM radars, capabilities to counter strategic ballistic missiles or their elements in flight trajectory, and not to test them in an ABM mode; and

(*b*) not to deploy in the future radars for early warning of strategic ballistic missile attack except at locations along the periphery of its national territory and oriented outward.

Art. 8. ABM systems or their components in excess of the numbers or outside the areas specified in this treaty, as well as ABM systems or their components prohibited by this treaty, shall be destroyed or dismantled under agreed procedures within the shortest possible agreed period of time.

Art. 9. To assure the viability and effectiveness of this treaty, each party undertakes not to transfer to other States, and not to deploy outside its national territory, ABM systems or their components limited by this treaty.

Art. 12. (1) For the purpose of providing assurance of compliance with the provisions of this treaty, each party shall use national technical means of verification at its disposal in a manner consistent with generally recognized principles of international law.

(2) Each party undertakes not to interfere with the national technical means of verification of the other party operating in accordance with paragraph (1) of this Article.

(3) Each party undertakes not to use deliberate concealment measures which impede verification by national technical means of compliance with the provisions of this treaty. This obligation shall not require changes in current construction, assembly, conversion, or overhaul practices.

Under the Interim Agreement, to be valid for five years, and also signed on May 26, both parties undertook:

in Article 1, "not to start construction of additional fixed land-based intercontinental ballistic missile (ICBM) launchers after July 1, 1972";
in Article 2, "not to convert land-based launchers for light ICBMs, or for ICBMs of older types deployed prior to 1964, into land-based launchers for heavy ICBMs of types deployed after that time"; and
in Article 3, "to limit submarine-launched ballistic missile (SLBM) launchers and modern ballistic missile submarines to the numbers operational and under construction on the date of signature of this Interim Agreement, and in addition launchers and submarines constructed under procedures established by the parties as replacements for an equal number of ICBM launchers of older types deployed prior to 1964 or for launchers on older submarines."

A protocol to the Interim Agreement contained the following provisions:

The United States may have no more than 710 ballistic missile launchers on submarines (SLBMs) and no more than 44 modern ballistic missile submarines. The Soviet Union may have no more than 950 ballistic missile launchers on submarines and no more than 62 modern ballistic missile submarines.
Additional ballistic missile launchers on submarines up to the above-mentioned levels—in the U.S. over 656 ballistic missile launchers on nuclear-powered submarines, and in the U.S.S.R. over 740 ballistic missile launchers on nuclear-powered submarines, operational and under construction—may become operational as replacements for equal numbers of ballistic missile launchers of older type deployed prior to 1964 or of ballistic missile launchers on older submarines.
The deployment of modern SLBMs on any submarine, regardless of type, will be counted against the total level of SLBMs permitted for the U.S. and the U.S.S.R.

The Soviet-American co-operation agreements signed at the same time were:

(*a*) an Environmental Protection Agreement on measures to prevent pollution and to protect environmental quality;

(*b*) a Medicine and Public Health Agreement;

(*c*) a Space Co-operation Agreement providing notably for the first joint space-flight by astronauts of the two countries in 1975;

(*d*) a Scientific and Technological Co-operation Agreement;

(*e*) an Agreement on Prevention of Incidents at Sea, aimed at ensuring safety of navigation by warships and aircraft of the two countries; and

(*f*) a communiqué announcing the two parties' intention to establish a joint Commercial Commission.

In addition, the two parties issued on May 29 a statement on the "Basic Principles of Relations between the United States of America and the Union of Soviet Socialist Republics," in which they expressed their agreement as follows:

(1) They [the U.S.A. and the U.S.S.R.] will proceed from the common determination that in the nuclear age there is no alternative to conducting their mutual relations on the basis of peaceful coexistence. Differences in ideology and in the social systems of the U.S.A. and the U.S.S.R. are not obstacles to the bilateral development of normal relations based on the principles of sovereignty, equality, non-interference in internal affairs, and mutual advantage.
(2) The U.S.A. and the U.S.S.R. attach major importance to preventing the development of situations capable of causing a dangerous exacerbation of their relations. Therefore, they will do their utmost to avoid military confrontations and to prevent the outbreak of nuclear war. They will always exercise restraint in their mutual relations, and will be prepared to negotiate and settle differences by peaceful means. Discussions and negotiations on outstanding issues will be conducted in a spirit of reciprocity, mutual accommodation, and mutual benefit.
Both sides recognize that efforts to obtain unilateral advantage at the expense of the other, directly or indirectly, are inconsistent with these objectives. The prerequisites for maintaining and strengthening peaceful relations between the U.S.A. and the U.S.S.R. are the recognition of the security interests of the parties based on the principle of equality and the renunciation of the use or threat of force.

Following approval of the treaty by the U.S. Senate, President Nixon ratified it on behalf of the United States on Sept. 30, 1972, while in the U.S.S.R. the treaty was approved by the Supreme Soviet and ratified by President Podgorny on Sept. 29. Instruments of ratification were exchanged in Washington on Oct. 3. [*25309A; 25585A*]

9. Earlier U.S.–Soviet Agreements

(a) The "Hot Line" Agreement of 1963

An agreement signed in Geneva on June 20, 1963, by the heads of the U.S. and Soviet delegations at the Geneva disarmament conference provided for the establishment of "a direct communications link between the two Governments" for use in an emergency, e.g. an abrupt shift in the East–West military balance. The communicating link established under this agreement was improved, under a further agreement signed in Washington on Sept. 30, 1971, by the proposed replacement of cable and radio teleprinter links by a satellite communication system comprising two circuits and a number of ground stations. [*19553A; 24884A*]

(b) Agreement on Reduction of Nuclear War Risk of 1971

An agreement to reduce the risk of outbreak of nuclear war was signed in Washington on Sept. 30, 1971, by the U.S. Secretary of State and the Soviet Foreign Minister.

In the agreement both parties undertook to notify each other immediately in the event of an "accidental, unauthorized, or any other unexplained incident involving a possible detonation of a nuclear weapon which would create a risk of outbreak of nuclear war"; "to take necessary measures to render harmless or destroy any such weapon"; to notify the other "in advance of any planned missile launches" extending "beyond its national territory in the direction of the other party." [*24884A*]

10

The Commonwealth-Commonwealth Regional Groupings and The Treaties of Great Britain

THE COMMONWEALTH

The Commonwealth is an association of independent sovereign States all of which have been, at one time, British territories. It is neither a formal alliance nor a federation of States since there exists no written Commonwealth Constitution and no central Government. Any former British territory, on attaining independence, may seek membership of the Commonwealth; this is granted only by the unanimous consent of the members.

The Head of the Commonwealth is the British Monarch, who is recognized, even by those member-countries which have their own Heads of State, as the symbol of the free association of member-nations of the Commonwealth. In those countries which owe allegiance to her as their Head of State, the Queen is represented by a Governor-General whom she appoints on the recommendation of the country in question.

One of the principal factors binding together the member-nations of the Commonwealth is the use of English Common Law as a basis for most judicial systems. Exceptions are the Canadian province of Quebec, where the judicial system is based on French law; Ceylon, where Dutch Roman law is applied (this is also the case in Rhodesia); and the Moslem countries of Africa and Asia, where Moslem civil law is applied.

Members

The members of the Commonwealth are Britain, together with her Dependent Territories, Protectorates and Protected States, and 32 independent States. The membership is given in the table on page 141.

Since the merging of the Colonial Office and the Commonwealth Relations Office in August 1966, to form the Commonwealth Office, the Dependent Territories of Britain (listed below) have become the responsibility of this Office.

Dependent Territories

Associated States
ANTIGUA
DOMINICA
GRENADA
ST. KITTS-NEVIS
ST. LUCIA
ST. VINCENT

Protectorate
BRITISH SOLOMON ISLANDS

Protected States
BRUNEI
TONGA

Colonies with Internal Self-Government
BAHAMAS
BRITISH HONDURAS

Other Colonies
ANGUILLA
BERMUDA
BRITISH ANTARCTIC TERRITORY

BRITISH INDIAN OCEAN TERRITORY
BRITISH VIRGIN ISLANDS
CAYMAN ISLANDS
FALKLAND ISLANDS AND DEPENDENCIES
GIBRALTAR
GILBERT AND ELLICE ISLANDS
HONG KONG (Colony and Leased Territories)
MONTSERRAT
PITCAIRN ISLAND
ST. HELENA AND DEPENDENCIES
SEYCHELLES
TURKS AND CAICOS ISLANDS

Anglo-French Condominium
NEW HEBRIDES

Notes: (1) Rhodesia declared its independence unilaterally on Nov. 11, 1965, but Britain, which does not recognize its independent status, still regards it as a colony with internal self-government.
(2) The Federation of South Arabia (Aden and Protectorates), a British Colony and Protectorate until Sept. 1, 1967, when its Government ceased to function, became independent outside the Commonwealth as the People's Republic of South Yemen on Nov. 30, 1967, which assumed the name of People's Democratic Republic of Yemen on Nov. 30, 1970.

Development of the Commonwealth

The Commonwealth began to evolve with the formation of self-governing dominions. The first of these was the Dominion of Canada, created, under the British North America Act of 1867, out of the provinces of Ontario, Quebec, Nova Scotia, and New Brunswick. Additional provinces acceded to the Dominion, in accordance with the provisions of the Act, as follows: Manitoba (1869), British Columbia (1871), Prince Edward Island (1873), Alberta (1905), Saskatchewan (1905), and Newfoundland (1949).

INDEPENDENT COUNTRIES WITHIN THE COMMONWEALTH

Country	Date of Independence	Political Status
Britain	—	Monarchy
Canada	1867	Monarchy
Australia	1900	Monarchy
New Zealand	1907	Monarchy
India	Aug. 15, 1947	Republic since Jan. 26, 1950
Sri Lanka (Ceylon)	Feb. 4, 1948	Republic since May 22, 1972
Ghana	March 6, 1957	Republic since July 1, 1960
Cyprus	Aug. 16, 1960	Republic since Aug. 16, 1960
Nigeria	Oct. 1, 1960	Republic since Oct. 1, 1963
Sierra Leone	April 27, 1961	Republic since April 19, 1971
Tanzania	Dec. 9, 1961	Republic since Dec. 9, 1962 (in union with Zanzibar since April 27, 1964)
Western Samoa‡	Jan. 1, 1962	Independent State under two Chiefs
Jamaica	Aug. 5, 1962	Monarchy
Trinidad and Tobago	Aug. 31, 1962	Monarchy
Uganda	Oct. 9, 1962	Independent Sovereign State on Oct. 9, 1963. Republic (officially) since Sept. 8, 1967
Malaysia	Sept. 16, 1963	Monarchy*
Kenya	Dec. 12, 1963	Republic since Dec. 12, 1964
Malawi	July 6, 1964	Republic since July 6, 1966
Malta	Sept. 21, 1964	Monarchy
Zambia	Oct. 24, 1964	Republic since Oct. 24, 1964
Gambia	Feb. 18, 1965	Republic since April 24, 1970
Singapore	Oct. 16, 1965	Republic since Dec. 22, 1965
Guyana	May 26, 1966	Republic since Feb. 23, 1970
Botswana	Sept. 30, 1966	Republic since Sept. 30, 1966
Lesotho	Oct. 4, 1966	Monarchy*
Barbados	Nov. 30, 1966	Monarchy
Nauru†	Jan. 31, 1968	Republic
Mauritius	March 12, 1968	Monarchy
Swaziland	Sept. 6, 1968	Monarchy*
Tonga	June 4, 1970	Monarchy*
Fiji	Oct. 10, 1970	Monarchy
Bangladesh	Dec. 22, 1971	Republic

* These Monarchies are headed by their own Monarchs. All other Commonwealth countries described as Monarchies owe allegiance to the British Queen.

† Special member without representation at Commonwealth Heads of Government conferences.

‡ Western Samoa became a member of the Commonwealth on Aug. 28, 1970.

Pakistan—a Commonwealth member since Aug. 15, 1947, and a Republic since March 23, 1956—withdrew from the Commonwealth on Jan. 30, 1972, in protest against recognition of the independence of Bangladesh (formerly East Pakistan) by Britain, Australia, and New Zealand. [25114]

The 6 self-governing provinces of Australia formed a dominion in 1900 known as the Commonwealth of Australia. New Zealand, which had obtained a unitary form of government in 1876, was designated a dominion in 1907, but did not adopt the principal sections of the Statute of Westminster (see below) until 1947. The Union of South Africa was formed from 4 self-governing colonies in 1910. Southern Ireland became in effect a self-governing dominion when the Irish Free State was established in 1921.

An *Imperial Conference of 1926,* adopting a report by an Inter-Imperial Relations Committee, defined the Dominions and Great Britain as "autonomous communities within the Empire, equal in status, in no way subordinate to one another in any aspect of their domestic or external affairs, though united by a common allegiance to the Crown, and freely associated as members of the British Commonwealth of Nations

. . . Every self-governing member of the Empire is now the master of its destiny. In fact, if not always in form, it is subject to no compulsion whatever . . . The British Empire is not founded upon negations. It depends essentially, if not formally, on positive ideals. Free institutions are its lifeblood. Free co-operation is its instrument."

The *Statute of Westminster of 1931* gave effect to the above definition and offered all former colonies the undisputed right to secede from the Commonwealth. Other provisions of the Statute are:

1. The Parliament of Westminster ceases to have the right of revision with regard to the legislation of the Parliaments of the Dominions.
2. A Dominion possesses full authority to make laws possessing extra-territorial validity.
3. When there are discrepancies between a Do-

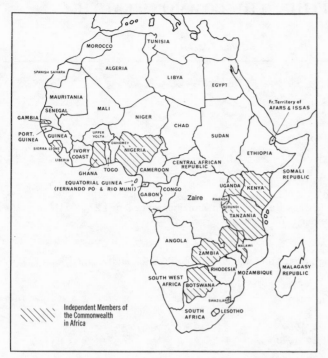

Independent Members of the Commonwealth in Africa

minion law and an existing law of the United Kingdom, this fact shall not render the Dominion law invalid. [106G]

Steps in the gradual decentralization of powers within the Commonwealth were:

1. The granting of complete independence in 1947 to Burma, Ceylon, India, and Pakistan—with Burma seceding from the Commonwealth and the other three States becoming independent members of it.

2. British recognition of the secession of the Irish Republic in 1949—although citizens of the Republic continued to enjoy in Britain substantially all rights and privileges of British subjects.

3. The acceptance of India as a Republic in 1949, with the British Sovereign being acknowledged as Head of the Commonwealth. (The monarchy remained merely a unifying symbol for the Commonwealth, but no longer had valid constitutional significance. Relations among Commonwealth members are no longer based on constitutional law, but on international law —i.e. multilateral treaties which also embrace non-Commonwealth States.)

4. The Canadian Citizenship Act of 1946 by which Canadians became Canadian citizens first, and British subjects only by consequence. This Act forced the other independent members of the Commonwealth to follow suit by establishing their own citizenships.

South Africa left the Commonwealth in 1961, not because it had become a Republic the previous year, but because its racial policies were at variance with the principles of all other Commonwealth members.

Organs

Questions of common interest to Commonwealth members are discussed at meetings of the Prime Ministers of Commonwealth countries. Such meetings generally take place in London. They are held in private and have no special rules of procedure. The agenda is decided at the first session, after which much of the discussion takes place at smaller meetings attended by interested groups. Decisions taken at the Prime Ministers' meetings are limited to matters of immediate constitutional importance, in particular questions of membership.

The Commonwealth Secretariat was set up in London in July 1965 in pursuance of a recommendation made by the Prime Ministers' Conference of July 1964. The Secretariat was to be "a visible symbol of the spirit of co-operation which animates the Commonwealth." Divided into departments dealing with International Affairs, Economic Affairs, and Administration, the Secretariat is responsible for disseminating information on questions of common interest; for aiding the various Commonwealth agencies, both official and unofficial, in the promotion of Commonwealth links in all fields; and for preparing and servicing the Prime Ministers' and other Ministerial meetings.

Commonwealth Co-operation

There is co-operation among member-countries of the Commonwealth in many spheres of activity. This takes the form of conferences (economic, educational, scientific, medical, etc.) and of work through specialized agencies.

Commonwealth Citizenship
Under a scheme devised at a meeting of Commonwealth representatives in February 1947, each Commonwealth country recognizes as British subjects (or Commonwealth citizens) both its own citizens and citizens of other Commonwealth countries. Although holders of this common status are not accorded equal rights throughout the Commonwealth, their rights are always superior to those of aliens.

Economic Co-operation
A system of tariff preferences, known as *Commonwealth Preference,* is in general operation between Commonwealth countries. A lower rate of customs duty, or none at all, is levied on Commonwealth goods, as opposed to the higher rate of duty on imports from foreign countries. (The Republic of Ireland and the Republic of South Africa, as former Commonwealth countries, still enjoy Commonwealth Preference.)

The *Commonwealth Economic Committee,* founded in 1925 as the Imperial Economic Committee, provides economic and statistical information on questions related to Commonwealth production and trade. The Committee is formed by two representatives of each Commonwealth member-country and two members representing the Dependent Territories.

The *Commonwealth Sugar Agreement,* concluded in 1951 between the British Ministry of Food and the sugar-producing Commonwealth countries, provided for sugar supplies to Britain and New Zealand at negotiated prices normally above world market prices. In 1968 it was given indefinite duration with provision for triennial reviews. The principal sugar-producing countries or areas in the Commonwealth are Australia, Fiji, Guyana, Mauritius, and the West Indies.

Educational Co-operation

Co-operation in the sphere of education is the concern of the following bodies:

Association of Commonwealth Universities, founded in 1913 as the Universities Bureau of the British Empire;

Commonwealth Education Liaison Committee, founded in 1959;

Commonwealth Education Liaison Unit, founded in 1960;

League for the Exchange of Commonwealth Teachers.

Agriculture and Forestry

The Commonwealth Agricultural Bureaus—3 Institutes and 11 Bureaus, each concerned with a particular aspect of agricultural science—collect and supply specialized information on agricultural science for research workers. The organization was founded in 1929.

Two bodies concerned with co-operation in the field of forestry are:

Commonwealth Forestry Association, founded in 1921;

Standing Committee on Commonwealth Forestry, founded in 1923.

Science and Medicine

The following bodies have been set up to aid collaboration between Commonwealth scientists:

Commonwealth Scientific Committee, founded in 1946;

Commonwealth Scientific Liaison Offices, founded in 1948.

The interests and principles of the medical profession are promoted throughout the Commonwealth by the Commonwealth Medical Association.

Civil Aviation and Telecommunications

Civil air communications and aeronautical research throughout the Commonwealth are the concern of the following bodies:

Commonwealth Air Transport Council, founded in 1945;

Commonwealth Advisory Aeronautical Research Council, founded in 1946;

The Commonwealth Telecommunications Board, formed in 1949, an advisory body on matters related to external telecommunications systems.

Other Commonwealth Organizations

A list of other bodies concerned with various aspects of Commonwealth co-operation is given below.

Commonwealth Committee on Mineral Processing, founded in 1960;

Commonwealth Committee on Mineral Resources and Geology, founded in 1948;

Commonwealth Consultative Space Research Committee, founded in 1960;

Commonwealth Council of Mining and Metallurgical Institutions;

Commonwealth Countries League, a women's organization founded in 1925;

Commonwealth Foundation, founded in 1965 to administer a fund for promoting professional co-operation throughout the Commonwealth;

Commonwealth Institute, founded in 1893 as the Imperial Institute. It functions as an information and education center;

Commonwealth Parliamentary Association, formed in 1911;

Commonwealth War Graves Commission, founded in 1917;

Federation of Commonwealth Chambers of Commerce, founded in 1911;

Royal Commonwealth Society, to promote understanding among the peoples of the Commonwealth.

The Sterling Area

The Sterling Area consists of countries whose central banks hold certain proportions of their gold and currency reserves in a pool in London, drawing on these reserves as needed.

Its members are Britain (including all dependent territories except, temporarily, Rhodesia); the Commonwealth, excluding Canada and the New Hebrides; and the following non-Commonwealth countries: Bahrain, Iceland, the Republic of Ireland, Jordan, Kuwait, Maldives, Oman, Pakistan, Qatar, Sikkim, South Africa, Southwest Africa, United Arab Emirates, Western Samoa, and Yemen (People's Democratic Republic). Most of these countries have concluded agreements with the United Kingdom designed to protect them against fluctuations in the sterling exchange rate.   [*Pages 23138; 23790; 25769*]

Botswana, Lesotho, and Swaziland have been in a monetary and customs union with South Africa since 1910, and a new agreement on the division of customs revenue between the 4 countries was concluded on Dec. 11, 1969.   [*23809B*]

COMMONWEALTH REGIONAL GROUPINGS

1. The Colombo Plan
(*A plan for the economic development of South and Southeast Asia*)

Members Within the Area: Afghanistan, Bangladesh, Bhutan, Burma, Cambodia, Ceylon, Fiji, India, Indonesia, Iran, Korea (South), Laos, Malaysia, Maldive Islands, Nepal, Pakistan, Philippines, Singapore, Thailand, Vietnam (South)

Members Outside the Area: Australia, Britain, Canada, Japan, New Zealand, United States

The Colombo Plan for Co-operative Economic Development in South and Southeast Asia was drawn up by the Commonwealth Consultative Committee on South and Southeast Asia, and published on Nov. 28, 1950. This plan, originally adopted for a 6-year period, was based on detailed development programs for India, Pakistan, Ceylon, Malaya, Singapore, North Borneo, and Sarawak, and formally came into operation on July 1, 1951. Already by February 1951 the scope of the scheme had been widened to include non-Commonwealth countries, and the U.S.A. had agreed to join Australia, Britain, Canada, and New Zealand in making available aid within the framework of the Colombo Plan.   [*11349A; 11621A*]

At a meeting of the Colombo Plan Consultative Committee (see below) in October 1955 it was decided that the Plan—originally scheduled to terminate on June 30, 1957—should continue in operation until 1976.   [*14657A*]

Organization

The principal organ of the Colombo Plan is the Consultative Committee, which directs the working of the Plan. The Committee, consisting of Ministers of the member-countries, meets annually to discuss the annual reports of the individual members, and to co-ordinate the schemes for aid. The meetings of the Committee are also attended by representatives of the Asian Development Bank, the World Bank (IBRD), the International Labor Organization, the U.N. Economic Commission for Asia and the Far East, the U.N. Development Program, the Asian Productivity Organization, the Commonwealth Secretariat, and the Colombo Plan Bureau.

The Council for Technical Co-operation in South and Southeast Asia is a consultative organ concerned specifically with the problems of technical co-operation. It is also responsible for the dissemination of information on the Colombo Plan as a whole. The Council, which meets in Colombo several times a year, is composed of representatives of the member-countries' Governments.

The decisions of the Council for Technical Co-operation are executed by the Colombo Plan Bureau. The work of the Bureau includes the keeping of records of all technical assistance given and received and of capital aid projects; the provision of information to member-Governments, in particular on the training facilities, experts, and equipment available; and the issuing of progress reports and statistics.

Forms of Aid

Although the bulk of aid within the framework of the Colombo Plan is provided by Australia, Britain, Canada, Japan, and the United States, economic co-operation among the other members of the Plan is encouraged.

Economic assistance is provided through capital aid in the form of grants and loans for national projects, and through technical aid in the form of experts, facilities for technical training, and the supply of special equipment.

2. The Caribbean Free Trade Association (CARIFTA)
Following a free trade agreement between Antigua, Barbados, and Guyana signed on Dec. 15, 1965, an enlarged Caribbean Free Trade Area was established between May 1 and Aug. 1, 1968, with the following membership: Antigua, Barbados, Dominica, Grenada, Guyana, Jamaica, Montserrat, St. Kitts-Nevis-Anguilla, St. Lucia, St. Vincent, and Trinidad and Tobago. It was joined by British Honduras on May 1, 1971. The aim of the partners in CARIFTA, which has a common currency, is economic integration, with the abolition of all internal tariffs and the preparation of a common external tariff.

The 12 member-countries of CARIFTA, together with the Bahamas, decided at the seventh meeting of the Heads of Government in Port of Spain, Trinidad, on Oct. 9–14, 1972, to establish a Caribbean Common Market which would come into being on May 1, 1973, and also agreed in principle to the formation of a Caribbean Community. [22884A; 25562A]

3. Proposed Political Union in Eastern Caribbean

A "Declaration of Grenada" signed in Grenada on July 25, 1971, and published on Nov. 1, 1971, provided for eventual political union of the Republic of Guyana and 5 of the West Indies Associated States—Dominica, Grenada, St. Kitts-Nevis, St. Lucia, and St. Vincent. [25012A]

TREATIES OF GREAT BRITAIN

ANZUK Agreements

In succession to an Anglo-Malaysian Defense Treaty (of Oct. 12, 1957), which was terminated on Oct. 31, 1971, agreements were signed between Australia, Britain, and New Zealand to implement as from Nov. 1, 1971, a decision made on April 16, 1971, to set up a joint ANZUK force for the defense of Malaysia and Singapore.

Under these agreements the five Governments decided to establish (1) an Integrated Air Defense System for Malaysia and Singapore under the responsibility of a joint Air Defense Council; (2) a Joint Consultative Council; and (3) continued stationing of Australian, New Zealand, and United Kingdom armed forces in Malaysia and Singapore. [24924B]

Important Bilateral Treaties Between Britain and Commonwealth Countries

1. Britain–Australia: Agreements on Atomic Testing Grounds in Australia

An agreement on the construction of a rocket-testing range in Central Australia (the Woomera range) was announced on May 13, 1947. The cost of maintaining the range, used in a joint British-Australian scheme for the development of guided weapons, is shared by the two Governments under an agreement of Sept. 13, 1953.

On April 4, 1955, it was announced that the Australian and British Governments had agreed on the establishment of a new atomic testing ground, to be known as Maralinga, in the South Australian desert. [8681A; 13136D; 14141B]

2. Britain–Maldives: Agreements Concerning an R.A.F. Airfield on the Island of Gan

Under an agreement of Jan. 1, 1953, Britain retained the right to establish and maintain defense facilities in the Maldives. On Jan. 3, 1957, an agreement was announced for the re-establishment, by Britain, of the wartime airfield on the island of Gan. An agreement of Feb. 14, 1960, granted Britain the continued use of the Gan airfield for 30 years retrospectively from December 1956, in return for a sum of £85,000, and this was reaffirmed under the independence agreement of July 26, 1965. [15295A; 20919A]

3. Defense Agreements with Uganda and Kenya

After British troops had helped to put down mutinies in the Uganda and Kenya Armies in January 1964, two new defense agreements were concluded by the British Government on March 3 and March 6, 1964, with the Governments of Uganda and Kenya respectively. The agreements provided for the continuation of British assistance in the command and training of the Uganda and Kenya Armies. Under the agreement with Kenya, Britain was granted training facilities for the Army, overflying and staging rights for the R.A.F., and port maintenance facilities at Mombasa for the Royal Navy. [19963A]

4. Britain–Malta: Defense Agreement

A 10-year defense agreement between Britain and Malta was initialed on July 21, 1964, when agreement was reached on the independence Constitution for the island. The defense agreement included provisions for mutual defense assistance, and for co-operation between the two armed forces. Malta granted the British Government the right to station armed forces in Malta and the use of facilities in the island for defense purposes. The British Government would consult the Maltese Government should any major changes be contemplated in the British forces in Malta, which might have significant effects on the defense or economy of Malta. [20309A; 21925A]

A new defense agreement was signed, after protracted negotiations, in London on March 26, 1972, and was to remain in force until March 31, 1979.

While the agreement renewed Britain's rights "for the defense purposes of the United Kingdom and NATO," Malta undertook not to permit "the forces of any party to the Warsaw Pact to be stationed in Malta or to use military facilities there." Britain undertook to pay Malta £12,750,000 immediately; £3,500,000 on Jan. 1, 1973; and £7,000,000 thereafter on each of April 1 and Oct. 1 of each year of the agreement. (These amounts included annual contributions of £8,750,000 to be paid to Britain by NATO, but they did not include further bilateral aid to Malta from NATO countries.) [25221A]

During and after the negotiations with Britain, Malta concluded trade agreements with Poland (Nov. 30, 1971) and the Soviet Union (Dec. 27, 1971) and an agreement for a long-term loan from China (April 8, 1972). [25153; 25278B]

5. Britain–Tonga: Treaty of Friendship

A treaty of friendship between Britain and Tonga was signed on Aug. 25, 1958, to replace the treaty of 1900 by which Tonga became a British-protected State while remaining self-governing. The treaty provided for greater autonomy for Tonga. [16369C]

6. Britain–Mauritius: Defense Agreement
A 6-year defense agreement between Britain and Mauritius was signed on March 12, 1968, providing for joint consultation on any request for assistance by the Government of Mauritius in the event of a threat to the island's internal security. It also provided for the continuation of existing British facilities in Mauritius, and for British help in equipping and training the Mauritius police and security forces. [22596A]

British Treaties with Countries Outside the Commonwealth

Treaties concluded by Britain within the NATO framework may be found in the chapter "North Atlantic Treaty Organization," page 93, except for those with the U.S.A., which are included in the section, "U.S. Defense Treaties," page 170. A number of other treaties involving Britain, not mentioned elsewhere in this book, are given below.

1. Anglo–Portuguese Alliance
A treaty of alliance concluded between King Edward III of England and King Ferdinand and Queen Eleanor of Portugal in 1373 provided for "perpetual friendship" between the two countries and mutual assistance "by sea and by land against all men."

This treaty, variously reinforced between 1386 and 1815, was reaffirmed by the Portuguese Government early in World War II and was invoked by the British Government in connection with a temporary agreement, announced on Oct. 12, 1943, on the use by Britain of facilities in the Azores. [6035A]

2. Treaty of Utrecht
Under the Treaty of Utrecht of 1713, which ended the War of the Spanish Succession and by which Spain's power in Europe was greatly reduced, Britain obtained the "full and intire propriety of the Town and Castle of Gibraltar, together with the port fortifications and forts thereunto belonging." However, if Britain should wish to "grant, sell, or by any means alienate" ownership of Gibraltar, the Treaty stated that Spain should be given first preference to it.

While the provisions of the Treaty have not been challenged by Spain, there have been repeated disputes between Britain and Spain, e.g. in 1854 and 1908, when Spain alleged that Britain had moved Gibraltar's frontier farther north, and since 1950 when Britain first granted increased rights of internal government to the people of Gibraltar—the Spanish Government considering the new political institutions in Gibraltar to be incompatible with the Treaty of Utrecht. [20947; 21843A]

3. The Cyprus Agreements
Agreement on the future of Cyprus was reached in London on Feb. 19, 1959, between the British, Greek, and Turkish Governments and representatives of the Greek and Turkish communities in Cyprus. This agreement followed a previous agreement reached in Zürich on Feb. 11, 1959, between the Governments of Greece and Turkey.

The documents embodying these agreements, published on Feb. 23, 1959, included:

(a) a Greco-Turkish Declaration on the "Basic Structure of the Republic of Cyprus";

(b) a Treaty of Guarantee between Cyprus on the one hand, and Britain, Greece, and Turkey on the other, whereby Britain, Greece, and Turkey undertook to recognize and maintain "the independence, territorial integrity, and security" of the Republic of Cyprus;

(c) a Treaty of Alliance between Greece, Turkey, and Cyprus, whereby the 3 countries undertook to "co-operate for their common defense" and to "resist any attack or aggression, direct or indirect, against the independence and territorial integrity of the Republic of Cyprus";

(d) a Declaration by the British Government in which it relinquished sovereignty over the island to the Republic of Cyprus, except for two areas (see below).

It was not until July 1960 that the British and Cypriot Governments reached final agreement on the areas of the bases remaining under British sovereignty, the agreement being embodied in the Treaty of Establishment, published on July 7, 1960. This treaty defined the areas of the two bases, Akrotiri and Dhekelia, and gave Britain the right to use 31 defense sites and installations, and 10 training areas and ranges in other parts of the island.

On April 14, 1964, Cyprus unilaterally abrogated the Treaty of Alliance with Turkey. [16643A; 16657A; 17727A; 20113A]

4. Britain–South Africa: Agreements on the Simonstown Naval Base
In 1898 the British naval base at Simonstown, 25 miles from Cape Town, was ceded to the British Admiralty for exclusive use as a naval base, but in 1930 an agreement was signed giving the freehold of the base to South Africa. On July 4, 1955, an agreement was announced, whereby the Simonstown Royal Naval Base was transferred to South African control, and a new naval command structure was set up to strengthen the defense of the sea routes round the Cape. Both the British and South African navies would work under the guidance of the Royal Naval Commander-in-Chief South Atlantic, and the Royal

Navy would continue to enjoy the facilities of the base.

On Jan. 25–27, 1967, negotiations between Britain and South Africa resulted in a new agreement on the future use of the Simonstown naval base, and on co-operation between Britain and South Africa in the defense of the Cape route. Under this agreement, the exact terms of which were not published, Britain withdrew the Commander-in-Chief South Atlantic, and the remaining British frigate from Simonstown, while the defense of the Cape route became primarily the responsibility of South Africa. [*14294A; 21948B*]

5. Britain–Nepal
(*a*) An agreement on the employment of Gurkha troops in the British Army was signed on Nov. 9, 1947.

(*b*) A Treaty of Peace and Friendship was signed on Oct. 30, 1950. The treaty, which laid down that each country would acknowledge and respect the independence of the other, replaced an earlier treaty of 1923, which had been made partially invalid through the independence of India and Pakistan. [*8987B; 11068C*]

6. Britain–Libya: Treaty of Friendship and Alliance
The 20-year Treaty of Friendship and Alliance signed by Britain and Libya on July 29, 1953, has been rendered worthless by Libya's request, in June 1967, for the withdrawal of all British forces from Libya and the liquidation of bases. [*13046D; 19986A; 21309A*] All remaining British forces were withdrawn from Libya by March 31, 1970. [*23836A*]

7. Britain–Venezuela: Settlement of Territorial Dispute
An agreement on procedure for the settlement of a territorial dispute between Britain and Venezuela, relating to some 60,000 square miles of territory in British Guiana (now Guyana), was signed on Feb. 17, 1966. Guyana became a party to the treaty on attaining independence on May 26, 1966. [*21324B*]

8. Treaties with Countries in the Persian Gulf Area
(*a*) *Britain-Bahrain.* A treaty of friendship, signed on Aug. 15, 1971, replaced earlier treaties of 1882 and 1892. [*24843A*]

(*b*) *Britain-Qatar.* A treaty of friendship came into force on Sept. 1, 1971, replacing a treaty of 1916 under which Britain had been responsible for Qatar's defense and foreign relations. [*24843A*]

(*c*) *Britain-United Arab Emirates.* A treaty of friendship, concluded on Dec. 2, 1971, replaced earlier 150-year-old treaties with the Trucial Coast sheikhdoms. [*25010A*]

Bilateral Agreements Between Commonwealth Countries

1. Australia–New Zealand
An agreement on integrated defense planning and buying of defense equipment was announced in Canberra and Wellington on Aug. 28, 1969. [*23548D*]

2. India–Bangladesh
A 25-year Treaty of Friendship and Co-operation, signed in Dacca on May 19, 1972, provided *inter alia* that neither country would participate in any military alliance directed against the other; both would refrain from aggression against each other; neither would give any assistance to a third party involved in an armed conflict against the other; and, in the event of an attack or threat of attack against either, both parties would immediately enter into consultations in order to take measures to eliminate the threat. [*25430*]

11

The French Community ("Communauté")

MEMBERS: French Republic (including Overseas Departments and Overseas Territories), Central African Republic, Chad, Congo (Brazzaville), Gabon, Madagascar, Senegal

The French Union, as defined under the 1946 Constitution of the Fourth Republic of France, was reconstituted as the French Community under the new Constitution of the Fifth Republic, published on Sept. 4, 1958.

Section XII of the Constitution deals with the Community. Its most important provisions are the following:

Art. 77. In the Community established by the present Constitution, the member-States enjoy autonomy; they administer themselves and manage their own affairs democratically and freely.

There is only one citizenship in the Community.

All citizens are equal before the law, whatever their origin, their race, or religion. They have the same duties.

Art. 78. The competence of the Community comprises foreign policy, defense, currency, and common economic and financial policy, as well as policy concerning strategic raw materials.

In addition, it comprises (unless excluded by special agreement) control of justice, higher education, the general organization of external and common transport, and telecommunications.

Special agreements may establish other common spheres of competence or regulate the transfer of competences from the Community to one of its members.

Art. 80. The President of the Republic presides over and represents the Community.

The organs of the Community are an Executive Council, a Senate, and a Court of Arbitration.

Art. 86. A change in the status of a member-State may be requested either by the Republic or by a resolution of the Legislative Assembly of the State concerned which has been confirmed in a local referendum, the organization and supervision of which is carried out by the organs of the Community. The terms of such a change in status are regulated by an agreement approved by the Parliament of the Republic and the Legislative Assembly concerned.

Under the same conditions a member-State of the Community may become independent. It then ceases to belong to the Community. *[Page 16533]*

Each overseas territory of France was given the choice of: (*a*) becoming a *département* of the French Republic; or (*b*) retaining the territorial status it then enjoyed; or (*c*) entering the French Community as an autonomous unit.

The Central African Republic, Chad, Congo (Brazzaville), Dahomey, Gabon, Ivory Coast, Madagascar, Mauritania, Niger, Senegal, the Sudan, and Upper Volta chose to join the Community. *[16529A]*

Early in 1960 the Mali Federation (comprising the Republics of Senegal and the Sudan) and Madagascar decided to ask for full independence while retaining membership in the Community. An amendment to the Constitution, enabling member-States to remain in the Community after attaining full independence, was approved by the French National Assembly on May 11, 1960.

The six present members of the Community in Africa gained their independence in June and August of 1960. The five remaining members of the old Community—Dahomey, Ivory Coast, Mauritania, Niger and Upper Volta—chose to leave the Community on attaining independence. (For dates of independence see table, page 149). (See also *Conseil de l'Entente*, page 189.) *[17359A; 17513A; 17569A; 17612A; 17799A]*

Development of the Community

The character of the French Community was radically altered by the new, independent status of all its members. This was recognized by the French Government which, on May 18, 1961, agreed upon the creation of new governmental machinery for dealing with the relations of France with French-speaking Africa and Madagascar. The new posts of Minister for Co-operation (to deal with technical assistance), Secretary of State for Political Affairs, and Secretary-General to the President were created. The function of the latter is to co-ordinate the activities of the President relating to the countries in question. A Council for African and Malagasy Affairs was also created. [18100B]

The powers exercised by the Community, as laid down in Article 78 of the French Constitution (see above), were transferred to each member-country on its attaining independence. The practical functions of the Community have thus been greatly reduced, and the bond between France and other Community members is now mainly restricted to a co-ordination of foreign policy in certain matters, and to co-operation in the fields of economy and education.

Mutual Defense Agreements

Agreements for co-operation between France and the newly-independent States were signed immediately after the various proclamations of independence. These agreements contained important provisions for mutual military aid. The mutual defense agreement between France and the Mali Federation, which may be taken as typical, stated that France and Mali would assist each other in defense matters; Mali would share with France in the defense of the Community and possibly of other African states; a Franco-Malian defense committee would be set up; Mali would obtain military equipment exclusively from France; and Malian nationals would be free to enlist in the French armed forces.

The defense agreements with the Central African Republic, Chad, the Congo Republic, and Gabon were supplemented in 1961, when these four States joined to form, with French co-operation, the "Defense Council of Equatorial Africa." [18363A]

France also has defense agreements with African countries outside the Community, namely Cameroon, Dahomey, Ivory Coast, Mauritania, Niger, and Togo.

Although all these defense agreements are still in force, the French military presence in Africa was drastically reduced in the year 1964–65. It was announced on Sept. 29, 1964, that by July 1965 it was intended to reduce the total of French forces in African States and Madagascar to about 6,600 officers and men, from an official total of 27,800 on Oct. 1, 1964. The remaining troops would be regrouped, and there would be four "support points," these being Dakar (Senegal), Abidjan (Ivory Coast), Fort-Lamy (Chad) and Diégo-Suarez, Ivato and Antsirabé in Madagascar. [20921A]

The Independence agreements signed by these States included no agreements on their continued membership in the Community.

Bilateral Agreements with France

	Independence Agreement Signed on	Proclamation of Independence	Co-operation and Mutual Defense Agreements Signed on
Community Members			
MADAGASCAR	April 2, 1960	June 26, 1960	June 27, 1960
*MALI FEDERATION	April 4, 1960	June 20, 1960	June 22, 1960
CHAD	July 12, 1960	Aug. 10, 1960	Aug. 11, 1960
			May 1, 1964
CENTRAL AFRICAN REPUBLIC	July 12, 1960	Aug. 12, 1960	Aug. 13, 1960
CONGO (BRAZ- ZAVILLE)	July 12, 1960	Aug. 14, 1960	Aug. 15, 1960
GABON	July 15, 1960	Aug. 16, 1960	Aug. 17, 1960
Former Members			
DAHOMEY	July 11, 1960	Aug. 1, 1960	
NIGER	July 11, 1960	Aug. 2, 1960	
UPPER VOLTA	July 11, 1960	Aug. 5, 1960	
IVORY COAST	July 11, 1960	Aug. 6, 1960	
MAURITANIA	Oct. 19, 1960	Nov. 27, 1960	

[17513A; 17569A; 17799A]

* After the secession of Senegal from the Federation of Mali (Aug. 20, 1960) and the subsequent French recognition of Senegal on Sept. 11, 1960, the Republic of Mali declared itself free from all links with France, claiming that the Franco-Malian agreements had been broken by France's recognition of Senegal. Senegal remains within the Community. [17359A; 17513A; 17569A; 17612A]

The Evian Agreements Between France and Algeria

After being a member of the French Community—divided into 5 autonomous territories comprising a total of 13 *départements* (as well as 2 *départements* of the Saharan territory under the control of the French Minister for the Sahara)—Algeria achieved its independence in 1962 after many years of warfare between French forces and the Algerian National Liberation Front.

On March 18, 1962, after several months of negotiations, a cease-fire agreement between France and the "Provisional Government of the Algerian Republic" was signed at Evian in France, together with a general declaration summarizing the agreements reached on the future of Algeria. The latter agreements included provision for a referendum on self-determination for the people of Algeria (held on July 1, 1962), and outlined the terms of Algerian independence.

Under the provisions concerning Franco-Algerian co-operation, Algeria guaranteed the interests of France and the rights acquired by individuals and organizations, while France, in exchange, undertook to provide technical, cultural and financial assistance to Algeria. Preferential treatment would be applied in certain spheres of trade, and Algeria would be part of the Franc Zone. In the *départements* of the Oases and Sahara the development of subsoil wealth would be carried on under Franco-Algerian co-operation, to be ensured by a technical body for co-operation which would include an equal number of French and Algerian representatives.

The military arrangements laid down in the agreements included the withdrawal of French troops from Algeria, and the leasing to France by Algeria of the naval base of Mers-el-Kébir and the air base of Bou-Sfer for a 15-year period. France was also granted the use of a number of other military areas required by her (including rocket and nuclear-testing installations in the Sahara).

The French Government, however, evacuated the Mers-el-Kébir base on Jan. 31, 1968, and the air base at Bou-Sfer on Dec. 29, 1970. [*22567A; 24000B*]

A convention signed in December 1967 provided for continued Franco-Algerian co-operation. [*25089*]

The Franc Zone

The Franc Zone provides for the free movement of currency among its members and a guaranteed franc exchange rate. Its members are France (with its Overseas *Départements* and Territories, except that of the Afars and Issas—formerly French Somaliland), Cameroon, the Central African Republic, Chad, the Congo (Brazzaville), Dahomey, Gabon, the Ivory Coast, Madagascar, Mauritania, Niger, Senegal, Togo, and Upper Volta.

12

The Americas

PAN-AMERICANISM AND THE FIRST REGIONAL SECURITY ARRANGEMENTS

1. The Monroe Doctrine

The idea of the unity of interests of the countries of the American continents, or of Pan-Americanism, received its first impetus from the so-called Monroe Doctrine which rejected all interference in American affairs by outside Powers.

The doctrine was proclaimed by President James Monroe in a Message to Congress delivered on Dec. 2, 1823, stating *inter alia:*

"The American continents, by the free and independent condition which they have assumed and maintain, are henceforth not to be considered as subject for future colonization by any European Power. . . . We would not view any interposition for the purpose of oppressing" the former colonies in the Americas or "controlling in any other manner their destiny by any European Power in any other light than as the manifestation of an unfriendly disposition toward the United States."

The doctrine was restated by President James K. Polk on Dec. 2, 1845, and by other U.S. Presidents later in the 19th century. It was formally recognized by Great Britain after President Theodore Roosevelt had pronounced the following corollary to the doctrine in May 1904: "In the Western Hemisphere the adherence of the United States to the Monroe doctrine may force the United States, however reluctantly, in flagrant cases of such wrongdoing or interference, to the exercise of an international police power."

2. The Earliest Pan-American Organizations

The first manifestation of Pan-Americanism was the First Congress of American States convened in Panama City by Simón Bolívar in 1826 which led to the signing of a "Treaty of Permanent Union, League and Con-federation" of Colombia, Central America, Mexico, and Peru.

An "International Union of American Republics" was set up at a First International Conference of American States in Washington in 1889–90. The fourth conference of this organization decided in Washington in 1910 to change its name to "Union of American Republics," and at the fifth conference in Santiago de Chile in 1923 it was decided to adopt the name of "Union of the Republics of the American Continents" and to establish the Pan-American Union as its permanent organ. This conference also formulated the Gondra Treaty providing for procedures for the peaceful prevention of conflicts.

At the 7th conference of the Union of the Republics of the American Continents in Montevideo in 1933 the United States joined the other member-States in signing a convention on the "Rights and Duties of States" declaring explicitly: "No State has the right to intervene in the internal or external affairs of another."

A Conference of American States held in Buenos Aires in December, 1936, adopted:

(*a*) a Pan-American Peace Pact, providing for consultation in the event of the peace of the American Republics being threatened or in case of war between American nations;

(*b*) a Pact for Co-ordination of Treaties, endorsing and amplifying existing treaties between American States; and

(*c*) a Non-Intervention Convention named the "Declaration of Inter-American Solidarity and Co-operation." [*2391C,D; 2392A*]

A further conference held in Lima in December 1938 issued the "Declaration of Lima" on inter-American solidary, under which regular meetings of American Foreign Ministers were agreed upon.   [3395A]

3. The Act of Chapultepec
The basis of later alliances between American States is the so-called Act of Chapultepec of 1945. This declaration on "reciprocal assistance and American solidarity" was issued on March 3, 1945, during an "Inter-American Conference on the Problems of War and Peace," convened by the Pan-American Union.

The declaration of the Act of Chapultepec contained the following provisions:

1. All sovereign States are juridically equal amongst themselves.
2. Every State has the right to the respect of its individuality and independence on the part of the other members of the international community.
3. Every attack against the integrity, territorial inviolability, sovereignty, or political independence of an American State shall be considered as an act of aggression against the other States which sign this declaration. Invasion by armed forces of one State into the territory of another, trespassing boundaries established by treaty and marked in accordance therewith, shall constitute an act of aggression.
4. In the case that acts of aggression occur or that there may be reasons to believe that an aggression is being prepared by any other State against an American State, the States signatory to this declaration will consult amongst themselves in order to agree upon measures they think it may be advisable to take.
5. This laid down that during the war against the Axis the American nations would, in the event of interference with the war effort of the United Nations, take any or all of the following actions: recall of diplomatic missions, breaking of diplomatic relations, interruption of economic, financial and commercial relations, breaking off of postal, telegraphic, radio-telephonic, etc., communications, and the use of armed force to prevent or repel aggression.   [7565A]

The signatories were Bolivia, Brazil, Chile, Colombia, Costa Rica, Cuba, the Dominican Republic, Ecuador, Guatemala, Haiti, Honduras, Mexico, Nicaragua, Panama, Paraguay, Peru, the U.S.A., Uruguay, and Venezuela. Argentina signed the Act on April 4, 1945.

4. The Treaty of Rio
A mutual defense treaty in pursuance of the Act of Chapultepec was adopted on Aug. 30, 1947, at an inter-American defense conference held at Petropolis near Rio de Janeiro. The treaty—known as the Treaty of Rio, or Inter-American Treaty of Reciprocal Assistance—was signed on Sept. 2, 1947, by 19 of the 21 American Republics, only Ecuador and Nicaragua—both of which had suffered recent *coups d'état*—withholding their signatures; Cuba withdrew from the treaty on March 29, 1960.

The treaty came into force on Dec. 3, 1948. Its principal terms are summarized below:

Art. 1. The signatories "formally condemn war and undertake in their international relations not to resort to the threat or use of force in any manner inconsistent with the U.N. Charter or of this treaty."

Art. 2. Consequently, they "undertake to submit every controversy which may arise between them to methods of peaceful settlement and endeavor to settle such controversies among themselves by means of procedures in force in the inter-American system before referring them to the U.N. General Assembly or the Security Council."

Art. 3. 1. The signatories "agree that an armed attack by any States against an American State shall be considered as an attack against all the American States," and consequently each of the signatories "undertakes to assist in meeting the attack in exercise of the inherent right of individual or collective self-defense recognized by Art. 51 of the U.N. Charter."
2. "On the request of the State or States directly attacked and until the decision of the organ of consultation of the inter-American system," each of the signatories "may determine immediate measures which it may individually adopt in fulfillment of the obligation contained in the preceding paragraph and in accordance with the principle of Continental solidarity. The organ of consultation shall meet without delay for the purpose of examining these measures and agreeing upon measures of a collective character that should be adopted."
3. These provisions shall apply "in case of any armed attack which takes place within the region described in Art. 4 or within the territory of an American State. When an attack takes place outside this area the provisions of Art. 6 shall be applied."
4. The above measures of self-defense "may be taken until the U.N. Security Council has taken measures necessary to maintain international peace and security."

Art. 4. This article defines the region to which the treaty refers, which extends from the North Pole to the South Pole, and includes Canada, Alaska, the Aleutians, Greenland, the Falklands, the South Orkneys, and Antarctica.

Art. 6. "If the inviolability or the integrity of the territory or sovereignty or political independence of any American State should be affected by an aggression which is not an armed attack or by an intra-Continental or extra-Continental conflict, or by any other fact or situation that might endanger the peace of America, the organ of consultation shall meet immediately in order to agree on the measures which must be taken in case of aggression to assist the victim of the aggression or, in any case, the measures which should be taken for the common defense and for the maintenance of the peace and security of the Continent."

Art. 7. "In the case of a conflict between two or more American States, without prejudice to the right of self-defense in conformity with Art. 51 of the U.N. Charter," the signatories, "meeting in consultation, shall call upon the contending States to suspend hostilities and restore matters to the *status quo ante bellum,* and shall take in addition all other necessary measures to re-establish or maintain inter-American peace and security and for the solution of the conflict by peaceful means. The rejection of the pacifying action will be considered in the determination of the aggressor and in the application of the measures which the consultative meeting may agree upon."

Art. 8. "The measures on which the organ of consultation may agree will comprise one or more of the following: recall of chiefs of diplomatic missions, breaking of diplomatic relations, breaking of consular relations, complete or partial interruption of economic relations or of rail, sea, air, postal, telegraphic, telephonic, radio-telephonic or radio-telegraphic communications, and the use of armed force."

Art. 11. "The organ of consultation referred to in this treaty shall be, until a different decision is taken, the meeting of the Ministers of Foreign Affairs of the signatory States."

Art. 20. "Decisions which require the application of the measures specified in Art. 8 shall be binding upon all the signatory States . . . except that no State shall be required to use armed force without its consent." [8881A]

The Treaty of Rio formed the basis of a series of bilateral treaties of assistance concluded by the U.S.A. with Brazil, Chile, Colombia, Cuba, Peru, and Uruguay after 1951 (see under "Defense Treaties of the U.S.A.").

Applications of the Treaty of Rio
The Treaty of Rio has been applied in the following disputes and civil conflicts in Latin America.

1948. Dispute between Costa Rica and Nicaragua. [9727A]
1950. Dispute between the Dominican Republic and Cuba and Guatemala. [10815A]
   Dispute between Haiti and the Dominican Republic. [10815A]
1954. Civil war in Guatemala. [13677A]
1955. Dispute between Costa Rica and Nicaragua. [14048A; 14142A]
1957. Border dispute between Honduras and Nicaragua. [15574B]
1959. Attempted invasion of Panama. [16817A]
   Attempted coup d'état in Nicaragua. [16898A]
1960. Dispute between Venezuela and the Dominican Republic. [17548A]
1962. Events in Cuba caused the treaty to be invoked twice in this year. [18713A; 19059A]
1963. Dispute between Haiti and the Dominican Republic.
   Dispute between Venezuela and Cuba. [20069A]
1964. Dispute between Panama and the U.S.A. [19927A]
   Venezuelan accusation of aggression by Cuba. [20336A]
1965. Civil war in the Dominican Republic. [20813A]

THE ORGANIZATION OF AMERICAN STATES (OAS)

Members: Argentina, Barbados, Bolivia, Brazil, Chile, Colombia, Costa Rica, Dominican Republic, Ecuador, El Salvador, Guatemala, Haiti, Honduras, Jamaica, Mexico, Nicaragua, Panama, Paraguay, Peru, Trinidad and Tobago, U.S.A., Uruguay, Venezuela
Observers: Canada, France, Guyana

The Organization of American States was formed in 1948 as a regional alliance, under the United Nations, to foster mutual understanding and co-operation among the nations of the Western Hemisphere. The Charter of the OAS was drawn up in treaty form at the ninth Inter-American Conference, held in Bogotá in April 1948, and was signed by all 21 American Republics (the present members of the OAS without Trinidad and Tobago, Barbados, and Jamaica, which joined in February and October 1967 and June 1969 respectively, and with Cuba, which was later excluded from the organization, see below, page 159). The Charter gave permanent legal form to the hitherto loosely and indefinitely organized Pan-American system.

The OAS Charter

A summary of the main provisions of the Charter of the Organization of American States is given below:

CHAPTER 1
Nature and Purposes

Art. 1. The American States "establish the international organization that they have developed to achieve an order of peace and justice, promote their solidarity, strengthen their collaboration, and defend their sovereignty, territorial integrity, and independence. The Organization of American States is a regional agency within the United Nations."

Art. 2. All American States ratifying the Charter are members of the Organization.

Art. 3. Any new political entity arising from the union of several member-States which, as such, ratifies the Charter shall become a member of the Organization, the States forming the new entity forfeiting their separate membership.

Art. 4. The Organization has the following aims: (a) to strengthen the peace and security of the continent; (b) to prevent possible causes of difficulties and ensure the pacific settlement of disputes arising among member-States; (c) to organize "solidarity action" by those States in the event of aggression; (d) to seek the solution of political, juridical, and economic problems arising among them; (e) to promote by co-operative action mutual economic, social, and cultural development.

CHAPTER 2
Principles

Art. 5. This reaffirms a number of principles, *inter alia* respect for the "personality and sovereignty of States," for the fulfilment of international obligations derived from treaties and other sources of international law, and for the human rights of the individual without distinction of race, creed, color, sex, or nationality. It also states that the solidarity of the American nations "requires their political organization on the basis of effective exercise of representative democracy"; that "aggression against one American State is aggression against all the others"; and that "the spiritual unity of the continent is based on respect for the cultural value of the American countries and demands their close co-operation"; and that "economic co-operation is essential to the common welfare of the continent."

CHAPTER 3
Fundamental Rights and Duties of States

Arts. 6–19. This section also enunciates various principles, *inter alia* that States are juridically equal (Art. 6); that each State has "the right to develop its cultural, political, and economic life freely and naturally" (Art. 13); that "no State or group of States has the right to intervene in any way, directly or indirectly, for any reason whatever, in the internal or external affairs of any other State" (Arts. 15–16); and that "the American States bind themselves not to use force except in self-defense or in accordance with existing treaties" (Arts. 18–19). Art. 17 stipulates: "The territory of a State is inviolable; it may not be the object, even temporarily, of military occupation or of other measures of force taken by another State. No territorial acquisitions or special advantages obtained either by force or other means of coercion shall be recognized."

CHAPTER 4
Pacific Settlement of Disputes

Arts. 20–23. All inter-American disputes, before being referred to the Security Council, shall be submitted to one or other of the following peaceful procedures: direct negotiation, good offices, mediation, investigation and conciliation, judicial procedure, arbitration, and those which the parties may especially agree upon at any time. A special treaty will establish the proper means of settling disputes and determine appropriate procedures.

CHAPTER 5
Collective Security

Art. 24. "Every act of aggression against an American State shall be considered an act of aggression against the other American States."

Art. 25. If the territorial integrity, sovereignty, or political independence of any American State is affected by an armed attack or other act of aggression, or by any extra-continental conflict, or by a conflict between two or more American States, the American States shall apply the measures and procedures established in the special treaties on the subject.

CHAPTER 6
Economic Co-operation

Art. 26. The member-States will co-operate to strengthen their economic structure, develop their agriculture and mining, promote their industry, and increase their trade.

Art. 27. If the economy of an American State is affected by serious conditions that cannot be satisfactorily remedied by its unaided efforts, it may place its economic problems before the Inter-American Economic and Social Council (see below) to seek the most appropriate solution of such problems.

CHAPTER 7
Social Co-operation

Arts. 28–29. The member-States will co-operate to achieve just and decent living conditions for their populations, and affirm the desirability of developing their social legislation on the following bases: "(a) all human beings, without distinction as to race, nationality, sex, creed, or social condition, have the right to attain material well-being and spiritual growth under circumstances of liberty, dignity, equality of opportunity, and economic security; (b) work is a right and a social duty . . . to be performed under conditions that ensure life, health, and a decent living standard both during working years and in old age or incapacity."

CHAPTER 8
Cultural Co-operation

Arts. 30–31. The member-States agree that (a) elementary education shall be compulsory and, when provided by the State, without cost; (b) higher education shall be available to all without distinction as to race, nationality, sex, language, creed, or social condition. They undertake to facilitate cultural interchange by all media of expression.

Chapters 9–15 (Arts. 32–101) deal with the structure and functions of the organs of the OAS (see below under separate heading). Chapter 16 (Art. 102) upholds the rights and obligations of the member-States under the United Nations Charter; and Chapters 17 and 18 (Arts. 103–112) contain miscellaneous provisions covering, *inter alia,* the diplomatic immunity of OAS officials, and the ratification and entry into force of the Charter. [*9293A*]

The Bogotá Charter of the OAS entered into force on Dec. 13, 1957.

The 1948 Bogotá Declarations

(a) A declaration condemning the existence of European colonies in the Western Hemisphere and establishing an inter-American body to study the problem and seek peaceful means of solving it was adopted at the Bogotá conference; the declaration was approved by 17 of the 21 countries represented, those abstaining being the U.S.A., Brazil, Chile, and the Dominican Republic.

The declaration considered "that the historical process of emancipation of America will not be completed so long as there remain on the continent peoples and regions subjected to colonial regimes or territories occupied by non-American countries," and described as a "just aspiration" that an end be put to colonialism and to occupation of American territories by extra-continental countries. There would be created, the declaration continued, an "American Commission of Dependent Territories" to centralize the study of the colonial problem, composed of one representative from each member-State, and it would be considered to be installed when two-thirds of those representatives had been named. Its site would be Havana and its functions would include study of the "colonial situation" and the seeking of peaceful means for "the abolition of colonialism as well as the occupation of American territories by extra-continental countries." It would submit a report on each territory to the Council, which would inform the member-States, the reports being subsequently considered at the first meeting of the Foreign Ministers. "The creation of this Commission," the declaration concluded, "and the exercise of its functions, shall not exclude or limit the rights and actions of interested States in seeking directly and by peaceful means the solution of problems affecting them."

(b) Another declaration reaffirming the faith of the American States in democracy and condemning Communism was also adopted.

This declaration said *inter alia* that "the present international situation demands urgent measures to safeguard peace and defend mutual respect among States, proscribing tactics of totalitarian hegemony irreconcilable with the tradition of the American countries and preventing agents at the service of international Communism or any totalitarianism from seeking to distort the free world of the peoples of this Hemisphere." It reiterated "the faith that the peoples of the New World have placed in the ideal and reality of democracy"; condemned the "interference of any foreign Power, or any political organization serving the interests of a foreign Power, in the public life of the nations of the American continent"; and promised that the American States would adopt within their respective territories the necessary measures to prevent and uproot activities directed or instigated by foreign Governments which tended to subvert their institutions through violence or to promote disorder in their internal political life. [9293A]

Amendments to the Charter

1. ACT OF RIO DE JANEIRO

The Act of Rio de Janeiro, embodying suggestions for the amendment of the OAS Charter, was signed by delegates of the 19 American nations (all OAS members except Venezuela) represented at the Second Special Inter-American Conference, held at Rio de Janeiro on Nov. 17–30, 1965. The principal sections of this document are given below:

The Second Special Inter-American Conference:
Reaffirms:
The principles and standards in effect that are embodied in Part One of the Charter of the Organization of American States;
Declares:
(1) That it is essential to forge a new dynamism for the Inter-American system and to avoid duplication of efforts and conflicts of jurisdiction among its organs, in order to facilitate co-operation between the American States and obtain a more rational utilization of the resources of the Organization;

(2) That it is essential to modify the working structure of the Organization of American States as defined in the Charter; and
Resolves: . . .
(3) To entrust to a Special Committee, composed of representatives of each of the member-States, the preparation of a preliminary draft proposal on amendments to the Charter of the Organization.
(4) The Special Committee shall use the following guidelines for the amendment of the Charter of the Organization:
(*a*) An Inter-American conference, as the highest body of the OAS, shall be convened annually at a different location and on a fixed date, for the purposes set forth in Article 33 of the Charter and to approve the program and budget of the Organization, to determine the quotas of the member-States, and to co-ordinate the activities of the organs and agencies of the inter-American system.
(*b*) The Meeting of Consultation of Ministers of Foreign Affairs shall be retained in the form established in Article 39 of the Charter.
(*c*) There shall be three Councils, directly responsible to the Inter-American Conference, as follows:
(i) The present Council of the Organization, which shall be permanent in nature and, in addition to the pertinent powers that may be assigned to it in the Charter of the Organization and inter-American treaties and agreements as well as those relative to the maintenance of peace and the peaceful settlement of disputes, shall be the executive body for the decisions the Inter-American Conference or the Meeting of Consultation does not entrust to the Inter-American Economic and Social Council, to the Inter-American Educational, Scientific, and Cultural Council, or to other organs;
(ii) The Inter-American Economic and Social Council (IA-ECOSOC), which shall meet at least once a year and shall have a permanent executive committee with a structure similar to that of CIAP (the Inter-American Committee for the Alliance for Progress). CIAP shall act as the executive committee of the IA-ECOSOC so long as the Alliance for Progress is in force; and
(iii) The Inter-American Educational, Scientific, and Cultural Council, which shall meet when convoked by the Inter-American Conference and shall have as its duties, in addition to promoting education, science, and culture, those assigned to the present Inter-American Cultural Council in Articles 73 and 74 of the OAS Charter. . . . The Inter-American Educational, Scientific, and Cultural Council shall have a permanent committee, and its activities in the fields of education and training should be closely co-ordinated, whenever pertinent, with those of the IA-ECOSOC.
(*d*) The Pan-American Union shall continue to function as the central and permanent organ of the OAS and the General Secretariat of the Organization, adapting its functions to the needs of the inter-American system.
(*e*) The Secretary-General and the Assistant Secretary-General of the Organization shall hold office for five years.
(*f*) The present Inter-American Juridical Committee of Rio de Janeiro shall be maintained as an advisory organ with the structure and functions deemed desirable by the Special Committee, and the situation of the Inter-American Council of Jurists shall be studied.
(*g*) A study shall be made of the advisability of locating the permanent headquarters of all the Councils in one place or having them geographically decentralized, as well as a study of the feasibility of proceeding similarly in the case of the other OAS organs and agencies. . . .

(*h*) The provisions of the Act of Washington, signed at the First Special Inter-American Conference on Dec. 18, 1964, regulating the admission of new members shall be included. [*22229A*]

2. DECLARATION OF BOGOTÁ

The Presidents of Chile, Colombia, and Venezuela, and personal representatives of the Presidents of Ecuador and Peru, met at Bogotá on Aug. 14–16, 1966, to consider the question of the reform of the OAS Charter with the emphasis on social and economic development. Those present on Aug. 16 signed the Declaration of Bogotá, which reasserted the principle of non-intervention in the internal affairs of American States; called on the rich nations of the world to assist in Latin American development; demanded "greater respect by the United States for the rules of international trade"; and advocated economic integration in the Americas, particularly in the form of closer relations between the Latin American Free Trade Association (LAFTA) and the Central American Common Market (see below). [*22229A*]

Structure of the Organization

Inter-American Conference
The supreme organ of the OAS is the Inter-American Conference, which meets in ordinary session every 5 years. A Special Inter-American Conference may be convened at the request of two-thirds of the OAS members. The Conference, in which each member-State has one vote, determines the policy and activities of the other OAS organs (for proposed changes in the organization of the Conference see under Act of Rio, above).

Meetings of Foreign Ministers
The Foreign Ministers of the OAS member-countries meet from time to time as circumstances demand. These meetings have a purely consultative function. Any member may request the OAS Council (see below) to convene a meeting of Foreign Ministers; the Council decides whether or not to do so by an absolute majority vote. Under Article 43 of the OAS Charter, a meeting of Foreign Ministers is called immediately in case of an armed attack on an American State, or within the region of inter-American security delimited by treaties in force. The meetings may be assisted by an Advisory Defense Committee, on which each member-State is represented by its highest military authority.

Council of the Organization
The Council, the permanent organ of the OAS, comprises representatives with ambassadorial rank from each member-State, and any other representatives appointed by the Governments. It deals with matters referred to it by the Inter-American Conference and the Foreign Ministers' meetings, and supervises the activities of the Pan-American Union (see below). In the event of an act of aggression, the Council acts as an organ of consultation. Its Chairman and Vice-Chairman are elected annually. (For the proposed revised status of the Council see under Act of Rio, above.)

Organs of the Council
The Council works through three organs: the Inter-American Economic and Social Council (IA-ECOSOC); the Inter-American Council of Jurists; and the Inter-American Cultural Council.

The Inter-American Economic and Social Council, which had been in existence since 1945, was incorporated into the OAS Charter in 1948. The aim of IA-ECOSOC is to promote economic and social improvement in American countries by the development of agriculture and industry. Meetings are held annually at ministerial and experts level. One of the main functions of IA-ECOSOC is to supervise the development of the Alliance for Progress (see below, page 161). The Act of Rio (see above) contains proposals for the revision of the structure of IA-ECOSOC.

The Inter-American Council of Jurists provides advice on juridical matters, promotes the development and codification of public and private international law, and studies the possibility of unified legislation among the member-States of the OAS. The Council, which meets at least every 2 years, consists of jurists representing each member-country of the OAS, the Secretary-General of the OAS, and the Director of the Department of Legal Affairs of the Pan-American Union. The Council of Jurists has a permanent 9-member committee, the Inter-American Juridical Committee. The Secretariat is the Department of Legal Affairs of the Pan-American Union.

The principal aim of the Inter-American Cultural Council is to promote cultural contacts and mutual understanding among the American nations, through educational, scientific and cultural exchanges. The Council, which meets twice yearly, comprises the Minister of Education from each member-country, the Secretary-General of the OAS, and its own Executive Secretary. It is served by a 5-member Committee for Cultural Action. The Secretariat is the Department of Cultural Affairs at the Pan-American Union (for the proposed Inter-American Educational, Scientific and Cultural Council see under Act of Rio, above).

Pan-American Union
The Pan-American Union, which has its seat in Washington, is the permanent Secretariat of the OAS. It is directed by a Secretary-General, elected by the OAS Council for 10 years. Under the proposed amendments to the Charter, however (see Act of Rio, above), the

Secretary-General and Assistant Secretary-General are to be elected for terms of 5 years only. The Pan-American Union is served by specialized departments dealing with economic, social, legal, cultural, administrative and scientific affairs, technical co-operation, statistics, and public information.

Specialized Organizations
A number of Inter-American Specialized Organizations of an intergovernmental nature exist within the framework of the OAS.

1. PAN AMERICAN HEALTH ORGANIZATION (PAHO).

Seat: Washington

This organization was founded in 1902 for the promotion and co-ordination of efforts to fight disease, to raise expectation of life, and to improve the physical and mental health of the American peoples. PAHO acts as a regional organization of the World Health Organization (see page 29). Its main tasks are the planning and co-ordination of programs for the extermination of infectious diseases and for the improvement of general hygiene; the strengthening of national health services; and the expansion of education and training facilities for health workers.

2. INTER-AMERICAN CHILD INSTITUTE (IACI).

Seat: Montevideo

The IACI was founded in 1927 to improve the health and living conditions of mothers and children.

3. INTER-AMERICAN COMMISSION OF WOMEN (IACW).

Seat: Washington

The purpose of the IACW, founded in 1928, is to work toward the extension of civil, political, economic, social, and cultural rights of women in the Americas.

4. PAN-AMERICAN INSTITUTE OF GEOGRAPHY AND HISTORY (PAIGH).

Seat: Mexico

In addition to the OAS countries, Canada is a member of this Institute, which encourages and co-ordinates geographical, historical, and related studies throughout the Americas, with the aim of promoting mutual understanding and opening up the natural resources available in individual countries of the Continents.

5. INTER-AMERICAN INDIAN INSTITUTE (IAII).

Seat: Mexico

The members of the IAII, founded in 1940, are Argentina, Bolivia, Brazil, Chile, Colombia, Costa Rica, Ecuador, El Salvador, Guatemala, Honduras, Mexico, Nicaragua, Panama, Paraguay, Peru, U.S.A., and Venezuela. The aim of the Institute is to promote the welfare of the native peoples of America. By making studies of Indian peoples, the Institute provides Governments with information relevant to the preparation of legislation, and also helps the Indians themselves to increase their consciousness of their cultural heritage. The IAII is a consultative authority for the Indian Bureaus in individual countries, and serves as the permanent committee of the Inter-American Indian Conferences.

6. INTER-AMERICAN INSTITUTE OF AGRICULTURAL SCIENCES (IAIAS).

Seat: Washington

The aim of the IAIAS is to improve agriculture and to conserve the natural resources of the soil, forests, and water, through education and research. It gives advice to Governments on the development of agricultural aid programs.

Special Agencies and Commissions
Other aspects of the work of the OAS are carried on though Special Agencies and Commissions all based in Washington.

1. INTER-AMERICAN STATISTICAL INSTITUTE (IASI).

The aims of the IASI, of which Canada is also a member, are to promote improvement in statistical methods; to encourage collaboration among statisticians; and to co-operate with national and international organizations in the promotion of statistical studies.

2. INTER-AMERICAN DEFENSE BOARD (IADB).

The purpose of the IADB is to bring about the fullest possible inter-American military co-operation, with the co-ordination of defense measures. An institution of the Board is the Inter-American Defense College, established in 1962 to provide special education for high-ranking officers of the Latin American armed forces.

3. INTER-AMERICAN COMMISSION ON HUMAN RIGHTS (IACHR).

This 7-member Commission, elected by the OAS Council, is the consultative organ on questions of human rights.

4. INTER-AMERICAN PEACE COMMITTEE (IAPC).

The 5-member Inter-American Peace Committee was founded in 1940 to ensure the peaceful settlement of disputes between member-States.

5. INTER-AMERICAN NUCLEAR ENERGY COMMISSION (IANEC).

The IANEC was established in 1959 to help the American Republics to develop and co-ordinate their researches in the peaceful uses of atomic energy.

6. SPECIAL CONSULTATIVE COMMITTEE ON SECURITY.

This Committee was founded in 1962 for the prevention of acts of subversion.

Protection of American States
Against Communism

In pursuance of the policies expressed in the Declaration on Communism of 1948 adopted at the Bogotá Conference (see above), further declarations were approved by OAS members as follows:

1. The "Declaration of Solidarity for Preservation of the Political Integrity of the American States against International Communist Intervention," presented by John Foster Dulles and adopted by 17 votes to 1 (Guatemala), with Argentina and Mexico abstaining, at the 10th conference of the OAS held in Caracas, March 1–28, 1954.

In its final form the Declaration specified that:

(1) The conference condemned the activities of international Communism as constituting intervention in American affairs; expressed the determination of the American States "to take the necessary measures to protect their political independence against the intervention of international Communism"; reiterated "the faith of the peoples of America in the effective exercise of representative democracy as the best means to promote their social and political progress"; and declared that "the domination or control of the political institutions of any American State by the international Communist movement, extending to this hemisphere the political system of an extra-continental power, would constitute a threat to the sovereignty and political independence of the American States. . . . and would call for consultation and appropriate action in accordance with existing treaties."

(2) The Governments agreed to take the following steps "for the purpose of counteracting the subversive activities of the international Communist movement within their respective jurisdictions": (i) to require "the disclosure of the identity, activities, and source of funds of those who are spreading propaganda of the international Communist movement, or who travel in the interests of that movement, or who act as its agents or on its behalf"; (ii) to exchange information with a view to implementing the resolutions adopted on this subject at inter-American conferences.

(3) "This declaration of foreign policy made by the American Republics in relation to dangers originating outside this hemisphere is designed to protect, and not to impair, the inalienable right of each American State freely to choose its own form of government and economic system, and to live its own social and cultural life." [13669A]

2. The "Declaration of San José," adopted unanimously (after the withdrawal of the Cuban delegation from the conference) at the meeting of OAS Foreign Ministers in San José (Costa Rica), Aug. 16–28, 1960.

The Declaration contained the following points:

(1) An "emphatic condemnation" of "intervention or the threat of intervention . . . from an extra-continental Power in the affairs of the American Republics," coupled with a declaration that "the acceptance of a threat of extra-continental intervention by any American State jeopardizes American solidarity and security."

(2) Rejection of "the attempt of the Sino-Soviet Powers to make use of the political, economic or social situation of any American State, inasmuch as any such attempt is capable of destroying hemispheric unity and jeopardizing the peace and security of the hemisphere."

(3) Reaffirmation of "the principle of non-intervention by any American State in the internal or external affairs of other American States," and of the right of each State "to develop its cultural, political, and economic life freely and naturally, respecting the rights of the individual and the principles of universal morality. As a consequence, no American State may intervene for the purpose of imposing upon another American State its ideology or political, economic, or social principles."

(4) "The inter-American system is incompatible with any form of totalitarianism and . . . democracy will achieve the full scope of its objectives in the hemisphere only when all the American Republics conduct themselves in accordance with the principles stated in the Declaration of Santiago de Chile."

(5) A declaration that "all member-States (of the OAS) are under obligation to submit to the discipline of the inter-American system, voluntarily and freely agreed upon. . . ."

(6) A declaration that "all controversies between member-States should be resolved by the measures of peaceful solution contemplated in the inter-American system."

(7) Reaffirmation of "faith in the regional system" and of "confidence in the Organization of American States, created to achieve an order of peace and justice that excludes any possible aggression, to promote solidarity among its members, to strengthen their collaboration, and to defend their sovereignty, territorial integrity, and political independence. . . ." [17691A]

3. A resolution on "the offensive of Communist Governments" in America, approved unanimously, in the absence of the Cuban delegation, at the conference of OAS Foreign Ministers in Punta del Este (Uruguay) held Jan. 22–31, 1962.

The resolution stated *inter alia*:

The Ministers of Foreign Affairs of the American Republics . . . declare that the continental unity and the democratic institutions of the hemisphere are now in danger.

The Ministers have been able to verify that the subversive offensive of Communist Governments, their agents, and the organizations which they control has increased in intensity. The purpose of this offensive is the destruction of democratic institutions and the establishment of totalitarian dictatorships at the service of extra-continental Powers. The outstanding facts in this intensified offensive are the declarations, set forth in official documents of the directing bodies of the international Communist movement, that one of its principal objectives is the establishment of Communist regimes in the underdeveloped countries and in Latin America; and the existence of a Marxist-Leninist Government in Cuba which is publicly aligned with the doctrine and foreign policy of the Communist Powers.

In order to achieve their subversive purposes and hide their true intentions, the Communist Governments and their agents exploit the legitimate needs of the less-favored sectors of the population and the just national aspirations of the various peoples. With the pretext of defending popular interests, freedom is suppressed, democratic institutions are destroyed, human rights are violated, and the individual is subjected to materialistic ways of life imposed by the dicatorship of a single party. Under the slogan of "anti-imperialism" they try to establish an oppressive, aggressive imperialism, which subordinates the subjugated nations to the militaristic and aggressive interest of the extra-continental Powers. By maliciously utilizing the principles of the inter-American system, they attempt to undermine democratic institutions and to strengthen and protect political penetration and aggression. The subversive methods of Communist Governments and their agents constitute one of the most subtle and dangerous forms of intervention in the internal affairs of other countries.

The Ministers . . . alert the peoples of the hemisphere to the intensification of the subversive offensive of Communist Governments, their agents, and the organizations that they control and to the tactics and methods they employ, and also warn them of the dangers this situation represents to representative democracy, to respect for human rights, and to the self-determination of peoples.

The principles of Communism are incompatible with the principles of the inter-American system.

Convinced that the integrity of the democratic revolution of the American States can and must be preserved in the face of the subversive offensive of Communism, the Ministers . . . proclaim the following basic political principles:

(a) The faith of the American peoples in human rights, liberty, and national independence as a fundamental reason for their existence, as conceived by the founding fathers who destroyed colonialism and brought the American republics into being.

(b) The principle of non-intervention and the right of peoples to organize their way of life freely in the political, economic, and cultural spheres, expressing their will through free elections, without foreign interference. The fallacies of Communist propaganda cannot and should not obscure or hide the difference in philosophy which these principles represent when they are expressed by a democratic American country, and when Communist Governments and their agents attempt to utilize them for their own benefit.

(c) The repudiation of repressive measures which, under the pretext of isolating or combating Communism, may facilitate the appearance or strengthening of reactionary doctrines and methods which attempt to repress ideas of social progress and to confuse truly progressive and democratic labor organizations and cultural and political movements with Communist subversion.

(d) The affirmation that Communism is not the way to achieve economic development and the elimination of social injustice in America. On the contrary, a democratic regime can encompass all the efforts for economic advancement and all measures for improvement and social progress without sacrificing the fundamental values of the human being. The mission of the peoples and governments of the hemisphere during the present generation is to achieve an accelerated development of their economies and to put an end to poverty, injustice, illness, and ignorance as was agreed in the Charter of Punta del Este.

(e) The most essential contribution of each American State in the collective effort to protect the inter-American system against Communism is a steadily greater respect for human rights, improvement in democratic institutions and practices, and the adoption of measures that truly express the impulse for a revolutionary change in the economic and social structures of the American republics." [18713A]

The conference decided on Jan. 31, 1962, by 14 votes to 1 (Cuba), with Argentina, Bolivia, Brazil, Chile, Ecuador, and Mexico abstaining—i.e. with the bare two-thirds majority required by the OAS Charter—to exclude Cuba from the Inter-American system, and this resolution was ratified by the Council of the OAS on Feb. 14 by 17 votes (including Argentina, Bolivia, and Ecuador) to 3 (Brazil, Chile, and Mexico). Cuba was also excluded "immediately" from the Inter-American Defense Board.

4. A resolution approved by the OAS Council in Washington on Oct. 23, 1962, by 19 votes to none (with Uruguay abstaining in the absence of governmental instructions).

This resolution, *inter alia,*

(1) called for "the immediate dismantling and withdrawal from Cuba of all missiles and other weapons with offensive capability";
(2) recommended that the OAS member-States, in accordance with Articles 6 and 8 of the Inter-American Treaty of Reciprocal Assistance, should "take all measures, individually and collectively, including the use of armed force, which they may deem necessary to ensure that Cuba cannot continue to receive from the Sino-Soviet Powers military material and related supplies which may threaten the peace and security of the continent, and to prevent the missiles in Cuba with offensive capability from ever becoming an active threat to the peace and security of the continent." [Page 19062]

5. A report by the OAS Council, issued on Feb. 24, 1964, indicting the Government of Cuba for "a series of actions . . . openly intended to subvert Venezuelan institutions and to overthrow the democratic Government of Venezuela through terrorism, sabotage, assault, and guerrilla warfare." [Page 20070]

6. A resolution adopted by the 9th consultative meeting of American Foreign Ministers in Washington on July 26, 1964, by 15 votes to 4 (Bolivia, Chile, Mexico, and Uruguay) with Venezuela, having brought a charge of aggression against Cuba, taking no part in the vote.

This resolution, based on a report by an investigating committee appointed by the OAS Council in December 1963, *inter alia,*

(1) declared "that the acts verified by the investigating committee constitute an aggression and an intervention on the part of the Government of Cuba in the internal affairs of Venezuela, which affects all of the member-States";

(2) condemned "energetically the present Government of Cuba for its act of aggression and intervention against the territorial inviolability, sovereignty, and political independence of Venezuela";

(3) requested member-countries, "in accordance with the provisions of Articles 6 and 8 of the Inter-American Treaty of Reciprocal Assistance, . . . (a) not (to) maintain diplomatic or consular relations with the Government of Cuba"; (b) to "suspend all trade, whether direct or indirect, with Cuba, except in foodstuffs, medicines, and medical equipment that may be sent to Cuba for humanitarian reasons"; (c) to "suspend all sea transportation between their countries and Cuba" except for transportation "necessary for reasons of a humanitarian nature." [20336A]

Convention on Kidnapping of Diplomats

A draft Convention outlawing the kidnapping of foreign diplomats was approved by the Foreign Ministers of the OAS member-States on Feb. 2, 1971, by 13 votes to 1 (Chile), with Bolivia and Peru abstaining and Barbados absent.

The Convention defined criminal acts against persons with diplomatic status as common crimes and not political acts; their perpetrators would therefore not be entitled to political asylum in any country whose Government had ratified the Convention but would be liable to extradition or trial. [24478A]

Promotion of Economic and Social Co-operation Among American States

An inter-American economic conference held under the auspices of the OAS in Buenos Aires from Aug. 15 to Sept. 4, 1957, approved the "Economic Declaration of Buenos Aires," which expressed the intention of the participating States to increase the volume of mutual trade, to reduce trade barriers, to endeavor jointly to solve the problems of producers of basic raw materials subject to excessive price fluctuations, to take measures to attract foreign capital and stimulate private investment, to establish sound financial and monetary systems in Latin America, and to increase technical co-operation through the OAS. [16423A]

On Aug. 16, 1958, the Brazilian Government proposed to all Latin American countries a plan known as "Operation Pan-America" for increased economic co-operation with a view to establishing, *inter alia*, an Inter-American Development Bank and eventually a Latin-American Common Market. A conference of Foreign Ministers of the OAS decided in Washington on Sept. 24, 1958, to recommend the establishment of a Special Commission for Economic Co-operation, and

such a commission was constituted in Buenos Aires from April 28 to May 9, 1959. [*Page 16378*]

The Act of Bogotá

At a meeting in Bogotá Sept. 5–12, 1960, the commission approved the *Act of Bogotá,* signed on Sept. 13, 1960, by all American Republics except Cuba and the Dominican Republic which, however, signed it later. Considering it opportune to give further practical expression to the spirit of Operation Pan-America, the Act contained the following recommendations:

Measures for Social Development

(1) Modernization and improvement of the legal and institutional systems of land tenure, agricultural credit, and taxation; acceleration of projects for land reclamation and improvement, land settlement, and the construction of farm-to-market and access roads; and governmental programs particularly designed to help small farmers.

(2) Expansion and improvement of schemes of housing and community services; strengthening of the existing facilities for mobilizing financial resources for housing, or, if necessary, the creation of new institutions for this purpose; expansion of those industries engaged in house-building; encouragement of pilot projects of "self-help" housing; and the purchase of land for low-cost and industrial housing projects.

(3) Development of all aspects of the educational system, particularly mass education aimed at eradicating illiteracy; instruction in agricultural, technical, and scientific subjects; and the training of professional personnel "of key importance to economic development."

(4) Improvement of health services, including the provision of medical services in remote areas, development of health insurance schemes, campaigns for the control or elimination of communicable diseases, especially malaria, and the provision of adequate water-supply facilities.

(5) More equitable and effective measures to achieve maximum domestic savings; improvement of fiscal and financial practices; and the allocation of tax revenues to an extent adequate for the above-mentioned measures of social development.

Creation of Special Social Development Fund

The Latin American countries welcomed the decision of the U.S. Government to establish a special inter-American fund for social development, with the Inter-American Development Bank as the primary mechanism for administering the fund.

Measures for Economic Development

(1) Provision of additional domestic and external resources for financing plans and projects of basic economic and industrial development, with special attention to loans on flexible terms and conditions, including repayment in local currency whenever advisable because of balance-of-payments conditions, and the strengthening of credit facilities for small and medium private business, agriculture, and industry.

(2) Special attention to the expansion of long-term lending.

(3) Examination of methods to deal with the problem of the instability of exchange earnings in countries relying heavily on exports of primary products.

It also provided for further meetings to implement the Act. [16423A; 17811A]

The Alliance for Progress

In a Message to Congress on March 14, 1961, President John F. Kennedy declared that the Act of Bogotá marked "an historic turning point in the evolution of the Western Hemisphere," and he requested massive aid to Latin America. The previous day, March 13, he had outlined a broad development plan for Latin America, which he called the "Alliance for Progress." It contained the following principal provisions:

(1) A "vast new ten-year plan for the Americas" should be initiated, for which, if the Latin American countries were ready to do their part, the U.S.A. would help to provide resources "of a scope and magnitude sufficient to make this bold development program a success."

(2) A ministerial meeting of the Inter-American Economic and Social Council would shortly be convened in order to help each country to formulate its own long-term development plans.

(3) The President would submit to Congress a request for the appropriation of $500,000,000 for aid to Latin America (see above).

(4) Support should be given to all projects of economic integration, such as the Central American Common Market and the free trade areas in South America.

(5) The U.S.A. was "ready to co-operate in serious, case-by-case examinations of commodity market problems."

(6) The U.S.A. would accelerate its "Food for Peace" emergency program.

(7) Latin American scientists would be invited to co-operate with the United States in scientific fields, and the U.S.A. intended to expand its science teacher training programs to include Latin American instructors.

(8) Technical training programs would be expanded, the Peace Corps made available wherever it was needed, and assistance given to Latin American universities, graduate schools, and research institutes.

(9) The United States reaffirmed its pledge "to come to the defense of any American nation whose independence is endangered."

(10) "Our friends in Latin America" were invited to "contribute to the enrichment of life and culture in the United States." [18035A]

The First Punta del Este Conference (1961)

President Kennedy's proposal for the establishment of an Alliance for Progress was approved by 20 member-countries of the OAS (i.e. all except Cuba) at a conference of the Inter-American Economic and Social Council at Punta del Este (Uruguay) on Aug. 5–17, 1961. The conference also issued (a) a "Declaration to the Peoples of America," and (b) a "Charter of Punta del Este" setting out the aims, methods, and execution of the Alliance for Progress.

The Declaration contained the following operative paragraphs:

This Alliance is founded on the principles that only under freedom and through the institutions of representative democracy can man best satisfy his aspirations, including those for work, home and land, health, and schools. The only system which guarantees true progress is one which provides the basis for reaffirming the dignity of the individual, which is the foundation of our civilization.

Therefore the countries signing this declaration . . . have agreed to work toward the following goals during the coming years:

(i) To improve and strengthen democratic institutions through application of the principle of self-determination by the people;

(ii) To accelerate economic and social development to bring about a substantial and steady increase in the average income as quickly as possible, so as to narrow the gap between the standard of living in Latin American countries and that enjoyed in the industrialized countries;

(iii) To carry out housing programs, both in the city and in the countryside, in order to provide decent homes for the American peoples;

(iv) To encourage, in accordance with the characteristics of each country, programs of integral agrarian reform leading to the effective transformation, where required, of unjust structures and systems of land tenure and use, with a view to replacing *latifundia* and dwarf holdings by an equitable system of property so that, supplemented by timely and adequate credit, technical assistance, and improved marketing arrangements, the land will become for the man who works it the basis of his economic stability, the foundation of his increasing welfare, and the guarantee of his freedom and dignity;

(v) To wipe out illiteracy; to extend the benefits of primary education to all Latin Americans; and to provide broader facilities, on a vast scale, for secondary and technical training and for higher education;

(vi) To press forward with programs of health and sanitation in order to prevent sickness, fight epidemics, and strengthen our human potential;

(vii) To assure to workers fair wages and satisfactory working conditions; to establish effective systems of labor-management relations and procedures for consultation and co-operation among government authorities, employers' associations, and trade unions in the interests of social and economic development;

(viii) To reform tax laws, demanding more from those who have most, punishing tax evasion severely, and re-distributing the national income in order to benefit those who are most in need, while at the same time promoting savings investment, and re-investment of capital;

(ix) To maintain monetary and fiscal policies which, while avoiding the calamities of inflation or deflation, will protect the purchasing power of the many, guarantee where possible price stability, and form an adequate basis for economic development;

(x) To stimulate private enterprise in order to encourage the development of Latin American countries at a rate which will help them to provide jobs for the growing populations, to eliminate unemployment, and to take their place among the modern industrialized nations of the world;

(xi) To find a rapid and lasting solution to the grave problem created by excessive price fluctuations in the basic exports of Latin American countries on which their prosperity so heavily depends; and

(xii) To accelerate the integration of Latin America so as to stimulate the economic and social development of the continent. This process has already begun through the General Treaty of Economic Integration of Central America and, in other countries, through the Latin American Free Trade Association.

This Declaration expresses the conviction of the nations of Latin America that these profound economic, social, and cultural changes can come about only through the self-help efforts of each country. Nonetheless, in order to achieve the goals which have been established with the necessary speed, it is indispensable that domestic efforts be reinforced by essential external assistance.

The United States, for its part, pledges its efforts to supply financial and technical co-operation in order to achieve the aims of the Alliance for Progress. To this end the U.S.A. will provide a major part of the minimum of $20,000,000,-000, principally in public funds, which Latin America will require over the next ten years from all external sources in order to supplement its own efforts. The U.S.A. will provide from public funds more than $1,000,000,000 during the twelve months which began on March 13, 1961, when the Alliance for Progress was announced, as an immediate contribution to the economic and social progress of Latin America. The U.S.A. intends to furnish development loans on a long-term basis, where appropriate, running up to 50 years and at very low or zero rates of interest.

For their part, the countries of Latin America agree to devote a rapidly increasing share of their own resources to economic and social development, and to make the reforms necessary to assure that all share fully in the fruits of the Alliance for Progress. The countries of Latin America will formulate comprehensive and well-conceived national programs for the development of their own economies as the contribution of each one of them to the Alliance for Progress. Independent and highly qualified experts will be made available to Latin American countries in order to assist in formulating and examining national development plans. [18378A]

During the following two years, however, the Alliance for Progress failed to achieve many of its objectives. Experts and leaders from the Latin American States criticized the United States for not having lived up to its promises, while U.S. spokesmen placed the blame on the Latin American countries themselves.

The annual report of the Alliance for Progress published on Nov. 11, 1963, showed that the actual growth rate of *per capita* income in Latin America in 1962 had been between 0.6 and 1 percent—as against 2.5 percent aimed at by the Alliance for Progress; this development had been due to a decline in Argentina's gross national product and a fall in Brazil's growth rate.

At a ministerial conference of the Inter-American Economic and Social Council in São Paulo on Nov. 12–16, 1963, President Goulart of Brazil called on the Latin American countries to unite in defense of their common interests in trade and aid, declaring that present trade conditions "represent a continual bleeding of our economies" since "our irreducible needs for imports, combined with falling export receipts, are in large measure responsible for the inflationary process which destroys the values of our national labors." All the Latin American countries, he stressed, were facing the same problem—of "breaking an agrarian structure that is manifestly archaic, in which the barriers of feudalism and intolerable privileges suffocate our effort for development, industrialization, and diversification." Deficits in the balance of payments forced the Latin American countries to negotiate loans or to obtain refinancing of debts in conditions which did not meet their interests, and the answer would not be found "in palliatives or false, superficial concessions" by the industrialized capital-exporting countries. "Our objectives," President Goulart declared, "must be the establishment of a new international division of labor, just and remunerative prices for our exports of raw materials, and expansion of our exports of manufactures and semi-manufactures."

A special session of the Inter-American Economic and Social Council in Washington on Jan. 29, 1964, set up an 8-man executive committee to provide new and more dynamic leadership for the Alliance for Progress. [19912A]

2nd Inter-American Conference at Rio (1965)

At a second special Inter-American Conference in Rio de Janeiro the U.S. Secretary of State on Nov. 22, 1965, read a message from President Johnson pledging U.S. support for the Alliance for Progress—which had until then totaled $4,000,000,000—beyond 1971, the terminal date agreed at Punta del Este in 1961. In return, the Latin American nations agreed to do more to promote their own economic development.

The conference also adopted the Economic and Social Act of Rio de Janeiro, reaffirming the principles and objectives of the "Declaration to the Peoples of America" and the Charter of Punta del Este (see above).

In Chapter I—Political Security and Economic and Social Development—the Act declared, *inter alia:*

To achieve the objectives of the Alliance for Progress, the obligation to co-operate in the solution of economic and social problems is essential, inasmuch as these problems can disturb relations among peoples, limit the opportunities to affirm the dignity of the individual, limit the full exercise of democracy, and endanger the peace and security of the nations.

In Chapter III—Mutual and External Economic and Social Assistance—the Act laid down:

(13) The member-States accept the obligation, within the framework of their constitutional processes and to the extent their resources permit, to help one another and to provide assistance, in the order of need, to the less developed countries of the system, with a view to achieving, on a national and regional level, the social and economic objec-

tives set forth in this Act, for the purpose of putting the countries of the hemisphere in a situation of development as soon as possible.

(14) The member-States undertake to avoid adopting policies, actions, or measures that might jeopardize the economic and social development of another member-State.

(15) The member-States recognize the necessity of co-operating individually and collectively in multi-national projects to accelerate the process of Latin American economic integration, particularly those projects originating in the organizations which have that purpose.

(16) The member-States agree to seek the solution of urgent problems that arise when the economic development or stability of any member-State is seriously affected by economic or trade measures adopted by other countries, by severe and continuing deficits in their balance of payments resulting from sharp drops in income from foreign sources, or by emergency situations, whatever their origin, that cause a shortage of essential goods and services.

The Act further contained provisions for the promotion of foreign trade by, *inter alia,* eliminating excessive tariffs, trade preferences, and other discriminatory practices, and lessening the fluctuations in earnings from export of primary products, and diversifying the export of manufactures and semi-manufactures from developing countries.

In Chapter V—Economic Integration—the Act stated:

(27) The American States recognize that the economic integration of the developing countries of the hemisphere should be one of the basic objectives of the inter-American system and, for that reason, will orient their efforts and take the measures that are necessary to accelerate the process of integration.

(28) With the object of strengthening and accelerating integration in all its aspects, special priority must be given to the preparation and execution of multi-national projects, and to the financing thereof, and the already existing economic integration agencies should co-ordinate their activities with a view to the earliest possible establishment of the Latin American common market. Likewise, the economic and financial institutions of the region should continue to give their fullest support to the organizations for regional integration.

(29) Within the framework of mutual assistance, the participation of the comparatively less developed countries in Latin American programs of multi-national economic co-operation should be encouraged, and the smooth, balanced development of Latin American integration promoted, with special importance attached to the needs of those countries and particularly to their infra-structure programs and programs for the promotion of new lines of production. [22229A]

A report issued by the Inter-American Committee on the Alliance for Progress in Washington on March 31, 1967, stated that during 1966 the *per capita* growth in goods and services in Latin America had been little more than 1 per cent on average, and that economic growth had barely kept ahead of Latin America's increasing population, which was expected to reach 250,000,000 by the end of 1967.

President Johnson asked the U.S. Congress on March 13, 1967, to increase aid to the Alliance for Progress by $1,500,000,000 over the next five years, in addition to the $1,000,000,000 already provided by the U.S.A. annually since 1961.

The Second Punta del Este Conference (1967)

The Punta del Este conference of American Presidents on April 14, 1967, adopted a "Declaration of the American Presidents," embodying an "Action Plan" for "Latin American Economic Integration and Industrial Development."

The aims of this Plan were defined as follows:

We, the Latin American Chiefs of State, agree to take action on the following points:

[A]

Beginning in 1970, to establish progressively the Latin American Common Market, which should be substantially in operation within a period of no more than 15 years.

[B]

The Latin American Common Market will be based on the improvement of the two existing integration systems: the Latin American Free Trade Association (LAFTA) and the Central American Common Market (CACM). The two systems will initiate simultaneously a process of convergence by stages of co-operation, closer ties, and integration, taking into account the interest of Latin American countries not yet associated with these systems, in order to provide their access to one of them.

The Plan envisaged a system of programmed elimination of duties and other restrictions from 1970 to not later than 1985 within the Latin American Free Trade Area, and of working toward integration in the Central American Common Market countries.

The Plan also stated:

The economic integration of Latin America demands a vigorous and sustained effort to complete and modernize the physical infrastructure of the region. It is necessary to build a land transport network and improve all types of transport systems to facilitate the movement of persons and goods throughout the hemisphere, to establish an adequate and efficient telecommunications system and interconnected power systems, and jointly to develop international watersheds, frontier regions, and economic areas that include the territory of two or more countries.

To this end it listed concrete proposals "for immediate implementation," including the completion of the Pan-American Highway.

On international trade conditions the Declaration stated *inter alia*:

The economic development of Latin America is seriously affected by the adverse conditions in which its international trade is carried out. Market structures, financial conditions, and actions that prejudice exports and other income from outside Latin America are impeding its growth and retarding the integration process. All this causes particular concern in view of the serious and growing imbalance between the standard of living in Latin American countries and that of the industrialized nations, and at the same time calls for definite decisions and adequate instruments to implement the decisions.

Individual and joint efforts of the member-States of the OAS are essential to increase the incomes of Latin American countries derived from, and to avoid frequent fluctuations in, traditional exports, as well as to promote new exports. Such efforts are also essential to reduce any adverse effects on the external earnings of Latin American countries that may be caused by measures which may be taken by industrialized countries for balance-of-payments reasons.

It outlined a program for overcoming these difficulties, *inter alia* by "the greatest reduction or the elimination of tariffs and other restrictions" without the more highly developed countries expecting reciprocity."

The Plan also listed proposals for the modernization of agricultural activities and for the adjustment of education to the demands of economic, social, and cultural development. [*22229A*]

Inter-American Development Bank (I.D.B.)

Members: All members of the Organization of American States with the exception of Trinidad and Tobago and Barbados.

An Inter-American Development Bank and a Fund for Special Operations were set up in April 1959. They represented the culmination of prolonged efforts by the Latin American countries for the creation of a development bank backed by the U.S.A., ever since the Marshall Plan was initiated in 1948 for the recovery of Western Europe. Until August 1958, however, the U.S. Government had always opposed such a scheme on the ground that private banks, the World Bank, and the U.S. Export-Import Bank were able to provide sufficient credit for sound development projects. The change in U.S. policy was the direct result of the meeting of the Foreign Ministers of the 21 American Republics in September, 1958.

The *Inter-American Development Bank,* founded to finance economic and social development projects and to provide technical assistance in member countries, opened with an authorized capital stock of

$850,000,000, of which $400,000,000 was to be paid in, the remaining $450,000,000 to be payable on call. The United States provided 37.5 percent of the payable capital, and 44.5 percent of that payable on call. By Dec. 31, 1965, the authorized capital of the I.D.B. was $2,150,000,000, of which $475,000,000 was paid in.

Loans from the capital resources are made for particular economic projects, and are repayable in the currencies lent.

The powers of the I.D.B. are vested in a Board of Governors, on which each member-country is represented by one Governor and one alternate. Executive powers are delegated to an Executive Board of seven Directors, six of whom are elected by Latin American countries and one nominated by the U.S.A.

At the Bank's 10th anniversary meeting at Punta del Este (Uruguay) on April 22, 1970, its achievements were criticized by the Peruvian Minister of Economic Affairs and Finance as "disheartening and incommensurate with what Latin America expected of economic and social progress," as the disparities in production, income, and living standards were "even more marked than at the beginning of the decade."

The *Fund for Special Operations* opened with a capital of $150,000,000, of which the United States contributed $100,000,000. The Fund makes loans on economically and socially useful projects which would not normally be acceptable to a bank. Repayments may be made in local currency. By 1966 the authorized capital of the Fund was $1,123,158,000. [*16772A; 21618A*]

A *Social Progress Trust Fund* came into being in June 1961, as an instrument for carrying out the program of the Alliance for Progress (see above). The Fund, which was set up by the U.S.A., included $500,-000,000 intended for long-range economic aid; $394,-000,000 of which were assigned to the I.D.B. The main uses of the fund are for land settlement and improved land use, housing, water supply, sanitation, and technical assistance. [*18234A*]

On Aug. 1, 1966, it was announced that a *Pre-Investment Fund for Latin American Integration* had been established. The $15,000,000 Fund is intended to finance the preparation of projects designed to promote and accelerate economic integration in Latin America. [*21618A*]

Of the loans made to Latin American countries in 1965 from capital resources and funds, 23 percent were for industry and mining, 21 percent for agriculture, 19 percent for water and sewerage, 15 percent for housing, 9 percent for transportation, 8 percent for electric power, 2 percent for education, 2 percent for pre-investment, and 1 percent for export financing.

THE ORGANIZATION OF CENTRAL AMERICAN STATES (OCAS)

Members: Costa Rica, El Salvador, Guatemala, Honduras, Nicaragua

An Organization of Central American States was first set up on Oct. 14, 1951, at the end of a conference held in San Salvador from Oct. 10–14, 1951, to discuss measures for common action by the five Central American Republics in regard to problems of mutual interest.

The Charter of San Salvador

The Organization came into being with the signing, by the five Republics (listed above), of the "Charter of San Salvador." It was officially stated that the object of the Organization would be "to promote by group action the strengthening of the bonds of fraternity among the Central American States, and to serve as an instrument for the study and solution of their common problems"; that periodic meetings of the Foreign Ministers would be held; that special committees, with representatives from each country, would be set up to study and report on matters of mutual interest; that these bodies would include a committee on economic relations (comprising the Finance Ministers of the five countries), which would report on the possibility of a Central American Customs Union, and a committee on educational and cultural matters (consisting of the Ministers of Education), which would consider the eventual standardization of educational courses and methods, together with the possibility of establishing a Central American University; and that the Organization would have a permanent secretariat with its headquarters in San Salvador. [*11830B*]

On Nov. 30, 1961, at a Conference of the Foreign Ministers of the Organization's member-countries, it was decided to prepare for the creation of a common supreme command with an integrated Latin-American army; integrated organs for security; a common defense council; and common organs to deal with economic and social matters.

The New Charter

At a meeting of Foreign Ministers of five Central American countries—Costa Rica, El Salvador, Guatemala, Honduras, and Nicaragua—held on Nov. 15–17, 1962, and attended also by an observer from Panama, it was provisionally agreed to set up a new Organization of Central American States (*Organización de Estados Centroamericanos,* abbreviated ODECA) superseding the organization of the same name set up in October 1951. The Charter of the new organiza-

tion, known as the San Salvador Charter (the same name as the Charter of the previous organization), was formally signed at a further meeting of Foreign Ministers held in Panama City, Dec. 12–14, 1962.

The new San Salvador Charter provided for the setting up of: (1) a Supreme Council of Heads of member-States; (2) a Council of Foreign Ministers; (3) an Executive Council with permanent headquarters in San Salvador; (4) a Legislative Council comprising three legislators from each member-country, to standardize legislation; (5) an Economic Council to pursue actively the aim of a common market similar to the European Economic Community; (6) a Cultural and Educational Council; (7) a Council of Defense Ministers to maintain collective security; and (8) a Central American Court of Justice. [*19264B*]

The new Charter, which came into force in 1965, was not signed by Panama, because of "international commitments and economic problems." (See also U.S.A.-Panama relations, page 173.) In addition to the organs mentioned above, there is a General Secretariat (the Central American Bureau), which serves to co-ordinate the work of the various organs and to prepare information.

Declaration of Central America

On March 18–19, 1963, a meeting between the Presidents of the member-countries of OCAS (or ODECA) and the Presidents of the U.S.A. and Panama took place in San José, Costa Rica. At the end of the meeting a "Declaration of Central America" was issued, in which it was stated:

The Presidents of the Republics of Central America and Panama are determined to improve the well-being of their peoples, and are aware that such a task demands a dynamic economic and social development program based on the carefully planned use of human, natural, and financial resources. It also depends on important changes of the economic, social, and administrative structure, within the framework of the principles that govern our democratic institutions.

The Presidents continued by pledging:

To accelerate establishment of a customs union to perfect the functioning of the Central American Common Market; to formulate and implement national economic and social development plans, co-ordinating them at the Central American level, and progressively to carry out regional planning for the various sectors of the economy; to establish monetary union and common fiscal, monetary, and social policies within the program of economic integration; to co-operate in programs to improve the prices of primary export commodities; to complete as soon as possible the reforms needed to achieve the objectives set forth in the Act of Bogotá and the Charter of Punta del Este, especially in the fields of agriculture, taxation, education, public administration, and social welfare; to take the above measures with a view to achieving the creation of a Central American economic community which will establish relationships with other nations or regional groups having similar objectives. [19309A]

OTHER AGREEMENTS BETWEEN THE ORGANIZATION'S MEMBER-STATES

Central American Defense Council

On July 2, 1965, the Governments of El Salvador, Guatemala, Honduras, and Nicaragua decided on the creation of a military bloc for the co-ordination of all defense measures against possible Communist aggression. Costa Rica and Panama were invited to join. The formation of this bloc is the task of a Defense Council, which has to prepare the plans for the co-ordination of the armed forces of the individual countries. The chairmanship of the Council is held by the Defense Ministers of each of the member-countries in turn.

The Central American Common Market (CACM)

Members: Costa Rica, El Salvador, Guatemala, Nicaragua

The Ministers of Economy of Costa Rica, Guatemala, Honduras, Nicaragua, and El Salvador, meeting in Guatemala City on Feb. 24, 1957, approved in principle two treaties designed to create a free trade area in Central America and a system of regional industries.

A 10-year multilateral trade treaty was designed to eliminate import and export duties on certain products embracing about 49 percent of inter-Central American trade on the basis of 1955 figures. In its original form the treaty laid down two lists of member-countries' products: (*a*) those which would have unhindered circulation within the projected free trade zone, and (*b*) those that might be subjected to quantitative export and import controls by member-countries. To this, the Ministers of Economy added a third classification—viz., products whose tariffs might be lowered gradually over several years to lessen the economic impact of the change. The treaty stated that the five countries would form a customs union after the creation of a free trade zone, "as soon as conditions are propitious."

The second treaty provided for the establishment of regional industries in areas where the most efficient use could be made of local resources and transport, and in such a manner as not to duplicate existing industries. It laid down, *inter alia,* that the industries concerned would have access to the free trade zone; that conflicting national interests would be resolved by a separate 5-nation pact to be signed for every regional industry established; and that such pacts would include the specific amounts of tariff reductions, tax-exemptions, fiscal benefits, and subsidies. [15468A]

A common market for Central America first came into effect on Jan. 8, 1959, when three out of the five countries which had signed the 5-nation treaty on the establishment of a free trade area had ratified it. It was brought within the framework of the Organization of Central American States in 1960. [16641A]

On Dec. 13, 1960, representatives of the Governments of El Salvador, Guatemala, Honduras, and Nicaragua signed, in Managua, the *General Treaty of Central American Economic Integration*. The 20-year treaty, which came into force in June 1961, established the Central American Common Market, and took precedence over all earlier free trade agreements between the contracting parties. The treaty provided for the immediate removal of internal duties on 95 percent of product classifications, and for the abolition of all tariff restrictions by June 1966. Provision was also made for the free movement of labor and capital throughout the treaty area. [18058C]

Costa Rica entered the Common Market in 1962, while Honduras withdrew in December 1970.

Treaties

The treaties on which the Central American Common Market system of equalization of duties and reduction of tariffs is based are the following:

(A) TRATADO MULTILATERAL DE LIBRE COMERCIO E INTERGRACIÓN ECONÓMICA CENTROAMERICANA.

This was signed in 1958 by El Salvador, Guatemala, Honduras, and Nicaragua, and in 1962 by Costa Rica.

It provides for the equalization of customs duties between the signatory countries, and for the removal of duties from regionally-produced goods, the latter to be completed by 1972.

(B) TRATADO DE INTEGRACIÓN ECONÓMICA CENTROAMERICANA.

This was signed in February 1960 by El Salvador, Guatemala, and Honduras; Nicaragua signed in December 1960, and Costa Rica in July 1962. When Costa Rica had added her signature in 1962, all five partners signed supplementary agreements establishing uniform duties for some 95 percent of all goods imported into their countries.

(C) TRATADO DE ASOCIACIÓN ECONÓMICA.

This treaty, between El Salvador, Guatemala, and Honduras, was signed in February 1960 and came into force in April 1960. It removed tariffs on groups of commodities in the trade between the three States, to the value of 50 percent of the total trade. The treaty is valid for 20 years with unlimited extension. A Development and Welfare Fund, with a capital of $5,500,-000 was set up under its terms.

(D) TRATADO DE INTERCAMBIO PREFERENCIAL Y DE LIBRE COMERCIO.

This treaty, signed by Costa Rica, Nicaragua, and Panama in 1961 and ratified in 1962, is aimed at speeding up economic integration through tariff reductions between the members.

By 1967 internal tariff dismantlement had been applied to 95 percent of all items of trade. The rates of a common external tariff had by then entered into force for more than 90 percent of items of trade.

Organization

The principal organ of the CACM is the Central American Economic Council, consisting of the Ministers of Economy of the member countries, which meets every three months. Its other organs are the Executive Council, composed of two government delegates from each of the member-countries, and the Permanent Secretariat in Guatemala City.

Institutions

There are a considerable number of Institutions which now function within the framework of the CACM. The most important of these is the Banco Centroamericano de Integración Económica (BCIE). Founded in 1960, the Central American Integration Bank came into operation on Sept. 2, 1961, with a capital of $40,000,000. On July 29, 1965, a Central American

Integration Fund, to finance regional infrastructure projects, was established when the U.S.A. placed a loan of $35,000,000 at the disposal of the members of the Bank. Each CACM member also contributed $1,400,000 to the Fund. In 1966 Mexico made a loan to the bank of $5,000,000.

A Camara Centroamericana de Compensación de Monedas (Central American Clearing House) was set up within the framework of the BCIE to encourage the use of Central American currencies within the area. The Clearing House began operations on Oct. 1, 1961.

The Unión Monetaria Centroamericana, a union of the Central Banks of the five Central American Republics, has been effective as a formal union since 1964. Its main organ is the Consejo Monetaria Centroamericano.

Other institutions are listed below with their dates of foundation:

Federación de Camaras de Comercio del Istmo Centroamericano.   Founded 1961.
Federación de Camaras y Asociaciones Industriales de Centroamerica.   Founded 1960.
Federación de Bancos de Centroamerica y Panama.   Founded 1965.
Instituto Centroamericano de Investigación y Tecnologia Industrial.   Founded 1955.
Escuela Superior de Administración Publica, America Central.   Founded 1954. Panama is a member.
Consejo Superior Universitario Centroamericano.   Founded 1948.
Instituto de Nutrición de Centroamerica y Panama.   Founded 1949.
Corporación Centroamericana de Servicios de Navegación Aerea.   Founded 1960.

Labor Council of Central America
A Labor Council of Central America, to orient and co-ordinate the labor and social policies of Costa Rica, El Salvador, Guatemala, Honduras, and Nicaragua, was established after the first conference of Central American Labor Ministers on April 20–23, 1964. At the conference El Salvador announced that from April 30, 1964, she would permit free transit of all Central American nationals in her territory. The conference adopted a resolution recognizing the importance of such mobility for the "full labor and social integration of the Central American economies." [20131B]

LATIN AMERICAN PARLIAMENT

At a meeting of representatives of Latin American countries and institutions held in Lima on Dec. 6–11,

1964, it was decided to set up a permanent Latin American Parliament with its headquarters in Lima.

The first session of the Parliament was held on July 17–18, 1965, and was attended by delegations from Argentina, Bolivia, Brazil, Chile, Colombia, Ecuador, Guatemala, Panama, Peru, Uruguay, and Venezuela. Under the statutes approved at the session, the Latin American Parliament is a permanent unicameral body, meeting in ordinary session once a year and in extraordinary session at the request of a majority of its members.

The functions of the Parliament are to promote Latin American integration in all fields, to protect human rights, to contend any form of colonialism, and to defend the peace.

LATIN AMERICAN FREE TRADE ASSOCIATION (LAFTA)

Members: Argentina, Bolivia, Brazil, Chile, Colombia, Ecuador, Mexico, Paraguay, Peru, Uruguay, Venezuela

The Treaty of Montevideo, creating a Latin American free trade area and establishing the Latin American Free Trade Association, was signed on Feb. 18, 1960, by Argentina, Brazil, Chile, Mexico, Paraguay, Peru, and Uruguay after ten months of negotiations. Colombia joined on Oct. 3, 1961, Ecuador on Nov. 3, 1961 and Venezuela on Sept. 1, 1966. Bolivia, which had taken part in the original negotiations for the treaty, but had declined to sign in 1960, eventually joined the Association on Feb. 8, 1967. Cuba was refused admission in September 1962. [*18752B; 21694B*]

The Treaty of Montevideo

The most important provisions of the Treaty of Montevideo are summarized below:

Arts. 2–3. The Free Trade Area would become effective not later than 12 years after the Treaty came into effect. During this period the Contracting Parties would gradually eliminate from the essential part of their reciprocal trade all types of restrictions and duties (i.e. customs duties and import charges of a fiscal, monetary, or exchange nature, but excluding service levies and charges) which affected the import of goods originating in the territory of any Contracting Party.

Arts. 4–7. National and Common Lists would be established at periodical negotiations between the Contracting Parties.

The National Lists would lay down the annual reductions in duties and other restrictions granted by each Contracting Party to the others; the weighted average of these annual reductions would be equivalent to at least 8 percent of the weighted average of the duties in force for other

countries as at Dec. 31 of the year preceding the negotiations, and the reductions would be continued cumulatively until the duties were essentially eliminated, details of the necessary calculations being laid down in the first Protocol to the Treaty. Any existing import restrictions would be relaxed to the extent required to permit the implementation of the duty reductions. National Lists would come into effect on Jan. 1 of each year, but for the initial lists the date would be decided by the Contracting Parties.

The Common List would cover goods on which the Parties had committed themselves by common agreement to eliminate entirely, over a period of not more than 12 years, all duties and other restrictions within the Area of the Association, subject to progressively enlarged minimum percentages of their total exchanges being included in the List and to the same scale of annual duty reductions being applied as described above for the National Lists.

Minimum percentages of the total trade among the Parties which would become subject to duty reduction under this heading would be 25 percent over the first three years, 50 percent over the second three-year period, 75 percent over the third three-year period, and the "essential part" of such trade during the fourth three-year period.

Art. 8. The inclusion of goods in the Common List would be definitive, and concessions granted on such products would be irrevocable; but concessions granted on goods contained in the National Lists might be withdrawn by agreement, against compensation.

Art. 11. If, as a result of the concessions granted, marked and persistent deteriorations develop in the exchange of goods incorporated in the liberalization program between one Contracting Party and the others as a group, the correction of these deteriorations will be examined by the . . . Parties at the request of the . . . Party concerned, with the aim of adopting measures of a non-restrictive nature to stimulate trade to the highest possible levels.

Arts. 15–17. The Parties would endeavor as far as possible to harmonize their import and export systems, as well as the treatment accorded to capital goods and services originating outside the Area. They would therefore gradually increase the co-ordination of their respective industrialization policies, especially by sponsoring agreements among representatives of the economic sectors concerned and by arranging among themselves agreements on the integration of industrial sectors. These agreements might contain, *inter alia,* provisions designed to harmonize the treatment given to the raw materials and components used in the manufacture of such products. The negotiations would be open to any Contracting Party interested and the results would be incorporated in protocols when found compatible with the general principles and objectives of the Treaty.

Arts. 18–20. "Most-favored-nation" treatment would be "immediately and unconditionally" accorded by each Party to goods originating in or consigned to any other Party, and similar provisions would apply to capital originating within the Area. Exceptions would be made in the case of advantages, concessions, and privileges granted or to be granted with the aim of promoting frontier traffic.

Art. 21. Each Party would accord to products originating within the Area not less favorable treatment with regard to internal imposts, duties, and taxes than that enjoyed by similar national products.

Art. 27. The Parties would endeavor "to co-ordinate their policies of agricultural development and the exchange of agricultural produce, with the object of securing the maximum yield from their natural resources, raising the standard of living of rural populations, and guaranteeing normal supplies for the benefit of consumers, without disrupting the customary production of each Contracting Party."

Art. 32. In order to create conditions favorable to the economic growth of economically less-developed countries within the Area:

(a) a Party might be authorized to grant special concessions to such a country with the object of stimulating the establishment or expansion of specified productive activities;

(b) a Party which "is, within the Area, relatively less developed economically" might: (i) carry out the program of reductions in duties and other restrictions under more favorable conditions, which would be specially arranged; (ii) adopt adequate measures for the purpose of correcting incidental imbalances in its payments position; or (iii) apply, when necessary, suitable measures to its domestic production of goods included in the liberalization program which were of "basic importance" to its economy;

(c) the Parties might: (i) undertake collective action in favor of a less-developed country by supporting and promoting, within and outside the Area, financial or technical measures to procure the expansion of already existing productive activities or to promote new activities, especially those designed to process its raw materials; or (ii) promote or support special technical assistance programs designed to raise the levels of productivity in specific sectors of production in such countries.

Art. 51. Products imported or exported by any Party would enjoy freedom of movement within the Area and would be subject only to the payment of the rates normally charged for services.

Art. 52. No Party might favor its exports by means of subsidies or similar measures. The exemption from duties or taxes levied on the product or its components when intended for domestic consumption, or the refund of such duties or taxes for exports ("drawback"), would not, however, be regarded as a subsidy. [*18370A*]

The treaty came into force on Jan. 1, 1962.

Organs

The principal organ of LAFTA is the Conference of Contracting Parties, whose main function is to bring about implementation of the Treaty of Montevideo. The Conference meets once a year in ordinary session and also meets in extraordinary session when convoked by the other main organ of the Association, the Permanent Executive Committee. The Executive Secretary is also General Secretary of the Conference.

Tariff Reductions

The year following the entry into force of the Treaty of Montevideo saw tariff reductions on some 2,500 articles, amounting to 27 percent of total duties. In the second year, however, the minimum 8 percent of tariff reductions provided for in the treaty was barely attained, the good results of the first year having been due to the inclusion, in the total of reductions, of many preferences already in force between LAFTA members.

Tariff reduction has continued to progress at a very slow rate, principally because of the unsatisfactory system, in use among LAFTA countries, of bilateral tariff bargaining on each item of trade. The trade among LAFTA member-countries still accounts for only about 10 percent of total foreign trade.

Stagnation of LAFTA

By the end of 1966 it was apparent that LAFTA had reached a state of stagnation. The 6th annual conference, held in Montevideo in November and December of that year, ended in disagreement. Argentina, Brazil and Mexico—the major industrial countries of LAFTA—refused to accept cuts in customs and import duties on industrial products. Venezuela, which had recently joined LAFTA, could not agree to the extension, to all LAFTA countries, of the favorable duties which she allowed the U.S.A. on 500 articles.

A Conference of Foreign Ministers of LAFTA countries, held in Montevideo in December 1966 to discuss the conversion of the Free Trade Association into a Common Market, also ended in disagreement. The Chilean Foreign Minister demanded the introduction of an across-the-board program of tariff reductions to replace the bilateral bargaining, and the establishment of a common external tariff. Argentina and Brazil, however, advocated a more gradual approach, and the Chilean proposals were rejected. Agreement was, however, reached on the setting-up of a permanent Council of Ministers as the supreme executive organ of LAFTA.

OTHER REGIONAL AGREEMENTS IN LATIN AMERICA

The Andean Group

Under the "Cartagena Agreement" signed in Bogotá (Colombia) on May 26, 1969, the Governments of Bolivia, Chile, Colombia, Ecuador, and Peru set up an Andean Common Market, in which all internal customs tariffs between the 5 member-countries were to be abolished by 1980. This Andean Subregional Integration Agreement came into force on Nov. 24, 1969, with the organization's headquarters in Lima (Peru). On Dec. 31, 1970, the group's member-countries decided to impose conditions on foreign investments in their countries.   [24939B]

River Plate Basin Development

A treaty for the economic integration and joint development of the Rio de la Plata region was signed in Brasilia on April 23, 1969, by the Foreign Ministers of Argentina, Bolivia, Brazil, Paraguay, and Uruguay. The treaty provided for the establishment of an Intergovernmental Co-ordinating Committee as the permanent body responsible for promoting and co-ordinating assistance from international institutions and for implementing decisions made by the five countries' Foreign Ministers.   [23400B]

BILATERAL AGREEMENTS IN LATIN AMERICA

Argentina and Chile
An arbitration agreement signed in Buenos Aires on April 5, 1972, between Argentina and Chile provided for reference to the International Court of Justice of any bilateral dispute not resolved by direct negotiation. The agreement superseded a 1902 treaty which had provided for arbitration by the British Crown in territorial disputes between the two countries. [25239A]

El Salvador and Honduras
El Salvador and Honduras agreed to the establishment of a demilitarized zone along their common frontier at a meeting of the Foreign Ministers of five Central American States under OAS auspices at San José (Costa Rica) on June 4, 1970.   [24056A]

The OAS had previously mediated in hostilities between the two countries in July 1969.   [23526A]

DEFENSE TREATIES OF THE U.S.A.

Many bilateral and multilateral agreements relating to defense have been concluded by the United States with partners throughout the world. Of these a number are direct defense treaties, while others are merely agreements on defense assistance.

BILATERAL TREATIES
The bilateral agreements are listed in alphabetical order. Where only one date is given, the agreement entered into force immediately after signature.

Argentina
Agreement relating to a military assistance program: May 10, 1964.

Australia
Mutual defense assistance agreement: exchange of notes Feb. 1 and Feb. 20, 1951; entry into force Feb. 20, 1951.

Agreement on a mutual weapons development program; Aug. 23, 1960.   [17651B]

Agreement relating to the establishment of a United States naval communication station in Australia: signed May 9, 1963; entered into force June 28, 1963. [19450A]

Belgium
Mutual defense assistance agreement under the North Atlantic Treaty: signed Jan. 27, 1950; entered into force March 30, 1950. (See also agreements with Britain, Denmark, France, Italy, Luxemburg, the Netherlands, and Norway.)   [10509A]

Bolivia
Military assistance agreement: exchange of notes March 21 and April 22, 1958; entry into force April 22, 1958.

Agreement on the furnishing of defense articles and services to Bolivia: April 26, 1962.

Brazil
Agreement for the establishment of the Joint Group on Emergency Supply Problems: July 24, 1951.

Military assistance agreement: signed March 15, 1952; entered into force May 19, 1953.   [12279C]

Agreement for the continuation of Joint Brazil–U.S. Military and Defense Commissions: exchange of notes Aug. 1 and Sept. 20, 1955; entry into force Sept. 20, 1955.

Britain
Arrangement relating to naval and air bases: Sept. 2, 1940.

Protocol concerning the defense of Newfoundland: March 27, 1941.

Mutual defense assistance agreement under the North Atlantic Treaty: Jan 27, 1950. (See also agreements with Belgium, Denmark, France, Italy, Luxemburg, the Netherlands, and Norway.)   [10509A]

Agreements concerning a long-range proving ground for guided missiles in the Bahamas: July 21, 1950, March 2, 1953, and April 1, 1957.   [10861D]

Agreements relating to the extension of the Bahamas Long Range Proving Ground by the establishment of additional sites in Ascension Island: June 25, 1956, and Aug. 25, 1959.   [14964B]

Agreement on the supply by the United States of intermediate range ballistic missiles: Feb. 22, 1958 (see page 109).   [16063A]

Agreement relating to the establishment and operation of a ballistic early warning station at Fylingdales Moor: Feb. 15, 1960.   [17283A; 18118A]

Agreement concerning the establishment in the Bahama Islands of a long-range aid to navigation station: June 24, 1960.

Agreement on the setting up of a missile defense alarm system station in Britain: July 18, 1961. [18228B]

Agreement relating to a weapons production program: June 29, 1962.

Polaris sales agreement: April 6, 1963 (see also page 109). [19389A]

Agreement concerning the availability of certain Indian Ocean islands for defense purposes: Dec. 30, 1966.

Agreement regulating the joint use of the British Indian Ocean Territory for defense purposes: April 1, 1967. [22107C]

Canada
Declaration regarding the establishment of a Permanent Joint Board on Defense: Aug. 18, 1940. [4214A]

Protocol concerning the defense of Newfoundland: March 27, 1941.

Agreement establishing a Joint Industrial Mobilization Committee: April 12, 1949. [9988B]

Agreement relating to the extension and co-ordination of the continental radar defense system: Aug. 1, 1951.

Agreement on the establishment and operation of a distant early warning system between the U.S. and Canada: May 5, 1955.

Agreement on the organization and operations of the North American Air Defense Command (NORAD): May 12, 1958. Extended March 30, 1968. [22662A; 16230B]

Agreement providing for the establishment of a Canada–U.S. Committee on Joint Defense: exchange of notes Aug. 29 and Sept. 2, 1958; entry into force Sept. 2, 1958. [16314A]

Agreement relating to the establishment, maintenance, and operation by the U.S. of aerial refueling facilities in Canada: June 20, 1958.

Agreement relating to the establishment, maintenance, and operation of short-range tactical air navigation (TACAN) facilities in Canada: May 1, 1959.

Agreement on the establishment of a ballistic missile early warning system: July 13, 1959.

Agreement for improving the air defense of the Canada–U.S. region of NATO: June 12, 1961. [18176D]

Agreement on the extension and strengthening of the continental air defense system (CADIN): Sept. 27, 1961.

Agreement establishing a Joint United States–Canadian Civil Emergency Planning Committee: Nov. 15, 1963.

There are, in addition, a number of agreements between the U.S. and Canada relating to air bases, radar stations, and communications facilities in particular regions of Canada.

Chile
Military assistance agreement: signed April 9, 1952; entered into force July 11, 1952. [12279C]

China (Taiwan)
Agreement relating to the presence of U.S. armed forces in China: exchange of notes Aug. 29 and Sept. 3, 1947; entry into force Sept. 3, 1947.

Mutual defense treaty: signed Dec. 2, 1954; entered into force March 3, 1955 (see page 200). [14007C]

Colombia
Military assistance agreement: April 17, 1952.

Agreement on Army, Navy and Air Force advisers: exchange of notes July 13 and Sept. 16, 1955; entry into force Sept. 20, 1955.

Agreement relating to the furnishing of military equipment, materials, and services to Colombia: April 3, 1961.

Congo–Kinshasa (Zaïre)
Military assistance agreement and provision for a military mission to Congo (Kinshasa): exchange of notes June 24 and July 19, 1963; entry into force July 19, 1963.

Costa Rica
Agreement on the furnishing of defense articles and services to Costa Rica for the purpose of contributing to its internal security: exchange of notes May 21 and June 18, 1962; entry into force June 18, 1962.

Cuba
Agreement for the lease to the U.S. of lands in Cuba for coaling and naval stations: signed Feb. 16 and Feb. 23, 1903; entered into force Feb. 23, 1903.

Under this agreement, confirmed by a treaty of 1934, the United States was granted complete jurisdiction and control over a military base on Guantanamo Bay at the southern tip of Cuba, in return for which the United States would recognize Cuban sovereignty over the area. After the deterioration in U.S.–Cuban relations in 1960, President Eisenhower issued a statement in November of that year, saying that the agreement on the Guantanamo Bay military base could be modified or abrogated only by agreement between the two parties, and that the U.S. Government had no intention of agreeing to modification or abrogation. [17787A]

Dahomey
Agreement on the furnishing of military equipment, materials, and services to Dahomey to help assure its security and independence: exchange of notes June 5 and June 13, 1962; entry into force June 13, 1962.

Denmark
Mutual defense assistance agreement under the North Atlantic Treaty: Jan. 27, 1950. (See also agreements with Belgium, Britain, France, Italy, Luxemburg, the Netherlands, and Norway.) [*10509A*]

Agreements concerning the defense of Greenland: (1) signed April 27, 1951; entered into force June 8, 1951; (2) signed and entered into force Dec. 2, 1960. [*11446A*]

Dominican Republic
Military assistance agreement: signed March 8, 1962; entered into force June 10, 1964.

Ecuador
Military assistance agreement: Feb. 20, 1952. [*12279C*]

Agreement on Army, Navy and Air Force advisers: exchange of notes July 29 and Aug. 24, 1955; entry into force Aug. 24, 1955.

El Salvador
Agreement on the furnishing of defense articles and services to El Salvador to contribute to its internal security: exchange of notes April 10 and April 13, 1962; entry into force April 13, 1962.

Ethiopia
Mutual defense assistance agreement: May 22, 1953.

Agreement on the utilization of defense installations in Ethiopia: May 22, 1953.

France
Mutual defense assistance agreement under the North Atlantic Treaty: Jan. 27, 1950. (See also agreements with Belgium, Britain, Denmark, Italy, Luxemburg, the Netherlands, and Norway.) [*10509A*]

Agreement on a weapons production program: Sept. 19, 1960.

Federal Republic of Germany
Mutual defense assistance agreement: signed June 30, 1955; entered into force Dec. 27, 1955.

Agreements on the training of German army and navy personnel: Dec. 12, 1956.

Agreement relating to a weapons production program: May 27, 1960.

Greece
Agreement on the use of certain Greek islands for training exercises by the U.S. fleet in the Mediterranean: exchange of notes Feb. 11 and Feb. 21, 1949; entry into force Feb. 21, 1949.

Agreement concerning military facilities: Oct. 12, 1953. [*13204C*]

Agreement concerning the status of United States forces in Greece: Sept. 7, 1956.

Agreement on a weapons production program: Feb. 15, 1960.

Guatemala
Military assistance agreement: June 18, 1955.

Agreement on the furnishing of defense articles and services to Guatemala to contribute to its internal security: exchange of notes May 25 and Aug. 2, 1962; entry into force Aug. 2, 1962.

Guinea
Military assistance agreement: June 29, 1965.

Guyana
Agreement on the future use of Atkinson Field: May 26, 1966.

Haiti
Military assistance agreement: signed Jan. 28, 1955; entered into force Sept. 12, 1955.

Honduras
Military assistance agreements: May 20, 1954, and Oct. 24, 1962. [*13677A*]

Agreement on Army and Air Force advisers: exchange of notes April 17 and April 25, 1956; entry into force April 26, 1956.

Iceland
Defense agreement pursuant to the North Atlantic Treaty: May 5, 1951. [*11454A*]

Agreement on the presence of defense forces in Iceland: Dec. 6, 1956. (See page 112.) [*15300B*]

India
Military assistance agreement: Jan. 13, 1965.

Indonesia
Agreement for a program of military assistance: Aug. 15, 1950.

Iran
Mutual defense assistance agreement: May 23, 1950. [*10751B*]

Agreement of co-operation: March 5, 1959 (see page 183). [*16748A*]

Israel
Mutual defense assistance agreement: exchange of notes July 1 and July 23, 1952; entry into force July 23, 1952.

Italy
Mutual defense assistance agreement under the North Atlantic Treaty: Jan. 27, 1950. (See also agreements with Belgium, Britain, Denmark, France, Luxemburg, the Netherlands, and Norway.) [*10509A*]

Agreement on a weapons production program: July 7, 1960.

Jamaica
Agreement on the furnishing of defense articles and services to Jamaica: June 6, 1963.

Japan
Mutual defense assistance agreement: signed March 8, 1954; entered into force May 1, 1954. [*13450B*]

Treaty of mutual co-operation and security: signed Jan. 19, 1960; entered into force June 23, 1960 (see page 199). [*17263A*]

Korea (South)
Mutual defense assistance agreement: Jan. 26, 1950.

Mutual defense treaty: signed Oct. 1, 1953; entered into force Nov. 17, 1954 (see page 200). [*13077A*]

Lebanon
Military assistance agreement: exchange of notes June 3 and June 6, 1957; entry into force June 6, 1957.

Liberia
Mutual defense agreement: exchange of notes Nov. 16 and Nov. 19, 1951; entry into force Nov. 19, 1951.

Agreement on military co-operation: July 8, 1959. [*17000B*]

Libya
Agreement relating to military bases in Libya: signed Sept. 9, 1954; entered into force Oct. 30, 1954. [*13790B*]

Military assistance agreement: June 30, 1957.

Luxemburg
Mutual defense assistance agreement under the North Atlantic Treaty: signed Jan. 27, 1950; entered into force March 28, 1950. (See also agreements with Belgium, Britain, Denmark, France, Italy, the Netherlands, and Norway.) [*10509A*]

Mali
Military assistance agreement: May 20, 1961.

Netherlands
Mutual defense assistance agreement under the North Atlantic Treaty: Jan. 27, 1950. (See also agreements with Belgium, Britain, Denmark, France, Italy, Luxemburg, and Norway.) [*10509A*]

Agreement on the stationing of U.S. armed forces in the Netherlands: exchange of notes Aug. 13, 1954; entry into force Nov. 16, 1954. [*13758A; 13931D*]

Agreement establishing an air defense technical center: Dec. 14, 1954.

Agreement on a weapons production program: exchange of notes March 24, 1960; definitive entry into force Jan. 2, 1962.

New Zealand
Mutual defense assistance agreement: June 19, 1952.

Nicaragua
Military assistance agreement: April 23, 1954. [*13677A*]

Agreement on Army and Air Force advisers: exchange of notes Jan. 17 and Feb. 9, 1957; entry into force Feb. 9, 1957.

Niger
Agreement on the furnishing of military equipment, materials and services to Niger to help assure its security and independence: exchange of notes May 22 and June 14, 1962; entry into force June 14, 1962.

Norway
Mutual defense assistance agreement under the North Atlantic Treaty: signed Jan. 27, 1950; entered into force Feb. 24, 1950. (See also agreements with Belgium, Britain, Denmark, France, Italy, Luxemburg, and the Netherlands.) [*10509A*]

Agreement on a weapons production program: Feb. 13, 1960.

Agreements on a shipbuilding program for the Norwegian Navy: (1) July 6, 1960; (2) exchange of notes Nov. 29, 1960; entry into force Jan. 31, 1961.

Pakistan
Mutual defense assistance agreement: May 19, 1954. [*13624A*]

Agreement of co-operation: March 5, 1959 (see page 183). [*16748A*]

Panama
Agreement on transit of U.S. troops across Panamanian territory for training purposes: exchange of notes July 18 and July 20, 1912; entry into force July 20, 1912.

Agreement on the furnishing of defense articles and services to Panama to contribute to its internal security: exchange of notes March 26 and May 23, 1962; entry into force May 23, 1962.

Paraguay
Military assistance agreements: (1) Aug. 25, 1962; (2) Feb. 10, 1964; (3) April 11, 1966.

Peru
Military assistance agreement: signed Feb. 22, 1952; entered into force April 26, 1952. [*12279C*]

Agreement on the furnishing of defense articles and services to Peru: exchange of notes Dec. 17 and Dec. 20, 1962; entry into force Dec. 20, 1962.

Philippines
Agreement concerning military bases: signed March 14, 1947; entered into force March 26, 1947 (see page 199). [*8538C*]

Mutual defense treaty: signed Aug. 30, 1951; entered into force Aug. 27, 1952 (see page 199). [*11715C*]

Agreements on military assistance: (1) exchange of notes June 26, 1953; entry into force July 5, 1953; (2) April 27, 1955. [*14297C*]

Agreement for the establishment of a Mutual Defense Board: May 15, 1958.

Portugal
Mutual defense assistance agreement: Jan. 5, 1951. [*11227E*]

Defense agreement: Sept. 6, 1951 (see page 112). [*11740B*]

Agreement on a weapons production program: Sept. 26, 1960.

Saudi Arabia
Agreement providing for a military assistance advisory group: June 27, 1953.

Senegal
Agreement on the furnishing of military equipment, materials and services to Senegal: July 20, 1962.

South Africa
Mutual defense assistance agreement: Nov. 9, 1951. [*11830D*]

Spain
Mutual defense assistance agreement: Sept. 26, 1953.

This agreement, concluded initially for 10 years, with two automatic extensions of 5 years, provided for material assistance on the part of the United States to support Spain's effective air defense, and to improve the equipment of her military and naval forces. In return the Government of Spain authorized the U.S. Government to develop, maintain, and utilize for military purposes, jointly with the Government of Spain, certain areas and facilities in territory under Spanish jurisdiction. The agreement was extended for 5 years on Sept. 26, 1963, when a joint declaration was issued under which, *inter alia,* the U.S.-Spanish defense agreement was recognized as "part of the security arrangements for the Atlantic and Mediterranean areas"; and both Governments recognized that "the security and integrity of both Spain and the United States are necessary for the common security." In an accompanying exchange of letters it was agreed to establish a joint U.S.-Spanish consultative committee on defense to meet monthly. [*13157A; 19736A*]

The agreement was, on June 20, 1969, extended for a further period of 18 months (from March 1969 to September 1970).

A new "Agreement of Friendship and Co-operation," signed in Washington on Aug. 6, 1970, contained a section on "Co-operation for Defense," under which the United States would have the continued use of three air bases, a naval base, and other facilities in Spain and would "support Spanish defense efforts." Both countries agreed to resort to "urgent consultations" in the event of "external threat or attack against the security of the West." At the same time the United States would make available to Spain credits of $120,000,000 for the purchase of military aircraft in the U.S.A., and funds of $63,000,000 for equipment for the Spanish land forces. [*24154A*]

Thailand
Military assistance agreement: Oct. 17, 1950.

An agreement on the withdrawal of about 6,000 U.S. military personnel (out of some 49,000 U.S. servicemen stationed in Thailand as a result of the Vietnam war) by July 1, 1970, was announced in Bangkok and Washington on Sept. 30, 1969. [*23600A*]

Trinidad and Tobago
Agreements on U.S. military bases in the area:
(1) exchange of letters Nov. 19, 1953 and July 19, 1954; entry into force July 19, 1954;

(2) Feb. 10, 1961 (agreement between the U.S.A. and the West Indies Federation) [*17998A*];

(3) exchange of notes Dec. 2 and Dec. 5, 1964; entry into force Dec. 5, 1964.

Uruguay
Military assistance agreement: signed June 30, 1952; entered into force June 11, 1953. [*12344A*]

Vietnam (South)
(see page 203).

MULTILATERAL TREATIES

The multilateral defense treaties in which the United States is concerned are listed in chronological order.

1. The Act of Havana
Signed on July 30, 1940, by representatives of all 21 American Republics, the Act of Havana provided for the collective trusteeship, by American nations, of European colonies and possessions in the Americas, should any attempt be made to transfer the sovereignty of these colonies from one non-American power to another. The Act came into force immediately. [*4191A*]

2. The Havana Convention
The corresponding "Havana Convention" embodied the agreements adopted in the Act of Havana. It was signed on July 30, 1940 by representatives of all the American Republics with the exception of Bolivia, Chile, Cuba, and Paraguay, and came into force for the United States on Jan. 8, 1942.

3. Inter-American Treaty of Reciprocal Assistance (Treaty of Rio)
Signed on Sept. 2, 1947, and entered into force on Dec. 3, 1948.

For details see page 152.

4. North Atlantic Treaty
Signed on April 4, 1949, and entered into force on Aug. 24, 1949.

For details see pages 94–6.

5. Agreement for Mutual Defense Assistance in Indo-China
Signed on Dec. 23, 1950, by Cambodia, France, Laos, the United States, and Vietnam. The agreement entered into force immediately. [*11429A*]

6. ANZUS Pact
Signed on Sept. 1, 1951, and entered into force on April 29, 1952.

For details see pages 194–5.

7. Southeast Asia Collective Defense Treaty
Signed on Sept. 8, 1954, and entered into force on Feb. 9, 1955.

For details see pages 196–7.

8. The Pacific Charter
Signed on Sept. 8, 1954, and entered into force immediately.

For details see page 197.

OTHER BILATERAL U.S. AGREEMENTS

Agreements on Civil Uses of Atomic Energy

Agreements for co-operation concerning civil uses of atomic energy have been concluded by the United States with the following countries and organizations, the dates given being those of the entry into force of these agreements:

Argentina	July 25, 1969.
Australia	May 28, 1957; extended and amended Sept. 14, 1960, and April 11, 1967.
Austria	Jan. 24, 1970.
Brazil	Nov. 9, 1966.
Britain	July 21, 1955; extended and amended Oct. 20 and Nov. 3, 1955; June 13, 1956; July 3, 1958; June 5, 1963; June 29, 1964; July 15, 1965; June 2, 1966; Sept. 10, 1970.
Canada	July 21, 1955; extended and amended June 26, 1956; May 22, 1959; June 11, 1960; May 25, 1962.
Colombia	March 29, 1963; extended and amended Feb. 24, 1967.
Denmark	July 25, 1955; extended and amended June 27, 1956; June 26, 1958; June 7, 1968.
Finland	July 7, 1970.
Greece	Aug. 4, 1955; extended and amended June 11, 1960; April 3, 1962; June 22, 1962; June 8, 1964; Sept. 27, 1968.
India	Oct. 25, 1963.
Indonesia	Sept. 21, 1960; extended and amended Jan. 12, 1966; June 10, 1970.
International Atomic Energy Agency	Aug. 7, 1959.
Iran	April 27, 1959; extended and amended June 8, 1964; March 18, 1969.
Ireland (Republic of)	July 9, 1958; extended and amended Feb. 13, 1961; Aug. 7, 1963; June 12, 1968.
Israel	July 12, 1955; extended and amended Aug. 20, 1959; June 11, 1960; June 22, 1962; Aug. 19, 1964; April 2, 1965; Aug. 23, 1966.
Italy	April 15, 1958; amended July 22, 1959.
Japan	July 10, 1968.
Korea (South)	Feb. 3, 1956; extended and amended March 14, 1958; July 30, 1965.
Norway	June 8, 1967; amended Dec. 23, 1969.
Philippines	July 19, 1968.
Portugal	July 19, 1969.
South Africa	Aug. 22, 1957; extended and amended June 12, 1962; July 17, 1967.
Spain	Feb. 12, 1958; extended and amended Nov. 29, 1965.
Sweden	Sept. 15, 1966; amended Oct. 22, 1970.
Switzerland	Aug. 8, 1966.
Taiwan	July 18, 1955; extended and amended Dec. 8, 1958; June 11, 1960; May 31, 1962; June 8, 1964; Aug. 25, 1966.
Thailand	March 13, 1956; extended and amended March 27, 1957; June 11, 1960; May 31, 1962; June 8, 1964.
Turkey	June 10, 1955; extended and amended April 27, 1961; June 3, 1965; May 11, 1966; May 20, 1971.
Venezuela	Feb. 9, 1960; amended Nov. 14, 1969.
Vietnam (South)	July 1, 1959; extended and amended June 9, 1964.

Environmental Agreement

U.S.A.–Canada

The Great Lakes Water Quality Agreement, signed in Ottawa on April 15, 1972, laid down a joint program for reducing pollution of Lakes Superior, Huron, Erie, Ontario, and Michigan. [252834]

THE 26 INDEPENDENT STATES IN THE AMERICAS

COUNTRIES	OAS	Commonwealth	LAFTA	OCAS	Central American Common Market	NATO	Defense Treaty or Military Assistance Agreements with U.S.A.
ARGENTINA	X		X				X
BARBADOS	X	X					
BOLIVIA	X		X				X
BRAZIL	X		X				X
CANADA		X				X	X
CHILE	X		X				X
COLOMBIA	X		X				X
COSTA RICA	X			X	X		
CUBA							
DOMINICAN REPUBLIC	X						X
ECUADOR	X		X				X
EL SALVADOR	X			X	X		
GUATEMALA	X			X	X		X
GUYANA		X					
HAITI	X						X
HONDURAS	X			X			X
JAMAICA	X	X					
MEXICO	X		X				
NICARAGUA	X			X	X		X
PANAMA	X						
PARAGUAY	X		X				X
PERU	X		X				X
TRINIDAD AND TOBAGO	X	X					X
UNITED STATES	X					X	
URUGUAY	X		X				X
VENEZUELA	X		X				

BRITAIN

1. Associated States with full internal autonomy, Britain retaining responsibility for Defense and External Affairs:

    ANTIGUA   (since Feb. 27, 1967)

    DOMINICA   (since March 1, 1967)

    GRENADA   (since March 3, 1967)

    ST. KITTS-NEVIS   (since Feb. 27, 1967)

    ST. LUCIA   (since March 1, 1967)

    ST. VINCENT   (since Oct. 27, 1969)

2. Colonies with internal self-government, Britain retaining responsibility for Defense, External Affairs, and Internal Security:

    BAHAMAS   (since Jan. 1, 1964)   — *Inside NATO Area: X*

    BRITISH HONDURAS   (since Jan. 1, 1964)

3. Colonies with Executive Councils and Legislatures:

    BERMUDA   — *Inside NATO Area: X*

    BRITISH VIRGIN ISLANDS

    CAYMAN ISLANDS

    FALKLAND ISLANDS (Malvinas)

    MONTSERRAT

    TURKS AND CAICOS ISLANDS

4. Colony under direct British rule:

    ANGUILLA   (since July 28, 1971)

FRANCE

1. French Overseas Territory (i.e. an integral part of the French Republic):

    ST. PIERRE ET MIQUELON   — *Inside NATO Area: X; Associated with EEC: X*

2. French Overseas *Départements* since March 19, 1946, and members of French Community:

    FRENCH GUIANA   — *Associated with EEC: X*

    GUADELOUPE   — *Associated with EEC: X*

    MARTINIQUE   — *Associated with EEC: X*

DENMARK

GREENLAND, with a Legislative Council in West Greenland and two members in the Danish Parliament.   — *Inside NATO Area: X*

NETHERLANDS

Integral parts of the Kingdom of the Netherlands Government with internal autonomy since Dec. 29, 1954:

NETHERLANDS ANTILLES (Aruba, Bonaire, Curaçao, Saba, St. Eustatius, St. Maarten)   — *Associated with EEC: X*

SURINAM (or Netherlands Guiana)   — *Associated with EEC: X*

UNITED STATES

PANAMA CANAL ZONE, leased in perpetuity from the Republic of Panama since 1903. Agreement on the conclusion of a new treaty, which would recognize Panama's sovereignty over the Canal Zone, was announced by President Johnson on Sept. 24, 1965.

PUERTO RICO, an autonomous Commonwealth (since 1952), associated with the U.S.A., which retains responsibility for Defense and External Affairs.

VIRGIN ISLANDS of the U.S.A., governed under the Revised Organic Act of the Virgin Islands of July 22, 1954, with a U.S.-appointed Governor and an elected Legislature.

13
The Middle East

THE ARAB LEAGUE

SEAT: Cairo

MEMBERS: Algeria, Bahrain, Egypt, Iraq, Jordan, Kuwait, Lebanon, Libya, Morocco, Oman, Qatar, Saudi Arabia, Sudan, Syrian Arab Republic, Tunisia, United Arab Emirates, Yemen (Arab Republic), Yemen (Peoples's Democratic Republic)

History

A union of the Arab peoples was envisaged during World War I, when the Arabs rose in revolt against their Turkish rulers. Under the Peace Treaty of 1919, however, the Arab-populated former Turkish territories were split into separate States and, with the exception of the Hedjaz and Yemen, placed under British or French mandate. The Hedjaz was subsequently conquered in 1925 by King Ibn Saud, ruler of Nejd, and his enlarged realm renamed Saudi Arabia in 1932.

Between 1932 and 1946 the British and French mandated territories (Iraq, Lebanon, Syria, and Transjordan) succeeded in gaining *de facto* independence. In 1943 and 1944 a series of bilateral meetings on the formation of an Arab union took place between the various Arab States. This revival of Pan-Arabism differed in its aims from the movement against the Turks during World War I in that it envisaged the mutual co-operation of individual Arab States rather than the formation of a single Arab realm.

A sufficient measure of agreement was reached in these bilateral talks to make possible the convening of a conference of Arab nations. The conference was held at Alexandria from Sept. 25 to Oct. 7, 1944, and was attended initially by delegates from Egypt, Iraq, Lebanon, Syria, and Transjordan, and later also by delegates from Saudi Arabia and Yemen and a representative of the Palestinian Arabs. On Oct. 7, 1944, a Protocol providing for the establishment of a League of Arab States was signed by the Egyptian, Iraqi, Lebanese, Syrian, and Transjordanian delegates.

A Pan-Arab Union Preparatory Committee, formed at the Alexandria Conference and consisting of the Foreign Ministers of Egypt, Iraq, Lebanon, Saudi Arabia, Syria, and Transjordan, and a Palestinian representative, met on Feb. 14, 1945, to approve and sign a constitution for the proposed Arab League.

The Pact

The "Pact of the Union of Arab States" was finally signed on March 22, 1945, by representatives of Egypt, Iraq, Lebanon, Saudi Arabia, Syria, Transjordan, and Yemen. Later adherents to the pact were Libya (March 28, 1953); the Sudan (Jan. 9, 1956); Tunisia and Morocco (Oct. 1, 1958); Kuwait (July 20, 1961); Algeria (Aug. 16, 1962); People's Democratic Republic of Yemen (i.e. South Yemen) (December 1967); Bahrain and Qatar, Sept. 11, 1971; Oman, Sept. 29, 1971; and United Arab Emirates (Dec. 6, 1971).

The main provisions of the pact are summarized below:

The League of Arab States: It was laid down that "a League of Arab States will be formed by those independent Arab countries who wish to join it"; that it would possess a Council on which all member-States would be on an equal footing; that the Council would organize periodical meetings to improve and strengthen mutual relations, co-ordinate their political programs with a view to mutual co-operation, and "safeguard by every possible means their independence and sovereign rights against all aggression"; that decisions of the Council would be binding on all member-States (disputes between member-States being referred to it for arbitration); that resort to force between member-States in settling disputes was forbidden; and that no State would be permitted to follow a policy prejudicial to the League of Arab States as a whole.

177]

Co-operation: The Arab States would co-operate closely on questions of economics and finance (commercial exchanges, customs duties, currency, agriculture, and industry), communications (by land, sea, and air), cultural matters, social and hygiene questions, and matters relating to nationality, passports and visas, extradition of criminals, etc. For these questions, commissions of experts would be formed, with a co-ordinating committee to direct their work.

Lebanon: The Arab States unanimously affirmed their respect for the independence and sovereignty of Lebanon within her existing frontiers.

Palestine: The declaration on Palestine stated: "The Committee considers that Palestine forms an important integral part of the Arab countries and the rights of the Arabs there cannot be infringed without danger to the peace and security of the Arab world. At the same time it considers that the engagements entered into by Great Britain, which include the cessation of Jewish immigration, the safeguarding of land belonging to the Arabs and the guiding of Palestine along the road to independence, constitute a portion of the rights acquired by the Arabs and that their execution will be a step towards the goal to which they aspire, towards the establishment of peace and security. It proclaims its support of the Palestine Cause for the realization of legitimate aspirations and the safeguarding of lawful rights. It sympathizes as deeply as anyone with the Jews for the horrors and sufferings they have endured in Europe through the actions of certain dictatorial States. But it is careful not to confuse the case of these Jews with Zionism, for nothing would be more arbitrary or unjust than to wish to resolve the question of the Jews of Europe by another injustice of which the Arabs of Palestine, no matter to what religion or confession they belong, would be the victims."

It was also laid down that the Arab League would study means of collaboration with international organizations; that its permanent headquarters would be in Cairo (though the Council could meet in other cities); that the Council would hold biennial meetings (in March and October); that member-States could withdraw from the League on one year's notice, or be expelled by unanimous vote for not fulfilling their obligations; and that the Pact could be modified by a two-thirds majority vote. [7190A]

Organization

The League Council is the supreme organ of the Arab League. It is composed of representatives of all the member-States, each of which has one vote, and a representative of the Palestinian Arabs. The Council is responsible for the functioning of the League and the realization of its objectives. It meets twice a year, in March and September.

The League Council is aided by nine Permanent Committees which deal with Political, Economic, Cultural, Social, Military and Legal Affairs, Information, Health, and Communications.

The other organ of the Arab League is the Secretariat, whose main officers are the Secretary-General, three Assistant Secretaries-General, a Military Assistant Secretary, and an Economic Assistant Secretary. Among the functions of the Secretary-General are the preparation of a draft budget, which he submits to the Council, and the convening of the Council sessions.

Subsidiary Bodies

A considerable number of subsidiary bodies have been set up under the Arab League. The most important of these are given below:

(1) THE ECONOMIC COUNCIL

Formed in 1950, the Economic Council consists of the Ministers of Economic Affairs of the member-countries.

(2) THE ARAB FINANCIAL ORGANIZATION

The Economic Council announced the creation of an Arab Development Bank in January 1959. The members of the bank, which is now known as the Arab Financial Organization, are Iraq, Jordan, Kuwait, Lebanon, Libya, Saudi Arabia, Egypt, and Yemen. The function of the organization is to finance development projects for which no private capital is available. The initial capital of £E20,000,000 ($55,000,000) was raised to £E25,000,000 ($68,500,000) in 1961. [16663B; 18043A]

(3) COUNCIL OF ARAB ECONOMIC UNITY

A Convention for Economic Unity was signed by Iraq, Jordan, Kuwait, Morocco, Saudi Arabia, Syria, the United Arab Republic, and Yemen in June 1957. The Council of Arab Economic Unity came into being seven years later, in June 1964. Its object is, *inter alia,* to reduce internal tariffs, to establish a common external tariff, and to bring about the co-ordination of economic policies.

(4) ARAB COMMON MARKET

An agreement on the creation of an Arab Common Market was initialed by the representatives of Jordan, Kuwait, Morocco, Syria, and the U.A.R. at a meeting of the Arab League Economic Council in June 1962. Although nothing further came of this agreement, a similar one was signed two years later, on Aug. 13, 1964, by representatives of Iraq, Jordan, Kuwait, Syria, and the U.A.R.

The agreement provided for (*a*) freedom of movement of persons and of currencies; (*b*) freedom of trade exchanges in local and foreign products; (*c*) freedom of residence, work, and the pursuit of economic activities; and (*d*) freedom of transport, transit, and the use of airports and harbors. In trade between the five countries there would be a first reduction in customs tariffs of 10 percent for industrial products and of 20 percent for agricultural produce, to be followed by similar reductions over the next ten or five years respectively. [20312C]

The provisions of the agreement were to be implemented within ten years of Jan. 1, 1965, when the Common Market was scheduled to come into operation. Any other member of the Arab League might join the Common Market at any time.

(5) ARAB LABOR ORGANIZATION

To co-ordinate labor conditions throughout the Arab world an Arab Labor Organization was set up in 1965.

The Organization also undertakes research work, technical assistance, and vocational training.

(6) JOINT DEFENSE COUNCIL

An Arab Supreme Defense Council, composed of the Foreign and Defense Ministers of countries adhering to the Arab League Collective Security Pact (see below), was set up in 1950 under the terms of that Pact. Its first meeting did not take place until September 1953.

(7) PERMANENT MILITARY COMMITTEE

The formation of a Permanent Military Committee was also provided for in the Collective Security Pact. Composed of representatives of Army General Staffs, the committee is responsible for the drafting of joint defense plans.

(8) ARAB UNIFIED MILITARY COMMAND

The establishment of a unified Arab military command was decided at a conference of Arab Heads of State held in Alexandria in September 1964 (see below). A Palestine Liberation Army, composed of Palestinian refugees, was also formed as a section of the Joint Arab Force.

Palestine Liberation Organization

The Palestine Liberation Organization (PLO), stated to be "the only legitimate spokesman for all matters concerning the Palestinian people," is separate from the Arab League, although it receives funds and support from the League. The PLO was set up at a congress of Palestinian Arab refugees in Jerusalem on May 28–June 3, 1964. Because of its revolutionary attitude and leanings toward Communism, the PLO has alienated certain of the more moderate Arab League members, and in 1966 both Tunisia and Jordan withdrew their support. [20335A; 21661A; 21817A]

Collective Security Pact

On June 17, 1950, a Collective Security Pact was signed by Egypt, Syria, Lebanon, Saudi Arabia, and Yemen.

The draft of the pact had been unanimously approved by the Council of the Arab League on April 13, 1950.

The main provisions of the pact were as follows: (1) An armed attack on one of the signatories would be regarded as aggression against all. In the event of such an aggression, the other signatories would provide, individually or collectively, all military and other aid consistent with existing obligations under the League Charter and Art. 51 of the U.N. Charter. (2) A permanent Joint Defense Council, consisting of the Foreign Ministers and Defense Ministers of the signatories, would be set up to co-ordinate defensive measures. Its decisions, reached by majority vote, would be binding on all members. (3) A permanent committee composed of the signatories' Chiefs of Staff would give technical advice on measures of collective defense. (4) An economic committee composed of the Ministers of National Economy would carry out economic measures complementary to the military decisions reached. (5) The signatories would give one another priority in the exchange of goods and services, and would co-operate in raising the economic level of the Arab world as a whole, measures envisaged for this purpose including the establishment of an Arab Central Bank and a Bureau of Statistics, the improvement of communications, the joint exploitation of the mineral wealth of the Arab countries, and the modernization of agricultural equipment. [10812A]

Subsequent signatories to the Collective Security Pact were Iraq on Feb. 2, 1951, Jordan on Feb. 16, 1952, Morocco on June 13, 1961, and Libya, Sudan, Algeria, Tunisia, and Kuwait on Sept. 10, 1964. The pact came into force on Aug. 24, 1952.

Arab Summit Conferences

Since 1964 the Heads of Arab States have four times met in conference to discuss questions of common political interest.

(1) The first such conference, which took place in Cairo Jan. 13–16, 1964, styled itself the "Council of the Kings and Heads of State of the Arab League." All 13 Arab League members were represented. A communiqué issued at the end of the conference stated, *inter alia*, that the meetings had resulted in "unanimous agreement . . . to stop all campaigns by information media, to consolidate relations among the sister Arab States in order to ensure constructive joint co-operation, and to ward off expansionist aggressive ambitions threatening all Arabs alike." It was decided that a meeting of Kings and Heads of State should be held at least once a year. [19975A]

(2) At the second Arab "summit conference," held at Alexandria, Sept. 5–11, 1964, the organization of the

meetings of Heads of State was worked out in some detail. It was agreed that a conference of Arab Heads of State should be held each year in September. A control commission, meeting monthly, would supervise the implementation of conference decisions. Every third meeting of this commission would be attended by the Prime Ministers of the Arab countries or their representatives.

Other decisions of the Alexandria conference included the setting up of a unified Arab military command (see above), an Arab Court of Justice, and an Arab council for research into the use of atomic energy for peaceful purposes. [20335A]

(3) In the course of their third conference, held in Casablanca Sept. 13–17, 1965, the Arab Heads of State signed a "solidarity pact," which was intended to put an end to propaganda attacks by one Arab State against another, and to bind the signatories not to support "subversive movements of any kind" against one another. [21011A]

(4) A fourth summit conference, scheduled to open in Algiers on Sept. 5, 1966, was indefinitely postponed, after it had been announced that the U.A.R. would not take part in a conference with "the reactionary Arab forces."

(5) A conference of Arab Heads of State held in Khartoum from Aug. 28 to Sept. 3, 1967 was boycotted by the Government of Syria. The conference dealt mainly with the aftermath of the Arab-Israeli war of June 1967. It reached agreement *inter alia* on the consolidation of Arab military strength, the need to eliminate "all foreign military bases from Arab territory" and "the principles of non-recognition and non-negotiation" in relations with Israel. [22275B]

(6) A meeting of Arab Heads of State or Government in Rabat (Morocco), opened on Dec. 21, 1969, broke down on Dec. 23, when President Nasser of the United Arab Republic (Egypt) withdrew because of his failure to obtain general Arab support for his proposal of a mobilization of all Arab resources against Israel. [23808A]

FEDERATION OF ARAB REPUBLICS

A Federation of the three Arab States of Egypt (until then the United Arab Republic), Libya, and Syria came into being on Jan. 1, 1972.

Plans for such a Federation had been agreed upon in Benghazi on April 17, 1971, and its draft Constitution announced thereafter.

Under this Constitution the institutions of the Federation consisted of:

(*a*) a Presidential Council consisting of the Presidents of the member-States and empowered to elect its President for a 2-year period;

(*b*) a Federal Ministerial Council (or Cabinet) appointed by the Presidential Council and responsible to the latter;

(*c*) a Federal Legislative Assembly, in which each member-country was represented by 20 members elected for 4 years by the national Parliaments; and

(*d*) a Constitutional Court with 2 members from each member-country.

The Federation was to have an annual Federal Budget; to pursue a unified foreign policy; and to possess competence in all matters concerning the conclusion of international treaties and agreements, and in matters relating to the organization of defense, with a military command to be established.

The Constitution also provided that, "in the event of internal or external disorders," the Federation would "have the right to intervene to re-establish order, even without a request from the republic concerned."

The Federation would have a common economic and financial policy, and would seek economic co-ordination between its member-countries and other Arab States.

Transitional provisions included the stipulation that international treaties and agreements concluded before the coming into effect of the Federal Constitution would remain in force; that a political Front embracing representatives of the political organizations of each member-republic would be set up by unanimous decision of the Presidential Council; and that membership of the Federation would be open to "Arab republics which believe in Arab unity and are ready to work for the advent of a unified Socialist Arab society."

The Federation was to have a single flag and emblem, a single national anthem and a single capital (as which the Presidential Council chose Cairo on Oct. 5, 1971). Islam would be the religion of each member of the Federation.

National referenda held in Egypt, Libya, and Syria on Sept. 1, 1971, resulted in overwhelming approval of the Federation proposals, official results being "yes" votes of 99.9 percent in Egypt, 98 percent in Libya, and 96.4 percent in Syria. [24820A; 24979C; 25094A]

OTHER AGREEMENTS IN FORCE BETWEEN ARAB COUNTRIES

Jordan—Saudi Arabia

On Aug. 29, 1962, it was announced that King Hussein of Jordan and King Saud of Saudi Arabia had concluded agreements on military, political, and economic co-operation. The agreements included the establishment of a joint Saudi-Jordanian military command. In a communiqué the two countries pledged themselves to work for the achievement of Arab rights in Palestine. [18957C]

United Arab Republic—Iraq

On May 26, 1964, the Presidents of the U.A.R. and Iraq signed an agreement providing for the establishment of a Joint Presidency Council with its headquarters in Cairo. The Council, meeting every three months, studies means to implement Arab unity, and to co-ordinate the political, economic, military, social, and cultural policies of the two countries. It was also agreed that a joint military command should be set up. [20156B]

On Oct. 16, 1964, after a meeting of the Joint Presidency Council, it was announced that the Presidents had agreed to set up a "unified political command," which would constitute the highest political authority of the two countries. It would consist of the two Presidents and at least six other representatives from each country. The main tasks of the Unified Political Command were stated to be the achievement of constitutional unity, and the supervision of foreign policy, the armed forces, defense, economic planning, culture and national guidance, education, and national security. [20388A]

Maghreb Permanent Consultative Committee
At a conference held in Tangiers on Nov. 26 and 27, 1964, the Economics Ministers of Algeria, Libya, Morocco, and Tunisia decided to establish a permanent joint consultative committee to harmonize economic development plans. The 9-member Maghreb Consultative Committee, which meets every three months, is served by an administrative secretariat and a number of specialized commissions. [20507A]

Maghreb Bilateral Treaties
Bilateral treaties between Maghreb countries were:

(1) A 20-year "treaty of solidarity and co-operation" between Algeria and Morocco, signed in Ifrane (Morocco) on Jan. 15, 1969 [23312B];

(2) a 20-year "treaty of brotherhood, good neighborliness, and co-operation" between Algeria and Tunisia, signed in Tunis on Jan. 6, 1970 [24068A];

(3) a "treaty of solidarity, good neighborliness, and co-operation" between Morocco and Mauritania, signed in Casablanca on June 8, 1970. [24125A]

Two further agreements, on the settlement of their border dispute and on joint exploitation of iron-ore deposits in the border area, were concluded by Morocco and Algeria on June 15, 1972. [25371A]

U.A.R.—Syrian Defense Pact
A joint defense agreement was signed by the Prime Ministers of the United Arab Republic and Syria on Nov. 4, 1966, in Cairo. The principal terms of the agreement are summarized below:

(1) A joint Defense Council, including the Foreign and Defense Ministers of each country, would meet at six-monthly intervals in Cairo and Damascus alternately.
(2) A joint military command would be set up, comprising a Chiefs of Staff Committee and a joint staff.
(3) Each country would regard any act of armed aggression committed against the other as an attack against itself, and would aid the other by taking all measures, including the use of armed force, necessary to defeat the aggressor.

(4) In the event of military operations, the Chief of Staff of the U.A.R. Armed Forces would undertake their direction.
(5) The terms of the agreement were declared not to be in conflict with the two parties' existing international obligations, especially those arising from the Arab League Charter and the U.N. Charter.
(6) The agreement would come into force after ratification by each country according to its constitutional procedures, and would run for an initial five-year period, with an option of renewal for further similar periods. [21710C]

U.A.R.—Jordanian—Iraqi Defense Pact
On May 30, 1967, shortly before the outbreak of the six-day Arab-Israeli war, a defense pact between the U.A.R. and Jordan was signed by King Hussein of Jordan and President Nasser of the U.A.R. in Cairo.

The Egyptian-Jordanian defense pact provided that each country would consider an attack on either State as an attack on both; that joint military operations would be undertaken in such an eventuality; that the Chief of Staff of the U.A.R. would command both the Egyptian and the Jordanian forces in the event of war; and that the two countries would set up (a) a Joint Defense Council, and (b) a Joint Command consisting of a Chiefs of Staff Council and a Joint General Staff. The treaty was concluded for five years and was automatically renewable for similar five-year periods unless one party gave notice of withdrawal one year before the expiration of the first or subsequent five-year periods. [22075A]

On June 4, 1967, Iraq joined the pact.

United Arab Emirates
The United Arab Emirates came into being as a sovereign independent State on Dec. 2, 1971, being then joined by the six Trucial Coast Sheikhdoms of Abu Dhabi, Ajman, Dubai, Fujairah, Sharjah, and Umm el Quwain, and three weeks later by the seventh, Ras al Khaimah. [25010A; 25024A]

A federal Constitution for the new State had been agreed upon in July 1971. [24731A]

ISLAMIC ORGANIZATION
An International Islamic Organization, replacing an earlier Afro-Asian Islamic Organization established in Jakarta in 1965, held a conference of Foreign Ministers of 22 Islamic countries in Karachi on Dec. 26–28, 1970. (At a previous meeting of Foreign Ministers in Jedda on March 23–26, 1970, Algeria, Libya, the Sudan, and the United Arab Republic were reported to have opposed a permanent association of Islamic States.) [24482A]

An Islamic Summit Conference held in Rabat on Sept. 22–25, 1969, was attended by representatives of 25 countries out of 36 invited. Those present included Iran and Turkey but not Iraq and Syria; India was, upon a decision by the conference, admitted as a full member but was subsequently asked to withdraw because the President of Pakistan had refused to attend a conference at which India would be represented. [23689A]

THE CONSTANTINOPLE CONVENTION ON FREE NAVIGATION OF THE SUEZ CANAL

On Oct. 29, 1888, Austria-Hungary, Britain, France, Germany, Italy, the Netherlands, Russia, Spain, and Turkey signed the Convention respecting the Free Navigation of the Suez Maritime Canal.

The fundamental provisions of this Convention are contained in Articles 1 and 4 as follows.

"The Suez Maritime Canal shall always be free and open, in time of war as in time of peace, to every vessel of commerce or of war, without distinction of flag. . . . The Canal shall never be subjected to the exercise of the right of blockade."

"The Maritime Canal remaining open in time of war as a free passage, even to the ships of war of belligerents . . . the High Contracting Parties agree that no right of war, no act of hostility, nor any act having for its object to obstruct the free navigation of the Canal, shall be committed in the Canal and its ports of access . . . though the Ottoman Empire should be one of the belligerent Powers." (In the terms of the Convention the legal successor to the Ottoman Empire is the United Arab Republic.)

The Convention also confirmed and completed the system of international operation embodied by the Universal Suez Canal Company, set up in 1863.

Egypt nationalized the Suez Canal Company in July 1956, an act which was regarded by many users of the Canal as a contravention of the 1888 Convention.

In April 1957, when the Canal was re-opened to navigation, after it had been obstructed for several months, the Egyptian Government issued a declaration in which it stated its intention to respect "the terms and spirit of the Constantinople Convention and the rights and obligations arising therefrom. . . ." [15545A]

CENTRAL TREATY ORGANIZATION (CENTO)

Members: Britain, Iran, Pakistan, Turkey
Associate Members: U.S.A.
Headquarters: Ankara

The Central Treaty Organization (CENTO) is both a defense alliance and an organization for regional co-operation in the economic, cultural, and technical fields.

The Pact of the Central Treaty Organization is identical with the earlier Baghdad Pact (Pact of Mutual Co-operation), of which the members were the four present members of CENTO with the addition of Iraq. The Baghdad Pact was first signed by Turkey and Iraq on Feb. 24, 1955, and came into force two days later. Britain joined the Pact on April 4, 1955, when she also signed a special defense agreement with Iraq. Pakistan joined on Sept. 23, 1955, and Iran on Nov. 3, 1955.

The name of the alliance was officially changed to Central Treaty Organization on Aug. 21, 1959, as a result of Iraq's withdrawal from the Baghdad Pact on March 24, 1959. [16748A; 16990C]

The CENTO Pact

The main provisions of the pact are given below:

Art. 1. Consistent with Art. 51 of the U.N. Charter, the parties will co-operate for their security and defense. Such measures as they agree to take to give effect to this co-operation may form the subject of special agreements with each other.

Art. 3. The parties undertake to refrain from any interference whatsoever in each other's internal affairs. They will settle any disputes between themselves in a peaceful way in accordance with the U.N. Charter.

Art. 5. This pact shall be open for accession to any member-State of the Arab League or any other State actively concerned with the security and peace in this region and which is fully recognized by both of the parties. Accession shall come into force from the date on which the instrument of accession of the State concerned is deposited with the Ministry of Foreign Affairs of Iraq. Any acceding State . . . may conclude special agreements, in accordance with Art. 1, with one or more States parties to the present pact.

Art. 7. This pact remains in force for a period of five years, renewable for further five-year periods. Any contracting party may withdraw from the pact by notifying the other parties in writing of its desire to do so six months before the expiration of any of the above-mentioned periods, in which case the pact remains valid for the other parties. [14105A]

Organization

The Council
The principal organ of CENTO is the Council, which meets at both the ministerial and the deputies level. On the Ministerial Council, which meets annually in each of the CENTO countries' capitals in turn, the member-countries are represented by Prime Ministers, Foreign Ministers or other senior Cabinet Ministers.

Fortnightly meetings of the Council are held at the level of deputies, the deputies being the Ambassadors of the CENTO countries resident in Ankara, and a special Turkish representative from the Ministry of Foreign Affairs.

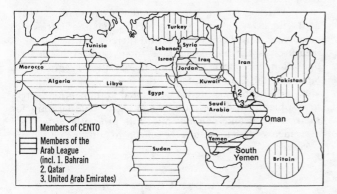

The U.S.A. is represented by an observer at all Council meetings, at both ministerial and deputies level.

Committees
The Council is assisted by the six Committees listed below:

Military Committee, generally composed of the Chiefs-of-Staff or Commanders-in-chief of the CENTO countries. The U.S.A. is represented on this Committee.

Permanent Military Deputies Group, composed of representatives of the four CENTO members and the U.S.A. with the rank of Lieutenant-General.

Counter-Subversion Committee. The U.S.A. is also represented on this Committee.

Liaison Committee, for the exchange of information on matters of security.

Economic Committee, composed of Ministers or senior officials of the four CENTO members and the U.S.A. The Committee is assisted by sub-committees on Communications and Public Works; Trade and Economics; Agriculture, Animal Production, and Animal Health; and Health.

Council for Scientific Education and Research.

Combined Military Planning Staff
Set up in January 1958, CENTO's combined Military Planning Staff is composed of officers from all three services in the 5 member-countries of the Military Committee (see above). Its three Divisions deal with Intelligence; Plans, Training, and Operations; and Logistics.

Secretariat
The Secretariat, headed by the Secretary-General, has four divisions: a Political and Administrative Division;

an Economic Division; a Public Relations Division; and a Security Organization. The Secretary-General acts as permanent Chairman of the Deputies' Council meetings.

Bilateral Defense Agreements of the U.S.A. with CENTO Countries

On March 5, 1959, bilateral defense agreements between the U.S.A. and Iran, Turkey, and Pakistan were signed in Ankara after some six months of negotiations. The treaties, consisting of a preamble and six articles, were all identically worded.

The preamble places each treaty within the framework of CENTO by reference to Article 1 of the Pact of Mutual Co-operation (Baghdad or CENTO Pact). Reference is also made to a declaration signed in London on July 28, 1958 (see below).

The treaty with Turkey is here quoted in full:

PREAMBLE

The Government of the United States of America and the Government of Turkey;

Desiring to implement the declaration in which they associated themselves at London on July 28, 1958;

Considering that under Article 1 of the Pact of Mutual Co-operation signed at Baghdad on Feb. 24, 1955, the parties signatory thereto agreed to co-operate for their security and defense, and that similarly, as stated in the above-mentioned declaration, the Government of the United States of America, in the interest of world peace, agreed to co-operate with the Governments making that declaration for their security and defense;

Recalling that, in the above-mentioned declaration, the members of the Pact of Mutual Co-operation . . . affirmed their determination to maintain their collective security and to resist aggression, direct or indirect;

Considering further that the Government of the United States is associated with the work of the major committees of the Pact of Mutual Co-operation signed at Baghdad on Feb. 24, 1955;

Desiring to strengthen peace in accordance with the principles of the Charter of the United Nations;

Affirming their right to co-operate for their security and defense in accordance with Article 51 of the U.N. Charter;

Considering that the Government of the United States regards as vital to its national interest and to world peace the preservation of the independence and integrity of Turkey;

Recognizing the authorization to furnish appropriate assistance granted to the President of the United States of America by the Congress of the United States in the Mutual Security Act of 1954, as amended, and in the Joint Resolution to Promote Peace and Stability in the Middle East; and

Considering that similar agreements are being entered into by the Government of the United States of America and the Governments of Iran and Pakistan respectively;

Have agreed as follows:

Art. 1. The Government of Turkey is determined to resist aggression. In case of aggression against Turkey, the

U.S. Government, in accordance with the U.S. Constitution, will take such appropriate action, including the use of armed forces, as may be mutually agreed upon and as is envisaged in the Joint Resolution to Promote Peace and Stability in the Middle East, in order to assist the Government of Turkey at its request.

Art. 2. The U.S. Government, in accordance with the Mutual Security Act of 1954, as amended, and related laws of the U.S.A., and with applicable agreements heretofore or hereafter entered into between the U.S. and Turkish Governments, reaffirms that it will continue to furnish the Government of Turkey such military and economic assistance as may be mutually agreed upon between the U.S. and Turkish Governments, in order to assist the Government of Turkey in the preservation of its national independence and integrity and in the effective promotion of its economic development.

Art. 3. The Government of Turkey undertakes to utilize such military and economic assistance as may be provided by the U.S. Government in a manner consonant with the aims and purposes set forth by the Governments associated in the declaration signed at London on July 28, 1958, and for the purpose of effectively promoting the economic development of Turkey and of preserving her national independence and integrity.

Art. 4. The U.S. and Turkish Governments will co-operate with the other Governments associated in the declaration signed at London on July 28, 1958, in order to prepare and participate in such defensive arrangements as may be mutually agreed to be desirable, subject to the other applicable provisions of this agreement.

Art. 5. The provisions of the present agreement do not affect the co-operation between the two Governments as envisaged in other international agreements or arrangements.

Art. 6. This agreement shall enter into force upon the date of its signature and shall continue in force until one year after the receipt by either Government of written notice of the intention of the other Government to terminate the agreement. [16748A]

The Joint Declaration mentioned in the bilateral defense treaties, was issued on July 28, 1958, at a meeting of the Ministerial Council of the Baghdad Pact, attended by the Prime Ministers of Britain, Iran, Pakistan, and Turkey, and the U.S. Secretary of State. It read as follows:

(1) The members of the Baghdad Pact attending the Ministerial meeting in London have re-examined their position in the light of recent events and conclude that the need which called the Pact into being is greater than ever. These members declare their determination to maintain their collective security and to resist aggression, direct or indirect.

(2) Under the Pact collective security arrangements have been instituted. Joint military planning has been advanced and area economic projects have been promoted. Relationships are being established with other free-world nations associated for collective security.

(3) The question of whether substantive alterations should be made in the Pact and its organization, or whether the Pact will be continued in its present form, is under consideration by the Governments concerned. However, the nations represented at the meeting in London reaffirmed their determination to strengthen further their united defense posture in the area.

(4) Article 1 of the Pact of Mutual Co-operation signed at Baghdad on Feb. 24, 1955, provides that the parties will co-operate for their security and defense and that such measures as they agree to take to give effect to this co-operation may form the subject of special agreements. Similarly, the United States, in the interests of world peace, and pursuant to existing Congressional authorization, agrees to co-operate with the nations making this declaration for their security and defense, and will promptly enter into agreements designed to give effect to this co-operation. [16340A]

Regional Co-operation for Development (RCD)

Members: Iran, Pakistan, Turkey
Headquarters: Tehran

The decision to form a regional co-operation group was made at a meeting of the Foreign Ministers of Iran, Pakistan, and Turkey, held in Ankara July 3–4, 1964. The group, it was stated, would be "parallel to but outside CENTO." Details of the organization, known as Regional Co-operation for Development (RCD) were worked out at a meeting of the three Heads of State, July 20–21, 1964.

Organization

The principal decision-making organ of RCD is the Ministerial Council, consisting of the three Foreign Ministers of the member-countries. Meetings are held at least three times a year.

The Ministerial Council is assisted by a Regional Planning Council, consisting of the Heads of the Planning Organizations of the member-countries. It is, in its turn, assisted by subcommittees dealing with aviation, culture, finance, joint ventures, land transport, petrochemicals, petroleum, shipping, technical co-operation, telecommunications, tourism, and trade.

The Secretariat, which is formed by the Secretary-General and six directors, was set up in September 1964.

Developments in Co-operation

A considerable number of schemes for co-operation between the three countries of RCD are already in operation. They include a Regional Cultural Institute, a tripartite Shipping Conference, a joint Chamber of Commerce and Industry, and an RCD commercial bank. A tripartite agreement on tourism and bilateral agreements on the abolition of visas for tourists were concluded at the first meeting of the Ministerial Council held in October 1964. [20437A; 20730A]

Turkish-Pakistani Agreement on "Friendly Co-operation"

An agreement on "friendly co-operation" between Turkey and Pakistan was signed in Karachi on April 2, 1954. The treaty, which remains valid for consecutive periods of five years if no notice of denunciation is given one year before the end of a five-year period, is open to other countries. It came into force on June 12, 1954.

The main provisions of the treaty are given below:

Art. 1. The contracting parties undertake to refrain from intervening in any way in the internal affairs of each other, and from participating in any alliance or activities directed against the other.

Art. 2. They will consult on international matters of mutual interest, and, taking into account international requirements and conditions, co-operate to the maximum extent.

Art. 4. Consultation and co-operation between the contracting parties in the field of defense shall cover the following points:

(*a*) Exchange of information for the purpose of deriving joint benefit from technical experience and progress.

(*b*) Endeavors to meet, as far as possible, the requirements of the parties in the production of arms and ammunition.

(*c*) Studies and determination of the manner and extent of co-operation which might be effected between them, in accordance with Article 51 of the U.N. Charter, should an unprovoked attack occur against them from outside.

Art. 5. Each contracting party declares that none of the international engagements now in force between it and any third State is in conflict with the provisions of this Agreement, and that this Agreement shall not affect, and cannot be interpreted as affecting, the aforesaid engagements. They undertake not to enter into any international engagement in conflict with this Agreement. [13519A]

Iran and Saudi Arabia—Continental Shelf Agreement

An agreement on the demarcation of the continental shelf between Iran and Saudi Arabia was signed in Tehran on Oct. 24, 1968. [23072A]

14

Africa

THE ORGANIZATION OF AFRICAN UNITY (OAU)

The Organization of African Unity was constituted at a conference of African Heads of State and Government in Addis Ababa held from May 23 to 26, 1963. Those attending the conference signed a Charter of the OAU, the principal provisions of which are as follows:

Establishment

Art. 1. The High Contracting Parties do by the present Charter establish an Organization to be known as the "Organization of African Unity."

The Organization shall include the continental African States, Madagascar, and all the islands surrounding Africa.

Purposes

Art. 2. (1) The Organization shall have the following purposes:

(*a*) To promote the unity and solidarity of the African and Malagasy States;

(*b*) To co-ordinate and intensify their co-operation and efforts to achieve a better life for the peoples of Africa;

(*c*) To defend their sovereignty, their territorial integrity, and independence;

(*d*) To eradicate all forms of colonialism from Africa; and

(*e*) To promote international co-operation, having due regard to the U.N. Charter and the Universal Declaration of Human Rights.

(2) To these ends, the member-States shall co-ordinate and harmonize their general policies, especially in the following fields:

(*a*) Political and diplomatic co-operation;

(*b*) Economic co-operation, including transport and communications;

(*c*) Educational and cultural co-operation;

(*d*) Health, sanitation, and nutritional co-operation;

(*e*) Scientific and technical co-operation; and

(*f*) Co-operation for defense and security.

Principles

Art. 3. The member-States, in pursuit of the purposes stated in Article 2, solemnly affirm and declare their adherence to the following principles:

(1) The sovereign equality of all member-States;

(2) Non-intereference in the internal affairs of States;

(3) Respect for the sovereignty and territorial integrity of each member-State and for its inalienable right to independent existence;

(4) Peaceful settlement of disputes by negotiation, mediation, conciliation, or arbitration;

(5) Unreserved condemnation, in all its forms, of political assassination, as well as of subversive activities on the part of neighboring States or any other States;

(6) Absolute dedication to the total emancipation of the African territories which are still dependent;

(7) Affirmation of a policy of non-alignment with regard to all blocs.

Institutions

Art. 7. The Organization shall accomplish its purposes through the following principal institutions:

(1) The Assembly of Heads of State and Government;

(2) The Council of Ministers;

(3) The General Secretariat;

(4) The Commission of Mediation, Conciliation, and Arbitration.

The Assembly of Heads of State and Government

Art. 8. The Assembly of Heads of State and Government shall be the supreme organ of the Organization. It shall, subject to the provisions of this Charter, discuss matters of common concern to Africa with a view to co-ordinating and harmonizing the general policy of the Organization. It may in addition review the structure, functions, and acts of all the organs and any specialized agencies which may be created in accordance with the Charter.

Art. 9. The Assembly shall be composed of the Heads of State or Government, or their duly accredited representatives, and shall meet at least once a year. At the request of any member-State, and upon approval by the majority of the member-States, the Assembly shall meet in extraordinary session.

The Council of Ministers

Art. 12. The Council of Ministers shall consist of Foreign Ministers or such other Ministers as are designated by the Governments of member-States.

The Council of Ministers shall meet at least twice a year. When requested by any member-State and approved by two-

Territories not yet granted
independence

Rhodesia, unilaterally declared
independent on Nov. 11, 1965,
but not internationally recognized
as independent

All independent countries, except
South Africa, are members of the
Organization of African Unity

thirds of all member-States, it shall meet in extraordinary session.

Art. 13. The Council of Ministers shall be responsible to the Assembly of Heads of State and Government. It shall be entrusted with the responsibility of preparing conferences of the Assembly.

General Secretariat

Art. 16. There shall be an Administrative Secretary-General of the Organization, who shall be appointed by the Assembly of Heads of State and Government on the recommendation of the Council of Ministers. The Administrative Secretary-General shall direct the affairs of the Secretariat.

Commission of Mediation, Conciliation, and Arbitration

Art. 19. Member-States pledge to settle all disputes among themselves by peaceful means and, to this end, decide to establish a Commission of Mediation, Conciliation, and Arbitration, the composition and the condition of service of which shall be defined by a separate protocol to be approved by the Assembly of Heads of State and Government.

Specialized Commissions

Art. 20. The Assembly shall establish such Specialized Commissions as it may deem necessary, including the following: (1) Economic and Social Commission; (2) Educational and Cultural Commission; (3) Health, Sanitation, and Nutrition Commission; (4) Defense Commission; (5) Scientific, Technical, and Research Commission.

The conference also appointed a committee of 9 members (Algeria, Congo-Kinshasa, Ethiopia, Guinea, Nigeria, Senegal, Tanganyika, Uganda, and the U.A.R.) charged with establishing a "Liberation Bureau" in Dar-es-Salaam to aid national liberation movements in their struggle to end remaining "forms of colonialism" in Africa. [*Pages 19466–68*]

The committee was enlarged to 11 members by the addition of Somalia and Zambia in 1967 and to 15 by that of the Congo (Brazzaville), Libya, Mauritania, and Morocco in June 1972. [*22991A; 25371A*]

Assemblies of Heads of State and Government

The second Assembly of Heads of State and Government, held in Cairo July 17–21, decided *inter alia* (*a*) to make Addis Ababa the seat of the Organization's permanent headquarters; (*b*) to approve a protocol providing for mediation, conciliation, and finally, arbitration in disputes between member-countries, as well as an undertaking by member-States to respect their frontiers as existing at the achievement of independence; and (*c*) to set up two permanent commissions—one of African jurists and another on communications. [*20253A*]

The third Assembly of Heads of State and Government, held in Accra Oct. 21–26, 1965, issued a Declaration on Subversive Activities containing the following main provisions:

(1) The OAU pledged itself to oppose collectively and firmly, by every means as its disposal, every form of subversion conceived, organized, or financed by any foreign Power against Africa as a whole or against OAU member-States.

(2) The declaration emphasized that member-States would tolerate neither subversion by one State against another nor the use of their territory for subversive activity directed from outside Africa against another member-State.

(3) All differences between two or more member-States should be settled by bilateral or multilateral consultations, on the basis of a protocol of mediation, conciliation, and arbitration as laid down in the OAU Charter, and there should be no reaction against a member-State by means of a radio or press campaign.

(4) Member-States should not give cause for dissension among themselves by fomenting or aggravating racial, religious, linguistic, ethnic, or other differences, and should combat all forms of activity of this kind.

(5) In regard to political refugees, the declaration enjoined member-States to observe strictly the principles of international law toward all nationals of member-States; to try to promote through bilateral or multilateral consultations the return of refugees to their home country with the consent both of the refugees themselves and their country of origin; and to continue to guarantee the safety of political refugees from dependent territories and support them in their struggle for the liberation of their countries.

It also adopted a resolution on political refugees which recalled the member-States' pledge to prevent refugees living in their territories from carrying out by any means whatsoever any acts harmful to the interests of member-States; requested all member-States never to allow the refugee question to become a source of disagreement among them; appreciated the assistance given to the refugee programs of African Governments by the U.N. High Commissioner for Refugees (UNHCR); requested African members of the U.N. Economic and Social Council to seek an increase in African representation on the executive committee of the UNHCR program on refugees; and requested those member-States which had not already done so to ratify the U.N. convention on refugees and to apply meanwhile the provisions of that convention to refugees in Africa. [21051A; 12074A]

The fourth Assembly of Heads of State and Government, held in Addis Ababa Nov. 5–9, 1966, decided *inter alia* to replace the Liberation Committee in Dar-es-Salaam by a new committee of 10 members, the executive of which would be placed under the direct control of the OAU Secretariat-General and would be excluded from any initiative of a political nature in its activities. [21738B]

The fifth Assembly of Heads of State and Government was held in Kinshasa (Congo) Sept. 11–14, 1967, without Malawi being represented. [22281A]

The sixth Assembly of Heads of State and Government, attended by representatives of all 40 member-States except Malawi, was held in Algiers, Sept. 13–16, 1968. [22991A]

The seventh Assembly, at which all 41 member-States (including Equatorial Guinea, independent since Oct. 12, 1968) were represented, took place in Addis Ababa, Sept. 6–9, 1969. [23607A]

The eighth Assembly, held in Addis Ababa from Sept. 1 to 3, 1970, was marked by the reconciliation of the Federal Military Government of Nigeria and the Governments of Gabon, the Ivory Coast, Tanzania, and Zambia, all of which had in 1967 recognized the secessionist regime in "Biafra," since defeated by the Federal Nigerian forces. [24191A]

The ninth Assembly, which took place in Addis Ababa from June 21 to 23, 1971, was not attended by the Central African Republic and Uganda, the latter being absent in protest against the transfer of the Assembly's venue from Kampala to Addis Ababa as the result of opposition to President Amin of Uganda by several member-States. The Assembly adopted, by 28 votes to 6, with 5 abstentions, a declaration rejecting a "dialogue" with the Government of South Africa as suggested by President Houphouët-Boigny of the Ivory Coast. [24737A]

The tenth Assembly, held in Rabat on June 11–15, 1972, reaffirmed its support for the OAU liberation committee by increasing its budget by 50 percent and its membership to 15 countries—Algeria, the Congo (Brazzaville), Egypt, Ethiopia, Guinea, Libya, Mauritania, Morocco, Nigeria, Senegal, Somalia, Tanzania, Uganda, Zaïre, and Zambia. The Assembly also adopted a resolution strongly supporting Egypt's de-

mand for the evacuation by Israel of all Egyptian territory occupied since July 1967.

During the years 1971–72 the OAU was instrumental in achieving reconciliation in a number of disputes between member-States, including those between Senegal and Guinea (on Senegal's alleged failure to suppress activities against the Guinean Government), between Guinea and Ghana (over the burial of the late ex-President Kwame Nkrumah), and between rival Angolan liberation movements. [25371A]

Scientific and Technical Commission

The OAU Scientific and Technical Commission (established under Art. 20 of the OAU Charter) on Jan. 1, 1965, absorbed the Commission for Technical Cooperation in Africa (CTCA), which had been established in Paris in January 1950.

The CTCA had reconstituted itself in Abidjan (Ivory Coast) Feb. 8–16, 1962, so as to comprise all independent African member-States, ending the full membership of Britain, France, and Belgium (which had founded the Commission and were to be invited to participate in the Commission's work at technical level), and excluding Portugal and South Africa. [18991B]

Civil Aviation Commission

An African Civil Aviation Commission open to all member-States of the OAU and of the U.N. Economic Commission for Africa was set up at a meeting of representatives of 32 African countries in Addis Ababa on Jan. 13–18, 1969. The new Commission's secretariat services would be provided by the International Civil Aviation Organization. [23318B]

REGIONAL ORGANIZATIONS IN AFRICA

1. EAST AND CENTRAL AFRICA
Conference of East and Central African States
Heads of State or Governments of East and Central African States began in 1966 to hold regular conferences to discuss problems of mutual interest.

The first of these conferences, held in Nairobi from March 31 to April 2, 1966, was attended by Heads of State, Ministers, or other representatives of 11 States (Burundi, Congo-Kinshasa (Zaïre), Ethiopia, Kenya, Malawi, Rwanda, Somalia, Sudan, Tanzania, Uganda, and Zambia). [21464A]

The second conference, held in Kinshasa on Feb. 12–14, 1967, was also attended by representatives of the

Central African Republic and the Congo (Brazzaville), whereas Ethiopia, Malawi, and Somalia were not represented. It issued a "Declaration of Kinshasa" expressing solidarity on African problems and in particular support for the "liberation movement in Africa" and the use of force against the Smith regime in Rhodesia. [*21928A*]

The fifth conference, held in Lusaka on April 14–16, 1969, and attended by representatives of 14 countries (i.e. those present at the first conference and also the Central African Republic, Chad, and Congo (Brazzaville), issued the "Lusaka Manifesto," defining the 14 States' attitude to "colonialism and racial discrimination . . . practiced in southern Africa."

The document contained *inter alia* the following passages:

Our stand toward southern Africa involves . . . a rejection of racialism, not a reversal of existing racial domination. . . .

If peaceful progress to emancipation were possible, or if changed circumstances were to make it possible in the future, we would urge our brothers in the resistance movements to use peaceful methods of struggle, even at the cost of some compromise on the timing of change. But while peaceful progress is blocked by the actions of those at present in power in the States of southern Africa, we have no choice but to give to the peoples of those territories all the support of which we are capable in their struggle against their oppressors. . . .

The actions of the South African Government are such that the rest of the world has a responsibility to take some action in defense of humanity.

South Africa should be excluded from the United Nations' agencies and even from the United Nations itself. It should be ostracized by the world community. It should be isolated from world trade patterns and left to be self-sufficient if it can.

The South African Government cannot be allowed both to reject the very concept of mankind's unity and to benefit by the strength given through friendly international relations. [*23333A; 23902A*]

The seventh conference, held in Mogadishu on Oct. 18–19, 1971, when all 14 countries were represented, approved the "Mogadishu Declaration" condemning any "dialogue" with the Government of South Africa (as had been advocated by President Houphouët-Boigny of the Ivory Coast) and reaffirming support for "armed struggle . . . for the liberation of southern Africa." The conference also adopted a "Declaration on Aggression against Zambia" pledging "all material and other aid" to that country against "aggressive actions on the part of the minority and colonialist regimes in southern Africa." [*25012B*]

2. EAST AFRICA

(a) *The East African Common Services Organization* was created in London in June 1962 to continue the services previously administered by the British East Africa High Commission.

The organs of the Organization, in which Kenya, Tanzania, and Uganda are equal partners, are (i) the East African Common Services Authority consisting of one elected Minister from each of the three countries; (ii) a Central Legislative Assembly consisting of 12 Ministers, 9 members from each country elected by that country's legislature, a Secretary-General, and a Legal Secretary.

The legislative powers of the Central Legislative Assembly were defined as covering civil aviation; customs and excise; inter-territorial research; university institutions; posts and telegraphs, telephones, and radio communications; railways, harbors, and inland water transport; merchant shipping; allocations from the distributable revenue pool; and public service commissions. [*18263A*]

(b) An *East African Economic Community* to come into force on Dec. 1, 1967, was established by a treaty signed in Kampala (Uganda) on June 6, 1967, by the Presidents of Kenya, Tanzania, and Uganda, with provision for the creation of an East African Development Bank. The Bank was formally brought into operation on July 3, 1968. [*22107A; 22538A; 22806B*]

The new Community, which took over the assets and liabilities of the Common Services Organization and adopted the Central Legislative Assembly as its own main organ, has largely superseded the older organization.

3. FRENCH-SPEAKING AFRICA
(see also French Community, page 148)

(a) The *Conseil de l'Entente* was established by Dahomey, Ivory Coast, Niger, and Upper Volta at Abidjan (Ivory Coast) May 29–30, 1959, as the supreme organ of a union which would involve (i) a customs union; (ii) co-ordination of the four countries' legislation in the spheres of finance, justice, public service, labor, communications, and public health; (iii) harmonization of tax legislation; and (iv) the creation of a "Solidarity Fund." [*Page 17054*]

Togo—which had been in a customs union with Dahomey after concluding an agreement on Aug. 20, 1960—became associated with the *Conseil de l'Entente* in 1966. [*18132A; 21438A*]

The four members of the Council achieved full independence outside the French Community in July 1960 and later signed co-operation agreements with France in economic matters and also in defense in April 1961—except in the case of Upper Volta which declined to sign a defense agreement. [*Page 17515; 18132A*]

(b) A *West African Monetary Union* comprising Dahomey, the Ivory Coast, Mali, Mauritania, Niger, Senegal, and Upper Volta was agreed upon in Paris on May 12, 1962. The new Union decided to retain, as a joint currency, the existing C.F.A. franc at the rate of 50 C.F.A. francs = 1 French (new) franc (with C.F.A. standing for *Communauté Financière Africaine*), and with a new joint note-issuing bank. Mali, however, withdrew from this Union on July 1, 1962. [*18844B; 18878E*]

(c) A *Central African Customs Union–Union douanière et économique de l'Afrique centrale* (UDEAC)–established in Brazzaville on Dec. 8, 1964, came into force on Jan. 1, 1966, between Cameroon and the members of an earlier Equatorial Customs Union embracing the Central African Republic, Chad, the Congo (Brazzaville), and Gabon, with headquarters at Bangui (Central African Republic). Chad withdrew from the organization on Dec. 31, 1968.   [*17054; 20896; 23359A*]

(d) A *Joint African and Malagasy Organization*, the *Organisation commune africaine et malgache* (OCAM), was established at Nouakchott (Mauritania) on Feb. 12, 1965, by 13 French-speaking African States (Cameroon, Central African Republic, Chad, Congo-Brazzaville, Dahomey, Gabon, Ivory Coast, Madagascar, Mauritania, Niger, Senegal, Togo, and Upper Volta), which were later joined by Rwanda. Congo-Kinshasa (Zaïre) was admitted to OCAM on May 26, 1965, and Mauritania withdrew on June 24, 1965.

The new organization superseded the *Union africaine et malgache de coopération économique* (UAMCE) set up in March 1964, which in turn had succeeded the *Union africaine et malgache* (UAM), also known as the "Brazzaville Group" of French-speaking African States created in Tananarive (Madagascar) in September 1961 by 12 former French territories.

A Charter for OCAM was approved by a conference of leaders of the organization's member-States at Tananarive, June 25–28, 1966. Defining increased co-operation between member-States as the main object of OCAM, the Charter laid down that any African independent and sovereign State accepting the Charter's provisions could be admitted to the Organization upon application. It provided for three organs of OCAM, as follows:

(1) The Conference of the Heads of State and Government as the supreme organ of the Organization, meeting once a year in ordinary session.

(2) The Council of Ministers, consisting of the Foreign Ministers of member-States, meeting once a year in ordinary session, responsible to the Conference, and implementing co-operation between member-States as directed by the Conference.

(3) The Administrative General Secretariat, appointed for two years by the Conference upon the proposal of the Council of Ministers, with its seat at Yaoundé (Cameroon) and its mandate being renewable.   [*21619A*]

At its formation, OCAM was characterized by its first President (M. Ould Daddah of Mauritania) as "an African grouping which has the aim, within the framework of the OAU, of reinforcing co-operation and solidarity among the African States and Madagascar in order to accelerate their development in the political, economic, social, technical, and cultural spheres."

Mauritius was admitted as a member on Jan. 20, 1970, when OCAM changed its name to *Common African, Malagasy, and Mauritian Organization (Organisation Commune Africaine, Malgache, et Mauricienne)*. [*23880C*] The Republic of Zaïre announced its withdrawal on April 19, 1972, and Congo (Brazzaville) on Sept. 22, 1972, the latter continuing to participate in OCAM's technical agencies.   [*25257A; 25564A*]

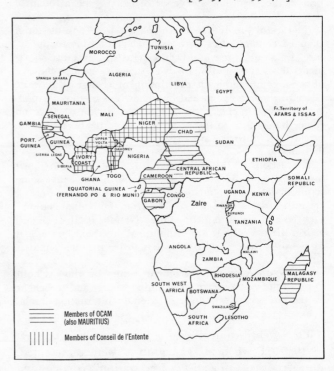

OCAM has established the following joint enterprises:

Air Afrique, a multinational airline with its head office in Abidjan and with the following 10 members: Central African Republic, Congo, Dahomey, Gabon, Ivory Coast, Mauritania, Niger, Senegal, Togo, and Upper Volta. [*25257A*]

Organization for the Development of Tourism in Africa (ODTA), Paris.

African and Malagasy Union for Postal Services and Telecommunications (UAMPT), Brazzaville.

School for Engineering and Agricultural Equipment (EIER), Ouagadougou.

African and Malagasy Sugar Agreement, Fort Lamy.

Inter-State School for Science and Veterinary Medicine, Dakar.

African and Malagasy Office for Industrial Property (OAMPI), Yaoundé.

African, Malagasy, and Mauritian Cultural Institute, Dakar.

Organization for Meat Marketing, Niamey.

African Institute of Information, Libreville.

(e) The charter of a *Union of Central African States* (UEAC) was signed in Fort Lamy on April 2, 1968, by the Presidents of the Central African Republic, Chad, and the Congo (now Zaïre), and on May 7, 1968, the 3 member-States of the UEAC concluded mutual defense and security agreements. On Dec. 8, 1968, however, President Bokassa of the Central African Republic announced that his country would leave the UEAC. [*22653A; 23359A*]

(f) An *Organization for the Development of the Senegal River* was set up in Nouakchott (Mauritania) on March 12, 1972, by the Governments of Mali, Mauritania, and Senegal for the joint economic development of the Senegal river and its tributaries. (This Organization superseded an earlier Organization of Riparian States of the River Senegal of which Guinea had also been a member, in addition to the above 3 countries, and which had been disbanded on Nov. 30, 1971.) [*25180B*]

(g) A treaty establishing a *West African Economic Community—Communauté économique de l'Afrique de l'Ouest* (CEAO)—providing for "an area of organized exchanges" to be constituted by Dahomey, the Ivory Coast, Mali, Mauritania, Niger, Senegal, and Upper Volta was signed in Bamako (Mali) on June 3, 1972. It superseded an earlier West African Customs Union (UDEAO), established by the same 7 States on June 3, 1966, and in force since Dec. 15, 1966. [*22084B; 25236B*]

4. WEST AFRICA

The establishment of a West African Common Market was approved at a conference held in Accra from April 27 to May 4, 1967, by Dahomey, Ghana, the Ivory Coast, Liberia, Mali, Mauritania, Niger, Nigeria, Senegal, Sierra Leone, Togo, and Upper Volta. [*22084B*]

BILATERAL TREATIES IN AFRICA

1. ETHIOPIA AND KENYA

A defense agreement, providing for mutual aid in the case of attack by a third party, was concluded between Ethiopia and Kenya in November 1963 and ratified by both countries on Dec. 27, 1963. [*19809D*]

A treaty delimiting the entire frontier between both countries was signed in Nairobi on June 9, 1970. [*24112B*]

2. GUINEA AND SIERRA LEONE

Under a defense agreement signed on March 26, 1971, Guinean troops were sent to Sierra Leone to prevent the latter country's Government from being overthrown. [*24559A*]

3. IVORY COAST AND SENEGAL

A Treaty of Friendship and Co-operation between the Ivory Coast and Senegal was signed in Abidjan on Dec. 15, 1971, together with an agreement on the establishment of a joint co-operation commission. [*25191C*]

4. SUDAN AND UGANDA

A mutual defense agreement between the Sudan and Uganda, providing for military aid against aggression by any external enemies, was signed in Khartoum on June 28, 1972. [*25236C*]

5. NIGERIA AND CHAD

A treaty of friendship, co-operation, and mutual assistance, together with an extradition treaty and an agreement on cultural relations, was initialed at Fort Lamy on Dec. 11, 1972. [*25711B*]

GROUPINGS IN AFRICA
DEPENDENT TERRITORIES

BRITAIN
Colonies:
Seychelles and the British Indian Ocean Territory, St. Helena and dependencies (Ascension Island and Tristan da Cunha).

FRANCE
(1) *French Overseas Territories* (i.e. integral parts of the French Republic):
French Territory of the Afars and Issas (formerly French Somaliland);
Comoro Islands.
(2) *French Overseas Département:*
Réunion.

PORTUGAL
Territories with the status of Overseas Provinces:
The Cape Verde Islands;
Portuguese Guinea;
São Tomé and Principe islands;
Angola (including the enclave of Cabinda);
Mozambique.

SOUTH AFRICA
(1) *South-West Africa (Namibia)*, administered by the Government of South Africa as an integral part of the Republic of South Africa under a mandate

	OAU	Commonwealth	Communauté	OCAM	Conseil de l'Entente	Defense Pact with France	Associate of EEC	Arab League	Maghreb Permanent Consultative Committee	East African Economic Community	West African Monetary Union	Central African Customs Union	West African Economic Community	West African Common Market
ALGERIA	X							X	X					
BOTSWANA	X	X												
BURUNDI	X						X							
CAMEROON	X			X		X	X					X		
CENTRAL AFRICAN REPUBLIC	X		X	X		X	X					X		
CHAD	X		X	X		X	X					X		
CONGO (BRAZZAVILLE)	X		X			X	X					X		
DAHOMEY	X			X	X	X	X				X		X	X
EQUATORIAL GUINEA	X													
ETHIOPIA	X													
GABON	X		X	X			X					X		
GAMBIA	X	X												
GHANA	X	X												X
GUINEA	X													
IVORY COAST	X			X	X	X	X				X		X	X
KENYA	X	X					X			X				
LESOTHO	X	X												
LIBERIA	X													X
LIBYA	X							X	X					
MALAGASY REPUBLIC	X		X	X		X	X							
MALAWI	X	X												
MALI	X						X						X	X
MAURITANIA	X					X	X				X		X	X
MAURITIUS	X	X		X										
MOROCCO	X						X	X	X					
NIGER	X			X	X		X				X		X	X
NIGERIA	X	X												X
RHODESIA														
RWANDA	X			X			X							
SENEGAL	X		X	X		X	X				X		X	X
SIERRA LEONE	X	X												X

	OAU	Commonwealth	Communauté	OCAM	Conseil de l'Entente	Defense Pact with France	Associate of EEC	Arab League	Maghreb Permanent Consultative Committee	East African Economic Community	West African Monetary Union	Central African Customs Union	West African Economic Community	West African Common Market
SOMALIA	×						×							
SOUTH AFRICA														
SUDAN	×							×						
SWAZILAND	×	×												
TANZANIA	×	×					×			×				
TOGO	×			×	×	×	×							×
TUNISIA	×						×	×	×					
UGANDA	×	×					×			×				
UNITED ARAB REPUBLIC	×							×						
UPPER VOLTA	×			×	×		×				×		×	×
ZAÏRE	×						×							
ZAMBIA	×	×												

granted by the League of Nations in 1919. The U.N. General Assembly decided on Oct. 27, 1966, to terminate South Africa's mandate and to take steps to establish an interim administration to prepare the territory for complete independence. [21797A]

(2) The following territories have been granted self-government by South Africa:

Territory of the Transkei, May 24, 1963.

Bophuthatswana, June 1, 1972.

Territory of the Ciskei, Aug. 1, 1972.

Lebowa, Oct. 2, 1972. [19532A; 25575A]

SPAIN

(1) *The towns of Ceuta and Melilla* on the North African coast are integral parts of Spain.

(2) *Overseas Province,* juridically part of metropolitan Spain:

Spanish Sahara.

15

South and East Asia and the Pacific Area

AUSTRALIAN–NEW ZEALAND AGREEMENT (ANZAC)

After a conference held in January 1944 in Canberra between Australia and New Zealand to discuss their common interests, and in particular joint policy regarding the Southwest Pacific region, a joint declaration, the Australian—New Zealand Agreement, 1944 (ANZAC), was signed on Jan. 21.

The two Governments agreed that a "regional zone of defense comprising the Southwest and South Pacific areas shall be established and that this zone should be based on Australia and New Zealand, stretching through the arch of islands North and Northeast of Australia to Western Samoa and the Cook Islands."

In regard to dependent territories, the two Governments declared that "the interim administration and ultimate disposal of enemy territories in the Pacific is of vital importance to Australia and New Zealand and that any such disposal should be effected only with their agreement and as part of a general Pacific agreement," and that "no change in the sovereignty . . . of any of the islands of the Pacific should be effected except as the result of an agreement to which they are parties." [6273A]

In implementation of a further decision of the ANZAC Agreement, a South Pacific Commission was set up on Feb. 6, 1947, with the aim of assisting the social welfare and economic development of island peoples in the South and Southwest Pacific. Its members are Australia, Britain, France, New Zealand, and the U.S.A., as well as the island territories in the South Pacific. [8458A]

ANZUS PACT

A tripartite security treaty between Australia, New Zealand, and the United States was signed on Sept. 1, 1951, in San Francisco, and came into force on April 29, 1952. The treaty is known as the Pacific Security Treaty or, more usually, the ANZUS Pact. The latter name derives from the initials of the three signatory countries.

The possibility of a pact between Australia, New Zealand, and the United States had been discussed in February 1951, when the American President's Republican adviser on foreign affairs, John Foster Dulles, visited the Australian and New Zealand capitals. On April 18, 1951, President Truman announced from Washington that the Australian and New Zealand Governments, in view of the impending re-establishment of peace with Japan (the Japanese peace treaty was signed on Sept. 8, 1951), had suggested to the United States an arrangement between the three countries which would "make it clear that no one of the three would be indifferent to an armed attack upon the others in the Pacific," and which would "establish consultation to strengthen security on the basis of continuous and effective self-help and mutual aid."

The Treaty

The text of the Pacific Security Treaty was released on July 12, 1951. The preamble ran as follows:

The parties to this treaty:
reaffirming their faith in the purposes and principles of the U.N. Charter and their desire to live in peace with all peoples and Governments, and desiring to strengthen the fabric of peace in the Pacific area;
noting that the United States has already arrangements pursuant to which its armed forces are stationed in the Philippines, and has armed forces and administrative responsibilities in the Ryukyus, and upon the coming into force of the Japanese peace treaty, may also station armed forces in and about Japan to assist in the preservation of peace and security in the Japan area;
recognizing that Australia and New Zealand, as members of the British Commonwealth of Nations, have military obligations outside as well as within the Pacific area;
desiring to declare publicly and formally their sense of unity, so that no potential aggressor could be under the

illusion that any of them stand alone in the Pacific area; and

desiring further to co-ordinate their efforts for collective defense for the preservation of peace and security pending the development of a more comprehensive system of regional security in the Pacific area;

declare and agree as follows . . .

The terms of the treaty were contained in 11 Articles summarized below:

Art. 1. The parties undertook, in conformity with the U.N. Charter, to settle by peaceful means any international disputes in which they might be involved, and to refrain in their international relations from the use of force in any manner inconsistent with the purposes of the United Nations.

Art. 2. In order more effectively to achieve the objectives of the treaty, the parties would maintain and develop their individual and collective capacity to resist armed attack "by means of continuous self-help and mutual aid."

Art. 3. The parties would consult together when, in the opinion of any one of them, the territorial integrity, political independence, or security of any of them was threatened in the Pacific.

Art. 4. "Each party recognizes that an armed attack in the Pacific area on any of the other parties would be dangerous to its own peace and safety, and declares that it would act to meet the common danger in accordance with its constitutional processes." Any such attack, and all measures taken as a result of such attack, would be reported to the U.N. Security Council. Such measures would be terminated when the Security Council had taken the necessary steps to restore and maintain international peace and security.

Art. 5. For the purpose of Art. 4, an armed attack on any of the three countries would be deemed to include "an armed attack on the metropolitan territory of any of the parties, or on the island territories under its jurisdiction in the Pacific, or on its armed forces, vessels, or aircraft in the Pacific."

Art. 6. The treaty would not affect the rights and obligations of the three countries under the U.N. Charter, or the responsibility of the United Nations for the maintenance of international peace and security.

Art. 7. The three countries would establish a Council, consisting of their Foreign Ministers or deputies, to consider matters concerning the implementation of the treaty. The Council would be organized so as to be able to meet at any time.

Art. 8. Pending the development of a more comprehensive regional security system in the Pacific, and the development by the U.N. of more effective means to maintain international peace and security, the Council, established under Art. 7, would maintain a consultative relationship with States, regional organizations, associations of States, and other authorities in the Pacific area which were in a position to further the purpose of the treaty and contribute to the security of the area.

Art. 9. The treaty would be ratified by the three countries in accordance with their respective constitutional processes. Instruments of ratification would be deposited with the Australian Government, and the treaty would enter into force as soon as the ratifications of the signatories had been deposited.

Art. 10. The treaty would remain in force indefinitely. Any party to the treaty could cease to be a member of the Council established under Art. 7 one year after notification to the Australian Government.

Art. 11. The treaty, drawn up in the English language, would be deposited in the archives of the Australian Government, which would make copies available to the other signatories. [*11690A*]

Organization

The Pacific Council
The organ of the ANZUS pact is the Council—known as the Pacific Council—set up under Article 7 of the treaty. It is composed of the Foreign Ministers (or their deputies) of the signatory powers. The Foreign Ministers generally meet once a year, but special Council meetings, attended by the deputies, are held in Washington more frequently. The Council has no permanent staff or funds.

Military Representatives
At the first meeting of the Pacific Council, held in Honolulu Aug. 4–6, 1952, it was decided to create a military organization. In this organization each of the three signatory countries is represented by a military officer, who attends Council meetings. The military representatives also hold their own meetings from time to time as required by circumstances. Their function is to advise the Council on military co-operation in the Pacific. [*12399A*]

AUSTRALIA—NEW ZEALAND FREE TRADE AREA

An agreement was signed in Wellington on Aug. 31, 1965, by Australia and New Zealand on the establishment of a limited free trade area. The agreement, covering commodities accounting for some 60 percent of the value of trade between the two countries, and including forestry and dairy products, will remain in force for a period of 10 years as from Jan. 1, 1966. [*20962B*]

SOUTHEAST ASIA TREATY ORGANIZATION (SEATO)

Members: Australia, Britain, France, New Zealand, Philippines, Thailand, United States

The Southeast Asia Treaty Organization, or SEATO, came into being with the signing of the Southeast Asia

Collective Defense Treaty in Manila on Sept. 8, 1954. The treaty came into force on Feb. 9, 1955.

The idea of "united action" in the Southeast Asia region was put forward by the U.S. Secretary of State, John Foster Dulles, in the spring of 1954, in view of the "grave threat to the whole free community" deriving from possible Communist domination of Indo-China.

The question of Southeast Asian defense was further considered at 5-Power military staff talks, held June 3–11, 1954, in Washington, between representatives of the United States, Britain, France, Australia, and New Zealand, and at top-level Anglo-American discussions in Washington June 25–28, 1954. An Anglo-American study group on Southeast Asian defense, which was set up at the last-mentioned meeting, ended its discussions on July 18. Earlier, on June 30, 1954, representatives of the ANZUS Powers (Australia, New Zealand, and the U.S.A.) held a meeting at which all three agreed on "the need for immediate action to bring about the early establishment of collective defense in Southeast Asia." [*13545A; 13621D; 13665A; 13668A*]

All these preliminary meetings led to a final 8-Power conference on collective security in Southeast Asia, which opened on Sept. 6, 1954, in Manila. Attended by delegations from Australia, Britain, France, New Zealand, Pakistan, the Philippines, Thailand, and the U.S.A., the meeting ended on Sept. 8, 1954, with the signing of the Southeast Asia Collective Defense Treaty. The treaty was accompanied by (*a*) a unilateral U.S. declaration in the form of an "understanding" that the pact was directed against Communist aggression; (*b*) a Protocol on Indo-China; and (*c*) the "Pacific Charter," a general statement of principles, signed by all eight contracting parties.

The texts of the Collective Defense Treaty and the other three documents are given below:

The Southeast Asia Collective Defense Treaty
PREAMBLE

The parties to this treaty: recognizing the sovereign equality of all the parties; retaining their faith in the purposes and principles set forth in the U.N. Charter, and their desire to live in peace with all peoples and Governments; reaffirming that, in accordance with the U.N. Charter, they uphold the principle of equal rights and self-determination of peoples; declaring that they will earnestly strive by every peaceful means to promote self-government and to secure the independence of all countries whose peoples desire and are able to undertake its responsibilities; intending to declare publicly and formally their sense of unity so that any potential aggressor will appreciate that the parties stand together in the area; and desiring further to co-ordinate their efforts for collective defense for the preservation of peace and security, have agreed as follows:

Art. 1. The parties undertake, as set forth in the U.N. Charter, to settle any international disputes in which they may be involved by peaceful means in such a manner that international peace, security and justice are not endangered, and to refrain in their international relations from the threat or use of force in any manner inconsistent with the purpose of the United Nations.

Art. 2. In order more effectively to achieve the objectives of this treaty, the parties, separately and jointly, by means of continuous and effective self-help and mutual aid, will maintain and develop their individual and collective capacity to resist armed attack and to prevent and counter subversive acts from without against their territorial integrity and political stability.

Art. 3. The parties undertake to strengthen their free institutions and to co-operate with one another in the further development of economic measures, including technical assistance, designed both to promote economic progress and social well-being and to further the individual and collective efforts of Governments toward these ends.

Art. 4. (1) Each party recognizes that aggression by means of armed attack in the treaty area against any of the parties, or against any State or territory which the parties by unanimous agreement may hereafter designate, would endanger its own peace and safety, and agrees that it will, in that event, act to meet the common danger in accordance with its constitutional processes. Measures taken under this paragraph shall be immediately reported to the U.N. Security Council.

(2) If, in the opinion of any of the parties, the inviolability or integrity of the territory or the sovereignty or political independence of any party in the treaty area, or of any other State or territory to which the provisions of paragraph (1) of this Article from time to time apply, is threatened in any way other than by armed attack, or is affected or threatened by any fact or situation which might endanger the peace of the area, the parties shall consult immediately in order to agree on the measures which should be taken for the common defense.

(3) It is understood that no action on the territory of any State designated by unanimous agreement under paragraph (1) of this Article, or on any territory so designated, shall be taken except at the invitation or with the consent of the Government concerned.

Art. 5. The parties hereby establish a Council, on which each of them shall be represented, to consider matters concerning the implementation of this treaty. The Council shall provide for consultation with regard to military and any other planning as the situation obtaining in the treaty area may from time to time require. The Council shall be organized so as to be able to meet at any time.

Art. 6. This treaty does not affect, and shall not be interpreted as affecting in any way, the rights and obligations of any of the parties under the U.N. Charter or the responsibility of the United Nations for the maintenance of international peace and security. Each party declares that none of the international engagements now in force between it and any other of the parties, or any third party, is in conflict with the provisions of this treaty, and undertakes not to enter into any international engagement in conflict with the treaty.

Art. 7. Any other State in a position to further the objectives of this treaty and to contribute to the security of the area may, by unanimous agreement of the parties, be invited to accede to this treaty. Any State so invited may become a party to the treaty by depositing its instrument of accession with the Philippine Government.

Art. 8. The treaty area is the general area of Southeast Asia, including also the entire territories of the Asian parties, and the general area of the Southwest Pacific, not including the Pacific area north of 21 degrees 30 minutes North latitude. The parties may, by unanimous agreement, amend this Article to include the territory of any State acceding to this treaty in accordance with Article 7, or otherwise to change the treaty area.

Art. 9. (1) This treaty shall be deposited in the archives of the Philippine Government. Copies thereof shall be transmitted by that Government to the other signatories.

(2) The treaty shall be ratified and its provisions carried out by the parties in accordance with their respective constitutional processes. Instruments of ratification shall be deposited as soon as possible with the Philippine Government, which shall notify all the other signatories of such deposit.

(3) The treaty shall enter into force between the States which have ratified it as soon as the instruments of ratification of a majority of signatories shall have been deposited, and shall come into effect with respect to each other State on the date of deposit of its instrument of ratification.

Art. 10. The treaty shall remain in force indefinitely, but any party may cease to be a party one year after notice of denunciation has been given to the Philippine Government, which shall inform the Governments of the other parties of each notice of denunciation.

Art. 11. The English text of this treaty is binding on the parties, but when the parties have agreed to the French text thereof and have so notified the Philippine Government, the French text shall be equally authentic and binding.

U.S. "Understanding"

The delegation of the United States of America, in signing the present treaty, does so with the understanding that its recognition of the effect of aggression and armed attack, and its agreement with reference thereto in Article 4, paragraph one, apply only to Communist aggression, but affirms that in the event of other aggression or armed attack it will consult under the provisions of Article 4.

Protocol on Indo-China

Designations of States and territory as to which the provisions of Articles 3 and 4 are to be applicable—The parties to the Southeast Asia Collective Defense Treaty unanimously designate for the purposes of Article 4 of the treaty the States of Cambodia and Laos and the free territory under the jurisdiction of the State of Vietnam.

The parties further agree that the above-mentioned States and territory shall be eligible in respect of the economic measures contemplated by Article 3. This protocol shall come into force simultaneously with the coming into force of the treaty.

The Pacific Charter

The delegates, desiring to establish a firm basis for common action to maintain peace and security in Southeast Asia and the Southwest Pacific, and convinced that common action to this end, in order to be worthy and effec-

tive, must be inspired by the highest principles of justice and liberty, do hereby proclaim:

(1) In accordance with the provisions of the U.N. Charter, they uphold the principle of equal rights and self-determination of peoples, and will earnestly strive by every peaceful means to promote self-government and to secure the independence of all countries whose peoples desire it and are able to undertake its responsibilities.

(2) They are each prepared to continue taking effective practical measures to ensure conditions favorable to the orderly achievement of the foregoing purposes in accordance with their constitutional procedures.

(3) They will continue to co-operate in the economic, social and cultural fields in order to promote higher living standards, economic progress, and social well-being in this region.

(4) As decreed in the Southeast Asia Collective Defense Treaty, they are determined to prevent or counter by appropriate means any attempt in the treaty area to subvert freedom or to destroy their sovereignty or territorial integrity. [*13761A*]

Organization

The principal organ of SEATO is the Council, set up under Article 5 of the Collective Defense Treaty. The function of the Council, which is composed of the Foreign Ministers of the eight signatory countries, is to decide the general policies of the Organization. Meetings are generally held once a year in the capital cities of the member countries.

In addition to the Council, the organization is composed of civil and military organs.

Civil Organs

At the first meeting of the Council, held in Bangkok Feb. 23–25, 1955, a permanent body of Council Representatives, with headquarters in Bangkok, was set up. This body, which consists of the Ambassadors of SEATO member-countries in Bangkok and a special Thai Ambassador, meets monthly to carry out the policies laid down by the Council and to make recommendations on the implementation of the treaty.

A Permanent Working Group, to assist the Council Representatives in Bangkok in carrying out preparatory work, was established at the second annual Council meeting, held March 6–8, 1956. The Working Group, which meets as required, consists of officers from the staffs of the Council Representatives.

A full-time executive Secretariat also came into being in 1956, although the post of Secretary-General was not created until the following year. The task of the Secretary-General is the co-ordination of SEATO's political, economic and cultural activities.

Various committees of experts meet at irregular intervals to give advice on specific subjects, such as economic aid, information, education, culture, labor, security, and counter-subversion.

The military activities of SEATO are directed by a group of Military Advisers, consisting of one high-ranking officer from each member-country. The Military Advisers' Group, which meets twice a year, makes recommendations to the Council on military co-operation.

The SEATO Military Planning Office, a permanent office with headquarters in Bangkok, was formed in January 1957. Its staff consists of the Chief and Deputy Chief, Military Planning Office (both of whom are senior officers in the armed forces of SEATO member-countries), Military Advisers' Representatives, and a number of planners, provided by the armed forces of all 8 member-countries.

Institutions

Among institutions founded to carry out the economic, cultural, and social objectives of SEATO are the Cultural and Economic Affairs Office, which administers the SEATO Cultural Relations Program and makes studies of economic problems and developments in the Treaty Area; the Medical Research Laboratory, the Cholera Research Laboratory, and the Clinical Research Center, founded in 1959, 1960, and 1963 respectively, for purposes of research into tropical diseases; a Rural Development Center, set up at Ubol in northeast Thailand; a graduate Asian Institute of Technology in Bangkok; and a number of vocational and technical training centers in Thailand, Pakistan, and the Philippines, set up to implement the SEATO Skilled Labor Program.

Internal Disagreements

The tenth meeting of the SEATO Council, held May 3–5, 1965, in London, saw a split in the alliance. France, which did not adhere to the common SEATO viewpoint on former Indo-China, and particularly Vietnam, refused to attend the Council as a full member, sending only an observer. At subsequent Council meetings—held in Canberra in June 1966 and in Washington in April 1967—France was again represented only by an observer. In May 1965, following the London conference, France severed another link with SEATO by withdrawing the 6 French officers holding staff posts in the Organization.

Pakistan too expressed disagreement with other SEATO members on certain matters. At the 10th meeting Pakistan made reservations on the Organization's political decisions on Vietnam and Laos, and also on the Malaysian-Indonesian dispute. Although Pakistan was fully represented at the 11th meeting of the Coun-

cil, this was not the case at the 12th meeting in 1967. [20876A]

While the Council continued to hold annual meetings—the latest being its 17th meeting of June 1972—without representatives of France and with only diplomatic representation of Pakistan, the value of the alliance was increasingly open to doubt. Mr. Thanat Khoman, the Thai Foreign Minister, said in May 1969 that SEATO's military capability was "a fiction," as it had no military structure, only a military framework; the only way to save SEATO from impotence, he said, was to "change the emphasis from military to political."

President Bhutto of Pakistan announced on July 16, 1972, that his country had withdrawn from SEATO.

BILATERAL MUTUAL DEFENSE TREATIES OF THE U.S.A.

The mutual defense treaties concluded by the U.S.A. in the Far East and the Pacific area are all similar in both content and wording. In each, the parties undertake to settle any international dispute in which they may be involved by peaceful means; to consult together at the threat of or in the event of an external armed attack; and to maintain and develop means to deter such an attack. The parties recognize that an armed attack on either would be dangerous to the peace and security of both, and declare their readiness to act to meet the common danger.

The full text of the mutual security treaty between the U.S.A. and South Korea (for further details see below under "U.S.A.—South Korea") is here given as an example:

PREAMBLE

The parties to this treaty, reaffirming their desire to live in peace with all peoples and Governments, and desiring to strengthen the fabric of peace in the Pacific area, to declare publicly and formally their common determination to defend themselves against external armed attack so that no potential aggressor could be under the illusion that either of them stands alone in the Pacific area, and to strengthen their efforts for collective defense for the preservation of peace and security pending the development of a more comprehensive and effective system of regional security in the Pacific area, have agreed as follows:

Art. 1. The parties undertake to settle any international disputes in which they may be involved by peaceful means . . . and to refrain in their international relations from the threat or use of force in any manner inconsistent with the purposes of the United Nations, or the obligations assumed by any party toward the United Nations.

Art. 2. The parties will consult together whenever, in the opinion of either of them, the political independence or security of either of the parties is threatened by external armed attack. Separately and jointly, by self-help and mutual aid, the parties will maintain and develop appropriate means to deter armed attack, and will take suitable measures in consultation and agreement to implement this treaty and further its purposes.

Art. 3. Each party recognizes that an armed attack in the Pacific area on either of the parties in territories now under their respective administrative control, or hereafter recognized by one of the parties as lawfully brought under the administrative control of the other, would be dangerous to its own peace and safety, and declares that it would act to meet the common danger in accordance with its constitutional processes.

Art. 4. The Republic of Korea grants, and the United States accepts, the right to dispose U.S. land, air and sea forces in and about the territory of the Republic of Korea as determined by mutual agreement.

Art. 5. This treaty shall be ratified by the Republic of Korea and the United States in accordance with their respective constitutional processes, and will come into force when instruments of ratification have been exchanged.

Art. 6. The treaty shall remain in force indefinitely. Either party may terminate it one year after notice has been given to the other party. [13077A]

U.S.A.–PHILIPPINES

The mutual defense treaty between the U.S.A. and the Philippines was signed in Washington on Aug. 30, 1951. The treaty, which was intended to reinforce the Pacific security arrangements embodied in the ANZUS pact (see page 194), entered into force on Aug. 27, 1952.

In this treaty it was stated that an armed attack would be deemed to include "an armed attack on the metropolitan territory of either of the parties, or on the island territories under its jurisdiction in the Pacific, or on its armed forces, public vessels, or aircraft in the Pacific." [11715C]

Agreement on Military Bases

On March 14, 1947 an agreement had been signed in Manila by representatives of the U.S.A. and the Philippines, providing for the establishment, for a 99-year period, of 23 American military, naval, and air bases in the Philippines. Under the agreement, which came into force on March 26, 1947, certain military bases, established before the Philippines' proclamation of independence in July 1946, would be maintained by the U.S.A., while others would pass to the control of the Philippine Government. [8538C]

In July 1956 the United States affirmed its recognition of the Philippine Government's sovereignty over all U.S. bases on Philippine territory. The agreement on military bases was revised by a memorandum signed on Oct. 12, 1959. Among the decisions embodied in the memorandum were the shortening of the leases granted to the U.S.A. for military bases from 99 years

to 25 years from Oct. 12, 1959; and an agreement that the U.S. Government would consult with the Philippine Government on the operational use of the bases, and before setting up long-range missile sites at American bases. [14987A; 17474A]

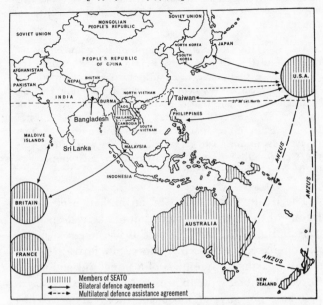

U.S.A.–JAPAN

A treaty of mutual co-operation and security between the U.S.A. and Japan was signed in Washington on Jan. 19, 1960, and entered into force on June 23, 1960. The treaty, which was concluded after some 18 months of negotiations, replaced the U.S.-Japanese defense pact signed at San Francisco on Sept. 8, 1951.

Under the 1951 treaty the United States had the right to dispose land, air, and sea forces in and about Japan, and to use those forces, at the request of the Japanese Government, "to put down large-scale internal riots and disturbances in Japan caused through instigation or intervention by an outside Power or Powers." The treaty also stated that Japan would not grant, without the prior consent of the United States, any bases, or the right of garrison, or transit of forces, to any third Power. [11724A]

Under the new treaty Japan is no longer treated as the weaker partner, but is placed on an equal footing with the United States.

The most important of the provisions peculiar to this treaty are contained in Articles 2, 6 and 10:

Art. 2. The parties will contribute toward the further development of peaceful and friendly international relations by strengthening their free institutions, bringing about a better understanding of the principles upon which these institutions are founded, and promoting conditions of stability and well-being. They will seek to eliminate conflict in their international economic policies and encourage economic collaboration between them.

Art. 6. For the purpose of contributing to the security of Japan and the maintenance of international peace and security in the Far East, the United States of America is granted the use by its land, air, and naval forces of facilities and areas in Japan. The use of these facilities and areas, as well as the status of U.S. armed forces in Japan, shall be governed by a separate agreement, replacing the administrative agreement under Article II of the Security Treaty between the U.S.A. and Japan signed at Tokyo on Feb. 28, 1952.

Art. 10. This treaty shall remain in force until, in the opinion of the Governments of the United States and Japan, there shall have come into force such United Nations arrangements as will satisfactorily provide for the maintenance of international peace and security in the Japan area. However, after the treaty has been in force for ten years, either party may give notice to the other party of its intention to terminate the treaty, in which case the treaty shall terminate one year after such notice has been given. [*17263A*]

The treaty was clarified by an exchange of Notes. In one of the Notes the United States agreed on prior consultation with the Japanese Government over (*a*) any envisaged increase in its forces in Japan; (*b*) any essential change in methods of arming and equipping forces (e.g. nuclear weapons); and (*c*) the use of Japanese bases for any action outside the treaty area. The treaty area was defined as the territory under Japanese rule at any time. The parties also agreed to consult together in the event of an armed attack or threat of attack against the islands over which Japan claims residual sovereignty. The principal islands in question are the Ryukyu Islands, the Bonin Islands, Volcano Island, and Marcus Island.

U.S.A.–SOUTH KOREA
The U.S.-South Korean mutual security treaty was initiated in Seoul on Aug. 8, 1953, shortly after the signing of the armistice at the end of the Korean war. The treaty was formally signed in Washington on Oct. 1, 1953, and entered into force on Nov. 17, 1954. [*13077A*]
For the provisions see above.

U.S.A.–TAIWAN
The mutual security treaty between the U.S.A. and Taiwan was signed on Dec. 2, 1954, and entered into force on March 3, 1955.

The following articles contain provisions which are peculiar to this treaty:

Art. 2. In order more effectively to achieve the objectives of this treaty, the parties separately and jointly, by self-help and mutual aid, will maintain and develop their individual and collective capacity to resist armed attack and Communist subversive activities directed from without against their territorial integrity and political stability.

Art. 3. The parties undertake to strengthen their free institutions, to co-operate with each other in the develop-

ment of economic progress and social well-being, and to further their individual and collective efforts toward these ends.

Art. 5. Each party recognizes that an armed attack in the West Pacific area directed against the territories of either of the parties would be dangerous to its own peace and safety, and declares that it would act to meet the common danger in accordance with its constitutional processes. Any such armed attack, and all measures taken as a result thereof, shall be immediately reported to the U.N. Security Council. Such measures shall be terminated when the Security Council has taken the measures necessary to restore and maintain international peace and security.

Art. 6. For the purposes of Articles 2 and 5, the terms "territorial" and "territories" shall mean, in respect of the Republic of China, Taiwan (Formosa) and the Pescadores; and in respect of the United States, the island territories in the West Pacific under its jurisdiction. The provisions of Articles 2 and 5 will be applicable to such other territories as may be determined by mutual agreement.

In an exchange of Notes, signed on Dec. 10, 1954, the Taiwan Government gave a formal undertaking that its forces would not attack the Chinese mainland without prior consultation with the United States. The Notes also stated that, while Taiwan's "inherent rights of self-defense" were assured as far as Formosa and the Pescadores were concerned, the use of force from either area would be a matter of joint agreement. [*14007C*]

THE 1954 GENEVA AGREEMENTS ON INDO-CHINA (VIETNAM, CAMBODIA, AND LAOS)

The 8-year war in Indo-China (1946–1954) between the Vietminh and France (with her three associated States—Cambodia, Laos, and Vietnam) was brought to an end by an armistice negotiated at the Geneva Conference, held between April 26 and July 21, 1954.

At the end of the conference the following documents were published: an 8-nation declaration "on the problem of restoring peace in Indo-China"; declarations by the French, Cambodian, and Laotian Governments; and a unilateral American declaration defining the position of the U.S. Government.

THE EIGHT-NATION DECLARATION
The declaration made by France, Britain, the Soviet Union, the People's Republic of China, Vietnam, Cambodia, Laos, and the Vietminh Government was worded as follows:

(1) The conference takes note of the agreements ending hostilities in Cambodia, Laos, and Vietnam, and organizing international control and supervision of the execution of the provisions of these agreements.
(2) The conference expresses satisfaction at the ending

of hostilities in Cambodia, Laos, and Vietnam. It expresses its conviction that the execution of the provisions set out in the present declaration and in the agreements on the cessation of hostilities will permit Cambodia, Laos, and Vietnam henceforth to play their part, in full independence and sovereignty, in the peaceful community of nations.

(3) The conference takes note of the declarations made by the Governments of Cambodia and Laos (see below) of their intention to adopt measures permitting all citizens to take their place in the national community, in particular by participating in the next general elections, which, in conformity with the Constitution of each of these countries, shall take place in 1955 by secret ballot and in conditions of respect for fundamental freedoms.

(4) The conference takes note of the clauses in the agreement on the cessation of hostilities in Vietnam prohibiting the introduction into Vietnam of foreign troops and military personnel, as well as of all kinds of arms and munitions. It also takes note of the declarations made by the Governments of Cambodia and Laos of their resolution not to request foreign aid, whether in war material, personnel, or instructors, except for the purpose of the effective defense of their territory and, in the case of Laos, to the extent defined by the agreements on the cessation of hostilities in Laos.

(5) The conference takes note of the clauses in the agreement on the cessation of hostilities in Vietnam to the effect that no military base at the disposition of a foreign State may be established in the regrouping zones of the two parties, the latter having the obligation to see that the zones allotted to them shall not constitute part of any military alliance and shall not be utilized for the resumption of hostilities or in the service of an aggressive policy. The conference also takes note of the declarations of the Governments of Cambodia and Laos to the effect that they will not join in any agreement with other States if this agreement includes the obligation to participate in a military alliance not in conformity with the principles of the U.N. Charter or, in the case of Laos, with the principles of the agreement on the cessation of hostilities in Laos, or, so long as their security is not threatened, the obligation to establish bases on Cambodian or Laotian territory for the military forces of foreign Powers.

(6) The conference recognizes that the essential purpose of the agreement relating to Vietnam is to settle military questions with a view to ending hostilities, and that the military demarcation line should not in any way be interpreted as constituting a political or territorial boundary. It expresses its conviction that the execution of the provisions set out in the present declaration and in the agreement on the cessation of hostilities creates the necessary bases for the achievement in the near future of a political settlement in Vietnam.

(7) The conference declares that, so far as Vietnam is concerned, the settlement of political problems, effected on the basis of respect for the principles of independence, unity, and territorial integrity, shall permit the Vietnamese people to enjoy the fundamental freedoms, guaranteed by democratic institutions, established as a result of free general elections by secret ballot. To ensure that sufficient progress in the restoration of peace has been made, and that all the necessary conditions obtain for free expression of the national will, general elections shall be held in July, 1956, under the supervision of an International Commission composed of representatives of the member-States of the International Supervisory Commission, referred to in the agreements on the cessation of hostilities. Consultations will be held on this subject between the competent representative authorities of the two zones from July 1955 onwards.

(8) The provisions of the agreements on the cessation of hostilities intended to ensure the protection of individuals and of property must be most strictly applied and must, in particular, allow everyone in Vietnam to decide freely in which zone he wishes to live.

(9) The competent representative authorities of the northern and southern zones of Vietnam, as well as the authorities of Laos and Cambodia, must not permit any individual or collective reprisals against persons who have collaborated in any way with one of the parties during the war, or against members of such a person's family.

(10) The conference takes note of the declaration of the French Government to the effect that it is ready to withdraw its troops from Cambodia, Laos, and Vietnam at the request of the Governments concerned and within a period which shall be fixed by agreement between the parties, except in the cases where, by agreement between the two parties, a certain number of French troops shall remain at specified points and for a specified time.

(11) The conference takes note of the declaration of the French Government to the effect that, for the settlement of all problems connected with the re-establishment and consolidation of peace in Cambodia, Laos, and Vietnam, it will proceed from the principle of respect for the independence, sovereignty, unity, and territorial integrity of Cambodia, Laos, and Vietnam.

(12) In their relations with Cambodia, Laos, and Vietnam, each member of the Geneva Conference undertakes to respect the sovereignty, independence, unity, and territorial integrity of the above-mentioned States, and to refrain from any interference in their internal affairs.

(13) The members of the Conference agree to consult one another on any questions which may be referred to them by the International Supervisory Commission in order to study such measures as may prove necessary to ensure that the agreements on the cessation of hostilities in Cambodia, Laos, and Vietnam are respected.

THE FRENCH, CAMBODIAN, AND LAOTIAN DECLARATIONS

France

The Government of the French Republic declares that it is ready to withdraw its troops from Cambodia, Laos, and Vietnam at the request of the Governments concerned and within a period which shall be fixed by agreement between the parties, except in the cases where, by agreement between the two parties, a certain number of French troops shall remain at specified points and for a specified time.

[The second paragraph of the French declaration was that referred to in paragraph (11) of the 8-nation declaration —see above.]

Cambodia

With the aim of assuring harmony and unanimity among the people of the Kingdom, the Royal Government of Cambodia declares itself willing to take all necessary measures to integrate all citizens, without any discrimination, in the national community, and to guarantee them the enjoyment of all rights and liberties provided for in the Constitution of the Kingdom. It also confirms that all Cambodian citizens will be able to participate freely, both as voters and candidates, in general elections to be held by secret ballot.

The Royal Government of Cambodia is resolved never to take part in an aggressive policy and never to permit the territory of Cambodia to be utilized in the service of such a policy. It will not join in any agreement with other States if this agreement carries for Cambodia the obligation to enter into a military alliance not in conformity with the principles of the U.N. Charter or with the principles of the agreement on the cessation of hostilities, or, as long as its security is not threatened, the obligation to establish bases on Cambodian territory for the military forces of foreign powers.

The Royal Government is resolved to settle its international disputes by peaceful means, in such a manner as not to endanger peace, international security, and justice.

During the period which will elapse between the date of the cessation of hostilities in Vietnam and that of the final settlement of political problems in Cambodia, the Royal Government will not solicit foreign aid in war material, personnel, or instructors, except for the purpose of the effective defense of its territory.

Laos

A declaration similar to the Cambodian was issued by the Royal Government of Laos, which undertook not to request foreign aid "except to the extent defined by the agreement on the cessation of hostilities."

It also stated that the Laotian Government would "promulgate measures with a view to setting-up, during the period between the cessation of hostilities and the holding of general elections, a special delegation attached to the administration of the provinces of Phong-Saly and Sam-Neua for the benefit of those Laotian nationals who did not participate in the fighting on the side of the Royal forces." (The two provinces were those which had been designated as "regrouping areas" for the Laotian rebel forces who had fought with the Vietminh.)

UNILATERAL U.S. DECLARATION

The unilateral declaration by the U.S. Government read as follows:

The Government of the United States, being resolved to devote its efforts to the strengthening of peace in accordance with the principles and purposes of the United Nations:

Takes note of the agreements concluded at Geneva on July 20 and 21, 1954, between (a) the Franco-Laotian Command and the Command of the People's Army of Vietnam (i.e. the Vietminh military authorities); (b) the Royal Cambodian Command and the People's Army of Vietnam; (c) the Franco-Vietnamese Command and the Command of the People's Army of Vietnam; and of paragraphs (1) to (12) inclusive of the declaration presented to the Geneva Conference on July 21, 1954;

Declares with regard to the aforesaid agreements and paragraphs that:

(1) It will refrain from the threat or the use of force to disturb them, in accordance with Article 2 (4) of the U.N. Charter dealing with the obligation of members to refrain in their international relations from the threat or use of force; and

(2) It would view any renewal of aggression in violation of the aforesaid agreements with grave concern and as seriously threatening international peace and security.

In connection with the statement in the declaration concerning free elections in Vietnam, my Government wishes to make clear its position, which it has expressed in a declaration made in Washington on June 29, 1954 (by President Eisenhower and Sir Winston Churchill) as follows: "In the case of nations now divided against their will, we shall continue to seek to achieve unity through free elections, supervised by the U.N., to ensure that they are conducted fairly."

With respect to the statement made by the representative of the State of Vietnam, the United States reiterates its traditional position that peoples are entitled to determine their own future and that it will not join in an arrangement which would hinder this. Nothing in this declaration is intended to, or does, indicate any departure from this traditional position.

We share the hope that the agreements will permit Cambodia, Laos and Vietnam to play their part, in full independence and sovereignty, in the peaceful community of nations, and will enable the peoples of that area to determine their own future.

Cease-Fire Agreements

The cease-fire agreements provided for, *inter alia,* the partition of Vietnam near the 17th parallel; elections in both parts of Vietnam; the supervision of the armistices; and the recognition, by the Vietminh, of the independence and political integrity of Cambodia and Laos.

Vietnamese Declaration

The Vietnamese Government, which strongly opposed the partitioning of Vietnam, issued a declaration on July 21, 1954, containing its own proposals for a cease-fire.

This declaration called for a settlement in the following stages, all of which would be under U.N. supervision: (1) a cease-fire throughout Vietnam, without any demarcation line being drawn; (2) the regrouping of the forces of both sides in specified areas; (3) the disarming of all irregular forces; (4) the disarming of the Vietminh forces, and the simultaneous withdrawal of all foreign troops from Vietnam; (5) elections throughout Vietnam when, in the opinion of the U.N., security and order had been re-established.

After protesting against "the rejection of these proposals without examination," the Vietnamese declaration registered four "solemn protests," as follows:

(1) Against "the haste with which the armistice agreement has been concluded by the French and Vietminh High Commands," in which connection it was stated that "many clauses of the agreement are of a nature which gravely compromises the political future of the Vietnamese people."

(2) Against "the fact that the armistice agreement abandons to the Vietminh certain territories which are still occupied by Vietnamese troops and which are essential for the defense of Vietnam against further Communist expansionism."

(3) Against "the action of the French High Command in arrogating to itself the right, without prior consultation with the State of Vietnam, of fixing the date of future elections."

(4) Against "the manner in which the armistice has been concluded and the conditions of the armistice, which take no account of the aspirations of the Vietnamese people." It was added that the Vietnamese Government reserved "full liberty of action to safeguard the sacred rights of the people of Vietnam to territorial unity, national independence, and liberty." [*13689A*]

Agreements Between the U.S.A. and the Indo-Chinese States

Certain agreements had been made between the U.S.A. and the countries of Indo-China before the conclusion of the Geneva Agreements of 1954. These were a mutual defense assistance agreement between the U.S.A. and the States of the French Union (France, Cambodia, Laos, and Vietnam), concluded on Dec. 23, 1950 (see also page 112); economic co-operation agreements between the U.S.A. and Vietnam (concluded on Sept. 7, 1951) and between the U.S.A. and Laos (concluded on Sept. 9, 1951); and agreements with Laos and Vietnam on economic and military aid under the U.S. Mutual Security Act of 1951, that with Laos coming into force on Dec. 31, 1951, and that with Vietnam on Jan. 3, 1952.

An agreement with South Vietnam providing for additional direct economic assistance was concluded on March 7, 1955, and a similar agreement with Laos came into force on July 8, 1955. Other agreements between the U.S.A. and South Vietnam were an agreement relating to the disposition of equipment and materials furnished by the U.S.A. (in effect May 10, 1955), and a treaty of amity and economic relations (in effect Nov. 30, 1961).

TREATIES AMONG NATIONS OF SOUTH AND EAST ASIA

A number of treaties, most of them aimed at friendly co-operation, have been concluded among Governments of non-Communist countries in Asia.

India–Bhutan
A treaty of "perpetual peace and friendship" was signed on Aug. 8, 1949. It provided, *inter alia,* that India would not interfere in the internal administration of Bhutan; the Government of Bhutan would be guided by the advice of the Indian Government in its external relations; India would return to Bhutan an area of 32 square miles in the Dewangiri district; and there would be freedom of trade and commerce between the two countries. [*10176C*]

India–Afghanistan
A treaty of peace and friendship, providing for closer commercial, cultural, industrial, and agricultural relations between the two countries, was signed on Jan. 4, 1950. Valid in the first instance for five years, the treaty can be terminated by either party at six months' notice. [*10460E*]

India–Nepal
A treaty providing for "everlasting peace and friendship" between the Governments of India and Nepal, was signed on July 31, 1950. The treaty states, *inter alia,* that the two countries recognize the "complete sovereignty, territorial integrity, and independence" of the other; that Nepal should be free to import from and through Indian territory the arms, ammunition, material, and equipment necessary for her security; and that each Government would "give to nationals of the other in its territory, national treatment with regard to participation in the industrial and economic development of such territory. . . ." [*10933A*]

Cancellation of the arms agreement by Nepal was announced on June 24, 1969. [*23608A*]

India–Sikkim
A treaty providing for the continuance of Sikkim as an internally autonomous Protectorate of India was signed on Dec. 5, 1950. Under the treaty India is responsible for the defense and territorial integrity of Sikkim, and has the right to take "such measures as it considered necessary for the defense of Sikkim or the security of India," including the stationing of Indian troops in Sikkim. Sikkim's external affairs are conducted by the Government of India. [*11147B*]

India–Philippines
A treaty affirming that there should be "perpetual peace and everlasting amity" between the two countries was signed on July 11, 1952. It is to remain in force unless terminated by either side at one year's notice. [*12354D*]

India–Burma
An agreement providing for the demarcation of the frontier between India and Burma was signed on March 19, 1967. [*23959A*]

India–Pakistan
1. *Settlement of Border Disputes.* Agreements were concluded between the Governments of India and Pakistan in September 1958 and October 1959 in regard to a number of border disputes. The latter agreement also laid down "ground rules" governing the conduct of army and police forces on both sides, and principles for provisional demarcation. [*16416A; 17095A*]

2. *The Indus Waters Treaty.* A treaty settling the long-standing dispute between India and Pakistan re-

garding the allocation of the waters of the Indus river system was signed on Sept. 19, 1960. Under the treaty, the waters of the three Eastern Rivers (Ravi, Beas, and Sutlej) are in general allocated to India, those of the three Western Rivers (Indus, Jhelum, and Chenab) to Pakistan. The treaty states that "both countries recognize their common interest in the optimum development of the rivers, and declare their intention to co-operate by mutual agreement to the fullest possible extent." Provision was made for the setting up of a Permanent Indus Commission, composed of one member appointed by each Government and with responsibility for implementing the provisions of the treaty. [*17655A*]

3. *The Tashkent Declaration* was signed at the end of a meeting between Prime Minister Shastri of India and President Ayub Khan of Pakistan, held at Tashkent in Uzbekistan (U.S.S.R.), Jan. 4–10, 1966, in an attempt to solve the Indo-Pakistani dispute which had reached a crisis with the outbreak of hostilities over Kashmir in August 1965. Under the declaration India and Pakistan pledged themselves, *inter alia,* to restore "normal and peaceful relations" between the two countries; to withdraw their armed forces, not later than Feb. 25, 1966, to the positions they held before the outbreak of hostilities; to repatriate captured prisoners of war; to restore diplomatic and economic relations between the two countries; to end hostile propaganda; and to deal with the question of refugees and illegal immigrants. [*21187A*]

4. *The Simla Agreement,* signed on July 3, 1972, and ratified by Pakistan on July 15 and by India on Aug. 1–3, came into effect on Aug. 4, 1972. It was designed to end conflict and confrontation between the two countries after the war which had led to the secession of Bangladesh from Pakistan. The agreement provided in particular for the withdrawal of armed forces to their side of the international border between the two countries, while in Jammu and Kashmir both sides would respect the line of control which had resulted from a cease-fire on Dec. 17, 1971—"without prejudice to the recognized position of either side" on the status of Jammu and Kashmir. [*25429A*]

Pakistan–Burma

1. A *treaty of "perpetual peace and friendship"* was signed on June 25, 1952. It provided for mutual co-operation in matters of common concern to both countries, and for periodical meetings of representatives of the two countries. [*12426B*]

2. An *agreement fixing the frontier between Burma and East Pakistan* in the area of the river Naaf was signed on May 9, 1966. [*21414B*]

Japan–Philippines

A treaty of friendship, commerce, and navigation was signed on Dec. 9, 1960. The treaty, valid initially for three years to be automatically extended unless either country gives six months' notice of termination, guarantees the rights of nationals of either country to reside and conduct business activities in the other. [*17934C*]

Japan–South Korea

A treaty on basic relations between Japan and South Korea was concluded on June 22, 1965. The treaty settled all issues between the two countries after a lapse of 55 years (South Korea was a Japanese colony from 1910 until the end of World War II). The treaty, *inter alia,* provided for the establishment of diplomatic relations; confirmed that "all treaties or agreements concluded between the Empire of Japan and the Empire of Korea on or before Aug. 22, 1910, are null and void"; and confirmed that "the Government of the Republic of Korea is the only lawful Government of Korea." [*20972A*]

Malaysia–Thailand

An agreement on armed forces' co-operation against Communist guerrillas in the Thai-Malaysian border region was signed in Bangkok on March 7, 1970. [*23900A*]

Indonesia–Malaysia

A treaty of friendship between Indonesia and Malaysia and another treaty establishing a boundary through the Straits of Malacca (between Sumatra and the Malay Peninsula) were signed in Kuala Lumpur on March 17, 1970. The treaty of friendship replaced an earlier treaty of April 17, 1959, and formally ended a period of "confrontation" between the two countries.

On Nov. 16, 1971, both Governments issued a declaration claiming sovereignty of the Straits, which they no longer considered to be an international waterway. [*16838B; 23962A; 25260A*]

ASIAN DEVELOPMENT BANK

On Dec. 4, 1965, 21 countries signed the Charter of the Asian Development Bank, a financial institution set up under the auspices of the United Nations Economic Commission for Asia and the Far East (ECAFE). The agreement came into force on Aug. 22, 1966.

Members: To date 37 countries have joined the Bank, of which 23 are regional and 14 non-regional countries.
Regional members: Afghanistan, Australia, Cambodia, Ceylon, Fiji, Hong Kong, India, Indonesia, Japan, South Korea, Laos, Malaysia, Nepal, New Zealand, Pakistan, Papua New Guinea, Philippines, Singapore,

Taiwan, Thailand, Tonga South Vietnam, Western Samoa

Non-regional members: Austria, Belgium, Britain, Canada, Denmark, Finland, France, German Federal Republic, Italy, Netherlands, Norway, Sweden, Switzerland, U.S.A.

Functions and Organization

The charter laid down that membership of the Asian Development Bank would be open to members and associate members of ECAFE as well as to other regional countries and non-regional developed countries which were members of the U.N. or any of its specialized agencies. (Communist China, North Korea, and North Vietnam were therefore not eligible for membership.)

The Bank would have 10 directors, of whom 7 would represent Asian or Australasian countries. The Bank's functions would be to further investment in development projects within the ECAFE region, to contribute to the harmonious economic growth of the whole area, to assist Asian member-countries in preparing and co-ordinating their development plans, and to provide technical aid for the preparation, financing, and execution of individual development projects.

It was laid down that 90 percent of the Bank's capital could be used for "hard" loans (at 5.5 percent interest for 25–30 years) and 10 percent for "soft" loans (low-interest and long-term). Member-countries such as Australia, Japan, and New Zealand, which, though members of ECAFE, were not underdeveloped countries, would not be entitled to draw any loans. A provision in the Charter authorized the Bank to administer trust funds for use as "soft" loan money. *[21186A]*

The decision-making organ of the Bank is the Board of Governors, on which each member-country is represented. The executive organ is the 10-man Board of Directors.

The Bank was inaugurated on Nov. 24, 1966, and began operations on Dec. 19, 1966. Its authorized capital was increased in November 1966 from $1,000,000,000 to $1,100,000,000. *[21766A]*

ASIAN AND PACIFIC COUNCIL (ASPAC)

Members: Australia, Japan, South Korea, Malaysia, New Zealand, Philippines, Taiwan, Thailand, South Vietnam
Observer: Laos

The Asian and Pacific Council (ASPAC) an organization of 9 non-Communist Asian and Pacific countries, came into being at a conference of the 9 countries in question, held June 14–16, 1966, in Seoul. Its main aim is to foster "greater co-operation and solidarity among the free Asian and Pacific countries."

At the Seoul conference it was agreed that annual meetings of the Council should be held at ministerial level in the capital city of each member-country in turn. The permanent organization of ASPAC has not yet been established, but the day-to-day administration of the Council is, in the interim, in the hands of a Secretariat, provided by the Thai Government, and a Standing Committee, consisting of the Ambassadors in Bangkok of the participant countries, under the chairmanship of the Thai Foreign Minister. A Sub-Committee assists the Standing Committee. *[21470A]*

At the second ministerial meeting of ASPAC member-countries, held on July 5–7, 1967, in Bangkok, it was decided to set up a social-cultural center in Seoul and a pool of technicians in Canberra. It was also agreed that steps should be taken by ASPAC countries towards the liberalization of trade, the co-ordination of economic plans, and the strengthening of the economic infrastructure.

From 1969 onwards ASPAC avoided any policy of confrontation with the Communist Governments in Asia.

The Thai Foreign Minister emphasized in June 1970 that ASPAC was "not a military organization, and not likely to become one." The Australian Foreign Minister, at a ministerial meeting in Manila in July 1971, advocated the opening of a dialogue with the People's Republic of China, and at the following meeting in Seoul President Park Chung Hee of South Korea declared on June 13, 1972, that ASPAC should "open its doors" to all countries in the Region, and that "confrontation" with the Communist countries should be replaced by "harmonious co-ordination." *[25465B]*

ASSOCIATIONS OF SOUTHEAST ASIAN COUNTRIES

There have, to date, been three attempts on the part of Southeast Asian countries to form themselves into regional associations.

Association of Southeast Asia (ASA)

Members: Malaysia, Philippines, Thailand

The Association of Southeast Asia (ASA) was established on July 31, 1961, at the end of a 2-day meeting between the Prime Minister of Malaya and the Foreign Ministers of Thailand and the Philippines.

The objectives of ASA were to promote economic, social, cultural, and administrative collaboration between the Southeast Asian nations, to which end various projects in the economic and social fields, including the establishment of an Organization for Asian Economic Co-operation, were initiated. A 3-year break in relations between Malaysia and the Philippines (September 1963–May 1966), however, prevented the proper functioning of the organization during this period. Eventually, on Aug. 29, 1967, the 3 ASA member-nations agreed to its dissolution. [18269B; 19715A]

"Maphilindo"

An agreement on the formation of a confederation of Malaya, the Philippines, and Indonesia, to be known as "Maphilindo," was made at a conference of the three Heads of State at Manila, July 31–Aug. 5, 1963. The "Manila Declaration," expressing the "common objectives and the decision of the Heads of Government to establish Maphilindo on the basis of regular and frequent consultations," was approved at this conference. [19715A]

With the worsening of relations between Malaysia and Indonesia after the formation of the Federation of Malaysia in September 1963, and the cessation of diplomatic relations between Malaysia and the Philippines, discussions on the projected confederation lapsed. It was not until June 1966, with the ending of the Malaysian-Indonesian "confrontation," that plans for an organization of regional collaboration were revived. [21493A]

Association of Southeast Asian Nations

Members: Indonesia, Malaysia, Philippines, Singapore, Thailand

The Foreign Ministers of Indonesia, Malaysia, the Philippines, Singapore, and Thailand signed on Aug. 8, 1967, in Bangkok, a declaration on the establishment of an Association of Southeast Asian Nations (ASEAN).

In the preamble to the Declaration, stress is laid on the importance of increased regional co-operation and of raising the standard of living in the contracting States. The Declaration itself emphasizes that all military bases of foreign Powers exist only on a temporary basis and with the express consent of the countries concerned, and may in no way be used for direct or indirect interference with the national independence and freedom of the region's States, or with their normal development. (This has been interpreted as a concession by the other four parties to Indonesia—which does not allow foreign bases.)

The Permanent Committee of the Association,

which will have its seat in Djakarta, was instructed to examine and decide how the member-States' agricultural and industrial potential could best be exploited and their trade expanded. The main fields of co-operation would be tourism, fisheries, and shipping. Membership was to be open to other countries in Southeast Asia.

The Association of Southeast Asian Nations is now responsible for joint development and trade projects initiated by the Association of Southeast Asia (see above).

South Pacific Forum

The South Pacific Forum held its first meeting in Wellington, New Zealand, Aug. 5–7, 1971, with Fiji, Tonga, and Western Samoa being represented by their Prime Ministers; Nauru by its Head of State; and the Cook Islands by their Premier. Also present were the Prime Minister of New Zealand and the Australian Minister of External Territories.

At a second meeting, held in Canberra on Feb. 23–25, 1972, it was decided to establish a South Pacific Bureau for Economic Co-operation at Suva, Fiji. [25011A; 25364B]

MEKONG RIVER DEVELOPMENT

An agreement on contributions totaling $22,815,000 for a hydroelectric development project at Nam Ngum (Laos) in the Mekong River area was signed in Washington on May 4, 1966, by Australia, Canada, Denmark, Japan, the Netherlands, New Zealand, and the United States.

A further agreement between Thailand and Laos, signed on the same day, provided for cement and power supplies by the former country during construction, and for the repayment by the latter on completion of the dam of funds invested and power consumed. [21390B]

An agreement providing for the implementation of the Prek Thnot power and irrigation development project on the Lower Mekong River, Cambodia's first multipurpose river scheme, was signed at the U.N. Headquarters in New York on Nov. 13, 1968, by the 10 co-operating Governments—Australia, Britain, Canada, Western Germany, India, Italy, Japan, Netherlands, Pakistan, and the Philippines—and by the Cambodian Government. The 10 Governments and the U.N. Development Program agreed to contribute $17,745,000 toward the $27,000,000 cost. [23043B]

DEPENDENT TERRITORIES IN THE PACIFIC AREA AND SOUTHEAST ASIA

AUSTRALIA

(1) *External Territories:*

Papua (southeast New Guinea), governed in an Administrative Union with New Guinea (see below).

Christmas Island (in the Indian Ocean), administered by an Official Representative of the Minister for Territories in Canberra.

Cocos (Keeling) Islands (in the Indian Ocean), administered as above.

Norfolk Island.

(2) *United Nations Trust Territory under Australian administration* (see pages 23–4):

New Guinea (including northeastern New Guinea; the Bismarck Archipelago; the Admiralty Islands; and the two northernmost Solomon Islands). New Guinea forms an Administrative Union with Papua (see above).

BRITAIN

(1) *Colonies:*

Gilbert and Ellice Islands, under the administration of the Western Pacific High Commission.

Pitcairn Islands Group, administered by the Governor of Fiji.

Hong Kong (consisting of the island of Hong Kong, Stonecutters Island, the Kowloon Peninsula, and the New Territories leased by China to Britain in 1898).

(2) *Protectorate:*

British Solomon Islands, under the administration of the Western Pacific High Commission.

(3) *Anglo-French Condominium:*

New Hebrides, jointly governed by British and French High Commissioners acting through Resident Commissioners.

FRANCE

Overseas Territories:

New Caledonia
French Polynesia (which includes Tahiti)
Wallis and Futuna Islands

NEW ZEALAND

Overseas Territories:

Cook Islands, an autonomous State in free association with New Zealand since 1965.

Niue, one of the Cook Islands under separate administration.

Tokelau Islands.

PORTUGAL

Overseas Provinces:

Macao (consisting of the Macao peninsula and the two adjacent islands of Taipa and Coloane).

Portuguese Timor (including the eastern portion of the island of Timor in the Malay Archipelago; and a number of adjacent territories).

UNITED STATES OF AMERICA

(1) *External Territories:*

American Samoa, administered by the U.S. Department of the Interior.

Guam, the largest island of the Marianas group (see below). The island has statutory powers of self-government, and its inhabitants have U.S. citizenship.

(2) *Trust Territory of the Pacific Islands,* administered by the United States under the U.N. trusteeship system (see pages 23–4):

Mariana Islands (except Guam, see above),
Caroline Islands,
Marshall Islands.

16

The "Third World": Attempts at Achieving a Union

Since the mid-1950s, delegations from countries of Asia, Africa, and, more recently, Latin America, have met in conference, from time to time, to define their common attitude with relation to international affairs, and to try to bring about closer solidarity in economic, cultural, and political fields. These countries, which represent the less privileged parts of the world, are sometimes referred to as the "Third World" or, since most of them form part of neither the Western (Capitalist) bloc nor the Eastern (Communist) bloc, as the "nonaligned" or "uncommitted" nations.

The Bandung Conference

A conference held at Bandung (Indonesia), April 18–23, 1955, was, as President Sukarno of Indonesia stated in the opening speech, "the first inter-continental conference of the so-called colored peoples in the history of mankind." It was attended by delegates of the Governments of Afghanistan, Burma, Cambodia, Ceylon, People's Republic of China, Egypt, Ethiopia, Gold Coast (now Ghana), India, Indonesia, Iran, Iraq, Japan, Jordan, Laos, Lebanon, Liberia, Libya, Nepal, Pakistan, the Philippines, Saudi Arabia, Sudan, Syria, Thailand, Turkey, North Vietnam, South Vietnam, and Yemen —as well as many unofficial observers from other countries. [14181A]

The decision to hold the conference had been made at a conference of the Prime Ministers of Burma, Ceylon, India, Indonesia, and Pakistan, held at Bogor (Indonesia), Dec. 28–29, 1954. The Prime Ministers agreed that an Afro-Asian conference should be held under their sponsorship, and that its basic purpose would be to make the countries concerned better acquainted with one another's point of view. [13977A]

Resolutions

The communiqué issued at the end of the Bandung Conference contained resolutions on economic and cultural co-operation; on human rights and self-determination; on problems of dependent peoples; and on world peace and co-operation.

The conference recognized the urgency of promoting economic development in the Asian-African region, and also the desirability of co-operation with countries outside the region. Recommendations were made for, *inter alia,* the early establishment of a special U.N. fund for economic development, and the allocation, by the International Bank (see page 27), of a greater part of its resources to Asian-African countries.

In the cultural field the conference condemned the alleged practice, on the part of colonial powers, of suppressing the national cultures of the peoples of Africa and Asia. This was described as a fundamental denial of the rights of man.

After declaring its full support of the fundamental principles of human rights and of the principle of self-determination of peoples and nations, as set forth in the U.N. Charter, the conference condemned the policies and practices of racial segregation and discrimination. In a Declaration on Problems of Dependent Peoples it was stated that colonialism, in all its manifestations, was an evil which should speedily be brought to an end.

The conference also adopted a Declaration on World Peace and Co-operation, in which it agreed that nations should live together in peace with one another as good neighbors, and develop friendly co-operation on the basis of the following principles:

(1) Respect for the fundamental human rights and for the purposes and principles of the U.N. Charter.
(2) Respect for the sovereignty and territorial integrity of all nations.
(3) Recognition of the equality of all races and nations, large and small.
(4) Abstention from intervention or interference in the internal affairs of other countries.
(5) Respect for the right of each nation to defend itself singly or collectively in conformity with the U.N. Charter.

(6) Abstention from the use of arrangements of collective defense to serve the particular interests of any of the big Powers; and abstention by any country from exerting pressure on other countries.

(7) Refraining from acts or threats of aggression or the use of force against the territorial integrity or political independence of any country.

(8) Settlement of all international disputes by peaceful means such as negotiation, conciliation, arbitration, or judicial settlement, as well as other peaceful means of the parties' own choice in conformity with the U.N. Charter.

(9) Promotion of mutual interest and co-operation.

(10) Respect for justice and international obligations.

The Five Principles

The principles listed above are an extension of the "Five Principles" of peaceful coexistence, or Panch Sila (from the Pali, in which it expresses a Buddhist concept). These principles were first enumerated in an agreement over Tibet—now superseded by China's action in that country—concluded between India and the People's Republic of China in April 1954, where they were given as follows:

(1) mutual respect for territorial integrity and sovereignty;

(2) mutual non-aggression;

(3) mutual non-interference in each other's internal affairs;

(4) equality and mutual benefit;

(5) peaceful coexistence. [13588A; 13611A]

Conferences of Non-Aligned Countries

1. The Belgrade Conference

An important international conference of 25 non-aligned countries took place in Belgrade, Sept. 1–6, 1961. Most of the countries were represented by Heads of State or Government although, in a few cases, only the Foreign Ministers attended.

The agenda for this conference had been fixed at a preparatory conference held in Cairo, June 5–13, 1961. Items considered included: a general exchange of views on the international situation; the rights of peoples to self-determination; non-interference in the internal affairs of States; the struggle against racial discrimination; general and complete disarmament; peaceful coexistence; and problems of economic development and co-operation.

The Belgrade Conference was attended by delegations from Afghanistan, Algeria, Burma, Cambodia, Ceylon, Congo (ex-Belgian), Cuba, Cyprus, Ethiopia, Ghana, Guinea, India, Indonesia, Iraq, Lebanon, Mali, Morocco, Nepal, Saudi Arabia, Somalia, Sudan, Tunisia, U.A.R., Yemen, and Yugoslavia.

At the end of the conference the delegates unanimously adopted a 27-point declaration containing their common views on international problems, and

an "Appeal for Peace," addressed particularly to the U.S.A. and the U.S.S.R.

The declaration included a demand for all dependent peoples to exercise their right to complete independence, and called for the ending of all armed action and repressive measures against them on the part of colonial powers. It condemned the maintenance of foreign bases in the territories of other countries, and stated that general, complete and internationally-controlled disarmament was "the most urgent task of mankind." It also stated that efforts should be made "to close, through accelerated economic, industrial and agricultural development, the ever widening gap in the standards of living between the few economically advanced countries and the many economically less developed countries." [18601A]

2. The Cairo Conference

A second international conference of non-aligned countries took place in Cairo, Oct. 5–10, 1964. A total of 47 countries attended as full participants; in addition to the 25 which attended the Belgrade Conference, delegations were sent by Angola (Government-in-exile), Burundi, Cameroon, Chad, Congo (Brazzaville), Dahomey, Jordan, Kenya, Kuwait, Laos, Liberia, Libya, Malawi, Mauritania, Nigeria, Northern Rhodesia (now Zambia), Senegal, Sierra Leone, Syria, Togo, Uganda, and the United Republic of Tanganyika and Zanzibar (now Tanzania). Observers were sent by Argentina, Bolivia, Brazil, Chile, Finland, Jamaica, Mexico, Trinidad and Tobago, Uruguay, and Venezuela.

The final communiqué of the conference was entitled "Program for Peace and International Co-operation." It included statements on the right to self-determination and independence, on peaceful coexistence and on denuclearization. Neo-colonialism and imperialism, in all forms, were condemned, particularly in South Africa. [20431A]

3. The Lusaka Conference

A third conference of non-aligned countries was held in Lusaka (Zambia) on Sept. 8–10, 1970, and was attended by representatives of 54 countries, i.e. those represented at the Cairo conference (except Angola's Government-in-exile, Burma, Cambodia, Dahomey, Malawi, and Saudi Arabia) and also Botswana, the Central African Republic, Equatorial Guinea, Gabon, Guyana, Jamaica, Lesotho, Malaysia, Rwanda, Singapore, South Yemen, Swaziland, and Trinidad and Tobago.

The conference had been preceded by two preparatory meetings in Belgrade (July 8–11, 1969) and Dar-es-Salaam (April 13–17, 1970), and had been further prepared by visits to African States during February 1970 by President Tito of Yugoslavia, who had proposed a "program of concrete actions to solve the problems which concern the international community as a whole and world peace, such as the liquidation of the vestiges of colonialism, establishment of democratic relations and co-operation on terms of equality, codification of the principles of coexistence, acceleration of the development of the developing countries, disarmament, strengthening of the United Nations and attainment of its universality."

Documents approved by the conference included the "Lusaka Declaration on Peace, Independence, Co-operation and the Democratization of International Relations," designed to constitute the "Charter of Non-Alignment."

This declaration no longer defined non-alignment as "an irreplaceable instrument for the solution of the dangerous contradictions of the contemporary world and the establishment of international relations based upon the principle of active and peaceful coexistence" but rather as "an integral part of the changes in the present structure of the international community in its entirety" and "the product of the anti-colonialist revolution." Instead of "rich" and "poor" countries, it distinguished between "oppressors" and "the oppressed," "aggressors" and "victims of aggression." It stated in particular that the immediate danger of a conflict between the super-Powers had diminished as the result of their tendency to negotiate, but that this did not contribute to the security of small, medium-sized, or developing nations, nor did it prevent the danger of local wars. At the same time the participants in the conference undertook "to continue their efforts to bring about the dissolution of the great military alliances." [24212A]

4. Foreign Ministers' Conference
At a conference of Foreign Ministers of non-aligned countries in Georgetown (Guyana) on Aug. 8–12, 1972, a "Declaration of Georgetown" was issued, calling for the extension of the process of *détente,* which had been successfully intensified in Europe, to all regions of the world, so that all military alliances would be dissolved, all foreign military bases evacuated and new areas of peace declared, especially in the Mediterranean and the Indian Ocean. The declaration also reaffirmed the non-aligned countries' support for African "liberation movements" and for nationalization policies in Latin American countries, and it called for an end to the war in Indo-China on the basis of peace proposals made by the Communist or pro-Communist forces in Vietnam, Laos, and Cambodia, and of the withdrawal of all foreign armed forces from these countries.

Afro-Asian Solidarity Council

The Cairo Conference
The decision to set up the Afro-Asian People's Solidarity Council, a permanent organization to promote and strengthen Afro-Asian solidarity, was taken at an Afro-Asian "solidarity conference" held at non-governmental level in Cairo from Dec. 26, 1957 to Jan. 1, 1958. All those nations which had taken part in the

Bandung Conference of 1955 were invited, and invitations also went to Morocco, Nigeria, Somaliland, and Uganda. A number of invitations were, however, refused on account of the pro-Communist character of the conference, which was organized by the Communist-front body known as the Asian Solidarity Committee.

The conference agreed that the Afro-Asian People's Solidarity Council should have its headquarters in Cairo, and meet at least once a year. All Afro-Asian peoples would be represented on the Council. [16000A]

The Conakry Conference
The second conference of the Afro-Asian Solidarity Council was held April 11–15, 1960, at Conakry in Guinea. It was attended by delegates from 50 countries, both Communist and pro-Western as well as neutral. In addition to passing a number of resolutions on various current situations, the conference recommended that an Afro-Asian governmental conference similar to the Bandung conference should be convened in the near future. It was also decided to enlarge the steering committee of the conference to 27, and to strengthen African representation on the permanent secretariat. [17554A]

The Moshi Conference
The third conference of the Council took place in Moshi (Tanganyika) Feb. 7–11, 1963. In the opening speech, President Nyerere of Tanganyika gave a warning against the "new colonialism" of the Communist States, whom he accused of using their economic strength to obtain political power in countries of Africa and Asia.

Among the resolutions adopted by the conference were a condemnation of British and French arms supplies to South Africa, and a demand for the release of political prisoners held there. The conference appointed a committee to prepare a conference of representatives from three continents to be held in Havana at the invitation of Dr. Fidel Castro, Prime Minister of Cuba. [20983A]

The Winneba Conference
The fourth conference of the Afro-Asian Solidarity Council, held at Winneba (Ghana), May 10–16, 1965, was the first to be attended by delegates from Latin America. In a general political resolution the conference accused the United Nations of deviating from the principles of its Charter and of reflecting the will of the imperialists instead of that of the people. A general declaration called for the immediate destruction of all nuclear weapons and the means of their production.

The conference decided to expand into a new organization which would embrace Latin America and hold its first conference in Havana in January 1966. It was, however, decided at the Havana Conference (see below), that the existing Afro-Asian Solidarity Organization should not be dissolved, but should continue to be maintained with its headquarters in Cairo. [20983A]

Second Afro-Asian Conference (postponed indefinitely)

At a conference of Asian and African countries held in Djakarta on April 10–16, 1964, it was decided that a second Afro-Asian conference, modeled on the Bandung Conference (see page 208), should be held, opening on March 10, 1965. It was eventually decided that the conference should take place in Algiers, and a standing committee was set up to make preparations. Because of delays in the preparations and internal political difficulties in Algeria at that time, the opening of the conference was repeatedly postponed, the last time until Nov. 5, 1965. It was finally indefinitely postponed after the People's Republic of China had announced her intention not to attend since, as she claimed, the new conflicts and tensions which had recently arisen among Asian and African nations would preclude the success of the conference and so impair rather than strengthen Afro-Asian solidarity. The postponement of the conference, *sine die*, was officially announced on Nov. 2, 1965. [20984A; 21115A]

Afro-Asian Organization for Economic Co-operation (AFRASEC)

The decision to establish a permanent Afro-Asian Organization for Economic Co-operation was made at the first economic conference of chambers of commerce in African and Asian countries, held in Cairo, Dec. 8–11, 1958. The objectives of the organization were stated to be (1) to supply information on the economic situation in Afro-Asian countries; (2) to eliminate customs and other trade barriers; (3) to lay down principles for sound commercial competition; (4) to promote contact and good understanding between Afro-Asian businessmen.

Among the Organs created were a Council, meeting every two or three years with a permanent Secretariat in Cairo, and a Consultative Committee (consisting of delegates from the Chinese People's Republic, Ethiopia, Ghana, India, Indonesia, Iraq, Japan, Libya, Pakistan, Sudan, and the U.A.R.), which was given the immediate task of drafting a charter for the organization.

The Consultative Committee decided that only those countries which participated in the Bandung Conference or had since acquired their independence,

could become members of the organization. At a conference held in Karachi, Dec. 5–9, 1963, decisions to admit seven more States to full membership of AFRASEC raised the total membership of the organization to 45. [16664B; 16842B; 19874B]

Three Continents Conference

The first "Solidarity Conference of the Peoples of Asia, Africa, and Latin America" took place in Havana between Jan. 3 and 15, 1966. The decision to hold such a conference had been taken at the Afro-Asian Solidarity Conference held at Moshi in February 1963 (see above). The declared main object of the "Three Continents Conference," as it is generally designated, was "to oppose the world-wide enterprises of imperialism with a global revolutionary strategy."

Over 500 delegates took part in the conference, which had a distinctly Communist character. Some represented the Governments of Communist countries (including both the Soviet Union and the People's Republic of China); others were representatives of national Communist parties and of other left-wing movements (many of the Latin American delegates belonged to this category); others represented "national liberation movements," such as the National Liberation Front of South Vietnam, the Pathet Lao of Laos, and the African National Congress of South Africa. Additional delegates represented the Governments of certain non-aligned African countries, including Algeria, Congo (Brazzaville), Guinea, and the U.A.R.

At its final plenary session, the conference adopted a general declaration; a general political resolution; and resolutions on the situation in various countries (Vietnam, Laos, the Dominican Republic, Angola, and the Congo-Kinshasa), on peaceful coexistence, and on the dismantling of military bases in foreign countries.

The general declaration stressed the need for social revolution to aid the "struggle" of the "national liberation movements." It also proclaimed the right of the peoples to have recourse to all forms of struggle to achieve complete political independence. In the general political resolution, "colonialism and neo-colonialism" were condemned, and the United Nations was accused of allowing itself to be the instrument of "U.S. imperialism."

Creation of New Organs

The conference approved the creation of a Three Continents Solidarity Organization, based in Havana and with a provisional executive secretariat headed by a Cuban. The executive secretariat was given the task of preparing the next "Solidarity Conference of the Peoples of Asia, Africa, and Latin America."

The conference also approved the formation of a committee to assist the "national liberation movements" in their struggle against "colonialism."

Latin American Solidarity Organization

On Jan. 18, 1966, delegates representing national revolutionary committees in 27 Latin American and Caribbean countries and territories announced the formation of a Latin American Solidarity Organization, with headquarters in Havana. The Organization, which would support revolutionary liberation movements in the Western hemisphere, would co-ordinate its work with that of the Three Continents Organization. A preparatory committee of representatives from Brazil, British Guiana (now Guyana), Colombia, Cuba, Guatemala, Mexico, Peru, Uruguay, and Venezuela was given the task of preparing a first "Solidarity Conference of Latin American Peoples," to be held in 1967. [*21219A*]

The policy of the Latin American Solidarity Organization was revealed at its first conference, held in Havana from July 31 to Aug. 10, 1967, as one of guerrilla warfare against all Latin American Governments other than that of Cuba, with the aim of seizing power, as Dr. Castro had done in Cuba in 1959, in order to establish Communism.

The conference, attended by delegates from 27 countries and by observers (including some from the Government of North Vietnam and from the National Liberation Front of South Vietnam), endorsed resolutions calling for guerrilla warfare, opposition to "servile Pan-Americanism" and the Organization of American States, and support for the Viet Cong and for the Black Power movement among U.S. Negroes. A resolution condemning "certain Socialist countries" which gave "credits and technical aid to dictatorships and oligarchies" was adopted in committee—against the wishes of representatives of various South American Communist parties—by 15 votes to 3 with 9 abstentions. The conference thus gave expression to the quarrel, as President Castro defined it, "between those who want to make revolution and those who in reality only wish to brake it" (i.e., the official Communist Parties advocating the use of means other than violence and guerrilla warfare).

SUPPLEMENT

This Supplement covers new treaties and agreements concluded, as well as changes in the membership of international groupings, during the period January to September 1973, and also a few earlier agreements not previously mentioned in this book. The index to this Supplement appears at the end of the regular index.

1. EARLY INTERNATIONAL AGREEMENTS AND THEIR LATER EXPANSION

Copyright Conventions (p. 3)
The Soviet Union acceded to the Universal Copyright Convention on May 27, 1973. [*26025A*]

2. WORLD WAR II

War Damages
An agreement between the U.S.A. and Hungary on the settlement of claims for war-damaged and nationalized American property in Hungary was signed on March 6, 1973. [*25827A*]

3. UNITED NATIONS

Membership (pp. 34–6)
Following the unanimous approval by the U.N. Security Council of the membership of the Federal Republic of Germany and the German Democratic Republic on June 22, 1973, and that of the Bahamas on July 18, the three countries were admitted to the United Nations at the opening of the twenty-eighth session on Sept. 18, 1973.

The German Democratic Republic had been given observer status at the United Nations in November 1972, as had the People's Democratic Republic of Korea in June 1973. [*25972C; 25751B*]

Membership of Specialized Agencies (pp. 34–6)
International Monetary Fund—Bahamas

World Bank—Bahamas
World Health Organization—People's Democratic Republic of Korea (North Korea)
Intergovernmental Maritime Consultative Organization—Thailand; German Democratic Republic
International Atomic Energy Agency—Mongolia; German Democratic Republic

The Economic and Social Council

Economic Commission for Western Asia
The U.N. Economic and Social Council on Aug. 9, 1973, adopted a resolution to establish an Economic Commission for Western Asia. Israel was not included in the membership of the new Commission, which, it was stated, was not an Arab body but would be open to other countries of the region.

Commodity Producers' Agreements (p. 24)

International Cocoa Agreement
After 16 years of negotiations, a three-year International Cocoa Agreement was adopted in Geneva on Oct. 21, 1972. The Agreement, the main features of which were an export quota system for producing countries, a fixed price range for cocoa and a buffer stock to support the agreed prices, also provided for the establishment of an International Cocoa Council to supervise its implementation. (In the course of 1973, however, the price of cocoa on the world market rose to more than double the maximum envisaged in the Geneva Agreement, a situation which, for the time being at least, rendered its main provisions inoperative.)

On the strength of signatures by countries representing some 70 per cent of consumption, the Agreement came into provisional effect on June 30 as a prelude to its formal implementation on Oct. 1, 1973. The inaugural meeting of the International Cocoa

Council was held in Geneva in July–August 1973. [26123A]

Organization of Arab Petroleum Exporting Countries (OAPEC)
The countries belonging to OAPEC now include Egypt, Syria and Iraq, bringing the membership up to 10.

Bilateral Agreements for the Prevention of Hijacking (pp. 29–30)

U.S.A.-Cuba
A five-year agreement between the U.S.A. and Cuba on the prevention of aerial and maritime hijacking was signed on Feb. 15, 1973, and entered into force immediately. Its provisions included the following:

(1) Any person who hereafter seizes, removes, appropriates or diverts from its normal route or activities an aircraft or vessel registered under the laws of one of the parties and brings it to the territory of the other party shall be considered to have committed an offence and therefore shall either be returned to the party of registry of the aircraft or vessel, to be tried by the courts of that party in conformity with its laws, or be brought before the courts of the party whose territory he reached for trial in conformity with its laws for the offence punishable by the most severe penalty according to the circumstances and seriousness of the acts to which this article refers.

(2) Each party shall try with a view to severe punishment in accordance with its laws any person who, within its territory, hereafter conspires to promote, or promotes, or prepares, or directs, or forms part of an expedition which from its territory or any other place carries out acts of violence or depredation against aircraft or vessels of any kind or registration coming or going to the territory of the other party or who, within its territory, hereafter conspires to promote, or promotes, or prepares, or directs, or forms part of an expedition which from its territory or any other place carries out such acts or other similar unlawful acts in the territory of the other party. [25827B]

Canada-Cuba
A similar agreement between Canada and Cuba was signed simultaneously with the U.S.-Cuban agreement. This contained undertakings by both Governments to prosecute hijackers or to return them to the countries in which the hijackings had been committed. [26033C]

Cuba-Mexico
An agreement on the prevention of aerial and maritime hijacking was signed by Cuba and Mexico on June 7, 1973. Under its terms the two parties undertook to try or to extradite hijackers other than those acting for political motives. [26068B]

Cuba-Venezuela
An agreement on the prevention of aerial hijacking was signed by Cuba and Venezuela on July 6, 1973. [26068B]

Atlantic Charter (p. 10)
In a speech on April 23, 1973, Dr. Henry Kissinger (then President Nixon's adviser on foreign affairs) put forward a proposal by the President for the formulation of a new Atlantic Charter. Such a Charter would link the countries of Western Europe with the United States and Canada and ultimately Japan, and would seek to bring about unity in economic and diplomatic fields as well as in defence. Dr. Kissinger said that it was hoped that toward the end of 1973 "we will have worked out a new Atlantic Charter setting the goals for the future." [25933A]

4. TREATIES AND AGREEMENTS ON NUCLEAR WEAPONS AND CO-OPERATION

Treaty of Tlatelolco (p. 38)
Protocol II of the Treaty for the Prohibition of Nuclear Weapons in Latin America (the Treaty of Tlatelolco) was signed by France (July 18, 1973) and China (Aug. 21, 1973). [26048]

5. EUROPE—STEPS TOWARD INTEGRATION AMONG NON-COMMUNIST STATES

European Economic Community

Trade Agreements with Non-Members (pp. 71–2)
The following further agreements were signed in April and June 1973.

A three-year non-preferential trade agreement with Uruguay was signed in Luxemburg on April 25, 1973. It provided for an effective increase of Uruguayan beef and veal imports by up to 30 per cent and a suspension, as far as possible, of import levies on Uruguayan refrigerated beef products. [26016C]

The agreement with Yugoslavia of March 19, 1970, was replaced by a new agreement for five years, signed in Brussels on June 26, to come into effect on Oct. 1, 1973; it provided *inter alia* for the maintenance of most-favoured-nation status for the two sides, and for free trade in industrial goods except cotton textiles from Yugoslavia, for which a limit was imposed. [26027A]

Adoption of Common Agricultural Policy by Acceding Members
The common agricultural policy [see pages 62–5] was officially adopted by Britain, Ireland and Denmark on Feb. 1, 1973.

[214

The adoption followed a compromise agreement reached a few days earlier on prices for cereals, pigmeat, poultry and eggs, and sugar. In this context Britain agreed, in view of the *de facto* devaluation of sterling against the Community's unit of account, to a new (reduced) reference rate for the purposes of the agricultural policy (involving a devaluation of sterling by 9.2 per cent since June 1972, when sterling had been allowed to float). [*25985A*]

European Free Trade Association (EFTA)

Special Relations Agreements (p. 77)
The Special Relations Agreement with the EEC negotiated by Norway during 1972 was signed in Brussels on May 14 and ratified by the Norwegian Parliament on May 25, 1973. Its main provision was the abolition, in five stages, of tariffs on industrial goods. [*25978A*]

European Space Agency
Final agreement was reached in Brussels on Aug. 1 on the establishment of a European Space Agency (ESA), to supersede the European Launcher Development Organization (ELDO) [see pages 81–2] and the European Space Research Organization (ESRO) [see pages 82–3]. Under the terms of the agreement, to which 11 countries were party (Belgium, Denmark, France, Western Germany, Italy, the Netherlands, Norway, Spain, Sweden, Switzerland and the United Kingdom), the new Agency was to come into being on April 1, 1974.

Under the main provisions of the agreement, it was intended that any new ventures envisaged by member-countries should be considered initially within its framework, although existing international or defence projects—such as the *Intelsat* [see page 39]—were to remain outside the context of the new Agency.

An agreement signed between ESRO and the American National Aeronautics and Space Administration (NASA) on Sept. 24, 1973, provided for a *Spacelab* (constructed under the auspices of the Space Agency at a total estimated cost of £130,000,000) to be launched into near-earth orbit at the end of 1979 or the beginning of 1980 by the American Space Shuttle—the reusable space transport system comprising recoverable booster and orbiter currently being developed—and used for manned or unmanned experiments. [*26104A; 26121B*]

European Science Foundation
Agreement was reached on Sept. 25, 1973, on the creation of a European Science Foundation to link the national research programmes of 16 countries. The new Foundation was expected to start functioning in 1975. [*26122B*]

Declarations and Conventions on Environment Problems (pp. 83–4)

Baltic Fishing Convention
A convention on fishing and the preservation of living resources in the Baltic Sea and the Danish Straits was signed at Gdansk (Poland) on Sept. 13, 1973, by the seven countries bordering the Baltic—Denmark, Sweden, Finland, the Soviet Union, Poland, the German Democratic Republic and the Federal Republic of Germany. The signatories agreed to set up an international commission for fishing in the Baltic, with its headquarters at Warsaw, which would co-operate with other international organizations having similar objectives. [*26121D*]

6. ORGANIZATION FOR ECONOMIC CO-OPERATION AND DEVELOPMENT (OECD)

Membership (p. 85)
New Zealand became a full member of the OECD on May 29, 1973. [*25962B*]

Agreement to Control Toxic Chemicals
Under the terms of an agreement announced on Feb. 14, 1973, the member-countries of the OECD undertook to control the use of polychlorinated biphenyls (PCBs), a group of toxic chemicals widely used in industrial processes and products. [*25770B*]

7. NORTH ATLANTIC TREATY ORGANIZATION (NATO)

Further Developments
At a meeting of the North Atlantic Council on Dec. 7–8, 1972, the Defence Planning Committee noted with concern the growing military capability of the Soviet Union and her allies, which it described as "greatly in excess of that required for purely defensive purposes," and endorsed the principle that "the overall military capability of NATO should not be reduced except as part of a pattern of mutual force reductions, balanced in scope and timing." The Committee adopted a five-year NATO Force Plan for 1973–77 in the light of each nation's force commitment for 1973.

The Eurogroup Ministers (i.e. the Defense Ministers of all the European members of NATO except France, Iceland and Portugal) met on Dec. 5, 1972. They reviewed the European Defence Improvement Programme [see page 105] and noted with satisfaction that its implementation was well under way.

The Committee on the Challenges of Modern Society [see page 105] met on Nov. 14–15, 1972. It endorsed a new project on urban transportation and sponsored the signing of a memorandum on the development of "clean" automobile engines by France, Western Germany, Italy, Britain and the U.S.A.

A ministerial meeting of the Defence Planning Committee was held at Brussels on June 7, 1973, during which the Committee reviewed the capabilities of NATO in the light of a further report on the Allied Defence Problems in the 1970s (*AD-70*). The report summarized progress in the preceding two years in improving NATO's effectiveness in each region, and also identified areas requiring further improvement. The Committee undertook to concentrate on these areas and to allocate more resources for the modernization and re-equipment of NATO forces. An increased need was recognized to improve co-operation in logistics and in the research, development and production of armaments. [*25697A; 25969A*]

Command Changes
A Standing Naval Force Channel (STANAVFOR-CHAN) was commissioned on May 11, 1973, to be under the operational command of the Commander-in-Chief, Channel Command. [*25970*]

8. THE COMMUNIST WORLD

Council for Mutual Economic Assistance (COMECON) (pp. 129–32)
An agreement between the COMECON and Finland —the first with a non-Socialist country—was signed on May 16, 1973. It provided for the establishment of a joint commission, with representatives from all the COMECON members and from Finland, to study the possibilities for the development of economic, scientific and technological co-operation. [*25993A*]

Bilateral Agreements (pp. 122ff)

Soviet Union-Cuba
A number of agreements for economic co-operation between the Soviet Union and Cuba were signed on Dec. 23, 1972. "Extraordinary assistance" provided by the Soviet Union for Cuba under these agreements included a deferment of payment of Cuba's accumulated debt; new credits for the years 1973–75; payment of special concessionary prices for Cuban sugar, nickel and cobalt; and aid for capital development. [*25663A*]

9. EAST-WEST TREATIES

Western Germany and Eastern Germany (p. 136)
The Treaty on the Basis of Relations between the Federal Republic of Germany and the German Democratic Republic was ratified by the German Federal Parliament on May 25 and by the East German *Volkskammer* on June 13, and came into force at midnight on June 20, 1973. [*25957A*]

Western Germany and Soviet Union
A 10-year "Agreement between the Government of the U.S.S.R. and Government of the Federal Republic of Germany on the Development of Economic, Industrial and Technical Co-operation" and a five-year agreement on cultural co-operation were signed on May 19, 1973. The first agreement included provisions for co-operation in the fields of industrial construction and manufacture and for the exchange of patents, licences and technical experts. Both agreements would apply to West Berlin in accordance with the 1971 four-Power agreement on Berlin [see page 134]. [*25975A*]

Western Germany and Czechoslovakia
A treaty normalizing relations between the Federal Republic of Germany and Czechoslovakia and declaring the Munich Agreement of 1938 to be null and void was initialled on June 20, 1973, by the Foreign Ministers of the two States. The text of the treaty is given below.

The Federal Republic of Germany and the Czechoslovak Socialist Republic;

In the historic recognition that the harmonious coexistence of the peoples of Europe constitutes a prerequisite for peace;

In the firm determination once and for all to put an end to the disastrous past in their relations, above all in connexion with the Second World War, which has inflicted immeasurable sufferings on the European peoples;

Recognizing that the Munich Agreement of Sept. 29, 1938, was imposed on the Czechoslovak Republic by the National Socialist regime under the threat of force;

In view of the fact that in both countries a new generation has grown up, which has a right to a secure [and] peaceful future;

With the intention of creating lasting foundations for the development of good-neighbourly relations;

Endeavouring to strengthen peace and security in Europe;

Convinced that peaceful co-operation on the basis of the aims and principles of the Charter of the United Nations is in accordance with the wishes of the peoples as well as the interest of peace in the world;

Have agreed as follows:

Art. 1. The Federal Republic of Germany and the Czechoslovak Socialist Republic consider the Munich Agreement of Sept. 29, 1938, as null and void under the terms of this treaty in regard to their mutual relations.

Art. 2. (1) This treaty does not affect the legal consequences arising with regard to private persons and legal entities from the laws applied in the period Sept. 30, 1938, to May 9, 1945. Excepted from this are the consequences of measures which both contracting parties consider as null and void by reason of their irreconcilability with the fundamental principles of justice.

(2) This treaty leaves unaffected the citizenship of persons

alive and dead resulting from the legal system of each of the two contracting parties.

(3) This treaty with its declarations on the Munich Agreement does not constitute a legal basis for material claims on the part of the Czechoslovak Socialist Republic and its natural and juristic persons.

Art. 3. (1) The Federal Republic of Germany and the Czechoslovak Socialist Republic are guided in their mutual relations, as well as in questions of guaranteeing security in Europe and in the world, by the aims and principles which are laid down in the Charter of the United Nations.

(2) Accordingly, in conformity with Articles 1 and 2 of the Charter of the United Nations, they will resolve all their differences by exclusively peaceful means, and in questions which concern European and international security, as well as in their mutual relations, will abstain from the threat of force or the use of force.

Art. 4. (1) In conformity with the foregoing aims and principles the Federal Republic of Germany and the Czechoslovak Socialist Republic reaffirm the inviolability of their common frontier at present and in the future, and reciprocally commit themselves to the unrestricted respect of their territorial integrity.

(2) They declare that they have no territorial claims of any kind against each other and likewise in the future will not raise any such claims.

Art. 5. (1) The Federal Republic of Germany and the Czechoslovak Socialist Republic will take further steps for the comprehensive development of their mutual relations.

(2) They are in agreement that an expansion of neighbourly co-operation in the fields of the economy, science, scientific and technological relations, culture, the protection of the environment, sport, traffic and their other relations is in their mutual interest.

Art. 6. This treaty requires ratification and enters into force on the day of the exchange of the ratification documents, which is to take place in Bonn. . . .

In an exchange of letters the two Ministers stated that Article 2 would be extended to cover West Berlin. However, owing to disagreement over the West German claim to represent West Berlin, the signature of the treaty was subsequently postponed. [25981A]

U.S.A. and Soviet Union

During a visit to the U.S.A. on June 17–25, 1973, by Mr. Leonid Brezhnev, General Secretary of the Central Committee of the Soviet Communist Party, a series of agreements between the U.S.A. and the Soviet Union was signed, the most important being an agreement on the Basic Principles of Negotiation on the Further Limitation of Strategic Offensive Arms, and an agreement on the Prevention of Nuclear War.

(a) The Agreement on the Basic Principles of Negotiation on the Further Limitation of Strategic Offensive Arms, signed on June 21, was worded as follows:

The President of the United States of America, Richard Nixon, and the General Secretary of the Central Committee of the CPSU, L. I. Brezhnev;

Having thoroughly considered the question of the further limitation of strategic arms, and the progress already achieved in the current negotiations;

Reaffirming their conviction that the earliest adoption of further limitation of strategic arms would be a major contribution in reducing the danger of an outbreak of nuclear war and in strengthening international peace and security;

Have agreed as follows:

(1) The two sides will continue active negotiations in order to work out a permanent agreement on more complete measures on the limitation of strategic offensive arms, as well as their subsequent reduction, proceeding from the Basic Principles of Relations between the U.S.A. and the U.S.S.R. signed in Moscow on May 29, 1972 [see page 138], and from the Interim Agreement between the U.S.A. and the U.S.S.R. of May 26, 1972, on Certain Measures with Respect to the Limitation of Strategic Offensive Arms [see page 138].

Over the course of the next year the two sides will make serious efforts to work out the provisions of the permanent agreement on more complete measures on the limitation of strategic offensive arms with the objective of signing it in 1974.

(2) New agreements on the limitation of strategic offensive armaments will be based on the principles of the American-Soviet documents adopted in Moscow in May 1972 and the agreements reached in Washington in June 1973; and in particular, both sides will be guided by the recognition of each other's equal security interests and by the recognition that efforts to obtain unilateral advantage, directly or indirectly, would be inconsistent with the strengthening of peaceful relations between the United States and the Union of Soviet Socialist Republics.

(3) The limitations placed on strategic offensive weapons can apply both to their quantitative aspects as well as to their qualitative improvement.

(4) Limitations on strategic offensive arms must be subject to adequate verification by national technical means.

(5) The modernization and replacement of strategic offensive arms would be permitted under conditions which will be formulated in the agreements to be concluded.

(6) Pending the completion of a permanent agreement on more complete measures of strategic offensive arms limitation, both sides are prepared to reach agreements on separate measures to supplement the existing interim agreement of May 26, 1972.

(7) Each side will continue to take necessary organizational and technical measures for preventing the accidental or unauthorized use of nuclear weapons under its control in accordance with the agreement of Sept. 30, 1971, between the United States and the Union of Soviet Socialist Republics.

(b) The text of the Agreement on the Prevention of Nuclear War, signed on June 22, was as follows:

The United States of America and the Union of Soviet Socialist Republics, hereinafter referred to as the parties;

Guided by the objectives of strengthening world peace and international security;

Conscious that nuclear war would have devastating consequences for mankind;

Proceeding from the desire to bring about conditions in which the danger of an outbreak of nuclear war anywhere in the world would be reduced and ultimately eliminated;

Proceeding from their obligations under the Charter of the United Nations regarding the maintenance of peace, refraining from the threat or use of force, and the avoidance of war, and in conformity with the agreements to which either party has subscribed;

Proceeding from the Basic Principles of Relations between the United States and the U.S.S.R. signed in Moscow on May 29, 1972;

Reaffirming that the development of relations between the U.S.A. and the U.S.S.R. is not directed against other countries and their interests;

Have agreed as follows:

Art. 1. The United States and the Soviet Union agree that an objective of their policies is to remove the danger of nuclear war and of the use of nuclear weapons.

Accordingly, the parties agree that they will act in such a manner as to prevent the development of situations capable of causing a dangerous exacerbation of their relations, as to avoid military confrontations, and as to exclude the outbreak of nuclear war between them and between either of the parties and other countries.

Art. 2. The parties agree, in accordance with Article 1 and to realize the objective stated in that Article, to proceed from the premise that each party will refrain from the threat or use of force against the other party, against the allies of the other party and against other countries, in circumstances which may endanger international peace and security. The parties agree that they will be guided by these considerations in the formulation of their foreign policies and in their actions in the field of international relations.

Art. 3. The parties undertake to develop their relations with each other and with other countries in a way consistent with the purposes of this agreement.

Art. 4. If at any time relations between the parties or between either party and other countries appear to involve the risk of a nuclear conflict, or if relations between countries not parties to this agreement appear to involve the risk of nuclear war between the U.S.A. and the U.S.S.R. or between either party and other countries, the United States and the Soviet Union, acting in accordance with the provisions of this agreement, shall immediately enter into urgent consultations with each other and make every effort to avert this risk.

Art. 5. Each party shall be free to inform the U.N. Security Council, the Secretary-General of the United Nations, and the Governments of allied or other countries of the progress and outcome of consultations initiated in accordance with Article 4 of this agreement.

Art. 6. Nothing in this agreement shall affect or impair:

(a) The inherent right of individual or collective self-defence as envisaged by Article 51 of the Charter of the United Nations;

(b) the provisions of the Charter of the United Nations, including those relating to the maintenance or restoration of international peace and security; and

(c) the obligations undertaken by either party towards its allies or other countries in treaties, agreements and other appropriate documents.

Art. 7. This agreement shall be of unlimited duration.

Art. 8. This agreement shall enter into force upon signature.

(c) A 10-year agreement on scientific and technical co-operation in the peaceful uses of atomic energy was signed on June 21.

This provided for co-operation to be concentrated in the spheres of controlled thermonuclear fission, fast breeder reactors, and research on the fundamental properties of matter. Under the terms of the agreement a U.S.-Soviet Joint Committee on Co-operation in the Peaceful Uses of Atomic Energy would be established.

Other agreements signed were:

(d) on June 19

an Agreement on Agricultural Co-operation;

an Agreement on Transportation;

an Agreement on Studies of the World Ocean;

a six-year Agreement on Cultural and Scientific Exchanges;

(e) on June 20

a Convention on Taxation (enabling nationals of either country to avoid paying double taxation in the other);

(f) on June 22

a protocol on the establishment of a Soviet trade mission in Washington and a U.S. commercial bureau in Moscow;

a protocol on the establishment of a U.S.-Soviet chamber of commerce;

(g) on June 23

a protocol on co-operation in air traffic.

The agreements on Agricultural Co-operation, Transportation and Studies of the World Ocean, all for five years, stated that co-operation would be "on the basis of mutual benefit, equality and reciprocity." Each provided for the setting up of a U.S.-Soviet joint committee for its implementation. [25997A]

Trade and Lend-Lease Agreements, 1972

At a session of the U.S.-Soviet Joint Commercial Commission [established under the Soviet-American co-operation agreements of May 1972—see page 138] held from Oct. 12–16, 1972, a series of agreements was reached covering trade and lend-lease obligations. The trade agreement provided *inter alia* for most-favoured-nation treatment between the two countries—this, however, being subject to congressional approval, without which the agreement would not enter into force. [25585A] Under a congressional move known as the Jackson Amendment, led by Senator Henry Jackson, the granting of most-favoured-nation status to the Soviet Union would be made conditional on the removal of restrictions on Jewish emigration from the Soviet Union. The U.S. Ways and Means Committee on Sept. 27, 1973, also voted to deny most-favoured-nation status until this condition was fulfilled.

[A "Jackson Amendment" was also adopted in regard to the ABM treaty [see page 137], in this case President Nixon being urged to seek a future treaty on the limitation of offensive nuclear weapons "which would not limit the United States to levels of intercontinental strategic forces inferior to the limits provided for the Soviet Union."] [25585A]

European Security Conference

A Conference on Security and Co-operation in Europe (CSCE) opened in Helsinki on July 3, 1973. The 35 participants were all the nations of Europe except Albania and Andorra, with the addition of the U.S.A. and Canada. Preparatory talks at ambassadorial level, held in Helsinki at intervals between Nov. 22, 1972, and June 7, 1973, ended with the adoption of an agenda for the CSCE. It was agreed that this should be grouped under four main heads: (1) Questions Relating to Security in Europe; (2) Cooperation in the Fields of Science and Technology, and of Environment; (3) Co-operation in Humanitarian and Other Fields; (4) Follow-up to the Conference. It was also decided that the CSCE should be held in three stages, the first at Foreign Ministerial level in July 1973 in Helsinki; the second, which would be carried out in specialized committees and subcommittees, in September 1973 in Geneva; and the third, the level of which would be decided during the second stage, in Helsinki in the spring or summer of 1974.

During the first stage of the CSCE, on July 3–7, 1973, the participating Foreign Ministers expressed their Governments' views on problems relating to security and co-operation in Europe, and put forward proposals on the questions on the agenda. A co-ordinating Committee was set up to prepare the organization of the second stage of the conference, which it was agreed would meet on Sept. 18, 1973. [25699A; 26013A]

10. THE COMMONWEALTH

At the Ottawa Conference of Commonwealth Heads of Government, held from Aug. 2 to 10, 1973, the Prime Minister of Canada, Mr. Pierre Trudeau, opened with the following speech on the nature of the Commonwealth:

Within the Commonwealth we have the opportunity and the means for both communication and understanding. In this forum of discussion each Commonwealth member is equal. None is senior; none is superior. None is distinguished by economic self-sufficiency; none is possessed of all political virtue. In our discussions during the next few days, I have no doubt that we will be able to demonstrate to one another and to the world the advantages of our dissimilarity, the richness of our diversity, the excitement of our variety. We will be able to do so because we are members of an association, not an institution. In this Commonwealth there is no structure to contain us, there are no fetters to chafe us. The Commonwealth is a reflection of its 32 members and of their desire to consult and co-operate with one another. There is no artificial adhesive. Nor is there any voting, any Constitution, any flag, any headquarters. This association is neither regional in nature, nor specialized in its interests. The Commonwealth is an organism and this fact guarantees both its vitality and its flexibility. . . .

None of us in the Commonwealth is so powerful or so self-sufficient that he is able to act independently of the opinion or the assistance of others. None of us disregards the value of consultation and co-operation. We are able in these gatherings of Heads of Government, and, by extension, in those other groupings to which we belong, to ensure that we understand one another's problems and one another's aspirations. That, to me, is the significance of our association. I am not, as this meeting, in search of a new role for the Commonwealth, or indeed any role. The Commonwealth is for many of us our window on the world. Over the years its importance will deepen largely because it has no specific role, but emphasizes instead the value of the human relations. . . . [26093A]

Membership (p. 141)

The Bahamas became an independent nation within the Commonwealth on July 9, 1973. [25994A]

Singapore Declaration of Commonwealth Principles

At the Commonwealth Conference held in January 1971 in Singapore, a Declaration of Commonwealth Principles was unanimously agreed on by the 31 delegations on Jan. 22. The Declaration stated *inter alia:*

. . . We believe in the liberty of the individual, in equal rights for all citizens regardless of race, colour, creed or political belief, and in their inalienable right to participate by means of free and democratic political processes in framing the society in which they live. We therefore strive to promote in each of our countries those representative institutions and guarantees for personal freedom under the law that are our common heritage.

We recognize racial prejudice as a dangerous sickness threatening the healthy development of the human race and racial discrimination as an unmitigated evil of society. Each of us will vigorously combat this evil within our own nation.

No country will afford to regimes which practise racial discrimination assistance which in its own judgment directly contributes to the pursuit or consolidation of this evil policy. We oppose all forms of colonial domination and racial oppression and are committed to the principles of human dignity and equality.

We will therefore use all our efforts to foster human equality and dignity everywhere, and to further the principles of self-determination and non-racialism. . . . [24441]

11. THE FRENCH COMMUNITY ("COMMUNAUTÉ")

Bilateral Agreements with France (p. 149)

The Malagasy Republic and France signed eight new co-operation agreements on June 4, 1973, replacing those in force since June 27, 1960. The agreement on military co-operation provided for the withdrawal of French ground forces based at Ivato by Sept. 1, 1973; the training of Malagasy units to run the naval installations at Diégo-Suarez; and unlimited French landing and harbouring rights for refuelling and repairs, renewable every year. [26011A]

France's defence agreement with Mauritania was regarded by the latter as void, following the signature on Feb. 15, 1973, of three new agreements covering cultural, technical and economic co-operation. No accord on military matters was reached during the negotiations. [26004A]

The Franc Zone (p. 150)

Mauritania withdrew from the franc zone on Feb. 15, 1973, following the Mauritanian Government's decision, first announced on Nov. 28, 1972, to create a national currency [25660B; 26004A]. The Malagasy Republic announced its withdrawal from the franc zone on May 22, 1973. [26011A]

12. THE AMERICAS

Bilateral Defence Treaties of the U.S.A.

Canada-U.S.A.
The agreement on the organization and operations of the North American Air Defence Command (NORAD —see page 171) was extended for two years from May 12, 1973. [25952A]

Regional Agreements in Latin America

The Andean Group (p. 169)
Venezuela joined the Andean Group as a full member on Feb. 13, 1973. In October of the previous year Mexico became a "working partner," co-operating with the Group in joint financial and industrial development. [25779A]

13. THE MIDDLE EAST

Egypt-Libya Merger
An agreement providing for political union between Egypt and Libya, which had been concluded at Benghazi on Aug. 2, 1972, and signed on Aug. 29, 1973, came nominally into force on Sept. 1, 1973, each country remaining for the time being, however, completely independent.

A joint declaration issued by the two Presidents provided *inter alia* for a unified political leadership, consisting of the two Heads of State, to assume responsibility for unity pending the formation of the new State; and for the formation of a Constituent Assembly, which would draw up a Constitution and nominate a Head of State. A referendum on the Constitution would be held when the document had been drawn up. However, no deadline was set for the completion of the Assembly's tasks, nor was it stated when and where the Assembly would meet. [26140A]

Other Agreements between Arab Countries (p. 180)

The Tripoli Charter
Egypt, Libya and Sudan on Dec. 28, 1969, signed the "Charter of Tripoli," under which the three countries proposed to establish a "revolutionary alliance" with the aim of promoting joint co-operation in foreign affairs, defence and economic affairs. Syria on Nov. 27, 1970, proclaimed its adhesion to the Charter. [23808A; 24309A]

14. AFRICA

The Organization of African Unity (OAU)

Assemblies of Heads of State and Government (pp. 187–8)
The eleventh Assembly was held in Addis Ababa on May 27–29, 1973.

In the course of the Assembly the disputes between Ethiopia and Somalia and between Uganda and Tanzania were the subject of OAU mediation. An eight-member "good offices committee" was formed to seek ways of reconciling Ethiopia and Somalia in their territorial dispute. In the case of Uganda and Tanzania, whose conflict dated from the previous September, when armed followers of former President Obote of Uganda had invaded Uganda from Tanzania, an agreement was reached, which was signed by the two Presidents on May 28.

Under the terms of the agreement, the Ugandan Government agreed to pay to Tanzania compensation for the deaths of 24 Tanzanian nationals in Uganda; both parties agreed to adhere strictly to the terms of the Mogadishu peace agreement [see below], and in particular to prevent their territories from being used as bases for subversion against each other; the Tanzanian Government assumed responsibility that ex-President Obote would not interfere in Uganda's affairs; and the Ugandan Government would not demand Dr. Obote's expulsion from Tanzania. [25955A]
[The Mogadishu peace agreement, signed on Oct. 5, 1972, provided for the withdrawal of troops from the Ugandan-Tanzanian border and for a cessation of all military activities by the two sides against each other.] [25543A]

French-speaking Africa

OCAM (p. 190)
Notice of withdrawal from OCAM was given by Cameroon on July 1, 1973, by Chad on July 3, 1973, and by the Malagasy Republic on Aug. 4, 1973. [26033B]

CEAO (p. 191)
At a conference on April 16–18, 1973, of Heads of State of six of the signatories of the treaty establishing

the West African Economic Community (CEAO) (Dahomey had previously announced its withdrawal from the proposed Community), it was decided that the treaty should come into force on Jan. 1, 1974. [25915A]

Dependent Territories

Portugal
Under an "Organic Law for the Overseas Territories," enacted on May 2, 1973, Angola and Mozambique were designated as States instead of overseas provinces, and were allowed greater autonomy "without affecting the unity of the nation." [25948A]

Bilateral Agreements

Nigeria-Mali
A treaty of friendship, co-operation and mutual assistance was signed by the Heads of State of Nigeria and Mali on March 3, 1973. It was agreed that a joint commission should be set up to plan for increased co-operation between the two countries. [25810B]

Egypt-Chad
A treaty of friendship between Egypt and Chad was signed on Feb. 22, 1973.

Libya-Burundi
A 10-year treaty of friendship and co-operation between Libya and Burundi, automatically renewable, was signed in Tripoli on Aug. 24, 1973.

15. SOUTH AND EAST ASIA AND THE PACIFIC AREA

The Vietnam Peace Agreement
An "Agreement on Ending the War and Restoring Peace in Vietnam" was signed in Paris on Jan. 27, 1973, by the Foreign Ministers of the U.S.A., North and South Vietnam and the South Vietnamese Provisional Revolutionary Government (PRG). The peace agreement consisted of a preamble and 23 articles under nine chapters, and was accompanied by four protocols dealing in detail with specific matters covered by the agreement.

The salient points of the agreement were as follows:

Chapter I. Article 1 stated: "The United States and all other countries respect the independence, sovereignty, unity and territorial integrity of Vietnam as recognized by the 1954 Geneva Agreements on Vietnam."

Chapter II. Articles 2 and 3 provided for a cease-fire throughout South Vietnam from midnight on Jan. 27, 1973, and the cessation of all United States military activities against North Vietnam at the same time. The cease-fire would be "durable and without limit of time."

Article 4 stated: "The United States will not continue its military involvement or intervene in the internal affairs of South Vietnam."

Articles 5 and 6 provided for the total withdrawal from South Vietnam of troops, military advisers and personnel, armaments, munitions and war material of the U.S.A. and other foreign allies within 60 days of the signing of the agreement, and for the dismantlement of all foreign military bases in South Vietnam.

Chapter III. Article 8 dealt with the return of prisoners of war, which, it was stated, should be "carried out simultaneously with and completed not later than the same day as the troop withdrawal." It also provided for cooperation in the passing of information on military personnel and foreign civilians missing in action and for the locating and care of graves of the dead.

Chapter IV. This chapter covered the exercise of the South Vietnamese people's right to self-determination and contained the following articles:

Art. 9. "The Government of the United States of America and the Government of the Democratic Republic of Vietnam undertake to respect the following principles for the exercise of the South Vietnamese people's right to self-determination:

"(a) The South Vietnamese people's right to self-determination is sacred, inalienable, and shall be respected by all countries.

"(b) The South Vietnamese people shall decide themselves the political future of South Vietnam through genuinely free and democratic general elections under international supervision.

"(c) Foreign countries shall not impose any political tendency or personality on the South Vietnamese people.

Art. 10. "The two South Vietnamese parties undertake to respect the cease-fire and maintain peace in South Vietnam, settle all matters of contention through negotiations, and avoid all armed conflict.

Art. 11. "Immediately after the cease-fire, the two South Vietnamese parties will:

"Achieve national reconciliation and concord, end hatred and enmity, prohibit all acts of reprisal and discrimination against individuals or organizations that have collaborated with one side or the other;

"ensure the democratic liberties of the people: personal freedom, freedom of speech, freedom of the press, freedom of meeting, freedom of organization, freedom of belief, freedom of movement, freedom of residence, freedom of work, right to property ownership, and right to free enterprise.

Art. 12. "(a) Immediately after the cease-fire, the two South Vietnamese parties shall hold consultations in a spirit of national reconciliation and concord, mutual respect and mutual non-elimination to set up a National Council of National Reconciliation and Concord of three equal segments.

"The council shall operate on the principle of unanimity. After the National Council of National Reconciliation and Concord has assumed its functions, the two South Vietnamese parties will consult about the formation of councils at lower levels.

"The two South Vietnamese parties shall sign an agreement on the internal matters of South Vietnam as soon as possible and do their utmost to accomplish this within 90 days after the cease-fire comes into effect, in keeping with the South Vietnamese people's aspirations for peace, independence and democracy.

"(b) The National Council of National Reconciliation

and Concord shall have the task of promoting the two South Vietnamese parties' implementation of this agreement, achievement of national reconciliation and concord and ensurance of democratic liberties.

"The National Council of National Reconciliation and Concord will organize the free and democratic general elections provided for in Article 9 (*b*) and decide the procedures and modalities of these general elections.

"The institutions for which the general elections are to be held will be agreed upon through consultations between the two South Vietnamese parties. The National Council of National Reconciliation and Concord will also decide the procedures and modalities of such local elections as the two South Vietnamese parties agree upon.

Art. 13. "The question of Vietnamese armed forces in South Vietnam shall be settled by the two South Vietnamese parties in a spirit of national reconciliation and concord, equality and mutual respect, without foreign interference, in accordance with the post-war situation.

"Among the questions to be discussed by the two South Vietnamese parties are steps to reduce their military effectives and to demobilize the troops being reduced. The two South Vietnamese parties will accomplish this as soon as possible.

Art. 14. "South Vietnam will pursue a foreign policy of peace and independence. It will be prepared to establish relations with all countries irrespective of their political and social systems on the basis of mutual respect for independence and sovereignty, and accept economic and technical aid from any country with no political conditions attached.

"The acceptance of military aid by South Vietnam in the future shall come under the authority of the Government set up after the general elections in South Vietnam provided for in Article 9 (*b*)."

Chapter V. Article 15, on the reunification of Vietnam, stated: "The reunification of Vietnam shall be carried out step by step through peaceful means on the basis of discussion and agreements between North and South Vietnam, without coercion or annexation by either part, and without foreign interference. The time for reunification will be agreed upon by North and South Vietnam.

"Pending the reunification:

"(*a*) The military demarcation line between the two zones at the 17th parallel is only provisional and not a political or territorial boundary, as provided for in Paragraph 6 of the final declaration of the 1954 Geneva conference.

"(*b*) North and South Vietnam shall respect the demilitarized zone on either side of the provisional military demarcation line.

"(*c*) North and South Vietnam shall promptly start negotiations with a view to re-establishing normal relations in various fields. Among the questions to be negotiated are the modalities of civilian movement across the provisional military demarcation line.

"(*d*) North and South Vietnam shall not join any military alliance or military bloc and shall not allow foreign Powers to maintain military bases, troops, military advisers, and military personnel on their respective territories, as stipulated in the 1954 Geneva Agreements on Vietnam."

Chapter VI. Articles 16 and 17 provided for the setting up of a four-party joint military commission, consisting of representatives of the four signatories of the agreement, and a two-party military commission representing the two South Vietnamese parties. These commissions would implement the provisions of the agreement concerning the cease-fire, the troop withdrawal and dismantlement of bases, and the return of prisoners of war. Under Article 18 an International Commission of Control and Supervision (ICCS) was to be established immediately after signature of the agreement.

Article 19 stated: "The parties agree on the convening of an international conference within 30 days of the signing of this agreement to acknowledge the signed agreements; to guarantee the ending of the war, the maintenance of peace in Vietnam, the respect of the Vietnamese people's fundamental national rights, and the South Vietnamese people's right to self-determination; and to contribute to and guarantee peace in Indo-China.

"The United States and the Democratic Republic of Vietnam, on behalf of the parties participating in the Paris Conference on Vietnam, will propose to the following parties that they participate in this international conference: the People's Republic of China, the Republic of France, the Union of Soviet Socialist Republics, the United Kingdom, the four countries of the International Commission of Control and Supervision, and the Secretary-General of the United Nations, together with the parties participating in the Paris Conference on Vietnam."

Chapter VII. Article 20, which was concerned with Cambodia and Laos, stated:

"(*a*) The parties participating in the Paris Conference on Vietnam shall strictly respect the 1954 Geneva Agreements on Cambodia and the 1962 Geneva Agreements on Laos [see below], which recognized the Cambodian and the Laos people's fundamental national rights, i.e. the independence, sovereignty, unity and territorial integrity of these countries. The parties shall respect the neutrality of Cambodia and Laos.

"The parties participating in the Paris Conference on Vietnam undertake to refrain from using the territory of Cambodia and the territory of Laos to encroach on the sovereignty and security of one another and of other countries.

"(*b*) Foreign countries shall put an end to all military activities in Cambodia and Laos, totally withdraw from and refrain from reintroducing into these two countries troops, military advisers and military personnel, armaments, munitions and war material.

"(*c*) The internal affairs of Cambodia and Laos shall be settled by the people of each of these countries without foreign interference.

"(*d*) The problems existing between the Indo-Chinese countries shall be settled by the Indo-Chinese parties on the basis of respect for each other's independence, sovereignty and territorial integrity and non-interference in each other's internal affairs."

Chapter VIII. Articles 21 and 22 were concerned with the relationship between the U.S.A. and North Vietnam.

Art. 21. "The United States anticipates that this agreement will usher in an era of reconciliation with the Democratic Republic of Vietnam as with all the peoples of Indo-China. In pursuance of its traditional policy, the United States will contribute to healing the wounds of war and to post-war reconstruction of the Democratic Republic of Vietnam and throughout Indo-China."

Art. 22. "The ending of the war, the restoration of peace in Vietnam, and the strict implementation of this agreement will create conditions for establishing a new, equal and mutually beneficial relationship between the United States and the Democratic Republic of Vietnam on the basis of respect for each other's independence and sovereignty, and non-interference in each other's internal affairs. At the same time, this will ensure stable peace in Vietnam and contribute to the preservation of lasting peace in Indo-China and South-east Asia."

Chapter IX. Article 23 provided for the immediate entry into force of the agreement after signature.

The four protocols to the agreement covered the cease-fire, the ICCS, the return of prisoners and the destruction of mines in territorial waters (this last being a bilateral agreement between the U.S.A. and North Vietnam). [*25781A*]

The Laos Peace Agreement

A peace agreement between the Government of Laos and the *Pathet Lao* was signed on Feb. 21, 1973. It comprised 12 Articles, of which the first laid down the general principles on which the future of Laos should be based.

Art. 1. "(*a*) The desires of the Lao people to safeguard and exercise their cherished fundamental national rights—the independence, sovereignty, unity and territorial integrity of Laos—are inviolable.

"(*b*) The declaration on the neutrality of Laos of July 9, 1962, and the 1962 Geneva Agreement on Laos [see below] are the correct bases for the Kingdom of Laos' foreign policies of peace, independence and neutrality. The parties concerned in Laos, the United States, Thailand and other foreign countries must strictly respect and implement this agreement. The internal affairs of Laos must be conducted by the Lao people only, without external interference.

"(*c*) To achieve the supreme objective of restoring peace, consolidating independence, achieving national concord and restoring national unity, and taking into consideration the present reality in Laos, which has two zones separately controlled by the two sides, the internal problems of Laos must be solved in the spirit of national concord and on the basis of equality and mutual respect, free from pressure or annexation by either side.

"(*d*) To safeguard national independence and sovereignty, achieve national concord and restore national unity, the people's democratic freedoms must be scrupulously observed, which comprise individual freedom, freedom of religion, speech, press, assembly, establishment of political organizations and associations, candidacy and elections, movement and residence, free enterprise, and the right to ownership of private property. All laws, regulations and institutions contrary to these freedoms must be abolished."

Articles 2 and 3 provided for a cease-fire throughout Laos from midnight on Feb. 22, 1973, with the cessation of foreign military involvement of any kind. Article 4 dealt with the withdrawal of military personnel and the dissolution of military and paramilitary organizations of foreign countries in Laos within 90 days. Article 5 provided for the return of prisoners of war within the same period.

Articles 6–10 contained provisions for political arrangements.

Art. 6. "Genuinely free and democratic general elections shall be organized to establish the National Assembly and a permanent National Union Government genuinely representing the people of all nationalities in Laos. The procedures and date of the general elections will be discussed and agreed upon by the two sides. Pending the general elections, the two sides shall set up a new Provisional National Union Government and a National Political Consultative Council within 30 days at the latest after the signing of this agreement, to implement the provisions of the agreement and handle State affairs."

Art. 7. "The new Provisional National Union Government will be composed of representatives of the Vientiane Government and of the Patriotic Forces [*Pathet Lao*], in equal numbers, and two intellectuals who stand for peace, independence, neutrality and democracy, who will be chosen by common agreement by the two sides. The future Prime Minister will not be included in the two equal numbers of representatives of the two parties."

Art. 8. The National Political Consultative Council will be an organization of national concord and will be composed of representatives of the Vientiane Government and of the Patriotic Forces in equal numbers, as well as a number of personalities who advocate peace, independence, neutrality and democracy, to be chosen by the two sides by common agreement. It will perform its duties in accordance with the principle of unanimity of the two parties. It has the responsibility to consult with and express views to the Provisional National Union Government on major problems relating to domestic and foreign policies; to support and assist the Provisional National Union Government and the two sides in implementing the agreement in order to achieve national concord; to examine and adopt together the laws and regulations for general elections; and to collaborate with the Provisional National Union Government in holding general elections to establish the National Assembly and the permanent National Union Government."

Article 9 provided for the neutralization of the towns of Luang Prabang and Vientiane, while Article 10 stated:

"(*a*) Pending the establishment of the National Assembly and the permanent National Union Government . . . the two sides will keep the territories under their temporary control, and will endeavour to implement the political programme of the Provisional National Union Government, as agreed upon by both sides.

"(*b*) The two sides will promote the establishment of normal relations between the two zones, and create favourable conditions for the people to move about, make their living, and carry out economic and cultural exchanges with a view to consolidating national concord and bringing about national unification at an early date.

"(*c*) The two parties take note of the declaration of the U.S. Government that it will contribute to healing the wounds of the war and to post-war reconstruction in Indo-China. The Provisional National Union Government will hold discussions with the U.S. Government in connexion with such a contribution regarding Laos."

Articles 11 and 12 covered the implementation of the agreement, providing for the setting up by the two sides of a Joint Commission for Implementation of the Agreement and the continued activities of the International Commission for Control and Supervision originally set up under the Geneva Agreements of 1954. [*25843A*]

The Laotian Government and the *Pathet Lao* on Sept. 14, 1973, signed an agreement implementing the peace agreement of Feb. 21, 1973 [see above], and aimed at bringing about a coalition Government. The agreement provided for the formation of a provisional national Government, headed by Prince Souvanna

Phouma and with portfolios equally divided between the two sides, and of a national political consultative council to advise the Government; the neutralization of Vientiane and Luang Prabang and the stationing there of troops and police by both sides; the withdrawal of all foreign troops and advisers within 60 days of the formation of the new Government; and the demarcation of the current cease-fire line with a number of specific points where the armies would particularly avoid confrontation.

The 1962 Geneva Agreement on Laos

An international agreement guaranteeing Laotian neutrality had been signed in Geneva on July 23, 1962. The agreement consisted of a Declaration and a Protocol, the main points being as follows:

The Declaration. The 13 participating countries other than Laos welcomed the neutrality statement of the Laotian Government (which had been agreed on July 8, 1962, and welcomed at a plenary session the following day, and which was incorporated in the preamble to the Declaration), and undertook *inter alia* that

"(*a*) they will not commit or participate in any way in any act which might directly or indirectly impair the sovereignty, independence, neutrality, unity or territorial integrity . . . of Laos;

"(*b*) they will not resort to the use or threat of force or any other measure which might impair the peace of . . . Laos;

"(*c*) they will refrain from all direct or indirect interference in the internal affairs of . . . Laos;

"(*d*) they will not attach conditions of a political nature to any assistance which they may offer or which . . . Laos may seek;

"(*e*) they will not bring . . . Laos in any way into any military alliance or any other agreement, whether military or otherwise, which is inconsistent with her neutrality, nor invite or encourage her to enter into any such alliance or conclude any such agreement;

"(*f*) they will not introduce into . . . Laos foreign troops or military personnel in any form whatsoever, nor will they in any way facilitate or connive at the introduction of any foreign troops or military personnel."

The Protocol. This was signed by the 14 participating countries including Laos, and contained provisions for the withdrawal of "all foreign regular and irregular troops, foreign paramilitary formations, and foreign military personnel." Article 5 noted that "the French and Laotian Governments would conclude as soon as possible an arrangement to transfer the French military installations in Laos to the Laotian Government", while Article 7 provided for the release within 30 days after the entry into force of the Protocol of "all foreign military persons and civilians captured or interned during the course of hostilities in Laos."

The Protocol would enter into force on signature. [*18919*]

Treaties among Nations of South and East Asia (p. 203)

India-Pakistan

An agreement was signed by India and Pakistan on Aug. 28, 1973, in New Delhi on the repatriation of Pakistani prisoners of war and civilian internees held since the 1971 conflict, as well as nationals of Bangladesh in Pakistan and Pakistanis in Bangladesh, with the exception of 195 prisoners of war. It was agreed that no trials of these 195 should take place during the repatriation period, but that on completion of repatriation Bangladesh, India and Pakistan would discuss and settle their fate.

16. THE THIRD WORLD: ATTEMPTS AT ACHIEVING A UNION

Conferences of Non-Aligned Countries (pp. 209–10)

The Algiers Conference

A fourth conference of non-aligned countries was held in Algiers on Sept. 5–9, 1973, and was attended by 76 full participants, 9 observers (i.e. entitled to participate on a consultative basis, but not to vote) and 3 guests. Also represented at the conference were the United Nations, the Organization of African Unity, the Arab League, the African, Asian and Latin American Solidarity Organization, and 14 "liberation movements" recognized by the OAU.

The conference was preceded by meetings of experts on Aug. 27 and of the Ministers of Foreign Affairs on Sept. 1–4, when a definite agenda was decided on and it was agreed to admit to full membership of the non-aligned group Argentina, Bangladesh, Bhutan, Malta (after an undertaking by Malta to evict foreign military bases upon expiry of the current agreements in 1979), Oman, Peru, Qatar, the Provisional Revolutionary Government of (South) Vietnam, and the Cambodian Government-in-exile.

During the conference the Algerian Government made strong efforts to give non-alignment a "new meaning," the Algerian Foreign Minister, M. Abdelaziz Bouteflika, defining the objectives of the conference as "the struggle for economic independence," co-operation on the basis of equality, and action on three fronts—(1) "maximum mobilization of our internal resources;" (2) the "strengthening of co-operation and trade exchanges . . . between developing and non-aligned countries in general;" and (3) the "democratization of relations between rich and poor countries." The need for a new appraisal of the idea of non-alignment had also been emphasized by other leaders of States in the "Third World."

At its closing session on Sept. 9 the conference approved:

(1) a political declaration, which *inter alia* demanded "the immediate and unconditional withdrawal of Israel from all occupied territories," and the recognition of the "inalienable right to independence of the non-aligned countries of Latin America still under colonial domination;" reaffirmed their solidarity with the liberation movements in Africa; and called for the holding of an international conference on disarmament;

(2) an economic declaration, which included a number of proposals for a common posture of non-aligned and other developing countries to be adopted in future trade negotiations;

(3) a number of resolutions on specified subjects, which included a call to boycott Israel, and the recognition of the "legitimacy and legality" of the Cambodian Government-in-exile.

It was decided that the next summit conference of the non-aligned countries should be held in Colombo (Sri Lanka) in 1976. [*26117A*]

ABBREVIATIONS OF MAIN ORGANIZATIONS AND GROUPINGS IN INDEX

AFRASEC	Afro-Asian Organization for Economic Co-operation
ASEAN	Association of South-East Asian Nations
CARIFTA	Caribbean Free Trade Association
CENTO	Central Treaty Organization
CERN	European Organization for Nuclear Research (*Conseil Européen pour la Recherche Nucléaire*)
CIAP	Inter-American Committee for the Alliance for Progress
CMEA	Council for Mutual Economic Assistance
COMECON	Council for Mutual Economic Assistance
EAEC	European Atomic Energy Community
EAGGF	European Agricultural Guidance and Guarantee Fund
ECA	Economic Commission for Africa
ECAFE	Economic Commission for Africa and the Far East
ECE	Economic Commission for Europe
ECLA	Economic Commission for Latin America
ECMT	European Conference of Ministers of Transport
ECOSOC	Economic and Social Council
ECSC	European Coal and Steel Community
EEC	European Economic Community
EFTA	European Free Trade Association
ELDO	European Launcher Development Organization
ENEA	European Nuclear Energy Agency
ESRO	European Space Research Organization
EURATOM	European Atomic Energy Community
FAO	Food and Agriculture Organization
GATT	General Agreement on Tariffs and Trade
IAEA	International Atomic Energy Agency
IA-ECOSOC	Inter-American Economic and Social Council
IBRD	International Bank for Reconstruction and Development
ICAO	International Civil Aviation Organization
IDA	International Development Association
IDB	Inter-American Development Bank
IFC	International Finance Corporation
ILO	International Labour Organization
IMCO	Intergovernmental Maritime Consultative Organization
IMF	International Monetary Fund
ITO	International Trade Organization
ITU	International Telecommunication Union
LAFTA	Latin American Free Trade Association
NATO	North Atlantic Treaty Organization
NEA	Nuclear Energy Agency
OAS	Organization of American States
OAPEC	Organization of Arab Petroleum Exporting Countries
OAU	Organization of African Unity
OCAM	Common African, Malagasy and Mauritian Organization
OCAS	Organization of Central American States
OECD	Organization for Economic Co-operation and Development
OEEC	Organization for European Economic Co-operation
OPEC	Organization of Petroleum Exporting Countries
RCD	Regional Co-operation for Development
SEATO	South-East Asia Treaty Organization
UDEAC	Central African Customs Union
UNCTAD	U.N. Conference on Trade and Development
UNCURK	U.N. Commission for the Unification and Rehabilitation of Korea
UNDP	U.N. Development Programme
UNFICYP	U.N. Peace-keeping Force in Cyprus
UNHCR	U.N. High Commissioner for Refugees
UNICEF	U.N. Children's Fund
UNIDO	U.N. Industrial Development Organization
UNITAR	U.N. Institute for Training and Research
UNMOGIP	U.N. Military Observer Group for India and Pakistan
UNRWA	U.N. Relief and Works Agency for Palestine Refugees in the Near East
UNTSO	U.N. Truce Supervision Organization (Palestine)
UPU	Universal Postal Union
WEU	Western European Union
WHO	World Health Organization
WMO	World Meteorological Organization

INDEX

The index entries for individual countries do not indicate their membership of international groupings, which can be ascertained easily from the lists of members, tables and maps in each relevant section of the text. Organizations and groupings are indexed under their full names, a list of abbreviations being found on page 226. The letters a and b after page numbers refer to the first or second column of the page concerned. Page numbers in *Italics* refer to maps.

Afghanistan
China (P.R.), Treaties, 128a
India, Treaty, 1950, 203b
Soviet Union, Treaty, 1931, 1955, 126b
Africa
Bilateral Treaties, 191a
Dependent Territories, 191b
European Economic Community, Association, *see under* European Economic Community
Independent Countries, 192–3
Regional Organizations, 188–91
East Africa, 189a
East and Central Africa, 188b
French-speaking Africa, 189b
West Africa, 191a
Afro-Asian Organization for Economic Co-operation (AFRASEC), 211a
Afro-Asian Solidarity Council, 210a
Albania
Bilateral Agreements, 122b, 128b
Council for Mutual Economic Assistance, Membership 1949–61, 129a
Soviet Relations, 116b
Warsaw Pact, 121a
Algeria
France, Co-operation Convention, 149b
——, Evian Agreements, 1962, 149b
Morocco, Treaties, 181a
Tunisia, Treaty, 181a
Alliance for Progress, 161–4
Charter of Punta del Este, 1961, 161a
Declaration to the Peoples of America, 161a
Economic and Social Act of Rio de Janeiro, 1965, 162b
Inter-American Committee, 155b
1967 Report, 163a
Second Inter-American Conference, Rio de Janeiro, 1965, 162b
Allied Control Council, Decisions on Germany, 6b
Allied Powers of World War II
European Advisory Commission, 6a
Joint Declaration, 1942, 10b
Peace Treaties, 1946–51, 7–8
Quebec Conference, 1944, 6a
American Commission of Dependent Territories *see under* Organization of American States
Andean Group, 169b
Anglo-French Alliance, Dunkirk, Treaty of, 41a

Anguilla,
Britain, Direct Rule, 176a
"Anschluss", Prohibition in Austrian State Treaty, 1955, 9a
Antarctica
Antarctic Treaty, 37a
Seals, Protection Agreement, 37b
ANZAC (Australia–New Zealand Agreement), 194a
ANZUK, 145a
ANZUS Pact, 194–5
Membership, 199
Arab League, 177–80
Collective Security Pact, 1950, 179a
Membership, 177a, *183*
Membership in Africa, 192–3
Pact of Union of Arab States, 1945, 177b
Subsidiary Bodies, 178b
Arab Republics, Federation of, 180a
Arab States
Bilateral Agreements, 180–1
Summit Conferences, 179b
Argentina
Chile, Arbitration Agreement, 170a
Euratom, Agreement, 1962, 77a
U.S.A., Atomic Energy Agreement, 175a
——, Defence Agreement, 170a
Asian Coconut Community, 24b
Asian and Pacific Council (ASPAC), 205a
Asian Development Bank, 204b
Association of South-East Asia (ASA), 205b
Association of South-East Asian Nations (ASEAN), 206a
Atlantic Alliance *see* North Atlantic Treaty Organization
Atlantic Charter, 1941, 10a
Atlantic Convention, 1962, 102a
Atomic Energy Agreements, 77a, 112b, 175a
Atomic Energy Commission *see under* United Nations
Australia
Bilateral Defense Agreements, 147b, 170b
Dependent Territories, 207a
ELDO, Membership, 81b
New Zealand (ANZAC) Agreement, 194a
——, Free Trade Area, 195b
OECD, Membership, 85

——, Development Assistance Committee, 92b
U.S.A., Agreements, 170b, 175a
Austria
Anschluss, Prohibition of, 1955, 9a
Austrian State Treaty, 1955, 8b
EFTA, *56,* 79b
Neutrality, 9a
South Tyrol Agreements, 7b
U.S.A., Atomic Energy Agreement, 175a

Baghdad Pact *see* Central Treaty Organization
Bahrain
Britain, Treaty, 147b
Bandung Conference, 1955, 208a
Bangladesh
India, Treaty, 147b
Belgium
Atomic Energy Agreements, 77a, 112b
NATO Agreements, 106–8, 170b
Belgrade Conference of Non-Aligned Countries, 1961, 209a
Benelux, 48–50
Economic Union Treaty, 1957–60, 49a
Labour Treaty, 1955, 49a
Membership, 48b, *51*
Pre-Union Treaty, 1949, 48b
Berlin
Allied Control Council, 6b
Enclaves, Agreement on, 135b
Four-Power Agreement on Status, 134b
Franco-German Treaty, 1963, 84b
Kommandatura, 1945–48, 7a
Transit Traffic, Agreement, 1971, 135b
Travelling and Visiting, Agreement, 135b
West Berlin "Independent Political Unit", 124a
Yalta Conference Provisions, 6a
Berne Copyright Convention, 3–4
Stockholm Conference, 1967, 3b
Bhutan
India, Treaty, 1949, 203a
Bogotá, Act of, 1960, 160b
Bogotá Declarations, 1948 *see under* Organization of American States
Bolivia
U.S.A., Defence Agreements, 170b
Brazil
Euratom, Agreement, 1961, 77a
U.S.A., Agreements, 170b, 175a

Brezhnev Doctrine, 118a
Briand-Kellog Pact, 1928, 14b
Britain
    Atomic Energy Agreements, 77a, 112b, 175a
    Bilateral Agreements and Treaties, 112, 145–7, 170–1, *199*
    Cyprus, Treaty of Establishment, 1960, 146b
    ———, Zurich and London Agreements, 146b
    Dependent Territories, 140b, 176a, 191b, 207a
    Euratom, Agreement, 1959, 76b
    European Communities, Membership, 58–61, *56*
    Indo-China, Geneva Agreements, 1954, 200–3
    NATO Agreements, 106–12
    Persian Gulf, Treaties, 147b
    Thailand, Peace Treaty, 7a
Brussels Treaty, 1948, 41–2
Buenos Aires, Economic Declaration of, 1957, 160a
Bulgaria
    Bilateral Treaties, 122–5
    Peace Treaty, 1947, 7b
Burma
    China (P.R.), Treaties, 120a
    India, Agreement, 203b
    Pakistan, Agreements, 204a

Cairo Conference of Non-Aligned Countries, 1964, 209b
Cambodia
    Czechoslovakia, Treaty, 1960, 124b
    Geneva Agreements, 1954, 200–3
    Multilateral Agreement for Mutual Defence Assistance, 1950, 174b, 203a
Cameroon
    France, Defence Agreement, 149a, 192
Canada
    Atomic Energy Agreements, 77a, 112b, 175a
    Bilateral Defence Agreements, 171a, 175a
    Euratom, Agreement, 1959, 77a
    NATO Agreements, 106–8, 171a
    Soviet Union, Protocol, 134b
Caribbean Free Trade Association (CARIFTA), 144b
    Eastern Caribbean, Proposed Political Union, 145a
Cartagena Agreement, 169b
Central African Customs Union, 190a
    Membership, 192–3
Central African Republic
    France, Defence Agreement, 149, 192–3
Central America, Declaration of, 1963, 158b, 165b
Central America, Labour Council of, 167b
Central American Common Market, 166–7

Basis for Latin American Common Market, 163b
    General Treaty of Central American Economic Integration, 1960, 166b
    Institutions, 167a
    Membership, 166a, 175b
    Treaties, 166b
Central American Defence Council, 166a
Central Treaty Organization, 182–4
    Baghdad Pact, 182b
    Membership, 182a, *183*
    Organization and Committees, 183b
    U.S.A., Bilateral Agreements, 183b
Chad
    France, Defence Agreement, 149, 192–3
    Nigeria, Treaties, 191b
Chapultepec, Act of, 1945, 143b, 152a
Chile
    Argentina, Agreement, 170a
    U.S.A., Defence Agreement, 171b
China, Nationalist see Taiwan
China (People's Republic of)
    Bilateral Treaties, *123*, 128–9
    Eastern Joint Institute for Nuclear Research, Withdrawal, 131b
    Indo-China, Geneva Agreements, 1954, 200–3
    Soviet Union, Ideological Controversy, 115–19
    U.N., Membership, 33b
Civil Aviation
    European Conference, 45a
    International Civil Aviation Organization, 29b
Civilians in Wartime
    Int. Red Cross Convention on Protection, 1948, 1b
Coffee
    International Coffee Organization, 25a
Colombia
    U.S.A., Atomic Energy Agreements, 175a
    ———, Defence Agreements, 171b
Colombo Plan, 144a
COMECON see Council for Mutual Economic Assistance
Cominform, 113b
Comintern, 113a
Commission for Technical Co-operation in Africa, 188b
Committee of Twenty see International Monetary Fund
Commodity Producers' Agreements, 24b
    Asian Coconut Community, 24b
    International Coffee Organization, 25a
    International Sugar Agreement, 25a
    Organization of Arab Petroleum Exporting Countries, 24b
    Organization of Petroleum Exporting Countries, 24b
    Pepper Community, 24b
Common African, Malagasy and Mauritian Organization (OCAM), 190a
    Joint Enterprises, 190b
    Membership, *190*, 190a, 192–3

Common Market see European Economic Community
Commonwealth
    Bilateral Agreements, 145–6
    Commonwealth Preference, 142b
    Economic Committee, 1926, 141a
    Membership, 141
        in Africa, *142*, 192–3
        in America, 175b
    Organizations, 142–3
    Regional Groupings, 144–5
    Sugar Agreement, 143a
    Westminster, Statute of, 141b
"Communauté" see French Community
"Communauté Financière Africaine," 190a
Communications Satellite Systems, 39a
    Intelsat, 39a
    Intersputnik, 39a
Communist Conferences (see also Three Continents Conference)
    Moscow, 1957, 113–14
    Moscow, 1960, 115–16
    Moscow, 1961, 116b
Communist International, 113a
Concordats, 4–5
Congo (Brazzaville)
    China (P.R.), Treaty, 1964, 128b
    ———, Military Agreement, 129a
    France, Defence Agreement, 1960, 149b, 192
Congo (Kinshasa) see Zaïre
"Conseil de l'Entente," 189b, *190*, 192–3
Constantinople Convention (on use of Suez Canal), 182a
Continental Shelf
    North Sea, Agreement, 83b
    Iran-Saudi Arabia, Agreement, 185b
    U.N. Convention, 18a
Copyright
    Conventions, 3b
    Stockholm Conference, 1967, 3b
Costa Rica
    U.S.A., Defence Agreement
Council for Mutual Economic Assistance (COMECON), 129–32
    Complex Programme, 131b
    International Bank for Economic Co-operation, 131a
    International Institute of Economic Problems, 131a
    Membership, 129a
Council of Europe, 43–8
    Conferences and Committees, 44–5
    Conventions and Agreements on European Co-operation, 47b
    European Commission of Human Rights, 45–6
    European Convention for the Peaceful Settlement of Disputes, 46b
    European Convention for the Protection of Human Rights, 45b
    European Court of Human Rights, 45–6
    European Social Charter, 46b

Membership, *46*, 48a
Organs, *42*
Statute, 44a
Cuba
  COMECON, Membership, 132b
  Exclusion from Inter-American System,
    159b
  Guantanamo Bay, Lease Agreement,
    171b
  Treaty of Rio, Withdrawal from, 1960,
    152a
  Venezuela, OAS Resolution on Cuban
    Aggression, 1964, 159b
Cyprus
  Britain, Treaty of Establishment, 1960,
    146b
  U.N. Peace-Keeping Force, 23b
  Zurich and London Agreements, 1959,
    146b
Czechoslovakia
  Bilateral Agreements, 122–4, 128b
  Soviet-Czechoslovak Treaty, 123a
  Soviet Invasion, 118–19
    NATO Reaction, 104b

Dahomey
  Bilateral Defence Agreements, 149a,
    171b, 192
Danube
  Freedom of Navigation, Peace Treaties,
    7–8
Denmark
  European Communities, Membership,
    58–61
  Greenland, Defence Agreements with
    the U.S.A., 172a
  NATO Agreements, 106b, 108a, 110–11,
    172a
  U.S.A., Atomic Energy Agreement, 175a
Dependent Territories
  Africa, *187*, 191b
  America, 176
  Britain, 140b, 176a, 191b, 207a
  Pacific Area and South-East Asia, 207
  United States, 176b, 207b
Disarmament *see under* United Nations
Dominican Republic
  U.S.A., Defence Agreement, 172a
Dumbarton Oaks Conference, 1944, 108
Dunkirk, Treaty of, 1947, 41a

**East African Common Services Organiza-
  tion,** 189a
East African Development Bank, 189b
East African Economic Community, 189b
  Membership, 192–3
East-West Treaties
  Berlin Agreements, 1971, 134–5
  G.F.R.-G.D.R., 1972, 135–7
  G.F.R.-Poland, 1970, 134a
  G.F.R.-Soviet Union, 1970, 133
  Soviet Union-Canada, 1971, 134b
  Soviet Union-France, 1971, 135b
  Soviet Union-U.S.A., 1963, 1971, 1972,
    137–9

Eastern Europe
  Bilateral Agreements, 122–8
  Defence Agreements, 122–3
**Eastern European Mutual Assistance
  Treaty** *see* Warsaw Treaty
  Organization
Eastern Germany *see* German Democratic
  Republic
**Eastern Joint Institute for Nuclear
  Research,** Dubna, 131b
Ecuador
  U.S.A., Defence Agreements, 172a
Egypt
  Bilateral Agreements, 127a, 180–1
  Defence Pact, 1967, 181b
  European Economic Community, Trade
    Agreement, 72a
  India, Atomic Energy Agreement, 77a
  Soviet Union, Treaty, 127a
El Salvador
  Honduras, Demilitarized Zone, 170a
  U.S.A., Defence Agreements, 172a
Environment
  Declarations and Conventions, 83–4
  Marine Pollution, 30
  U.S.A.-Canada, Great Lakes Agreement,
    175b
Ethiopia
  Defence Agreements, 172a, 191a
Eurisotop, 76a
Eurochemic, 91b
Eurocontrol, 80a
Eurofima, 80a
**European Agricultural Guidance and
  Guarantee Fund,** 64b
**European Atomic Energy Community
  (Euratom),** 74–7
  Establishment, 1957, 56a
  Eurisotop, 76a
  European Nuclear Energy Agency,
    Co-operation, 76a
  International Atomic Energy Agency,
    Co-operation, 76a
  Joint Research Centres, 75b
  Membership, 51b, *56*
  Non-Member-Countries, Agreements,
    76a
  Supply Agency, 75–6
  Treaty, 74–5
**European Coal and Steel Community
  (ECSC),** 53–5
  High Authority, 51b, 54b, 65a
  Membership, 51b, *56*
  Schuman Plan, 53b
  Switzerland, Consultation Agreement,
    55a
  ———, Transport Charges, 55a
European Commission, 52a
European Commission of Human Rights,
  45–6
European Communities
  Advisory Committees, 53a
  Council of Ministers, 51b
  Court of Justice, 52b
  Enlargement, 58–61
    Approval by Six, 61a

European Coal and Steel Community
  see separate entry
European Commission, 52a
European Communities Bill, 60
European Economic Community *see*
  separate entry
European Parliament, 52
  Headquarters, 53a
  Membership, 51b, *56*
  Merger of EEC, ECSC and Euratom,
    Treaty, 1965, 51b
  Norway, Withdrawal of Application,
    60b
  Treaty of Brussels, 58–60
**European Conference of Ministers of
  Transport,** 79b
**European Convention for the Protection
  of Human Rights and
  Fundamental Freedoms,** 45b
European Court of Human Rights, 45–6
European Cultural Convention, 47b
European Development Fund, 58b
European Economic Community (EEC)
  Agricultural Policy, 62–5
  "Agriculture 1980" Plan, 64
  Anti-Trust Policy, 66–7
  Arusha Convention, 70a
  Association, 67–71
  Barre Plan, 72a
  Budget, 72b
  Capital, Freedom of Movement of, 66a
  Cartels, 67a
  Competition Policy, 66–7
  Davignon Report, 74a
  Economic and Monetary Union, 72–3
  European Agricultural Guidance and
    Guarantee Fund, 64b
  European Development Fund, 58b
  European Free Trade Association,
    Special Relations Agreements, 79b
  European Investment Bank, 58a
  European Social Fund, 58a
  Fisheries, 64a
  Labour Policy, 65a
  Mansholt Plan, 64
  Membership, 51b, *56*
  Messina Resolution, 55b
  Monetary Agreements, 72a
  Paris Summit, 74a
  Political Union, 74a
  Rome, Treaty of, 56–7
  Tariff Preferences, 72a
  Trade Agreements (Non-members), 71–2
  Value Added Tax, 67a
  Werner Report, 72–3
  Yaoundé Conventions, 69
European Free Trade Association, 77–9
  Convention, 78
  Membership, *56*, 77a
  Special Relations Agreements, 79b
  Tariff Reductions, 78b
**European Fund and Multilateral Clearing
  System,** 90–1
European Investment Bank, 58a
**European Launcher Development Organ-
  ization (ELDO),** 81–2

British Withdrawal, 82a
ESRO, Merger, 83b
European Monetary Agreement, 87b
European Organization for Nuclear
    Research (CERN), 80–1
ESRO, Formation, 82b
European Parliament, 52
European Recovery Programme, 85a
European Security Conference, Proposed,
    106a
European Social Charter, 46b
European Social Fund, 58a
European Space Research Organization
    (ESRO), 82–3
ELDO, Merger, 83b
Installations, 83a
Membership, 82b
U.S.A., Memorandum of Agreement,
    83a
Evian Agreements (France-Algeria), 1962,
    149b

Faroe Islands
EFTA Convention applied, 79a
Finland
EFTA, 56, 79a
Peace Treaties, 7b
Soviet Union, Mutual Assistance Pact,
    7b, 126a
——, Treaty, 1971, 126a
Fishing
U.N. Convention, 18a
Five Principles
Enunciation, 1954, 209a
Moscow Declaration, 1957, 114a
Franc Zone, 150b
France
Algeria, Co-operation Convention, 150b
——, Evian Agreements, 149b
Atomic Energy Agreements, 112b
Bilateral Defence Agreements, 149,
    172a, 192–3
Bilateral Treaties, Western Europe, 84
German Federal Republic, Treaty of
    Co-operation, 1963, 84
——, Treaty on the Saar, 1956, 9b
Indo-China
    Agreement for Mutual Defence
        Assistance, 1950, 174b, 203a
    Geneva Agreements, 1954, 200–3
NATO, Agreements, 106–8, 110–12
——, Withdrawal from, 103b
Overseas Territories, 176, 191b, 207b
SEATO, Partial Withdrawal from,
    198a
Soviet Union, Co-operation Principles,
    135b
U.N. Disarmament Committee, Boycott
    of, 22a
French Community, 148–50
Membership, 148, 192–3

Gabon
France, Defence Agreement, 149, 192

General Agreement on Tariffs and Trade
    see under United Nations
Geneva Agreements on Indo-China, 200–3
Geneva Disarmament Committee, 19b, 20a
Geneva Protocol, 1925, 3a
Genocide, U.N. Convention, 1948, 14b
Georgetown Conference of Non-aligned
    Countries, 210a
German Democratic Republic
Bilateral Agreements, 123, 123–5, 128b
German Federal Republic, Treaty,
    135–7
Mongolia, Treaty, 124b
Soviet Union, Recognition by, 123b
U.N. Membership, Proposed Applica-
    tion, 33
German Federal Republic
Atomic Energy Agreements, 77a, 112b
Establishment, 7a
France, Treaties, 1956, 1963, 9b, 84
Full Sovereign Status, Paris, 1954, 7a
German Democratic Republic, Treaty,
    135–7
NATO Agreements, 106–8, 110–12
——, Membership, 7a, 93–4
Poland, Treaty, 1970, 134a
Soviet Union, Treaty, 1970, 133
U.N. Membership, Proposed Applica-
    tion, 33
U.S.A., Defence Agreements, 172a
Germany (see also German Democratic
    Republic and German Federal
    Republic)
Allied Control Council, Decisions, 1945–
    47, 6b
Concordat, 1933, 4b
Potsdam Conference, 1945, 6b
Yalta Conference, 1945, 6a
Ghana
China (P.R.), Treaty, 1961, 128b
Gibraltar, 146a
Gondra Treaty, 1923, 151b
Grenada, Declaration of, 145a
Greece
Atomic Energy Agreements, 112b, 175a
Cyprus, Zurich and London Agree-
    ments, 146b
European Economic Community,
    Association, 67–8
NATO, Adherence, 1952, 95a
——, Agreements, 106–8, 110–12, 172a
U.S.A., Defence Agreements, 172a
Greenland see under Denmark
Group of Ten see International Monetary
    Fund under United Nations
Guatemala
U.S.A., Defence Agreements, 172a
Guinea
China (P.R.), Treaty, 1960, 128b
Sierra Leone, Defence Agreement, 191b
U.S.A., Defence Agreement, 172b
Guyana
Atkinson Field Agreement, 1966, 172b
Venezuela, Treaty with Britain, 147a

Hague Conferences and Conventions,
    1899, 1907, 2–3
Haiti
U.S.A., Defence Agreement, 172b
Havana
Act of, 1940, 174b
Convention, 1940, 174b
Helsinki Convention, 1962, 50b
High Seas, U.N. Convention, 1958, 18a
Hijacking Conventions see International
    Civil Aviation Organization
    under United Nations
Holy See see Vatican
Honduras
El Salvador, Demilitarized Zone, 170a
U.S.A., Defence Agreements, 172b
Human Rights
European Commission of, 45b
European Convention for the Protection
    of Human Rights and Funda-
    mental Freedoms, 45b
European Court of, 45b
Universal Declaration and Covenants,
    1948, 15–17
Hungary
Bilateral Agreements, 122, 123, 124–5,
    128
Peace Treaty, 1947, 8a
Roman Catholic Church, Recognition
    by, 5b

Iceland
EFTA, Special Relations Agreement,
    56, 77a, 79
NATO, Agreements, 110–12, 172b
U.S.A., Defence Agreements, 172b
India
Atomic Energy Agreements, 77a, 175a
Bangladesh, Treaty, 147b
Bilateral Agreements, 172b, 203–4
Pakistan, Agreements, 203–4
——, U.N. Military Observer Group,
    23b
Soviet Union, Treaty, 127
Thailand, Peace Treaty, 7a
Indo-China
Geneva Agreements, 1954, 200–3
SEATO Protocol, 1954, 197a
U.S.A., Agreement for Mutual Defence
    Assistance, 1950, 174b, 199, 203a
Indonesia
China (P.R.), Treaty, 128b
Malaysia, Treaty, 204b
U.S.A., Atomic Energy Agreement, 175a
——, Defence Agreement, 172b
Indus Waters Treaty, 1960, 203–4
Industrial Property, Convention on
    Protection, 1883, 3a
Intellectual Property
Conventions, 3–4
International Bureau, 4a
Stockholm Conference, 1967, 3–4
World Organization, 3b
Intelsat, 39a
Inter-American Conference, 155–6

Inter-American Defence Board, 157b
Inter-American Development Bank, 164
Inter-American Treaty of Reciprocal
    Assistance, 1947, 152a
International, First, Second, Third, 113a
International Atomic Energy Agency
    (IAEA) see under United Nations
International Communications Satellite
    System, 39a
International Investment Bank, 130–1
International Monetary Fund (IMF) see
    under United Nations
International Postal Convention, 1874, 31a
International Red Cross, 1
International Telecommunication Union,
    31a
International Trade Organization, 31b
Intersputnik, 39a
Iran
    European Economic Community, Trade
        Agreement, 71a
    Saudi Arabia, Continental Shelf
        Agreement, 185b
    Soviet Union, Treaties, 1921, 126
    U.S.A., Atomic Energy Agreement, 175a
    ———, Defence Agreements, 172b
Iraq
    CENTO, Withdrawal from, 182b
    Defence Pact, 1967, 181b
    Egypt, Agreement, 180b
    Soviet Union, Treaty, 127b
Ireland
    European Communities, Membership,
        51b, 56, 58–61
    U.S.A., Atomic Energy Agreement, 175a
Islamic Organization, 181b
Israel
    European Economic Community, Trade
        Agreement, 71a
    U.S.A., Atomic Energy Agreement, 175a
    ———, Defence Agreement, 172b
Italy
    Atomic Energy Agreements, 112b, 175a
    Lateran Treaty, 1929, 4b
    NATO Agreements, 109–12
    Peace Treaty, 1947, 7b
    South Tyrol, Agreements with Austria,
        7–8
    Trieste Agreement, 1954, 8a
    U.S.A., Defence Agreements, 172b
Ivory Coast
    France, Defence Agreement, 149, 192
    Senegal, Treaty, 191b

Jamaica
    U.S.A., Defence Agreement, 172b
Japan
    Korea (South), Treaty, 1965, 204b
    Peace Treaty, 8
    Philippines, Treaty, 1960, 204b
    Ryukyu and other Islands, Return of, 8
    Soviet Union, Yalta Conference Secret
        Protocol, 1945, 6a
    U.S.A., Defence Agreements, 172b, 199,
        199–200

Joint African and Malagasy Organization
    see Common African, Malagasy and
    Mauritian Organization (OCAM)
Jordan
    Defence Pact, 1967, 181b
    Saudi Arabia, Agreements, 1962, 180b

Kenya
    Britain, Defence Agreement, 145b
    Ethiopia, Defence Agreement, 191a
Kidnapping of Diplomats, Convention,
    160a
Kinshasa, Declaration of, 189a
Korea (see also Korea, Democratic Peo-
    ple's Republic of, and Korea,
    Republic of)
    U.N. Commission for the Unification
        and Rehabilitation of Korea, 23a
Korea, Democratic People's Republic of
    (North)
    Bilateral Treaties, 125a, 128b
Korea, Republic of (South)
    Japan, Treaty, 1965, 204b
    U.N. Command, 23b
    U.S.A., Atomic Energy Agreements, 175a
    ———, Defense Agreement, 173a
    ———, Mutual Defense Treaty, 173a,
        198–9, 199, 200a

Laos
    Geneva Agreements, 1954, 200–3
    Multilateral Agreement for Mutual
        Defence Assistance, 1950, 174b,
        199, 203a
Lateran Treaty, 1929, 4b
Latin America (see also Alliance for
    Progress, Andean Group, Latin
    American Free Trade Association,
    Latin American Solidarity
    Organization)
    Action Plan for Latin American Eco-
        nomic Integration and Industrial
        Development, Punta del Este,
        1967, 163–4
    Bilateral Agreements, 170a
    Nuclear Weapons, Treaty on Prohibi-
        tion, 38a
    Regional Agreements, 169–70
    Tlatelolco, Treaty of, 38a
Latin American Free Trade Association,
    168–9
    Basis for Latin American Common
        Market, 163b
    Membership, 165, 168a, 175b
    Treaty of Montevideo, 1960, 168a
Latin American Parliament, 167–8
Latin American Solidarity Organization,
    212
Law of the Sea see Maritime Law
Lebanon
    European Economic Community, Trade
        Agreement, 71b
    U.S.A., Defence Agreement, 173a

Liberia
    U.S.A., Defence Agreements, 173a
Libya
    Britain, Treaty, 1953, 147a
    U.S.A., Defence Agreements, 173a
Lima, Declaration of, 1938, 151b
London
    Conference on Constitution of Council
        of Europe, 44a
    Nine-Power Conference, 1954, 41b, 95b
    Six-Power Conference, 1948, 7a
Lusaka Conference of Non-Aligned
    Countries, 209–10
Lusaka Declaration on Peace, Independ-
    ence, etc., 210a
Lusaka Manifesto, 189a
Luxemburg
    NATO Agreements, 108, 110–11

Madagascar
    France, Defence Agreement, 149, 192
Maghreb
    Bilateral Treaties, 181a
Maghreb Permanent Consultative Com-
    mittee, 181a
    Membership, 192–3
Malagasy Republic see Madagascar
Malaysia
    Indonesia, Treaty, 204b
    Thailand, Agreement, 204b
Maldive Islands
    Britain, Agreement on use of Gan Air-
        field, 1953, 145a, 199
Mali
    China (P.R.), Treaty, 1964, 128b
    U.S.A., Defence Agreement, 173a
Malta
    Britain, Agreement, 145b
    European Economic Community,
        Association, 70–1
Maphilindo, 206a
Marine Pollution Conventions, 30
Maritime Law (see also Intergovernmen-
    tal Marine Consultative Organiza-
    tion under United Nations, and
    Nuclear Treaties)
    Declaration of Paris, 1856, 1a
    Geneva Convention, 1906, 1b
    Hague Convention, 1907, 3a
    Int. Red Cross Convention, 1948, 2b
    U.N. Conventions, 1958, 18a
Marshall Plan, 85a
Mauritania
    France, Agreements, 149, 192
    Morocco, Treaty, 181a
Mauritius
    Britain, Defence Agreement, 146a
Mekong River Development Scheme, 206b
Messina Resolution see under European
    Economic Community
Mogadishu Declaration, 189a
Mongolia
    Bilateral Treaties, 124a, 128a
Monroe Doctrine, 151a
Montevideo, Treaty of, 1960, 168a

Morocco
  Algeria, Treaties, 181a
  European Economic Community,
    Association, 70b
  Mauritania, Treaty, 181a
Moscow Declaration, 1957, 113b

Nassau, Bahamas, Kennedy-Macmillan
  Meeting, 1962, 102–3
Nepal
  Britain, Agreement and Treaty, 1947–
    50, 147a
  China, Treaties, 128a
  India, Treaty, 1950, 203b
Netherlands
  Antilles and Surinam, 176
  NATO Agreements, 108, 110–12
  U.S.A., Atomic Energy Agreement, 112b
  ——, Defence Agreements, 173a
New Zealand
  Australia (ANZAC) Agreement, 194a
  ——, Free Trade Area, 195b
  Dependent Territories, 207b
  U.S.A., Defence Agreement, 173a
Nicaragua
  U.S.A., Defence Agreements, 173a
Niger
  Bilateral Defence Agreements, 141, 149,
    173a
Nigeria
  Chad, Treaty, 191b
Non-Aligned Countries, Conferences, 209–
  10
Nordek
  Draft Treaty, 51a
Nordic Council, 50–1
  Helsinki Convention, 1962, 50b
  Membership, 50a, *51*
  Nordic Institute of Theoretical Atomic
    Physics, 50b
North Atlantic Treaty Organization, 93–
  112
  AD-70 Study, 104a
  Anti-Submarine Warfare Research
    Centre, La Spezia, 102b
  Civilian and other Agencies, 98–9
  Committee on the Challenges of
    Modern Society, 105b
  Communications Satellite, 105b
  Council, 98–9
    Establishment, 96–7
    Removal from Paris to Brussels, 104a
    Temporary Committee (TCC), 96–7
  Defence Committee, 96b
  Defence Expenditure, 105–6
  Defence Ministers' Special Committee,
    103a
  Defence Research Director's Committee,
    103a
  Economic Problems, 106
  German Federal Republic, Membership,
    7a, 93–4
  Intermediate-Range Ballistic Missiles
    (IRBMs), 102a, 109a
  Membership, 93

  Military Committee, 100–1
    Establishment, 96b
    French Withdrawal, 103–4
    Removal from Washington to Brus-
      sels, 104a
  Military Organs, 100–1
  Missile Training Range, Crete, 102b,
    112b
  Multi-national Allied Task Force, 102b
  Parliamentarians' Conference, 97a, 102a
  Polaris Submarines, 102b, 109a
  Political Committee, 102a
  Regional Planning Groups, 96b
  Standing Group, 96b, 104a
  "Three Wise Men", 97a, 106a
  Treaty, 1949, 94–6
  U.N. Disarmament Committee, Repre-
    sentation on, 22a
  Western European Union, Members'
    Military Contribution, 42a
North Sea Continental Shelf, 83b
Norway
  Atomic Energy Agreements, 77a, 175a
  Bilateral Defence Agreements, 173b
  NATO Agreements, 108, 110–11, 173b
  Soviet Union, Spitsbergen Treaty,
    1920, 127a
Nuclear Research
  Eastern Joint Institute, Dubna, 131b
  Euratom Research Centres, 75b
  European Nuclear Energy Agency
    (ENEA), 91–2
  European Organization for Nuclear
    Research (CERN), 80b
  Inter-American Nuclear Energy
    Commission, 158a
  Nordic Institute of Theoretical Atomic
    Physics, 50b
  Nuclear Energy Agency, 91–2
Nuclear Treaties
  Nuclear Non-Proliferation, 38
  Latin America, Prohibition of Nuclear
    Weapons, 38a
  Seabed Arms Control, 38b
  Test-Ban, 37–8

Oder-Neisse Frontier
  Guaranteed by Soviet Union and other
    Warsaw Pact Members, 124b
  Poland-G.D.R., Agreement, 123a
  Potsdam Conference, 1945, 6b
Operation Pan-America, 1958, 160a
Organization of African Unity (OAU),
  186–8
  African Civil Aviation Commission,
    188b
  Assemblies, 187–8
  Charter, 186–7
  Disputes, Solution of, 188b
  Liberation Bureau, 188a
  Membership, *187*, 192–3
  OCAM, Relations with, 190b
  Scientific and Technical Commission,
    188a

Organization of American States, 153–64
  Alliance for Progress, 161–4
  American Commission of Dependent
    Territories, 154b
  Bogotá, Declarations, 1948, 154–5
  ——, Declaration, 1966, 156a
  Charter, 153–4
  Communism, Declarations against, 158–
    60, 155a
  Council, 155b, 156a
  Cuba, Exclusion, 159b
  Inter-American Conference, 155b, 156a
  Inter-American Council of Jurists, 155b
  Inter-American Cultural Council, 155b
  Inter-American Economic and Social
    Council, 155–6
  ——, São Paulo Conference, 1963, 162
  Inter-American Educational, Scientific,
    and Cultural Council, 155b
  Inter-American Juridical Committee,
    155b
  Kidnapping Convention, 160a
  Membership, 153b, 165, 175b
  Pan-American Union becomes General
    Secretariat, 155–6
  Rio de Janeiro, Act of, 1965, 155
  San José, Declaration of, 1960, 158
  Special Agencies and Commissions, 157b
  Special Commission for Economic
    Cooperation, 160a
  Specialized Organizations, 157
  Washington, Act of, 1964, 156a
**Organization of Arab Petroleum Ex-
  porting Countries (OAPEC),** 24b
Organization of Central American States,
  165–7
  Charter, 165
  Declaration of Central America, 1963,
    165–6
  Membership, *165*, 165a, 175b
**Organization for Economic Co-operation
  and Development,** 85–92
  Committee for Monetary and Foreign
    Exchange Matters, 91a
  Convention, 86–7
  Development Assistance Committee, 92b
  Development Center, 92b
  Eurochemic, 91b
  European Fund and Multilateral Clear-
    ing System, 90–1
  European Monetary Agreement, 87b
  European Nuclear Energy Agency, 91–2
  ——, Euratom, Co-operation with,
    76a .
  Membership, 85, *87*
  Nuclear Energy Agency, 91–2
  Structure, 88–9
**Organization for European Economic
  Co-operation,** 85a
**Organization of Petroleum Exporting
  Countries (OPEC),** 24b
Outer Space Treaty, 1966, 39–40

Pacific Charter *see under* South-East Asia
  Treaty Organization

Pacific Security Treaty *see* ANZUS Pact
Pact of Paris, 1928, 14b
Pakistan
    Atomic Energy Agreements, 77a
    Burma, Agreements, 204a
    China (P.R.), Border Treaty, 1963, 128b
    Commonwealth, 141b
    India, Agreements, 203–4
    ———, U.N. Military Observer Group, 23b
    SEATO, Withdrawal, 198
    Turkey, Agreement on Friendly Cooperation, 1954, 185
    U.S.A., Defence Agreements, 173b, 183b
Palestine
    Arab League Declaration, 1945, 178a
    Liberation Organization, 179a
    U.N. Relief and Works Agency for Palestine Refugees, 22b
    U.N. Truce Supervision Organization, 23a
Panama
    U.S.A., Defence Agreements, 173b
Pan-American Union (*see also* Organization of American States)
    Establishment, 1923, 156b
    Inter-American Conference on the Problems of War and Peace, 1945, 152a
Pan-Americanism (*see also* Organization of American States), 151–3
    Chapultepec, Act of, 1945, 152a
    Declaration of Inter-American Solidarity and Co-operation, 1936, 151b
    Gondra Treaty, 1923, 151b
    Inter-American Treaty of Reciprocal Assistance, 1947, 152a
    Lima, Declaration of, 1938, 151b
    Monroe Doctrine, 1823, 151a
    Pact for Co-ordination of Treaties, 1936, 151b
    Pan-American Peace Pact, 1936, 151b
    Rio, Treaty of, 1947, 152
Panch Sila *see* Five Principles
Paraguay
    U.S.A., Defence Agreements, 173b
Paris
    Agreements, 1954, 7a, 41b, 95b, 119b
    Congress of, 1856, 1a
    Declaration of, 1856, 1a
    Declaration of, 1962 (NATO), 102a
    Union of, 1883, 3a
Patents
    Convention on Patent Application, 3a
    Council of Europe Conventions, 48a
Peace Treaties of World War II, 7–9
Pepper Community, 24b
Persian Gulf
    Britain, Treaties, 147b
Peru
    U.S.A., Defence Agreements, 173b
Philippines
    India, Treaty, 1952, 203b
    Japan, Treaty, 1960, 204b
    U.S.A., Atomic Energy Agreement, 175a
    U.S.A., Defence Treaty and Agreements, 173b, 199a

Poland
    Bilateral Agreements, 122–5, *123*
    German Federal Republic, Treaty, 134a
    Potsdam Conference Provisions, 1945, 6b
Portugal
    Concordat, 1940, 4b
    EFTA, Special Relations Agreement, *56*, 79b
    Great Britain, Anglo-Portuguese Alliance, 1373, 146a
    NATO Agreements, 108, 110–12
    Overseas Provinces, 191b, 207b
    U.S.A., Atomic Energy Agreement, 175a
    ———, Defence Agreements, 173b
Potsdam Conference, 1945, 4b
Prisoners of War
    Hague Convention, 1907, 2–3
    International Red Cross Conventions, 1929, 1948, 1–2
Prussia
    Allied Control Council, Decree ending Prussian State, 1947, 7a
Punta del Este
    Charter of 1961, 161a
    Conference of American Presidents, 1967, 163–4
    Conference of OAS Foreign Ministers, 1961, 161
    Declaration to the Peoples of America, 161a
    Inter-American Development Bank, Anniversary Meeting (1970), 164b

Qatar
    Britain, Treaty, 147b

Red Cross *see* International Red Cross
Refugees
    Council of Europe Agreement on Abolition of Visas, 48a
    Council of Europe Committee of Advisers, 44b
    U.N. Convention, 1951, 25b
    U.N. High Commissioner, 25b
    ———, OAU Representation, 188b
    U.N. Relief and Works Agency for Palestine Refugees, 22b
Regional Co-operation for Development, 184–5
Rio, Treaty of, 1947, 152
Rio de Janeiro
    Act of, 1965, 155
    Economic and Social Act of 1965, 162b
    Second Inter-American Conference, 1965, 162b
River Plate Basin Development, 170a
Roman Catholic Church
    Concordats, 4b
Romania
    Bilateral Agreements, 122, *123*, 124
    Peace Treaty, 1947, 8a
Rome, Treaty of, 56–7
Rumania *see* Romania

Saar
    Franco-German Treaty, 1956, 9b
San Francisco Conference on International Organization (UNCIO), 1945, 11a
San José
    Declaration of, 1960, 158
    Declaration of Central America, 1963, 165–6
San Salvador *see* Charter *under* Organization of Central American States
Saudi Arabia
    Bilateral Agreements, 173b, 180b, 185b
Schuman Plan, 53b
Security Council *see under* United Nations
Sea, Law of, *see* Maritime Law
Seals, Protection Agreement, 37b
Senegal
    Bilateral Defence Agreements, 174a, 192
    Ivory Coast, Treaty, 191b
Senegal River, Organization for the Development of, 191a
———, Organization of Riparian States, 191a
Sick and Wounded Combatants
    Geneva Convention, 1864, 1906, 2b
    Int. Red Cross Convention, 1948, 1
Sierra Leone
    Guinea, Defence Agreement, 1916
Sikkim
    India, Treaty, 1950, 203b
Slavery
    U.N. Convention on Abolition, 1957, 17b
Social Charter *see* European Social Charter
Solidarity Conference of the Peoples of Asia, Africa, and Latin America, 211b
South Africa
    Botswana, Lesotho, Swaziland: Monetary and Customs Union, 144a
    Britain, Simonstown Agreements, 1930–1967, 146–7
    Self-governing Territories, 191a
    U.S.A., Atomic Energy Agreement, 175a
    ———, Defence Agreement, 174a
South-East Asia Treaty Organization, 195–8
    Collective Defence Treaty, 196–7
    Institutions, 198a
    Membership, 195b, *199*
    Pacific Charter, 197
South Pacific Commission, 194a
South Pacific Forum, 206b
South Tyrol
    Austro-Italian Agreements, 7–8
Soviet-Chinese Controversy, 115–19
Soviet Union
    Bilateral Treaties and Agreements, 122–8
    China (P.R.), Ideological Controversy, 115–19

Convention of the Expansion of Hong Kong, 1898, 118b
Finland, Peace Treaties, 1940, 1947, 7b
———, Treaty of Friendship, 1971, 7b, 126a
Indo-China, Geneva Agreements, 1954, 200–3
Iran, Treaties, 1921, 1927, 126
Japan, Yalta Conference, Protocol, 1945, 6a
Norway, Spitsbergen Treaty, 1920, 127a
Treaty of Aigun, 1858, 118b
Treaty of Peking, 1860, 118b
Treaty of Shimonoseki, 1895, 118b
Treaty of St. Petersburg, 1881, 118b
Troop Stationing, Treaties, 122–3
U.S.A., Hot Line Agreement, 139a
———, Nuclear War Risk, Agreement on Reduction of, 139b
———, ABM Systems, Treaty on, 137
Yugoslavia, Reconciliation, 119b
Space
Astronauts, Agreement on Rescue and Return of, 40
International Liability Convention, 40b
Outer Space Treaty, 39–40
Spain
Britain, Treaty of Utrecht, 1713, 146a
Concordat, 1953, 4–5
European Economic Community, Trade Agreement, 71b
France, Military Co-operation Agreement, 84b
Overseas Provinces, 193b
U.S.A., Atomic Energy Agreement, 175a
———, Other Agreements, 174a
Sterling Area, 143–4
Stockholm
Conference on Intellectual Property, 1967, 3–4
Treaty of, 77a
Sudan
Uganda, Defence Agreement, 191b
Suez Canal see Constantinople Convention
Sugar
Commonwealth Sugar Agreement, 143a
International Sugar Agreement, 25a
Sweden
EFTA, Special Relations Agreement, 796
U.S.A., Atomic Energy Agreement, 175a
Switzerland
EFTA, 56, 79b
U.S.A., Atomic Energy Agreement, 175a
Syria
Egypt, Defence Agreement, 181a

Taiwan
U.S.A., Atomic Energy Agreement, 175a
———, Defence Agreements, 171b, 200
Tanzania
China (P.R.), Agreements, 128–9
German Democratic Republic, Treaty, 1964, 124b

Tashkent Declaration, 1966, 204a
Territorial Sea
U.N. Convention, 1958, 18a
Thailand
Malaysia, Armed Forces Agreement, 204b
Peace Treaty, 1946, 7a
U.S.A., Atomic Energy Agreement, 175a
———, Defence Agreements, 174a
Three Continents Conference, Havana, 1966, 211b
Tibet Agreements, 128a, 209a
Togo
France, Defence Agreement, 149a, 193
Tonga
Britain, Treaty, 145b
Trieste, Free Territory
Agreement on Division between Italy and Yugoslavia, 1954, 7b
Trinidad and Tobago
U.S.A., Military Bases Agreements, 174a
Trust Territories see under United Nations
Trusteeship Council see under United Nations
Tunisia
Algeria, Treaty, 181a
Turkey
Bilateral Agreements, 175b, 183–5
Cyprus, Zurich and London Agreements, 1959, 146b
European Economic Community, Association, 68–9
NATO, Adherence, 1952, 94a
———, Agreements, 108–12
U.S.A., Atomic Energy Agreements, 175a

Uganda
Britain, Defence Agreement, 1964, 145b
Sudan, Defence Agreement, 191b
United Arab Emirates, 181b
Britain, Treaty, 147b
United Arab Republic see Egypt
United Kingdom see Britain
United Nations, 10–36
Atomic Energy Commission, 19b
Charter, 11–14
Conventions, 14–19
Disarmament Commission and Committee, 19b
Economic and Social Council, 24–5
Economic Commissions for Africa, Asia and the Far East, Europe, and Latin America, 24b
Asian Development Bank, 204b
Food and Agriculture Organization, 29a
Membership, 34–6
General Agreement on Tariffs and Trade, 31–2
Dillon Round, 32a
International Trade Organization, 31b
Kennedy Round, 32a
Membership, 34–6
General Assembly, 20–3
Group of 77 see U.N. Conference on Trade and Development
Inter-Governmental Maritime Consultative Organization, 30
Conventions, 30
Membership, 34–6
International Atomic Energy Agency, 32
Euratom, Co-operation with, 76a
Membership, 34–6
Nuclear Non-Proliferation Treaty, Inspection Agreement, 38a
U.S.A., Atomic Energy Agreement, 175a
International Bank for Reconstruction and Development, 27
Membership, 34–6
International Civil Aviation Organization, 29–30, 45a
Hijacking Conventions, 29–30
Membership, 34–6
International Court of Justice, 25–6
International Development Association, 28a
Membership, 34–6
International Finance Corporation, 28a
Membership, 34–6
International Labour Organization, 28b
Membership, 34–6
International Law Commission, 19b
International Monetary Fund, 27–8
Membership, 34–6
Committee of Twenty, 28a
Group of Ten, 27b
Special Drawing Rights, 27–8
International Telecommunication Union, 31a
Membership, 34–6
Organs (Diagram), 20–1
Peace-keeping Bodies, 23
U.N. Command in South Korea, 23b
U.N. Military Observer Group for India and Pakistan, 23b
U.N. Peace-keeping Force in Cyprus, 23b
U.N. Truce Supervision Organization (Palestine), 23a
Secretariat and Secretary-General, 26a
Security Council, 12–13, 23
Specialized Agencies, 27–32
Membership, 34–6
Trust Territories, 23b, 207
Trusteeship Council, 23–4
U.N. Children's Fund, 26b
U.N. Commission for the Unification and Rehabilitation of Korea, 23a
U.N. Conference on International Organization, 1945, 11a
U.N. Conference on Trade and Development, 22
Group of, 77, 22
U.N. Development Programme, 25a
U.N. Educational, Scientific, and Cultural Organization, 28–9
Membership, 34–6
Universal Copyright Convention, 3b

U.N. High Commissioner for Refugees, 25b
  OAU Representation, 188a
U.N. Industrial Development Organization, 27a
U.N. Institute for Training and Research, 26b
U.N. Relief and Works Agency for Palestine Refugees in the Near East, 22b
U.N. Trade and Development Board, 22a
Universal Postal Union, 31a
  Membership, 34–6
Women, Declaration on Elimination of Discrimination against, 17
World Health Organization, 29
  Membership, 34–6
World Meteorological Organization, 30b
  Membership, 34–6
United States
  Atomic Energy Agreements, 112b, 175
  Bilateral Defence Agreements, 107b, 109–12, 170–4, 183–4, 198–200, *199*
  Canada, Great Lakes Agreement, 175b
  Dependent Territories, 176b, 207b
  ESRO, Memorandum of Agreement, 1964, 83a
  Euratom, Agreement, 76b
  European Economic Community, Trade Agreement, 71b
  Indo-China, Agreement for Mutual Defence Assistance, 1950, 174b, 203a
  Japan, Defence Agreements, 172b, 199–200
  ——, Ryukyu and Other Islands, Return, 8
  Multilateral Defence Agreements, 106–7, 174b
  Mutual Defense Assistance Act, 1949, 104b
  Mutual Security Act, 1951, 107b
  NATO Agreements, 106–12

Soviet Union, Hot Line Agreement, 139a
——, Nuclear War Risk, Agreement on Reduction of, 139b
——, Limitation of ABM Systems, Treaty on, 137
Spain, Agreements, 174a
"United Action for Peace" Resolution, 1950, 19b
Vandenberg Resolution, 1948, 93a
Universal Copyright Convention, 1952, 3b, 4a
Uruguay
  U.S.A., Defence Agreement, 174b
Utrecht, Treaty of, 1713, 146a

Vandenberg Resolution, 1948, 93a
Vatican
  Concordats, 4–5
Venezuela
  Britain, Agreement on Guyana Territory, 1966, 147a
  U.S.A., Atomic Energy Agreement, 175b
Vietnam, Democratic Republic of (North)
  China (P.R.), Treaty, 1965, 128a
  Geneva Agreements, 1954, 200–203
  Support Agreements, 125
Vietnam, Republic of (South)
  Geneva Agreements, 1954, 200–203
  Multilateral Agreement for Mutual Defence Assistance, 1950, 174b, *199*, 203a
  U.S.A., Atomic Energy Agreement, 175b

Warsaw Treaty Organization, 119–22
  Membership, 119b, *123*
  Strength of Forces, 121b
  Troop-stationing Agreements, 122–3, *123*
  U.N. Disarmament Committee, Representation, 22a
  Warsaw Pact, 120

West African Common Market, 191a
  Membership, 192–3
West African Customs Union, 191a
West African Economic Community (CEAO), 191a
  Membership, 192–3
West African Monetary Union, 190a
  Membership, 192–3
Western European Union, 41–2
  European Economic Community, Co-operation with, 42b
  Membership, 41, *42*
  Organization (Diagram), *43*
Western Germany *see* German Federal Republic
Woomera Rocket Testing Range
  Britain, Agreement, 145a
World Health Organization (WHO) *see under* United Nations
World Meteorological Organization *see under* United Nations
World Bank *see* International Bank for Reconstruction and Development *under* United Nations

Yalta Conference, 1945, 6a, 11a
Yaoundé Convention *see under* European Economic Community
Yemen
  Bilateral Treaties, 124b, 128b
Yugoslavia
  Bilateral Agreements, 122
  CERN, Membership terminated, 81a
  COMECON, 129b
  EFTA, 79a
  European Economic Community, Trade Agreement, 71b
  OECD, 87b
  Soviet Reconciliation, 119b
  Trieste Agreement, 1964, 7b

Zaïre
  U.S.A., Defence Agreement, 171b

INDEX TO SUPPLEMENT

Andean Group, 220a
Angola
    State, Designation as, 221a
Atlantic Charter, 1973 Proposal, 214b
Bahamas
    Commonwealth, Membership, 219b
    U.N., Membership, 213a
Baltic Fishing Convention, 215b
Burundi
    Libya, Treaty, 221a
Cameroon
    OCAM, Withdrawal, 220b
Canada
    Cuba, Hijacking Agreement, 214a
    U.S.A., Defence Agreement (NORAD), 220a
Chad
    Egypt, Treaty, 221a
    OCAM, Withdrawal, 220b
Cocoa, International Agreement, 213b
Common African, Malagasy and Mauritian Organization (OCAM)
    Withdrawals, 220b
Commonwealth
    Definition, 219a
    Membership, 219b
    Singapore Declaration of Common Principles (1971), 219b
"Communauté" see French Community
Communist Countries
    Bilateral Agreements, 216a
Council for Mutual Economic Assistance (COMECON)
    Finland, Agreement, 216a
Cuba
    Hijacking Agreements, 214a
    Soviet Union, Agreement, 216a
Czechoslovakia
    G.F.R., Treaty, 216b
Dependent Territories
    Portugal, 221a
East-West Treaties
    G.F.R.–Czechoslovakia 216b
    G.F.R.–G.D.R., Ratification of Basic Treaty, 216a
    G.F.R.–Soviet Union, 216b
    Soviet Union–U.S.A., 217–18
        Jackson Amendments, 218b
Economic Commission for Western Asia, 213b
Egypt
    Chad, Treaty, 221a
    Libya, Projected Merger, 220a
    OAPEC, Membership, 214a
    Tripoli, Charter of, 220b
Environment
    Baltic Fishing Convention, 215b
    OECD, Toxic Chemicals Agreement, 215b
European Economic Community
    Common Agricultural Policy, Adoption by Three, 214b
    Trade Agreements, 214b
European Free Trade Association
    Special Relations Agreements, 215a
European Science Foundation, 215a
European Security Conference, 219a
European Space Agency, 215a

European Space Research Organization (ESRO)
    NASA, Agreement, 215a
Finland
    COMECON, Agreement, 216a
Fishing
    Baltic Convention, 215b
French Community
    Bilateral Agreements, 219b
    Franc Zone, 220a
German Democratic Republic
    G.F.R., "Basic" Treaty, Ratification, 216a
    IAEA, Membership, 213b
    U.N., Membership, 213a
Hijacking Agreements, 214a
Hungary
    U.S.A., War Damages Settlement, 213a
India
    Pakistan, Repatriation Agreement, 224b
Intergovernmental Maritime Consultative Organization (IMCO)
    Membership, 213b
International Atomic Energy Agency (IAEA)
    Membership, 213b
Iraq
    OAPEC, Membership, 214a
Jackson Amendments, 218b
Korea, People's Democratic Republic of
    U.N., Observer Status, 213a
    World Health Organization, Membership, 213b
Laos
    Geneva Agreement, 1962, 223
    Peace Agreements, 224a
Latin America
    Andean Group, 220a
    Nuclear Weapons, Treaty for the Prohibition of, 214b
Libya
    Burundi, Treaty, 221a
    Egypt, Projected Merger, 220a
    Tripoli, Charter of, 220b
Malagasy Republic
    Franc Zone, Withdrawal from, 220a
    France, Agreement, 220a
    OCAM, Withdrawal from, 220b
Mali
    Nigeria, Treaty, 221a
Mauritania
    Franc Zone, Withdrawal from, 220a
    France, Defence Agreements, 220a
Mexico
    Andean Group, Co-operation, 220a
    Cuba, Hijacking Agreement, 214a
Mongolia
    IAEA, Membership, 213b
Mozambique
    State, Designation as, 221a
National Aeronautics and Space Administration (NASA)
    ESRO, Agreement, 215a
Nigeria
    Mali, Treaty, 221a
Non-Aligned Countries
    Algiers Conference, 224b
North Atlantic Treaty Organization (NATO)

    Command Changes, 216a
    Further Developments, 215–16
Norway
    EFTA, Special Relations Agreement, 215a
Nuclear Weapons
    Treaty of Tlatelolco, Signature of Protocol II, 214b
OCAM see Common African, Malagasy and Mauritian Organization
Organization of African Unity (OAU)
    Assembly of Heads of State, 220b
Organization of Arab Petroleum Exporting Countries (OAPEC)
    Membership, 214a
Organization for Economic Co-operation and Development (OECD)
    Membership, 215b
    Toxic Chemicals, Agreement, 215b
Pakistan
    India, Repatriation Agreement, 224b
Singapore Declaration of Common Principles, 219b
Soviet Union
    Bilateral Treaties, 216–18
    Cuba, Agreement, 216a
    United States, Treaties and Agreements, 217–18
    Universal Copyright Convention, Accession to, 213a
Space Research
    European Space Agency, 215a
    NASA–ESRO Agreement, 215a
Sudan Tripoli, Charter of, 220b
Syria
    OAPEC, Membership, 214a
Tlatelolco, Treaty of, 214b
Tripoli, Charter of, 220b
United Nations (see also Table in main part of book, pp. 34–6)
    Economic and Social Council
        Economic Commission for Western Asia, 213b
    Membership, 213a
        IAEA, 213b
    Specialized Agencies, 213
United States
    Bilateral Defence Treaties, 220a
    Cuba, Hijacking Agreement, 214a
    Hungary, War Damages Settlement, 213a
    Jackson Amendments, 218b
    Soviet Union, Treaties and Agreements, 217–18
Universal Copyright Convention
    Soviet Union, Accession to, 213a
Uruguay
    EEC, Trade Agreement, 214b
Venezuela
    Andean Group, Membership, 220a
    Cuba, Hijacking Agreement, 214b
Vietnam
    Peace Agreement, 221–3
War Damages
    U.S.–Hungarian Settlement, 213a
West African Economic Community (CEAO), 221a
Yugoslavia
    EEC, Trade Agreement, 214b

Treaties and alliances of the world
Keesing's Contemporary archive

12141
341 Kee